Economic Report of the President

Transmitted to the Congress
February 1996

TOGETHER WITH
THE ANNUAL REPORT
OF THE
COUNCIL OF ECONOMIC ADVISERS

UNITED STATES GOVERNMENT PRINTING OFFICE

WASHINGTON : 1996

For sale by the U.S. Government Printing Office
Superintendent of Documents, Mail Stop: SSOP, Washington, DC 20402-9328
ISBN 0-16-048501-0

DAVID FADD

CONTENTS

* For a detailed table of contents of the Council's Report, see page 13.

(iii)

ECONOMIC REPORT
OF THE PRESIDENT

ECONOMIC REPORT OF THE PRESIDENT

To the Congress of the United States:

FIFTY YEARS AGO, the CONGRESS passed and President Truman signed the Employment Act of 1946, which committed the U.S. Government to promote policies designed to create employment opportunities for all Americans. I am proud that my Administration has made President Truman's commitment a reality. Over the past 3 years, we have created a sound economic foundation to face the challenges of the 21st century.

Strong Economic Performance

Overall, the American economy is healthy and strong. In the first 3 years of this Administration nearly 8 million jobs were created, 93 percent of them in the private sector. The so-called "misery index"—the sum of the inflation and unemployment rates—fell last year to its lowest level since 1968. Investment has soared, laying the basis for future higher economic growth. New business incorporations have set a record, and exports of American-made goods have grown rapidly. Ours is the strongest and most competitive economy in the world—and its fundamentals are as sound as they have been in three decades.

This turnaround occurred because of the hard work and ingenuity of the American people. Many of the new jobs are high-wage service sector jobs—reflecting the changing structure of the economy. The telecommunications, biotechnology, and software industries have led the high-tech revolution world-wide. Traditional industries, such as manufacturing and construction, have restructured and now use technology and workplace innovation to thrive and once again create jobs. For example, in 1994 and 1995, America was once again the world's largest automobile maker.

Our 1993 economic plan set the stage for this economic expansion and resurgence, by enacting historic deficit reduction while continuing to invest in technology and education. For over a decade, growing Federal budget deficits kept interest rates high and dampened investment and productivity growth. Now, our deficit is proportionately the lowest of any major economy.

Today, our challenge is to ensure that all Americans can become winners in economic change—that our people have the skills and the security to make the most of their own lives. The very explosion of technology and trade that creates such extraordinary opportunity also places new pressures on working people. Over the past

3

two decades, middle-class earnings have stagnated, and our poorest families saw their incomes fall. These are long-run trends, and 3 years of sound economic policies cannot correct for a decade of neglect. Even so, we are beginning to make some progress: real median family income increased by 2.3 percent in 1994, and the poverty rate fell in 1994 for the first time in 5 years.

Addressing Our Economic Challenges

I am firmly committed to addressing our economic challenges and enhancing economic security for all Americans. People who work hard need to know that they can and will have a chance to win in our new and changing economy. Our economic agenda seeks both to promote growth and to bring the fruits of that growth within reach of all Americans. Our overall strategy is straightforward:

- *Balancing the budget.* In the 12 years before I took office, the budget deficit skyrocketed and the national debt quadrupled. My Administration has already cut the budget deficit nearly in half. I am determined to finish the job of putting our fiscal house in order. I have proposed a plan that balances the budget in 7 years, without violating our fundamental values—without undercutting Medicare, Medicaid, education, or the environment and without raising taxes on working families. The plans put forth by my Administration and by the Republicans in the Congress contain enough spending cuts in common to balance the budget and still provide a modest tax cut. I am committed to giving the American people a balanced budget.

- *Preparing workers through education and training.* In the new economy, education is the key to opportunity—and the education obtained as a child in school will no longer last a lifetime. My Administration has put in place the elements of a lifetime-learning system to enable Americans to attend schools with high standards; get help going to college, or from school into the workplace; and receive training and education throughout their careers. We expanded Head Start for preschoolers; enacted Goals 2000, establishing high standards for schools; created a new direct student loan program that makes it easier for young people to borrow and repay college loans; gave 50,000 young people the opportunity to earn college tuition through community service; and enacted the School-to-Work Opportunities Act. Now we must continue to give our people the skills they need, by enacting my proposals to make the first $10,000 of college tuition tax deductible; to give the top 5 percent of students in each high school a $1,000 merit scholarship; and to enact the GI Bill for Workers, which would replace the existing worker training system with a flexible voucher that workers could use at community colleges or other training facilities.

- *Increasing economic security.* We must give Americans the security they need to thrive in the new economy. We can do this through health insurance reforms that will give Americans a chance to buy insurance when they change jobs or when someone in their family is sick. We can do this by encouraging firms to provide more extensive pension coverage, as I have done through my proposals for pension simplification. In addition, we should make work pay by increasing the minimum wage and preserving the full Earned Income Tax Credit (EITC), which cuts taxes for hard-pressed working families to make sure that no parents who work full-time have to raise their children in poverty.
- *Creating high-wage jobs through technology and exports.* We must continue to encourage the growth of high-wage industries, which will create the high-wage jobs of the future. We have reformed the decades-old telecommunications laws, to help spur the digital revolution that will continue to transform the way we live. We must continue to encourage exports, since jobs supported by goods exports pay on average 13 percent more than other jobs. My Administration has concluded over 200 trade agreements, including the North American Free Trade Agreement and the Uruguay Round of the General Agreement on Tariffs and Trade, seeking an open world marketplace and fair rules for exporters of American goods and services. As a result, merchandise exports have increased by 31 percent.
- *A government that is smaller, works better, and costs less.* A new economy demands a new kind of government. The era of big, centralized, one-size-fits-all government is over. But the answer is not the wholesale dismantling of government. Rather, we must strive to meet our problems using flexible, non-bureaucratic means—and working with businesses, religious groups, civic organizations, schools, and State and local governments. My Administration has reduced the size of government: as a percentage of civilian nonfarm employment, the Federal workforce is the smallest it has been since 1933, before the New Deal. We have conducted a top-to-bottom overhaul of Federal regulations, and are eliminating 16,000 pages of outdated or burdensome rules altogether. We have reformed environmental, workplace safety, and pharmaceutical regulation to cut red tape without hurting public protection. And we will continue to find new, market-based ways to protect the public.

The Need to Continue with What Works

As *The Annual Report of the Council of Economic Advisers* makes clear, this is a moment of great possibility for our country. Ours is the healthiest of any major economy. No nation on earth is better positioned to reap the rewards of the new era. Our strategy of deficit reduction and investment in our people has begun to work. It would be a grave error to turn back.

Our Nation must reject the temptation to shrink from its responsibilities or to turn to narrow, shortsighted solutions for long-term problems. If we continue to invest for the long term, we will pass on to the next generation a Nation in which opportunity is even more plentiful than it is today.

William J. Clinton

THE WHITE HOUSE
FEBRUARY 14, 1996

THE ANNUAL REPORT
OF THE
COUNCIL OF ECONOMIC ADVISERS

LETTER OF TRANSMITTAL

COUNCIL OF ECONOMIC ADVISERS,
Washington, D.C., February 14, 1996.

MR. PRESIDENT:

The Council of Economic Advisers herewith submits its 1996 Annual Report in accordance with the provisions of the Employment Act of 1946 as amended by the Full Employment and Balanced Growth Act of 1978.

Sincerely,

Joseph E. Stiglitz
Chairman

Martin N. Baily
Member

Alicia H. Munnell
Member

Fifty Years of the Council of Economic Advisers

The Council of Economic Advisers celebrates its 50th anniversary this year. The Council was established by the Congress in the Employment Act of 1946. Over the years, it has provided every President since Harry Truman with rigorous and independent economic analysis and advice.

The Council's 50-year tradition and reputation as a high quality, professional organization allows it to attract to government service some of the most distinguished economists in the country. For instance, a number of Council Members or staff have earned or went on to earn the Nobel Prize or John Bates Clark award.

Consistent with the mandate of the Employment Act, the Council prepares each year an *Economic Report of the President*; provides the President with advice and analysis on a full range of domestic and international economic issues; monitors key macroeconomic indicators and advises the President on how to interpret them; and publishes a monthly digest of economic statistics in conjunction with the Joint Economic Committee of the Congress.

The Council's mission within the Executive Office of the President is unique: it serves as a tenacious advocate for policies that facilitate the workings of the market and that emphasize the importance of incentives, efficiency, productivity, and long-term growth. This perspective has been essential to formulating and advocating creative approaches for effectively addressing America's economic challenges. The Council has also been important in helping to weed out proposals that are ill-advised or unworkable, proposals that cannot be supported by the existing economic data, and proposals that could have damaging consequences for the economy.

CONTENTS

LIST OF CHARTS—CONTINUED

LIST OF BOXES

CHAPTER 1

Economic Policy for the 21st Century

The American economy has performed exceptionally well over the past 3 years. The combined rate of unemployment and inflation fell to its lowest level since 1968. Productivity in the manufacturing sector has increased by an average of 4 percent per year. Investment has soared, laying the basis for increased productivity in the future, while exports have boomed: equipment investment and merchandise exports both have climbed more than 25 percent since the beginning of 1993. Yet despite these encouraging developments, many Americans remain concerned about the state of their own economic affairs. Their dissatisfaction reminds us of the many challenges that remain.

In 1992, more than 9 million Americans were unemployed, and the unemployment rate was above 7 percent. In parts of the country, such as California, nearly one-tenth of the labor force was without a job. By late 1995, however, the unemployment rate had dropped to 5.6 percent, and the economy was poised to reach the target the Administration had set for it: 8 million new jobs in 4 years.

Before the Administration could move ahead with its own positive economic agenda (which this *Report* describes), it had to address some of the economic problems it had inherited. The economy suffered from multiple infirmities—a weakened banking system, increasing poverty, and lackluster overall performance—but the most visible problem was the soaring budget deficit. The first step required to set the economy on the right course was to reduce the Federal budget deficit. By cutting the Federal Government's borrowing needs, deficit reduction has contributed to lower interest rates for businesses and consumers, thereby spurring investment and growth.

The Omnibus Budget Reconciliation Act of 1993 (OBRA93), which embodied the President's deficit reduction plan, put the country solidly on the road to fiscal responsibility. For over three decades the country had been gradually reducing the burden of the debt that had financed victory in World War II: the ratio of debt to gross domestic product (GDP) fell from 82 percent in 1950 to 27 percent in 1980. Within 12 years much of this progress was lost, and the debt to GDP ratio soared to 50 percent by 1992 (Chart 1–1). Following passage of OBRA93, the debt to GDP ratio has stabilized.

Chart 1-1 **Federal Debt-to-GDP Ratio**
After falling throughout the early postwar era, the Federal debt as a percent of GDP rose in the 1980s and has now leveled off.

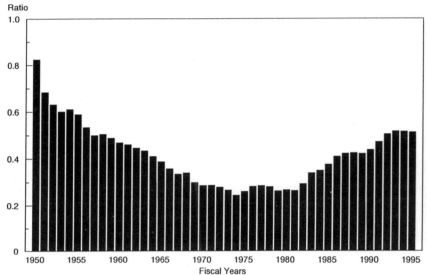

Fiscal Years
Note: The GDP measure used is pre-January 1996 benchmark revision.
Source: Office of Management and Budget.

Since OBRA93, the deficit has been cut nearly in half, from $290 billion in fiscal 1992 to $164 billion in fiscal 1995. The drop is even more dramatic when compared with the deficits that would have occurred without OBRA93 (Chart 1–2). The deficit has been reduced in dollar terms for 3 consecutive years for the first time since the Truman Administration. The decline in the deficit as a percentage of national output has been particularly striking: at 2.3 percent of GDP, the fiscal 1995 deficit is the lowest since fiscal 1979 and less than half the fiscal 1992 level of 4.9 percent. The Federal Government is now running a primary budget surplus: in other words, were it not for the interest payments on the inherited debt, there would be no deficit. And the general government deficit is now a smaller percentage of GDP than in any of the other major industrial economies (Chart 1–3).

This restoration of fiscal responsibility, achieved without sacrificing crucial investments in our Nation's human, physical, and natural resources, provided the background for the current bipartisan resolve to eliminate the deficit within 7 years. A later section of this chapter discusses the right way and the wrong way to elimi-

Chart 1-2   **Federal Budget Deficit**
Budget deficits would have remained large relative to the size of the economy without
deficit reduction initiatives. Instead, deficits have fallen sharply.

Percent of GDP

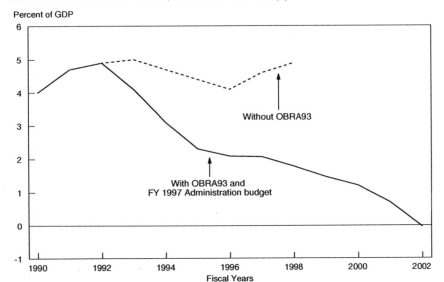

Note: The GDP measure used is pre-January 1996 benchmark revision.
Sources: Office of Management and Budget and Congressional Budget Office.

Chart 1-3   **General Government Deficits of the Group of Seven Countries in 1994**
The United States has the lowest general government deficit-to-GDP ratio of
any major industrialized country.

Percent of GDP

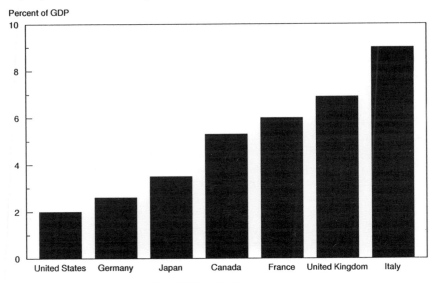

Note: General government includes Federal, State and local.
Source: Organization for Economic Cooperation and Development.

21

nate the deficit, and Chapter 2 of this *Report* examines budgetary issues in more detail.

ECONOMIC CHALLENGES

The economy's recent performance notwithstanding, pressing challenges remain. In the short run, as discussed in Chapter 2, the principal economic challenge is to maintain full employment with low inflation. In the long run, the two paramount challenges are to increase productivity growth and to ensure that all Americans share in the benefits of a stronger economy. Since 1973, productivity growth has been relatively sluggish: its pace in the economy as a whole is significantly slower than it was during the two and a half decades immediately following World War II. Output per hour grew by an average of 2.9 percent per year between 1960 and 1973, but has grown by only 1.1 percent per year since then. The cumulative impact of this productivity shortfall, compounded over decades, is dramatic: output per hour would be over 40 percent higher today if the pre–1973 rate of productivity growth had been maintained. Slower productivity growth since 1973 has resulted in stagnating real wages. Because of the difficulties in measurement, the extent of the weakness in wages may be overstated, but concern over slow wage growth is genuine and cannot be ignored.

Some evidence suggests that the tide may now be turning. In 1994 real median family income rose for the first time since 1989. But a 20-year trend cannot be corrected in one year. Indeed, even with the 1994 improvement, real median family income was just 2.5 percent above its 1973 level. More needs to be done. The Administration's economic policies are intended to boost growth and living standards well into the 21st century.

The negative effects of slower productivity growth have been sharpened for low-income Americans by a marked increase in income inequality. Between 1966 and 1979 Americans all across the income distribution enjoyed the benefits of economy-wide growth in real incomes: families in the poorest fifth of the population saw their real incomes grow by 20 percent, while families in the top fifth experienced real income growth of 28 percent. But since 1979 family incomes have grown apart. Between 1979 and 1993 real family incomes in the bottom fifth *fell* by 15 percent, while the incomes of the top fifth rose by 18 percent (Chart 1–4).

It is too soon to tell for sure, but we may be beginning to succeed in sharing the benefits of growth and reducing poverty. The poverty rate, for example, fell in 1994 for the first time in 5 years. But we must do more to reduce inequality and poverty: despite an improvement in 1994, over one-fifth of American children still live in poverty.

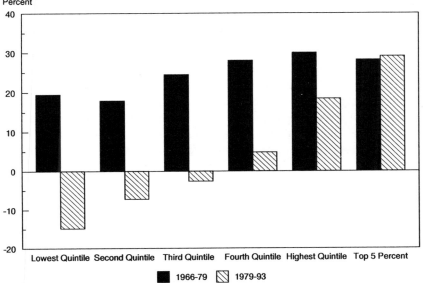

Chart 1-4 **Changes in Average Real Family Income by Quintile**
Real incomes have fallen or stagnated for most American families since 1979.

Percent

Lowest Quintile   Second Quintile   Third Quintile   Fourth Quintile   Highest Quintile   Top 5 Percent

■ 1966-79   ▨ 1979-93

Note: Family income is deflated by the CPI-U-X1.
Source: Department of Commerce.

PRINCIPLES FOR RAISING LIVING STANDARDS

The Administration's economic policies address the twin problems of slow productivity growth and rising income inequality. Three principles guide the Administration's efforts to solve these long-run problems: *embracing change, creating opportunity,* and *promoting personal responsibility.* These principles reflect core American values, and as such they provide the basis for a national consensus for addressing our economic challenges.

Putting this consensus into practice requires a variety of partnerships—between workers and firms, between the public and the private sector, between individuals and their communities, and between the Federal Government and State and local governments. Competition is the driving force of a market economy, but companies compete more effectively when workers and managers cooperate. The public and private sectors can cooperate in solving environmental problems and in meeting skill shortages. And the Federal Government can work with the States to meet the need for infrastructure investment and a social safety net.

Much of the current debate over the economy and the budget stems from different conceptions of the roles that markets, governments, and individuals should play in improving our society. Private enterprise lies at the very heart of our modern economy. Indi-

23

viduals and corporations provide the initiative and innovation that have enabled the market economy to bring unrivaled prosperity to our Nation, and the underlying dynamism of markets is fundamental to continued improvements in living standards.

Yet unfettered markets occasionally fail to yield desirable outcomes or to meet important national objectives. For example, in a completely unregulated marketplace, firms may produce too much of some "goods," such as pollution, and too little of others, such as basic research and development. This failure to produce the "right" amounts of certain goods and services is due to the presence of *externalities*. Externalities arise when the actions of one firm or individual produce costs or benefits for others without that firm or individual being charged for the costs or compensated for the benefits. In such cases the government has a special role. The government has an obligation to perform that role as efficiently as possible, minimizing the burden on the economy and the intrusions in the lives of its citizens. Not every market "problem" calls for government action. In order to raise living standards, government actions therefore must meet two criteria: they must address some serious imperfection in the private marketplace, and they must be designed so that their benefits outweigh their costs.

A variety of government programs have proved extremely successful in raising living standards. We take for granted many of the government services—such as retirement and disability benefits (Social Security), health insurance for the aged (Medicare), and unemployment insurance—that the market had failed to provide (Box 1–1). Before Medicare was enacted in the 1960s, for example, many elderly Americans lacked health insurance, whereas today almost all have it.

Medicare is a good example of a government program that filled a gap in the range of services provided by the private sector. But government programs can and do go awry. Indeed, government is sometimes part of the problem, not part of the solution. For example, the construction of high-density public housing projects may have contributed to some of the problems facing America's inner cities. Chapter 4 of this *Report* describes some of the efforts the Administration has made to make government work better, while Chapter 5 examines the role of policy in making markets work better.

In sum, government has a place, but government must know its place. We now turn to exploring what government's place should be with regard to the three principles enunciated above: embracing change, creating opportunity, and promoting personal responsibility.

24

Box 1–1.—Programs That Raise Living Standards

Many public sector programs have been extremely successful in improving living standards:

- *Social Security.* The Social Security system, created in 1935, provides monthly benefits to retired workers and their dependents and to survivors of insured workers. The program has dramatically reduced old-age poverty: only 12 percent of elderly Americans now live in poverty, down from almost 30 percent in 1966. The Social Security Administration is also remarkably businesslike. A leading financial news publisher recently ranked the quality of the agency's telephone customer service above those of several private companies renowned for their excellent customer service. And administrative costs only amount to about 1 percent of Social Security outlays.
- *The G.I. bill.* The first G.I. bill of rights, signed by President Franklin D. Roosevelt on June 22, 1944, transformed American society. It provided education benefits for all honorably discharged World War II veterans who had served at least 90 days during the war. Almost 8 million received education benefits under the first G.I. bill; more than 10 million veterans have received benefits under its extensions. The G.I. bill also provided loan guarantees for veterans to buy a home or a farm.
- *Student grants and loans.* The government provides various forms of financial assistance to students. Pell grants provide aid to financially needy students for educational costs at participating postsecondary institutions. Under the Perkins loan program, the Federal Government contributes the capital for qualifying institutions to make long-term, low-interest loans to needy students. Under the Stafford loan program, commercial loans to students are backed by the government. And the new direct lending program for college students is designed to provide educational finance in a less costly, less cumbersome fashion. Under the program, the government provides loans to students directly, rather than guaranteeing loans from financial intermediaries, and offers a variety of repayment schemes (including a new option to link repayments to students' incomes). Chapter 7 discusses the role of government in education.

EMBRACING CHANGE

Our continued prosperity and well-being depend on our embracing, not retreating from, the constant succession of new opportunities and challenges of an ever-changing world. During the past few years American firms have been through a technological revolution. They have taken a hard look at what they do, how they do it, and what they must do differently. The result: in many sectors American firms are the most competitive in the world. U.S. computer firms continue to lead the industry at a breakneck pace of technical innovation, of which the explosive growth of the Internet and the increasing popularity of the World Wide Web are merely the newest manifestations. When firms and workers embrace change as these industries have done, the economy as a whole benefits in the form of higher real incomes, lower prices for goods, a wider variety of products, and enhanced opportunities.

But while embracing change raises growth and average living standards, not everyone is made better off. In a rapidly changing economy some will find themselves without the skills required for the new jobs being created. When workers with outdated skills lose their jobs, they face the threat of prolonged unemployment or reemployment at much lower wages. Estimates suggest that about one-third of full-time workers who lose their jobs and are subsequently rehired at another full-time job take a pay cut of 20 percent or more. By providing retraining, and by establishing one-stop career development centers where workers can find out about both training and job opportunities, the government can increase the efficiency of the economy even as it reduces the burden on those who otherwise would be harmed by economic change.

This Administration has actively promoted change, by opening up markets here and abroad, by sponsoring research and development, by devising tax policies to stimulate the growth of new enterprises, and by easing the burden of government regulation. Critics sometimes claim that open trade and investment harm the economy. But as Chapter 8 of this *Report* argues, outward-looking trade and investment policies remain the best choice for America. They boost living standards by encouraging firms to innovate and become more competitive, by stimulating the flow of ideas across national borders, and by providing a wider variety of goods—at lower prices—to consumers and firms.

This Administration has not only promoted change for others— the workers and firms affected by its policies—but has embraced it in its own practices. The Administration recognizes that what the Federal Government does, and how it does it, is sometimes the result of a seemingly haphazard accumulation of functions rather than a coherent, concerted response to a present need. Programs inaugurated yesterday with great optimism in response to yesterday's exigencies too often survive long after their usefulness has passed. In an era of difficult budget choices, those programs that have outlived their purpose, or whose benefits no longer justify their costs, have to be cut back or eliminated to make room for programs that may be needed for success in the 21st century. Efforts to reinvent government over the past 3 years are explored in more detail below.

CREATING OPPORTUNITY

The Administration is committed to extending opportunity to all Americans. Opportunity means allowing each individual to live up to his or her full potential, and ensuring that those who suffer temporary setbacks have a chance to bounce back. The commitment to opportunity is not only a fundamental American value; it is also necessary for achieving faster growth rates and higher standards of living.

Education and training are essential tools for expanding opportunity. Educational opportunities must be available at all stages of a person's life: from the preschool years through high school or college, and continuing through one's career. But these opportunities are not universally available. Children from low-income families, for example, do not enter formal schooling with the same readiness as their more economically advantaged peers—a disparity that Head Start (a government program that provides a range of preschool services to young children and their families) helps redress. And the difficulties involved in borrowing against future income highlight the importance of government student loan programs. Although college is an investment that usually pays high returns to the student and to society, private lenders view these loans without collateral as simply too risky. Chapter 7 of this *Report* examines the government's role in the student loan market.

Opportunity entails more than just education and training: having learned the requisite skills, Americans should have the opportunity to obtain jobs. During the Great Depression, when the unemployment rate soared to over 25 percent, our economy failed to offer the opportunity to work to millions of Americans, unemployed through no fault of their own. The Employment Act of 1946 committed the government to combating unemployment. The act declared that "it is the continuing policy and responsibility of the Federal Government to use all practicable means . . . to foster and promote . . . conditions under which there will be afforded useful employment opportunities, including self-employment, for those able, willing, and seeking to work. . . ." The Administration's macroeconomic policies, described in Chapter 2, have provided opportunity to millions of Americans by fostering job growth and reducing unemployment.

Opportunity in the labor market requires much more than active education, training, and macroeconomic policies. It also requires policies that make work pay for low-skilled workers and eliminate labor market discrimination for all. Today a full-time, year-round minimum wage worker with a family does not earn enough to stay out of poverty. To help these low-income working Americans and their families, in 1993 the President and the Congress expanded the Earned Income Tax Credit (EITC), and the President has since proposed an increase in the minimum wage from $4.25 to $5.15 an hour.

All forms of discrimination contradict a fundamental tenet of American society: that every American should have a fair chance to succeed. Our Nation has made tremendous strides in reducing discrimination, but the job is not finished. "Audit" studies, in which white and minority job seekers are given similar resumes and sent to the same sets of firms for interviews, indicate that discrimination remains a problem in the labor market. Our civil rights statutes and affirmative action programs combat such discrimination and seek to ensure equal opportunity, and the Administration is fully committed to promoting opportunities in employment, education, and government contracting for Americans subject to discrimination or its lingering effects.

Finally, opportunity also means that those who suffer temporary setbacks have the ability to put themselves back on the right track. The EITC can help, and it does more than help those who directly benefit: it also provides an enhanced sense of security to the millions of other Americans who know they might need assistance at some time in their careers.

PROMOTING PERSONAL RESPONSIBILITY

It is each individual's responsibility to make use of the opportunities that society offers, and not to abuse the protections that society affords. The Administration is firmly committed to designing policies and programs to bolster personal responsibility. But ultimately it is up to each and every American to assume responsibility for his or her own life.

Policies must encourage people to assume responsibility for their own lives, not discourage them from it. And policies intended to address other challenges—for example, ensuring equity—must be carefully designed to minimize any adverse impact on individual incentives. A number of government programs provide, or can be thought of as providing, insurance. Yet a problem common to all types of insurance is *moral hazard*: having the insurance makes the insured-against event more likely to occur. For example, fire insurance reduces the incentives for homeowners to take precautions against fire, and thus may make fires more likely. In the policies they write, private insurance companies include mechanisms, such as deductibles and copayment provisions, aimed at minimizing moral hazard. Similarly, government programs that compensate for misfortune—such as employment and disability insurance, and welfare programs—must be designed so as to promote responsibility, minimize adverse incentive effects, and diminish moral hazard, including dependence on government programs.

In summary, an appropriate role for policy—an effective partnership between the public and the private sector—is crucial to raising living standards. Markets are the engine of prosperity, but sometimes government must help markets to work more efficiently.

THE ADMINISTRATION'S ECONOMIC POLICIES

Embracing change, creating opportunity, and promoting personal responsibility—these principles are a common thread running through the Administration's economic policies. Those policies are intended to bolster, not replace, the underlying strength of markets in building a better society and raising living standards. Raising living standards entails more than just raising incomes; it also includes providing educational opportunities for our children, protecting the environment, and supplying security against devastating adversity. The Administration's economic policies include expanding markets; investing in human, physical, and technological capital; making government more efficient; and reducing the budget deficit.

EXPANDING MARKETS

Promoting Competition

Competition is the driving force of efficiency and innovation. But as we all know, life is often more comfortable with less rather than more competition. Over 200 years ago, Adam Smith recognized that, "People of the same trade seldom meet together, even for merriment and diversion, but the conversation ends in a conspiracy against the public, or in some contrivance to raise prices." It is all too easy to advocate competition for others while seeking protection from competition for oneself. Such protection is often rationalized by claims of "unfair" competition. Economists have long criticized such self-serving arguments and have advocated strong antitrust laws to secure the advantages of effective competition: lower prices, greater efficiency, increased output, more rapid growth, and enhanced innovation. Under the leadership of the Justice Department's Antitrust Division, the Administration has implemented an aggressive policy to prevent unhealthy concentrations of market power and promote competition.

29

Competition policy issues in telecommunications provide a trenchant example of how ongoing change in the economy necessitates change in economic policies. The telecommunications sector not only has grown by leaps and bounds during the past 3 years, but has also provided a spur to changes in other sectors. Government has played a long and useful role in telecommunications, from its financing of Samuel Morse's first telegraph line between Baltimore and Washington to the development of what has become the Internet. But the 60-year-old legislation that regulated the industry until this year was out of tune with the times and stifled innovation. Passage of the new telecommunications bill in February 1996 is expected to stimulate competition and ease access to the information superhighway.

Most analysts agree that the telecommunications regulatory structure needed reform. But effective reform proved more complicated than simply repeating a mantra of deregulation: an unregulated private monopoly can be just as stifling, if not more so, than a regulated one. Deregulation done the wrong way could result in the growth of firms with market power that suppress competition and innovation; equally important, deregulation that permitted excessive media concentration could hamper the public's access to the full panoply of viewpoints. To avoid these pitfalls, the new legislation is designed in a way that fosters competition, recognizing that today's bottlenecks to competition might be removed in a few years. Chapter 6 details the constructive approach the Administration has taken to regulatory reform in this and other areas.

Promoting Exports

Both theory and evidence demonstrate that outward-looking trade and investment policies raise wages and living standards: jobs supported by merchandise exports pay 13 percent more than the national average. Chapter 8 of this *Report* presents the rationale for the Administration's continued support of "compete, not retreat" trade policies. It also explores what trade policy can achieve (higher living standards) and argues that the trade balance is not the proper measure by which to judge the success of trade policies.

The Administration's trade policy record includes several historic trade agreements that have opened foreign markets. Over the past 3 years the Administration has brought the Uruguay Round to a successful close; created the North American Free Trade Area with our largest and third-largest trading partners; reached agreement with 33 other countries to seek a Free Trade Area of the Americas by 2005; set the vision for achieving free trade and investment in the Asia-Pacific by 2020; concluded 20 bilateral trade agreements with Japan; and promoted macroeconomic and trade policies that have contributed to strong export growth (Chart 1–5). The Administration's aggressive support of intellectual property rights has benefited not only American firms, which lead the world in research and innovation, but also other innovative firms throughout the world, providing a spur to innovation everywhere. U.S. living standards have benefited and will continue to benefit from the Administration's efforts to promote trade.

Chart 1-5 **Merchandise Exports**
Goods exports have grown by 26 percent in real terms since the Administration took office.

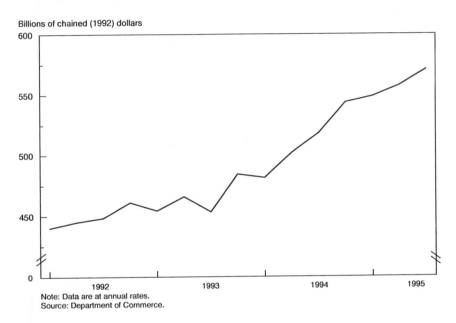

Billions of chained (1992) dollars

Note: Data are at annual rates.
Source: Department of Commerce.

INVESTING IN PHYSICAL, HUMAN, AND TECHNOLOGICAL CAPITAL

Increases in productivity are largely the consequence of investment: in physical capital (plant, equipment, and infrastructure), human capital, and in the development of new technology. Government can promote all three. Through the sound macroeconomic policies of the kind pursued during the past 3 years, the government can create an economic climate conducive to physical capital investment. But the government must play an even more direct role in making investments in people and in technology.

Investing in People

Preserving and extending lifelong investments in people has been central to the Administration's economic strategy. Investments in people are estimated to account for approximately a fifth of the annual increase in productivity achieved over the past three decades, and economic studies have demonstrated the high returns of *public*

31

investments in this area. As Benjamin Franklin once put it, "An investment in knowledge pays the best interest." Early childhood programs such as Head Start, seem to produce fewer repeated grades, a lower likelihood of being assigned to special education classes, and a higher likelihood of graduating from high school.

The Administration has expanded investments in education and training not only as a pro-growth policy, but also as an essential ingredient in breaking the vicious cycle of poverty. As Chapter 7 of this *Report* argues, past cutbacks in public support for education have aggravated trends in inequality. Between 1980 and 1994 the average tuition at public 2-year colleges increased by 70 percent, and that at public 4-year colleges by 86 percent, while the value of the maximum Pell Grant—the primary Federal program for low-income students—fell by more than 25 percent in real terms. The results of these changes are not unexpected. Returns to education have risen sharply in the past 15 years, but the expected response—increased enrollments—has occurred disproportionately among the children of the better off: over the same time period, the gap in enrollment rates between high-income and low-income children has actually increased.

This Administration is working to revitalize the Federal role in education and training. It has supported rigorous academic standards and comprehensive school reform through the Goals 2000: Educate America Act, which provides funding for the implementation of voluntary content standards and local educational innovation; created a new direct lending program for college tuition, to reduce costs and inefficiencies and make the terms of repayment less onerous; and encouraged a smooth transition from school to the workplace through the School-to-Work Opportunities Act. That piece of legislation is especially important because it funds programs to prepare high school students for today's careers. The Administration has also begun to transform the Nation's unemployment system into a reemployment system, by creating one-stop career centers and proposing a system of skill grants (job training vouchers) for low-income and dislocated workers. The Administration's policies to improve both the quantity and quality of expenditure on education and training are examined in more detail in Chapter 7 of this *Report*.

Investing in Research and Development

The Federal role in research and development and technology—both in conducting research and in disseminating the ideas that research generates—dates back to the 19th century. That investment has produced impressive returns: from a more productive agricultural sector to the underpinnings of what is today one of America's largest export sectors, aeronautics, and to the basic science that has given rise to one of America's most prominent high-technology sectors, biotechnology. Recent studies suggest that half or more of all increases in productivity are due to improvements in technology, and these studies have verified the high total returns to such investments—returns far in excess of those from investments in plant and equipment. As the 21st century approaches, our technology programs must be both strengthened and reoriented to emerging sectors. The Administration has promoted public sector investments in technology through programs such as the Advanced Technology Program and the Manufacturing Extension Partnerships (at the Department of Commerce's National Institute of Standards and Technology) and the Technology Reinvestment Project (at the Department of Defense's Advanced Research Project Agency).

MAKING THE GOVERNMENT MORE EFFICIENT

The Administration recognizes the need for change not only in *what* the government does, but also in *how* it does it.

Reinventing Government

The reinventing government initiative was undertaken to improve the efficiency of government, learning from the private sector wherever possible, while acknowledging the differences between public and private sector activities. The National Performance Review, headed by the Vice President, has focused on making government agencies more performance- and customer-oriented, developing performance measures, and ensuring that those measures are used for evaluation. These efforts are already beginning to bear fruit, in the form of better customer service and greater efficiency.

The Administration is committed to continuing the reinvention of the Federal Government, eliminating outmoded programs designed for the 19th and 20th centuries, and promoting new ones designed for the 21st. For example, the Department of Agriculture has reduced the number of its agencies from 43 to 29 and is in the process of closing or consolidating 1,200 field offices. It has also plowed under a bumper crop of paperwork: America's farmers this year will fill out 3 million pages fewer of government forms than in years past. Meanwhile the Administration has cut the overall Federal workforce by 200,000 positions. As a percentage of total employment in the United States, Federal employment is smaller today than at any time since the early 1930s.

In its efforts to reinvent regulation, the Administration has attempted to ensure that each regulation it reviews is consistent with its identified objectives, and that the benefits from the regulation justify its costs. Many of the proposals for reinventing government are intended to reduce those costs by fundamentally changing our regulatory philosophy. In its regulatory role, government should seek to facilitate compliance, not to act as a disciplinarian. And regulations should be as market-friendly and performance-oriented as possible. They should encourage innovation and cost-effective ways of achieving the objectives of the regulation. They should take advantage of incentives and market mechanisms, rather than try to suppress them.

One set of regulations that the Administration has examined is those affecting some private sector pensions. Two objectives of these regulations are to prevent pension plans from becoming a vehicle for tax evasion, and to keep them from discriminating against low-wage workers. But in the aggregate these provisions have discouraged firms from offering pensions, thus failing to encourage national saving. The Administration therefore proposed simplified pension arrangements. The proposal would provide substantial safe harbors from nondiscrimination rules if employers match employee contributions; this should reduce the costs to small businesses of administering pension plans.

Other strides have been made in reducing the burden of environmental regulations and those affecting the banking and telecommunications sectors. The proposals recognize the fundamental changes in the economy that call for reform of regulatory structures, but also the need for real safeguards to be kept in place to promote competition and innovation, and to protect consumers and the environment. These reforms are described in greater detail in Chapters 5 and 6.

Protecting the Environment

Americans want to know that the air they breathe, the water they drink, and the rivers and lakes in which they swim and fish are safe. They want to be sure that the places where they live and work do not harbor threats to their health from contamination by dangerous chemicals, and that the Nation's natural resources are properly protected and managed. Protecting the environment is one of the best investments we can make on behalf of our children. Preserving and improving our environmental heritage is an essential part of maintaining and raising overall living standards.

The country has made enormous progress in this area. The air we breathe today is cleaner than before the Clean Air Act was passed. Substances that pose real dangers to human health and the environment, such as lead and DDT, have been eliminated or their use sharply reduced. Rivers and lakes have been restored to health: 25 years ago Lake Erie was all but dead; today life thrives in it again. With U.S. leadership, the international community has made considerable progress in phasing out substances that damage the earth's stratospheric ozone layer, which shields us from dangerous radiation.

But the battle is far from over. Air quality in some locations remains unacceptably poor. The outbreak of water poisoning in Milwaukee in 1993, and other episodes in which drinking water in our major cities has failed to meet quality standards, do more than just raise anxiety. Chemical runoff from cities, subdivisions, and farms into our rivers and lakes is a constant challenge. Pressures from economic development and increased demand still threaten the Nation's wetlands, fisheries, and other natural resources.

Although we all enjoy the benefits of cleaner air and cleaner water, as individuals—whether managers of steel companies or of oil refineries, or the producers or the drivers of automobiles—we have little incentive to spend our own money to make these things happen. Few are willing to shoulder all the costs of something for which all share the benefits. Acceptable environmental quality cannot be achieved without collective action. With appropriate policies—including cooperation with States and localities, partnerships with the private sector that engender creative solutions as well as set standards, and careful assessment of the advantages and disadvantages of alternative government action—environmental protection can be secured at an affordable cost.

The Administration is improving the way in which we protect the environment, making government a partner rather than an overseer. The Environmental Protection Agency is eliminating 1,400 pages of obsolete regulations and revising 9,400 more. In the process it is cutting paperwork requirements by 25 percent, saving private industry about 20 million hours of labor per year. Chapter 5 of this *Report* examines environmental policy in more detail.

Devolution

The Administration has been examining not only what roles government should play, but also at what level—Federal, State, or local—government should play its role. It has reexamined the partnership between the Federal Government and the States and localities, to ensure that public funds are used most efficiently. In some areas, such as national defense, the Federal Government has a clear responsibility that cannot be delegated. Other areas have traditionally been matters of local responsibility. Chapter 4 of this *Report* reviews the basis on which different responsibilities should be assigned to different levels of government, and stresses that what is usually required is a careful balancing of roles and responsibilities between the different levels.

Redesigning Welfare Policies

The government has a crucial role to play in increasing economic independence, rewarding work, and ensuring that children are not trapped in poverty. This is important not only for social cohesion; it is an economic imperative as well. Each year that a child spends in poverty raises the probability of that child later dropping out of school. And dropouts tend to contribute less to national income: in

1994, mean annual earnings for a full-time, year-round worker aged 25 to 34 who had dropped out of high school were $18,679. Mean earnings for high school graduates in that age range were $23,778.

Although individuals must ultimately be responsible for their own actions, opportunities at least partially affect our behavior. The limited economic opportunities available to dropouts make recourse to antisocial behavior all the more likely. On any given day in 1992, 25 percent of men aged 18 to 34 who lacked a high school diploma were in prison, on probation, or on parole, compared to only 4 percent of high school graduates. This is not merely a tragic outcome for those young men: increased crime imposes a wider social cost, in the form both of greater expenditure by the criminal justice system and of reduced personal security for all of us.

The policies adopted in the past to reduce income inequality and poverty are in need of reform. Everyone agrees that the current welfare system is broken. Welfare dependency does enormous harm to individuals and families, by discouraging work and undermining personal responsibility. Welfare recipients are robbed of their dignity, and administrators spend too much time determining eligibility and to little time helping families get back on their feet.

Figuring out how to fix the welfare system, however, is a great challenge. With no easy answers, the Administration has worked to give States the flexibility they need to experiment with new approaches to welfare. As of February 1996, 37 States have received waivers allowing them to pursue a wide range of reforms. For example, Wisconsin has received a waiver to impose stringent work requirements and time-limited benefits.

In order to help move parents from welfare to work, the Administration has proposed to impose a time limit nationwide. Within 2 years, parents would be required to work. Within 5 years, they would lose their benefits. Children would receive vouchers for support if their parents' benefits were terminated. Chapter 4 of this *Report* discusses many of these issues in more detail.

REDUCING THE DEFICIT

Before it could pursue the rest of its economic agenda, the Administration had to bring the Federal budget deficit under control. One of the most detrimental legacies left by previous Administrations was the perilous state of public finances. The large budget deficits run up during the 1980s and early 1990s, and the associated increase in public debt, were restricting the private investment that is so crucial to growth and were deepening our indebtedness to foreigners.

Borrowing to finance the deficit absorbs funds that could otherwise be used to finance investment in plant and equipment—investment that would increase the productivity of the American economy. Combined with a low rate of private saving, government borrowing forces America to borrow more abroad, increasing our indebtedness to foreign countries. As discussed in Chapter 8, one of the fallouts from previous Administrations' economic policies was that the United States went from being the world's largest creditor country to being the world's largest debtor country in the space of a few years.

Deficit reduction can right many of these wrongs and provide the springboard for faster economic growth. But throughout the recent debate over the budget, the Administration has stressed that there is a right way and a wrong way to reduce the deficit. Deficit reduction is not an end in itself, but a means to the end of higher living standards for all Americans. How the deficit is cut may determine whether or not those ends are accomplished.

Deficit reduction done the wrong way will reduce living standards and worsen inequality. Cutting spending to reduce the deficit requires hard choices. In making these hard choices, we must assess what the government does now and what it should do in the 21st century. The Federal budget is not just a bland accounting statement—it is an expression of the Nation's priorities and values and should reflect a vision of where the country is going and the problems it faces. Some proposed budget cuts, such as those that would reduce equality of educational opportunity, represent attacks on fundamental American values. Others, such as in programs that protect the environment and Americans' health and safety, would have adverse effects on living standards in the future, and thus undermine the very purpose of deficit reduction.

Deficit Reduction and Public Investment

Investment is a key factor in stimulating growth. Reducing the deficit should lower interest rates and stimulate private investment. Cutting the deficit by cutting high-return *public* investments makes little sense: it merely substitutes one worthwhile investment for another. Indeed, deficit reduction that reduces high-return public investments—like those in research and development, technology, education, and training—may compromise long-term economic growth. Deficit reduction should not be achieved by running down our public infrastructure, by failing to invest in research and development, or by neglecting education and training.

Deficit Reduction and the Social Safety Net

Deficit reduction financed through ill-conceived and excessive cutbacks in social programs is also counterproductive. Reducing inequality not only is essential to keep from shredding the common fabric of our Nation, but may also be important in the more limited objective of promoting economic growth.

Economic growth would suffer if opportunities were reduced for those Americans—and especially the children—at the bottom of the income distribution. We would only worsen the inequality in our society by reducing support for the most vulnerable members of society while handing out large tax benefits to the richest. The better course is to ensure that all Americans who work hard and play by the rules have a chance to escape poverty. To do so would increase national output at the same time that it reduces inequality.

Deficit Reduction and Health Care

As the President has long emphasized, growth in health care expenditures must be contained. Failing to do so would not only pose the renewed threat of large budget deficits; it could also force unacceptable cuts in other programs that are vital to the country. It would be wrong, however, for the richest country in the world to abandon its commitment to increase access to basic health care.

Ongoing changes in our health care system not only allow us to take advantage of structural reforms (such as more extensive use of managed care), but also offer the hope that market forces will help contain rising health care costs. The restraint exercised by health maintenance organizations, for example, should serve to increase the relative supply of health care services in other segments of the market and, through the usual workings of supply and demand, help bring down costs. But more is needed, and experiments could provide the information required to implement effective reforms in the coming decade—reforms that would protect the elderly even as they reduce the growth rate of public expenditures. Possible demonstration initiatives include reforming the reimbursement system, developing a system of regional hospitals specializing in certain high-cost treatments, and cutting administrative costs at hospitals.

Deficit Reduction and Taxes

Fifteen years ago, marginal tax rates and the progressivity of the tax system were dramatically reduced. Some suggested that these policies would so spur economic growth that tax revenue would actually increase. The outcome of that experiment is now a matter of record: not only did this response not occur, but the national debt quadrupled in the span of a dozen years. Chapter 3 of this *Report* reviews the arguments and evidence concerning the efficacy of new tax proposals.

In developing its tax proposals, this Administration has emphasized fairness. The Administration has proposed tax cuts for the middle class and argued forcefully against increasing taxes on low-income families through a reduction in the EITC. And the Administration objects to proposals that would give a disproportionate share of tax relief to upper income individuals.

At the same time, the Administration has argued that existing expenditure and tax provisions that benefit particular sectors of the economy, and that cannot be justified in terms of some market failure, should be reduced. Although the Administration succeeded in persuading the Congress to eliminate some of the most obvious examples—the subsidies for mohair and honey, for example, and the tax deductions for lobbying expenses—billions of dollars in corporate subsidies and other loopholes remain.

APPROACHING THE 21ST CENTURY

The U.S. economy has changed profoundly in this century. It will continue to change as we enter the 21st century. Advances in technology will continue at a rapid pace. The globalization of economies will also continue. American firms will face competition from abroad, and all the evidence indicates that they can and will rise to the challenge. Lower priced imports and increased export sales will play a role in increasing living standards, as the United States is able to exploit its comparative advantage on an increasingly global scale.

Some sectors of the economy, such as the services sector, will expand, while others will contract. In 1850, the majority of Americans worked on farms; by 1950 only 12 percent did. In 1900, 20 percent of the workforce was employed in manufacturing; by 1950 this had increased to 24 percent. The manufacturing share has since declined and now stands at 16 percent. Today, the main growth sectors of the economy include service industries such as telecommunications services. Service industries in the private sector accounted for 46 percent of employment in 1950; today they account for 63 percent.

People naturally tend to recall the past in a softened light that obscures its blemishes, and to see in the future adversities that may never materialize. For some, the prospect of a future in which the service economy dominates even more than it does today is one that raises anxieties. To be sure, some of the service sector jobs that are being created are not good jobs. On the other hand, many new service sector jobs—in computer programming and management consulting, for example—are high-tech, high-wage jobs.

Markets and government will need to respond to ongoing changes in the economy. For government, change will require rebalancing: more emphasis on new problems, less emphasis on those of the past. The best combination of policies to address the problems of 2030 will be markedly different from those that got us through the problems of 1930 or 1830. Ideological and extremist solutions reflect neither the realities of today nor the tradition of American pragmatism. Rather, the problems of the 21st century need to be addressed with a balanced perspective. Markets are at the core of our economy, but they do not always operate fully efficiently and do not adequately meet all the needs—even all the economic needs—of Americans. It is then that the government can often help. In the face of increased income inequality, for example, it can make greater efforts to enhance educational opportunity so that the vicious cycle of poverty is not perpetuated.

Government cannot solve all of society's problems, and it certainly cannot solve the more persistent problems overnight. But even if the benefits do not manifest themselves immediately, government must continue to invest in the future. Only by making such investments can the long-term problems of slow productivity growth and increasing inequality be addressed. This Administration firmly believes that government—through selective, focused, and well-designed policies—can help American workers and families achieve higher living standards and develop a more humane, more just society.

CHAPTER 2

Macroeconomic Policy and Performance

ECONOMIC PERFORMANCE DURING the past 3 years has been exceptional. The economy has grown fast enough to create nearly 8 million new jobs and reduce the unemployment rate sharply. Long-term interest rates have declined and remain relatively low. And inflation, at its lowest average level since the Kennedy Administration, is no longer the factor it once was in economic decisions. This strong performance has been helped by macroeconomic policies conducive to sustainable economic expansion.

A major part of this Administration's macroeconomic strategy has been its effort to reduce the Federal budget deficit. Reducing the deficit is important because government borrowing to finance budget deficits raises real interest rates, crowding out business investment that is vital for raising productivity and economic growth. And to the extent that budget deficits spill over into current account deficits, they lead to a transfer of national wealth abroad.

But reducing the deficit is not an end in itself. Rather, it is a way to create economic conditions favorable to this Administration's ultimate goal of raising economic growth and thus the standard of living of all Americans. Once we recognize that deficit reduction is a means to achieving higher living standards, it becomes apparent that *how* we reduce the deficit is important. This Administration has supported responsible deficit reduction that preserves and enhances investments in people, businesses, and the environment.

Thus far during the Administration's tenure, the reduction in the Federal budget deficit has been impressive. For the first time since the Truman Administration the deficit has declined for 3 years in a row. The deficit for the past 2 calendar years has been less than the interest paid on the national debt, so that, except for interest payments, the budget has been in surplus. And the structural budget deficit—the deficit adjusted for the effects of the business cycle—has declined since 1993. This reflects a sharp break with the failed attempts to reduce the budget deficit during the 1980s. The commitment to balance the budget over the next 7 years represents a continuation of efforts to get the government's fiscal house in order.

41

This chapter first considers the role the government plays in setting macroeconomic policy. It next reviews macroeconomic developments during 1995 and argues that all signs point to the current expansion continuing into the foreseeable future. The chapter then considers the effects on the economy and the implications for monetary policy of the move to a balanced budget over the next 7 years. The chapter ends with a brief analysis of the outlook for the economy and presents the Administration's forecast for the 1996–2002 period.

THE TWIN ROLES OF MACROECONOMIC POLICY

Since the end of World War II, the Federal Government has played an important role in stabilizing fluctuations in the economy in the short run and in fostering a climate for maximum economic growth with low unemployment over the long run.

The government supports sound macroeconomic performance in two broad ways. First, its macroeconomic policies cushion the economy from the short-term ups and downs of the business cycle, helping to keep economic expansions from faltering. Both monetary policy and fiscal policy are important elements of these short-run stabilization efforts. Monetary policy stabilizes the economy through the adjustment of credit conditions, as reflected in interest rates and credit availability. Fiscal policy, in principle, can use changes in discretionary spending or the tax code to stabilize the economy, but in practice the time lags involved in legislating and implementing such changes tend to reduce their usefulness. Furthermore, in present circumstances, the commitment to eliminate the budget deficit limits any potential for using discretionary fiscal policy. As a result, the ability of fiscal policy to dampen economic fluctuations depends largely on its role as an "automatic stabilizer" whereby outlays and tax revenues change in a way that reduces the amplitude of the business cycle.

Second, the government's macroeconomic policies help lay the groundwork for the private sector to generate long-term growth with low unemployment. Policies that encourage businesses to invest can raise productivity, increasing the economy's potential output. As discussed below, the Administration's success at bringing down the deficit has helped redress the investment shortfall that developed during the 1980s. As the budget moves toward balance over the next 7 years and the government reduces its drain on national saving, real interest rates should fall and investment and growth should rise. Box 2–1 discusses how microeconomic policies designed to address market failures also can enhance long-run macroeconomic performance.

Box 2-1.—Microeconomic Policies Can Improve Long-Run Macroeconomic Performance

Microeconomic policies can reinforce macroeconomic policies. Policies that support research and development, along with policies that encourage education and training, complement increased capital investment in raising potential output. Indeed, as noted elsewhere in this *Report*, public expenditures on research and development are complementary to private expenditures, so that these expenditures can actually induce increased private investments. Targeted tax policies—such as the research and experimentation tax credit and the targeted capital gains tax cut for small and emerging businesses included in the Administration's 1993 budget—can encourage research and development expenditures and increase the flow of capital to new enterprises.

Other microeconomic policies designed to make the labor market work more efficiently—such as training programs, the school-to-work program, and, more broadly, the Administration's reemployment policies—can help reduce frictional unemployment (unemployment caused by workers moving from job to job) and thereby lower the rate of unemployment associated with stable inflation. Accordingly, microeconomic policies have payoffs in terms of macroeconomic performance.

These twin roles are often complementary. For instance, macroeconomic policies that keep the economy on an even keel in the short run can also spur the economy's growth in the long run by creating an environment in which businesses and individuals are more certain about the future. Freed from having to worry about how to insulate themselves from short-term economic fluctuations, businesses and individuals can plan for the long term. They are thus more likely to make the investments that lead to increased productivity and higher output.

IMPLICATIONS OF THE POLICY MIX

In pursuing these goals of short-run macroeconomic stabilization and long-run maximum growth, fiscal and monetary policy need to act in concert. Monetary policy must reflect changes in aggregate demand relative to the economy's potential output. For example, a shift to a more expansionary fiscal policy when the economy already is operating at full employment and full capacity would require monetary policy to offset the effects of the fiscal expansion. Should it fail to do so, the prospect of an overheated economy and rising inflation is likely to trigger an increase in long-term interest rates, as financial markets react to the change in the economic outlook. In either case, the shift in fiscal policy will be met with a financial market response that generally cushions its effects on aggregate demand. But without deliberate monetary tightening, changes in interest rates may not be sufficient to stem a rise in inflation.

Although monetary policy can offset the effects on aggregate demand from a shift in fiscal policy, changes in the mix of fiscal and monetary policies will invariably alter the composition of output and its potential level in the long run. During the early 1980s, changes in fiscal policy put the country on a path to large and rising budget deficits (over and above what would have been expected given the cyclical weakness of the economy) and left the Federal Reserve little choice but to restrain the overheating economy by further tightening monetary policy.

The high real interest rates that resulted from the burgeoning deficits and tight money of the early 1980s were in large part responsible for skewing the composition of output away from fixed investment. Private fixed investment as a share of gross domestic product (GDP) fell from over 18 percent in 1979 to under 15 percent by 1989 (to compare 2 years when the economy was operating close to capacity). The relative decline in private fixed investment net of depreciation was even sharper, from about 8 percent to about 5 percent of GDP. At the same time, personal consumption expenditures increased as a share of GDP from 62 percent in 1979 to 66 percent in 1989. The effects on investment of the increase in the budget deficit likely would have been somewhat less marked if private saving over this period had risen so as to offset the decline in public saving. But instead both personal and business saving as a share of GDP fell over the 1980s, exacerbating the effects of deficits on interest rates and thus on investment.

High real interest rates during the early 1980s also contributed to a sharp rise in the value of the dollar as foreign investors, attracted by high yields, bought dollar-denominated assets. The appreciation of the dollar in turn caused a rapid swing of the current account balance into substantial deficit. Growing current account deficits quickly transformed the United States from the world's largest creditor country into the world's largest debtor by the late 1980s. Although access to foreign capital moderated the rise in interest rates and the decline in investment, the resulting buildup in our international indebtedness required that a portion of the economy's output be used to service the foreign debt. In addition, the appreciation of the dollar, combined with the decline in investment's share of output, had strong adverse effects on U.S. international competitiveness.

Today, with this Administration committed to eliminating the budget deficit—and with substantial deficit reduction already achieved over the past 3 years—the environment is vastly different from that of the 1980s. The imbalances that resulted from the fiscal extremism of that decade can now be corrected. In contrast with earlier policies that raised interest rates, restrained investment, and impeded our international competitiveness, our progress in reducing the budget deficit has lowered interest rates, increased investment, and improved our competitiveness. As discussed later in this chapter, further deficit reduction over the next several years quite possibly will require monetary policy once again to stabilize short-run movements in the economy, this time to prevent a tightening fiscal stance from pushing the economy's growth rate below its potential. Such an accommodative stance of monetary policy should, in concert with deficit reduction, further enhance the climate for private investment and ensure that the economy remains on a healthier growth path over the long term.

OVERVIEW OF 1995:
RETURNING TO POTENTIAL GROWTH

Economic growth decelerated considerably in the first half of 1995 before regaining momentum in the third quarter. Some moderation in growth was anticipated because the robust expansion of the preceding 2 years had greatly reduced the slack in the economy. Between January 1993 and December 1994, the civilian unemployment rate fell from 7.1 to 5.4 percent, and capacity utilization in the industrial sector rose from 81.3 to 85.1 percent. Even after accounting for the economy's tightening capacity constraints, however, the moderation in growth was greater than expected. Following the rebound in the third quarter, evidence suggested that the economy was once again growing at its potential rate. This moderate pace of growth was fully reflected in the path of the unemployment rate, which, after falling by more than a percentage point over the course of 1994, remained virtually unchanged during 1995.

The moderate growth and reduced pace of job creation during 1995 were evidence that the economy had entered a new phase: it had moved from recovery following the 1990–91 recession to sustained growth. Thus, with the economy operating near full capacity by late 1994, significantly higher growth in the short term probably could not have been accommodated without a rise in inflation. The increase in short-term interest rates over the course of 1994 and early 1995 represented an attempt to restrain demand pressures and hold growth close to its long-run potential.

EXPLAINING THE MODERATION IN GROWTH DURING THE FIRST HALF OF 1995

The moderation in economic growth during the first half of 1995 was to a large degree the consequence of the rise in interest rates during 1994 and, to a lesser extent, the result of the crisis in Mexico that began in December 1994. Higher interest rates caused a weakening in interest-sensitive spending and an associated buildup in inventory that led producers to restrain output. The economic crisis in Mexico induced a sharp deterioration in the U.S.-Mexico trade balance, further moderating growth.

At the beginning of 1994, and increasingly over the course of the year, many observers believed that the slack in the economy that had emerged during the recession of 1990–91 had disappeared. As already noted, this led to concern that continued growth at anywhere near the heated pace of 1993 would lead to an increase in inflation. These concerns were evident in rising yields on long-maturity bonds beginning late in 1993 and continuing through most of 1994. The Federal Reserve responded by raising the Federal funds rate by 3 percentage points between February 1994 and February 1995.

Despite these rate increases, the economy continued to grow at a rapid pace through the end of 1994, while the unemployment rate dropped another three-quarters of a percentage point in the last half of the year. Housing starts, one of the more interest-sensitive indicators, did not peak until December 1994. Similarly, motor vehicle sales continued at a rapid pace through year's end, and, anticipating continued strength, automakers boosted production in the first quarter of 1995.

Higher interest rates did not affect economic growth until the beginning of 1995, and then their impact was reinforced by the economic crisis in Mexico. The slackening economy was evident as housing starts dropped in the first 3 months of the year. Although housing activity stabilized and then moved higher over the balance of 1995, the fall in starts translated into declines in residential investment during both the first and the second quarter. Motor vehicle sales also weakened, resulting in a buildup of inventory that reached uncomfortable levels by the end of the first quarter. In response, automakers cut production sharply in the second quarter, restraining GDP growth by almost 1 percentage point at an annual rate.

The magnitude of the moderation during the first half of the year seems clear in retrospect but was harder to read at the time. The advance estimate of first-quarter GDP showed a 2.1 percent (chain-weighted) annual rate of growth—a decline from the pace of 1994, but not a dramatic one. First-quarter growth was not revised down to its current estimate of a 0.6 percent annual rate until the benchmark revisions of January 1996. (Box 2–2 presents an overview of the recently released benchmark revisions of the national income and product accounts.) Although scattered indications of weakness, such as the declines in motor vehicle sales and housing starts, were beginning to accumulate early in the year, the first solid evidence was the May employment report (published in June), which showed the first substantial drop in payroll employment in over 3 years.

Partly as a result of the moderation in growth, interest rates fell steadily throughout the year. In response, the housing and automobile sectors retraced much of their decline during the second half of 1995. By the end of the third quarter, reduced automobile production and a pickup in sales had worked off much of the inventory overhang. Home sales and housing starts also had returned to stronger levels.

A review of economic performance sector by sector provides a more detailed picture of the economy as the expansion continued during 1995.

CONSUMPTION EXPENDITURES

During the first quarter of 1995, consumption expenditures grew by 0.8 percent at an annual rate, after averaging 3.0 percent during 1994. The drop in spending growth was concentrated in durable goods, which fell by nearly 9 percent at an annual rate, with weakening demand for automobiles fueling the decline. Higher interest rates, as discussed above, are likely to have been the primary reason for the retrenchment by consumers. Spending on durables recovered sharply in the second and third quarters, offsetting some weakening in spending on nondurable goods and pushing overall consumption growth back to a solid pace of about 3 percent at an annual rate for the second and third quarters of 1995.

As the year progressed, households continued to take on debt at a rapid rate, raising concerns that they might soon have to reduce their spending in order to meet debt obligations. Rising delinquency rates on consumer loans, especially credit card lending, suggested that an increasing number of households were encountering difficulties managing their debts. Household debt (consumer and mortgage debt) grew faster than disposable personal income, continuing the pattern of the past several years. The burden of this debt, as measured by debt service as a share of disposable personal income, also rose during the year, although it remained below the value reached during the late 1980s. The rise in the debt-service ratio during 1995 occurred despite a general decline in interest rates over the year, and reflected mainly the sharp rise in the overall debt level. As debt contracts are adjusted or renewed, however, the recent decline in interest rates should moderate the rise in debt service. Furthermore, consumption expenditures in the long term

Box 2-2.—The Comprehensive Revision of the National Income and Product Accounts

Early in 1996, the Bureau of Economic Analysis released new estimates of the national income and product accounts. These comprehensive revisions have been done about once every 5 years and incorporate definitional changes, statistical changes, and updated source data in an effort to portray the evolving U.S. economy more accurately. The latest revision incorporates three major improvements:

- Measures of real output and prices are estimated using "chained dollars," which more accurately account for the shifting mix of products purchased and sold in the economy (see *Economic Report of the President 1995* for a detailed discussion of chain-weighted GDP).
- Government investment is estimated separately from government consumption expenditures, allowing a more accurate description of government activities and improving the overall measurement of gross investment and national saving.
- Depreciation of fixed capital is estimated using a new methodology that better reflects the service lives of different types of assets.
- The revised estimates of real GDP show average annual growth of 3.2 percent over the period 1959 to 1994, 0.2 percentage point higher than had previously been reported using fixed (1987) weights. Between 1959 and 1987 growth averaged 3.4 percent per year, 0.3 percentage point higher than reported earlier, whereas between 1987 and 1994 it averaged 2.3 percent, 0.1 percentage point lower than reported earlier. Most of the change in growth rates for real GDP, as well as that of its components, is attributable to the shift from fixed weights to chain weights. Boxes 2-3 and 2-6 discuss other aspects of the revised data.

are related to overall net worth as well as to consumer indebtedness. Hence the stock market gain of over 30 percent during 1995 should help sustain consumer spending into 1996.

BUSINESS FIXED INVESTMENT

Business fixed investment grew solidly during the first three quarters of 1995. The growth rate of business equipment investment fell back only slightly from its torrid pace in 1994 and was sustained by rapid investment in computers, which grew even faster during the first three quarters of 1995 than in 1994. Investment in structures continued its recovery from the recession of 1990–91, and grew almost as fast as equipment investment in 1995 (Chart 2–1). The extremely slow recovery of structures investment following the recession appears to have been due in part to the oversupply of office buildings and retail space that characterized the runup and subsequent collapse of the real estate market during the late 1980s and early 1990s. The vacancy rate for office space has fallen for 3 years and is now at its lowest point in 8 years.

Chart 2-1   **Real Business Fixed Investment**
Investment in durable equipment and in structures continued to grow robustly in 1995.

Percent change from four quarters earlier

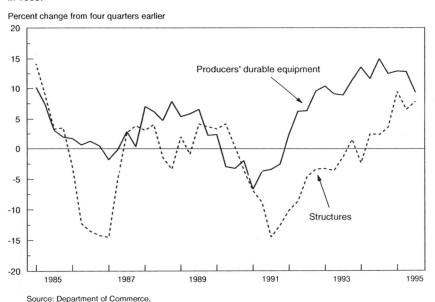

Source: Department of Commerce.

It has long been recognized that reported measures of gross investment for the U.S. economy understate actual gross investment because government investment in equipment and structures has always been treated in the same fashion as government consumption, with both reported together as government purchases. The recently revised national income and product accounts now report government investment separately from government consumption and thus provide a more complete view of investment in the economy (Box 2–3).

INVENTORIES

The buildup of excess inventories during the first quarter of 1995 led some producers to cut back output in the second quarter so as

Box 2–3.—New Measures of Government Investment

The Bureau of Economic Analysis now measures government expenditures for equipment and structures as investment, similar to the treatment of such expenditures by the private sector. Previously, government expenditures for fixed assets were considered to be "current account" purchases. This treatment understated gross investment and saving for the economy and ignored the service flow (or "output") of these assets over their lifetimes. The new approach is more consistent with international standards and will permit more accurate comparison of U.S. data with those of other countries.

The new treatment of government investment has three important effects. First, it increases the share of GDP accounted for by gross investment expenditures. Second, it reduces the government deficit measured on a current account basis and thus increases measured saving of the public sector. Because of these effects, gross domestic investment and national saving as a share of GDP each are reported about 3 percentage points higher compared with the earlier approach, to 18 percent and 15 percent, respectively, over the period 1970 to 1995. Finally, the new approach partly accounts for services provided by the government capital stock and thus raises the measured output of the government sector and the economy. For recent years, GDP is about 1.8 percent higher, due to the service flow of the government capital stock.

A rough way of measuring the importance of government investment is to compare it to total investment. Between 1959 and 1994, total government investment as a share of private nonresidential fixed investment plus government investment fluctuated between 20 and 40 percent, while government nondefense investment varied between 14 and 23 percent. Thus, even leaving aside investment for defense purposes, the earlier approach to measuring the economy's fixed investment misclassified a significant portion of spending aimed at augmenting and maintaining the Nation's productive capacity.

The new approach does not measure government investment in human capital or the environment. Investments in education or a cleaner environment are hard to measure, but also yield returns over time just as certain as those from investments in highways and office buildings.

to reduce inventories relative to sales. Producers continued to pare inventories, especially in the automotive sector, during the third quarter. By late in the year much of the earlier overhang had been worked off. By year's end, however, automobile industry data showed the inventory-to-sales ratio moving back up, although it remained below the levels reached earlier in the year.

RESIDENTIAL INVESTMENT

As alluded to above, a decline in residential investment during the first half of the year was a major factor in slowing the rate of economic growth. The rise in mortgage interest rates in 1994 had a lagged effect on the housing market, which began to lose its footing in early 1995 as housing starts and home sales both fell during the first quarter. Residential investment, which had shown hints of weakness toward the end of 1994, declined abruptly during the first half of 1995. By June, however, declining mortgage rates had revived the housing sector, as both starts and sales regained some ground. The improvement held firm over the summer and was reflected in a bounceback in residential investment during the third quarter.

NET EXPORTS

After declining during the last quarter of 1994, the net export deficit (imports minus exports of goods and services) rose sharply during the first half of 1995. The rise was due in part to the severe contraction of the Mexican economy that began at the end of 1994 following the peso crisis, and which resulted in a sharp fall in U.S. exports to Mexico. The U.S. merchandise trade balance with Mexico deteriorated from a surplus of about $1 billion in 1994 to a deficit over the first half of the year of about $8 billion.

By the latter part of the year, however, other factors, notably strong U.S. competitiveness and the lagged effects of earlier movements in exchange rates reestablished the trend toward a shrinking external deficit (see Chapter 8 for further discussion of exchange rates and the current account balance). By the third quarter, exports of goods and services were once again growing briskly, outpacing a slowing rate of growth for imports of goods and services. As a result, net exports contributed importantly to growth during the third quarter.

INFLATION

Inflation remained remarkably low and stable during 1995 (Table 2–1). The consumer price index (CPI) increased by 2.5 percent over the 12 months of 1995—down 0.2 percentage point from its year-earlier pace. Inflation as measured by the CPI has now run at less than 3 percent per year for the past 4 years, for the first time since the 1960s. This impressive record suggests that a regime change has taken place, whereby households and businesses have come to expect low inflation for the foreseeable future.

TABLE 2–1.—*Measures of Inflation*

Measure	1994	1995
	Percent change	
GDP chain-type price index	2.3	[1]2.7
Non-oil import prices	3.8	2.3
CPI-U:		
All items	2.7	2.5
All items less food and energy	2.6	3.0
PPI:		
Finished goods	1.7	2.2
Finished goods less food and energy	1.6	2.5
Intermediate materials less food and energy	5.2	3.1
Crude materials	−.5	4.1
Employment cost index:[2]		
Total compensation	3.3	2.6
Wages and salaries	2.9	2.8
Benefits	4.0	2.1

[1] Preliminary.
[2] For private industry workers.
Note.—Inflation as measured by the GDP price index and the employment cost index is computed from third quarter to third quarter; by non-oil import prices, from November to November; and by the CPI-U and PPI, from December to December.
Sources: Department of Commerce and Department of Labor.

The increase in the CPI during 1995 was held down by a decline in energy prices and a slowing in the rise of food prices, which increased almost a percentage point less than a year earlier. Core inflation, as measured by the CPI excluding food and energy, increased at a 3.0 percent annual rate over the 12 months of 1995, up 0.4 percentage point from the year-earlier rate. Inflation seemed to be proceeding at a faster pace during the first 5 months of the year but eased off thereafter. The early runup and the subsequent moderation largely reflected the pattern of used car prices, airfares, and automobile finance charges.

Hourly compensation in the private sector, as measured by the employment cost index, increased 2.6 percent in the year ending in the third quarter, versus a 3.3 percent increase during the year-earlier period. A slowdown in benefit costs—especially for health insurance and retirement programs—accounted for almost all of the deceleration. The increase in wages and salaries, in contrast, was little changed from its year-earlier pace. Overall, the evidence suggested an absence of any wage pressures as the expansion continued. The absence of significant acceleration in inflation, either for prices or for wages, especially as the unemployment rate remained around 5.6 percent for the year, led some observers to suggest that the unemployment rate consistent with stable inflation had fallen (Box 2–4). A possible decline in the sustainable unemployment rate raises important challenges for macroeconomic policymaking (Box 2–5).

Box 2–4.—Has the Sustainable Rate of Unemployment Fallen?

As the economic expansion continued during 1995, and unemployment remained well below 6 percent without sparking a rise in inflation, some economists suggested that the minimum sustainable unemployment rate or so-called NAIRU (Non-Accelerating-Inflation Rate of Unemployment) has declined.

During the 1980s, the core rate of inflation increased when the unemployment rate was below 6 percent and decreased when it was above 6 percent (Chart 2–2). In contrast, for over a year now the unemployment rate has fluctuated narrowly around 5.6 percent, yet the core rate of inflation has remained roughly stable rather than risen. (Wage inflation, as measured by the employment cost index, also has remained stable.) This recent evidence strongly argues that the sustainable rate of unemployment has fallen below 6 percent, perhaps to the range of 5.5 to 5.7 percent. The Administration's forecast falls on the conservative end of this range by projecting the unemployment rate at 5.7 percent over the near term.

Explanations for why the sustainable rate of unemployment may have fallen generally focus on structural changes in the U.S. economy that may have restrained increases in wages and prices. For example, increased domestic and international competition, a decline in unionization, and increased concern about job security are possible reasons why, at current levels of unemployment, wage and price pressures have been so subdued. In addition, since the sustainable unemployment rate is related to frictional unemployment, and since such job mobility is high among young workers, the recent fall in the labor-force share of young workers may have contributed to the possible decline in the sustainable rate, just as the increase in young workers during the 1970s contributed to its rise.

EMPLOYMENT AND PRODUCTIVITY

During 1995, the economy managed to create enough jobs not only to replace those lost as a result of corporate restructuring and downsizing, but also to provide employment for new entrants. As a result, the unemployment rate remained roughly constant.

A deceleration in the pace of job creation accompanied the economy's move from economic recovery to sustained economic expansion. Growth in payroll employment dropped to 146,000 per month

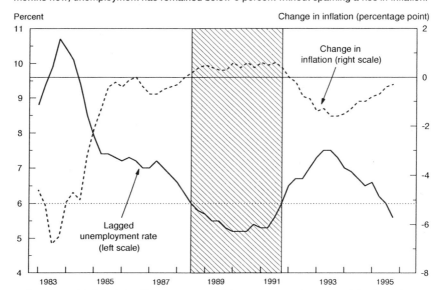

Chart 2-2 The Sustainable Rate of Unemployment in the 1980s
In the 1980s, inflation picked up when the unemployment rate fell below 6 percent. For over 17 months now, unemployment has remained below 6 percent without sparking a rise in inflation.

Note: Change in inflation is the difference between the eight-quarter percent change in the CPI excluding food and energy and its eight-quarter lagged value. Unemployment rate is lagged four quarters.
Sources: Department of Labor and Council of Economic Advisers.

in 1995—down from 294,000 per month a year earlier. Coming on the heels of a strong fourth quarter of 1994, job gains remained solid in the first quarter, slowed in the second, and then averaged 138,000 per month during the third and fourth quarters. The moderate pace of job growth in the second half is about what can be expected as the economy grows at its potential rate.

Official statistics show that 7.7 million jobs have been created since this Administration took office, but the best estimate is considerably stronger. Analysis of forthcoming revisions to estimates of payroll employment indicates that the job gains between March 1994 and March 1995 were stronger than currently estimated. As a result, after the revisions are announced this June, measured job growth through the end of 1995 should exceed 8 million. Over 50 percent of job growth in the private sector during 1995 occurred in "high wage" industries—those with an average wage above an employment-weighted median for all industries in 1993. For the past 3 years, the share of employment growth concentrated in these industries has continually risen.

The unemployment rate fluctuated in a narrow band around 5.6 percent during 1995, as increases in the number of jobs fully absorbed increases in the labor force. The growth rate of the labor force from 1994 to 1995 differed little from the growth rate of the population—a pattern that has persisted since 1989. Over this pe-

Box 2-5. Macroeconomic Policy and the Sustainable Unemployment Rate

A controversial issue in macroeconomic policy is whether the benefits from further reducing the unemployment rate when the economy is operating near full capacity outweigh the costs of possibly increasing the inflation rate. This controversy centers on how the sacrifice ratio (the change in unemployment associated with a given change in inflation) varies as inflation is reduced or increased. For example, in terms of output and unemployment, is the loss from reducing inflation by 1 percentage greater than the benefit from increasing inflation by 1 percentage?

The view that the unemployment rate must change by more when inflation is reduced than when it is increased, and the related view that a small increase in inflation may spark runaway inflation, have been used as a basis for cautious policy. For instance, some economists urge waiting until the evidence is overwhelming that the sustainable rate of unemployment has fallen before allowing an additional decline in the actual unemployment rate. The argument is that the cost of returning to the initial low rate of inflation if the sustainable rate has not changed vastly outweighs the benefit of learning whether it has in fact changed.

Much empirical work suggests, however, that for small changes, increases and decreases in inflation exhibit the same sacrifice ratio. And, small increases in inflation historically have not triggered runaway inflation. Thus, if policymakers reduced unemployment in the belief that the sustainable rate had fallen but were wrong and inflation increased, inflation is unlikely to "take off," and the cost of returning inflation to its earlier level would roughly equal the benefit of having temporarily lowered the unemployment rate. The gain, of course, if policymakers were right and the sustainable rate had fallen would be lower unemployment with unchanged inflation.

Furthermore, the sustainable rate itself is determined, in part, by institutional arrangements that result from the overall economic environment. As the economy gradually moves to lower inflation, arrangements that tend to amplify wage and price movements, such as cost-of-living clauses, become less common. In such an environment, gradual reductions in the unemployment rate that cause little change in inflation can actually reinforce market participants' views that the sustainable rate has fallen.

riod the labor force participation rate has remained virtually flat, in sharp contrast to rising participation rates during the 1970s and 1980s (Chart 2–3). Because the participation rate is cyclical, rising toward the end of an expansion, one might have expected the earlier trend to reassert itself as the current expansion matured. Instead, the stagnant participation rate has been one of the more enduring features of this expansion.

Chart 2-3 **Labor Force Participation Rates**
The overall participation rate has recently fallen below its trend rate of increase. A slower rise in the rate for women accounts for most of this break from trend.

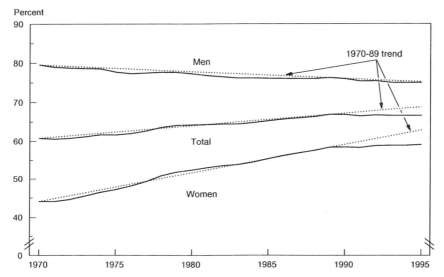

Note: Data refer to persons 16 years and over. Pre-1994 participation rates are corrected for effects of the revised Current Population Survey questionnaire.
Sources: Department of Labor and Council of Economic Advisers.

The stalling of the rise in the overall labor force participation rate is due mainly to a deceleration in the participation rate for women; the participation rate for men has fallen no faster than in earlier years. The flattening out of the female participation rate is probably the result of long-term demographic trends. As Chart 2–4 shows, the ratio of children per woman aged 20 to 54 fell between the late 1960s and the early 1980s, echoing the earlier pattern in the birth rate. The decline in this ratio allowed an increasing fraction of women to enter the labor force between the mid-1970s and mid-1980s, but its subsequent flattening in the late 1980s has limited further increases in participation.

While the increase in the overall labor force participation rate has slowed since the late 1980s, productivity growth appears to be little changed. Labor productivity has grown at an estimated 1.1 percent annual rate since the last business cycle peak in the second

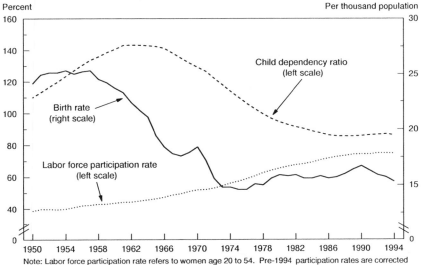

Percent   Per thousand population

Note: Labor force participation rate refers to women age 20 to 54. Pre-1994 participation rates are corrected for effects of the revised Current Population Survey questionnaire. The child dependency ratio is the ratio of children age 14 and under to the female civilian population age 20 to 54. The birth rate is the number of live births per thousand population.
Sources: Departments of Health and Human Services and Labor, and Council of Economic Advisers.

quarter of 1990, about the same as the trend rate during the entire post–1973 period (Chart 2–5). The figures discussed here are new estimates of productivity using the recently revised GDP data. See Box 2–6 for details about these estimates and Box 2–7 for a discussion of the relationship between productivity and real wages.

Table 2–2 shows the relative contributions of productivity and labor force growth to output growth, both over the past few decades and as projected for the next several years. In the past, the relative importance of these determinants of long-run growth have varied substantially across time periods. During the 1960–73 period, output growth was fueled by a rapid increase in both the working-age population and productivity. Productivity growth slowed dramatically after 1973, but was partially offset in the mid- and late 1970s by an increasing rate of labor force participation. From 1981 to 1995, the growth rate of the working-age population slowed dramatically, but was countered by stabilization in the length of the workweek and other factors. The Administration forecast of 2.3 percent average GDP growth for the next 7 years reflects projections of 1.2 percent average growth in productivity and 1.1 percent average growth in the labor force. Measured productivity is expected to grow a bit faster than in the recent past as further deficit reduction boosts investment, and planned adjustments to the CPI, which affect productivity measures, are implemented.

TABLE 2–2.—*Accounting for Growth in Real GDP, 1960–2002*

[Average annual percent change]

Item	1960 II to 1973 IV	1973 IV to 1981 III	1981 III to 1995 III	1995 III to 2002
1) Civilian noninstitutional population aged 16 and over	1.8	1.8	1.1	1.0
2) PLUS: Civilian labor force participation rate [1]	.2	.5	.3	.1
3) EQUALS: Civilian labor force [1]	2.0	2.4	1.4	1.1
4) PLUS: Civilian employment rate [1]	.0	–.4	.1	.0
5) EQUALS: Civilian employment [1]	2.0	2.0	1.5	1.1
6) PLUS: Nonfarm business employment as a share of civilian employment [1][2]	.1	.1	.1	.1
7) EQUALS: Nonfarm business employment	2.1	2.1	1.7	1.2
8) PLUS: Average weekly hours (nonfarm business sector)	–.5	–.7	.0	.0
9) EQUALS: Hours of all persons (nonfarm business)	1.6	1.3	1.6	1.2
10) PLUS: **Output per hour (productivity, nonfarm business)**	2.9	1.1	1.1	1.2
11) EQUALS: Nonfarm business output	4.5	2.5	2.8	2.4
12) LESS: Nonfarm business output as a share of real GDP [3]	–.3	.0	–.2	–.1
13) EQUALS: Real GDP	4.2	2.5	2.5	2.3

[1] Adjusted for 1994 revision of the Current Population Survey.

[2] Line 6 translates the civilian employment growth rate into the nonfarm business employment growth rate.

[3] Line 12 translates nonfarm business output back into output for all sectors (GDP), which includes the output of farms and general government.

Note.—Data may not sum to totals due to rounding.

Except for 1995, time periods are from business-cycle peak to business-cycle peak to avoid cyclical variation.

Sources: Council of Economic Advisers, Department of Commerce, and Department of Labor.

Chart 2-5 **Actual and Trend Labor Productivity**
Smoothed for cyclical fluctuations, labor productivity has grown at a steady
1.1 percent average annual rate since 1973.

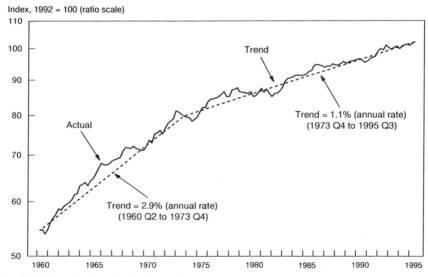

Index, 1992 = 100 (ratio scale)

Note: Data are for the nonfarm business sector.
Source: Provisional estimates calculated by the Council of Economic Advisers from data provided by the Departments of Commerce and Labor.

INCOMES

Income growth during the first three quarters of 1995 moderated a bit from its pace during 1994, reflecting mainly the deceleration in employment growth. Real disposable income increased at an annual rate of 2.4 percent for the first three quarters, just below the 2.6 percent rate over 1994. The slight decline from the year-earlier pace was due to a pause in income growth during the second quarter, which accompanied the overall moderation in economic growth.

Corporate profits increased in 1995, at about the same pace as 1994. The pattern over the year followed that of overall economic growth, with profits softening during the first half and rebounding strongly during the third quarter. Other components of national income likewise increased at more moderate rates during 1995, with the exception of rental income which declined through the third quarter.

MONETARY POLICY AND INTEREST RATES IN 1995

Monetary policy changed little during 1995. After raising the Federal funds rate by half a percentage point (to 6.0 percent) in February, the Federal Reserve held it constant until July, when it lowered the rate by a quarter of a percentage point. In late December, the Federal Reserve cut the rate another quarter percentage point, so that 1995 ended with the Federal funds rate at 5.5 percent, exactly where it had begun the year. In line with the relative

Box 2–7. Productivity and the Real Wage

Do employees benefit on average, either directly through an increase in compensation or indirectly through lower prices, from increases in their productivity? Conventional economic theory says that they should, at least over long periods. Historically, the evidence has borne this out. During the past few years, however, questions increasingly have been raised about whether the benefits of recent productivity gains have indeed gone to employees.

Some observers point out that hourly compensation (wages plus benefits) adjusted for changes in consumption prices has not kept pace with productivity in recent years. This "real consumption wage," however, is not the appropriate measure for assessing whether firms are remunerating employees for increases in productivity. Because firms hire an additional employee only if the cost of doing so is less than or equal to the value of that employee's output, a more appropriate measure to compare with productivity is compensation adjusted for output prices. This "real product wage" has tracked productivity in recent years (Chart 2–6).

The real consumption wage has risen recently by less than the real product wage because prices for goods and services that employees consume have risen by more than prices for goods and services they produce. A large part of this divergence likely is due to computer prices, which have fallen relative to most other prices. Because spending on computers represents a smaller share of personal consumption expenditures than computer production does of aggregate output, the decline in their price has restrained output prices by more than it has consumption prices.

Although the divergence between consumption and output prices explains much of the gap between productivity and the real consumption wage, pre-benchmark data also had shown a small gap between productivity and the real product wage. The new GDP data eliminate this gap.

Employees, of course, care more about the purchasing power of their wages (the real consumption wage) than about any "wage-productivity gap." And the stagnation of wages over the past two decades, particularly for the lower part of the income distribution, is cause for concern. Ultimately, however, the only way in the long run to raise real wages is to raise productivity.

Chart 2-6 Measures of Real Compensation and Labor Productivity
The real product wage has kept pace with productivity, whereas the real
consumption wage has not.

Index, 1979=100

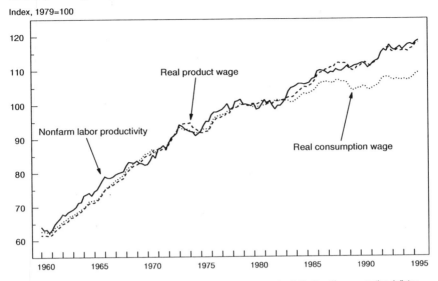

Note: Wages are compensation per hour in the nonfarm business sector divided by the consumption deflator
for the real consumption wage and by the nonfarm business deflator for the real product wage.
Sources: Departments of Commerce and Labor, and Council of Economic Advisers.

constancy of the Federal funds rate, other short-term interest rates declined only modestly during 1995, with the rate on 3-month Treasury bills dropping just half a percentage point compared with the end of 1994.

In contrast, longer term rates declined sharply over the course of the year. At the end of 1995, yields on 30-year, 10-year, and 3-year Treasury securities had fallen more than 2 percentage points from their peaks in late 1994. As a consequence, the spread between long- and short-term interest rates narrowed sharply, and the yield curve (which plots rates of interest for debt of different maturities) was remarkably flat at the end of 1995 (Chart 2–7).

The flatness of the yield curve is consistent with several explanations. The most probable is that investors expect short-term interest rates, including the Federal funds rate, to decline further. Certainly, evidence from the futures market for Federal funds supports this hypothesis and suggests that, as of February 5, 1996, investors expected a decline in the Federal funds rate on the order of half a percentage point to occur by July 1996 (Chart 2–8).

An expected decline in short-term nominal interest rates could reflect an expected decline in real interest rates or an expected decline in future inflation, or both. Real short-term interest rates might be expected to decline because the tightening stance of fiscal policy (as the deficit is reduced) increases the probability that eco-

Chart 2-7   **The Yield Curve**
The yield curve flattened in 1995 as long-term interest rates declined by more
than short-term interest rates.

Percent

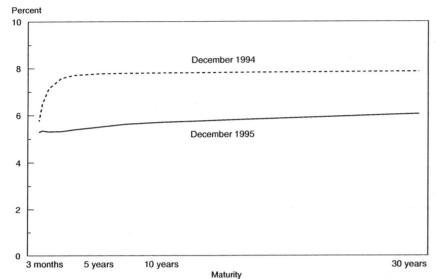

Note: Interest rates are yields on Treasury securities adjusted to constant maturities.
Source: Department of the Treasury.

Chart 2-8   **Federal Funds Rate**
The futures market for Federal funds anticipates a decline in the Federal
funds rate over the first half of 1996.

Percent per year

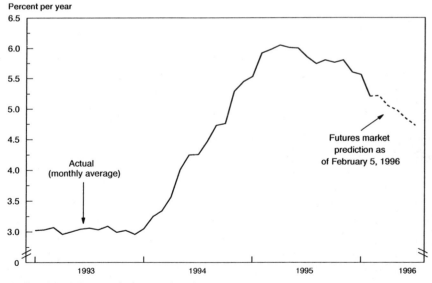

Note: February is average for first week of month.
Sources: Board of Governors of the Federal Reserve System and Chicago Board of Trade.

nomic growth will slow in the short run, and thus makes it more likely that the monetary authorities would have to lower real short-term interest rates to stabilize output. On the other hand, if output is not fully stabilized and falls below its potential, the rate of inflation should decrease. In this case, much of the expected decline in future nominal interest rates would reflect a drop in the expected premium for inflation.

The superb performance of the stock market—both the Dow industrial average and the broader S&P 500 index rose by more than 33 percent during 1995—seems to favor the view that *real* short-term interest rates are expected to fall. In general, equity prices should move positively with the current level and expected real growth rate of dividends, and inversely with the real rate of interest. Although dividend growth was very strong over the year, these gains probably were not sufficient, even with an associated permanent shift upward in the level of expected future real dividends, to explain the phenomenal gains in stock prices during 1995. More likely, investors anticipated that a decline in real short-term interest rates would be forthcoming.

FISCAL POLICY IN 1995

The budget deficit for fiscal 1995 was $164 billion, substantially below estimates made earlier in the year. The budget deficit has now declined for 3 years in a row, for the first time since the 1940s. Were it not for the interest payments on debt accumulated during past Administrations, the budget last year would have been in surplus (see Chart 2–9). The sharp decline in the budget deficit has slowed the rise in the national debt sufficiently that the ratio of the national debt to GDP has remained roughly constant for the past 2 fiscal years.

Part of the improvement in the deficit is likely to be associated with the state of the business cycle. Tax revenues relative to expenditures tend to rise during an expansion and fall during a recession. To assess changes in fiscal policy, economists adjust the budget deficit (or surplus) for economic conditions. On this basis, the Administration's progress in reducing the deficit also was evident during 1995, as the cyclically adjusted, or structural, budget deficit continued to decline (Chart 2–10).

The progress in reducing the deficit was made possible by the Omnibus Budget Reconciliation Act of 1993, which cut constant-dollar government purchases of goods and services over the past 2 years. Furthermore, as part of the ongoing efforts of this Administration to downsize government, the Federal workforce has been reduced substantially. Between January 1993 and November 1995, Federal civilian employment (excluding the Postal Service) has declined by about 215,000, leaving the Federal workforce smaller

Chart 2-9 Federal Budget Receipts and Non-Interest Outlays
The Federal budget excluding net interest payments was in surplus last fiscal year.

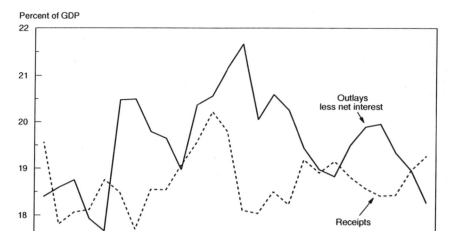

Note: The GDP measure used is pre-January 1996 benchmark revision.
Source: Office of Management and Budget.

Chart 2-10 Federal Budget Deficit
As the Federal budget deficit has declined over the past 3 years, the deficit adjusted
for the business cycle--the so-called structural deficit--also has fallen.

Note: The GDP measure used is pre-January 1996 benchmark revision.
Sources: Office of Management and Budget and Congressional Budget Office.

64

than at any time since the mid-1960s. Moreover, as the next few years unfold, the drop in employment should approach the target of 272,911 agreed to as part of the Federal Workforce Restructuring Act of 1994.

Two government shutdowns occurred late in the year and temporarily interrupted the disbursement of some Federal spending. Because most of this spending was restored once the shutdowns ended, the overall stance of fiscal policy was largely unaffected. However, the shutdowns did exact a significant budgetary cost and lowered real GDP growth by roughly 0.25 to 0.5 percentage point at an annual rate during the fourth quarter of 1995.

The Congress also failed to pass legislation acceptable to the Administration for an extended increase in the debt ceiling on Federal borrowing authority, forcing the Secretary of the Treasury to take extraordinary actions to ensure that the United States did not default for the first time in its history. As this *Report* went to press, the Congressional leadership had made a commitment in a letter to the President to pass a mutually acceptable debt limit increase by February 29. Passage of a straightforward long-term extension of the debt ceiling still is required to avoid a potential future default.

WHAT CAUSES ECONOMIC EXPANSIONS TO END?

The current economic expansion began in March 1991 and, as of February 1996, had run for 59 months, a little longer than the 50-month average for expansions since the end of World War II and the third-longest of the 10 postwar expansions (Chart 2–11). As the expansion continued past the postwar average, some reports pointed to its age and raised the possibility that it might soon falter, with the economy dipping into recession. Expansions, however, do not end simply because they have somehow reached the end of their "normal" life span. Rather, expansions end because of changes in economic conditions or policies.

The length of postwar economic expansions has varied substantially, with the shortest one, in 1980–81, lasting only 12 months and the longest, that of 1961–69, 106 months. Such large differences make the average length of expansions a relatively uninformative guide to the life expectancy of the current expansion (Box 2–8). A far better way to judge whether the expansion is about to end is to assess whether the economic symptoms that often precede a downturn—rising inflation, rising interest rates, financial imbalances, banking sector troubles, or an inventory overhang—have begun to appear, and if so, whether monetary or fiscal policies could successfully offset these symptoms. In the early 1960s, for example, the Kennedy and Johnson Administrations ju-

Chart 2-11 **Length of Economic Expansions**
The current expansion has run for 59 months, slightly longer than the average postwar expansion.

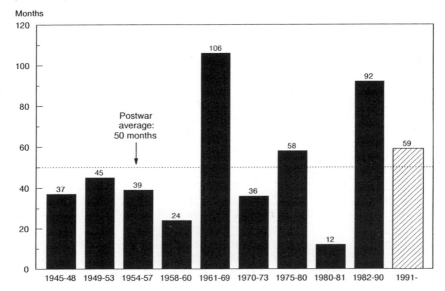

Sources: National Bureau of Economic Research and Council of Economic Advisers.

diciously applied tax policy as a tool of aggregate demand management to abort an impending downturn.

Box 2–8.—Duration Analysis of Business Cycles

Economists have used statistical methods to determine whether the end of an expansion or a recession becomes more likely the longer it goes on. Most findings show that, for business cycles since World War II, expansions are not significantly more likely to end simply because they get older, whereas recessions are (Chart 2–12). Although this difference between expansions and recessions is consistent with several explanations, the most likely reason is that policymakers since World War II have more actively engaged in countercyclical monetary and fiscal policies. With policymakers attempting to sustain expansions, events that precipitate downturns—such as oil price shocks or policy mistakes—are as likely to occur early as late in an expansion, so the length of an expansion does not affect the chance that it will soon end. On the other hand, if the pressure on policymakers to stimulate the economy grows stronger the longer a recession persists, then a recession that has lasted a while will be more likely to end in the next month than a recession that has just begun.

Chart 2-12 **Probability that an Expansion or a Contraction Will End**
The longer a contraction lasts, the higher the probability that it will end in the next month.
This is not true for expansions--they do not exhibit "duration dependence."

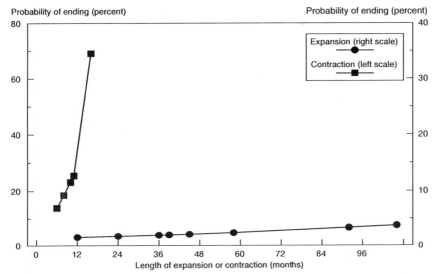

Note: Each data point represents one or more post-World War II expansions or contractions.
Sources: Diebold, F., G. Rudebusch, and D. Sichel (1993), "Further Evidence on Business-Cycle Duration Dependence," in Stock, J. and M. Watson, eds., NBER Studies in Business Cycles, vol. 28, University of Chicago Press; National Bureau of Economic Research; and Council of Economic Advisers.

ECONOMIC SYMPTOMS PRECEDING A DOWNTURN

The onset of most recessions since World War II has followed a sustained increase in the core rate of inflation (Chart 2–13). The rise in inflation sometimes has been precipitated by external events—such as foreign crises that have raised oil prices—and sometimes has resulted from overly stimulative fiscal or monetary policies. In the case of a foreign price shock, core inflation may rise if the foreign price increase gets incorporated into the process of setting domestic wages and prices. In the case of overly stimulative policies, core inflation may rise if the economy is pushed to operate at a level above full capacity (the unemployment rate is forced below its sustainable level).

A common pattern is that a sustained increase in the core rate of inflation eventually triggers an increase in short-term interest rates. In general, a greater ongoing acceleration of prices can lead to a sharper subsequent downturn. For example, during the late 1970s, although the Federal Reserve had begun to tighten policy just prior to the pickup in core inflation, the bulk of its tightening came only as inflation was rising rapidly. As a result, the subsequent tightening was much greater than it might have been if tightening had started somewhat earlier. Accordingly, one of the most important factors in assessing the chance that an expansion will end is the recent evidence on the core rate of inflation.

Chart 2-13 **Changes in Core Inflation**

A sustained rise in core inflation has preceded most postwar recessions.

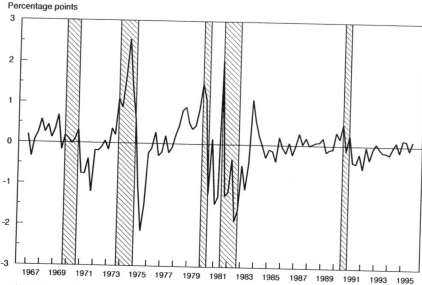

Percentage points

Note: Data are differences in four-quarter percent changes in the CPI less food and energy. Shaded areas denote recessions.
Sources: Department of Labor and Council of Economic Advisers.

After trending downward from its recent peak in 1990, core infla-tion has been low and stable over the past 2 years (Chart 2–14). In addition, during 1995 interest rates fell, especially during the last part of the year. As they did so, the interest-sensitive housing and automobile sectors recovered from their slackening earlier in the year. Thus, with inflation stable and interest rates likely to de-cline further, the evidence strongly supports continuing economic expansion.

The 1990–91 recession, however, did not follow the typical pat-tern of rising interest rates preceding a downturn (although it did follow the pattern of a prior increase in core inflation). When that downturn arrived, some short-term interest rates had been falling for a full year. But a distinguishing feature of the period preceding that recession was the weakened condition of financial institutions, especially savings and loan associations and banks. Unlike in the late 1980s and early 1990s, when savings and loan associations and many banks were in financial difficulty due in part to the col-lapse of an overheated real estate market, banks today are on a more stable footing. The better financial situation of the banks sug-gests that the system should be able to adapt more easily today to any adverse shift in interest rates or real estate values, thereby limiting the consequences for the overall economy.

Chart 2-14 **Core Inflation Rate**
Core inflation has remained low and roughly stable for the past 3 years.

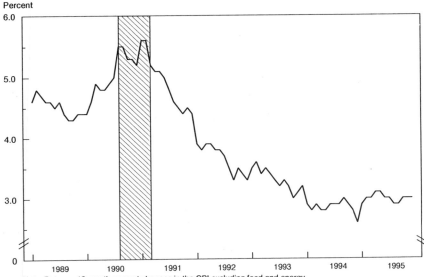

Note: Data are 12-month percent changes in the CPI excluding food and energy.
Shaded area denotes recession.
Source: Department of Labor.

Finally, a sharp rise in inventories can often signal that spending has unexpectedly fallen, and can lead firms to cut production, possibly precipitating a recession. After a buildup of inventory during the early part of last year, the subsequent moderation in production helped to reduce the overhang. As a result, inventories presently are at more manageable levels.

SHORT-RUN MACROECONOMIC EFFECTS OF REDUCING THE BUDGET DEFICIT

As the budget moves toward balance over the next 7 years, two factors will help to ensure that deficit reduction sustains economic growth in the short run. First, a forward-looking response of financial markets to deficit reduction can accelerate the decline in real long-term interest rates, bringing forward the investment dividend associated with balancing the budget. Second, an accommodative monetary policy can validate the market's response and reinforce its positive effects on short-run growth. But such a response by financial markets that is backed-up by monetary policy ultimately depends on the credibility of the deficit reduction itself.

The Response of Financial Markets

Cutting the deficit reduces the government's claim on the output of the economy, either directly through lower purchases of goods and services or indirectly through reduced transfer payments, freeing up resources for use by the private sector. Thus, the critical question for the outlook is whether or not spending by the private sector will rise and take advantage of the newly available resources, thereby sustaining growth in the short term. The answer depends largely on whether financial markets adjust sufficiently in response to deficit reduction so as to support the level of aggregate spending.

Adjustments in financial markets can stimulate spending in the economy in two major ways. First, deficit reduction raises private investment spending, primarily through a decline in real long-term interest rates, that is, long-term interest rates adjusted for expectations of future inflation. Second, deficit reduction spurs international competitiveness, leading to an improvement in the current account balance. Part of this improvement comes through expansion of exports to our trading partners and part comes through shifts by consumers and businesses away from imports and toward more competitive U.S. products. How much of the stimulus comes through investment and how much through net exports depends on the response of interest rates and interactions between interest rates and exchange rates. In the end, however, the stimulus will depend largely on the magnitude and timing of the decline in real long-term interest rates.

Some increase in spending could occur purely as a result of a fall in nominal interest rates that reflects entirely a drop in expectations about future inflation, leaving real rates unchanged. This might happen, for example, if qualifying standards for access to mortgage credit are specified in nominal terms, so that a decline in nominal interest rates allows more individuals or businesses to borrow even though real interest rates have not declined. Overall, though, a rise in aggregate spending due to this effect is likely to be far less important than the rise in spending accompanying a drop in real interest rates.

Deficit reduction can lower real long-term interest rates through three channels. First, a shrinking deficit directly lowers real long-term interest rates through a "portfolio" channel, as reduced government borrowing over time lowers the supply of government bonds relative to other assets. Second, a shrinking deficit lowers real long-term interest rates through an "aggregate demand" channel, as the shift to a contractionary fiscal policy weakens aggregate spending and money demand. Third, a shrinking deficit lowers real long-term interest rates through a "term-structure" channel. More prudent fiscal policy diminishes the likelihood that monetary policy in the future may have to restrain an overheating economy and lowers expected real short-term interest rates. Since long-term interest rates depend on the current and expected future levels of short-term rates, an expected decline in future short-term rates will be reflected in a decline in long-term rates.

The Importance of Forward-Looking Expectations

When market participants are forward-looking and anticipate (correctly) that the monetary authority will accommodate future credible deficit reduction, real long-term interest rates fall by more than when market participants either do not view future deficit reduction as credible or believe that monetary accommodation will not be forthcoming. To understand why credible deficit reduction accompanied by appropriate monetary accommodation leads to greater declines in long-term interest rates, we have to understand the relationship between short-term and long-term interest rates. Market participants investing their funds for say, 10 years, have a choice of buying a 10-year bond, or buying a 1-year bond, and rolling it over next year into another 1-year bond, and so forth. Adjusting for the differences in risk, the two investment strategies should yield the same return. In the absence of risk, this would mean that the long rate would simply equal the average of expected short rates over the 10-year period.

Deficit reduction that is viewed as credible and likely to be accompanied by future monetary accommodation leads investors to expect a future decline in short-term rates. Because long-term bonds must yield the same return (up to a risk premium) as a series of successive short-term bonds, long-term rates also will decline, typically by more than current short-term rates. In addition, credible deficit reduction that is accompanied by a more stable and certain fiscal policy, could further lower real long-term interest rates through a reduction in the "risk premium." With investors more certain about the future, long-term investments become less risky and the premium paid on such investments falls. On the other hand, if market participants believe the deficit reduction is not credible, then they will not expect additional future declines in real short-term interest rates and the risk premium will not fall, so that the decline in current real long-term rates will be less. In this case, a larger drop in current short-term interest rates would be necessary to lead to a sufficient decline in long-term rates so as to sustain aggregate spending and ensure full employment.

The evidence over the past 3 years, which witnessed deficit reduction combined with economic recovery, shows that interest rate declines can more than offset the contractionary effects when market participants are forward looking. In particular, the decrease in long-term interest rates occurred in anticipation of the deficit reduction, and had the desired effects of stimulating investment—not only in offsetting the shift to a contractionary fiscal stance, but in supporting the economic recovery.

71

The success thus far of financial markets in ensuring that deficit reduction does not compromise near-term growth does not mean that appropriate monetary policy is unimportant. Monetary policy—which operates with long and variable lags—needs to anticipate both the pattern of deficit reduction and other events which affect the level of aggregate economic activity. If monetary policy, for instance, follows a rule and responds to increases in the unemployment rate above its sustainable level only after the increases have occurred, then paths of more rapid deficit reduction would be accompanied by higher average levels of unemployment. But with a pre-announced schedule of credible deficit reduction, the shifting fiscal stance could be incorporated into monetary policymaking, taking account of normal lags. And, with investors expecting future deficit reduction, the market does much of the work of accelerating the decline in interest rates, so that relatively little change may be required in monetary policy to sustain growth in the short run.

Analysis using macroeconometric model simulations confirm these patterns. In one simulation, with monetary policy following a feedback rule (but not fully offsetting the effects of deficit reduction on the output gap) and with investors perfectly anticipating future changes in interest rates, long-term interest rates fall much more quickly than short-term interest rates—mirroring the pattern observed during 1995. In another simulation, investors are not forward-looking and monetary policy fails to accommodate the effects of deficit reduction and instead holds constant the rate of increase in the money supply. Although market forces lead to a decline in short-term and long-term interest rates and an associated increase in investment, in this simulation the decline in rates is not sufficient to sustain the economy at full employment. The message from this analysis is that the combination of credible deficit reduction and a well-designed monetary policy that anticipates future deficit reduction can avoid potential contractionary effects on the economy.

FORECAST AND OUTLOOK

The economic expansion is forecast to continue throughout 1996, as the effects of recent declines in long-term rates boost spending. Over the 7-year forecast horizon, output is projected to track potential output and the rate of inflation is expected to remain roughly constant (Table 2–3).

Real GDP is projected to grow at its potential rate of 2.2 percent during 1996 (on a fourth-quarter-over-fourth-quarter basis), as investment in both the housing and the business sectors responds to lower interest rates and as consumption spending is supported by recent gains in stock market prices. Inflation, as measured by the

TABLE 2–3.—*Administration Forecast*

Item	Actual 1994	Actual 1995	1996	1997	1998	1999	2000	2001	2002
	Percent change, fourth quarter to fourth quarter								
Nominal GDP	5.9	¹4.1	5.1	5.1	5.1	5.1	5.1	5.1	5.1
Real GDP (chain-type)	3.5	¹1.5	2.2	2.3	2.3	2.3	2.3	2.3	2.3
GDP price index (chain-type)	2.3	¹2.5	2.8	2.7	2.7	2.7	2.7	2.7	2.7
Consumer price index (CPI-U)	2.6	2.7	3.1	2.9	2.8	2.8	2.8	2.8	2.8
	Calendar year average								
Unemployment rate (percent)	6.1	5.6	5.7	5.7	5.7	5.7	5.7	5.7	5.7
Interest rate, 91-day Treasury bills .... (percent)	4.3	5.5	4.9	4.5	4.3	4.2	4.0	4.0	4.0
Interest rate, 10-year Treasury notes (percent)	7.1	6.6	5.6	5.3	5.0	5.0	5.0	5.0	5.0
Nonfarm payroll employment (millions)	114.0	116.6	118.3	119.8	121.2	122.6	124.1	126.0	127.9

¹ Estimates.
Note.—The figures for 1994 and 1995 reflect the benchmark revisions to GDP announced in January 1996 and may differ from those used to prepare the Administration's 1997 budget.
Sources: Council of Economic Advisers, Department of Labor, Department of the Treasury, and Office of Management and Budget.

CPI, is expected to increase to 3.1 percent in 1996 from 2.7 percent in 1995, as food and energy prices, which had held down the overall rate of price increase last year, are expected to rise in line with overall inflation this year. The core rate of inflation is expected to remain roughly unchanged during 1996, consistent with our forecast that unemployment is likely to remain relatively unchanged, and that at current unemployment rates, pressures for increasing inflation are weak or nonexistent.

Although true inflation is expected to remain constant from 1996 onward, inflation as measured by the CPI is expected to edge lower as revised procedures gradually remove part of the upward biases in current CPI inflation figures. CPI inflation is likely to slow by 0.2 percentage point in 1997, when the Bureau of Labor Statistics (BLS) will implement procedures to correct for problems associated with bringing new stores into the survey sample. CPI inflation is expected to slow by another 0.1 percentage point in 1998, when the BLS updates the CPI market basket to reflect more recent data on expenditure patterns. As a result of these adjustments, CPI inflation is expected to fall from 3.1 percent in 1996 to 2.8 percent in 1998 and thereafter. Some of these CPI adjustments pass through to the GDP price index and, given the growth rate of nominal GDP, raise estimates of real GDP growth. Consequently, real GDP growth is projected to rise to 2.3 percent from 1997 onward.

The impetus from the decline in interest rates in the second half of 1995 is expected to keep aggregate demand growing at the economy's potential rate for 1996. Over the medium term, interest rates are expected to edge lower as projected reductions in the Federal deficit reduce demands on capital markets. The projected decline in interest rates is expected to sustain growth at its potential rate as deficit reduction further restrains Federal spending.

The unemployment rate is projected at 5.7 percent in the near term and is expected to remain at that level throughout the forecast period. Economic growth of 2.3 percent over the forecast horizon is expected to generate enough jobs to employ all the new entrants implied by the expected 1.1 percent annual growth rate of the labor force. This unemployment rate is also expected to be consistent with long-term stability of the inflation rate.

As always, the forecast has risks. A basic assumption is that monetary policy will be calibrated to offset the ongoing effects of fiscal contraction. Obviously, monetary policy may not achieve this goal. Monetary policy has long lags, and so the course of fiscal policy must be properly anticipated. But fiscal policy depends on budgetary and other policy decisions of the Congress, and at present future Congressional action remains uncertain, despite bipartisan consensus toward achieving a balanced budget.

In the short term, the economy may hit a pothole in the first quarter of 1996, resulting at least in part from the effects of the government shutdown and bad weather in the eastern United States during January. But even if this should come to pass, the economy is expected to rebound, and the growth rate over the four quarters of 1996 is likely to be unaffected. The economy also faces the risk that foreign economic growth may stall, reducing foreign demand for U.S. exports. Still, the U.S. economy's export performance in 1995, in the face of economic weakening in three of our major trading partners, was impressive. Increased exports to strengthening economies in Canada, Japan, and Mexico would help offset any losses elsewhere.

CONCLUSION

As the year 1995 ended, the economy was fundamentally sound. None of the imbalances that typically precede a recession were evident. All signs pointed to continued economic expansion at a sustainable pace. Unemployment was expected to stay low, the inflation rate was expected to remain low and stable, and business investment was expected to continue powering the economy as interest rates declined.

The economy during 1995 made the transition from economic recovery, during which growth was driven by removing slack from labor and capital markets, to a period where growth is and will continue to be determined by expansion of the economy's capacity. Although the transition to sustained growth was not entirely smooth, the economy rebounded smartly during the second half of 1995 from the earlier bump in the road and should continue to expand during 1996.

Perhaps the best news during the year was that inflation remained low and stable despite an unemployment rate that in the past was associated with rising inflation. The stability of inflation even as the unemployment rate was essentially unchanged at about 5.6 percent appears to signal a shift in the economic environment. The improved economic environment also was apparent in bond and stock markets, as long-term interest rates fell and stock prices soared, reflecting in part an outlook for inflation reminiscent of the early 1960s.

The bipartisan commitment to balance the budget over the next 7 years was the major macroeconomic policy event of the year, and represents a continuation of Administration efforts to redress the fiscal imbalance inherited from the past. As the deficit is further reduced, private investment should increase, helping to raise living standards. And, deficit reduction that is credible means that the decline in interest rates needed to sustain growth in the short run is likely to be forthcoming with only modest accommodation from monetary policy. A significant portion of the decline in long-term interest rates during 1995, particularly over the second half of the year, probably reflected investors' perception that credible further deficit reduction was on the horizon. The Administration's success in reducing the deficit over the last 3 years certainly demonstrates the firmness of its commitment to restoring balance to the Federal budget.

CHAPTER 3

Making Fiscal Policy Choices Within and Across Generations

THE ROLE OF GOVERNMENT in a modern market economy was discussed in Chapter 1. That discussion largely centered on what government should do. This chapter shifts the focus to how government should be financed. Although these decisions are interrelated, separating them permits more detailed analysis of each. In particular, this chapter examines the tradeoffs between equity and efficiency that are pervasive in government finance.

The primary means of obtaining resources to fund government activities is the tax system. Even if public goods and services are financed initially by debt, the costs of debt service in later years and the ultimate repayment of the debt are covered through taxes. Decisions regarding the design of tax systems incorporate compromises between the sometimes competing concerns of economic efficiency and equity, as well as reflect competition among entities seeking favorable treatment. The current U.S. tax system reflects these considerations in various ways both large (the proportion of revenue raised by various components of the tax system) and small (provisions affecting single industries).

Recently numerous policymakers and others have called for an overhaul of the tax system because the current system is complex and sometimes has inappropriate economic incentives. In thinking about major or minor reforms to the tax system, it is important to judge them on several criteria: equity, economic efficiency, revenue adequacy, and simplicity. One should also remember that the details of tax proposals can affect greatly the extent to which a reform would satisfy these criteria.

As if the fiscal policy environment facing today's policymakers were not challenging enough, demographic trends are likely to make future fiscal policy choices even more difficult. Today the United States has 3.3 workers for every retiree. Under reasonable projections, by 2030 that number is expected to fall to 2.0. This will have major implications for government transfer programs such as Social Security and Medicare. Private sector institutions may also come under stress from these large and largely predictable demographic changes. How the U.S. economy adjusts to these changes may be the single greatest economic challenge facing today's children as they grow older. The second part of this chapter examines the policy implications of these demographic changes.

THE STRUCTURE OF THE TAX SYSTEM

The Federal Government raises revenues from payroll taxes, individual and corporate income taxes, estate and gift taxes, and excise taxes on a wide range of commodities. Revenues from each component of the tax system are the product of established tax rates (e.g., cents per gallon, percentages of taxable income) applied to defined tax bases (e.g., gallons of gasoline, dollars of taxable income). In some cases, tax bases are easy to define, while in others (such as taxable income) the definitions can be quite lengthy and complex. Statutory rules and administrative interpretations affect the amounts raised, as do the levels of compliance.

For over 200 years, Americans have debated the appropriate base for taxation of individuals. Some have claimed that income is the most appropriate base, because it provides a measure of an individual's (or household's) ability to pay tax. Others have claimed that consumption is a more appropriate tax base, because it measures how much of the resources available to society are claimed (or consumed) by an individual or household. Economics generally cannot settle this debate over what is, at heart, a philosophical concern. However, economists can contribute to the debate by analyzing the consequences of choosing alternative tax bases. For instance, generally the broader the tax base, the lower the rate required to raise a given amount of revenue. Since income in any period equals consumption plus saving, a broad-based consumption tax is assessed on a smaller base than a comprehensive income tax. In effect, a consumption tax exempts saving from taxation, whereas an income tax does not. This means that to raise the same revenue, lower tax *rates* can be applied to an income base than to a consumption base. But this simple arithmetic ignores possible supply responses to different tax systems (e.g., changes in saving behavior or labor supply). Economic analysis can provide insight into the likely magnitudes of these responses, contributing further to the policy debate.

The Federal tax system (like most State and local systems) has evolved into a hybrid, incorporating elements of both a consumption tax and an income tax. Elements of consumption taxation are the various excise taxes and the favorable tax treatment provided to capital income under both the individual income tax (e.g., individual retirement arrangements, pensions, favorable treatment of capital gains income, favorable treatment of investment in owner-occupied housing) and some provisions of the corporate income tax (e.g., immediate expensing of certain investments and accelerated depreciation). These provisions either partly or completely exempt the normal returns to capital investments from tax, either directly through a low or zero tax rate on this income (as with capital gains income; Box 3–1), or by allowing a deduction of all or part of an investment from taxable income. Table 3–1 lists a number of consumption tax components of today's income tax (individual and corporate), along with the amount of tax expenditure associated with each. (A tax expenditure is the revenue loss due to preferential provisions of tax law, such as special exclusions, exemptions, deductions, credits, deferrals, or preferential tax rates. These revenue losses are measured against a comprehensive income tax base.) Taken together, these components mean that the existing tax system is part income tax, part consumption tax.

Contrary to what some have claimed, taxes collected at all levels of government—Federal, State, and local—have been a fairly constant proportion (between 26 and 30 percent) of gross domestic product (GDP) for the last 30 years, despite numerous major changes in the Federal and State tax structures. By this same measure, the United States ranks among the lowest taxed of the countries of the Organization for Economic Cooperation and Development (OECD) (Table 3–2).

Federal revenues as a fraction of GDP have not changed dramatically over the past few decades (mostly fluctuating between 17 and 20 percent). However, the same cannot be said for the composition of revenues. Three major changes in revenue composition are illustrated in Table 3–3: an increased reliance on payroll taxes (Social Security, Medicare, and unemployment insurance), a reduced reliance on the corporate income tax, and a reduced reliance on excise taxes. Increased payroll taxes reflect changes in the Social Security system as well as the creation of Medicare. The reduction in corporate tax revenues reflects both lower corporate income tax rates and, more important, a reduction in recent years in domestic corporate profits as a share of the economy, as business organizational structures and financing arrangements have evolved. Through this period, the significance of the individual income tax has ebbed and flowed without any discernible pattern. Over time, tax base and rate changes have combined to more or less maintain the relative importance of the individual income tax as a Federal revenue source.

The level of taxation is important, but so is the distribution of the tax burden among individuals of different incomes. The recent debate over the tax system reveals considerable confusion about the share of taxes borne by taxpayers at various income levels. The Office of Tax Analysis of the Treasury Department estimates that, in 1995, effective tax rates for households generally increased with family economic income, which is a broad measure of income (Box

Box 3–1.—Taxation of Capital Gains Income

A capital gain (or loss) is the difference between what a tax-payer sells an asset for and the purchase price. Under current law, capital gains income is favored compared with other forms of income, and especially other forms of capital income:

- Capital gains income for individuals is never taxed at more than 28 percent, whereas other income is taxed at rates up to 39.6 percent. This preferential rate provides those facing the highest marginal tax rate with a benefit equivalent to excluding 30 percent of the gain.

- Capital gains income is not taxed until the asset generating the gain is sold with the timing of the sale at the option of the owner. Other forms of income (e.g., labor and interest income) are taxed as earned. This feature provides two distinct advantages to capital gains income. First, for assets held many years, deferral of tax liability significantly reduces the tax burden on capital gains assets compared with assets that generate income taxed annually. Second, taxpayers can strategically time sales of assets with accumulated gains and choose to realize gains in a year when they face a temporarily low tax rate.

- Under the "step-up in basis at death" provision, the income tax liability on assets with accumulated gains is forgiven when the asset holder dies. Heirs claim a new tax basis for these assets: the fair market value at the time of the previous owner's death. Each year more than $25 billion in capital gains income escapes taxation permanently through this provision.

- Taxpayers may defer gains from the sale of one primary residence by purchasing another of greater value. Moreover, those age 55 and over may exclude up to $125,000 of gain on personal residences from taxation.

- The 1993 budget act contained a provision excluding half of the gains on equity investments in certain "small" businesses held at least 5 years.

The tax advantages enjoyed by capital gains income tend to benefit disproportionately those taxpayers with the highest incomes, who tend to have the largest asset holdings. The 1 percent of the population with the highest adjusted gross incomes report over half the total capital gains realized and Treasury Department estimates that for a recent year, about 12,000 taxpayers realized gains over $1 million.

TABLE 3–1.—*Selected Consumption Tax Elements of the Income Tax*

[Billions of dollars]

Consumption tax elements	Estimated tax expenditure at FY 1996 level
Expensing of:	
Small investments	1.1
Research and development costs	2.6
Timber-growing costs	0.4
Multiperiod agricultural production costs	0.1
Accelerated depreciation of:	
Nonresidential real property	4.4
Machinery and equipment	20.9
Exclusion of:	
Pension contributions and earnings (employer plans)	59.0
Interest on life insurance savings	11.2
Deduction of IRA contributions and deferral of earnings	6.4

Source: Office of Management and budget.

TABLE 3–2.—*Tax Share of GDP in Selected OECD Countries, 1994*

Country	Percent of GDP
Group of Seven	
United States	31.5
Japan	32.3
Germany	46.5
France	48.9
Italy	44.9
United Kingdom	36.4
Canada	42.2
Australia	32.9
Austria	47.5
Belgium	51.1
Denmark	60.0
Finland	53.1
Greece	35.4
Ireland	41.6
Netherlands	51.4
Norway	55.3
Portugal	45.7
Spain	39.0
Sweden	58.4

Source: Organization for Economic Cooperation and Development.

3–2). These data (shown in Table 3–4) indicate that the Federal tax system maintains some degree of progressivity. (A progressive tax system is one where the proportion of income paid in taxes rises with a person's income.) This overall progressivity reflects the fact that the more progressive elements in the tax system outweigh the effects of the less progressive elements. When State and local taxes are factored into the analysis, this overall progressivity is reduced but not eliminated.

The Federal tax system has become somewhat less progressive over the past few decades, as payroll taxes came to account for a greater proportion of overall revenues. But the tax changes made

81

TABLE 3–3.—*Composition of Federal Receipts*

[Percent of total receipts]

Fiscal year	Individual income taxes	Corporation income taxes	Social in- surance taxes and contribu- tions	Excise taxes	Other [1]
1950	39.9	26.5	11.0	19.1	3.4
1955	43.9	27.3	12.0	14.0	2.8
1960	44.0	23.2	15.9	12.6	4.2
1965	41.8	21.8	19.0	12.5	4.9
1970	46.9	17.0	23.0	8.1	4.9
1975	43.9	14.6	30.3	5.9	5.4
1980	47.2	12.5	30.5	4.7	5.1
1985	45.6	8.4	36.1	4.9	5.0
1990	45.3	9.1	36.9	3.4	5.4
1995 [2]	43.7	11.2	36.0	4.3	4.8

[1] Includes estate and gift taxes, customs duties and fees, and Federal Reserve earnings transferred to the Treasury.
[2] Estimate.
Note.—Detail may not add to 100 percent because of rounding.
Source: Office of Management and Budget.

Box 3–2.—Family Economic Income

The Treasury Department uses a broad measure of economic well-being, called family economic income, when performing distributional analyses on tax proposals. Family economic income combines the incomes and taxes of related family members who form a single economic unit. This fairly comprehensive measure of income starts with adjusted gross income as reported to the Internal Revenue Service and then adds an estimate of unreported income; deductions claimed for individual retirement account (IRA) and Keogh contributions; employer-provided fringe benefits such as health coverage; earnings on pensions, IRAs, Keoghs, and life insurance policies; tax-exempt interest; nontaxable cash transfer payments; and imputed rent on owner-occupied housing. Capital gains are computed on an accrual basis, with the inflation component removed (if possible). Inflation adjustments are also made to the incomes of borrowers and lenders.

---

in the 1990 and 1993 budget acts tended to increase progressivity, both in the income tax and overall.

Chart 3–1 shows Gini coefficients for the before-tax distribution of income in the United States and for the distribution after tax and transfer programs are included. (The Gini coefficient is a measure of income inequality, indicating the extent to which the actual income distribution differs from equal incomes for all. A coefficient of 0.0 indicates exactly equal incomes and a coefficient of 1.0 maximum income inequality.) The smaller Gini coefficient for after-tax incomes indicates that the Federal tax and transfer system acts to reduce income inequality. In general, the after-tax data tell a story

TABLE 3–4.—*Projected Effective Federal Tax Rates, 1996*

Family economic income class [1]	Effective tax rate [2]
0–$10,000	8.0
$10,000–$20,000	8.8
$20,000–$30,000	13.3
$30,000–$50,000	17.5
$50,000–$75,000	19.9
$75,000–$100,000	21.1
$100,000–$200,000	22.0
$200,000 and over	23.7
Total	20.1

[1] Family economic income (FEI) is defined as the sum of adjusted gross income, unreported income, IRA and Keogh deductions, nontaxable transfer payments, employer–provided fringe benefits, tax–exempt interest, inside build–up on tax–favored investments, imputed rental value of owner–occupied housing, and inflation–adjusted capital gains and losses accrued during the year. FEI aggregates the incomes for all family members.
[2] Effective tax rate equals total taxes divided by family economic income.
Note.—Estate and gift taxes and custom duties are excluded. It is assumed that: individual incomes taxes are borne by the people who pay them; corporate income taxes are borne by all owners of capital; excise taxes on purchases by individuals are borne by the purchaser and those on business purchases are borne by individuals in proportion to total consumption; and payroll taxes are assumed borne by employees.
Source: Department of the Treasury.

similar to the before-tax measures, with substantial increases in income inequality occurring in the 1980s.

Chart 3-1 **Gini Indexes for Before- and After-Tax Income of Households**
After-tax income inequality, as measured by the Gini index, is less than before-tax inequality. Both before- and after-tax incomes became more unequal in the 1980s.

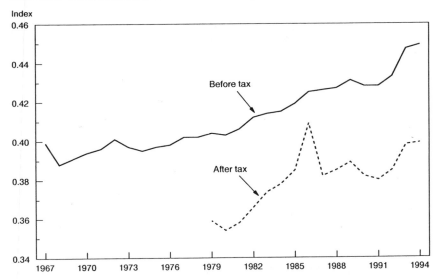

Note: Different methods are used in calculating the two Gini indexes shown. For details see Current Population Reports, Series P60-188. After-tax income is definition 14.
Source: Department of Commerce.

When considering the distributional consequences of government actions, it would be desirable to incorporate all aspects of the tax-and-transfer system. However, distributional analysis for some important government transfer programs (such as Medicare, Medicaid, Food Stamps, and others) and discretionary spending is not as completely developed as the analysis for the tax system. Steps to integrate both tax and transfer programs into the same distribution tables can, in principle, lead to more informed decisionmaking. In contrast, omitting tax components such as the earned income tax credit from a distributional analysis of a tax proposal may be misleading.

CHARACTERISTICS OF A WELL-DESIGNED TAX SYSTEM

Three main traits define a well-designed tax system: fairness, economic efficiency, and simplicity. As with almost everything else in government finance, design of a tax system requires tradeoffs among these desirable properties. Policymakers need to be aware how the various components of the existing tax system contribute toward meeting these objectives and how any potential reform of the tax system measures up.

FAIRNESS

Fairness is generally characterized as horizontal and vertical equity. Horizontal equity means similar tax treatment (i.e., tax payments of equal size) for similarly situated taxpayers. Economists generally view taxpayers as similarly situated when they have similar abilities and similar levels of human capital and financial wealth. However, economists may not agree about the type of adjustments necessary to reflect other personal circumstances (e.g., health status). Components of a tax system that do not meet the basic standards of horizontal equity will appear unfair.

Vertical equity is often associated with a progressive tax system. For the overall tax system to be progressive requires that at least some major revenue-raising components be progressive. The individual and corporate income taxes are generally judged to be the most progressive elements in the portfolio of taxes that make up the U.S. tax system. These elements more than offset the effects of the other, less progressive elements.

Horizontal and vertical equity can be thought of as objective, measurable indicators of fairness. But the *perceived* fairness (a less measurable indicator) of a tax system is also key to its acceptance by the public, which in turn is a very important determinant of the level of compliance.

EFFICIENCY

To be economically efficient, a tax system should not impede economic growth and should avoid excessive interference with private economic decisionmaking. In general, a tax characterized by a broad base and a low tax rate will cause less distortion of economic decisionmaking than one with a narrower base and higher rates that raises a similar amount of revenue. Minimal distortion means that competitive prices can better serve as reliable market signals, promoting an efficient allocation of resources and, hence, overall economic efficiency. These efficiency effects can be quite large and, if economic decisions affected by the tax are sensitive (elastic) to the tax rate, these distortions can be quite costly to the economy. A key issue in this regard is *how* sensitive various economic decisions are to contemplated changes in tax rates. For instance, many economists believe that the interest elasticity of saving is relatively low, so that reducing taxes on returns to a broad range of saving may not elicit much additional private saving. In fact, unless revenues are made up elsewhere, aggregate national saving may actually be reduced, as the increased Federal deficit (lower public sector saving) resulting from lower tax revenues more than offsets any increased private saving.

Correcting Market Failure. A tax system can also be used to address market failure: the under- or overprovision of goods by the private sector. For instance, a tax subsidy for research activities may offset the tendency for private organizations to undertake too little research because they cannot appropriate for themselves all the benefits of that activity. In the case of negative externalities, or spillover effects (e.g., pollution), a tax on the activities generating the externality may discourage them. It may be possible to design a revenue-neutral "tax swap" where, for example, revenues generated by a pollution tax can be used to reduce the rate of a distortionary tax elsewhere in the tax system. Judicious choice of the elements of such a tax swap can, in principle, enhance economic efficiency.

Direct Spending Versus Tax Expenditures. The government often has a choice of methods to promote activities considered desirable (e.g., because they yield positive externalities): it can do so either through the tax system (tax expenditures) or through direct spending programs. Two key issues in assessing the relative merits of these alternative approaches are *targeting* and *administrative costs*. The essential goal in targeting is "bang for the buck": how much extra stimulation of the desired activity can be accomplished per dollar of forgone tax revenue or dollar of direct expenditure. Some beneficiaries of either tax expenditures or direct expenditures would have undertaken the desired activity anyway, but claim the benefit nonetheless. This concern may be addressed in a direct

85

spending program by screening mechanisms to identify subsidized activities that would not have been undertaken without the subsidy. Of course, such mechanism requires administrative resources (e.g., the cost of obtaining the required information). However, direct spending programs are not always better at targeting. In some situations, the tax system may be more effective than spending programs at targeting subsidies, especially where income is a criterion for targeting.

Sometimes the administrative costs of providing incentives through the tax code can be lower than those for direct spending provisions. Because tax incentives piggyback on the existing structure of the tax system, the added administrative costs of providing an additional subsidy may be minimal. In contrast, spending programs may require a bureaucratic structure to deliver the subsidy, increasing administrative costs. For some cases, then, the savings in administrative costs associated with a tax subsidy can outweigh its somewhat inferior targeting, compared with a well-designed direct spending program. In other cases, however, the overall cost to the Internal Revenue Service of administering tax expenditure programs can be quite substantial. Moreover, the costs of tax administration for particular incentives may be hidden in the overall budget for the Internal Revenue Service. The administrative costs of direct spending programs, however, are explicitly accounted for.

The annual review process to which appropriated expenditures are subjected may be another advantage of direct spending programs over tax expenditures. This regular review is especially important in today's austere fiscal environment to ensure that obsolete programs do not remain on the books. Tax code provisions do not generally undergo annual scrutiny (although a handful routinely expire and must be renewed by the Congress). A determination that tax subsidies are desirable policy should be subject to the same criterion that spending programs are: do the society-wide benefits delivered exceed the social costs of the forgone revenues?

Corporate Subsidies and Loopholes. Subsidies can take the form of tax preferences or direct Federal payments, or more subtle forms such as import quotas that limit competition with domestically produced goods, below-market-rate sales or credits, or implicit government guarantees. Recently many observers have called for a reexamination of these subsidies, with an eye toward trimming those that lack adequate justification.

One strength of a market economy is that the incentives provided by prices and profits—not government subsidy—generally lead to the efficient supply of essential goods and services. The argument for government intervention must be predicated on the undersupply, absent government help, of valuable goods and services. Such is the case for many expenditures on research and technology development where large spillovers benefit other individuals and firms. Government support for research activity can offset a tendency for the private sector to underinvest in research. But other subsidies do not generate such spillover benefits and are much more difficult to justify on efficiency grounds.

Some might argue that government subsidies are necessary to prevent profits in an industry from falling below the normal rate of return, threatening the industry's existence. However, with or without subsidies, industries whose products are valued by consumers will survive. The only issue is their ultimate scale of operation and absent a significant market failure, such as associated with an externality, market prices provide appropriate signals for expansion or contraction. Market entry and competitive markets tend to ensure that private, risk-adjusted rates of return, taking into account all available government subsidies, are equated across activities through adjustments in prices and aggregate supply. Removing unwarranted subsidies would begin a process of exit from the industry, driving up the returns for those that remain until they reach competitive levels. In the end, ironically, because the value of government subsidies is likely to get capitalized in the value of scarce resources associated with an industry, the benefit of current subsidy payments may accrue not to the current subsidy recipient but to a previous owner of the scarce resource.

The bottom line is that unwarranted business subsidies lower economic efficiency. In contrast, subsidies that compensate for market failures, such as large positive spillovers, increase economic efficiency (as described in detail in Chapter 1).

Many business subsidies are hidden and receive scant attention from policymakers, in part because they do not show up in annual appropriations bills or on lists of tax expenditures, and because they confer relatively subtle benefits. However, hidden subsidies can be brought to light and undone in many ways. User fees can be set to cover the full costs of service provision. Auctions can be used to transfer resources to the private sector (e.g., portions of the electromagnetic spectrum). Other hidden subsidies could include below-market interest rates on government provision of credit to businesses and the implicit Federal guarantee provided to government-sponsored enterprises. Addressing these subsidies could increase overall economic efficiency (for instance, well-designed auctions would ensure that resources are allocated to those who can best use them), eliminate a source of unfairness, and raise substantial Federal revenues.

Other Efficiency Effects. Two other effects of the tax system contribute to economic efficiency: the provision of macroeconomic automatic stabilizers and the provision of a form of society-wide income insurance. Automatic stabilizers are mainly associated with the income tax components of the tax system (i.e., the individual and corporate income taxes). As the economy expands sharply, progressive tax rates ensure that individual income tax revenues grow even faster than the economy. Similarly, since corporate profits follow the business cycle, an economic expansion leads to increased corporate income tax revenues. These increased revenues exert a contractionary effect by lowering the Federal deficit (or increasing the surplus). The same effect happens in reverse when the economy slumps: tax revenues fall, widening the deficit (or reducing the surplus). The tax system thus helps stabilize the swings of the broader economy. Although any tax that raises additional revenue when incomes increase may function as an automatic stabilizer, progressive taxes are likely to be more effective automatic stabilizers than proportional or regressive taxes.

A progressive component of the tax system, such as the individual income tax, can also provide a form of income insurance in an economy where income fluctuations are unpredictable. This occurs because a progressive income tax can substantially reduce the variability of after-tax incomes without reducing average income very much. If incomes increase, in part because of an earner's good fortune, a progressive income tax system claims more than a proportional share of this increase. These additional revenues can be thought of as providing income insurance to those whose incomes are low, in part because of bad luck, by reducing their tax burden more than proportionally. The progressive rate structure of the income tax (including the earned income tax credit) accomplishes a significant amount of this income insurance.

This income insurance has the direct benefit of reducing the income risk borne by individuals themselves, shifting it to society as a whole, but it also provides an indirect benefit. Because households will be willing to bear more risk if they have access to income insurance, they will undertake investments (in both financial and human capital, including increased labor mobility) with greater risk and greater expected return. Aggregated over all individuals, the effect of undertaking such investments is a higher expected national income. Private markets will not offer such income insurance because the inherent difficulty of separating effort and luck from an individual's ability subjects private purveyors to adverse selection: those who expect poor outcomes would be more likely to purchase the insurance. The income tax system, in contrast, applies to virtually all economically active people, mitigating concerns with adverse selection.

SIMPLICITY

The third element of a desirable tax system is simplicity, as measured both by the cost of compliance to taxpayers and by the administrative cost to the government. Recent studies have suggested high costs of compliance (e.g., one study reports total compliance and administrative costs of around $75 billion, or around 6 percent of revenues). These estimates may be overstated, however, because it is difficult for taxpayers (especially businesses, for which the costs may be especially high) to separate out tax compliance costs from accounting and business planning costs they would incur anyway. However, even if true compliance costs (those above costs incurred for ordinary business reasons) are only half those reported, the concern is well-founded, because resources used to comply with the tax system do not increase output but are simply the costs associated with transferring resources from one party to another. A well-designed tax system attempts to minimize the sum of administrative and compliance costs, subject, of course, to the system attaining the other objectives.

ASSESSING THE CURRENT TAX SYSTEM

With respect to horizontal equity, the current U.S. tax system has some shortcomings. Different types of income are taxed differently, the composition of a household or family can affect its tax liability but not its ability to pay tax, and some forms of consumption are favored over others. Many of these departures from horizontal equity result from decisions by the Congress and partly reflect the difficulty in determining whether individuals are truly in "similar" positions in terms of ability to pay taxes.

Evaluating the current system in terms of vertical equity is more difficult, because economic reasoning provides no objective guide to what the degree of progressivity should be. We do know that the current tax system is progressive and that the tax-and-transfer system accomplishes a significant amount of redistribution. But observers disagree about whether the overall system exhibits an appropriate degree of progressivity.

Survey data provide one way to analyze the perceived fairness of the tax system. Public opinion polls often find that a substantial portion of Americans view their tax system as unfair. This may reflect the concern that others are able to exploit loopholes and avoidance mechanisms to reduce their tax payments. Whatever their origin, these feelings that the tax system is unfair have attracted the attention of policymakers and tax administrators. One concern is that, absent corrective action, these perceived inequities could lead to erosion of the present level of compliance.

Concerns with efficiency often focus on the possible adverse incentive effects of high marginal tax rates. Some advocates of the reforms that lowered the highest individual marginal tax rates in 1981 and 1986 argued that they would unleash supply-side responses that would lift the economy to new heights and, as a result, would raise rather than lower overall tax revenues. The evidence does not support these claims. Far from raising total tax revenues, the tax reductions of 1981 were followed by reduced individual and corporate income tax revenues as a share of GDP. Even though payroll taxes were increased, this led to the first huge peacetime budget deficits in the United States. These deficits crowded out private investment and led to the fiscal morass from which we are now just emerging. Moreover, the statistical evidence shows no significant break in the pace of productivity increases or labor force participation rates with either the 1981 or the 1986 tax changes. Whatever can be said for these tax changes, it cannot be claimed that they had marked effects on economic growth.

The minor effects of these tax rate reductions on labor supply are consistent with other evidence. Conventional estimates suggest that primary earners in a household generally change their behavior very little in response to relatively small changes in tax rates. The response of secondary earners is generally found to be larger. However, since secondary earners work fewer hours than primary earners, the overall labor supply response to a change in marginal tax rates is often quite limited. Similarly, conventional estimates of the response of saving behavior to changes in after-tax rates of return suggest that changes in individual income tax rates should not have a major effect on our low national saving rate.

Since 1986, marginal rates for individuals with the very highest incomes have been raised modestly in order to reduce the Federal deficit. Some have claimed that these rate increases (e.g., in 1993) would do severe harm to the economy by creating a disincentive for individuals to work and save. Again, these forecasts turned out to be false, just as did the earlier, supply-side forecasts of rapid economic growth from tax reductions.

Some critics claim that increases in marginal tax rates fail to raise the predicted revenues. One recent study estimated that the rate increases on high-income individuals in the 1993 budget act raised less than half the revenues predicted by the Treasury. But as Box 3–3 argues, subsequent analysis indicates that the 1993 provisions did raise the revenues predicted.

The current income tax system is often characterized as complex. A large part of the complexity results from eight decades of statutory and administrative modifications to address economic situations unforeseen when the income tax was originally enacted. Another part stems from tax initiatives intended to address important policy concerns. Policymakers should periodically review existing law to determine which provisions have outlived their usefulness and which can be streamlined or otherwise simplified. This Administration, as part of its National Performance Review and other efforts, has proposed several simplifications. One example is the pension simplification initiative announced in June 1995 and incorporated in the Administration's 1997 budget proposal. Other examples include simplified forms, greater use of electronic filing, and increased access to filing individual tax returns by telephone.

The Administration recognizes that the current tax system has some real and perceived problems. Some progress toward addressing them was made in the 1993 budget act. Further steps proposed in the budget for fiscal 1996 are described in Box 3–4.

EVALUATING REFORM PROPOSALS: THE FLAT TAX

Several proposals for a so-called flat tax have been offered over the past few years. In its most basic form, a flat tax applies a single tax rate on all business activities and individuals. This discussion focuses on the flat tax in its prototypical form, which may differ in some details from any particular legislative proposal.

The prototype flat tax is effectively a consumption tax—that is, a tax on wage income plus a tax on consumption from existing wealth at the time the tax is imposed. As such, a flat tax shares many of the benefits and shortcomings of other consumption taxes.

On the business side, all new investment could be immediately expensed under a flat tax, effectively exempting the normal returns to investment from tax. All types of business organizations would be subject to the flat tax: sole proprietorships, partnerships, and corporations. No deduction would be allowed for interest or dividends paid. Purchases from other businesses could be deducted, as could wage payments. However, the cost of fringe benefits (except for employer-provided pensions) would not be deductible.

For individuals, a flat tax would provide a standard deduction and some level of personal exemption for dependents. These amounts are intended to be large enough to exempt many households from tax. But few, if any, other deductions would be allowed. Moreover, individuals who run a business likely would have to file both a business and an individual return, with wage compensation from the business appearing as income on the individual return.

The prototypical flat tax would be less progressive than the current income tax. Its single tax rate would be set far below the highest marginal rate in the present individual income tax. Therefore, for the same amount of total revenue, it would raise less revenue from upper income households than the taxes it would replace (generally the individual and corporate income taxes). It follows that lower and middle-income households would see their taxes raised. If the earned income tax credit were repealed as part of the

91

Box 3–3.—Revenue Effects of the 1993 Tax Rate Increases

The Omnibus Budget Reconciliation Act of 1993 (OBRA93) raised income tax rates on higher income taxpayers. The marginal tax rate on couples with taxable income over $140,000 (over $115,000 for single taxpayers) was raised from 31 to 36 percent, and a 39.6 percent marginal rate was imposed on taxpayers with taxable incomes above $250,000. A taxable income of $140,000 roughly corresponds to an adjusted gross income of $200,000, so these rate increases apply to the 1.2 percent of the population with the highest incomes.

The Treasury Department predicted that these rate changes would raise $16 billion in the initial year. But some claim that revenues from these high-income taxpayers were as much as 50 percent smaller than predicted, as taxpayers reacted to the changes. The data generally do not support these claims and show that the revenues came in as predicted.

Analysts claiming substantial revenue shortfalls point to the difference between income growth among a "control group" not affected by the tax change and that of the affected group. This technique has several shortcomings. First, the Treasury Department estimates that taxpayers shifted at least $20 billion in income from early 1993 to late 1992 in anticipation of higher tax rates for 1993. This estimate is corroborated by data from the Bureau of Economic Analysis, which show a $20 billion spike in personal income in the fourth quarter of 1992. Such income shifting (which is to be expected when taxpayers can choose the timing of income receipts) is sufficient to explain the revenue shortfall claimed by critics of the OBRA93 tax increases. This is true even after accounting for another income shift: some wage and salary payments moved from 1994 to 1993 in response to a scheduled increase in the Medicare payroll tax.

Second, the incomes of taxpayers affected by the OBRA93 tax rate changes are notoriously hard to predict. Year-to-year income variations for those in the top 1 percent of the income distribution are large, because of the large share (over 50 percent in 1993) of nonwage income (interest, dividends, capital gains, and business income) in these taxpayers' total income. Predictions of income for this group on the basis of changes in a lower income control group's income are very imprecise.

Thus, although the marginal rate increases in OBRA93 may affect economic behavior over the longer term, the evidence to date suggests that they raised the revenues predicted.

Box 3-4.—Tax Proposals in the Middle Class Bill of Rights

The Administration's Middle Class Bill of Rights contains a three-part tax package: a tax credit of $500 per child, a tax deduction for postsecondary training and education, and an expansion of individual retirement accounts to all middle-class families. These proposals would encourage taxpayers to save and invest in themselves and their children.

The proposed child tax credit is meant to partly compensate for the failure of the personal exemption for dependent children to keep pace with inflation and income growth over the last 50 years. The $500 credit would apply to taxpayers with children under age 13 and would be nonrefundable (that is, it would not exceed the amount of tax otherwise due). It would be phased out for families with adjusted gross incomes (AGIs) between $60,000 and $75,000.

Taxpayers, their spouses, and dependents would be eligible for the proposed deduction for postsecondary training and education. When fully phased in, the measure would allow taxpayers to deduct up to $10,000 per year in qualifying educational expenses (generally those paid to institutions and programs eligible for Federal assistance). The deduction would be phased out for married couples with AGIs between $100,000 and $120,000.

The expanded IRA is intended to encourage households to save more. The proposal doubles the existing income limits on deductible IRAs for taxpayers with employer-provided pension coverage. IRA contributions up to $2,000 would be completely deductible for joint filers with AGIs below $80,000, with the amount deductible phased out for those with AGIs up to $100,000. In addition, these income limits and the maximum deductible contribution ($2,000) would be indexed for future inflation. The proposal would also permit taxpayers to make withdrawals from an IRA before age 59½ without payment of the 10 percent excise tax for the following purposes: to buy a first home, to pay for postsecondary education, to defray large medical expenses, or to cover expenses during spells of long-term unemployment. Finally, the Administration proposes a new form of IRA to which contributions would not be deductible but whose earnings would never be subject to income tax.

proposal, the tax burden of lower income working families would be raised substantially.

Often the tax rate contained in flat tax proposals is between 15 and 20 percent. Revenue estimates generally conclude that such proposals would raise significantly less revenue than the taxes they would replace, increasing future Federal budget deficits. One example is the Treasury Department analysis of H.R. 2060 (the Armey-Shelby flat tax proposal). At its proposed 17 percent rate, this tax plan would raise about $138 billion less per year (at 1996 income levels) than the taxes it would replace. Proponents of a flat tax respond that lower tax rates will so stimulate economic growth, and therefore raise tax revenues, that the projected shortfalls will vanish. However, these claims are generally not supported by the available evidence, including the historical record of the 1980s. A prudent reading of the economic literature suggests that the effects of a shift to a flat tax on economic growth are likely to be small.

Other shortcomings of a flat tax have received much less attention. For instance, since a flat tax effectively exempts capital income from taxation at the individual level, it would create strong incentives for entities to recharacterize payments to individuals as capital income. Similarly, since businesses would be taxed on gross receipts from the sale of goods and services but not on interest income, they would have an incentive to relabel payments they receive from other entities as interest. This distinction between the taxation of payments labeled "interest" and other payments creates an enormous potential loophole, and the concern is magnified when multinational firms enter the picture (because firms outside the United States would be subject to completely different tax regimes). This is a problem that could be solved, but only at the expense of introducing some complexity in distinguishing between payment types. Such a solution, though, undercuts one of the main arguments for the flat tax, namely simplicity. In addition, it indirectly points out that defining the tax base often is a major source of complexity, rather than the tax rate schedule.

The flat tax would change the relative desirability of many assets. Owner-occupied housing has received particular scrutiny in this regard. Housing would become much less tax-advantaged under a flat tax that eliminates the deduction for mortgage interest. The result could be a sizable drop in housing values. But owner-occupied housing is only one type of asset that could be affected in this manner. For example, existing plant and equipment or tax-exempt bonds could also suffer a marked decline in value. The impact on these assets indicates that tax reform proposals must be attentive to short-run effects; designing adequate transition rules is a crucial task.

A flat tax would apply to more types of organizations than the current tax. In addition to requiring separate business and individual tax returns for sole proprietorships and partnerships, a flat tax could require many currently tax-exempt entities to file.

Finally, since much middle-class saving is in the form of pensions and IRAs and is thus already effectively exempt from income tax, a flat tax would provide little additional benefit to saving for many middle-income families. Instead, it would skew much of the benefit of exempting capital income to the very wealthiest in society.

Although the flat tax discussed here is not the answer, reforms of the current tax system can certainly be found that can meet these three traditional tests. Our challenge is to design policies that recognize the inherent tradeoffs among them and that reflect deeply held American values. Moreover, decisions made today regarding tax reform are not made in a static economy. Any reforms made must not only be appropriate for today's economy but, more important, must also be flexible enough to address the long-term challenges affecting tomorrow's economy.

LONG-TERM DEMOGRAPHIC CHALLENGES

Both Republicans and Democrats agree that the Federal budget should be balanced over the next 7 years. Balancing the budget will require many tough choices, but putting our fiscal house in order is an important first step toward meeting the many challenges that stem from the aging of the population that is projected to begin in the early part of the next century.

DEMOGRAPHIC TRENDS

The median age in the United States in 1995 was 33 years. By 2015 it is projected to be 37, and by 2030 it will be 39. The elderly as a share of the population is projected to increase from roughly 13 percent today to over 20 percent by 2035 (Chart 3–2).

This aging of the U.S. population is the result of two demographic forces: a decline in fertility (lifetime births per woman of childbearing age) since the 1950s and 1960s (Box 3–5), and an increase in life expectancy. Whereas the average woman in 1950 had three children over her lifetime, the average woman today has only two. This decline in fertility means fewer children today and fewer workers tomorrow. With the increase in life expectancy, more people survive to age 65, and those who do live longer beyond 65. The result is an increase in the share of the over–65 population. Between 1950 and 1995, life expectancy at birth increased roughly 7 years for men and 8 years for women; life expectancy at age 65 increased 2.5 years for men and 4 years for women over this same period. In the future, life expectancy is projected to continue to increase, although at a somewhat slower rate.

The total dependency ratio—the ratio of dependents (children and elderly) to workers—can be used to summarize the effects on the economy of the decline in fertility and the increase in life ex-

Chart 3-2 **Past and Projected Population Shares by Age**
The U.S. population is aging. By 2030 more than 20 percent of the population
will be age 65 and over, and only 25 percent will be under age 20.

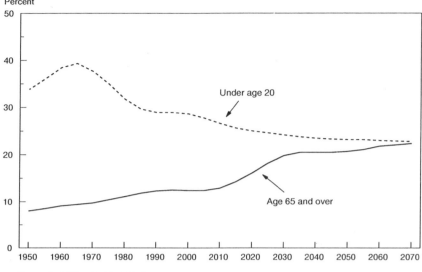

Source: Social Security Administration.

Box 3-5.—Changes in Fertility Over Time

Chart 3-3 reports changes in the total fertility rate, defined as the number of children a woman would bear in her lifetime (assuming she survives her entire childbearing period) if she were to experience the average birth rate by age observed in the selected year. It seems clear that the baby bust associated with the Great Depression and World War II, and the postwar baby boom that followed it, were temporary blips in a long-run trend of declining fertility. Without the postwar baby boom, elderly dependency ratios would be climbing steadily and by 2070 would reach the levels currently projected. The cycle of baby bust and baby boom actually observed accounts for the path of dependency between now and then: relatively little change over the next 20 years, as the relatively small cohort born in the 1930s and 1940s reaches retirement, followed by the rapid increases associated with the retiring of the baby-boom generation.

Chart 3-3   **Past and Projected Fertility Rates**
The baby boom of the 1940s and 1950s appears to be a temporary
aberration in a long-run trend of declining fertility.

Births per woman

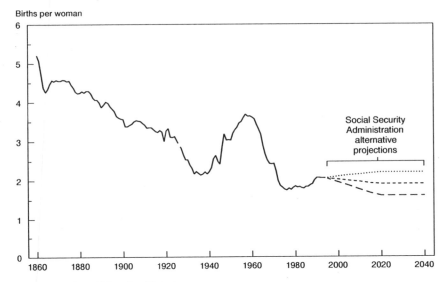

Note: Data prior to 1920 are for whites only.
Source: Data prior to 1920: Coale, A. and M. Zelnick (1963), "New Estimates of Fertility and Population in the U.S.,"
Princeton University Press; all other data: Social Security Administration.

pectancy. The ratio is a rough measure of how many nonworking
people must be supported by the output of the economy's workers.
Chart 3–4 reports trends in the total dependency ratio and its two
major components: the elderly dependency ratio, calculated as the
ratio of the population over 65 to the population aged 20 to 64, and
the youth dependency ratio, the ratio of those under 20 to those
aged 20 to 64.

The chart reveals that the total dependency ratio is currently
quite low by recent historical standards, because the youth dependency ratio is relatively low and the elderly dependency ratio has
risen very little recently. In contrast, in the 1960s the ratio of children to workers was very high, and in the future (after 2010) the
ratio of elderly to workers is expected to be high. Although the
total dependency ratio is expected to climb significantly in the future, it will be climbing from a relatively low level and is not projected to reach the high rates experienced—and supported without
great difficulty—in the mid-1960s. From this perspective, the expected aging of the population does not look so threatening.

Yet children demand different resources from society than the elderly, so it is worth separating elderly dependency from total dependency. Looking only at the elderly dependency ratio does show
a dramatically different picture. The ratio of elderly to the working-
age population rose slowly between 1950 and 1995, is expected to

Chart 3-4 **Past and Projected Elderly and Youth Dependency Ratios**
The projected increase in total dependency is smaller than the projected
increase in elderly dependency.

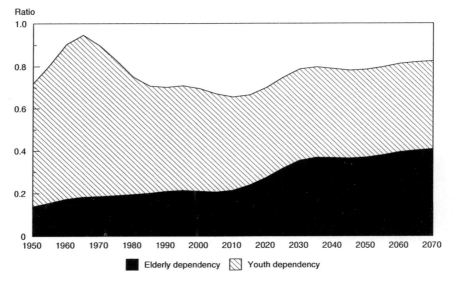

Note: Elderly dependency is the ratio of the population age 65 and over to those age 20-64; youth dependency
is the ratio of the population under 20 to those age 20-64.
Source: Social Security Administration.

stay roughly constant between 1995 and 2010, and then is expected
to increase sharply, by roughly 75 percent, in the years between
2010 and 2035.

ECONOMIC EFFECTS OF AN AGING POPULATION

Much public discussion of the impact of demographic changes on
the economy has focused on the potential effects of aging on government programs like Social Security and Medicare. This focus,
although certainly not misplaced, may give the impression that the
aging of the population would have little impact in an economy
with no government programs for the aged. This is clearly not the
case. Population aging has broad economic implications in any
economy, regardless of the breadth of government support for the
elderly.

As discussed above, the aging of the U.S. population stems from
increased life spans and declining fertility. Increased life expectancy—which accounts for only a small fraction of the change in dependency over the next 40 years—has relatively direct effects on
individuals. Although living longer is undoubtedly a good thing
(and something in which we invest many research dollars), it does
require individuals to make certain adjustments. People need to
generate enough resources to support themselves over more years
of life. They can do this by working more years (if they are able

to, Box 3–6), by increasing their saving rate while working, by reducing their consumption when retired, or by receiving greater transfers from those of working age during their retirement.

Box 3–6.—Will Increases in Longevity Permit Increased Work Effort?

The impact of an older population will depend, in part, on the ability of the elderly to remain active and economically productive. An important question, therefore, is whether tomorrow's 65-year-olds will be healthier than today's. If so, delaying retirement may be a viable option for many people. Advances in medical technology not only save lives but also improve lives by reducing the severity of disabling illnesses. For example, cataract surgery preserves vision, and hip replacements preserve the ability to walk, permitting people to remain independent and active. On the other hand, to the extent that medical advances extend life without reducing disabilities, increasing years of work would not be a viable response to the increase in longevity.

Which of these effects dominates the other is still uncertain. Still, so long as the first effect is present, some individuals can extend their working years, and the *average* work span can thus increase.

The decline in fertility rates from the levels of the 1960s means that the current generation of workers now has fewer children to care for; they can therefore consume more. This corresponds to the finding that the total dependency ratio is quite low now relative to the 1960s. As members of this generation age, however, they will also find that they have fewer children in the workforce. This corresponds to the increase in the elderly and total dependency ratios expected in the early part of the next century. Since workers today generally do not support their parents' retirement directly, this reduction in the ratio of workers to elderly should not have large *direct* effects. But it may have a number of indirect effects.

People can save for their retirement by purchasing homes and by investing in financial assets, either directly or through a pension fund, if they have one. When they retire, they support themselves with the income they earn on these assets, and with money they receive from selling them, and of course with benefits they receive from programs such as Social Security and Medicare. The value of those assets may be affected, however, by the number of workers in the next generation. For example, if the number of workers in the United States declines, the total value of what can be produced may also decline (relative to what could have been produced by a constant number of workers). The result might be to reduce the value of U.S. financial assets. Similarly, an economy with fewer people of working age has less demand for houses, leading some analysts to predict that housing values will not increase by as much as they might otherwise, or might actually decline. On the other hand, at our current rate of productivity growth, future generations will undoubtedly be better off than current generations. And this Administration has focused on policies devoted to improving productivity—policies like job training, education, and technology investment—which should make future generations even better off. Furthermore, some researchers have found that slow growth in the workforce could actually spur productivity growth, substantially offsetting or even eliminating the effects of aging on output and on the value of assets (Box 3–7).

Box 3–7.—Linking Productivity Growth to Demographics

Demographic developments and the rate of productivity growth have a number of potential links. Some observers argue that population aging will lead to slower productivity growth because of two factors. First, as the growth rate of the labor force slows, so does growth in demand for new capital goods. Innovation could become less profitable as the fixed costs of innovation are spread over fewer goods. Second, the aging of the population means that the average age of the workforce will rise. If innovators tend to be young, productivity growth could suffer.

On the other hand, many analysts believe that the incentives to innovate are strongest when labor is scarce. This theory, that "necessity is the mother of invention," predicts that as labor force growth slows, labor-saving technology will be developed to keep economic output from falling.

Finally, the actual effects of population aging in the United States will depend on international factors. If the United States were a small economy that traded freely with the rest of the world, the effects of population aging would be small: demographic changes in the United States would have little effect on the value of tradeable assets, which would largely reflect values established in international markets. But the United States is not a small economy—its population and income are too large for its demographic changes not to have significant worldwide effects. Furthermore, the demographic changes observed here are not confined to the United States—if anything, the countries that are our current principal trading partners are aging faster than we are (Box 3–8). If current trading patterns continue, we are likely to see lower returns to saving as labor force growth in the United States and in the rest of the industrialized world declines. If, however, conditions for trade between the United States and what are today's developing countries improve substantially over the next few decades, as they have over the past decade, it is possible that high-yielding investment opportunities in these countries will keep the rate of return on savings relatively high.

Chart 3-5 **Elderly Dependency Ratios in Europe, Japan, and the United States**
Elderly dependency is projected to rise higher and faster in Japan than in the United States or Europe.

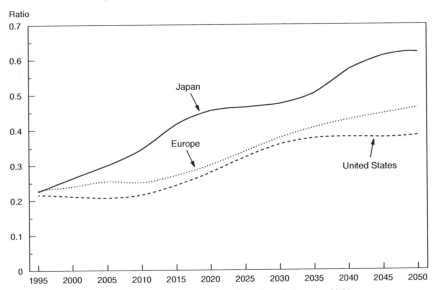

Note: Elderly dependency is the ratio of the population age 65 and over to those age 20-64.
Source: United Nations.

EFFECTS OF DEMOGRAPHIC CHANGE ON THE
FEDERAL BUDGET

Government support programs make up a large fraction of the retirement income of the elderly. These programs have worked successfully to reduce poverty among the aged (Chart 3–6) and enhance the health and economic security of both the aged and their families. Social Security and the insurance value of Medicare alone represent roughly half of all income (including the value of Medicare) received by elderly households. These programs also account for a significant portion of Federal expenditures—over 30 percent in 1995.

Chart 3-6   **Poverty Rate of the Elderly**
The percent of America's elderly who are poor has fallen by more than half since the 1960s and is near an all-time low.

Percent

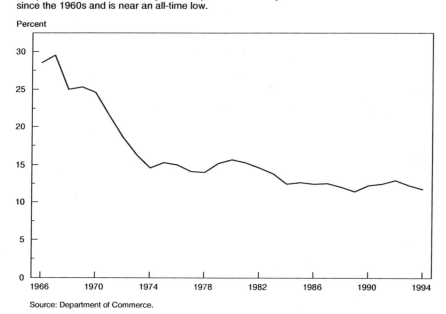

Source: Department of Commerce.

Social Security

The largest program for the elderly is Social Security. This program has traditionally been financed on a pay-as-you-go basis; that is, most of the payroll taxes collected from the current generation of workers (largely the baby-boom generation) are used to pay current benefits. However, Social Security is now developing a trust fund that will permit some advance funding in the future, at least temporarily. Accumulated assets in the trust fund are currently equal to roughly 1.5 years of benefits.

As currently structured, then, Social Security is mainly an intergenerational transfer program. The aging of the population will make such a transfer between workers and retirees more difficult. The Social Security actuaries consider three different scenarios for the program's future: one in which the Social Security program is in relatively good financial shape, with relatively high birth rates and real growth in income, and relatively slow growth in longevity; one in which the system is in relatively bad financial shape; and an intermediate scenario, which we focus on here.

Small differences in growth rates, compounded over decades, result in large differences in estimates of *levels* of expenditures and receipts. This means that we need to be cautious in interpreting any particular scenario. On the other hand, we need to be at least aware of some of the potential risks. How policy responds will depend on our degree of risk aversion and the consequences of delay. Under the Social Security actuaries' intermediate assumptions, benefits are expected to increase from the current 11.5 percent of payroll to 17.3 percent by 2030; Social Security income (tax collections plus interest on the trust fund assets) climb more slowly: from 12.6 percent now to 13.1 percent in 2030. Total income is projected to exceed benefits until 2020. After that, redemption of trust fund holdings can help finance benefits for an additional 10 years, until the trust fund finally runs out in 2030.

Clearly, steps need to be taken to ensure the long-term solvency of Social Security, and a bipartisan effort will be required. The Quadrennial Advisory Council on Social Security was charged with developing ways to balance Social Security in the long run, and is expected to release its recommendations in the near future.

Even without any changes to the program, the rate of return that people will receive on their Social Security contributions is declining. In the early years of the program, the benefits conferred on retirees far exceeded their contributions. Since then rates of return have declined because of statutory increases in tax rates, increases in the number of years that workers' wages have been subject to tax, and the slowdown in labor productivity growth, although these have been offset somewhat by increases in life expectancy. (Productivity growth affects the rate of return received on Social Security contributions because the calculation of a worker's initial benefit level reflects the productivity gains that occurred over his or her working years.) Even at current levels, Social Security, by providing returns that are fully indexed for inflation, offers a kind of economic security that is simply not available elsewhere in the market. And, increases in productivity growth beyond what is currently projected could lead to higher rates of return on Social Security contributions in the future.

Medicare

Government expenditures on Medicare, the program that provides health insurance for the elderly, are also projected to grow over the next 75 years. The projected expenditure growth over the first 25 years of that period is primarily due to projected increases in the cost of providing health care. For the remainder of the projection period, however, most of the growth is attributable to increases in enrollment stemming from the retirement of the baby-boom generation.

Medicare is composed of two parts. Part A covers inpatient hospital services, and Part B covers primarily physician and outpatient hospital services. Part A is financed by a 2.9 percent payroll tax, shared equally by employers and employees. Most of the taxes are used to finance current benefits, but like Social Security, at least until recently, some tax revenue was retained in a trust fund to finance future health care benefits. According to the 1995 Annual Report of the Board of Trustees of the Hospital Insurance Trust Fund, the trust fund for Medicare Part A is projected to be exhausted by the year 2002. Medicare reforms proposed by this Administration should extend the life of the Medicare Part A trust fund through at least 2011. Medicare Part B is financed partly from general revenues, but partly from premiums paid by beneficiaries. Expenditures on Part B are also expected to increase with the aging of the population.

Many policymakers have called for a commission, similar to the Quadrennial Advisory Council for Social Security, to develop recommendations to ensure the long-term solvency of the overall Medicare program.

Medicaid

Medicaid, the program that provides health care to low-income people with little wealth, is not exclusively a program for the elderly. But Medicaid does pay for nursing home care for elderly and other Americans who have depleted their assets. In 1995 roughly one-third of total Medicaid expenditures went to the elderly (with the remaining two-thirds split about equally between people with disabilities and the nonelderly, nondisabled poor).

The aging of the population is bound to lead to a significant increase in the number of people needing long-term care assistance. Not only will the number of old people increase, but so will the average age of those over 65. People over 85 made up about 11 percent of the elderly population in 1995; according to the Social Security Administration's projections, by 2050, they will make up over 16 percent. Older people are much more likely to be in a nursing home: in 1993, 31 percent of those 85 and older spent time in a nursing home, compared to just 7 percent of the general population over 65. If this rate of nursing home utilization is maintained, population aging will bring significant increases in the nursing home population and in expenditures on long-term care.

MAINTAINING VALUABLE PROGRAMS

The aging of the population will pose significant challenges for the economy and in particular for the government. Although changes to these programs are inevitable, certain features should be maintained. Medicare and Social Security do provide unique benefits that the private sector cannot provide. In particular, because Medicare and Social Security cover all Americans, they are not subject to the adverse selection problems that can plague the private annuity and health insurance markets. And Social Security and Medicare provide income streams that generate constant real purchasing power (Box 3–9). Administrative costs (which are less than 1 percent of benefits for Social Security) are far lower than for most private insurance plans or pensions. Social Security and Medicare are programs of universal participation that have received a great deal of public support. To maintain this support, it is important that these programs remain universal, but it is also important that they be put on a sound financial footing.

CHAPTER 4

Devolution

THE APPROPRIATE ROLE of the Federal Government in the U.S. economy has been a fundamental issue in this past year's debate over the budget. At issue are both the role for government in general and the division of responsibility between Federal and State governments. Chapter 1 of this *Report* addressed the question of the broader role of government. This chapter addresses how responsibilities might best be apportioned among the levels of government.

This Administration has dedicated itself from the outset to making government work better. Improving the efficiency of government requires a rational division of responsibility among Federal, State, and local entities. Today many support the notion that, in several policy areas, authority ought to be devolved from Federal agencies to States, localities, and individuals, to foster more creative and responsive solutions to the problems of diverse communities.

This Administration has been at the forefront of efforts to empower State and local governments by removing impediments to innovation and experimentation in public health, welfare, public housing, and environmental protection, and by reducing the proliferation of Federal unfunded mandates. But devolution of responsibilities must be done carefully, to ensure that national objectives are still met. In particular, a profound national interest lies in maintaining a social safety net, to guarantee at least a minimum standard of living for today's vulnerable families, and in promoting investment in education, research, and infrastructure, to ensure high living standards for tomorrow's families. The Federal Government also has a clear interest in ensuring that all of its expenditures, including those over which States and localities have some degree of control, are spent in the manner intended. Devolution that merely inserts an extra level of bureaucracy makes little sense: in many cases it is far better to empower individuals directly than to dispense funds to State and local governments on their behalf.

FACTS ON FEDERALISM

Despite major changes in our economy and in government programs over the past 25 years, the roles of the States and the Federal Government in the economy have remained relatively stable.

TRENDS OVER TIME

Total government expenditures—Federal, State, and local—have rose slowly as a share of gross domestic product (GDP) over the past three decades, from roughly 28 percent in the early 1960s to over 34 percent today (Chart 4–1).

Chart 4-1 **Expenditures by All Levels of Government**
Government expenditures in relation to the broader economy have climbed slowly over the past three decades.

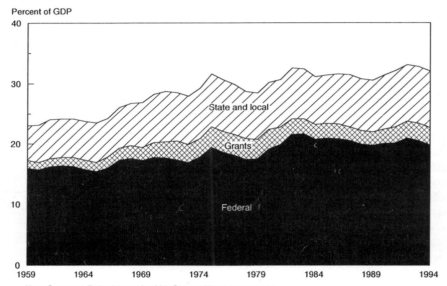

Note: Grants are Federal grants-in-aid to State and local governments.
Source: Department of Commerce.

The Federal Government accounts for the largest share of this spending. In 1993, if expenditures on State and local grants are included, the Federal Government accounted for 69 percent of total government spending. As Chart 4–2 shows, this share has not changed dramatically over the past 25 years: the Federal share of expenditures rose from 67 percent to 72 percent between 1970 and 1984, but has shrunk back to 69 percent since then.

COMPOSITION OF SPENDING

The Federal Government's major responsibilities include national defense, Social Security, and Medicare. States and localities have

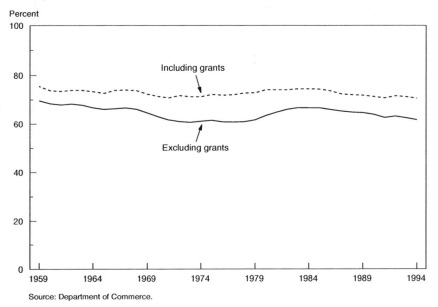

Chart 4-2 **Federal Expenditures as a Share of Total Government Expenditures**
The Federal Government's share of all government expenditures has been
relatively stable.

Percent

Including grants

Excluding grants

1959   1964   1969   1974   1979   1984   1989   1994

Source: Department of Commerce.

primary responsibility for public education, police and fire protection, and sewerage and sanitation. Highways are generally maintained by States and localities, but funds for new construction are largely provided by the Federal Government. Medicaid and some welfare programs are jointly financed by the Federal and State governments but administered by the States. Table 4–1 documents the current division of responsibility between the Federal Government and State and local government.

This division of responsibility has evolved gradually. Public roads and support for the needy, for example, are two areas where responsibility has traditionally rested with States and localities, but in both areas the Federal Government has assumed an increasingly important role. The Highway Revenue Act of 1956 created the Highway Trust Fund and dedicated the revenue received from taxes on diesel fuel and gasoline to this fund. These funds were used to build the interstate highway system, which has changed the face of America.

The growth of the Federal role in welfare arose in part out of the widely shared view that all children, no matter where they were born or who their parents were, should be entitled to certain basic standards of nutrition, housing, and health—common decency in a country as rich as the United States demanded no less. Although the acceptance of this national obligation was fundamentally a

109

TABLE 4–1.—*Composition of Government Spending, 1993*

Spending by function	Percent of non-interest expenditures	Percent of expenditures financed with Federal grants
Federal Government:		
National defense	26.6	
Social security	23.4	
Medicare	13.2	
Veterans benefits and services, welfare and social services, and housing subsidies	9.0	
Civilian and military retirement	4.9	
Other	22.9	
State and local government:		
Education	37.5	4.7
Medicaid	15.9	57.9
Welfare and social services	8.0	58.0
Highways	7.5	26.1
Police and fire protection	6.2	.8
Corrections	3.7	.7
Water, sewerage, and sanitation	1.5	15.5
Other	19.6	19.7

Note.—Data are on a national income and product accounts (NIPA) basis, and are as published in the Survey of Curent Business, September 1994. No later data are available.

In this table, Federal grants-in-aid to State and local governments are not included in Federal Government expenditures.

Source: Department of Commerce.

moral decision, it was supported by self-interest, in the recognition that the cost to society of *not* providing these minimal standards—in terms of lost wages, higher crime rates, and the like—could be very high.

THE RATIONALE FOR A FEDERAL ROLE

The reasons for the creation and expansion of these Federal programs provide considerable insight into the forces that drive the expanded Federal presence in American society. Yet a sensible allocation of responsibilities for governments in the future must be based on more than historical precedent.

Some might make the case that the Federal Government should do nothing other than national defense. After all, States and localities are better able to tailor their programs to meet the different needs and preferences of their residents, and competition among the States may enhance efficiency and innovation, just as it does in the private sector. But this view ignores the benefits of Federal action in a number of areas. The enumeration of powers given to the Federal Government under the Constitution suggests that our forefathers, even in the early infancy of the Republic, recognized the advantages of Federal involvement across a broad range of endeavors. The economic strength of the United States rests in part on our vast national market, fostered not only by the free flow of commerce without artificial trade barriers, but also by national standards and a national transportation and communications system.

Economists have sought to identify some general principles that would elucidate a "rational" division of responsibilities between levels of government. At least four categories of arguments justifying Federal action can be identified.

THE NEED FOR UNIFORMITY

Although diversity among State government programs is often desirable, in some cases the benefits of uniform government action across the States tip the scale toward Federal involvement. Uniformity of standards and regulations may improve efficiency. For example, uniform rules for interstate commerce preserve one of America's strengths: our large national market. Conflicting State regulation could fragment this market and impede producers' ability to take advantage of economies of scale. Likewise, uniformity in minimum safety net benefits would guarantee that all needy Americans, regardless of where they lived, enjoyed at least a certain level of well-being, and would avoid distorting and inefficient movements of households in response to differences in benefits.

DIRECT SPILLOVERS

Actions taken or not taken by States sometimes affect residents of other States. Residents of a State might be willing to tolerate pollution of their ground water, but the contaminated water could seep across State boundaries and harm residents of other States. States may also engage in activities that unintentionally benefit the residents of other States. For example, one State's successful innovation in its schools can lead the way for other States to reform their education systems, and States' efforts to prevent communicable diseases can benefit the health of nonresidents. Similarly, when States invest more in education, and incomes rise as a consequence, they confer a positive benefit on all taxpayers: the Federal Government reaps some of the rewards of the higher incomes in the form of higher Federal tax revenues. When the policies of one State affect the residents of others, for good or for ill, States may lack the right incentives to provide an appropriate level of public services, because the effects of policies on nonresidents may not factor strongly in their decisionmaking.

THE EFFECTS OF POLICY-INDUCED MOBILITY

The freedom of people and firms to move at will from State to State promotes competition among State governments. Although this competition can enhance the efficiency of government, it can also make it difficult for States to pursue certain worthwhile policies. For example, the fear of welfare-induced migration may cause States to reduce welfare benefits to a level below what they would otherwise provide. Similarly, State competition for jobs may limit the generosity of unemployment insurance programs.

INEQUALITY OF RESOURCES

States that are poorer than the average, or that are experiencing temporary downturns, are able to raise less revenue, yet have to spend more than other States to provide services for the needy. Clearly, only the Federal Government can transfer resources among the States. Not only does such redistribution help poorer States, but financial assistance from the Federal Government that increases during economic downturns can also help to stabilize regional economies. This assistance can be given through a number of channels: direct transfers of cash or in-kind benefits to lower income individuals, grants to lower income States or localities, matching grants to State or local programs for the needy, or direct provision of public services in poor communities. The role of the Federal Government in transferring resources to States and localities is more complicated, both in theory and in practice, than is often recognized, and will be discussed at greater length below.

These rationales for a Federal role are not mutually exclusive, and sometimes it is their interaction that makes a strong case for a Federal role in policy. For example, national safety standards, when desirable, might evolve on their own, were it not for spillovers. States could simply agree to a set of voluntary standards, and each State would weigh the benefits and costs of complying. In doing so, however, it would ignore the costs it might impose on others. A State might adopt more lax safety regulation for its cars, but then when its cars cross over into another State, the other State bears part of the costs. Federal action is therefore needed to ensure uniform national standards that avoid these spillover effects.

DEVOLUTION OF POLICYMAKING RESPONSIBILITY

Determining which level of government should be responsible for a particular program or activity is a delicate balancing act. It requires weighing the benefits of innovation, greater responsiveness, and competition that State and local control offers against the rationales for Federal involvement just outlined. Sometimes the answer is simple and obvious: either purely Federal control and financing or purely State control and financing. But many cases call for a sharing of responsibilities.

All government activities have three basic elements: policymaking, financing, and administration. These activities can be apportioned between the Federal Government and State and local governments in various ways. The current debate centers largely on how the policymaking role for programs that receive financing from the Federal government should be shared. At one extreme, the Federal Government could provide funds to States with no strings attached—States would not even be told on which programs to spend the money. Such an arrangement, used in other countries and in the past in the United States (where it was called "general revenue sharing"), is not currently under consideration. Instead the debate has focused on whether to convert existing programs into block grants (grants that can be used to fund programs in broad policy areas) and on how much discretion to allow States in determining how those grants should be used.

This Administration strongly supports enhancing the role of States and localities in policymaking. In many areas—job training, community development, and welfare, for example—enhanced flexibility for States and local communities is likely to yield better results. But it is important that this enhanced flexibility be provided in a way that protects the national interest. For all the reasons cited earlier, some Federal role in policy may need to be maintained. Furthermore, the Federal Government has a significant role in financing programs, it also should have some role in policy in order to ensure accountability.

ENSURING GOVERNMENT ACCOUNTABILITY

The Administration is committed to ensuring that government funds are spent wisely, whether the Federal Government or States and localities are doing the spending. A problem with revenue-sharing arrangements or pure block grants is that the level of government making the policy decisions is no longer the one responsible for financing the program. This separation of functions may increase the likelihood that taxpayer money is not well spent. Indeed, some evidence suggests that States spend money they receive from the Federal Government differently from funds they raise themselves—and restrictions on spending imposed by the Federal Government do not account for all of the difference. Thus, the availability of Federal highway money results in more spending on highways than States would otherwise undertake, even though, at the margin, most States pay 100 percent of each additional dollar of highway spending (Box 4–1). Evidently, State taxpayers are content to give government officials more discretion over funds coming from Washington than over funds contributed by their own State tax dollars.

This is a two-edged sword. On the one hand, it means that the Federal Government can influence the pattern of State spending more easily than it might otherwise: Federal money may not just

Box 4–1.—Federal Grants and the "Flypaper Effect"

The Federal Government provides substantial grants to States and localities—over $228 billion in 1995. Most of this grant money can be used for projects that these governments might otherwise fully fund themselves, and most do not require that the State or locality contribute any matching funds. Because these grants can simply serve to free up State and local government funds for other uses, they can be viewed as equivalent to pure transfers of cash from the Federal Government. From an economic perspective, then, one would expect States and localities to spend these grants in the same manner as they would any other increase in income. For example, States might allocate 5 to 10 cents of each grant dollar to increases in their spending, and the rest would simply be used to reduce State taxes.

Researchers have consistently found, however, that Federal grants have much larger effects on State and local government spending than this logic would suggest. Recent studies find that the actual increase is on the order of 40 to 65 cents on the dollar. This result has been dubbed the "flypaper effect": the money sticks where it hits. Moreover, not only does State and local spending increase when Federal grants increase, but the money tends to remain in the program area for which the grant was intended: grants for education tend to increase education spending, grants for infrastructure tend to increase infrastructure spending, and so on. Some of the grant money is used to finance other areas of government and to finance tax cuts, but such "leakages" are much smaller than economic theory would predict.

substitute for State money, as many critics of block granting have feared. (And, as is discussed later in the chapter, it is precisely the Federal Government's desire to influence patterns of State spending that justifies a Federal role at all.) On the other hand, if the substitution of Federal for local funding leads to less diligent monitoring by taxpayers, the money may not be well spent.

Federal actions can also impose costs on the States. And just as States may spend Federal money more readily than money raised through State taxes, so the Federal Government may spend State money more readily than funds raised through Federal taxes. Federal legislation that raises States' costs—so-called unfunded mandates—has recently received considerable attention. Legislation passed in 1995 attempted to address some of the most important problems posed by unfunded mandates (Box 4–2).

Box 4-2.—The Unfunded Mandates Reform Act

The Unfunded Mandates Reform Act, enacted in early 1995, will restrict the ability of the Congress to impose costly mandates on States, localities, and tribal governments. This legislation requires the Congressional Budget Office (CBO) to analyze the costs of any proposed mandates on State and local governments. Mandates certified by the CBO as costing States and localities $50 million or more in any of the first 5 years after becoming effective are not permitted. However, majority votes in both the House and the Senate can waive this prohibition. The CBO also is required to estimate the cost of any mandate on private companies which exceeds $100 million in any year over this same 5-year period.

The unfunded mandates legislation was enacted to restore equilibrium to the relationships between Federal, State, and local governments. For too long, Washington has placed overly burdensome mandates on States and localities. The new law rectifies this imbalance but also permits mandates that are in the national interest. For example, some unfunded mandates may be designed to control cross-jurisdictional externalities. A State that dumps garbage in a river, polluting the shores of a neighboring State, causes an externality every bit as important as that generated by a private firm. The law provides a flexible way of addressing unfunded mandates: it requires the disclosure of relevant information, without being overly prescriptive. With a majority vote, the Federal Government could, for instance, still proscribe States from dumping garbage in ways that adversely affect neighboring States. To do so imposes costs on States, but these are costs that they should rightly bear.

The legislation also requires Federal agencies to assess the qualitative and quantitative costs and benefits of any proposed regulatory actions that would result in annual expenditures of $100 million or more by State, local, and tribal governments or the private sector before promulgating such actions. Agencies must ". . . [1] identify and consider a reasonable number of regulatory alternatives and [2] from those alternatives select the least costly, most cost-effective or least burdensome alternative that achieves the objectives of the proposed rule," or explain their decisions if a different action is adopted. Finally, the legislation requires the Advisory Commission on Intergovernmental Relations, an independent agency, to make recommendations on paring existing mandates.

DEVOLUTION AND THE PROVISION OF PUBLIC SERVICES

In many cases, government action can correct inefficiencies in the private market—so-called market failures—and so improve the overall allocation of resources. As discussed in Chapter 1, to correct market failures, government may need to provide certain goods directly (so-called public goods), adopt or enforce standards that apply to other goods (such as safety standards), or encourage, through subsidies or regulation, private firms to provide goods that would otherwise be underprovided (i.e., those with positive externalities). All of these activities can be viewed as providing public services.

State and local governments have many advantages in providing these public services. They can more easily address the differing needs and preferences of particular communities. For example, building codes should reflect local weather and geological conditions, and communities should be able to choose their own level of community services. Having a number of communities with different mixes of services (and of taxes to pay for them) improves overall efficiency, if people can choose to live in the jurisdiction that best meets their needs and desires.

Competition among localities can enhance this efficiency by making it easier for people to hold their local government accountable for the decisions it makes. For example, if a city, by operating efficiently, is able to maintain a high level of public services with relatively low taxes, residents of nearby cities may demand equally efficient government from their policymakers—and use the threat of relocation to the efficient city to make their demands resonate.

But the problems described above require some Federal role in the provision of many public services. Uniformity of regulations or of standards, such as safety standards, can improve the effectiveness and efficiency of certain policies. A uniform set of minimum water and air quality regulations ensures that all Americans, regardless of where they live, have clean air to breathe and water to drink. Cross-jurisdictional spillovers also can be important. Some types of public services, like national defense and subsidies to scientific research, need to be provided by the Federal Government because the spillovers from government action are so large. Public services and goods, like national defense, that can only be provided effectively at the national level are called *national public goods*. Those whose benefits accrue exclusively to residents of a particular locale are called *local public goods*.

Between purely local and purely national public goods are many intermediate cases: many public services create some spillovers, but still much of the benefit accrues within the community. Highways are a prominent example. Many highways are used primarily by residents of the State where the highway is located. But these highways also provide significant benefits to out-of-State residents who travel on them and who purchase goods that have been transported on them. If State residents had to pay for all the costs of building highways in their State, their choices regarding highway construction might take into account only the benefits they expect for themselves. Thus they would construct fewer roads with smaller capacity than would be socially desirable.

MATCHING GRANTS

One method used to solve this problem is the categorical matching grant, in which the Federal Government pays a fraction of the overall costs of the program. For example, the Federal Government could match additional State spending on a 1-to-1 basis, or on a 2-to-1 or 4-to-1 basis. Ideally, the match rate would be set so that the fraction of the total costs paid by the States equals the fraction of the total benefits that accrue to their residents. Under such a financial arrangement, the decision on the *level* of expenditures can be delegated to the States. Because the spillover effects are taken into account in the "price" States have to pay, they will set the level of expenditures at an efficient level.

In practice, however, a large share of Federal grants for public infrastructure, education, and social services is not in the form of matching grants, but rather in the form of categorical unmatched grants (grants that provide funds for particular purposes, such as education of the disabled or tuberculosis control, but do not require States or localities to put up any of their own money). Furthermore, while there are grant programs that do require States to spend their own funds in order to receive Federal money, many are in the form of capped matching grants, which place a ceiling on the total amount that the Federal Government will pay. From an economist's perspective, capped matching grants are much like categorical grants. Once the cap on Federal grants is reached, State and local governments bear the full cost of additional projects. And since, for many capped matching grant programs, States likely do spend more than the amount required to receive the maximum allowable Federal grant, the grants probably do little to change the incremental costs of projects, but simply allow States and localities to shift resources to other projects. Capped matching grants may thus insufficiently address the problem of underspending arising from cross-jurisdictional spillovers. Surprisingly, however, evidence indicates that categorical grants and capped matching grants do stimulate a significant amount of additional investment in the targeted activities (Box 4–1), although they also serve to free up State funds for other purposes. Open-ended matching grants, which

117

would change the marginal cost to States, could have significantly greater effects on State spending decisions, because they would affect the prices faced by the States at the margin.

PUBLIC SERVICES AND DIFFERENCES IN LOCAL RESOURCES

One of the rationales cited above for a Federal role in provision of public goods is that some jurisdictions lack the resources to finance public services at a level deemed adequate by the Nation as a whole. But a lack of sufficient State resources to provide services does not necessarily imply that the Federal Government should provide those services instead. In principle, the Federal Government could, instead of providing grants for public services to poor States, provide income transfers to poor individuals. Just as individuals, not the government, should decide how their income is spent, so too individuals should decide for themselves about the level of consumption of local public goods.

If taxpayers closely monitored their policymakers, the level of public services would not depend on whether resources were transferred to State and local governments or directly to taxpayers, and the transfer of resources to the States would simply substitute for State governments levying taxes. But the evidence cited earlier suggests that the way money is distributed does matter. Direct transfers to individuals force State and local policymakers to justify their choices of public services.

This general principle has two exceptions. First, Americans believe that society has a special responsibility to children, regardless of the economic condition of their parents. Providing *services* that go directly to children, rather than providing cash to their parents, may be a more effective way of making sure that it is children who ultimately benefit. More generally, society may not care so much about inequality of income as about inequality in the consumption of certain goods, and so may prefer to provide these goods instead of cash. To the extent that these goods are public services—like health care, clean water, decent schools, good job opportunities, and safe places for children to play—Federal funding of such services for poor neighborhoods is warranted.

A second reason why it may be better for the Federal Government to provide direct financing for public services is to save on administrative costs. Indirect financing, through Federal transfers to citizens residing within the jurisdiction, involves two steps: disbursing funds to individuals and collecting the money once again at the State or community level. Because each step has its costs, direct transfers to State and local governments may save on overall transaction costs.

BETTER GOVERNMENT THROUGH COMMUNITY AND INDIVIDUAL EMPOWERMENT

Over time, a large number of Federal programs have evolved primarily to meet certain perceived needs that were not being adequately addressed at the State and local level. Although these programs direct attention and resources to real problems, in some cases they leave too little discretion to States and localities in allocating the funds, and Federal paperwork requirements lead States and localities to devote too large a share of their resources toward administrative costs. Furthermore, in some cases these funds could be more effective if they were used to empower *individuals,* by providing them the wherewithal and the information to make appropriate choices, rather than having government—Federal, State, or local—in the driver's seat.

This Administration has put forward a new approach to Federal grants:

- The Federal Government would provide States and local governments with greatly enhanced flexibility: funds from numerous programs would be consolidated, and regulations would be pared back.
- Accountability would be ensured not by restrictions on the use of funds but by performance measures. Programs that live up to their stated goals could receive more funding.
- Individuals benefiting from government programs would also be given as much discretion as possible to choose how those funds should be spent, reducing the possibility that they would be spent unwisely.

One example of this new approach is the Administration's proposed G.I. Bill for America's Workers (Box 4–3). Under the current Job Training Partnership Act, States are provided the funds to obtain training for dislocated workers. Under the Administration's proposal, funds would instead be dispensed directly to individuals, in the form of "skill grants" which they could use for tuition at private or public institutions. States and localities would create one-stop career development centers, which would provide individuals with the information necessary to make good choices about how to use their skill grants, would track participant earnings and job retention, and would work with businesses to help match newly trained workers with jobs. Allowing individuals to make informed choices about what skills to obtain and where to obtain them will ensure that only those institutions that provide high-quality, relevant training will survive.

The Administration has also encouraged legislative efforts, such as the proposed Local Empowerment and Flexibility Act, that would waive programmatic regulations for local communities that have a federally approved "Local Flexibility Plan" from certain Federal laws and regulations that impede their efforts to meet their plan. Similarly, as part of its overhaul of environmental regulation, the Administration has initiated Project XL, which gives responsible companies and other regulated parties the flexibility to replace the requirements of the current regulatory system with their own alternative strategies to achieve better bottom-line environmental results.

These efforts are similar to the project currently under way to revitalize distressed communities: The Empowerment Zone and Enterprise Community (EZ/EC) initiative provides block grants, tax subsidies, and regulatory flexibility to a number of designated communities that have formulated innovative strategic development plans. A major element of these plans, and of the EZ/EC initiative, is the inclusion of performance benchmarks, so that policymakers can learn what works and what does not.

In cases where local control has not done the job, a reconsideration of the intergovernmental partnership is in order. Public housing is one example of a program that needs major change (Box 4–4). In its plan to reorganize the Department of Housing and Urban Development (HUD), the Administration proposed providing greatly increased flexibility to well-performing housing agencies and overhauling those public housing agencies that are chronically troubled. In some cases, residents of severely distressed units will be provided with rental vouchers, which could be used to obtain private housing. After all, individuals have the best incentive to ensure that the dollars they receive for housing are well spent.

DEVOLUTION AND THE SAFETY NET

This country has reached a general consensus that providing a minimum level of subsistence for our most vulnerable citizens, regardless of where they live, is an essential government role. But because differences exist across States—in job opportunities, in family characteristics, and even in views on the appropriate level of support for the poor—States also have a role in providing and administering the safety net.

At the same time, safety net programs—programs that provide assistance to those meeting certain income or asset tests, such as Aid to Families with Dependent Children (AFDC) or Medicaid—present several problems that require some Federal role. One problem stems from the mobility of the population. For example, whenever one State chooses to expand its welfare program—by raising benefits or relaxing eligibility criteria—it may encourage poor people from other States to move in. As they do, the welfare program becomes more expensive, forcing the State either to reduce benefits or eligibility, raise taxes, or both. If the State raises taxes to pay

Box 4–3.—Rethinking Devolution: The Job Training Partnership Act

The history of the Job Training Partnership Act (JTPA) shows that simply shifting accountability and policy discretion to the States does not always improve performance. When enacted in 1982, JTPA was designed as a block grant to the States. JTPA reduced the role of the Federal Government, enhanced the role of the States, and retained a strong role for policymaking and initiative at the local level. However, the program became the subject of a growing number of reports. The General Accounting Office concluded that Federal dollars were being misused, while the Department of Labor's Office of the Inspector General found a serious lack of uniform control and guidance. JTPA's problems led the previous Administration and a coalition in Congress to reassert Federal accountability through a set of new rules and regulations enacted in 1992.

The 1992 legislation was an understandable response, but it made JTPA less flexible. The dilemma facing JTPA is one of the reasons why the present Administration has proposed a G.I. Bill for America's Workers. The new bill is based on a different model, one that replaces bureaucratic accountability with market-driven accountability based on individual empowerment, informed customer choice, and competition among providers. It establishes appropriate and complementary roles for all three levels of government—Federal, State, and local—in the design, implementation, and oversight of effective workforce development systems. It also provides for the close participation of businesses, labor organizations, and local elected officials to facilitate effective training and placement.

for the more expensive welfare program, residents with higher incomes may migrate to other States with lower taxes, again making it harder for the State to finance its established level of benefits. Accordingly, States and localities are discouraged from providing safety net benefits. This phenomenon—sometimes labeled the "race to the bottom"—limits the ability of States to offer their residents welfare benefits that are as generous as they would like in the absence of migration.

The severity of this problem depends on how prone people are to move in response to differences in the generosity of welfare benefits across States. The evidence is inconclusive. Some researchers have found that low-income households are indeed more likely to move from low-benefit to high-benefit States, whereas others have found no evidence of welfare-induced migration. Even when welfare bene-

Box 4-4. Rethinking Devolution: The Case of Public Housing

Since 1937 the Federal Government has invested some $90 billion in Federal housing. The legacy of that investment is mixed. Public housing does provide affordable shelter for approximately 1.3 million households. But many public housing projects are in abject disrepair.

One problem with the current system is the lack of accountability. The discipline of the real estate market seldom extends to public housing. Instead, local public housing agencies administer the public housing stock, subject to the rules and regulations of a distant Federal bureaucracy. Under the reorganization plan for the Department of Housing and Urban Development, well-performing public housing agencies will be given greater flexibility to improve their housing stock, through modernization or demolition, and to attract and retain a broader range of families by setting their own rules for admission to public housing.

But public housing agencies that exhibit persistent management deficiencies will be overhauled. And some projects, such as Chicago's infamous Cabrini-Green, will be demolished. In many cases, residents of demolished units will be given rental vouchers to live in better housing in the private market. Vouchers permit tenants to demand quality housing, and also make it easier for them to seek out gainful employment and jobs that maximize their income, regardless of where they are located. In other communities, a new form of public housing is being tested. Instead of mammoth apartment buildings, small-scale, townhouse-style housing is being constructed that would provide housing to residents with a wide range of incomes. Instead of purely public ownership and management, this housing will be owned and managed by partnerships between public entities and for-profit and non-profit developers.

fits are found to affect migration, the effects are generally small and slow to happen. But even if the effects are small on average, they could be substantial for neighboring States with population centers in close proximity. Furthermore, the studies examining the effects of differences in AFDC benefit levels on migration were all done within the context of the current AFDC program, which does impose some limits on the differences across States. For instance, although average benefit levels and eligibility requirements vary widely, States are required to provide coverage for all families meeting the State income and asset requirements. Interstate competition might be more of a problem if some States imposed rigid time limits on welfare recipiency or denied benefits to certain families while others did not.

Some State legislatures have taken the position that welfare-induced migration occurs and should be discouraged. As a result, under waivers granted by the previous Administration, California and Wisconsin were permitted to create "two-tier" welfare systems, in which new residents on AFDC could receive a different level of benefits than longer term residents of those States. However, some have questioned the legality of the two-tier system: California's waiver was voided by the Court of Appeals, and Wisconsin's is the subject of pending litigation.

Disparities in State resources—particularly in relation to the demands put upon them—provide another rationale for a Federal role. Poorer States feel that they cannot afford the same level of safety net protection that wealthier States can. As in the case of public services, this rationale does not necessarily imply that the Federal Government should finance the safety net programs. Just as the government can help provide public services in two ways, it also has two ways of helping individuals: directly, and indirectly by first giving it to States and communities. The direct method can save on transaction costs, and the resulting empowerment of individuals may enhance the efficiency of the funds. On the other hand, in cases where benefit recipients also require other government help—for example, in finding child care or getting job training—transfers to States or communities to fund such services may prove more effective.

Some States have historically been poorer than others, and these differences are not likely to change any time soon. But in addition to these persistent disparities, shorter term disparities arise from fluctuations in the business cycle. In the past, Federal funding has acted in part as a form of insurance against these shocks, with those States experiencing increases in their poverty population receiving greater Federal funding. To some extent States can insure themselves against *temporary* economic shocks if they maintain "rainy day" funds or if they permit themselves to borrow during hard times. However, political constraints that States face, such as balanced budget requirements, may reduce their ability to insure their safety net programs against adverse economic shocks.

THE FEDERAL ROLE IN THE SAFETY NET

All these considerations argue for a strong Federal role in safety net programs. And in fact, most safety net programs are either federally run or run jointly by the Federal and State governments. The Federal Government finances and makes policy decisions for Food Stamps and Supplemental Security Income (SSI, the cash assistance program for the low-income aged, blind, or disabled);

123

States do have an administrative role in both, however, and many States supplement SSI benefits with their own funds. Medicaid and AFDC—which along with Food Stamps are the largest programs for the nonelderly poor—are administered by the States, but States and the Federal Government share responsibility for funding and for policymaking. Other safety net programs, like housing subsidies and energy assistance, are provided by both the Federal Government and the States.

The Federal share of spending on safety net and social service programs increased with the introduction of Medicaid, SSI, and Food Stamps: from roughly 44 percent of the nationwide total in 1960 to over 70 percent in 1976, and has remained relatively stable since then.

Under current law the Federal Government provides open-ended matching grants to States for Medicaid and AFDC, with the Federal share of expenditures in 1995 varying, from 50 percent to 79 percent, according to State income. This open-ended matching reduces the States' marginal price of providing benefits, giving States an incentive to provide higher levels of benefits than they otherwise would. Federal matching also helps offset the problems of States offering lower benefits for fear of becoming welfare magnets or because of insufficient resources. Yet despite their significantly higher Federal matching rates, poorer States still tend to pay lower AFDC benefits (Table 4–2).

Although the theoretical arguments supporting a Federal role in welfare are strong, almost all observers, including welfare program participants themselves, agree that the welfare system is not working well. For too long, it has undermined the values of work and personal responsibility, not strengthened them.

Welfare policy presents a dilemma with which the Nation has been struggling for 60 years: providing adequate support to low-income families who fall upon hard times, and especially to their children, without generating dependency. Despite a broad consensus that the goal of welfare reform should be to move people from welfare to work, how best to accomplish this goal is still unclear.

In such uncertain circumstances, the potential value of innovation and experimentation is high, and States have shown increasing interest in trying new approaches. This Administration has used waivers effectively to allow States to engage in valuable experimentation. The Administration has made clear that it is open to States' proposals for alternative approaches to providing welfare support. Since January 1993 the Administration has approved welfare demonstration projects in 37 states. In an average month these demonstrations will cover more than 10 million people, or approximately 73 percent of all AFDC recipients.

TABLE 4–2.—*Typical Maximum AFDC Payments for a Family of Three*

[Dollars per month]

State	Three-person family typical maximum	State	Three-person family typical maximum
Alabama	164	Montana	375
Alaska	923	Nebraska	364
Arizona	347	Nevada	348
Arkansas	204	New Hampshire	550
California	607	New Jersey	424
Colorado	356	New Mexico	381
Connecticut	581	New York	577
Delaware	338	North Carolina	272
District of Columbia	420	North Dakota	431
Florida	303	Ohio	341
Georgia	280	Oklahoma	307
Hawaii	712	Oregon	460
Idaho	317	Pennsylvania	403
Illinois	377	Rhode Island	554
Indiana	288	South Carolina	200
Iowa	426	South Dakota	430
Kansas	403	Tennessee	185
Kentucky	262	Texas	188
Louisiana	190	Utah	426
Maine	418	Vermont	656
Maryland	373	Virgin Islands	240
Massachusetts	579	Virginia	291
Michigan	459	Washington	546
Minnesota	532	West Virginia	253
Mississippi	120	Wisconsin	517
Missouri	292	Wyoming	360

Note.—"Typical maximum" is amount paid for basic needs to a family (including one adult) with no income or special needs in State's highest caseload area.

Source: Department of Health and Human Services.

In their reform efforts, many States have sought to reduce welfare dependency by beginning to experiment with time limits on families' welfare benefits. Others have sought to facilitate the movement from welfare to work by setting strict job search or work requirements, or by providing subsidies to private employers who hire welfare recipients. Many States require recipients to sign "personal employability plans" or "self-sufficiency agreements," with specific goals and deadlines. Failure to meet the deadlines can result in reduction or denial of benefits.

The Administration has reinforced these state welfare reform efforts with other policies that reward work over welfare. In 1993 the President's economic plan cut the taxes of 15 million working families through the earned income tax credit. The Administration has also proposed raising the minimum wage to ensure that, in combination with the Earned Income Tax Credit, a single parent with two children working full-time would escape poverty. The Administration has also strengthened collection of child support, enabling more single parents to support themselves through a combination of child support and work, instead of welfare.

MOVING FORWARD: WELFARE REFORM

The Administration has called for comprehensive, bipartisan welfare reform legislation to impose time limits, work requirements,

125

and tough child support enforcement nationwide. Many in the Congress, believing that the waiver process is still too burdensome and uncertain, have proposed converting AFDC into a block grant program, providing States the flexibility to design their own approaches to welfare reform without the need for waivers from Washington, and putting an end to the open-ended entitlement funding structure.

Converting AFDC to a pure block grant could have a number of effects. First, under pure block grants, States would no longer receive additional funding for increases in benefits arising from economic downturns or population growth, making it more difficult to provide needed benefits. Second, under a block grant program, States would receive a fixed amount of money from the Federal Government, independent of the level of State expenditures. The elimination of the Federal matching program would mean that States would no longer receive extra Federal money when they raised benefits, nor lose Federal support when they cut benefits. This change in incentives (which would be greater for low-income States since they now have the most generous Federal match rates) might induce some States to cut their welfare spending.

On the other hand, converting AFDC to a block grant program would also mean that States that managed to get people off welfare and into jobs would realize all the resulting welfare savings. Under the current program most State job training expenditures are not matched, even though the Federal Government receives a large fraction of the resulting welfare savings.

In any reform of the welfare system, the Administration has consistently argued for crucial safeguards to promote work and responsibility and to protect children. It has insisted on a strong maintenance-of-effort requirement so that States keep their welfare spending at adequate levels, and sufficient resources to pay for child care so that recipients can leave welfare and go to work. Finally, the Administration has required that additional resources be made available to States during economic downturns. Under the current system, this occurs automatically through the Federal match, but an adequately financed contingency fund with an effective trigger mechanism could also accomplish this goal.

Because the current system frustrates taxpayers and recipients alike, the Administration plans to work with the Congress to enact a bipartisan welfare reform bill. As part of its 7-year balanced budget proposal, the Administration has proposed repealing the AFDC program and replacing it with a new Federal program with strict time limits on welfare benefits. The new program would require parents to go to work after 2 years or lose their benefits; after 5 years benefits would end unconditionally. States would enjoy new flexibility to tailor their welfare systems to local conditions. At the same time, the plan would provide vouchers to protect children whose parents reach the time limit. Because the Federal government would continue to match State welfare spending, States would be protected in the event of economic downturns or caseload growth.

MOVING FORWARD: MEDICAID

This Administration has insisted upon maintaining the Federal entitlement to Medicaid, for two main reasons. First, this Administration believes that all Americans should be guaranteed access to quality medical care, regardless of income or State of residence. Second, the Medicaid program is not performing badly: it needs reform, not repeal. Although overall Medicaid expenditures have been increasing at a rapid rate, part of this increase is attributable to legislated increases in the eligible population.

This Administration's insistence upon maintaining the guarantee of health care coverage for poor families in no way contradicts its commitment to flexibility, innovation, and experimentation. The President's plan expands State flexibility in administering Medicaid programs, but maintains protection for beneficiaries and for States facing population growth or economic downturns. To this end, the Administration is committed to working in partnership with the States to test new approaches to Medicaid through the waiver process. The Administration shares States' interest in developing innovative delivery systems, improving quality of care, and expanding coverage to uninsured Americans. To date, the Administration has approved 12 comprehensive health care reform demonstrations. These waivers have allowed States to greatly increase their use of managed care, to subsidize health insurance for employed but uninsured workers, and to expand Medicaid eligibility by eliminating asset tests and increasing income limits. Furthermore, the Administration has granted 14 States Medicaid waivers as part of larger welfare reform projects. These waivers enable States to continue providing essential health care services while encouraging independence from welfare. The Administration's 7-year budget plan would give States further flexibility to modify their programs. In particular, it would no longer require States to obtain a waiver in order to expand coverage to any person whose income is at or below 150 percent of the poverty line, to use managed care plans to provide health insurance to their Medicaid population, or to move people from nursing homes to home- and community-based settings. The plan also repeals the Boren Amendment, thus allowing States greater flexibility in establishing their provider payment rates.

THE CHALLENGES OF DEVOLUTION

This Administration is committed to making government more efficient and effective. Designing government programs so that activities are performed at the appropriate government level—Federal, State, or local—is one of the most difficult challenges associated with this task. Although in many areas the answers are clear—national defense is a Federal responsibility, whereas sewage treatment and water supply are local responsibilities—in many other areas the advantages of Federal responsibility must be balanced against the advantages of State and local responsibility. Federal grants to fund certain public services can reduce the problems of spillovers, but if the sense of accountability for Federal funds is different from that for funds raised through State or local taxes, Federal grants may be spent unwisely. Restrictions on the use of Federal funds may reduce this problem, but they may also impose significant administrative burdens and severely limit State innovation.

One approach to solving this problem is to ensure accountability through results-oriented measures, rather than through conventional rules and regulations. A results-oriented approach allows States much more flexibility without severely hampering efficiency. The Administration has proposed using this approach in housing, job training, the environment, welfare, and numerous other policy areas. Subjecting government expenditures to this discipline is likely to be the best way to improve government efficiency. Furthermore, when possible, government should use the private market directly. For example, individuals can be provided housing vouchers that permit them to live wherever they choose, and those in need of job training can receive funds to pay for training at the institution of their choice. In this way, individuals are provided the wherewithal to choose what is best for them, and only those providers that bring desirable services to market at the lowest cost—whether it be rental housing or job training—will survive.

States must also be provided with greater flexibility where no consensus has emerged on how to accomplish the goal. In these cases, experimentation and innovation by the States could prove invaluable. But this enhanced flexibility must be provided in a way that protects the national interest and advances the objectives of the programs. What is appropriate in one program may not be appropriate in another. In some cases the solution may entail Federal regulation as a "default option," with wide latitude for waivers to allow for State and local adaptation. In other cases, block grants with little Federal policy involvement may be called for.

Devising policies that ensure accountability and that protect the national interest, while also allowing for flexibility, adaptability, and innovation at the State, local, and individual levels is a great challenge. What worked in the past may no longer work today. Carefully balancing the advantages and disadvantages to find the right mix of policies is vital if government is to work at its best.

CHAPTER 5

Economic Efficiency and Regulatory Reform

OUR LIVING STANDARDS depend on more than just our monetary income. We benefit from open spaces and clean rivers and lakes. We gain a sense of security from safer airplanes, cars, food, and toys for our children. We benefit from safer workplaces and from safer financial institutions.

Over the years the U.S. Government has enacted a number of laws and issued a number of regulations designed to protect consumers, workers, and investors. These efforts are important for improving our environment, public health, and safety. Reducing the corrosion of factory equipment by polluted water, or the loss of agricultural productivity due to air pollution, also lowers business costs. In some cases, efforts to correct environmental or safety problems may stimulate other productivity improvements.

But regulation also inevitably imposes costs, and these can be substantial. They include not only direct expenditures to enforce and comply with regulation, but also indirect costs, such as loss of flexibility and choice for consumers and businesses, diversion of investment from other productive activities, and delays in redeveloping inner cities where hazardous waste sites are located.

To best serve the public interest, regulation should impose the least burden necessary to achieve its objective, and its benefits should justify its costs. A major theme of this Administration has been *reinventing regulation*: taking a new look at regulation and the regulatory process to ensure that regulations meet legitimate social needs, and where necessary changing both content and process to improve efficiency and effectiveness.

This chapter begins by surveying the broad and continuing debate over the scope and design of regulation. It identifies the rationales for regulation and the basic principles of effective and efficient regulation of threats to human health, safety, and the environment. The balance of the chapter then illustrates the application of these principles in the context of ongoing efforts to restructure regulations affecting the environment and natural resources.

RATIONALES FOR GOVERNMENT REGULATION

The fundamental strength of a market economy is that the pursuit of private gain serves the public interest by stimulating efficiency and innovation. But private gain and public interest are not always so firmly tethered: they can and do diverge. In the absence of regulation, polluters do not have an incentive to pay adequate attention to the environmental damage they cause. Workplaces may be unsafe. Consumers may be unwittingly exposed to defective or unsafe products and services.

Economists refer to such divergences between public and private interest as *externalities,* because in each case the amount paid for a good or service fails to reflect its full cost to society—some costs remain "external" to the transaction. Externalities are a form of *market failure.* Government action is needed to correct this market failure, by confronting economic actors with the full costs of their behavior. Correcting externalities improves economic efficiency and the quality of life. The United States has long used regulations as a way of better aligning public and private interests within the market. For example, legislation in the area of food and drug safety was enacted in the 1930s. Internalization of externalities is an important role of government in modern society, to be set alongside the provision of public goods like national defense and the maintenance of a social safety net.

Although this chapter focuses on regulation, governments have a variety of other tools to address market failure. These include direct changes in incentives through subsidies or fees; changes in legal liability standards; provision of information about products, markets, and technologies; support for the development of new technologies; and voluntary, cooperative ventures with the private sector.

Changes in our economy and our society call for changes in regulatory policies. When pressures mount for both land development and the preservation of undeveloped natural areas, new tensions in land use and resource protection policies will have to be addressed. As States demand a greater say over their own affairs, Federal-State partnerships grow, leading to tensions between the objectives of consistency and flexibility. Regulation also must adjust to reflect changes in technology. For example, it is important to focus on the risks posed by contaminants, not just the ability to measure their concentrations in human tissues and the environment.

The Administration's strategy of reinventing regulation addresses these varied and sometimes conflicting concerns. It encompasses not just deregulation and reform of the content of regulation, but also a rethinking of *how* government regulates. The goal is to devise a regulatory system that both works better and is more responsive to public concerns.

Efforts to reinvent regulation are taking a variety of forms. One important step is better targeting of regulatory efforts to where the need is greatest. Another is a shift in emphasis from prescribing methods of compliance to specifying desired outcomes. Still another is harnessing economic incentives through market-based regulatory mechanisms. The process of regulating can be improved through reduced paperwork burdens and streamlined reporting requirements, better dissemination of information to the public, and increased opportunities for public participation in the regulatory process.

EVALUATING REGULATORY PERFORMANCE: PRINCIPLES AND PRACTICE

Evaluating regulatory reforms requires consideration of the benefits and costs of alternatives. This can raise a number of questions. What range of consequences from regulation should be considered? How does one address benefits or costs that are uncertain or inherently difficult to quantify? How should concerns about fairness be dealt with? How should regulators balance the need for consistency in rulemaking with the advantages of flexibility? How can the assessment process itself obtain high-quality analysis without creating an excessive administrative burden, and without imposing excessive societal costs from the delay of necessary actions?

SETTING REGULATORY PRIORITIES

Executive Order 12866, which the President signed on September 30, 1993, reflects the Administration's basic philosophy and principles for regulatory planning and review. The order stipulates a number of criteria that should apply both to assessments of "significant" new regulations (including but not limited to regulations with an expected annual economic effect of $100 million or more) and to reevaluations of existing regulations. The order requires that Federal regulations address real needs while avoiding undue economic burdens. In assessing the need for regulation, agencies should consider a variety of alternatives, including alternatives to new regulation. The assessment should use the best reasonably available information, including information about risks and costs and the uncertainties surrounding them, and it should encompass both quantitative and qualitative benefits and costs. To the extent compatible with existing statutes, agencies should show that the chosen regulatory approach maximizes net benefits (including economic, environmental, public health and safety, and other advantages, as well as distributional impacts and equity), and that those benefits justify the costs. The means of regulating should be cost-effective, imposing the least possible cost on society to achieve the objective (after taking into account the potential for technical innovation, requirements for verifying compliance, and equity concerns). Federal agencies should also reduce regulatory inconsistency and overlap; they should coordinate their activities with State, local, and tribal governments; and they should provide significant opportunities for contribution by the public to regulatory review.

The criteria for regulatory planning and review established in the order recognize that some benefits and costs are difficult to quantify but nevertheless important. The order acknowledges the importance and limitations of benefit-cost evaluations for obtaining good regulatory outcomes. The Administration opposes legislative changes that would burden the regulatory system with rigidly prescribed assessment methods, unnecessary costs and delay, and excessive opportunities for litigation.

DESIGNING EFFECTIVE REGULATORY POLICIES

To make regulation less burdensome, the order states that, wherever possible, agencies specify regulatory goals in terms of *performance standards,* which specify desired outcomes, rather than *design standards,* which prescribe methods of compliance. Performance-based regulation lowers the cost of compliance by allowing a variety of compliance options and encouraging technical innovation. In contrast, the input-oriented, design standards approach tends to raise the cost of achieving regulatory objectives by limiting flexibility. For example, standards for atmospheric pollutants could specify a desired reduction in emissions or in the damages caused by emissions, and a means for determining whether that reduction has been achieved. This obviates the need to mandate investment in specific pollution abatement technology such as scrubbers for power plants.

Performance standards may require greater effort on the part of regulators to ascertain the level of compliance. They also require public confidence in the approach. The applicability of performance standards in practice is limited by constraints on the ability to monitor compliance and public acceptance. Improved measurement capacities and increased confidence in the approach can be expected to increase its applicability, yielding significant improvements in the cost-effectiveness of regulation.

Even with performance standards in place, the total cost to the economy of complying with regulation may be higher than necessary. The total cost can be reduced if those who face lower compliance costs undertake more of the total effort required. Regulations can employ economic incentives toward this end, rather than rigid requirements. Society further benefits from incentive-based policies because they can provide a strong inducement to the development of new technologies that reduce the cost of compliance for all.

Tradeable emissions allowances for pollution control illustrate these points. A tradeable emissions regime sets a limit on total emissions from all sources and a nominal emissions limit for each source. Sources can then vary their actual emissions above or below that limit through voluntary exchange of emissions allowances with other emitters. Those that can comply at lower cost can cheaply cut emissions below their nominal limit, then sell their unused allowances to emitters with higher costs, who can then exceed their nominal emissions levels. A further advantage of allowances is that they essentially put a price on allowed emissions, providing an incentive for the development of lower cost options for pollution control and prevention.

Although regulation is necessary to curb negative externalities such as pollution, in some cases government policy itself contributes to externalities. Then the challenge to designing effective policies includes reducing these government-induced distortions. For example, ill-designed subsidies can contribute to environmental harm. These include agricultural commodity programs that encourage overuse of soil, water, and chemical fertilizers, and access to forests on government land at less than their opportunity cost. Reducing or eliminating distorting subsidies offers an opportunity to improve the environment and market performance simultaneously.

REGULATION AND DEVOLUTION

The question of who should regulate can be as important as how to regulate. This question has no easy answer. Many of the arguments parallel those raised in Chapter 4 on the devolution of expenditure programs. If regulatory authority goes to that level of government whose jurisdiction best corresponds to the scope of the externality, this can help ensure a solution that is tailored to the problem. For example, plans to clean up and rehabilitate contaminated industrial sites might be better made at the State or the local level. State and local decisionmakers may be better able to assess the benefits and costs of additional cleanup—greater public safety, cleaner sites, but increased expense and delay—and to ensure that resources are used most efficiently.

Devolution of regulatory responsibility may not be appropriate, however, for several reasons. Broader, cross-jurisdictional environmental interests may be at stake. For example, protecting wetlands and endangered species habitats is a national as well as a local issue. The impacts of pollution may transcend local boundaries. Federal regulation of air and surface water pollution is intended in part to address the fact that some of these problems spill over city limits and State lines. State or local authorities might have a weak interest in preventing or containing damages outside their jurisdictions. Devolution of regulatory authority might also compromise protection because of limits on local regulatory capacity (such as inadequate resources for monitoring or lack of enforcement experience), or because States or localities are in competition with each other for economic development opportunities. In addition, disparate State or local regulatory standards can increase costs of compliance by, for example, requiring excessive product differentiation.

Problems can arise when the impacts of externalities are felt by one group of people, but political decisions are made by others. By the same token, however, problems can arise when the beneficiaries of policies to address externalities do not have a stake in balancing the costs and benefits of policy intervention. This can happen when decisions are made by States or localities but costs are borne at the Federal level. Conversely, the imposition of requirements on State and local governments without the funding to meet those requirements—so-called unfunded mandates—has become a point of contention. Some mandates could be seen as undue restrictions on local discretion, but others may appropriately compensate for market or policy failures at the State or local level. For example, if a mandate restricts the ability of States or localities to impose externalities on others, it can be justified on the same economic grounds that apply to the regulation of private entities that generate externalities. It can be difficult in practice to ascertain into which category a particular mandate falls. In any case, the Federal Government should be aware of the costs it imposes on other levels of government. As noted in Chapter 4, legislation passed in 1995 ensures that this information will be available during congressional debates.

REGULATORY ASSESSMENT IN PRACTICE

The capacity to estimate the consequences of regulation has grown enormously since the early days of benefit-cost analysis. And even imprecise analyses can at least be useful in placing bounds around potential benefits and costs. Nevertheless, a number of methodological questions persist and are addressed in newly updated guidelines issued by the Office of Management and Budget. The following examples illustrate these issues and the means available to address them.

The primary purpose of much regulation is to reduce an identified threat to human health, safety, or the environment. However, there are gaps in current knowledge about the nature and magnitude of the hazards that different substances and practices pose to different parts of the population, and about the costs of reducing those hazards. With limited information, analysts will be able to describe only a few possible scenarios; in other cases a more complete characterization of outcomes and probabilities may be possible. Such information may include measures of central tendency (e.g., the median risk), upper and lower bounds, measures of the uncertainty of possible outcomes, and effects on different populations. Where the level of risk depends on more than one factor (e.g., both exposure and toxicity), statistical techniques can combine these factors in a way that accurately describes the overall risk without putting excessive emphasis on those outcomes that are very unlikely.

The valuation of risk reduction is an important element of many regulatory assessments. It is complicated, however, by the fact that typically there are no markets that directly value the reductions in risk achieved through regulation. Instead, indirect methods must be employed. For example, the assessment of many health and safety regulations centers on the question, By how much will this regulation reduce the risk of illness or premature death? It is possible in principle to assign an economic value to the reduced risk of premature mortality by posing the question, How much would members of the affected public willingly pay for this reduction in the probability of earlier death? This makes the issue analogous to the willingness to pay for insurance—and quite different from placing a monetary value on a specific person's life. (Even the notion of putting a monetary value on risk reductions of this kind remains controversial for many.) The question can be approached by examining, for example, how much more people pay for safer but costlier products, or by estimating the wage premiums offered for riskier occupations. However, debate continues about the reliability and applicability of this information to the assessment of other kinds of risks. Among the questions at issue are the degree to which the risks in question are assumed voluntarily or involuntarily, and the extent to which valuations should reflect the age of those affected and the latency of the risk (that is, the lag with which any ill effects are likely to occur).

Discounting future benefits and costs is another complicated methodological issue. Benefits received now or soon are generally worth more to people—have higher present value—than the same benefits received later. An important question here is the extent to which the costs of regulation displace private consumption or investment. Displacement of investment implies a loss of future consumption possibilities. Higher market returns on investment imply a larger consumption displacement. The weighing of long-term benefits and costs should also attempt to account for changes in the *relative* scarcity of resources and the potential for irreversible losses that result in a sacrifice of future as well as current benefits.

Analysis of issues with very long-term consequences, such as climate change and depletion of the stratospheric ozone layer, involves yet another complicated issue: tradeoffs among the interests of different generations that may give rise to ethical considerations. One way to introduce ethical elements into the analysis is through intergenerational discount rates that explicitly reflect assumptions about society's attitudes toward such tradeoffs. Discount rates derived from ethical considerations about fairness to future generations were calculated in one study to range between 0.5 and 3.0 percent (in real terms) for an advanced industrial economy. This range is generally below rates of return to private capital, but not necessarily below real short-term yields on government bonds.

SETTING REGULATORY PRIORITIES FOR THE ENVIRONMENT AND NATURAL RESOURCES

Over the past 25 years environmental regulation has succeeded in reducing a number of threats to human health and the environment. For example, emissions of lead into the air, which pose serious threats to human health, have fallen sharply (Table 5–1), and lead paint has been banned. As a consequence, blood lead levels have dropped sharply. Air quality in many cities has improved considerably (Chart 5–1). The past quarter century has also seen efforts to protect valuable natural resources such as wetlands, and the ban on the pesticide DDT has reduced serious threats to species like the bald eagle. The agreement to phase out the production of substances that deplete stratospheric ozone is an important first step toward greater international cooperation in protecting the global environment. Nevertheless, concerns about local environmental quality remain. For example, the frequency with which concentrations of fecal coliform bacteria in rivers and streams are found to exceed standards shows little decline. And other regional and global problems have come to the fore, such as the global loss of biodiversity, marine pollution, stress on fisheries, and the threat of global warming.

It is important to consider the costs of environmental policies as well as their benefits. Direct public and private expenditures associated with the regulations of the Environmental Protection Agency (EPA) have been estimated to be between 1.6 and 1.8 percent of GDP since the mid-1970s, a small but significant share of total economic activity. In absolute terms, current-dollar expenditures in 1992 and 1993 were slightly over $100 billion, or almost as much as total personal expenditures for religious and philanthropic activities. These estimates exclude indirect costs associated with environmental regulations, and the costs of other regulations to restrict land and natural resource use. They also do not indicate the marginal cost of stricter regulation.

138

TABLE 5–1.—*Atmospheric Emissions of Lead, by Source, 1970–94*

[Thousand short tons]

Year	Total	Non-transportation fuel combustion	Transportation	Industrial processes
1970	219.5	10.6	180.3	28.6
1975	158.5	10.3	135.2	13.0
1980	75.0	4.3	65.5	5.1
1985	20.1	.5	16.2	3.4
1990	5.7	.5	1.9	3.3
1994	5.0	.5	1.6	2.9

Note.—Detail may not add to totals because of rounding.
Source: Environmental Protection Agency.

Chart 5-1 **Air Quality in Urban Areas**
Air quality has improved markedly in just the last decade.

Days per year of "good" or "moderate" air quality

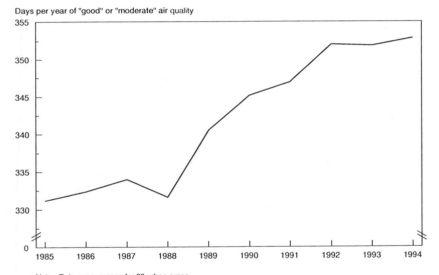

Note: Data are averages for 23 urban areas.
Source: Environmental Protection Agency.

Satisfying public concern for protection of the environment and natural resources without imposing an undue burden on the economy is a challenge. Part of the Administration's response is through programs like EPA's Common Sense Initiative. This program is a pilot collaborative effort among government, business, and the public to identify areas for improvement in how regulations are structured and implemented, and how technologies can be improved to help protect the environment. Another new initiative is EPA's Project XL, which invites companies to propose their own environmental performance standards, to increase flexibility and improve environmental performance. The Army Corps of Engineers has streamlined permitting procedures related to protection of wetlands to reduce regulatory burdens on activities involving small tracts of land.

Beyond these efforts, resources devoted to regulation can be used more efficiently through careful evaluation of benefits and costs, keeping in mind the uncertainties inherent in such evaluations and the need to consider qualitative or subjective factors such as distributional equity and environmental justice, as noted above. Three recent regulatory reform initiatives—the reauthorization of the Safe Drinking Water Act, the reform of waste management programs, and shifts in the focus of agricultural land retirement programs—illustrate efforts to target regulation better.

THE SAFE DRINKING WATER ACT

The unanimous reauthorization by the Senate of the Safe Drinking Water Act in the fall of 1995 is a good example of bipartisan legislative reform to increase the role of benefit-cost assessments in setting more rational priorities. The previous version of the act put EPA on a regulatory treadmill, requiring new standards for 25 substances every 3 years, regardless of the threat they posed. A study by the Congressional Budget Office estimated the cost of reducing cancer risk under standards that various administrations have been required to promulgate for different contaminants under the act. The estimates ranged from less than $1 million to over $4 billion per expected cancer death avoided. Although other important health benefits besides reduced risk of cancer are also tied to drinking water standards, a range this wide suggests that much could be gained from better targeting of regulatory efforts on those substances that pose the greatest risk.

The Senate revisions to the act would explicitly allow EPA to consider the balance between potential public health benefits and the costs when establishing drinking water standards. EPA would be able to target those threats to public health that scientific assessments indicate are more important. EPA could also modify standards whose benefits do not justify the costs, so long as the alternative standard chosen maintains or increases health benefits. This general approach—protecting public health and environmental values, but also providing greater latitude for balancing benefits and costs—is an instructive example of how such balancing provisions could be incorporated in other environmental laws and regulations.

HAZARDOUS WASTE

There are several important Federal programs for disposal of hazardous wastes and cleanups of waste contamination. The Comprehensive Environmental Response, Compensation, and Liability Act (CERCLA, otherwise known as the Superfund program) established a program to clean up major disused contaminated sites. CERCLA also requires those responsible to restore, replace, or provide compensation for the loss, injury, or destruction of natural resources (Box 5–1). The Resource Conservation and Recovery Act (RCRA) established a program that regulates ongoing management of hazardous and solid wastes, as well as cleanups of facilities covered by the permitting requirements of the act. The Federal Government also is subject to these laws and cleans up sites managed by Federal agencies or contractors.

CERCLA and RCRA require that cleanups and waste management protect human health and the environment. To achieve this goal, CERCLA currently contains a strong preference for remedies that are permanent and involve treatment of contaminants, as opposed to lower cost alternatives that contain the contamination and limit human exposure or environmental damage, without a full long-term cleanup. CERCLA currently puts only limited weight on cleanup costs as one of a number of factors to be balanced in selecting remedies. In addition, remedies must satisfy a variety of other Federal and State statutory requirements directly or indirectly related to site cleanups; these can impose stricter standards than CERCLA itself would require. Some standards for hazardous waste disposal under RCRA require threats to human health and the environment to be "minimized," regardless of the level of risk posed by the waste or the cost of compliance. This requirement could imply the need for waste management efforts to intensify as technical capacity improves, regardless of background environmental quality or the hazard posed by the material.

The advantages of reform in waste cleanup could be substantial. The Administration estimated that its 1994 CERCLA reform proposals (discussed below) could reduce cleanup costs by 19 to 25 percent (including savings at Federal facilities). A review of CERCLA cleanup decisions by researchers at the University of Tennessee found that increasing the flexibility of remedy selection could reduce the cost of actual site cleanup by anywhere from 20 percent to more than 50 percent without compromising the basic statutory goal of protecting human health and the environment. Since governments and private parties spend several billion dollars each year on CERCLA site remediation, the total savings could be substantial. Significant cost savings could also be realized from reforms of RCRA. For example, EPA has estimated that billions of dollars in cumulative cost savings could be obtained by increasing the flexibility with which one category of materials—contaminated materials excavated during site cleanups—is handled, without an unacceptable increase in risk.

Improving the balance between the benefits of risk reduction, on the one hand, and the costs of cleaning up old waste and managing new waste, on the other, calls for both legislative and administrative changes. These should build upon the basic principles laid out earlier in this chapter. Cleanup remedies and regulations for managing new wastes should protect human health and the environment. Policies should reflect sound assessments of the risks involved. Decisionmakers should have greater flexibility in designing remedies and waste management policies, and greater weight should be given to costs than in the past. Decisions should take into account the concerns of affected communities and the potential for redevelopment of contaminated sites. And regulatory actions should be able to proceed without bogging down in red tape. The policy debate seems to center not so much on these basic principles as on how reforms should be implemented and how tradeoffs should be structured to achieve the stipulated goals.

During the 1994 debate on CERCLA reform, the Administration proposed legislation that would have given more weight to cleanup costs in choosing remedies, limited requirements for more stringent cleanups due to other statutes, and required greater consideration of the likely future uses of the site (e.g., residential versus industrial) in assessing risks and selecting remedies. The reforms would have limited the preference for permanent treatment to so-called "hot spots," such as portions of sites with high concentrations of contaminants. Under this approach, greater use could be made of remedies that prevent the spread of contaminants or avoid human exposure without requiring the more expensive removal or destruction of contaminants. Although this legislation was supported by industry and environmental interests, the 103d Congress failed to vote on it before adjourning.

Legislation introduced in the 104th Congress proposes more sweeping changes to the remediation process. The Administration opposes changes to the remediation process that provide inadequate protection, fail to give due weight to State and community interests, or pose an excessive administrative burden. Meanwhile the Administration is pursuing a number of administrative reforms to strengthen the reliability of risk assessments, put greater emphasis on sites of greater risk, and compare the potential risk reductions and costs of alternative remedies. For example, high-cost remedies will be subject to additional review to determine whether a lower cost remedy would meet the cleanup goals. A finding of high cost and limited risk reduction would provide a rationale for waiving more restrictive remedy requirements.

The Administration organized public discussions on reinventing RCRA. These generated a variety of suggestions for the management of newly created wastes: disposal restrictions could be made more risk-based, barriers to economically and environmentally sound recycling could be lowered, and there could be more flexibility in determining what substances will be regulated as hazardous wastes. The Administration currently supports carefully targeted legislative efforts to relax restrictions on certain low-risk types of waste disposal. Through rulemaking, EPA is attempting to exclude certain low-risk materials from RCRA hazardous waste requirements.

As indicated previously, cost savings also can be obtained from increased regulatory flexibility in handling materials produced in the course of cleanups. Even if these materials have low levels of contamination, under current law they must be treated the same as the most hazardous industrial process wastes. When large volumes of these materials become subject to strict cleanup standards, they can pose a significant cost burden. Reform can be achieved without jeopardizing human health and the environment by combining some relaxation of waste disposal requirements with a requirement that a cleanup plan be approved by Federal or State regulators.

AGRICULTURAL LAND RETIREMENT PROGRAMS

Over the last decade, agricultural policies have reflected a broadening of priorities to include concerns for environmental quality and market efficiency as well as farm income. This can be seen in changes in commodity programs that give farmers greater planting flexibility and provide greater incentives to respond to market prices rather than government support prices. Removal of market price distortions and planting restrictions can stem the overuse of chemicals and fertilizers on program crops and can encourage the adoption of environmentally beneficial crop rotations.

Concern for environmental quality is also reflected in government programs to idle cropland. These programs have been used since the 1930s both to control agricultural output and to achieve environmental goals. Program eligibility guidelines requiring the removal of land from production impose costs on society by reducing output, raising consumer prices, and distorting agricultural input markets. But idling certain tracts of land can also provide environmental benefits, for example by maintaining soil productivity through erosion control, reducing water pollution from sediment and chemical runoff, and increasing area for wildlife habitat. The net benefits of land retirement programs depend on whether they are designed primarily to control agricultural production or to protect the environment.

Box 5-1.—Natural Resource Damages

In addition to authorizing the cleanup of contaminated sites, CERCLA provides authority for certain "trustees" (Federal agencies, State governments, and Indian tribes) to seek compensation on behalf of the public for damages to public natural resources and ecosystems caused by contamination with hazardous substances. The 1990 Oil Pollution Act provides similar authority to address damages from oil spills. The laws require trustees to restore, replace, or acquire the equivalent of the damaged or destroyed resources. Trustees must also obtain compensation for interim losses incurred by the public while recovery, restoration, or replacement is taking place.

Natural resources and ecosystems support recreation and commercial ventures (such as fisheries) and provide a variety of important ecological functions such as waste absorption and species habitat. Beyond these more or less tangible benefits, the very existence of natural areas can be a source of value for people. However, quantifying the economic value of natural resource damages can be challenging. Even where the physical effects on ecosystems (such as fish kills or beach contamination) can be measured with some precision, the corresponding loss of benefits to people may be much more uncertain. The EPA and the National Science Foundation are supporting a research program to improve our understanding of the value of ecological resources, as part of the Administration's larger effort to expand and strengthen environmental research. The Administration has also issued revised rules for assessing damages under the Oil Pollution Act. Under these rules, economic assessment would determine the scale of investment when direct comparisons are not possible between the damaged resources and the resources being provided to compensate for the damages.

The Department of Agriculture's annual acreage reduction programs (ARPs) have historically required farmers to set aside a portion of their assigned crop base acreage in order to receive direct government payments and other benefits. Current law, however, gives the Secretary of Agriculture limited discretion over how and when planting restrictions are imposed. In many years, over 10 percent of U.S. cropland has been idled under the ARPs. By limiting supply and raising market prices, ARPs reduce deficiency payments and shift the cost of farm income support from taxpayers to consumers. The use of acreage restrictions to limit supply can also cause overuse of other inputs. By raising prices, ARPs create incentives to farm the land remaining in production more intensively.

This can have unfortunate environmental consequences if more fertilizer and pesticide are applied to the remaining acreage.

The Conservation Reserve Program (CRP), established in 1985, allows farmers to enter into long-term land retirement contracts with the Agriculture Department. Farmers receive "rental payments" from the government for taking environmentally sensitive land out of production. The primary goal of the legislation was to reduce soil erosion and its adverse environmental consequences, although control of agricultural output was also a key objective at the time (about one-quarter of the land enrolled in CRP may not be highly erodible, although much of this land provides wildlife habitat and other environmental benefits). Landowners bid competitively for CRP contracts. Bid selection is based on the cost of the rental payments and on an environmental benefit index. Tracts of land receive an index score that indicates the potential environmental benefits of idling those acres.

Agricultural land idled under all Federal programs has declined considerably since the late 1980s, and the CRP has supplanted annual ARPs as the main land retirement program. The 1990 Farm Bill extended the CRP, placing greater emphasis on curbing water pollution and other environmental problems. It also established the Wetlands Reserve Program (WRP) to protect and restore wetlands through long-term and permanent easements. These targeted programs complement the conservation efforts of private land trusts (Box 5–2).

Recent Administration initiatives have continued to emphasize the goal of environmental protection over that of controlling agricultural supply. For the current Farm Bill the Administration recommended that ARPs be made a discretionary tool to be used only when supply and demand are critically out of balance. Eliminating annual ARPs could also reduce the costs of operating the CRP and the WRP if the annual set-aside programs bid up the price of agricultural land, making environmental easement contracts more costly to acquire. In 1995 the Department of Agriculture allowed the early release of over 683,000 acres from CRP contracts, using a new bid selection system to replace those acres with more environmentally sensitive cropland.

How costs and environmental benefits are weighed in ranking CRP bids also affects the geographic distribution of land enrolled in the program. Most CRP acreage is currently in the Great Plains, the Mountain States, and the Corn Belt. But as more recent signups have placed more weight on water quality and habitat protection, enrollment has shifted toward the Great Lakes States, with the Corn Belt also still accounting for a large share. If funding for the CRP is reduced, decisionmakers may face more difficult tradeoffs between targeting the program for greater environmental benefit and maintaining income support for current beneficiaries. Research to estimate the economic value of environmental improvements from land retirement can provide better information on the nature of these tradeoffs.

CREATING COST-EFFECTIVE POLICIES: ECONOMIC INCENTIVES FOR ENVIRONMENTAL PROTECTION

Policymakers can create and enhance economic incentives for protecting the environment in a number of ways. Laws that specify liability for environmental damages, such as those in the Superfund program, can create incentives for increased care before the fact. Economic theory also has long advocated the use of charges or fees that induce more sparing use of nonmarket environmental resources.

The use of tradeable allowances or harvest quota shares is another approach for limiting the use of environmental resources (in this case limiting pollution discharges) or the use of natural resources such as ocean fisheries that are subject to excessive exploitation. As described earlier, this approach sets a limit on total use of the resource (a limit on the total fish harvest or waste discharge) and nominal limits on individual users. Users can, however, exceed their nominal limit by purchasing allotments from others, who then use less than their allotments. The market price that emerges for the use of the resource creates incentives to limit that use, just as a user fee does. Unlike a fee, however, trading can be used without a revenue transfer from the private sector to the government. The ability to trade allotments helps to ensure a cost-effective outcome, since those who can comply with the constraint on total resource use most economically—that is, those with the most efficient harvesting operations or lowest pollution control costs—assume the greatest share of responsibility for meeting the limit. The approach also creates incentives to devise new technologies that lower compliance costs, since all participants would like to reduce their allowance purchases or increase their allowance sales. Finally, regulators can use their flexibility in the initial allotment of allowances or quota shares to treat distributional or equity concerns that may arise from the limit on resource use.

This section discusses several examples of the use of pollution trading or tradeable harvest quotas in practice. The discussion focuses on the use of emissions trading for air pollution control and tradeable fishing quotas for regulation of overfishing. However, the approach has a number of other potential applications. For example, the Administration's 1994 assessment of the Clean Water Act reauthorization estimated compliance cost savings of several hun-

Box 5-2.—Land Trusts and the Tax System

Land trusts are private, voluntary, nonprofit conservation organizations that complement Federal and State programs by preserving 14 million acres of scenic areas, farmland, and wildlife habitat—more land than is held in State parks and recreation areas in the entire United States. Land trusts are established by national organizations such as the Nature Conservancy, the Conservation Fund, and the National Audubon Society as well as by groups at the local, State, and regional levels. Land is preserved through outright purchase, purchase of development easements, leases, and land management agreements.

Land acquired by land trusts is often purchased later by Federal resource management agencies. This acquisition sequence has several advantages. Local organizations may have better information about the environmental characteristics of particular tracts of land and more flexibility in conducting timely transactions with private landowners. Resale of land to the Federal Government, in turn, provides trusts with revenue to continue their preservation activities. Federal tax policy also affects land preservation activities. Land trusts try to acquire land through donations or below-market-value purchases, relying on incentives provided by the income, property, and estate tax codes to obtain properties or land use rights.

Federal interaction with land trusts raises two policy questions. First, do Federal agencies pay fair market value for land purchased from trusts? A recent report by the General Accounting Office suggests that they do. Second, should incentives for land preservation be altered directly through targeted programs such as the WRP, or more indirectly through changes in tax codes? Direct land retirement programs have some advantages over increases in broad-based tax incentives in their ability to target properties and set priorities for land preservation. For example, the WRP ranks easement bids according to cost, significance of ecological functions, and geographic location, among other criteria. In contrast, income or property tax credits or estate tax deferrals are available to all owners of eligible lands. Eligibility can be conditioned on providing environmental benefits, but the lands eligible for the tax incentive may not be the most ecologically desirable or cost-effective locations for such efforts. On the other hand, the greater budgetary visibility of direct programs may make them more difficult to sustain.

dred million to several billion dollars per year from expanded water pollution trading. EPA is developing a framework for expanded use of effluent trading. Expanded use of trading programs to protect wetlands and species habitats, provided they are ecologically sound, can also achieve regulatory goals while providing cost-reducing flexibility in the timing and location of protection efforts.

AIR POLLUTION TRADING

Precursors of today's air pollution emissions trading programs were established in the 1970s. An example is the "offset" program, which allows new pollution sources in areas with poor air quality, provided they reduce other emissions sources in the area by more than their own emissions. Another example is the "bubble" program. This program subjects a group of individual sources in close proximity to a single common limit on total emissions, and allows the sources to trade emissions rather than comply with individual limits. Even though subject to numerous restrictions, these programs have delivered emission reductions at lower cost.

A more comprehensive approach to emissions trading was implemented in the national program that allows power plants to trade sulfur dioxide emissions (a precursor to acid rain) under the 1990 amendments to the Clean Air Act. This program, whose initial phase began in 1995, allows firms to save money by complying with performance standards rather than strict emissions controls requiring the use of specific technologies. The shift to performance standards makes possible a broader range of cost-effective compliance strategies, such as blending coals with different sulfur contents. This flexibility has also created competition among compliance options, lowering the costs of both fuel switching and removal of sulfur from stack exhausts. These benefits have been achieved even though the initial phase of the program has so far resulted in limited trading of allowances among firms. This phase requires only a limited number of plants to participate and sets sulfur dioxide standards that are less restrictive than standards in the second phase will be. Under these circumstances, electricity producers have been able to achieve the benefits of more flexible regulation without extensive reliance on allowance trading with other producers. In the second phase of the program, beginning in 2000, performance standards will be tighter and more plants will be involved. Consequently, emissions trading among firms seems likely to become more important.

Local and regional efforts along these lines are emerging as well. In 1994 Southern California implemented a regional emissions trading market for nitrogen oxides, which also cause acid rain and contribute to haze and ground-level ozone pollution. Known as the Regional Clean Air Incentives Market, or RECLAIM, the Southern

California program is broadly similar to the national market for sulfur dioxide emissions discussed above, but with some distinctive features. For example, the program sets limitations on the location of emissions that are traded, to help prevent "hot spots." The RE-CLAIM program for nitrogen oxides is part of a larger compliance strategy that seeks to lower total emissions in the region toward levels needed to achieve mandated air quality standards. Under such an approach, regulators can simultaneously improve the environment, enhance cost-effectiveness, and provide flexibility for economic growth in the region. Other areas (notably the Northeast) are in the process of developing their own nitrogen oxide trading programs.

Programs like the national sulfur dioxide allowance market and RECLAIM, which establish an aggregate emissions limit for a whole class of emitters, entail setup costs to establish allowable aggregate emissions limits, initial allocations of allowances, and trading rules. EPA has proposed an "open markets" system for trading of allowances for both nitrogen oxides and volatile hydrocarbon emissions in the absence of these elements. Under this approach, various types of emitters can participate in a variety of cost-reducing trades. For example, a paint shop switching to a lower volatility paint for 6 months could sell the short-term emissions reductions to a refinery with a temporary need to cover surplus emissions. A similar approach to bilateral trading could be an important complement to international efforts aimed at protecting the stratospheric ozone layer (Box 5–3).

Regulators face an important challenge in using the open market approach: how will Federal and State air quality regulators obtain adequate assurance that proposed emissions reductions are credible? EPA's proposal reflects several approaches. The agency's preferred approach is a "buyer beware" plan whereby the user of an open markets emission reduction credit ultimately is responsible for the quality and integrity of the credit. This approach provides maximum environmental security by giving buyers strong incentives to check the legitimacy of credits, but it could also deter buyers from participating in the market, since they would incur a liability if sellers fail to live up to their obligations. EPA has identified alternative liability arrangements, such as placing more liability on sellers (with a system of spot checks to detect inadequate performance) and using third-party verification through brokers, who would be able to absorb legal liability for the quality of credits and provide warranties to buyers.

TRADEABLE FISHING QUOTAS

Overfishing—the consequence of unrestricted access to ocean fish stocks—has put heavy pressure on many of the world's fisheries.

Box 5–3.—Protecting the Stratospheric Ozone Layer: An Incentives-Based Approach

Methyl bromide is a pesticide that is damaging to the stratospheric ozone layer which shields the earth from harmful ultraviolet radiation. Recent adjustments to the Montreal Protocol, the international treaty governing ozone layer protection, place the first global limits on methyl bromide. Industrial countries must phase out methyl bromide production and use by 2010, except for certain essential uses such as treatment of imports and exports (currently less than 10 percent of global use). Use by developing countries (currently about 20 percent of the world total) will be frozen in 2002, with additional controls to be negotiated in the next 2 years.

Interim reductions by industrial countries en route to a phaseout will also be required. By limiting the total quantity of methyl bromide available, rising methyl bromide prices will automatically and cost-effectively allocate the remaining supply to more highly valued uses. The signatories to the Montreal Protocol will review the expanded use of market-based measures for controlling methyl bromide. One option, an international trading system, could allow some countries to reduce their methyl bromide use more slowly, by purchasing allowances from countries that have reduced use ahead of schedule.

Current U.S. law requires more stringent control on methyl bromide use than do the adjustments to the Montreal Protocol. The Clean Air Act bans, without exemption, all U.S. methyl bromide production and use by 2001. U.S. agricultural producers have expressed concern that they will be placed at a competitive disadvantage if other countries are allowed to continue methyl bromide use. The Administration supports legislative changes necessary to allow for continued methyl bromide use beyond 2001, in cases where alternatives do not exist, to safeguard U.S. agricultural competitiveness.

Without limits on access, anyone with the necessary skills and financing can enter the industry. The exercise of individual self-interest in this case leads to serious economic waste from excess entry and damage to the resource, since individual boat operators do not take into account the long-term consequences of depletion in their own harvesting decisions. Any unilateral exercise of forbearance simply expands the catch available to others.

Traditionally, fisheries management has attempted to cope with this problem through such measures as limited fishing seasons and restrictions on allowable gear. These efforts slow depletion of stocks in a costly manner by requiring the use of less efficient technology and creating market gluts during the abbreviated fishing seasons. And in any event these efforts often are overwhelmed by technical advances in harvesting methods.

A promising alternative is the use of individually transferable quotas (ITQs). In a manner analogous to air pollution trading programs, ITQs operate by setting a limit on the total allowable harvest and creating tradeable rights to a share of the harvest. With trade in ITQs, the harvest is undertaken by the most efficient operators, and since the quota rights can be used at any time during the year, the harvest rate does not glut the market. The sale of ITQs also provides a temporary financial buffer for less efficient operators, who are induced to leave the industry as overcapitalization declines.

Several challenges must be addressed in establishing an ITQ program. These include determining the initial size of the quota, allocating the quotas, and addressing the effects of an ITQ for one fish species on others; setting up a monitoring program; and dealing with the plight of fishing communities whose residents might not remain competitive in the ITQ market.

ITQs are currently being used by two East Coast regional fishery management councils, on a larger scale in an Alaskan fishery, and in other countries. The effects of harvest limits and pressures to increase harvest efficiency are shown in the decline of excess capital applied in the East Coast fisheries: the number of vessels has decreased by more than 50 percent. Similarly, in one application in British Columbia the decreased economic waste is indicated by an increase in the net overall economic return to the fishery of 65 percent.

TECHNOLOGY DIFFUSION FOR POLLUTION CONTROL IN AGRICULTURE

Government can play a role in improving environmental quality not only by internalizing externalities, but also by correcting market failures in the provision of information. Improved production techniques and management practices can improve efficiency and cut waste and pollution, in effect substituting one clean input—information—for other, polluting inputs. However, information has certain aspects of a public good—it is difficult for individual suppliers to restrict its use to those who have paid for it. As a result, private markets may undersupply information about environmentally beneficial technologies. Information problems can also constrain the adoption of new technologies by farmers. In such cases, the government may be able to improve efficiency by collecting and providing information about resource-conserving practices.

U.S. agricultural policy has a long tradition of emphasizing education, technical assistance, and subsidies to achieve economic and environmental goals. Technology transfer programs dating back to the 1930s have encouraged farmers to adopt soil conservation practices to maintain soil productivity through erosion control. The traditional extension and technology transfer system has increasingly emphasized technologies aimed at off-site environmental damages. Integrated pest management and conservation tillage are examples of the environmentally beneficial practices that have been promoted.

More recent programs have aimed at curbing water pollution from agriculture through provision of public information and financial incentives for farmers. Demonstration programs have been set up to encourage the adoption of best management practices (BMPs). An assumption underlying such voluntary environmental programs is that technological options can reduce both production costs and pollution. In theory, if these practices do reduce costs through more efficient use of water, fertilizer, and pesticides, demonstration programs will encourage their long-term adoption. Programs frequently include short-term subsidies to encourage initial adoption.

The adoption of BMPs has yielded some impressive results. For example, one study found that depending on field conditions, corn farmers in Nebraska who adopted soil nitrogen testing could reduce their use of fertilizer up to 25 percent with no loss in yields. In this case, the soil testing procedure substitutes information for chemical fertilizer applications. Moreover, farmers who participated in the Department of Agriculture's educational programs appeared to have made more effective use of nitrogen testing results than did nonparticipants.

Although the history of government programs to promote BMPs is still somewhat limited, useful lessons have already emerged. First, familiarity with new management practices has been found to encourage adoption, especially for BMPs that represent minor changes in current operations. Second, although profitability is a prime consideration in BMP adoption, it is not the only one. The belief that a BMP improves water quality has been found to be an important incentive for adoption, particularly in areas where agriculture has impaired ground water used for drinking. Third, significant regional differences exist in the perceived profitability and adoption rates of BMPs. Thus, no single set of practices may be widely adopted, and a decentralized approach may be needed to promote environmental technologies in agriculture. There may also be a role at the State level for research that tailors BMPs to local environmental conditions.

152

CONCLUSION

Without regulation to protect health, safety, and the environment, the quality of life Americans enjoy would be significantly lower than it is today. At the same time, regulation and the regulatory process must keep pace with changes in knowledge, technology, the economy, and social priorities. Reinventing regulation to work more cost-effectively and to address the greatest needs is a crucial step down this path. The efforts made thus far to enhance the performance of environmental regulation illustrate how broad are the opportunities for improvement.

CHAPTER 6

Promoting Competition in
Traditionally Regulated Industries

AT THE CENTER OF THE SUCCESS OF our economy is the market, and at the core of the success of the market is competition: it is competition that drives down costs and prices, induces firms to produce the goods consumers want, and spurs innovation and the expansion of new markets abroad.

In stark contrast to the gains from competition are the inefficiencies that result from monopoly. Monopolists typically set an artificially high price and restrict output, and often have weaker incentives to innovate than do competitive firms. The disadvantages of monopoly are sufficient to warrant government action to ensure competition or regulate the conduct of monopolies. Part of this Administration's commitment to strengthen the private sector involves ensuring that robust competition prevails where competition is possible, and guarding against the abuse of market power in those limited instances where it is not.

Powerful market forces, coupled with increased recognition of the costs of regulation, are strengthening the consensus to reform regulation in order to promote competition in two of our country's major regulated industries: electric power and telecommunications. Regulatory policy needs to respond to the forces of change in these industries, and important reform initiatives are under way.

At the Federal level the Congress, with the Administration's support, has recently passed sweeping legislation to rewrite the Communications Act of 1934 and other rules governing competition in telecommunications services. The Federal Communications Commission, which helped foster competition in telephone equipment and long-distance service, is developing policies for the interconnection of telephone networks that will promote competition in local telephone service as well. And the Federal Energy Regulatory Commission is trying to ensure access to electric utilities' transmission lines for all power generators. Various States also are moving to promote competition in intrastate phone service and in electricity. The stakes are high. Electricity and telecommunications are critical elements of an economy's infrastructure, and in the United States each sector accounts for over $200 billion in annual sales or, collectively, over $800 per U.S. resident.

Regulatory reform enjoys broad support, but disagreement exists over how best to make the transition from regulated monopoly to competition, and over the role of government once that transition is complete. Although the debate is often couched in terms of "regulation" versus "deregulation," implying that deregulation by itself will encourage competition and thus efficiency and innovation, what is at issue is something far more subtle, namely, the form and nature of regulation, with profound effects on both efficiency and equity. It cannot be overemphasized that immediate blanket deregulation is not a panacea. Well-designed regulations and antitrust safeguards are likely to result, ultimately, in more competitive markets with more innovation than immediate deregulation could provide. Moreover, until competition develops, it is important to maintain safeguards to protect consumers and to prevent incumbent monopolists from stifling the growth of competition.

This chapter discusses the challenges facing regulatory and antitrust policies in the telecommunications (Box 6–1) and electric power (Box 6–2) industries. It begins by discussing the growing consensus for increased reliance on competition in traditionally regulated industries, then provides an overview of the main challenges to successful regulatory reform. The two subsequent sections elaborate on these challenges in the telephone industry, which accounts for most telecommunications revenues, and in the electric power industry.

FROM REGULATED MONOPOLY TO COMPETITION

Public policy has historically taken two approaches to the problem of monopoly power: antitrust and regulation. The Congress passed the first antitrust law, the Sherman Act, in 1890. Antitrust policy seeks to encourage free market competition wherever possible by prohibiting parties from stifling competition through certain mergers, collusive practices, or unreasonable exclusion of competitors. Antitrust policy does not outlaw monopoly or monopoly prices, but instead seeks to prevent monopoly by promoting competition.

But the main policy approach in public utility industries like electricity, gas pipelines, and telephones has been regulation of private monopolies. (Some countries have tried government ownership as an alternative, but with few exceptions these have proven less effective than private ownership and regulation.) The first Federal law permitting regulation of monopoly, the Interstate Commerce Act, dates back to 1887.

Usually the stated reason for resorting to regulation of a monopoly rather than promoting competition through antitrust is that the industry in question is believed to be a *natural monopoly*—an in-

Box 6–1.—The Telecommunications Industry

The boundaries of the telecommunications industry are not clearly defined. In the broadest sense, the industry spans the entire backbone of our information economy. Some divide the industry into three segments: "conduit" (including local and long-distance telephone service; cable television; wireless services; emerging services that combine data, voice, and image transmissions; and communications equipment); "content" (such as broadcast television and radio and cable programming); and "computers" (computer hardware and software, and computing and processing services). In this chapter, "telecommunications" generally refers to conduits, especially telephones, cable television, and wireless services.

Telephone service generated about $150 billion in revenues in 1994, television and radio broadcasting almost $42 billion, and cable television about $28 billion. Cable television, although small compared with the telephone industry, is an important component of the telecommunications industry. Almost two-thirds of American households with televisions—more than 60 million households—subscribe to at least basic cable service, and the industry employs about 112,000 people.

The telecommunications equipment market includes a vast array of hardwares, from sophisticated equipment to facsimile machines to public pay phones. This market is growing rapidly: its sales of more than $63 billion in 1994 are projected to rise to almost $100 billion by 1997.

dustry in which product demand can be supplied most efficiently by a single firm. Natural monopolies arise mainly from large fixed costs relative to the size of the market: for example, the cost of running telephone or video cables to a home, or the cost of electric transmission lines. Such conditions create large economies of scale; that is, unit costs drop significantly with the volume of firm's output. In such cases the judgment may be made that competition is not workable and that the market is best served by a single monopoly firm that can fully exploit economies of scale but is prevented by price regulation from exercising monopoly power over customers.

The last 25 years have witnessed a sea change in attitudes toward regulating industries on grounds of natural monopoly. Economic studies have increasingly questioned the extent of economies of scale, challenging the view that many such industries are ubiquitous natural monopolies. More important, there has been a growing awareness of the major inefficiencies spawned by the regime of regulated monopoly.

165-967 96 – 6

Four main types of electric utilities operate in the United States: investor-owned utilities, which are typically privately owned, regulated monopolies; non-Federal publicly owned utilities, which are nonprofit State and local government agencies established to serve their communities and nearby customers at cost; cooperative utilities, which are owned by and provide electricity to their members; and Federal power agencies, which are primarily electricity producers, wholesalers, and transmitters. Although only about 250 out of the 3,204 electric utilities nationwide in 1994 were investor-owned, they are by far the most economically significant group, earning almost 80 percent of all electricity revenues. Over 99 percent of investor-owned utilities' revenues accrued to the 179 largest utilities.

Total electricity revenues in 1994 were $203 billion, or about 3.2 percent of gross domestic product (GDP). Of that sum, residential users accounted for almost $85 billion, commercial users for about $63 billion, and industrial users for $48 billion. The electric utility industry is one of the most capital-intensive in the United States; the 179 largest investor-owned utilities alone had almost $575 billion in assets in 1994, amounting to almost 5 percent of the gross capital stock of all industries.

Competition typically offers important advantages over monopoly: it encourages innovation, which lowers costs and increases the variety of products available to consumers. And *regulated* monopolists generally have weaker incentives than unregulated monopolists to cut costs, to launch new products, and to respond to changing customer demands. In addition, there are administrative costs of regulation and, more important, the potential for losses due to protracted disputes between the regulated firm, customers, and regulators, which can cause long delays in adjusting prices or in authorizing new investments.

The bottom line is that competition need not be perfect for it to be preferable to regulated monopoly. The advantages of competition can easily outweigh the disadvantage of not fully exploiting economies of scale.

ADAPTING REGULATION TO INCREASE COMPETITION

Although regulation has been the primary tool for addressing monopoly in infrastructure industries, these industries have also been subject to antitrust rules in some aspects of their operation, such as interconnection in the case of the telephone industry. Regulation and antitrust have had an uneasy coexistence, given their somewhat inconsistent thrusts: antitrust encourages competition but for the most part does not attempt to control a firm's prices, investments, and technology choices, whereas regulation does attempt to control such decisions and often restricts entry into the industry as well, thereby reducing competition. The difficulties in reconciling these approaches, and the distortions that stem from regulating monopolies, have created growing support for moving toward a more integrated competition-cum-antitrust regime.

Regulatory reforms in the 1970s and 1980s demonstrated that largely unregulated competition yields more efficient performance in such traditionally regulated industries as air transport and trucking, natural gas production, and long-distance telephone service. More recently, technological advances have further increased the scope for competition in local telephone and cable service and in the electric power industry. Regulatory regimes should adapt to changing conditions, to help shrink the boundaries of the regulated sector and rely more on competition.

Removing Legal Entry Barriers

The need for regulatory reform is nowhere more glaring than in telecommunications, with its blistering pace of technological change. Several technologies may in the future offer economical alternatives to today's local telephone network. Cable companies are experimenting with upgrading their existing lines to deliver telephone service. Wireless technologies now used mainly for mobile communications might also be used for ordinary telephone service if costs fall sufficiently. Fiberoptic lines, now used principally by companies that specialize in providing access to long-distance carriers, could be extended to homes and businesses. Mobile telephone service from low-orbiting satellites could eventually provide basic local service. Similarly, large-scale competition to cable companies in delivering video services may come from various sources including satellites, wireless land-based technologies, or telephone companies upgrading their networks. Meanwhile the rapid technological change that is blurring industry boundaries in telecommunications is also leading to the emergence of hybrid services such as multimedia, which defy easy classification into traditional industry definitions.

With so much uncertainty about the shape of the communications networks of the future, and with significant potential for competition, the best course is to leave their evolution to be determined by the private sector. Policymakers should not attempt to prejudge the outcome by assuming that local telephone and cable service are natural monopolies best provided by regulated franchise monopolists. Attempts to preserve artificial industry lines for the sake of maintaining regulation under traditional monopoly franchises become arbitrary, futile, and counterproductive.

159

For many years, local telephone and cable monopolies were sheltered from competition by legal restrictions: States granted monopoly franchises to local phone companies, municipalities could grant monopoly cable franchises, and, with some exceptions, Federal law restricted phone companies' ability to offer cable service. During the past few years a broad consensus has arisen, both in the Congress and in the executive branch, that it is desirable to try to eliminate existing regulatory and artificial technical barriers to competition in these industries. A number of States have started to open up their local telephone markets to competition. The recently passed telecommunications legislation requires immediate removal of all State and local laws and regulations that unduly prevent entry into telecommunications and cable services.

In electric power generation, the advent of smaller, more efficient gas-fueled generators, coupled with falling prices for natural gas, led to greatly reduced economies of scale. In addition, since the 1980s it has been demonstrated that independent generators can be successfully integrated into utility-owned transmission grids. These and other developments have prompted growing interest in further promoting competition in electricity generation. Although States now retain monopoly franchises for electric utilities virtually everywhere moves to relax legal barriers to competition are gathering steam. Many States are considering initiatives to permit some competition, and some, like California, have developed concrete proposals.

Assigning Spectrum Licenses Through Auctions

A major step taken by this Administration to promote competition and market forces in telecommunications is the recent, highly successful use of auctions to assign certain licenses for use of the so-called "spectrum"—the range of electromagnetic wave frequencies used in wireless communications services, including radio and television broadcasting, paging, and mobile telephones. The huge sums of revenues raised in recent auctions have focused attention on budget and equity issues. Auctions for other parts of the spectrum, if appropriately designed, could raise billions of additional dollars. When the government does not auction off but simply assigns spectrum licenses for free, it is giving away public resources worth billions of dollars. But more than revenue is at stake. Auctions can help promote economic efficiency, by ensuring that spectrum is deployed in the highest-return uses, including emerging growth industries that entail innovative technologies and services.

Assigning spectrum efficiently has taken on increased urgency as the value of spectrum has risen with the growth of wireless technologies. Wireless technologies are among the most promising avenues for delivering new services and for eventually providing competition to wireline local telephone and cable monopolies. The exciting potential of wireless technologies is evidenced by the rapid growth of cellular telephone systems (Chart 6–1) and of direct broadcast satellite television service, which since its inception in June 1994 has already attracted almost 2.5 million subscribers.

Chart 6-1   **Growth in the Cellular Communications Industry**
The cellular telecommunications industry has grown dramatically, illustrating the market potential for wireless technologies in general.

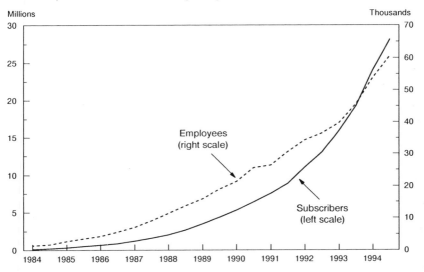

Note: Data are for end of year, except 1995 are as of June 1995.
Source: Cellular Telecommunications Industry Association.

The Federal Communications Commission (FCC), charged with managing spectrum use by the private sector, traditionally assigned licenses without charge, using hearings to judge which applicants would best serve the public interest. These trial-like hearings resulted in large wasteful expenditures by applicants and long delays in assigning licenses. In 1981 the Congress authorized the FCC to use lotteries in certain cases. Lotteries reduced the delay in assigning licenses, and the ability of lottery winners to resell licenses allowed users that valued spectrum highly to try to obtain licenses in a secondary market. However, using the secondary market can entail inefficiently large transaction costs, especially in assembling suitable blocks of licenses. The lotteries also created windfall profits for lottery winners—windfalls that became transparent when certain lottery winners resold their licenses at huge profits.

To avoid such inefficiencies and windfall gains to a lucky few, economists have long urged the use of auctions to allocate scarce public resources such as the spectrum. Spectrum auctions have also been advocated by the National Telecommunications and Information Administration (NTIA) of the Department of Commerce, the Council of Economic Advisers, and the FCC. In 1993 the Congress gave the FCC limited authority to use auctions in assigning spectrum licenses to provide services for which subscribers pay fees (in contrast to advertising-financed broadcasting), such as personal communication services (PCS; these are advanced mobile two-way voice and data communications services).

Designing good rules for PCS and other spectrum auctions presents novel and difficult problems. Bidders are often interested not in a single license but in suitable blocks of licenses, which makes the values of different licenses interdependent. Interdependence arises, for example, because aggregating licenses over adjoining regions allows a PCS device to use the same spectrum frequency over a wider area and makes boundary coordination easier. Interdependence can also arise because a bidder may be able to reconfigure its planned network to use a different set of frequencies as prices for some frequencies increase. Designing auction rules to help bidders cope with such interdependence in license values can both promote economic efficiency and bring in greater auction revenue.

To date, the FCC—in consultation with economists—has developed innovative auction rules and has conducted very successful auctions. For example, in the largest auction to date, winners were able to assemble suitable aggregations of PCS licenses over frequency bands and regions, as needed to form efficient communications networks. The auctions have attracted participation by numerous entrepreneurial companies and promise to speed up the availability of innovative services to consumers. In the short time since their inauguration in July 1994, spectrum auctions have raised over $15 billion for U.S. taxpayers.

DEREGULATION IS NOT ENOUGH: CHALLENGES TO REGULATORY REFORM

Removing legal barriers to entry into traditional monopoly industries, although critical, is unlikely by itself to ensure the rapid development of competition or an efficient and equitable transition. To promote these and other goals, regulatory reform must address several difficult and important challenges, which are outlined below and discussed further in the later sections on the telephone and electric power industries.

Promoting and Preserving Competition

Preventing regulated monopolists from distorting competition in related markets. A common and difficult problem arises in bringing competition to traditionally regulated industries when, whether for jurisdictional or technological reasons, a vital "bottleneck" segment will continue for some time under the control of a regulated monopoly. For example, competition is envisaged in electric power generation, but for the time being transmission and distribution will remain regulated monopolies. Similarly, competition is expected to develop more slowly in certain elements of local telephone networks, notably the final set of wires to a customer's premises (the "local loop"), which will therefore remain regulated longer.

The difficulty posed by such a mixture of regulation and deregulation is that a price-regulated bottleneck monopolist has strong incentives to provide its own affiliates in unregulated segments better access to the bottleneck than it offers to rivals. (This and related issues are explored further in the section on the telephone industry below.) Such discrimination can inefficiently exclude rivals from the potentially competitive segments, harming both the would-be rivals and consumers. Preventing such access discrimination (and cross-subsidization, which, as discussed later, also distorts competition) could be approached in alternative ways, all of which have certain limitations.

Relying solely on regulation to prevent the regulated monopolist from favoring its unregulated operations over rivals raises problems. Firms can devise many clever technological games to circumvent regulation, such as varying the quality of connections provided to competitors. An alternative approach is to separate the regulated and unregulated parts of a monopolist's business into different companies. This was done in the Department of Justice's landmark case that resulted in the 1982 consent decree and the 1984 breakup of the American Telephone and Telegraph Company (AT&T, then the dominant U.S. telephone services provider). The seven regional Bell operating companies (RBOCs) created under the 1982 consent decree were allowed to offer regulated regional telephone service but were barred from the largely unregulated long-distance market.

Such forced structural separation helps promote level-playing-field competition in the unregulated markets, but it may sacrifice economies of scope—efficiencies in joint ownership and operation of related segments of an industry. How to prevent discrimination without unduly sacrificing economies of scope is a central challenge in assessing whether and under what safeguards the RBOCs should be permitted to offer long-distance service while they still dominate local telephone networks; and whether electric utilities should be allowed to sell unregulated power in competition with rivals while they still control the vital transmission grids.

Preventing monopolists from unreasonably denying interconnections. One way in which network monopolists can stifle competition is by denying potential competitors interconnection with their net-

163

works. The telephone industry exhibits strong positive network externalities—a user's benefit from the network increases greatly as additional users are connected. This feature marks an important distinction between telephones and, say, textiles. A new textile producer does not need much cooperation from other textile producers, but an entrant to local telephone service needs the incumbent's cooperation to let its customers communicate with the incumbent's customers. With its much larger customer base, the incumbent could hamper entry even by efficient entrants, by denying interconnection or by providing connections of poor quality or at an exorbitant price. Ensuring suitable and fairly priced interconnection may require government intervention.

Restricting mergers between likely potential competitors. Regulation must be forward looking: it must consider the market not only as it is today but also as it is likely to evolve. In most traditionally unregulated industries, it is actual competitors—the firms already present in a market—that largely determine the prospects for present and future competition. But in traditionally regulated monopolies, future competition must largely come from the outside. Mergers between regulated monopolists that are likely potential competitors therefore can significantly reduce the likelihood of future competition.

For this reason, the Administration opposes excessive loosening of restrictions on mergers and cross-ownership between cable and telephone companies in the same local area. Although there are technological challenges in using telephone wires to deliver video, and cable wires to deliver telephone service, cable and telephone companies nevertheless are likely potential competitors because both have wires to the home. Thus, consolidations among them could delay competition.

Antitrust enforcers could attempt to block such anticompetitive consolidations, but reviewing and challenging a potentially large number of transactions in different regions on a case-by-case basis would be quite costly. Maintaining clear prohibitions may be the better course as long as such mergers promise no significant economies, and as long as local cable and telephone companies remain among each other's most likely potential competitors.

Improving the Regulation of Remaining Monopoly Segments

As noted earlier, although promoting competition is generally the preferred approach, some segments of telephone and electric utilities' operations will continue to be regulated for some time. In those segments it is important to devise better ways to regulate prices. Traditionally, utilities have been subject to cost-of-service regulation, under which prices are set to cover the regulated firm's costs plus a "fair rate of return" on capital. Such regulation, however, reduces incentives to innovate or to contain costs, because the firm realizes essentially the same profits regardless of its efforts: success at cutting costs is penalized by reducing the allowed prices.

Performance-based regulation (PBR) loosens the link between the firm's controllable costs and its allowable price. For example, pure price-cap regulation places a ceiling on the firm's price at some initial level based on estimated cost, then lets the cap change only with conditions outside the firm's control, such as the rate of inflation. The firm then has an incentive to cut costs, because to do so increases its profit. On the other hand, the firm also has an incentive to cut costs by shading quality, and regulators must guard against such attempts. Recognizing that suitably designed PBR can often create better incentives than pure cost-based regulation, ultimately benefiting both the firm and consumers, many States are moving toward PBR in telephone service and in the transmission and distribution of electricity.

Protecting Consumers and Investors During the Transition

Protecting consumers. When should an incumbent monopolist's prices be deregulated? Setting a fixed date reduces investors' uncertainty, but at the risk that competition may not have developed enough by that time to substitute for regulation in disciplining prices. For example, critics of rapid deregulation of cable television rates point out that substantial actual competition (not merely potential competition) is needed to discipline prices, and argue that the requisite competition will develop more slowly than proponents of quick deregulation assume. In electricity, many economists favor some temporary regulation of the prices that utilities can charge, even if reforms are instituted to make generation competitive, because it will take time to build new plants and reduce existing utilities' dominant share of generation assets.

A complicating factor in deregulating prices is that competition often develops faster for some customers than others, typically faster for large business customers than for residential users. It therefore may be appropriate to deregulate prices on a phased basis, starting with those customers for whom competition develops earliest. But if the utility has large (current or past) fixed costs that are common to all of its operations, which regulators allow to be recovered through regulated rates, it becomes important to ensure that deregulating one group's prices will not shift onto others an increased share of these common costs. One way to prevent this is to deregulate some prices, but on condition that the utility agrees not to raise prices to its remaining captive customers. Competition should increase overall benefits, not be used as a cover for cost shifting among customers.

Protecting investors. Nor should competition be a cover for unreasonably shifting costs from customers to utility investors. To meet their obligation to serve all customers in their monopoly franchise areas, electric utilities have made costly investments in long-lived generating plant and other assets—with the regulators' implicit promise of a guaranteed return. Opening up utilities' traditional monopoly franchises to competition at a time when they have significant excess capacity would greatly reduce the value of such investments, and subject utilities to so called "stranded costs." As discussed further in the section on the electricity industry below, it is important to ensure that, in the transition to competition, utilities are not saddled with these stranded costs.

Promoting Universal Service and Other Social Goals

Promoting universal service—reasonably priced access to essential services for all customers—has been a longstanding goal of regulators in both the telephone and the electric power industries. Traditionally this and other social goals (such as assisting certain disadvantaged customers and reducing environmental pollution) have been pursued by imposing obligations on and regulating the price structure of utilities.

These regulations, however, have spawned inefficiencies. Moving to competition and letting prices respond to market forces, so that they more accurately reflect true costs, are likely to reduce these inefficiencies and cut the cost to society of providing universal service by lowering overall costs and prices. But doing so may require devising alternative ways of funding service to those consumers who would not be able or willing to pay the prices that might emerge under competition.

Reassessing Jurisdictional Boundaries

In both the telephone and the electric power industries, State and Federal regulators share jurisdiction. This can lead to differing regulatory objectives and inconsistent policies. As is discussed in Chapter 4, a main advantage of decentralizing regulatory jurisdiction is to allow States the flexibility to pursue social and economic policies tailored to different local preferences and conditions. As markets become more competitive, the scope for pursuing such goals through regulation may decline, although the States will play a major role in ushering in an efficient and equitable transition to competition.

On the other hand, decentralizing regulation also has its drawbacks. Efficient networks in telecommunications and electricity often involve facilities used to serve several States, which can lead to inconsistent policies when such networks are regulated at the State level. Multiple State regulatory regimes also can increase firms' uncertainty and costs of compliance. For these and other reasons, jurisdictions such as the European Union have been moving to harmonize the regulation of network industries. As the United States attempts to increase competition in such industries, it too

166

will have to reassess what jurisdictional boundaries are most efficient. In any event, regulators must work across jurisdictional boundaries to foster cooperative and consistent public policy goals.

PROMOTING COMPETITION IN TELEPHONE SERVICE

The 1984 breakup of AT&T was a landmark event in fostering competition in parts of the U.S. telephone industry. As explained earlier, a regulated monopolist operating in related, unregulated markets has incentives to stifle competition in such markets. To prevent such behavior, the breakup aimed to separate local telephone service, which many viewed as a natural monopoly that would remain regulated, from manufacturing of telephone equipment and from long-distance service, which were viewed as potentially competitive and could eventually be deregulated. AT&T retained its equipment manufacturing and long-distance service divisions. Seven new regional Bell operating companies inherited AT&T's regulated local-service monopolies, each within its region, and were prohibited from entering the less regulated markets for equipment and long-distance service.

Today the long-distance market is relatively competitive, whereas local service remains largely a regulated monopoly, in most cases provided by the RBOCs (Box 6–3). The new telecommunications legislation aims to increase competition further in equipment manufacturing and long-distance service and allows the RBOCs back into these markets under certain conditions. The legislation also aims to introduce competition in local telephone service, by removing State barriers to entry and by requiring local telephone companies to grant entrants reasonable access to their networks. These legislative and related regulatory initiatives, together with technological advances discussed previously, promise to foster increased competition throughout the telephone industry.

The terms for allowing the RBOCs to enter long-distance service have been one of the most contentious issues in the debate over telecommunications reform and may have the greatest economic consequences. Telephone service is by far the largest telecommunications industry (see Box 6–1), and establishing appropriate conditions for allowing entry by the RBOCs into the other markets is critical to achieving the legislation's goals.

Allowing immediate, unrestricted entry by the RBOCs while they still control vital local telephone networks would have been unlikely to promote efficiency and consumer welfare in the way that unrestricted entry normally does. To clarify this point, the next part of this section explains the incentive—and the ability—of a price-regulated monopolist in local telephone service to distort competition in related, unregulated markets such as long-distance service that are dependent on access to the monopolist's bottleneck facilities. We then analyze further the issues of RBOC entry into long-distance and of local competition. The final part of this section discusses the relation between increased competition and universal service.

UNBUNDLING POTENTIALLY COMPETITIVE SERVICES FROM REGULATED MONOPOLY SERVICES

As noted above, traditional cost-of-service regulation sets prices so as to allow the regulated monopolist a "fair rate of return" on its investment. Under such regulation, a monopolist can gain from engaging in related businesses that are potentially competitive. As long as regulation is not too stringent, the more businesses the monopolist is engaged in, the more likely it is to successfully conceal profits from the regulators, because overstating costs slightly in many businesses is more likely to escape detection than overstating costs dramatically in a single monopoly business. Moreover, by ex-

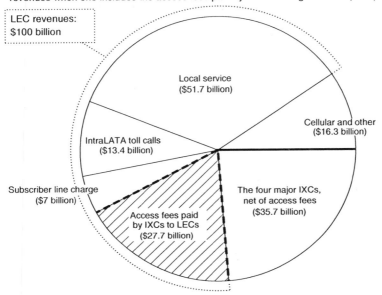

Chart 6-2 **Telephone Industry Revenues in 1994**
Local exchange carriers (LECs) account for two-thirds of all telephone industry
revenues when one includes the access fees paid by interexchange carriers (IXCs).

LEC revenues:
$100 billion

Local service
($51.7 billion)

Cellular and other
($16.3 billion)

IntraLATA toll calls
($13.4 billion)

Subscriber line charge
($7 billion)

The four major IXCs,
net of access fees
($35.7 billion)

Access fees paid
by IXCs to LECs
($27.7 billion)

Note: Access fees are not double-counted as net IXC revenues. Some cellular revenue accrues to LECs.
Source: Federal Communications Commission.

cluding all rivals from potentially competitive businesses, the monopolist can prevent regulation of these segments from becoming
more stringent: the exclusion of competitors denies regulators a signal of the true costs in those businesses.

To promote competition, regulators can mandate unbundling—
that is, they can require the firm to offer the monopoly service separately from other services, at a regulated price. But problems
arise if, as is often the case, regulators allow the monopolist to
offer the potentially competitive services at unregulated (or less
tightly regulated) prices, on the theory that competition will keep
these unregulated prices low. For example, a local telephone company's access charges to long-distance carriers might be regulated,
but not its long-distance prices to consumers. Such partial regulation induces the monopolist to favor its unregulated affiliates over
rivals in ways that are difficult for regulators to prevent. The mo-
tive of this favoritism may be largely to shift profits to unregulated
affiliates, but the effect can be to stifle competition.

Cross-Subsidization and Discrimination in Bottleneck Access

One way that such profit shifting occurs is through
misattribution of costs incurred by a firm's unregulated businesses
to the regulated business. This is sometimes referred to as cross-
subsidization. Under cost-based regulation, shifting costs to the
regulated business allows the firm to argue for higher regulated

169

rates. In principle, cross-subsidization may be a problem whenever a regulated firm also operates in unregulated markets; but it is more likely to escape regulatory detection when the markets are related, since there is more scope for interaffiliate transactions and for mischaracterizing costs as common to both businesses.

Discrimination poses an even greater threat to competition. The monopolist controlling the price-regulated bottleneck facility may try to evade regulation through what is known as "tying." Suppose that customers seek to purchase an unregulated service, the provision of which hinges on access to the bottleneck service. The monopolist can then require, as a condition of access to the bottleneck, that customers also purchase from it the unregulated service at a high price. To implement such tying, the monopolist reduces competition in the unregulated market by discriminating against competitors in the technological and other nonprice terms it grants them for access to the bottleneck.

AT&T's behavior before its breakup is consistent with these incentives. The monopoly local telephone service was a major customer of equipment and a vital input into long-distance service. AT&T's prices for long-distance service and equipment were regulated more lightly than those for local service, creating incentives for AT&T to favor its less regulated affiliates. Indeed, AT&T's local affiliates were alleged to have paid its equipment affiliate Western Electric inflated prices for possibly inferior equipment. AT&T is also alleged to have discriminated against long-distance rivals in various ways, including offering poorer connections to local networks and imposing unnecessary delays in honoring requests.

Resulting Inefficiencies and Harm to Consumers

When it occurs, cross-subsidization inflates the reported cost of regulated services, leading to higher prices. For this reason regulators consistently try to keep the cost accounting of unregulated and regulated businesses as separate as possible. Prices of unregulated services—whose costs are underreported—could fall, but need not (for example, if underreporting involves fixed rather than variable costs). Even if prices do fall, they will be artificially below cost, and consumption of unregulated services will be inefficiently high. Also, sales may be diverted away from more efficient competitors in the unregulated markets, because the regulated firm attains an artificial advantage through the cross-subsidies.

Discrimination in access terms raises the prices of *unregulated* services, because the excluded competitors might have been more efficient, and because even equally efficient competitors could curb the monopolist's prices more effectively than can regulation alone. Consumers also are denied the variety and innovation that competitors might have offered. Finally, such potentially more efficient or innovative competitors are denied profit opportunities. These losses resulting from discrimination can far exceed the gain to the regulated monopolist: the monopolist is willing to exclude a rival that would generate large benefits to consumers (say, by offering a superior alternative), as long as exclusion yields even a modest increase in its own profit.

ENTRY BY THE REGIONAL OPERATING COMPANIES INTO LONG-DISTANCE

The Department of Justice sought AT&T's breakup, which separated the ownership of the regulated-monopoly local telephone service from other services, because it believed that regulation alone could not, without imposing undue burdens, prevent the many ways in which AT&T could use its control of local telephone service to inefficiently favor its affiliates. (The Justice Department and AT&T at one point tried to negotiate a settlement without divestiture; the result was a draft consent decree which for its length and complexity became known as Quagmire II, or the Telephone Book decree.)

Maintaining the consent decree's prohibition of RBOC entry into other markets may forgo some economies of scope that could be realized therefrom, but it is likely to be more effective than regulation alone in curbing access discrimination by the RBOCs against competitors in these other markets. The new legislation attempts to achieve the best of both worlds, by linking the RBOCs' entry authority to the emergence of competition in their local markets—competition that should reduce their control of local networks and ability to discriminate against competitors.

Arguments in Favor of Entry: The Drawbacks of Separation

Consumers could well benefit from one-stop shopping for all their telephone needs; for example, an integrated provider could offer simplified calling plans. The RBOCs could provide such one-stop shopping if allowed into long-distance, although in principle this could be provided even without RBOC entry. For example, the new legislation requires all incumbent local telephone companies to sell local service to other companies at discounted wholesale prices. When authorized, long-distance or other companies could resell such local service together with long-distance and other services.

Some economists contend that RBOC entry into long-distance service is particularly important for lowering prices because the long-distance industry is far from perfectly competitive. Although there is some debate about how competitive the long-distance industry already is, the real issue is why entry would be more profitable for the RBOCs than for other firms. This could be the case either because the RBOCs could use such entry to circumvent local rate regulation (a "bad" reason), or because they have special cost advantages in offering long-distance service (a "good" reason).

A clear such cost advantage arises because any RBOC could link its existing networks to provide long-distance service at lower cost than could other entrants deploying entirely new facilities. Indeed, the separation between local area service and long-distance service (see Box 6–3) can be arbitrary and artificial: the boundaries of "local areas" at times do not track economic or technological realities. This highlights a general problem with using structural separation to prevent a regulated bottleneck monopolist from stifling competition in potentially competitive markets. Where to draw the boundaries depends on where the monopoly bottleneck lies, but the bottleneck can shift location as technology changes. For local telephone networks, most agree that the bottleneck includes the local loop, but experts disagree over whether it includes additional upstream elements such as switches. The issue of where the bottleneck lies is relevant also for policy toward promoting local competition.

Arguments Against Entry: Preventing Access Discrimination

Combining local and long-distance service within a single firm is likely to offer some economies of scope, but such economies also existed at the time of AT&T's breakup. The policy judgment then was that breakup was needed to protect competition in the potentially competitive segments, given the incentive and ability of local network monopolists to stifle it, and that the gains from competition would outweigh the loss of economies of scope. On many counts the breakup has succeeded: today the equipment and the long-distance markets are reasonably competitive. Opponents fear that if the RBOCs are allowed to reenter these markets before they face competition in their core local phone markets, regulation alone could not prevent them from inefficiently excluding competitors.

Long-distance service still hinges on access to local networks, which for now are still largely monopolies controlled by the RBOCs. Although cross-subsidization by the RBOCs from their regulated local phone service to their unregulated businesses may be less of a threat today, access discrimination against other providers of long-distance service and perhaps of central-office switching equipment remains a real concern.

Cross-subsidization may now be less of a threat because, in order to improve regulated firms' incentives, States are replacing pure cost-of-service regulation of local phone rates with performance-based regulation. Such regulation also reduces the regulated firm's incentives to cross-subsidize, because higher costs of the regulated business are not passed through as fully or as rapidly in higher regulated rates as under pure cost-of-service regulation. As added protection, the new legislation requires the RBOCs to manufacture equipment and provide long-distance service through separate sub-

sidiaries for some time, to help regulators detect cross-subsidization.

However, preventing RBOC discrimination against long-distance
companies in access to local networks remains a thorny challenge.
Performance-based regulation of local rates leaves intact incentives
to discriminate against long-distance rivals, in order to raise prices
in the unregulated long-distance market. Requiring long-distance
service to be offered through a separate subsidiary does not eliminate discrimination incentives, because the subsidiary's profits accrue to common shareholders. Finally, regulators today may be
more attuned to the dangers of discrimination, but preventing
through regulation all avenues of technological discrimination in
network access is still likely to be difficult.

Allowing the regulated RBOCs to provide unregulated long-distance service gives them incentives to discriminate against long-
distance rivals. Allowing them to manufacture switches and other
network equipment could enhance their ability to discriminate, by
making it easier for them to retain proprietary control of important
technical information needed to interface with long-distance and
other unregulated services that rely on the network. If, as is likely,
regulation alone cannot adequately curb such discrimination, then
allowing the RBOCs to enter these other markets while they retain
monopolies over local networks could reduce prices temporarily in
those markets; but it could threaten rivals' long-run viability, raising the specter of ultimately reducing competition and causing
higher prices and less innovation.

Competitive Safeguards

Local competition can greatly help prevent access discrimination.
It provides alternative ways of reaching some customers. It also offers regulators a useful yardstick for policing discrimination: claims
that certain network services cannot be provided to competitors
will ring hollow if a local network competitor finds no difficulty providing such services. Although competition is coming to local networks, the RBOCs' dominance is unlikely to disappear overnight
even if regulatory entry barriers are relaxed. Potential entrants
have encountered technological problems, for example, in delivering
telephone service over cable lines. Wireless connections may eventually offer alternatives to the local loop for reaching a customer's
premises, but those currently available are higher in cost, less secure, and of lower quality than wireline connections.

Since local competition is both critical to safeguarding competition in long-distance and related markets but is in a nascent stage,
the new legislation not only imposes regulatory safeguards against
discrimination and other abuses but, importantly, links the RBOCs'
authority to enter these other markets to the emergence of local
competition. In broad brush terms, the new legislation provides the

following process for authorizing RBOC entry into long-distance (i.e. interLATA) service. Such service, as well as the manufacturing of equipment, must be offered through a separate subsidiary. An RBOC may offer long-distance service immediately on enactment of the legislation in any State where it currently provides no local service. But an RBOC must receive FCC approval to offer service originating in any State where it does provide local service (and likely controls many local networks). FCC approval is granted only after the following requirements are met.

Within 6 months of the new law's enactment the FCC will formulate rules for interconnection and network unbundling, discussed further below, that all incumbent local exchange companies must follow in dealing with new local competitors. At a minimum, an RBOC must offer terms, including prices, which the State public utility commission certifies are consistent with the FCC rules. Moreover, if a new local competitor has requested interconnection from an RBOC, then before being eligible to offer long-distance service the RBOC must have *fully implemented* a binding interconnection agreement with the competitor. That agreement must satisfy the FCC rules; the competitor must use predominantly or exclusively its own facilities; and it must provide local exchange service to both business and residential customers in the State (pure access providers, for example, do not suffice). In short, the local competitor is intended to have a significant presence.

Because these requirements help promote local competition but do not guarantee its imminence or durability, the new legislation provides further safeguards. Before authorizing RBOC entry, the FCC must consult with the Department of Justice regarding the likely competitive implications and give the Department's evaluation "substantial weight." This procedure offers an important safeguard, given the leading role that the Department's Antitrust Division has played in bringing competition to long-distance telephone service through the AT&T breakup, and given its analytical expertise in competition matters. Finally, the FCC must determine that RBOC entry would be in the public interest. Preservation of competition requires that antitrust enforcers and regulators have the latitude to make judgments of this kind, because no mere checklist could hope to capture all the relevant contingencies.

IMPLEMENTING LOCAL COMPETITION

As mentioned earlier, in order to foster local competition the new legislation would require existing local exchange companies to cooperate with entrants. Even a full facilities-based entrant (one that serves its customers entirely through its own physical facilities) would still require interconnection to the incumbent's network—to enable its customers to communicate with the incumbent's customers, to let customers keep their telephone numbers if they switch to the entrant, and to access common signaling facilities and data bases. The new legislation requires incumbent carriers to provide such cooperation on reasonable terms.

Other entrants might lease some or all facilities from the incumbent. A *reseller* of local services would lease all network facilities in bulk but undertake all customer-related functions such as marketing and billing ("retailer" might therefore be a better term). It could offer to customers a package of local and other services such as interexchange service or cellular service. A *partial facilities-based* entrant would lease some elements and supply the rest itself; it might, for example, install its own switches but use the incumbent's local loops. Both types of entrants require unbundling of the local exchange carrier's integrated functions. A reseller would require unbundling of netwcrk functions from marketing and other customer-related functions. A partial facilities-based entrant would additionally require unbundling of some network functions. To accommodate such entrants, the new legislation requires incumbents to unbundle their networks and provide nondiscriminatory access to all the unbundled components.

Inevitably the new legislation provides only a framework and leaves such "details" as the pricing of interconnection and unbundled services to be determined later by the FCC and State regulatory commissions. But these details will be crucial. To stay in business, a reseller must be able to buy the local network services at a sufficient discount below retail rates, reflecting the fact that it undertakes costly retailing functions otherwise performed by the incumbent. (The new legislation requires incumbents to offer their services to resellers at wholesale rates, defined as retail rates less the costs avoided by incumbents.) If the discount is too small, even an efficient reseller will be unprofitable. A partial facilities-based entrant likewise needs reasonably priced access to the facilities it wishes to lease.

Determining the proper discount to resellers has already raised controversy, embroiling regulators in defining and measuring the costs a local phone company could avoid by delegating some retailing functions. In long-distance there is already an active market in capacity resale, as multiple owners of facilities compete to provide capacity. But until competition arrives in local networks, implementing resale of local service through mandated discounts will be difficult. Mandated unbundling of physical network elements, as opposed to just retailing functions as with resale, is likely to be even harder. There are many joint and common costs, network congestion is important in determining efficient prices, and unbundling certain elements may pose technical problems.

In short, introducing competition into local networks will be a complex process, requiring continued active involvement by State regulators, the FCC, the Justice Department, and possibly the courts. Nevertheless, by defining the broad rules and providing for active government involvement in implementing agreements and refereeing disputes, the new legislation holds the promise of stimulating ubiquitous, vigorous competition with potentially enormous benefits to businesses and

REPLACING CROSS-SUBSIDIES AND PROMOTING UNIVERSAL SERVICE

A longstanding policy goal in the United States has been universal service: widespread access to telephone service at reasonable prices. Such a goal can be defended on narrow economic grounds because the benefits of having a telephone on one's premises accrue not only to the subscriber but also to others who might be interested in calling that subscriber. Encouraging telephone subscription by people who would not otherwise have a phone on their premises can therefore also benefit others. Support for universal service, however, is based also on broader social considerations— that all members of a society should be entitled to a certain level of key services.

Where attaining universal service is thought to require government intervention, because without it prices would be deemed too high in certain regions or to certain customer groups, economists generally advocate the use of targeted, explicit subsidies, financed through broadly based taxes. Traditional regulatory policy has not taken this route. Instead, regulators have used the rate structure of regulated telephone monopolists to promote universal service and other goals. Many economists believe that this rate structure is inefficient and incompatible with a move toward increased competition in telephone service.

The new legislation requires the formation of a Federal-State Joint Board, representing regulators and consumers, to thoroughly review the existing system of Federal support for universal service and recommend reforms within 9 months of the law's enactment. Within 15 months of enactment, the FCC is to establish a specific timetable for implementation of reforms. This envisaged reform for the most part promises to better harmonize the goals of promoting competition and universal service.

Cross-Subsidies and the Tension with Competition

Cross-subsidization arises when the price in one market does not cover the incremental cost of serving that market, and the deficit is financed by charging a price significantly above incremental cost in another market. The different markets can be for different products (e.g., long-distance versus local calls) or different identifiable customer groups (e.g., residential versus business customers of local calls). As discussed earlier, cross-subsidies can arise from attempts by a regulated monopolist to evade cost-based regulation by misattributing costs of its unregulated business to the regulated business. But cross-subsidies also can be mandated by regulators.

For many years regulators, with the support of the Congress, used cross-subsidies between regulated monopolists to pursue universal service goals. Through a complicated nationwide pooling of telephone costs and revenues, local telephone companies, especially in high-cost rural areas, received substantial subsidies to keep their rates low. The subsidies were financed by setting prices of long-distance calls and of telephone equipment artificially high. In addition, long-distance rates were set by geographic averaging: rates for routes of the same distance were set equal despite different traffic densities and therefore different costs. There may also have been subsidies from business to residential customers generally.

This system was administered by AT&T, whose affiliate companies provided most local telephone service nationwide and virtually all long-distance service. The system came under strain once AT&T's virtual monopoly began to erode. The growth of competition in supplying customer premises equipment (such as telephone sets) in the 1970s and later in long-distance service reduced the funds available for cross-subsidies. In response, after the breakup of AT&T the FCC introduced fixed monthly fees for all telephone subscribers, reducing the need for subsidies; the FCC and State regulators also instituted explicit access fees for all long-distance carriers originating and terminating calls on local carriers' networks. These access fees are still used to finance subsidies to rural carriers.

The inflated access fees, however, prompted large long-distance customers to bypass the local exchange and instead use private lines to connect their premises directly to an interexchange carrier. Such bypass again threatens the revenue used to cross-subsidize other services. Some local telephone companies have also alleged that revenue from high-volume local business customers cross-subsidizes basic local service to residential customers, so that permitting entry into local service also will threaten cross-subsidies: entrants will siphon off lucrative business customers and reduce the revenue available for subsidizing rates to other customers.

Universal service and other social goals that may be threatened by competition can be pursued through diametrically different approaches, as discussed below. One is to try to maintain a broad monopoly charged with meeting these social objectives, by legally prohibiting entry or by requiring all entrants to make substantial contributions to cover the incumbent's cost of providing below-cost services. The other is to permit widespread competition and develop alternative, market-based ways of funding legitimate social goals.

Joint Costs, Natural Monopoly, and Cream Skimming

Defenders of retaining monopoly might paint the following picture of local telephone service. Serving the different markets—be they different customers or different services—is largely a natural monopoly, because it entails large fixed and common costs. The markets are therefore most efficiently served by a single firm, but to cover the fixed costs, prices in some or all markets will have to exceed the incremental costs of serving those markets. Entry could then be profitable but economically inefficient, because an entrant could engage in *cream skimming*—targeting only the monopolist's more lucrative markets where the gap between prices and incremental costs is greatest, thus saddling other groups with a higher proportion of the common costs.

Charging different price-cost margins, which are vulnerable to cream skimming, can be efficient if demands in different markets exhibit different degrees of price sensitivity. The fixed costs are then best covered by charging higher margins where demands are less price-sensitive, as this pricing pattern minimizes the inefficiency from reduced consumption due to prices that exceed marginal costs (economists call this "Ramsey pricing"). For example, if demand for local service were less price-sensitive than demand for long-distance service, it might make sense to charge higher margins for local calls to finance the common costs, such as for wires to the home, entailed in providing local and long-distance service.

Distortions in the Current System

If the view of the industry just outlined—as a ubiquitous, multimarket natural monopoly that is pricing efficiently to recover common costs but is vulnerable to cream-skimming entry—were accurate, policymakers would face a tradeoff: restricting entry would better allow exploitation of scale and scope economies, but would deny the benefits of competition and impose regulatory costs. Many economists, however, challenge this portrait of the local telephone service industry. They are skeptical about characterizing too many costs as "fixed and common" and the industry as a ubiquitous natural monopoly. Moreover, to the extent there do exist fixed and common costs, current regulated prices do *not* recover such costs efficiently. Rather, the current price structure sends wrong signals about the true costs, thereby distorting the decisions of entrants and consumers.

Distorted entry decisions. Access fees charged by local network operators to long-distance companies far exceed marginal costs. These high fees cross-subsidize service in rural areas and perhaps

178

basic local service nationwide, which may be priced below its marginal cost. Such pricing can distort entry decisions in two ways: artificially high prices can encourage inefficient entry, and artificially low prices can discourage efficient entry.

Regarding possibly inefficient entry, inflated access fees may have provided an artificial stimulus to the growth of so-called competitive access providers: companies that bypass local networks and link businesses directly to long-distance companies. Regarding the discouragement of efficient entry, there may be greater potential for competition in local services than is currently evident. Artificially low prices for the subsidized incumbent's services (such as to rural areas) can make it unprofitable for entrants to compete for providing such services, even if the entrants are more efficient. This comes about because under the current system only incumbents are eligible for certain subsidies.

Distorted consumer decisions. The current rate structure also distorts consumer decisions. High long-distance rates subsidize telephone subscription but discourage calling; raising the fixed charge for telephone subscription and reducing the prices for calls would stimulate calling. The benefits from lower toll rates and expanded calling would make many consumers better off even after paying higher fixed charges. Cross-subsidies from long-distance to local service are sometimes defended on the grounds that low-income individuals use local service relatively intensively, but the correlation between income and long-distance versus local calling may not be strong, and some studies have indicated that high toll bills often lead to low-income subscribers being disconnected for nonpayment. Better ways can be found to assist those with low incomes.

Lack of transparency. A vital ingredient of any sound economic policy is to make costs and objectives explicit and transparent. The goals and methods of telephone cross-subsidies are now opaque; as a result, the true extent of cross-subsidies needed to ensure universal service or other legitimate social goals remains unclear. In some cases, cross-subsidies may instead reflect regulatory capture—some groups may simply be more adept than others at manipulating the regulatory process so as to procure subsidies for themselves. Competition is likely to reduce the cost to society of providing universal service by lowering costs and most prices and by introducing new technologies. It may well reveal that most people would have affordable access to basic telecommunications services even without subsidies.

Challenges for Reform

The rapid changes in technology and the accompanying changes in regulation described earlier imply that protecting universal service by maintaining regulated monopolies is likely to become both increasingly inefficient and untenable. Many economists favor giving competition freer rein and letting prices adjust to better reflect true costs. Any legitimate social goals served by the current regulated price structure should be addressed through other means that are more transparent, more targeted to explicit goals, and do not distort competition. A strong collaborative effort between Federal and State regulators should be established in pursuit of these goals.

What should be included in universal service? For many years there was only one basic service to be universalized or not: a telephone was a telephone. Today, however, telephone and other telecommunications networks are evolving to permit a much broader range of enhanced services. As conditions change, it will be important to review, perhaps on an evolving basis, the range of services targeted for universal service and to be clear about what is meant by "sufficiently affordable" prices.

Increasingly, we have realized the potential of modern communications to affect other aspects of life, from health (via telemedicine) to education. Access to computers and the Internet can put at the instantaneous disposal of every child in America resources superior to those available in even the best schools only a couple of decades ago. This Administration, through the National Telecommunications and Information Administration, has been striving to ensure that all Americans have access to advanced information services, for example, through public institutions such as schools and libraries. The new legislation includes the provision of such access as a core principle to guide universal-service reform.

Who should be eligible for support? For example, should all rural residents be eligible or only low-income consumers wherever they reside? And how much should prices be allowed to vary so as to reflect differences in the cost of providing service? Another reform principle adopted by the new legislation is that all consumers should have access to telecommunications and information services that are "reasonably comparable" in quality, variety, and rates to those available in urban areas. It goes further, however, with regard to interexchange and interstate telecommunications services (which include, at a minimum, telephone service), by requiring the rates charged to residential subscribers in rural areas to be "no higher" than those charged in urban areas. Many economists would hesitate to recommend such a stringent requirement.

How should universal service be funded? Once the goals have been clearly identified, funding mechanisms should be devised that do not distort competition. At present, subsidies to serve ostensibly unprofitable markets are not offered to all comers on an equal footing but are largely reserved for incumbent monopolists and financed through surcharges on long-distance and other services. Alternative financing methods would be less distorting and more

180

compatible with competition. An example might be a universal service fund, financed by charges levied on all telecommunications carriers, or even more broadly. All eligible consumers could draw on the fund, to help them pay for the provider of their choice. Alternatively, the right to provide subsidized service to a designated group could be allocated through competitive bidding among all qualified potential providers.

In the absence of explicit mechanisms to fund universal service or other social goals, regulators might feel compelled to meet such goals by imposing obligations on entrants. Such obligations could easily stifle competition. For example, regulators might be led to require entrants to offer a configuration of services, regional coverage, and rate structure very similar to that of the incumbent local monopolist. But entry is more likely to occur and to be more valuable if entrants have flexibility in choosing their technologies and mix of services to best exploit their comparative advantage. Revamping the funding of universal service therefore is an integral part of a successful move toward increased competition in telephone service. Consistent with this goal, the principles in the new legislation call for making support mechanisms explicit and predictable; requiring all providers of telecommunications services to make nondiscriminatory support contributions; and making all interested carriers eligible for support to provide service in designated areas, with the exception of any area served by a rural telephone company.

PROMOTING COMPETITION IN ELECTRICITY

The Nation's major electric utilities have historically been vertically integrated, engaged in both the generation and the delivery of electricity. Delivery is over high-voltage transmission lines from generators to substations, and from there over local distribution lines to users. The Federal Energy Regulatory Commission (FERC) regulates interstate transmission services and interstate wholesale power transactions (sales to utilities for resale), whereas the States regulate their investor-owned utilities' retail sales. In the past the supply of electricity within a given geographic area was seen as a natural monopoly, and State public utility commissions awarded utilities exclusive franchise areas. They required utilities to serve all consumers in their franchise areas at regulated, bundled rates, covering generation and delivery, based on cost of service.

A major crack in the vertically integrated structure of the industry came with the Public Utilities Regulatory Policy Act (PURPA) of 1978, which required utilities to buy power from nonutility generating companies that employed renewable energy sources or co-generation (co-generation uses steam both to generate power and

to heat adjoining buildings). Although its primary goals were to reduce dependence on imported oil and encourage renewable energy
sources, PURPA played a major role in promoting competition in
power generation. By giving rise to a class of nonutility generating
firms, PURPA created momentum for efforts to unbundle generation from delivery. Moreover, experience with PURPA demonstrated that independents could build generators on time and on
budget and could be reliably integrated into the transmission grid,
subject to utilities' control. Nonutility generating firms have grown
rapidly since PURPA's enactment. Their share of nationwide generating capacity has doubled from 3.6 percent in 1987 to 7.2 percent
in 1995; since 1990 they have contributed over half of all new investment in generating plant.

An obvious reason for some independents' growth is obligations
imposed on utilities to purchase power from PURPA-qualifying facilities. Although PURPA required purchases at prices that were
supposed to reflect utilities' expected costs were they to supply
power from their own sources, regulators in a few States calculated
these prices in ways that led to artificially high purchase prices.
But technological change also played a major role in the growth of
independents. The advent of small, efficient, natural gas-fueled
generators, coupled with falling gas prices, drastically reduced the
capital cost and minimum efficient scale of generating plants, making it easier for independents to finance plants (because of shorter
construction lags and lower financing needs) and to build plants
under contract to serve a particular utility. Market innovations in
the financing of power plant construction by independents also
were important.

Asymmetrical regulatory treatment also contributed to the independents' growth. Independents had stronger incentives than utilities to cut costs, because only they were exempt from cost-based
regulation. The Energy Policy Act of 1992 expanded this exemption
to a broader class of independents than PURPA had covered, allowing such independents to enter the wholesale power market, where
they could sell power to utilities at unregulated market rates (unlike PURPA, however, the 1992 Act did not oblige utilities to purchase from the independents). In addition, some utilities may have
refrained from building their own plants, fearing that regulators
would later reject some of the costs when it came to resetting their
rates. And regulators in some States required utilities to look first
elsewhere, to nonutility generating firms or to other utilities with
excess capacity, to supply their incremental generating capacity
needs before building more plants themselves. In this the regulators' intent was to foster competition, as part of an effort to curb
the rise in electricity prices following the oil shocks of the 1970s.

These changes expanded wholesale competition among generating firms to sell power to utilities. Pressure is growing to allow retail competition as well: for generating companies or utilities to sell directly to final customers in the franchise area of a different utility, paying regulated rates to use the utilities' existing transmission and distribution lines. This pressure comes mainly from large customers, who, among other things, can credibly threaten to bypass their local utility by generating their own electricity using small natural gas plants, or through municipalization (discussed later in this section). Promoting increased wholesale competition and introducing retail competition present three major challenges, which are discussed below.

UNBUNDLING GENERATION FROM TRANSMISSION AND DISTRIBUTION

To deliver power to final consumers, generating firms require access to the transmission and distribution facilities that utilities own and operate. These facilities appear to be natural monopolies, likely to remain subject to price regulation. This gives rise to a by-now familiar problem: if utilities are also permitted to generate their own power and sell it at unregulated rates, they will have an incentive to evade regulation by favoring their own generators and realizing profits through unregulated power sales. Such favoritism could involve cross-subsidizing the unregulated power generation business from the regulated transmission and distribution business or, more important, discriminating against outside generators in providing access to transmission and distribution networks.

If there were no significant economies of scope between generation and other functions, an obvious way to prevent discrimination would be to require separate ownership of regulated transmission and distribution assets and of unregulated generation assets. However, as discussed below, transmission and generation may be subject to important economies of scope. The challenge to policymakers and market participants is to devise solutions that balance potentially conflicting goals: preventing access discrimination, but without comprising the reliability of electricity supply, sacrificing economies of scope, or imposing excessive regulation.

The technological relationship between the generation and transmission of electricity is more complex than that between production and transportation in most other industries. Modern alternating-current transmission networks require tight and rapid balancing between power generated into and power withdrawn from the transmission grid. Storing electricity in significant volumes is generally impractical, and failure to balance power inflows and outflows can result within seconds in serious deterioration of system operation and widespread damage to equipment. The system is much less tolerant than, say, gas pipelines, which can accommodate imbalances for longer periods through external storage and by changing the degree of gas compression within the pipelines. Moreover, electricity flows cannot be easily routed within an integrated transmission network; rather, power flows automatically and instantaneously along the path of least impedance. Imbalances at one point on the grid therefore can have widespread and unpredictable consequences throughout the network.

Although network operations are largely computerized, unforeseen contingencies can require central intervention by the grid operator: transmission constraints may result from unforeseen demand surges or equipment failures, requiring some generating sets to be unexpectedly dispatched and others turned off. In addition, there are common costs in operating a transmission network, such as maintenance of reserves, and charging individual generators for such costs requires a central authority. Operating such a complex system therefore requires the grid operator to have substantial control over at least some generating assets, and over some network functions that entail common costs.

Until now such complications have been addressed within the context of a vertically integrated industry, and through regional power pools and other voluntary associations. However, moving to a more competitive regime may require devising alternative institutions. Vertical integration opens the possibility that utilities would use their control of transmission to discriminate in favor of their own generating plant. And, as explained below, reliance on voluntary cooperation to resolve regional transmission issues may be more difficult in a competitive environment.

The FERC has addressed the issue of expanding transmission access by requiring utilities situated between one utility seeking to purchase power and another utility or independent power producer seeking to sell power to allow use of their transmission lines to complete the sale. At first efforts to expand access were episodic; for instance, approvals of utilities' merger requests were made contingent on their granting transmission access. The 1992 Energy Policy Act explicitly authorized the FERC to require wholesale transmission access upon request. The FERC is in the midst of an important rulemaking to establish a comprehensive framework for implementing open, nondiscriminatory wholesale transmission access: a utility would have to grant access to outsiders seeking to consummate wholesale transactions on the same terms as to its own generating facilities.

Important as these initiatives are, some observers believe that more will have to be done. Defining and policing against discriminatory access may be difficult when an integrated utility runs the grid. In addition, increased competition will strain the current system of informal coordination between utilities, each operating transmission facilities that are connected into regional grids. Connecting such systems offers important advantages: it provides alternative transmission paths and economizes on redundant facilities, and it facilitates power sales to resolve temporary local imbalances between supply and demand or to benefit from differences in the cost of power over a wider region. Such informal coordination worked reasonably well in an era when utilities had exclusive franchises, but may become increasingly frayed in a competitive environment.

To address these concerns, some observers have proposed, and California regulators have recently endorsed, the formation of an "independent system operator." Investor-owned utilities and independent nonpublic generating companies would bid competitively to sell power into a regional grid. Utilities would retain ownership of transmission facilities but would turn over their operation under contract to an independent entity, which would manage the system on a regional basis. The operator would have authority over decisions such as how to respond to unforeseen contingencies and, under FERC oversight, how to price certain network services and allocate certain common costs. Although promising, this model also raises some questions. Can an operator be truly independent of utilities while they retain ownership of transmission and distribution? And will such a system cope well with coordinating investments in transmission and generation, given that different generating firms that rely on the grid can often have diverging interests?

In short, moving toward a more competitive market in electric power generation will require innovations in both regulation and market institutions. Maximizing the benefits from competition will also require implementing pricing policies that more accurately reflect transmission congestion and the costs of generation at different times (peak and off-peak). Finally, the gains from increased competition beyond those already being realized from today's wholesale competition may be modest in the short run, because much of utilities' expenses are associated with past investments, and with fuel expenses, which cannot be greatly reduced.

Nevertheless, some efficiency gains could materialize even in the short run: from increased utilization of excess capacity, from superior operation and maintenance of existing plants, and from boosting labor productivity. In the longer run the gains may be greater, since generation accounts for about half of the cost of electricity to the end user, and increased reliance on competition rather than regulation could allow both better operating decisions and better investment decisions regarding the amount, mix, and speed of construction of new plant.

STRANDED COSTS

Allowing competition would put pressure on utilities' prices and customer base, threatening to create stranded costs. Stranded costs are those unamortized costs of prior investments that are scheduled for recovery through regulated monopoly rates but would not be recovered under competition. Stranded costs for the industry as a whole have been estimated at $135 billion—well over half the total equity value of all investor-owned utilities. Many of the vulnerable utilities are concentrated in California, New York, New England, Pennsylvania, and Texas (Chart 6–3 provides a breakdown by region). Many of these utilities would be threatened with bankruptcy if unfettered wholesale and, especially, retail competition were allowed without providing utilities assistance in covering stranded costs.

Chart 6-3 **Potentially Stranded Costs of Investor-Owned Electric Utilities by Region**
Northeastern electric utilities have the highest potentially stranded costs, both in dollars and as a percent of equity.

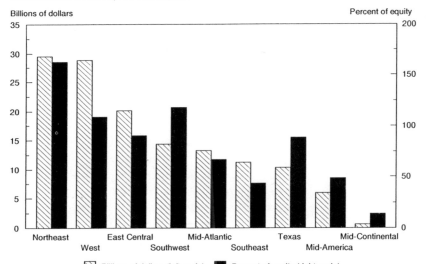

Note: Data are estimated present values of total costs minus revenues from 1996 through 2005, assuming a move to competition. Some utilities located in Texas are included in the "Southwest," and not in the "Texas" category.
Source: Moody's Investors Service.

One source of stranded costs is past investments that turned out differently than expected. In some cases nuclear power proved more expensive than projected, and gas prices much lower; therefore some investments in nuclear generators led to higher generating costs than those of modern gas-based plants at today's gas prices. Second, in many regions utilities overestimated power demand, leading them to build excess generating capacity. If this capacity were fully used under the pressure of competition, it would drive the price of power down to the short-run marginal cost, and thus well below average cost (which includes sunk capital costs). Although such pricing promotes short-run efficiency, it would impose large losses on some utilities. Finally, stranded costs also arise from regulatory obligations imposed on some utilities but not on other suppliers, including requirements to buy power from PURPA-qualifying facilities at prices above today's market prices, to invest in pollution control equipment, and to fund demand conservation programs.

In unregulated markets the possibility of stranded costs typically does not raise an issue for public policy—it is simply one of the risks of doing business. However, there is an important difference between regulated and unregulated markets. Unregulated firms bear the risk of stranded costs but are entitled to high profits if things go unexpectedly well. In contrast, utilities have been limited to regulated rates, intended to yield no more an a fair return on their investments. If competition were unexpectedly allowed, utilities would be exposed to low returns without having had the chance to reap the full expected returns in good times, thus denying them the return promised to induce the initial investment. A strong case therefore can be made for allowing utilities to recover stranded costs where these costs arise from after-the-fact mistakes or changes in regulatory philosophy toward competition, as long as the investments were initially authorized by regulators.

The case for allowing recovery is even stronger where stranded costs arise from regulatory obligations imposed on utilities. Several States, notably California, required utilities to purchase power from qualifying facilities under PURPA at long-term contract prices based on high estimates of future oil and gas prices, even after utilities resisted purchasing all the capacity offered at the high prices. Utilities also were required to fit coal-fired generators with costly pollution control equipment, again with the expectation that costs would be recovered through regulated rates. Utilities should be allowed to recover such costs mandated by regulation.

To be sure, utilities should be granted recovery only of costs prudently incurred pursuant to legal and regulatory obligations to serve the public. Investments made after utilities are notified that competition is coming and are relieved of their obligation to serve should not qualify; and utilities must try to mitigate their losses. But recovery should be allowed for legitimate stranded costs. The equity reason for doing so is clear, but there is also a strong efficiency reason for honoring regulators' promises. Credible government is key to a successful market economy, because it is so important for encouraging long-term investments. Although policy reforms inevitably impose losses on some holders of existing assets, good policy tries to mitigate such losses for investments made

187

based on earlier rules, for instance, by grandfathering certain investments when laws and regulations change.

Because stranded costs are sunk, economic reasoning suggests that they should be recovered through mechanisms that do not artificially reduce power consumption. One possibility is a charge levied on transmission, but as a fixed fee rather than a marginal charge: customers would be required to pay specified amounts, based perhaps on their past consumption, regardless of their future use of electricity.

Since stranded costs reflect policy decisions, recovery should be borne broadly by all parties on whose behalf the stranded costs were incurred, including customers that switch to other suppliers. Consistent with this principle, the FERC proposed that wholesale customers departing a utility be assessed a contribution toward stranded costs. Although the FERC proposal would directly apply to stranded costs resulting only from increased wholesale competition, it could also serve as a model for States contemplating retail competition, and serve as the FERC approach to recovering stranded costs resulting from retail competition in the unlikely event that the State lacked authority to address the issue.

Most State discussions of initiatives to foster retail competition in fact have included, as an integral part, mechanisms to recover stranded costs. But some retail customers threaten to bypass this process, for example, by resorting to "municipalization." A municipal utility within the franchise area of an investor-owned utility may generate none or only some of its required power, and as a power reseller it qualifies for FERC-mandated wholesaler access to outside suppliers. Although municipal utilities typically serve legitimate functions, they might at times provide a loophole for avoiding fair sharing of stranded costs. A municipality might extend its boundaries to encompass the premises of a large industrial customer served by the investor-owned utility; that customer becomes eligible to buy power from outside suppliers, using the municipal utility as conduit. Such actions raise important issues of equity and cost-shifting, both for the local utility and for other customers in its franchise area that may be stuck with a larger share of stranded costs. The FERC has stated that municipalization should not be a vehicle to escape responsibility for stranded costs.

COMPETITIVE PARITY, UNIVERSAL SERVICE, AND ENVIRONMENTAL PROTECTION

For competition to work well, it must take place on a level playing field: competition will be distorted if producers are given selective privileges, or subjected to selective obligations imposed to further even legitimate social goals. This principle raises several issues as we move toward increased competition.

As competition grows, increasing distortions may result from some entities having access to special privileges such as federally tax-exempt bonds or other preferential treatment. Accordingly, re-examining special privileges of various entities may become more important.

On the other hand, producers should not be subjected to selective obligations. New ways must be found, as in the telephone industry, to address universal service, assist low-income consumers, and meet other social goals currently addressed through obligations on regulated monopoly utilities. Continuing to impose such requirements only on some producers would place them at a competitive disadvantage and imperil their ability to meet these obligations. Accordingly, these obligations would be better financed through more broadly based mechanisms.

Increased competition in electricity can also affect the environment. To reap the advantages of more efficient electricity markets and a cleaner environment, environmental policy will need to respond to any risks that restructuring may pose for environmental quality. But policy toward restructuring should also recognize those risks and, where possible, facilitate appropriate responses. For example, the burden of funding renewable energy sources or energy conservation programs to reduce pollution should be shared broadly, not placed solely on vertically-integrated utilities. Symmetrical treatment of all players will address environmental concerns more effectively and provide competitive parity.

CONCLUSION

Our telecommunications and electricity sectors are undergoing sweeping transformations, which hold the promise of increased reliance on market forces and competition, with potentially large dividends for consumers and business. To facilitate such transformations, regulatory and competition policy must adapt. Unnecessary legal restrictions on entry must be removed, and regulation must be reformed to better address those industry segments where monopoly power will persist. But blanket deregulation will not ensure an equitable, efficient, and durable transition to competition. To ensure a successful transition and protect important social goals, government will have to play an evolving but ongoing role.

189

CHAPTER 7

Investing in Education and Training

THE FEDERAL GOVERNMENT HAS BEEN a vital partner in education for more than 200 years. Even before the Constitution was adopted, the Ordinance of 1785 set aside a section in every township in the new territories west of Pennsylvania to support a school. In 1862 the first Morrill Act authorized Federal land grants to States for the establishment of colleges. As World War II came to an end, a grateful Nation offered the G.I. bill, which eventually served nearly 8 million returning veterans—and fundamentally changed the educational landscape of the country. Today, Federal educational loans and grants open the doors to college for millions of students who could not otherwise attend, and Federal grants to low-income schools help more than 6 million children learn to read and to do math.

Learning is a lifelong process, not limited to those between the ages of 5 and 25. From early childhood education to college to training for the unemployed, this Administration has sought to complement the efforts of State and local governments in responding to the new demands of the labor market. The Nation is in the midst of an educational renewal, and families, teachers, local school districts, colleges, States, employers, and the Federal Government all have a role to play in the transformation.

The renewed Federal interest in education and training is in part a response to the two challenges outlined in Chapter 1: the slowdown in the growth of productivity and the increase in earnings inequality. Education and training policy is one of the few policy levers available to address both problems simultaneously.

One of the most dramatic changes in our economy during the past 15 years has been the increased economic payoff to skills, as reflected in the increased inequality in earnings between high school and college graduates. In 1979 full-time male workers aged 25 and over with at least a bachelor's degree earned on average 49 percent more per year than did comparable workers with only a high school degree. By 1993 the difference in wages had nearly doubled, to 89 percent. To the extent that this rise in the payoff to education reflects an increase in the value of skill, improving our schools and expanding access to postsecondary training stimulate economic growth. Based on estimates from the Bureau of Labor Statistics, the rise in the average educational attainment of the workforce accounted for one-fifth of the annual growth in productivity between 1963 and 1992. International evidence reveals that, all else equal, those nations with the highest school enrollment rates in the early 1960s tended to enjoy the most robust growth in subsequent decades.

Education and training policies can also help address the problem of growing inequality. A primary goal of Federal policy must be to ensure that educational opportunities are not restricted to those whose parents can finance an education out of their own pockets. Federal programs such as Head Start, which helps low-income children prepare for school; Title I of the Elementary and Secondary Education Act, which provides supplemental Federal assistance to low-income schools and school districts; and Federal financial aid for college students are all designed to support those who would otherwise not have an equal opportunity to invest in learning.

The sharp rise in family income inequality should not be allowed to cause greater inequity in access to educational opportunities. The widening disparity in earnings prospects between the more and the less educated makes such efforts to equalize educational opportunities even more imperative. Since the 1980s the Nation's track record in equalizing educational opportunity has been mixed. In elementary and secondary schools, racial gaps in test scores in mathematics, reading, and science have closed somewhat, even as mean scores have risen for whites as well as blacks and Hispanics. The black-white gap in high school graduation rates has also narrowed since the mid-1970s, as high school graduation rates rose for blacks.

However, gaps in college enrollment rates between low- and high-income youth and between minority and white, non-Hispanic youth have widened since the late 1970s (Chart 7–1). Although all groups have responded to changes in the labor market by attending college at higher rates, the increases have been larger for middle- and higher income youth than for low-income youth. Because blacks and Hispanics are overrepresented at the bottom of the income distribution, the racial and ethnic enrollment gaps have widened as well.

The widening gaps in college enrollment are troubling for at least two reasons. First, they may imply an increasing perpetuation of inequity from one generation to the next—with access to higher education increasingly allocated on the basis of ability to pay, not ability to learn. In this country, which values the principle that children's success in life should not be held hostage to their parents' lack of resources, this is unacceptable. A second reason is that low enrollments deprive the economy of the skills of those unable to finance those investments. The labor market is demanding high-

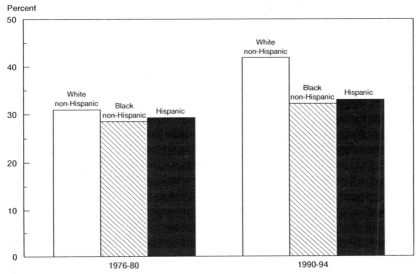

Chart 7-1   **College Enrollment Rates of Young High School Graduates**
Enrollment rates have increased for white, black, and Hispanic high school graduates, but the increase in white enrollment has been larger.

Note: Data are for high school graduates age 18 to 24.
Source: Department of Education.

er levels of skill, and the economy will grow more quickly if we succeed in producing more skilled workers.

Education and training policy can contribute to reversing the growth of inequality in the country in two ways. First, by targeting educational resources more effectively, education and training policy may enable more of our citizens to benefit from the rising payoff to skill. Second, a robust supply response that creates an abundance of skilled labor and causes less-skilled labor to become relatively more scarce may slow the rise in the price of skill in the labor market, reducing the growth of wage inequality and possibly even reversing it somewhat.

In short, the Administration's education and training policies are predicated on the three principles outlined in Chapter 1. They encourage students and schools to *embrace change* by developing the skills demanded by the new labor market. They *create opportunity* by targeting resources to the disadvantaged, providing greater opportunity to participate fruitfully in that market. And they *promote personal responsibility,* by stressing to young people and workers that they are responsible for making their own educational choices, and by requiring them to share some portion of the cost: through their efforts in school, through the earnings they forgo to remain in school, through their participation in the Federal Work Study program, and through their obligation to repay educational loans.

This chapter first reviews the good news on the extent to which the Nation has responded to the rise in the value of education since the early 1980s, as well as the sobering news on how far we still have to go. The chapter then examines the evidence from the economics literature on the payoff to investments in schooling and training. Finally, we describe the Federal role in education and training policy in complementing State and local efforts.

AMERICANS ARE RESPONDING TO THE DEMAND FOR SKILLS

Americans have always placed a high value on education, seeing it as a ladder of opportunity. Therefore, the country was ready to respond when *A Nation at Risk,* the 1983 report of a commission appointed by the Secretary of Education, sounded the alarm over declining nationwide test scores. Since then a number of States and local school districts have launched ambitious reform projects. After a decade of effort, progress clearly has been made:

- Students are spending more time on homework than they did at the end of the 1970s. The proportion of 13-year-olds reporting that they had no homework or that they had not done their homework declined from 38 percent in 1980 to 25 percent in 1992.
- The proportion of 11th- and 12th-grade students taking advanced placement courses grew by 138 percent between 1984 and 1992.
- In 1992 the average public high school graduate had completed 49 percent more courses in algebra or higher mathematics, 33 percent more coursework in science, and 8 percent more coursework in English than his or her counterpart in 1982.
- Between 1980 and 1993, the proportion of students in grades 10 through 12 remaining in school rose for whites, blacks, and Hispanics. The decline in the dropout rate was particularly steep for blacks.

The hard work of students, parents, teachers, and school administrators has borne fruit in the form of higher test scores and higher college enrollment rates. Some year-to-year fluctuations notwithstanding, most of the trends suggest that progress is being made:

- As measured by scores on the National Assessment of Educational Progress, average mathematics proficiency rose for nearly every age, gender, and racial or ethnic group between 1978 and 1992.
- Average mathematics scores on the Scholastic Aptitude Test (SAT) rose by 13 points overall and by 28 points for blacks between 1980 and 1994. These gains are particularly impressive given the large increase in the proportion of high school stu-

dents taking the SAT, which would have tended to reduce average scores.

- The proportion of college-age youth (those 18 to 24 years old) enrolled in college grew by more than one-third between 1980 and 1994, from 26 percent to 35 percent.

- The numbers of associate, bachelor's, and doctoral degrees awarded grew by 28 percent, 25 percent, and 29 percent, respectively, between 1980 and 1993, even though the population of college-age youth declined by 15 percent.

However, much remains to be done. Although average scores have been rising in mathematics and science, much of the gain has occurred in lower level computational skills rather than in higher level problem solving. Reading and writing test scores declined slightly for the weakest students during the late 1980s. Perhaps most disturbing, students in the United States continue to lag behind their counterparts in many Asian and European countries in math and science (Chart 7–2).

Chart 7-2 **Mathematics Proficiency of U.S. and Foreign Students**
The median performance of U.S. 13-year olds in 1991 was below that of students in several other countries.

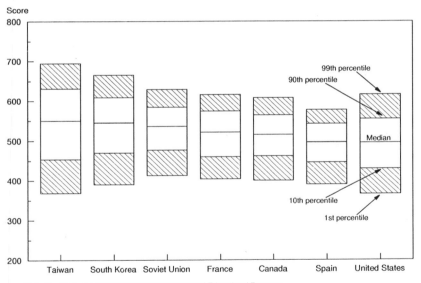

Note: Test instrument is International Assessment of Educational Progress.
Source: Department of Education.

Although it is tempting to extrapolate from current trends and to assume that the rise in skill-related earnings inequality will continue unabated, economic historians tell us that the payoff to education has fluctuated over the past 50 years, rising and falling with changes in supply and demand. For example, the ratio of the average earnings of a college graduate to the average for high school graduates is today roughly what it was in 1940. Economic theory predicts that positive shifts in demand will be met by increases in the quantity supplied. Although Americans have responded by enrolling in college in record proportions, so far the demand for skill has outpaced the Nation's ability to produce more skilled workers. But the demographic tide is gradually turning, as the number of 18- to 24-year-olds is expected to rise by 20 percent over the next 15 years. Eventually the rise in the labor market value of skill, and the wage inequality it has brought about, may be dampened if these new workers are better equipped to meet the demands of the labor market. The remainder of this chapter discusses the role of government policy in aiding that response.

DO EDUCATION AND TRAINING LEAD TO HIGHER EARNINGS?

Throughout the 1980s the gap in real annual earnings widened between American workers with different levels of education (Chart 7–3). Labor economists have argued for decades over whether education actually *causes* differences in earnings, or whether those with better earnings prospects—because of more favorable family backgrounds or greater native ability—simply consume more education. After literally hundreds of studies of the economic importance of education, most economists now agree that education does, indeed, lead to higher earnings (although they may disagree about the size of the effect). Each additional year of formal schooling is associated with a 5 to 15 percent increase in annual earnings later in life. Even without counting the other benefits offered by education—a more active citizenry, breakthroughs in science and the arts, less reliance on social welfare programs—such benefits are often large enough to justify the public and private investments involved (Box 7–1).

Questions of causation are difficult to resolve, however, because unlike natural scientists working in the controlled setting of the laboratory, researchers cannot simply assign people randomly to different educational careers. Even if one tried to perform such an experiment, those assigned to lower levels of educational attainment or training could always decide to pursue their options elsewhere. This implies that random assignment experiments can only evaluate the *incremental* impact of specific programs over that of opportunities available elsewhere—not the full value of the training. The more options available for education and training, the smaller will be the incremental impact of any specific program— even if the training itself is quite worthwhile. Therefore, in addition to using experimental evidence, economists have exploited sev-

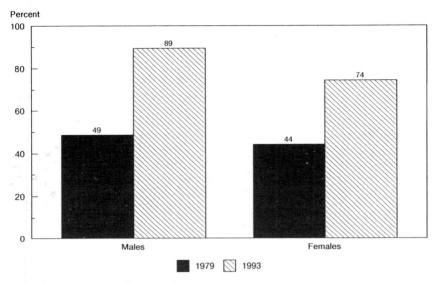

Note: Data are for year-round, full-time workers, age 25 and over.
Source: Department of Labor.

eral other sources of variation in educational attainment in study-ing the effect of additional education and training on earnings.

COMPARING THE EARNINGS OF SIMILAR WORKERS WITH VARYING EDUCATIONAL ATTAINMENT

For decades survey researchers have collected information not just on education and earnings but on other characteristics, such as standardized test scores, parental education, and family income, which might be related to both educational attainment and future earnings. In analyzing these data, economists have attempted to control for prior differences in earnings prospects between the more and less educated, by studying the relationship between education and earnings only among those who might be expected to have similar earnings given their other characteristics.

In such studies, more than 75 percent of the estimated impact of education typically remains even after controlling for test scores prior to entering college. One recent study compared the earnings 14 years after high school of a sample of graduates of the high school class of 1972 who had attended different types of postsecond-ary institutions. Although those who had attended 4-year institu-tions had higher earnings than either community college students or those with no postsecondary training, they also had higher grades, higher standardized test scores, and more favorable family

Box 7-1.—Is a College Education a Worthwhile Investment?

Calculating the return on any investment involves assessing both costs and benefits. Here we do some back-of-the-envelope calculations of the economic return to a college education.

Although a college education certainly yields other benefits, earnings differentials after college—the additional wages that a college graduate earns compared with a high school graduate—are perhaps the easiest to measure. It remains to be seen how today's college graduates will fare over the next 45 years of their careers; absent that information, the most straightforward approach is to assume that the difference in earnings observed among people of various ages and educational attainments today will persist into the future.

A college education clearly has high costs as well. In addition to the $10,000 in average educational costs per year of college, students forgo potential earnings while in school. Since a full-time college student would typically miss 9 months of work experience in a year, three-quarters of the average annual earnings of an 18- to 24-year-old male high school graduate, or $12,200, is a reasonable estimate of earnings forgone for each year of full-time college study. Therefore the total cost of a year in college is the combination of educational costs and forgone earnings, approximately $22,200.

If these measures of costs and benefits are accurate, the internal rate of return on 4 years of college for a male, 13 percent, is higher than that for most financial instruments. Even if one attributes only 75 percent of the earnings difference between high school and college graduates to schooling, the internal rate of return is still 11 percent. Despite the high costs, then, a college education continues to be a worthwhile investment.

backgrounds upon graduating from high school—all characteristics that would have predicted higher earnings for them even if they had not attended college. Comparing those who had similar family backgrounds and academic characteristics in high school, the researchers found that a year of community college was associated with an increase in earnings of 4 to 7 percent, roughly the same as that associated with a year in a 4-year college.

STUDIES USING TWINS

Admittedly, however, many of the characteristics that affect earnings are difficult to measure. Such easily quantifiable variables as family income or years of education received by one's parents may not fully capture the myriad differences in family background.

Rather than attempt to collect information on a seemingly infinite list of characteristics, some survey researchers have gone to great lengths to follow the experience of pairs of identical twins. Because identical twins growing up in the same household share a variety of environmental and genetic factors, analyzing differences in their earnings and educational attainment eliminates the need to measure the subtle ways in which backgrounds may differ between families.

The conclusion of this research is that, even among identical twins, those with more education tend to earn more. In some studies, the difference in earnings associated with a year of education has been as great as the 5 to 15 percent earnings difference per year of education observed in the broader population. For example, a recent study of this type found that each year of education was related to a difference in earnings of between 12 and 16 percent.

NATURAL EXPERIMENTS

Just as individuals from different families may differ in ways that are not easily measured, identical twins may have different experiences growing up that would lead one twin to attend school longer and to earn more in the labor market than his or her sibling. A third approach, therefore, is to identify laws or institutional differences that may have an effect on educational attainment but are expected to have no independent effect on earnings.

Compulsory schooling laws provide one such opportunity. Many States once had regulations that allowed only those turning 6 during the current calendar year to enter first grade in the fall. In other words, 5-year-olds with their 6th birthdays falling on or before December 31 could begin classes in the fall, while those born on January 1 or later had to wait an additional year. Because compulsory schooling laws specify a minimum *age* of mandatory attendance (usually age 16 or 17) and not a minimum *grade level*, those born during the first calendar quarter reached the age at which they could drop out after having completed a year less of school than those born in the last calendar quarter. As long as the earnings of those born at different times of the year do not vary systematically for reasons unrelated to educational attainment, the interaction between compulsory schooling laws and calendar quarter of birth provides a "natural experiment" for measuring the impact of education on earnings. Researchers have found that those with birthdays in the first calendar quarter were indeed slightly more likely to drop out at lower grade levels than those born later in the year. Moreover, each year of additional education was associated with a 5 to 10 percent increase in hourly wages later in life.

The study of compulsory schooling laws is particularly important because it identifies the payoff to a year of schooling only for those who are constrained by such laws to remain in school, rather than describing the average return to education for all who remain. Therefore, the results suggest that even those who would have dropped out earlier than compulsory schooling laws allowed seemed to benefit from additional schooling. This is a strong argument for measures to deter high school students from dropping out (Box 7–2).

RANDOM ASSIGNMENT EXPERIMENTS

Even though, as noted above, random assignment experiments can identify only the incremental impact of specific programs and not the value of training itself, some programs do indeed seem to raise the earnings of those who are assigned to them. The primary advantage of being able to randomly assign some subjects to training and others to a comparison group is that one can expect that any resulting difference in average earnings for the two groups is due to the incremental training provided and not to some other difference between the two groups. Although the studies are usually conducted on a small scale, random assignment evaluations have often found that education and training raise the earnings of participants. For instance, in recent years the Center for Employment Training (CET) in San Jose, California, has achieved impressive results in two different random assignment evaluations. Out-of-school youth receiving an average of 4.1 months of training at CET earned 40 percent more per year (approximately $3,000 per year in 1993 dollars) than the control group during the third and fourth year after being assigned. The total cost of the program per enrollee was $4,200. In a separate random assignment evaluation of a program for minority single female parents, participants earned $1,500 (again in 1993 dollars) more than the control group in the second year after training. Earnings increases remained large in the fifth year of the study, by which time those who had received training and job placement services were still earning 16 percent more than the control group.

Education and training for experienced workers yield economic benefits as well. A recent random assignment evaluation of the Job Training Partnership Act (JTPA), a Federal program providing training for economically disadvantaged clients, found that participation increased the earnings of adult male participants by 7 percent and those of adult female participants by 10 percent. These earnings gains were one and one-half times greater than the costs of producing them.

LEARNING OR SORTING?

Although labor economists would generally agree that education and training do lead to higher earnings, it is more difficult to deter-

Box 7–2.—New Opportunities for Potential Dropouts

One of the eight goals set out in the Goals 2000 Act is to raise high school graduation rates to 90 percent by the year 2000. Indeed, dropping out of high school is not a good financial decision. A male youth who finishes the last 2 years of high school will reap a net lifetime earnings increase of $99,000 (stated in present value terms at a 3 percent discount rate). Even when one considers the cost to taxpayers of 2 additional years of public secondary education ($5,600 per year), the internal rate of return for a male completing high school is 9.5 percent. Persuading young people to remain in high school seems a particularly worthwhile investment.

Between 1987 and 1989 the Department of Labor conducted a random assignment evaluation of JTPA programs for out-of-school youth. The average youth assigned to JTPA did not receive higher earnings during the 30-month evaluation than did those assigned to the control group, many of whom participated in other non-JTPA education and training programs. In other words, the availability of JTPA programs did not seem to add much to the existing array of services for out-of-school youth.

In response, the Department of Labor is exploring alternative strategies. For instance, rather than providing training to students once they drop out of school, the department is funding a replication of a promising high school dropout prevention program. The Quantum Opportunities Program (described in more detail in the 1995 *Economic Report of the President*) will be replicated with over 1,000 participants at seven sites around the country.

The Labor Department is also conducting a major evaluation of the Job Corps program, a comprehensive, residential job training program for high school dropouts. Treatment and control subjects will be followed for 5 to 6 years to determine the impact of the program on employment and other social outcomes.

The Labor Department has also experimented with "geographic targeting," saturating high poverty communities in inner cities and rural areas with job training, work opportunities, school-to-work programs, and sports and recreation activities. The aim is to reach enough young people in a neighborhood to reverse the effect of peer pressure. Although the saturation approach made random assignment difficult, a nonexperimental evaluation is yielding promising results.

mine *why* they matter. Do employers pay their highly educated workers more because of the skills they have learned, or do the more educated earn more because educational attainment provides other signals to an employer about them, such as their perseverance or level of motivation? The question is very difficult to resolve empirically, since it is difficult to measure acquired skill as distinct from educational attainment. For instance, we infer the extent of a physician's training not by directly measuring his or her medical knowledge but by observing his or her educational credentials.

It is likely that some portion of the observed payoff to schooling is due to both the "skills" and the "sorting" explanations. However, it appears that technological change has increased the value of some skills more than others. Even if sorting accounts for some portion of the value of education, higher level problem-solving skills have almost certainly increased in value with the availability of computers. Furthermore, it would be difficult to attribute the large increase in the payoff to schooling, even among those who have been in the labor market for decades, to an increase in the value of education as a signal. Greater success in producing these skills not only would raise the earnings of those benefiting, but also would contribute to economic growth. Moreover, when it comes to improving the earnings prospects of the disadvantaged, whether it is the skill learned or the credential acquired that opens the door, such investments improve the prospects of those who may lack the resources to invest in themselves and reduce the perpetuation of poverty.

THE PAYOFF TO PUBLIC INVESTMENT IN EDUCATION

Since the publication of *Equality of Educational Opportunity* (commonly known as the Coleman Report) in 1966, researchers have struggled with the question of whether increased expenditure on schools improves student performance. The debate is often quite contentious because of the large differences in expenditure per pupil between rich and poor school districts. For example, during the 1992–93 school year, New Jersey spent more than $9,400 per pupil in public elementary and secondary schools, while Alabama and Mississippi spent less than $3,900. Regional differences in the cost of living can explain only a small part of such variation. Furthermore, given the importance of local financing of public education, expenditure per pupil can differ by a factor of two or three even between districts in the same State.

Typically, analysts compare average test scores in high-spending and low-spending districts to learn about the effect of additional resources on scores. Not surprisingly, the high-spending districts have higher average scores. However, since high-spending districts also tend to have higher average family income and parental education, the differences in student performance may be caused not by differences in the level of spending but by differences in family resources. When analysts compare test scores in high- and low-spending districts with similar family incomes and parental education, the results are often considered provocative: districts that spend more are often found *not* to have higher test scores.

However, additional resources could have other beneficial impacts. The standardized tests used in much of the research may not reliably measure the kinds of improvements that parents or policymakers would expect schools to produce with additional resources. The benefits of new courses in American history, geometry, or calculus or improved learning opportunities for the disabled—valuable as they may be—would not be captured by such measures.

Consistent with this hypothesis, studies of the long-term impacts of school expenditure on earnings and educational attainment—in contrast to those that focus on test scores—yield more optimistic evidence that public investment in elementary and secondary schooling does generate benefits later in students' lives. For instance, better paid and better educated teachers and smaller classroom size have been associated with greater educational attainment and higher payoffs to education later in life, even if they have not had large effects on the particular test scores used. One recent study concluded that the payoff was not only positive but financially lucrative: a 10 percent increase in expenditures from kindergarten through 12th grade would produce additional lifetime earnings valued at 1.2 times the additional cost (in present value terms). Admittedly, studies of this kind remain few, and some authors have reported less positive results, but some evidence suggests that past increases in spending on education did bear fruit, even if the results did not register on the particular tests used.

But the debate over such findings often misses a more relevant question: rather than continue to debate how much of a difference additional resources have made in the past, we should be asking how programs and incentives could be structured today to ensure even greater benefits from resources invested now and in the future. It is difficult to believe that a knowledgeable school principal could not find a way to use additional resources to improve student learning, as long as the incentives in the environment rewarded such gains. The task of policymakers should be to create an environment in which incentives dictate that resources be invested profitably.

On this question, Federal, State, and local governments are already a step ahead of the academic debate. Many of the educational reforms being pursued today seek to produce more decentralization and greater accountability, both of which are designed to create an environment in which resources are used more efficiently. The charter school movement is a good example. Minnesota was the first State to pass a law allowing for charter schools in 1991. Since then 19 other States have enacted laws permitting the development of charter schools. A charter school is usually the brainchild of a committed group of teachers or set of parents who want the flexibility to try a different approach. Typically, they apply to the local school board or the State department of education for a charter allowing them to open a new school with public funding. Since charter schools are public schools, they do not charge tuition. Such charters typically waive many of the regulatory requirements imposed on other public schools for 3 to 5 years, at which time they are subject to review.

Charter schools enhance accountability in two ways. First, charter contracts often specify benchmarks for performance, such as scores on specific State assessments. In exchange for the freedom to innovate, charter school organizers are expected to produce results. Some contracts are more specific in spelling out such performance expectations than others. As States develop better assessment tools under the Goals 2000: Educate America Act (described below), these performance expectations can be more explicitly stated. Second, the presence of charter schools is intended to encourage innovation by nearby public and private schools, through the demonstration of successful educational strategies and through the threat of lost enrollment.

The Department of Education has helped to nurture the charter school movement by providing seed money for the establishment of charter schools. In the 1995 fiscal year, the Federal Government provided nearly $6 million in grants to help cover startup costs for charter schools. The Administration hopes to increase this commitment significantly over the next few years.

But the establishment of charter schools represents only one way in which States and local school districts are seeking to provide better incentives for schools and teachers. School report cards, performance bonuses for schools, magnet schools, and other forms of public school choice are also being tested.

Publicly funded vouchers for use at private schools are another, more radical approach. But vouchers have several problems. Their advocates fail to recognize the many ways in which education for children differs from conventional goods. The primary risk of vouchers is that they may produce a dramatic increase in social stratification. The cost in terms of the resulting damage to social mobility and social cohesion could exceed any benefit in terms of better school performance. Because they are public schools dependent upon public support, charter schools can be more carefully planned to serve all children's interests by locating them in urban areas, by insisting on open admissions policies, by holding them directly accountable for results, and—when oversubscribed—by requiring them to establish lotteries for admission. Charter schools provide a framework for an improved educational system, with parents and teachers working together to develop new and creative solutions to the challenges they face, and demanding accountability of all participants in the educational process.

Some approaches to accountability are better suited to some environments than others. For instance, school report cards are better indicators of school performance when mobility between schools is low and when one can control for differences in student characteristics. Charter schools and magnet schools provide better incentives when the quality of local transportation is good and parents are engaged and well informed. Still another approach, which several European countries employ, raises the stakes for students, through more widespread use of achievement tests as a criterion for high school graduation and college admission, or even by employers in their hiring decisions (Box 7–3). Given the diversity of circumstances around the country, it is appropriate that each State and school district pursue its own strategy for encouraging more decentralization and accountability. The next section discusses the various ways in which the Federal Government has chosen to complement these efforts.

THE FEDERAL ROLE IN EDUCATION AND TRAINING

The environment facing providers of education and training is changing. Today parents and taxpayers increasingly expect results from their investments. In partnership with State and local policymakers, Federal policy is helping to create this new environment in several ways: by providing seed money to States developing content standards in core subject areas, by supporting States in the development of assessment tools for measuring progress, by helping States to invest in their teachers, and by supporting the establishment of charter schools. But in addition to these efforts the Federal Government serves many other roles in our education and training system, such as guaranteeing student loans, channeling resources to low-income schools and school districts, helping disadvantaged children prepare to enter kindergarten, and helping States develop new pathways from school to the world of work. As mentioned at the outset of this chapter, the Federal Government has played a vital role in education since before the Constitution was signed. There are at least five reasons why.

Box 7–3.—Raising the Stakes for Students

Despite recent gains, American youth continue to perform poorly in science and mathematics relative to their counterparts in many other industrialized countries. American students also seem to spend less time on their studies than students in other countries. The Organization for Economic Cooperation and Development has suggested that one of the causes of the poorer U.S. performance is the lack of connection between high school achievement and employment or schooling opportunities.

Unless they are planning to attend a selective college, high school students in America often have little incentive to do well academically. Surveys suggest that employers have difficulty collecting and interpreting transcripts from many different schools. And except for the most competitive colleges, a student's performance in high school has little impact on his or her chances of admission to college. The skills developed in school may well matter later in students' careers, but many students may fail to see a connection between performance in school and immediate prospects for a job or college admission.

In contrast, many European countries require students graduating from high school to take tests in various subject areas. Universities use these scores in making admission decisions, as do employers in their hiring decisions. Some precedent for such high-stakes testing exists in the United States—the Regents Examination in New York is an example. By raising the stakes for high school performance—or, possibly more important, making the actual consequences more visible—these tests may induce students to work harder.

An achievement test may also strengthen the incentives of students and teachers to work together. Absent an external standard, schools judge individual students relative to their classmates. But the relative scale gives students an incentive to discourage their peers from "wrecking the curve." In contrast, an external standard unites teachers, students, and their classmates in a common objective: to perform well.

To focus attention on the value of high school achievement, the Administration has proposed providing $1,000 scholarships to the top 5 percent of every high school class, public and private, for use at college. Although the reward is still based on a relative standard, the goal of the awards will be to make the new realities of the labor market more salient, giving students in school a more immediate reason to strive harder.

First, Americans are a mobile people. Between 1993 and 1994 alone, 6.7 million Americans moved from one State to another. The consequences of a good—or a bad—educational system therefore extend well beyond the borders of a single State. For this reason, education is a national concern as well as a local one.

One consequence of that mobility is that the Federal Government has a distinct advantage in administering educational loan programs. The average cost of a year at a public 4-year college is approximately $10,000, not counting room and board, earnings forgone while attending school, college expenditures on sponsored research, or scholarships and fellowships. Even though States often pay a large share of these costs through subsidies to public institutions, relatively few families have the resources to finance such large investments out of pocket. Moreover, because an education cannot be repossessed like a car or a house, private lenders have not been willing, absent government guarantees, to lend at reasonable rates, even to the most promising student. Given the mobility of the population, the Federal Government is in the best position to guarantee these loans and to pool the risk associated with them.

Second, the Federal Government must share the responsibility of guaranteeing equality of opportunity for all children. The commitment to equal opportunity is founded upon both moral imperatives and economic interests. The commitment to opportunity for all children has long been a fundamental American value. The economic interest is also clear. Without intervention by higher levels of government, many communities would not be able to invest to the full extent worthwhile in their children's educations. Although many State governments do target resources on the most disadvantaged schools and school districts, as argued in Chapter 4, Federal involvement may be necessary to avert a "race to the bottom" in the provision of State services to the disadvantaged. And even if there were no race to the bottom, differences in resources would mean children in disadvantaged communities or poor States might receive an inadequate education. The Federal Government can help to equalize access to educational opportunities across States and school systems.

Indeed, some progress has been made over the past decades. As already mentioned, black youth have closed part of the gap in test scores with their white classmates in elementary and secondary school. Nevertheless, students continue to come out of our school system with enormous disparities in basic skills. One recent study has suggested that differences in basic skills among youth emerging from our school system may account for a significant share of the difference in average earnings between black and white males in their late 20s.

Third, the Federal Government must play a role in research and evaluation and in informing local decisionmakers about the payoffs to alternative strategies. This is true of research and innovation in education no less than in other areas. How much does classroom size matter? Which teaching techniques produce better student performance? Which training programs best meet workers' and employers' needs? To deploy a school's resources wisely, teachers and administrators must know which strategies work best for which youth. The answers to these questions are public goods, of value to educators everywhere. Although some school districts have conducted evaluations of their own, no individual school or school district has a sufficient incentive to invest, to the full extent worthwhile, in the kind of careful, expensive random assignment evaluation necessary to resolve critical issues. The Federal Government— through the Departments of Education and Labor, in particular— has an important role in promoting, analyzing, and disseminating this knowledge.

Fourth, the Federal Government has a critical role to play in encouraging States to set content standards in education and to develop testing methods that are consistent with those standards. Just as industries have found it essential to set national standards to support a national market for their goods, so it is with education: the national labor market is more effective and efficient when employers in California know that a job applicant graduating from school in New York was held to a reasonably stringent set of standards. The recently enacted Goals 2000: Educate America Act provides seed money to States to develop standards and assessments.

Fifth, the Federal Government has a particularly important role to play as a catalyst in developing a national response whenever change occurs as suddenly as it has in the labor market over the last 15 years. It performed this role admirably in the post-Sputnik era, leading reforms in the math and science curricula of our Nation's schools. It is playing that role today in a number of areas. For instance, the School-to-Work Opportunities Act allows the Departments of Education and Labor to jointly offer relatively small, short-term grants to States to begin developing pathways to careers for high school students. Although the Federal funding is short-term, scheduled to be phased out by 2001, the presumption is that thereafter States and local governments will continue to finance the experiments that worked and drop those that did not. Similarly, in response to an evolving labor market in which some workers find themselves in need of retooling, the Administration has been working to transform the unemployment system into a reemployment system. A third example is the Federal Government's encouragement of charter schools. In these and other areas the

Federal Government acts as a catalyst, providing startup funds to encourage States to think in new ways about the problems presented by a changing world.

Federal efforts—in particular, research and evaluation and the encouragement of standards and assessments—complement States' systemic reform efforts. With the knowledge gained from rigorous experimental evaluations of alternative educational interventions, school principals will make better decisions. With well-defined standards and assessments, parents and local school administrators will have better information to back their demands for accountability from the schools. Teachers, too, will have a clearer idea about where to invest in their own training and classroom preparation, so that they can effectively teach the material defined in content standards at the State and local level.

ONGOING EFFORTS IN EDUCATION AND TRAINING

State and local governments have traditionally borne most of the burden of financing elementary and secondary education. As recently as 1920, the Federal Government provided only 0.3 percent of nationwide funding for public education from kindergarten through 12th grade. (Currently, 9 out of 10 youth attend public elementary and secondary schools.) With the advent of the Great Society programs of the 1960s and the growth in Federal aid to low-income school districts, the Federal share rose, reaching a peak of 10 percent in 1980. That share has generally declined over the past decade and a half, however. In 1992–93 the Federal Government provided only 7 percent of total funding for public elementary and secondary education, with State and local governments roughly splitting the remaining 93 percent.

The Federal Government has traditionally played a larger role in higher education than in elementary and secondary education. In 1993 Federal spending accounted for approximately 25 percent of the revenues of all American institutions of higher education. (Of that 25 percent, 9 percent went to provide student grants and loans, 12 percent was for sponsored research, and the remaining 4 percent for direct appropriations and unrestricted grants.) In part, the greater Federal role in higher education may reflect the fact that highly educated people are more likely to move across State lines. In 1990, 49 percent of 25- to 34-year-olds with a bachelor's degree, but only 33 percent of those with less education, lived outside their State of birth.

EARLY CHILDHOOD EDUCATION

The Head Start program, begun in 1965, provides educational, nutritional, and health services to children up to the age of 5; 90 percent of program beneficiaries must be from families with incomes below the poverty level. The program has enjoyed bipartisan support, as reflected in the fact that funding for Head Start more than doubled between 1989 and 1995. In the 1995 fiscal year, the Head Start program cost $3.5 billion and provided funds to approximately 2,000 programs and 750,000 children. In addition to increased funding, the Administration has sought to improve program quality by increasing the number of expanded day slots for children from families with working parents and by seeking to improve the quality of program staff.

Evaluations of Head Start have reported short-term gains in IQ among children enrolled in the program; enrollees are also less likely in their later school careers to repeat grades or be assigned to special education classes. The long-term impacts of Head Start are more difficult to assess, given the long lag between investments and results. One recent evaluation reported sustained improvements in cognitive test scores for white participants, whereas initial favorable impacts seemed to diminish for black youth. Early benefits may wither if they are not nurtured in elementary school. Evaluations of Head Start have also pointed to its significant improvement in the delivery of preventive health services to children from low-income families, as reflected in measures such as immunization rates.

Despite recent additional investments in Head Start, children from high-income families remain much more likely to start school having had the benefit of early childhood education. In 1993 only 33 percent of children from the poorest 20 percent of families were enrolled in preschool or kindergarten, compared with 59 percent of children with family incomes in the top quintile. Because Head Start still serves fewer than 40 percent of eligible families, the Administration has proposed its continued expansion. If we are to reach the goal of equal access to high-quality early childhood education, the Head Start program deserves continued and expanded bipartisan support.

ELEMENTARY AND SECONDARY EDUCATION

To sustain the gains achieved in early childhood programs, elementary and secondary schools must provide challenging and engaging curricula that set high expectations for all their students. Three major initiatives over the past 2 years—the Goals 2000: Educate America Act, the reauthorization of the Elementary and Secondary Education Act, and the School-to-Work Opportunities Act—

were designed to complement and support the reform efforts of State and local school officials.

The Goals 2000: Educate America Act

The Goals 2000: Educate America Act, passed by the Congress in 1994, is the centerpiece of the Administration's effort to support State and local school reform to raise standards of achievement. Its purpose is twofold: to provide grants to States to set rigorous standards for academic achievement, and to support local grass-roots efforts to ensure that all students meet those standards. In the first round of grants every State but two applied for funding to support statewide systemic reform efforts as well as promising local initiatives. In the first year of the program, total funding for State grants was $90 million. States were required to distribute 60 percent of these grants directly to school districts, to support innovative programs to improve student achievement in core subjects. The remaining 40 percent could be used for statewide planning, such as the development of academic standards and better statewide assessment tools. In the second year of the program, 33 States have so far received grants totaling $274 million, of which States are obligated to pass 90 percent along to school districts.

As argued above, educational investments are most likely to pay off when the objectives are clear and when some measure exists for tracking the progress of students and schools. Accordingly, States applying for funding under the second year of the program must develop or adopt challenging content and performance standards and a means of assessing whether the standards were met. States must also outline their plans for helping teachers develop their abilities to teach to the challenging standards. States, school districts, and schools are given a great deal of flexibility in their planning to achieve these goals. Indeed, the act expressly proscribes Federal mandates, direction or control of a school's curriculum or program of instruction or the allocation of State or local resources.

According to a survey by the Council of Chief State School Officers in May 1995, 47 States were working on more rigorous content standards and means of assessment. In Vermont, for example, the assessments encompass a broader range of student achievement than do standardized tests. The mathematics standards are typically the furthest along, drawing on the efforts of the National Council of Teachers of Mathematics during the mid-1980s. Perhaps it is no coincidence that mathematics test scores have shown the greatest gains since 1980.

In addition to providing grants for systemic reform, the Goals 2000: Educate America Act codified into law eight national goals, for improving high school graduation rates, student achievement and citizenship, math and science performance, adult literacy, teacher education, school safety, school readiness, and parental participation. The act also provided funding for the National Education Goals Panel, to monitor the Nation's progress toward meeting those goals. The panel, an autonomous body established in 1990, is charged with publishing regular progress reports and with making suggestions to Federal, State, and local governments that will further the achievement of those goals.

The Improving America's Schools Act

Whereas the Goals 2000: Educate America Act intends to provide momentum and direction to State education reform efforts, the Improving America's Schools Act (IASA) seeks to better coordinate Federal aid with those State reform efforts. The most important part of this act was its reauthorization of the Elementary and Secondary Education Act (ESEA) of 1965. The most significant budgetary change was the overhaul of Title I (formerly Chapter 1) of the ESEA, which provides grants to States and local school districts for the education of disadvantaged students. The program, for which $6.7 billion was appropriated in 1995, was improved in five important ways.

First, the act allows more schools with high proportions of students from poor families to use their Title I grants for schoolwide reform programs. Until the IASA was enacted, only schools in which more than 75 percent of children came from poor families had been allowed to use the money for schoolwide programs. The IASA lowered the threshold further: eventually it will allow schools with more than 50 percent poor children to use Title I grants for schoolwide reforms. This corrects a longstanding problem that prevented some students and teachers even in high-poverty schools from using equipment purchased with Chapter 1 funds.

Second, States and local educational authorities are required to monitor the progress of students in Title I programs using the same standards and assessments used for other students. State and local educational authorities are given greater authority to intervene in schools that fail to show progress. Both measures should allow local administrators to better coordinate Title I programs with State and local reform efforts.

Third, the IASA eliminated the perverse penalty imposed on low-income schools that succeeded in raising test scores. Prior to the IASA, while poverty rates determined school eligibility, resources were distributed among individual schools according to the performance of their students. Low-income schools that raised their performance could actually lose funds. Thirteen percent of principals in a survey of elementary schools reported that their Chapter 1 (now Title I) program had lost some funding as a result of improved performance. Under the reauthorization, disbursement within local educational authorities depends only upon the number and percentage of poor children, not on their academic performance.

Fourth, school districts are required to involve parents and communities in the education of their children, and to use 1 percent of their Title I money for such programs. Research consistently finds that close parent and teacher collaboration is needed to help students learn.

Fifth, Title I establishes two new, better targeted formulas for disbursing money to poor districts and schools. As part of its 1996 budget, the Administration proposed distributing an additional $1 billion through the more targeted of the two new formulas, combining $700 million that was to have been distributed under the old formula with $300 million in new money.

The IASA includes other legislation intended to improve teaching and learning. For instance, the Eisenhower grants (Title II of the ESEA) are designed to support the efforts of schools and communities to develop high-quality teacher training in all core subject areas, with particular emphasis on math and science. The Safe and Drug-Free Schools Act (Title IV of the ESEA) provides funds to States and communities to support prevention of drug abuse and violence in their schools. In combination with the Goals 2000: Educate America Act, the IASA for the first time also grants the Secretary of Education waiver authority to give States and local schools more flexibility in implementing their reforms.

Promoting Uses of Technology in Education

The Administration has supported the creative use of technology in schools. The Technology Learning Challenge, funded under Title III of the ESEA, provides challenge grants to partnerships of schools, colleges, and the private sector for the development and demonstration of educational technology. In 1995 the initial challenge grant competition for elementary and secondary education attracted over 500 proposals and resulted in 19 grants totaling $10 million. The challenge grants have been matched by $70 million in private sector contributions in the first year. For example, the Capital School District in Dover, Delaware, received a challenge grant to bring educational curricula and communication links into students' and teachers' homes. Using a device connected to their telephone or cable lines, students use their family television sets to communicate with their teachers and classmates, and so replace passive television watching with learning time. The project, intended eventually to reach all 16 of Delaware's school districts, also receives considerable support from the State government and private sources.

During 1995 the President and the Vice President appealed to a group of firms to bring Internet access to schools in California. The goal of the privately funded effort is to establish Internet access to all elementary and secondary schools and set up local area networks within 20 percent of them by the end of this school year. Before this effort, California ranked near the bottom in the ratio of students to computers available in schools, even though it is home to much of the computer industry.

The Star Schools program provided $25 million in matching grants in fiscal 1995 for projects using telecommunications technology in distance learning. For instance, a Star Schools grant supported the development of software to allow teachers from around the country to contribute and draw from a data bank of lesson plans in various topic areas such as math and science.

The IASA also provided $10 million in funding in fiscal 1995 for six regional technology consortia. For instance, the South Central consortium is made up of the Kansas State Board of Education and colleges of education at Texas A&M University, University of Oklahoma, University of Missouri-Columbia, and University of Nebraska-Lincoln. The consortia are intended to provide consulting services to States and school districts interested in finding new uses for technology in their schools.

To give teachers, school administrators, and researchers around the country better access to the inventory of educational research maintained by the Educational Resources Information Center (ERIC), the Administration created the AskERIC service. Educators and researchers are able to send questions to the service by electronic mail and receive a response within 48 hours.

Although the Federal investment in each of these programs is relatively small, the lessons learned from experimenting with the uses of technology in education may eventually have much broader applications in elementary and secondary schools around the country.

The School-to-Work Initiative

Young people leaving high school often lack the skills and the social networks to make the transition to work. A successful transition means that a young person soon finds a job that puts him or her on a career ladder at the hiring firm or imparts skills that make him or her more widely employable. The experience of other countries and some of the experiments in the United States have shown that programs that help young people learn skills in the context of an actual workplace make successful transitions from school to work more likely. For instance, Germany's apprenticeship system is often given credit for the low unemployment rates for youth in that country.

The School-to-Work Opportunities Act, passed in 1994, provides States and communities with funds to assist young people in making the transition to work after secondary schooling. Through the combined efforts of the Departments of Education and Labor, the

Federal Government is to act as a catalyst, providing venture capital to States for the development and implementation of school-to-work systems. In 1994 the Federal Government gave 52 development awards—one to each State, the District of Columbia, and Puerto Rico—to assist in the initiation of these systems. Also included were eight implementation awards: funds competitively awarded to States with operating school-to-work systems. The States receiving the implementation awards in 1994 were Kentucky, Maine, Massachusetts, Michigan, New Jersey, New York, Oregon, and Wisconsin. By the end of 1995, 27 States had received school-to-work implementation grants, as had almost 90 urban and rural communities. Since the inception of the program, the Departments of Labor and Education have provided $345 million to advance the school-to-work initiative.

For example, the Socorro High School for the Health Professions in El Paso, Texas, combines a traditional college preparatory course of study with applied health occupations classes. In the first 2 years of the 4-year program, students take an introductory course in the health professions, a health occupations laboratory, enhanced mathematics, and a foreign language, in addition to standard subject matter. In the 11th grade, students spend half of each school day in clinical rotations; they undertake 12 unpaid 3-week rotations, formally observing health care providers and administrators at work. Students also visit local colleges to learn about postsecondary education in health fields. In the last year of the program students work between 15 and 20 hours per week in competitively allocated, year-long internships. Students receive performance evaluations from supervisors in these internships; those receiving positive evaluations are typically hired as part-time regular employees. The program receives guidance from the El Paso Hospital Council, a coalition of senior executives from all the major health care facilities in the city. More than three-quarters of the students in the Socorro program are from low-income bilingual families; the school receives funds from Title I of ESEA and the Job Training Partnership Act.

An apprenticeship program in rural Pickens County, South Carolina, accepts exemplary students for youth apprenticeships. The program offers high school courses at the district career center, where students learn skills from agricultural mechanics to graphic communications to welding. Even in traditional subject areas, students apply their knowledge in situations that simulate the workplace. During their senior year advanced vocational students work as apprentices for 20 hours a week, earning an average of $6 per hour at local businesses while taking classes both at their high school and at the district career center. After graduating from high school, the apprentices continue to work part-time while studying for an associate degree at a technical college in the area. Local businesses and large corporations with local establishments have taken apprentices in the program. The Partnership for Academic and Career Education (PACE), a consortium of businesses and educators, assists with curriculum development, provides staff development opportunities, and contributes materials to area high schools. The Department of Education recognized PACE with the first Award for Technical Preparation Program Excellence in 1991.

Both these programs have some degree of employer involvement, a critical component of success. Employers can be counted upon to maintain their investments in apprenticeships and worker training only to the extent that they learn that it is in their economic interest to do so. If employers are expected to share the costs, they must be rewarded with some of the benefits. Some evidence suggests that there are indeed benefits to be shared. A recent study of small manufacturing firms in Michigan that received training grants from the State government significantly raised productivity by reducing wastage. Another survey of manufacturing firms that introduced formal training programs in 1983 suggested that these firms enjoyed faster productivity growth than other firms. How these benefits are shared will depend upon turnover rates among trained workers. The experience of those firms that have been willing to participate in the school-to-work initiative, or have invested in incumbent workers, will have an important impact on future investment in education and training by the private sector.

POSTSECONDARY EDUCATION AND TRAINING

As described above, many young people seem to have responded to the rising payoff to college. The proportion of 18- to 24-year-olds enrolled in college increased by one-third between 1980 and 1994. Moreover, college students are increasingly likely to earn degrees in the fields where earnings are rising the most, such as in engineering, the sciences, and the health occupations. But not all young people have reacted similarly. Although college enrollment rates have increased for most groups, differences in college enrollment rates by race and by family income have widened since 1980.

One possible cause of the widening gaps in college enrollment rates is the dramatic increase in the cost of a college education, at public as well as at private institutions. Between 1980 and 1994 the real average tuition at public 2-year and 4-year colleges rose by 70 percent and 86 percent, respectively. Over the same period, however, the value of the maximum Pell grant, the primary Federal grant program for low-income students, fell by more than 25 percent in real value. Not counting parental borrowing, the maximum amount a dependent undergraduate student could borrow over 4 years of college also declined by 5 percent in real value

(Chart 7–4). Even if one takes State and institutional need-based aid into account, the net cost at a public 4-year college for the average youth with family income in the bottom quartile rose between 1987 and 1993.

Chart 7-4   **Real Change in Maximum Pell Grant, Loan Limit, and Tuition, 1980-94**
Inflation-adjusted college tuition and fees have increased, while the maximum Pell grant and Federal student loan limit have decreased.

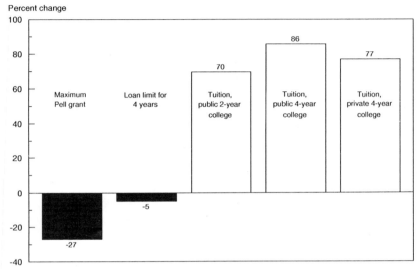

Note: Tuition includes tuition and required fees. The CPI-U-X1 is used to adjust all values.
Sources: Department of Education and The College Board.

The college entry decisions of young adults, particularly those from low-income families, seem to be quite sensitive to increases in tuition. A number of studies have attempted to measure this price sensitivity by comparing enrollment rates in high- and low-tuition States. These studies suggest that a $100-per-year difference in college tuition levels is associated with a 1.2 to 1.6 percent difference in college enrollment rates among 18- to 24-year-olds. Some recent evidence also suggests that those States that have raised tuition see slower rates of growth in enrollment, and that the gaps in enrollment rates between high- and low-income youth have grown most in those States that have raised tuition.

Rising costs were not the primary cause of rising tuition at public institutions. Educational expenses per full-time student (including costs of instruction, administration, student services, libraries, and operation and maintenance of physical plant, but excluding sponsored research and scholarships and fellowships) rose by only 15 percent in real terms between 1980 and 1992 at public 4-year colleges and by only 12 percent at public 2-year colleges. Rather,

217

public tuition rose primarily because State and local taxpayers were paying a smaller percentage of the cost than they had in the past. As enrollments have risen and as other demands on State budgets have grown, States have responded by raising tuition rather than increasing their appropriations proportionately.

Reforming Student Aid Policy

Given the forces at work, the Nation faces a number of difficult choices in the financing of higher education. In addition to a continuing increase in the demand for a college education, demographic trends indicate a 20 percent increase over the next 15 years in the population of traditional college-age youth. In some States, such as California, the demographic shift will be even more pronounced. Unless State budgets for higher education grow, public tuitions are likely to continue rising, not because costs are rising, but because State appropriations will be spread over larger enrollments. This will make a college education even less accessible for many Americans. Therefore Federal student loan and grant programs are likely to be more critically important than ever before.

To meet these new challenges, the Administration's direct lending program has sought to provide educational financing in a less costly, less cumbersome manner, with more flexible terms of repayment. The Federal Government issues loans to students through the financial aid offices of colleges, bypassing the more than 7,500 private lenders, 41 guaranty agencies, and 90 secondary market participants that make up the Federal Family Education Loan (FFEL) program.

Under the FFEL program, the Federal Government guarantees a return to banks that provide financing for student loans. Under the direct lending program, on the other hand, the Federal Government provides the capital. Whether or not direct lending saves taxpayers money depends on whether the Department of Education can service the loans for less than the subsidies it pays the private banks to carry the loans. Based on the prices it has already negotiated with private contractors to service the loans, the Administration believes that the program can deliver substantial budgetary savings. At the time the Student Loan Reform Act was passed in 1993, gradual conversion to direct lending was projected to save more than $4 billion over 5 years.

However, the debate over the cost savings generated by direct lending has overshadowed discussion of the quality of service received by students and colleges participating in the program. On this question there seems to be little disagreement, at least among the colleges and students themselves. Direct lending clearly provides more timely, more accessible service to students and universities. After the first year of direct lending, in which 104 schools participated, a survey funded by the Department of Education revealed that 61 percent of participating schools reported themselves very satisfied and an additional 28 percent were satisfied. The General Accounting Office (GAO) also evaluated the program. Officials interviewed at 11 of the 17 schools examined by the GAO described themselves as greatly satisfied with direct lending, and the remaining 6 reported being generally satisfied. None of the schools reported serious misgivings. The GAO report also cited a number of ways in which direct lending helped students and universities: parents and students do not have to file separate loan applications to banks; students receive their loans more quickly; students know whom to contact for deferments or other questions, because their loans are not resold; and each college works with a single lender, the Federal Government, rather than hundreds of financial intermediaries.

More Flexible Options for Repayment

The average student borrower completing 4 years of undergraduate education today leaves school approximately $11,000 in debt. As loan burdens grow with ever-rising tuitions, flexibility in the terms of repayment can lighten the burden significantly. The direct lending program offers four different repayment options to provide such flexibility: the standard plan, the extended plan, the graduated plan, and income-contingent repayment. Private banks also can offer some choice in the form of repayment.

Under the standard repayment plan, borrowers pay fixed nominal monthly payments over a 10-year term. At an annual interest rate of 8.25 percent, a borrower with the average debt for someone finishing a bachelor's degree pays $135 per month. Under the extended repayment option the same borrower would pay $107 per month, with payments spread over 15 years.

Under both the standard and the extended plan, the nominal payment is fixed over the term of the loan, so that the real value of the payment actually declines over time. However, a declining real payment schedule may impose unnecessary hardship since young college graduates often earn significantly more after a few years on the job than they did immediately out of college. The graduated plan therefore attempts to ease their debt burden by matching payments more closely to this expected rise in earnings. For instance, a borrower with $11,000 in debt would make payments of $77 per month during the first 2 years and end with a $175 monthly payment during the 15th year.

The income-contingent option is even more flexible: monthly payments are calculated on the basis of the borrower's adjusted gross income, as reported by the borrower and verified by the Internal Revenue Service. The above graduate starting his or her career making $18,000 and enjoying annual earnings increases of 5 percent would begin by paying $90 per month and end, after 15 years, paying $121 per month. Borrowers whose earnings are so low that they still have loan balances after 25 years of repayment will have those balances forgiven. Income-contingent student loans may thus be viewed as an innovative form of "forward-looking" means testing (Box 7–4). Although it is too early to tell, more flexible terms of repayment may also lower default rates by helping to deter borrowers from getting behind in their payments early in their careers.

Box 7–4.—Income-Contingent Student Loans as Forward-Looking Means Testing

Means testing in student aid programs "taxes" the income and assets of parents and students at a high rate by providing less aid for those with higher incomes or more assets. Because the implicit taxes apply for every year that one has a child in college, the marginal tax rates on savings can approach 50 percent for families with two children attending college for 8 years. In other words, for every dollar in savings above a threshold, parents may lose 50 cents in financial aid, lowering parents' incentive to save. In the past these very high tax rates did not apply to very many families, because many families' incomes were too high to qualify for any aid. However, as tuition levels rise, the marginal tax rates apply to an increasing number.

High marginal tax rates are an inevitable result of "backward-looking" means testing, in which financial aid is distributed according to the recent past income and assets of applicants and their parents (usually a single year of income and assets). In contrast, the income-contingent loan program may be thought of as a form of "forward-looking" means testing. It has three advantages: it targets resources on those with low earnings after they leave college (rather than just low family incomes in the year before they enter college); it provides some "insurance" to students from middle- and higher income families who may be anxious about their future labor market prospects given a large debt; and it broadens the base of income used for means testing from a single year to the student's whole career. Because parents' savings are not taxed when means testing is forward-looking, parents may even save more to contribute to their children's education. Moreover, this forward-looking means testing is more suited to the needs of older workers seeking to return to school, since the traditional backward-looking financial aid formulas were often designed with traditional college-age dependent students in mind.

In a time of rising tuition and strained public budgets, publicly guaranteed loans make the most of public resources while ensuring that young people use the Nation's educational resources prudently. The availability of the income-contingent repayment scheme protects those with very low or highly variable earnings later in their careers. If tuition levels continue to increase, limits on student borrowing under both the direct lending and the FFEL programs may need to be raised in coming years. At present, dependent undergraduate students (those who are unmarried, not veterans, with no dependents, and less than 24 years of age) can borrow only $2,625 during their first year in college, $3,500 during the second year, and $5,500 per year during the junior and senior years. Parents are allowed to borrow more under the Parental Loans for Undergraduate Students (PLUS) program. However, since payments on PLUS loans begin immediately, many parents may be reluctant or unable to take on the additional burden. Tuition expenses alone exceed the $2,625 limit at a group of public 4-year institutions that together enroll 42 percent of all undergraduate students. As a result, unless borrowing limits are raised, an increasing number of dependent students will not even be able to borrow enough under the Federal programs to pay their college tuition and living expenses.

Default Rates

Ever since the inception of the Federal student loan programs, defaults have been a significant concern. This concern was heightened, however, when default claims paid to lenders exceeded $2 billion for the first time in 1989. Under this Administration, the Department of Education has made lowering student loan default rates a high priority. Default rates differ markedly according to the institution the borrower attended. Therefore the Department of Education has imposed standards to preclude schools whose attendees have high default rates from receiving federally guaranteed loans: postsecondary institutions can lose eligibility to participate if they have a default rate in excess of 25 percent for 3 consecutive years. (The default rate is calculated as the percentage of loans going into repayment in a given year that default by the end of the following year. This threshold has been lowered from 35 percent in 1991 and 1992.) Approximately 250 schools have been declared ineligible to participate in the loan programs based upon their 1992 default rates. An additional 190 schools have appealed the calculation of their default rates, and it is anticipated, based on past appeals, that many of these institutions will also lose eligibility. Although it is difficult to distinguish the impact of regulatory efforts from the effects of an improving economy, the default rate has been cut nearly in half over the past few years: from 22

221

to 12 percent for debts going into repayment in the years 1990 and 1993, respectively.

Future Challenges

A college education is becoming both more expensive and more important for a successful career. The combination of these two trends is making parents and students increasingly anxious. The Federal Government provides a number of separate grant, loan, and work-study programs for college students, but this variety of programs may itself add to the lack of transparency in the financial aid process, increasing families' anxiety. Students and their parents could make better decisions regarding college if they knew more about how much they could borrow or receive in grants and how much they were likely to have to finance out of their own income and savings. Complicated means tests necessarily make it difficult for students to anticipate the exact mixture of grants and loans they will receive. Even so, there could be much better information about the size of the total package available. Moreover, parents and students who are worried about rising debt burdens may find that the more flexible options for repayment now available help relieve their concern.

BETTER OPTIONS FOR THOSE ALREADY IN THE LABOR FORCE

As different skills appreciate or depreciate in value, workers must have the opportunity to react to these changes in the labor market. As proposed in the G.I. Bill for America's Workers, the Administration has also been working to reinvent how the Nation delivers education and training services to those already in the workforce. Both the Congress and the Administration have proposed consolidating many of the separate education and training programs now administered by the Departments of Labor and Education and providing block grants to the States. These reforms are intended to convert our unemployment system into a re-employment system. Although the proposals differ in some details—particularly in the level of funding—they are similar in at least two important dimensions.

First, States would coordinate the delivery of employment and training services through one-stop career development centers. The goal of the one-stop centers would be to allow workers to find out about employment opportunities, apply for jobless benefits, learn about available training programs, and receive assistance in financing that training all in one place. Sixteen States have already received multiyear implementation grants from the Department of Labor to begin integrating an array of education, training, and employment programs into the one-stop centers. The remaining

States, which are at an earlier stage in the process, have all received grants to plan the transition to the one-stop concept.

Second, the Congress and the Administration have both proposed consolidating more than 70 existing training programs and giving training recipients the ability to choose the program that best meets their needs. Under the Administration's proposal, dislocated and low-income workers would be eligible for so-called skill grants of up to $2,620 per year to complete an associate degree, enough to cover tuition, supplies, and fees at a typical community college. Other proposals would provide the funding to States in the form of block grants but would also encourage States to allow recipients more discretion in choosing the training program that is right for them. Unlike the current system, in which government agencies often choose what training workers will receive and who will provide it, grants could be used by workers themselves to find the best match among eligible training providers. But any worker, regardless of his or her income or employment status, could use the centers to learn about training and education options and would receive guidance in applying for educational loans.

Both reforms are intended to enhance accountability among providers: training providers that do not attract workers' interest would be allowed to founder and the more successful programs to flourish. Accountability will be enhanced if the quality of information available to workers for assessing different programs, such as graduation rates or placement rates (using, for instance, unemployment insurance wage records to track the employment histories of graduates of each program), can be improved. By voting with their feet, workers themselves will be empowered to shut down ineffective training programs and expand those that meet the changing needs of the labor market—decisions that may be more difficult for program administrators to make.

The $10,000 tax deduction for tuition expenses in the Middle Class Bill of Rights (described in Chapter 3, Box 3–4) will also lower the cost of further training for those workers going back to school, as well as for families with dependent children struggling with large tuition increases.

CONCLUSION

Ever since the Nation's founding, the Federal Government has been a partner in education and training. It has served as a clearinghouse for research and evaluation results, contributed to equality of educational opportunity by targeting resources to low-income schools and college students, and guaranteed educational loans for college students. No other layer of government could assume these responsibilities as effectively and efficiently.

In addition to these traditional responsibilities, the Federal Government must also help coordinate a national response to the dramatic changes in the labor market. The Federal Government has responded by providing funds to States interested in developing new pathways from school to work. To add focus and momentum to school reform efforts, the Department of Education has offered seed money to States for the development of voluntary content standards in core subject areas and has encouraged States to develop testing tools for measuring their progress. Federal grants have supported the startup of charter schools and investments in educational technology. In these new endeavors, the Federal role is properly understood as that of a catalyst—vital but temporary.

Progress has been made. Despite some year-to-year fluctuations, test scores in math and science have risen for all age groups since 1980. High school graduation and college enrollment rates have also risen. But this is no time to drastically scale back those efforts. The shift in demand has continued to outpace the increased output of more skilled workers: earnings differences between the more and the less educated continue to widen. Someday the increase in supply may begin to overtake the increasing demand of the labor market and dampen future increases in wage inequality, but at least until that day arrives, the Federal Government must continue to support State and local efforts to transform their educational systems.

In the midst of efforts to balance the Federal budget, it is important to keep in mind that the objective of deficit reduction is to spur long-term economic growth by freeing up more of the Nation's savings for productive investment. To cut investment in education and training simply for the sake of balancing the Federal budget in the short term runs counter to that goal. Education and training have always been a major source of U.S. growth; as the economic returns have increased, these undertakings should represent a larger share of the Nation's investment portfolio, not a smaller one. As families and communities respond to the rise in the payoff to skill by investing in themselves, the Federal Government should not shrink from the task of encouraging and complementing their efforts.

CHAPTER 8

The United States in the World Economy

AMERICA HAS LONG LED THE WORLD in championing open trade and competition. The result has been an unprecedented period of worldwide growth in incomes and trade. The expansion of international trade that supported postwar growth in incomes has been accompanied by dramatic transformations in the economies of the United States and other countries. In 1960, trade—exports plus imports—was equivalent to just 9 percent of U.S. gross domestic product (GDP); that figure is now 23 percent. Twelve million American workers now owe their jobs to exports, and the opportunities for global sales represent a critical part of firms' investment, research and development, and hiring decisions. The importance of exports to the U.S. economy has been strikingly apparent in the last 3 years; U.S. exports of goods and services have grown by 20 percent, accounting for about one-third of real GDP growth.

Not only the size but also the geography of the international market has changed since the 1950s. Developing countries that adopted market-oriented policies grew significantly faster than those that clung to closed markets and statist policies. Now many of these successful emerging economies have become major markets. Whereas in 1970, 29 percent of U.S. exports went to developing countries, in 1995 these same countries absorbed 41 percent of U.S. exports. These will be the major growth markets into the next century and will generate huge demands for capital goods, infrastructure, and an increasing variety of consumer goods.

But a high-income, highly competitive economy poses challenges as well as opportunities. Technological change, business reorganization, and international competition have at times required painful adjustments of workers and firms. Critics of international trade often point to the trade deficit, "lost" domestic production due to imports, or expanding income differentials as evidence that foreign trade and investment are harmful to the United States.

Americans have legitimate concerns about job security and standards of living, and the Administration is strongly committed to fostering better jobs and greater economic security. But neither job security nor future income growth will be enhanced by closing the American economy to foreign competition. As the 21st century

225

approaches, the Administration firmly believes that economic isola-
tion would lead only to economic decline, and that the most promising way forward is to rise to the challenges of the international
market. We can and must compete, not retreat, in the face of global
competition.

The Administration has pursued an aggressive trade policy to
open markets abroad. Despite historic reductions in trade barriers
and the striking growth in U.S. exports, many countries still maintain formal trade barriers, or more subtle administrative or collusive barriers, that prevent other nations' firms from competing on
an equal basis. This Administration has insisted that other countries live up to their obligations under international and bilateral
agreements and has attacked remaining barriers that discriminate
against U.S. exports.

This chapter explains why outward-looking, competitive policies
remain the best choice for America and examines the Administration's record in promoting open competition across the globe. Special attention is given to the role of trade policy and to the proper
measure of its success. This chapter also discusses the causes and
consequences of the trade deficit and effective policy for reducing
it.

THE BENEFITS OF OUTWARD-LOOKING, MARKET-OPENING POLICIES

Open, competitive trade promotes the economic welfare of all
countries that engage in it, and does so in four ways. It secures the
benefits of national comparative advantage, allowing each trading
economy to devote more of its resources to producing those goods
and services that it can produce most efficiently. It sharpens domestic competitive pressures, spurring productivity gains. It quick-
ens the flow of technology and ideas, allowing countries to learn
from each other. And it broadens the variety of inputs available to
producers and final goods available to consumers, boosting efficiency and standards of living.

Nations that engage in trade benefit from the logic of comparative advantage, as each imports those goods that are produced
more cheaply abroad, and exports those goods that are produced
more cheaply at home. Box 8-1 offers a simple example that illustrates this traditional argument favoring free trade. Critics argue,
however, that many industries of increasing importance in the
world economy (including many high-technology industries) are
characterized by economies of scale in production, and that these
scale economies undermine the simple comparative advantage argument. But although economies of scale do complicate the story,
they do not invalidate the principle of comparative advantage or

226

lessen its importance, as Box 8–2 explains. Now more than ever, unimpeded access to a world market is crucial.

Box 8–1.—Comparative Advantage and Living Standards

The classic argument for free trade is based on the principle of comparative advantage. Suppose U.S. workers are much better at producing computer software and somewhat better at producing shoes than workers in Thailand. Comparative advantage states that trade between the two countries—with the United States exporting software and Thailand exporting shoes—can still boost living standards in both.

A simple analogy may help illustrate this abstract and seemingly implausible intuition. Imagine a lawyer who happens to be a very good typist—so good that she is somewhat faster than her secretary. Even though the lawyer is better than her secretary at both practicing law and typing, it makes sense for her to spend all her time on the law and leave the typing to her secretary. A greater combined total of lawyering and typing will get done in the same amount of time than if each did some or all of the other's work, and the incomes of both workers will be greater than they would otherwise.

Similarly, by allowing countries to focus their resources on what they do *relatively* well, international trade boosts living standards. Especially when an economy is near full employment, the primary impact of trade is on the allocation of jobs among industries rather than the overall number of jobs. Trade allows employment to be shifted into relatively more productive, better jobs. This effect is manifest in U.S. wage data: jobs in the United States supported by goods exports pay 13 percent more than the national average. This is not surprising, given that U.S. comparative advantage lies in highly specialized manufacturing and service activities, not in low-skill, low-wage sectors. Comparative advantage in high-skill industries, however, appears to provide only a partial explanation for the higher wages paid in export jobs. Even after plant size, location, industry, and skill category are controlled for, exporting plants seem to pay higher wages than nonexporting plants.

The second argument in favor of open competition is that exposure to the challenges of the international marketplace strengthens competitive pressures in the domestic economy, stimulating efficiency and growth. An open trade regime effectively increases the number of both actual and potential competitors in the domestic market by including those located beyond the Nation's borders. This encourages domestic producers to innovate and become more

Box 8–2.—The New Trade Theory

Over the past 15 years, economists have formalized new models of international trade that offer theoretical justifications for protectionism. These models, often referred to collectively as the "new trade theory," have prompted a reexamination of the costs and benefits of open trade.

The new trade theory assumes that certain industries enjoy increasing returns to scale or generate positive spillover benefits to society as a whole, for which the industry is not compensated. Increasing returns actually *raise* the gains from trade: they make it even more efficient to sell to a global market. But in some cases, unilateral protection can raise social welfare. Under the right conditions, for example, temporary protection can secure a permanent cost advantage for a domestic firm by discouraging foreign producers from entering the market. If the monopoly rents that then accrue to the domestic firm are large enough to offset the costs of capturing them, the nation as a whole benefits.

These sophisticated arguments for protectionism do not necessarily invalidate the case for free trade. Even with scale economies, if all countries adopt protectionist policies in the hope of making their national champion the global monopolist, the costs will be even higher than in the absence of increasing returns. With access to foreign markets blocked, all hope of any firm exploiting the increasing scale returns is lost; the traditional losses from protectionism (arising from ignoring comparative advantage) are then compounded by the failure to produce at efficient scale. In a sense, therefore, protectionism is even more costly with increasing returns than without them.

But perhaps the greatest challenge in the new trade theory sweepstakes is targeting only those industries and firms that best meet the theory's narrow conditions. In practice, selection would be complicated by political pressures from special interests, who are likely to exaggerate the positive spillovers their industries contribute. And the costs of an erroneous choice may prove counterproductive: granting protection in inappropriate cases may outweigh the benefits of granting it in appropriate ones. In sum, the new trade theories provide a possible theoretical justification for protectionist policies in some limited cases. But practical considerations suggest that the potential gains, if any, are likely to be small.

competitive. Consumers, both at home and abroad, reap the benefits.

A third, related argument is that access to international markets stimulates the flow of information across borders. Domestic firms engaged in international competition assimilate new ideas about production methods, product design, organizational structure, and marketing strategy, allowing them to employ their resources more efficiently. Open competition thus boosts productivity.

Finally, trade expands the menu of goods and services available to both producers and consumers. Firms gain access to a wider variety of inputs, and consumers get to choose from a broader assortment of final goods and services. By expanding the choices available to all, trade boosts efficiency and improves living standards.

One can also gauge the benefits of open markets by assessing the cost of the alternative, namely, protectionism. It is impossible to protect all industries; protecting some inevitably distorts market signals and imposes higher costs on other industries and on domestic consumers. For example, extending protection to the steel industry imposes a cost on automobile manufacturers, who pay more for steel, and on consumers, who pay more for a new car than they would if steel were available at the lower world price. Because the impact of such restrictions is both indirect and spread over a large number of consumers, the total cost may be difficult to discern. But it is nevertheless quite real, and it is likely to grow over time. By raising the relative price of the protected sectors' output, and thus drawing capital and labor into those sectors and away from others, protectionist policies prevent the most efficient long-run use of an economy's resources. These distortions may be particularly harmful when restrictions are imposed on inputs used by industries that are characterized by economies of scale in production (that is, by lower average costs per unit at higher levels of output; Box 8–2).

Finally, every protectionist action invites retaliatory reaction. The costs of a tit-for-tat escalation are so high that in the long run all countries are likely to lose from the adoption of restrictive policies. The experience of the 1930s provides a grim demonstration: the major industrial countries responded to the onset of the Great Depression by raising trade barriers against each other, which provoked retaliation in kind and succeeded only in weakening their economies still further. A better strategy is for all to strive for a regime of open and fair competition, rather than to focus on any possible (and in any case usually illusory) short-term gains from protection.

Many of the same advantages that accrue from an open trade regime also accrue from international investment flows. Inward flows of foreign direct investment can boost efficiency and cross-border learning. Direct investment in the opposite direction—that by domestic firms in countries overseas—also promotes such learning and is closely linked to export expansion: approximately three-fifths of U.S. exports are sold by U.S. firms with operations abroad, and several recent studies have confirmed that foreign direct investment is more likely to increase trade than reduce it.

THE EVIDENCE ON OPEN ECONOMIES

Trade affects growth through various channels, but the cause-and-effect relationship is difficult to establish in practice: even if expanded trade is statistically associated with growth in income, does the expansion in trade *cause* the expansion in income, or vice versa? There can be no definitive answer, but careful studies generally conclude that trade liberalization establishes powerful direct linkages between the domestic and the world economy, unencumbering the flow of ideas and technology across borders, bolstering competitive pressures.

A recent economic analysis, which controlled for other national characteristics such as education, starting income, and political instability, found that the open economies in a sample of 79 countries grew by an average of 2.5 percentage points more per year (over a 20-year period) than did the closed economies. A comprehensive study of productivity across manufacturing industries in Germany, Japan, and the United States recently concluded that trade restrictions generally hurt productivity by reducing competitive pressures; productivity growth is the single most important factor underlying sustained increases in income. Other studies have found that protection of industries that produce intermediate inputs reduces growth. For example, one recent study found that, across a sample of over 70 countries, a 10-percentage-point increase in the tariffs on capital goods and intermediate products was associated with a decline in real growth of GDP per capita of 0.2 percentage point per year. For the United States, such a reduction in growth over the 10-year period through 1994 would have lowered GDP per capita by $500 from its actual 1994 level of $26,558.

Even when trade restrictions are used to curtail unfair foreign competition, they can still impose costs on consumers. The U.S. antidumping and countervailing duty laws, for example, are intended to offset the effects of unfair foreign competition: antidumping laws seek to counter unfair pricing by foreign firms, while countervailing duties seek to compensate for the anticompetitive effects of foreign government subsidies. The concern is a legitimate one: U.S. living standards could be diminished by certain types of predatory foreign behavior. But many analysts believe that many of the cases filed under these statutes have little to do with preventing unfair competition, and the duties make consumers and domestic businesses pay higher prices for imported goods and inputs. In any case, a recent study found that the net cost of the 163 antidumping duty orders and 76 countervailing duty orders in place in the United States in 1991 was $1.6 billion.

TRADE AND WAGE INEQUALITY

Over the past 15 years the real earnings of low-skilled U.S. workers have fallen sharply while those of highly skilled workers have risen: between 1980 and 1994, real average annual earnings for high school dropouts aged 25 to 34 fell by 18 percent, while those for college graduates rose by over 3 percent. Over the same period, imports have risen as a percentage of GDP. Are these two trends related? Is increased trade hurting low-skilled workers, and if so, is this an argument for protectionism?

In theory, increased trade could worsen inequalities in wages even while raising aggregate income. The U.S. economy has a relative abundance of skilled labor, and so U.S. comparative advantage is in producing skill-intensive goods. Traditional models of trade therefore suggest that the United States would tend to export goods requiring relatively large amounts of skilled labor and import goods requiring relatively large amounts of unskilled labor. International trade would in effect increase the supply of unskilled labor to the U.S. economy, lowering the wages of unskilled American workers relative to those of skilled workers, thus aggravating wage inequality.

Economic theory does not, however (except under extremely restrictive assumptions), tell us how great the resulting gap in wages will be. Moreover, careful examination of the channels through which trade should affect wages suggests that other factors bear a larger responsibility for the widening of wage differentials. Foreign workers do not compete with American workers directly, but rather through the products that they produce and sell. The argument that imports drive down wages for unskilled labor is predicated on a relationship between the relative prices of goods and the prices of inputs used to produce them. If competition from developing countries lowers the prices of goods requiring unskilled labor as their major input, the wages of unskilled workers will be driven down, widening income disparities. The problem with this argument is that there has been no such change in relative goods prices: over the 1980s the average relative price of goods that require substantial inputs of unskilled labor actually increased.

If trade, or factors such as immigration that affect the relative supply of workers, were the predominant cause of wage disparities, one would expect to see domestic producers taking advantage of the lower cost of unskilled workers by using more of them. Yet just the

231

opposite has occurred. In almost all industries, employment of skilled workers has increased relative to that of unskilled workers, despite the higher cost of skilled workers. This suggests that factors affecting the demand for different kinds of workers, such as technological changes that have increased the demand for skilled workers, have been the more powerful force in influencing relative wages.

Yet even if the effect is small, trade may indeed have some adverse impact on wage inequality. In many ways the effects of trade are similar to those of technological advance: both raise national income but can worsen inequality. Yet just as a neo-Luddite crusade against technology is not the solution to increased inequality due to technological progress, neither is protectionism the answer to wage inequality resulting from expanded trade. Several recent studies show that protection can impose costs on the economy that far outweigh the targeted benefits. Moreover, import protection cannot promise continuing reductions in inequality over time. At best, a strategy of import protection would narrow the wage gap temporarily at the risk of slowing the rate of productivity and income growth generally.

Ultimately, the only lasting solution to the increase in wage inequality that results from increased trade is the same as that for wage inequality arising from any other source: better education and increased training, to allow low-income workers to take advantage of the technological changes that raise productivity. In addition, programs such as the earned income tax credit and the minimum wage can be effective in raising the after-tax wages of low-income workers.

U.S. TRADE POLICY IN THE 1990s

Governments play a decisive role in determining the rules of competition in international markets. Just as governments must be responsible for regulating domestic markets, they must also be responsible for the rules that govern international trade and investment. This is a responsibility that cannot be shirked—even the absence of a formal trade policy is itself a policy. The objective is therefore to structure government involvement so as to help, not hurt economic performance.

The United States has led international efforts to liberalize world trade and investment, and this Administration has actively sought to eliminate foreign market barriers to U.S. exports. Regardless of their effects on the overall trade balance, these market-opening policies raise U.S. incomes by securing the gains from international trade. As already noted, the expansion of market opportunities is especially important in industries characterized by economies of scale (e.g., those with high fixed costs). The opportunity to sell in a larger market allows these fixed costs to be spread over a larger number of units, reducing average cost.

Opening up markets to U.S. exports also increases world demand for our products by removing artificial barriers to their consumption by foreigners. Stronger demand raises the prices that our products command on world markets, and so improves our terms of trade with the rest of the world. The terms of trade (defined as the ratio of the average price of our exports to that of our imports) affects U.S. real incomes. An increase in the terms of trade means that, for any given volume of exports, Americans can purchase more foreign goods. Even a small change in the terms of trade can have a huge effect: a 1 percent rise in the terms of trade corresponds to a real increase in income of more than $7 billion.

Open markets benefit all participants in international trade, even those whose own national markets are closed to foreign competition. Open markets are a public good, the benefits of which are available to all. As with any public good, countries have some incentive to "free ride"—to seize a share of the benefits without assuming any of the costs (the case of trade may be special, however, in that every country may have an incentive to adopt open trade policies regardless of what other countries do). The negotiators in the Uruguay Round of the General Agreement on Tariffs and Trade (GATT) recognized the importance of ensuring every nation's participation in lowering trade barriers: in almost all respects, membership in the new World Trade Organization (WTO), created under the 1994 Uruguay Round agreement, requires adherence to all of its rules. Indeed this is one of the reasons why the Administration strongly supported the Uruguay Round agreement.

Even those nations that have adopted the general rules of the trading system often come under pressure to intervene in particular instances—to protect industries going through difficult adjustments to foreign competition, to skew the rules in favor of domestic companies, or to try to influence foreigners to purchase from domestic firms. An aggressive policy to protect American interests from such practices abroad helps ensure that U.S. firms do not lose out, and that foreign governments are less inclined to try to bend the rules. The strengthened dispute settlement process within the WTO, together with the United States' own Section 301 legislation, which addresses unfair or unjustified foreign practices, are the most important tools that the United States uses to enforce our rights in the trade and investment arenas.

THE ADMINISTRATION'S TRADE STRATEGY

This Administration has embraced an outward-oriented, protrade, progrowth economic strategy. In its first 3 years in office, this Administration has concluded over 200 trade agreements and done more to promote trade and open markets abroad than any previous Administration (Box 8–3). We are using all the tools available to us—multilateral, regional, and bilateral—to advance our protrade agenda. This multilevel approach to trade policy has become particularly important as the nontraditional aspects of trade policy have assumed increasing importance (Box 8–4), and as global trade patterns have shifted toward emerging markets. Recognizing that success is measured not by the number of agreements signed, but by concrete results, the Administration has taken great pains not only to reach mutually beneficial agreements with our trading partners, but also to follow through in implementing, monitoring, and enforcing those agreements.

In assessing the results of the Administration's trade policies to date, it is important to recognize what trade policy can and cannot do. Trade policy can raise U.S. income and productivity, but it cannot significantly affect the overall trade balance. That is determined by domestic saving and investment and by government fiscal policy. Although the overall trade *balance* may not change, trade policy can alter the composition (both the sectoral breakdown of products traded and the shares of individual trading partners) and the overall *level* of trade. But U.S. trade policy should not be judged by whether our trade is in balance in any particular product or with any particular country. Even if our overall trade were balanced, there is simply no reason to expect (or desire) that our imports of cabbages or computers will match our exports of cabbages or computers, or that our sales to Japan or Zambia will cancel out our purchases from those countries, in any given year or even over an extended period. As we have already seen, it is precisely the ability to specialize, to concentrate on what we produce most efficiently, and to sell it in those markets that offer the highest returns, that is the fundamental source of the gains from international trade.

Multilateral Initiatives

The Uruguay Round trade agreement was signed in April 1994. The agreement went into force on January 1, 1995, with some provisions phased in over a 10-year period. The 1995 *Economic Report of the President* describes the agreement in detail.

Over nearly five decades, a series of GATT negotiating rounds has developed basic principles for the international trading system, which have guided trade negotiations in other spheres and have informed (and been informed by) U.S. trade policy. These principles include nondiscrimination, transparency, and reciprocity. Nondiscrimination is defined by two precepts: the most-favored-nation (MFN) precept requires that the most favorable concessions that a country gives to any trade partner be applied to all its trade part-

Box 8–3.—The Administration's Trade Achievements

Over the last 3 years the Administration has:

- Brought the Uruguay Round of multilateral trade negotiations to a successful close after 7 years. The Uruguay Round agreement cuts global tariffs by an average of 40 percent and extends international trade rules to agriculture, services, and intellectual property rights. The United States will eventually gain an estimated additional $100 billion to $200 billion in income per year from the agreement.
- Through the North American Free Trade Agreement (NAFTA), created a free-trade area encompassing our largest and third-largest trading partners. NAFTA has helped maintain and indeed increase U.S. exports to Mexico despite a financial crisis and recession there.
- Reached agreement with 33 other countries—including some of the world's biggest emerging markets—to seek a Free Trade Area of the Americas by 2005. Trade with countries in the hemisphere already accounts for roughly 40 percent of U.S. exports.
- Articulated a vision for achieving free trade and investment by 2020 in the fastest-growing region of the world: the Asia-Pacific. At the 1995 Asia-Pacific Economic Cooperation summit in Osaka, Japan, the leaders of the 18 member countries detailed the steps they will take to make this vision a reality.
- Negotiated 20 bilateral trade agreements with Japan. In those goods sectors covered by these agreements for which precise data are available, U.S. exports to Japan have grown nearly 80 percent since this Administration took office.
- Established a National Export Strategy under the leadership of the Trade Promotion Coordinating Committee, which for the first time coordinates the Federal Government's efforts to assist U.S. exporters through advocacy, export financing, and business counseling.
- Promoted macroeconomic and trade policies that have contributed to strong export growth. Exports of goods and services have grown 20 percent in real terms since the Administration took office.

ners; national treatment requires that a country's laws and regulations treat foreign products no differently from domestic products. Transparency ensures that the rules governing trade are explicit and that due process is followed in applying them, and reciprocity refers to the balancing of concessions from different countries. In addition, the GATT process has endorsed the use of safeguards—escape clauses and other forms of temporary relief from import surges—to protect against job dislocation during transitions.

The Uruguay Round agreement called for negotiations in three service sectors to be extended beyond the Round's conclusion: financial services, telecommunications, and maritime transport. The WTO's major negotiating effort in 1995 focused on the first of these. As the extended negotiating period for financial services drew to a close, the United States concluded that many offers—especially those from several emerging economies—provided inadequate new market access or did not formally protect even existing market access. The United States therefore announced that it would take an MFN exemption (that is, that it would not apply MFN treatment to all WTO members), allowing the United States to grant differential market access for new entrants and the new activities of foreign financial services suppliers. The United States also indicated that, while reserving its legal right to do so, it had no intention of imposing new restrictions on foreign firms. The participants in the negotiations nonetheless reached an interim agreement on July 28, to be reconsidered by the end of 1997. The United States is a party to the agreement and is entitled to all the commitments made by all participants.

WTO negotiations on telecommunications liberalization were initiated at the meeting of trade ministers of the WTO member countries in Marrakesh in April 1994. The talks are scheduled to conclude by April 30, 1996. As of January 1996 there were 48 WTO members participating, 33 of which had submitted offers detailing the liberalization they are prepared to undertake. The telecommunications negotiations are taking place at a critical point in the evolution of the global telecommunications industry. As Chapter 6 has described, the telecommunications sector was long considered a natural monopoly and has been heavily regulated or state owned in most countries. In recent years, however, technological change has greatly increased the scope for entry and competition. At the same time, systems of regulation and public ownership that were designed to protect consumers have in many cases become obstacles to competition and further progress, from both domestic and foreign firms. Thus deregulation and trade liberalization are closely intertwined, and the outcome of the trade negotiations depends on legislative reform in the major participating countries.

The goals of the United States in these negotiations are to ensure market access and national treatment for U.S. telecommunications firms abroad and to secure agreement on procompetitive regulatory principles in the participating countries. Competition in this sector requires that all entrants be able to connect to existing networks on equal terms. It also requires safeguards to ensure competition and the independence of regulators from the operating companies they oversee. The United States has indicated that if there is a critical mass of high-quality offers from industrial and developing countries, it will be willing to lift restrictions on foreign ownership in the U.S. telecommunications industry and to guarantee national treatment for foreign firms operating in the United States. However, if offers of sufficient quality are not forthcoming, the United States has reserved the right to amend or withdraw its existing offer or to take an exemption to the MFN requirement, as it did in financial services.

Regional Initiatives

The Administration has promoted the creation of regional trade agreements as stepping stones toward global free trade. The Administration has set ambitious goals for free trade in the two most dynamic markets of the world: the Asia-Pacific and Latin America. The combination of rapid growth and unprecedented liberalization is likely to make export and investment opportunities in these markets a key engine of growth for the U.S. economy over the next decade, and developing countries already account for over 40 percent of U.S. exports.

Regional initiatives founded on the principles of openness and inclusivity serve to strengthen the multilateral trading system. The principle of inclusivity encourages members of a regional agreement to pursue additional liberalization with nonmembers, including possible accession to the agreement. Regional free-trade agreements that do not raise external barriers and that welcome new members can set off a virtuous cycle of liberalization. As the market encompassed by a free-trade area expands and becomes increasingly dynamic, other countries become more interested in joining.

The GATT has always recognized the "desirability of increasing freedom of trade by the development, through voluntary agreements, of closer integration between the economies of the countries parties [sic] to such agreements" (Article XXIV), as long as such agreements do not result in an increase in the parties' external barriers. This restriction helps to ensure that preferential regional agreements create more trade among the participants (and others) than they divert from nonparticipants. In general, cheaper imports improve the well-being of the member countries and create trade. But regional liberalization *may* reduce trade with nonmember countries, since imports from such countries do not benefit from the reduction of trade barriers. Trade diversion arises when countries within a regional agreement switch from importing goods from the lowest-cost nonmember to importing from other members. Minimizing such distortionary trade diversion is a key objective in well-designed regional agreements.

Regional agreements often achieve deeper and broader economic integration than multilateral agreements because, as neighbors, members have substantial interests in common. Such agreements therefore often become models for future multilateral liberalization in new areas such as services, investment, and environmental and labor standards. The expansion of regional free-trade areas has also encouraged nations to find more common ground in multilateral negotiations. The U.S. regional initiatives in North America and the Asia-Pacific, for example, were an impetus for the successful conclusion of the Uruguay Round.

The North American Free Trade Agreement. NAFTA liberalizes trade with our two closest neighbors—who are also our largest and third-largest trade partners—over a period of 10 to 15 years. The impact of NAFTA on bilateral trade flows is difficult to isolate because Mexico experienced a severe financial crisis during 1995 (Box 8–5). In NAFTA's first year U.S. merchandise exports to Mexico and Canada grew by 16 percent—over twice as fast as U.S. exports to the rest of the world. Although U.S. exports to Mexico fell as Mexico entered recession, they remained higher during 1995 than they had been in 1993, before NAFTA. And despite the recession Mexico continued to honor its commitments to the United States, cutting tariffs on U.S. products in accordance with NAFTA's provisions—even as it increased tariffs on many goods from non-NAFTA partners by 15 percentage points. In part because of this, the U.S. share of Mexico's imports has grown from 69 percent in the first 9 months of 1994 to 74 percent over the same period in 1995. The performance of U.S. exports to Mexico in 1995 stands in sharp contrast to what happened after the previous Mexican financial crisis, in 1982, when the Mexican Government imposed 100 percent duties and import permit requirements on products from the United States and other countries. U.S. exports to Mexico were cut in half during that episode, and it took 6 years for U.S. exporters to recover their pre-1982 position. In contrast, U.S. exports to Mexico during the current episode fell by less than 10 percent and remain higher than before NAFTA.

In some instances, expanded trade with Mexico and Canada has displaced workers in the United States. Consequently, the President made it a priority to include a strong transitional program of trade adjustment assistance as part of the legislation implementing NAFTA. This program provides support to displaced workers in industries experiencing large increases in imports from, or whose plants have relocated to, Mexico or Canada, regardless of whether the job losses are directly related to NAFTA. In addition, the Department of Commerce's Economic Development Administration, through its Trade Adjustment Assistance program (which predates NAFTA), has provided assistance to a significant number of firms adversely affected by increased imports from Mexico and Canada.

NAFTA will serve both as a model for future multilateral liberalization in areas such as investment and as a vehicle for further regional liberalization. The Administration is committed to conducting negotiations with Chile on accession to NAFTA. Since Chile's population is only about one-seventh the size of Mexico's, the economic impact on the United States from Chile's accession is likely to be comparatively small. But Chile's accession will provide opportunities for American businesses to expand operations in this fast-growing market (which has grown by 7 percent per year on average

Box 8–5.—Mexico's Financial Stabilization

In December 1994 Mexico faced a balance of payments crisis. Investors lost confidence in Mexico's ability to maintain the exchange rate of the peso within its trading band, in part because of Mexico's large current account deficit, which had reached almost 8 percent of GDP in 1994. Intense pressure on the peso in foreign exchange markets threatened to exhaust Mexico's international reserves, compelling the Mexican Government to float the peso.

The President responded swiftly to Mexico's crisis, leading a $50 billion multilateral effort to assist in Mexico's stabilization and making available $20 billion in U.S. credit. This effort helped attenuate the impact of the crisis on other emerging markets. At the same time, the newly inaugurated Mexican President took the difficult steps essential to restoring stability and growth in Mexico. Government spending was cut, resulting in a budget surplus of 1.5 percent of GDP in the first three quarters of 1995. The Mexican Government also implemented a tight monetary policy, and because a lack of timely information was seen as having contributed to the crisis, Mexico took steps to make key financial and economic data more transparent and more widely available to investors.

Together these measures have begun to work, setting the stage for a return to growth. Nearly all of the $29 billion stock of *tesobonos*—short-term, dollar-denominated government debt—has been retired. Mexico's international reserves have risen from $6 billion at the beginning of 1995 to $16 billion at year's end. Monthly inflation has fallen to 2 to 3 percent from a high of 8 percent. As of mid-January 1996 the peso had stabilized, after an additional sharp decline in November, and the stock market had staged a partial recovery. Interest rates have declined from over 80 percent at the height of the crisis to below 40 percent. In addition, Mexico appears to have largely regained access to the international capital markets after only 7 months—far less than the 7 years it took Mexico to regain the trust of foreign investors after the debt crisis of 1982.

The financial crisis engendered a severe recession in Mexico, leading to a contraction of 7 percent in the first three quarters of 1995. But U.S. support, Mexico's tough stabilization policies, and the strong economic foundation that had been laid by the preceding 7 years of structural reform in Mexico should accelerate a return to sustainable growth.

since 1988), help encourage sound economic policies in the region, and serve as an important step on the road to creating a Free Trade Area of the Americas.

The Free Trade Area of the Americas (FTAA). In December 1994 in Miami, leaders from 33 Western Hemisphere countries joined with the President in embracing the goal of achieving free trade in the Western Hemisphere by 2005. Even though the FTAA will take years to achieve, by securing a commitment to work toward a hemispheric free-trade area now, hemispheric leaders set a high standard for the region, ensuring that subregional trade agreements will evolve in a manner consistent with the FTAA and the multilateral system.

The United States should reap significant benefits from establishment of the FTAA. It will create a market of over 850 million consumers with a combined income of roughly $13 trillion. Latin America is one of the fastest-growing regions in the world. Total exports of countries in the hemisphere grew nearly 17 percent on a year-over-year basis in the first half of 1995. Import growth was also strong at over 18 percent. Total trade flows in the hemisphere are estimated to have reached over $2 trillion in 1995. The FTAA will also level the playing field for U.S. exporters, reducing Latin American trade barriers that are currently three times higher on average than U.S. barriers. The increase in growth and improved access to new ideas that freer trade will bring should also promote U.S. goals of development and democracy in the region.

Trade ministers from throughout the hemisphere met in Denver in June 1995 to lay out a road map for achieving the leaders' vision of regional free trade. They agreed that trade liberalization should be consistent with WTO principles and comprehensive in scope. The Denver Ministerial established working groups in seven important areas: tariffs and nontariff barriers, customs procedures and rules of origin, investment, standards and technical barriers, sanitary and phytosanitary measures, antidumping and countervailing duties, and smaller economies. Each working group is responsible for compiling an inventory of regulations and regimes in its assigned area and undertaking a variety of other projects to prepare the foundations for the negotiated dismantling of trade and investment barriers. In March, trade ministers will meet again in Cartagena, Colombia. At the Cartagena Ministerial four additional working groups will be established, covering government procurement, IPR, services, and competition policy.

Asia-Pacific Economic Cooperation (APEC). The 18 members of APEC include some of the largest and most dynamic economies in the world today. Indeed, APEC is a unique combination of some of the world's most important established markets and some of its most important emerging markets. With a combined population of

241

2.1 billion and $13 trillion in combined annual income (over half of world income), the members make up the largest consumer market in the world. More than 30 percent of global trade takes place between APEC countries. The Asia-Pacific region continues to grow at a faster pace than any other region in the world: in 1994 China grew by 12 percent in real terms, Singapore by 10 percent, and South Korea, Malaysia, and Thailand by more than 8 percent. Over the next decade the developing East Asian economies are projected to invest between $1.2 trillion and $1.5 trillion in infrastructure, generating enormous opportunities for sales of American goods and services. Already APEC accounts for over 60 percent of U.S. merchandise exports, and these exports have grown 35 percent since the beginning of the Administration. U.S. exports to the Asian countries of APEC have grown 55 percent since the beginning of this Administration.

APEC was formed in 1989 as an informal group of 12 nations focused on increasing economic cooperation in the region. Initially only the members' designated APEC ministers attended the group's meetings. In November 1993, however, the President hosted the first summit of the leaders of the APEC countries. At that meeting, held at Blake Island in Washington State, the Asia-Pacific leaders embraced the President's vision of a Pacific community based on shared strength, peace, and prosperity, as well as his determination to make APEC relevant to the everyday problems of businesses throughout the region. Having set their course in 1993, APEC leaders again met in Bogor, Indonesia, in 1994, where they made a momentous commitment. The Bogor Declaration set a goal of achieving free trade and investment between the member economies over the next 25 years. For the industrialized countries in APEC the benefits come even sooner: full implementation is scheduled to occur within 15 years.

This year at Osaka, Japan, the APEC leaders put in place a work program and a liberalization process to make the vision of freer and fairer trade a reality, and meanwhile to deliver some concrete measures of immediate value to business. The leaders adopted an Action Agenda for implementing free trade and investment in the region by 2020 (Box 8–6). The Action Agenda covers 15 broad areas for liberalization and sets out 135 specific actions that members should take to open their markets and reduce the costs of doing business. The agenda's broad scope covers market access issues such as tariffs, quotas, and services. It also includes new areas that are the source of some of the most pernicious market barriers in Asia, such as IPR protection and investment, and other issues of growing importance to the region such as competition policy and deregulation. In each of these areas the Action Agenda sets out key objectives, benchmarks, time frames, and specific actions. The principles embodied in the Action Agenda ensure that liberalization in each country will be comprehensive, covering all products, services, and investment, and require each country to achieve results that are balanced and comparable to those of other APEC members. In the coming months, each member will detail the specific steps it will take to begin implementing the Action Agenda, to be presented at the next meeting of the APEC leaders in Manila in 1996. Implementation could begin as early as January 1997—only 2 years after APEC leaders made the commitment to achieve free trade.

The Transatlantic Trade and Investment Initiative. The U.S.-European relationship is one of the oldest and most durable in international affairs. To further strengthen this partnership, the United States and the European Union initiated a Joint Action Plan at their Madrid summit in December 1995. The summit declaration included the commitment to foster a Transatlantic Marketplace. As part of this effort, the United States and the European Union have pledged to seek agreements on mutual recognition of testing data and standards certification, to cooperate and assist each other on customs procedures, to begin work on a comprehensive agreement on cooperation in science and technology, and to initiate a joint study on market barriers confronting transatlantic trade. The two sides will draw heavily on the advice of the private sector. Their cooperation will also extend to environmental and labor issues.

The OECD Multilateral Agreement on Investment. After 4 years of intensive work, the ministers of the member countries of the Organization for Economic Cooperation and Development (OECD) agreed in May 1995 to launch negotiations toward a multilateral agreement on investment. The aim is to conclude negotiations by 1997. At the negotiators' first meeting in September 1995, broad consensus was reached on ensuring a high standard of principles (including full national and MFN treatment of investment). Exceptions to such treatment will be limited in number and narrowly drawn. In future negotiations the United States hopes to establish international legal standards governing expropriation, freedom from performance requirements (such as the requirement that a foreign subsidiary's products contain at least a specified minimum local content, or that a specified minimum quantity be exported), guaranteed access to binding international arbitration of disputes between private investors and national governments, and the right to unrestricted investment-related transfers across borders. If these principles are adopted, the multilateral agreement on investment would establish a high standard for future work on investment issues in Asia.

Bilateral Initiatives

Disputes and negotiations between one country and another are inevitable in international trade relations. The United States ac-

Box 8–6.—The APEC Action Agenda

The Action Agenda details steps that APEC members will take to dismantle key trade barriers that currently impede foreign businesses. Examples include:

- *Tariffs:* According to one estimate, automobile sales to Indonesia, Malaysia, and Thailand combined could equal U.S. auto sales to Canada and Mexico combined by 2000. Under NAFTA, U.S. car exports to Canada face no tariffs; those to Mexico face a 10 percent tariff, which will be eliminated by 2003. But tariffs on U.S. car exports to Indonesia, Malaysia, and Thailand range between 30 and 60 percent. The Action Agenda stipulates that members will progressively lower these tariffs. Some members will start reducing tariffs as early as January 1997.
- *Air transport:* Demand for air transport services in Asia is projected to grow by 8.5 percent annually through the end of the decade. This is a key opportunity for U.S. carriers, whose costs per passenger-mile are half those of their Japanese competitors. Yet barriers are high. APEC has commissioned a group of experts to develop options to lower barriers to competition in this fast-growing market.

The Action Agenda also contains a variety of measures that will reduce the cost of doing business in the region:

- *Infrastructure database:* APEC is assembling an infrastructure opportunity database, which will provide information on the Internet—in English—on all government procurement open to foreign bidding. APEC has already launched a pilot home page on the World Wide Web that includes projects from Hong Kong, the United States, Japan, and Australia.
- *Customs harmonization:* APEC is working to promote uniform customs classifications and procedures and to establish common forms for manifests, travel documents, and the electronic transmission of business documents. Businesses can look forward to the day when a single customs form is accepted in all APEC countries.
- *Standards harmonization:* APEC is developing so-called mutual recognition agreements in toys and some food products, which will enable companies to sell their products throughout the APEC countries after a single laboratory test.

tively engages in bilateral consultations, negotiations, and dispute settlement procedures to defend U.S. commercial interests and to ensure that trade agreements are implemented, market access is expanded, and offending foreign practices are addressed. The focus of U.S. bilateral agreements is to open foreign markets to producers from all countries, not just those from the United States. These agreements are designed to support a more open, less distorted world trade regime. This Administration has also insisted on agreements that lead to tangible market opening, not simply agreements in form. The Administration's trade agreements specify qualitative and quantitative indicators of progress, agreed to by both countries, and the Administration has actively reviewed and monitored the agreements it has reached, comparing actual progress made against these indicators.

Japan. Japan remains among the most important of our economic partners. The Administration's goals in our relationship with Japan are to increase both access for and sales by non-Japanese firms in the Japanese market, to stimulate demand-led growth in the Japanese economy, and to raise standards of living in both Japan and the United States. To these ends, in 1993 the Administration signed the Framework for a New Economic Partnership with Japan. The Framework laid out macroeconomic goals and identified areas for sector-specific and structural negotiations. In the past year alone the Administration has signed new agreements under the Framework in automobiles and auto parts (discussed below), financial services, and investment. These agreements bring to 20 the number of trade agreements that the Administration has concluded with Japan.

The sectoral agreements with Japan are beginning to produce results. The Framework set up mechanisms, including qualitative and quantitative criteria, for both countries to use in reviewing the progress made on these agreements. Although it is still too early to judge the effects of the 1995 agreements, the results from the agreements concluded in 1993 and 1994 have generally been positive. By any measure, growth of U.S. exports to Japan has been striking, especially given that country's continuing economic stagnation. Overall U.S. exports to Japan were 20 percent higher in the period from January through November 1995 than in the previous year, and 47 percent higher than when the Administration took office. Growth of U.S. exports to Japan has been even stronger in those goods sectors covered by the Administration's trade agreements with Japan (Chart 8–1).

After 2 years of negotiations to open Japan's markets in automobiles and auto parts to U.S. and other foreign suppliers, an agreement was reached in the summer of 1995 to increase Japanese purchases of foreign automobiles and parts. Under the agree-

Chart 8-1 **Merchandise Exports to Japan**
Exports in goods sectors covered by Administration trade agreements with Japan
have increased at a faster rate than other U.S. exports to Japan since 1993.

Index, January 1993=100

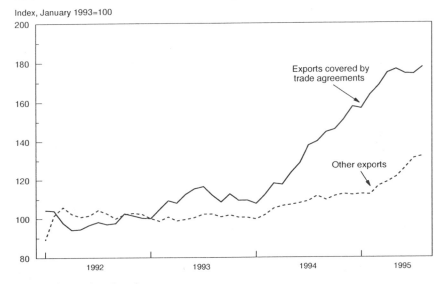

Note: Data are 6-month moving averages.
Sources: Department of Commerce and Council of Economic Advisers.

ment, Japan promised to improve foreign automakers' access to Japanese dealerships. U.S. industry expectations are for access to 1,000 new outlets and the annual export of 300,000 U.S.-made vehicles to Japan by 2000. Also in connection with the agreement, the Japanese Big Five automakers announced plans for their U.S. assembly plants that are expected to increase those plants' purchases of North American auto parts by $6.75 billion by 1998. Japan also agreed to deregulate the repair and replacement market for auto parts in Japan, which will make it much easier for foreign firms to sell auto parts in the Japanese aftermarket. Finally, the Japanese Government will increase the budget of the Japan Fair Trade Commission and consider U.S. suggestions for improved antitrust enforcement.

The two countries also signed an investment agreement in July 1995. Despite the abolition of most formal barriers to foreign direct investment in Japan, Japan has absorbed only 1 percent of world foreign direct investment—remarkably little for an economy that accounts for about 16 percent of world output. A tangible market presence is increasingly important for overseas sales in many industries, and for many service industries it is indispensable for conducting business. Efforts to facilitate foreign direct investment in Japan were therefore an important part of the Framework negotiations. Under the United States-Japan Investment Arrangement,

Japan will review the few remaining restrictions on foreign investment, make foreign investors eligible for low-interest loans from the Japan Development Bank, and ensure that foreign-owned firms are eligible for government-funded employment programs. Japan has also pledged to make land available to foreign investors in designated foreign access zones, and the Keidanren (Japan's major business organization) has pledged to facilitate foreign contacts with its members.

China. China is an increasingly important player in the world economy. China's share of world trade has tripled since market reforms were launched in the late 1970s, making it the world's 10th-largest exporter. The Chinese economy has recently recorded some of the fastest growth rates in the world (12 percent in 1994 and roughly 10 percent in 1995). Already the world's most populous country, China may have the world's largest economy by early in the next century. U.S. exports to China continue to grow quickly, as incomes, and hence demand for high-quality U.S. goods, increase. This Administration is committed to encouraging further economic liberalization and to integrating China more fully into the world economy. Success at these efforts will support U.S. foreign policy objectives of democratization, economic reform, and development in China. Although great progress has been made on these fronts, there is still a long way to go.

China's accession to the WTO is an important goal for both the United States and China, with negotiations under way since 1988. The United States and other WTO members have stipulated that China must join the organization on commercial terms. Every country that has joined the GATT in the past has agreed to adhere to the basic principles of the multilateral trading regime, such as transparency of the trade regime and uniform application of trade rules. The United States is working with China to reach these world trade standards in a variety of forums, including bilateral trade initiatives on market access, protection of intellectual property, and services.

In February 1995 the United States reached a bilateral agreement with China on IPR protection. The new agreement lays out specific enforcement measures for China to undertake, and consultations between China and the United States have been occurring frequently to ensure that these measures are being carried out. In addition to creating a new enforcement structure, the agreement increases market access for U.S. audiovisual products, software, books, and periodicals by placing a ban on quotas and by allowing U.S. companies to set up joint ventures in several urban areas around the country.

Chinese pirating of U.S. software and audiovisual materials and infringements of U.S. trademarks and patents had become a concern to the United States as exports of pirated goods began turning up in Southeast Asia, Latin America, and even Canada and the United States. China has more than 29 factories with the capacity to produce 75 million compact discs annually—in a domestic market that, according to estimates, can absorb only 5 million. Under the new agreement, task forces have been set up to raid illegal retail and manufacturing establishments as well as to provide border control. As of the end of 1995, implementation of the agreement has been mixed. Although China has attacked piracy at the retail level, massive production, distribution, and export of pirated materials continue. In particular, China has yet to halt production of pirated CDs.

Korea. Although Korea is the fifth-largest manufacturer and a rapidly growing exporter of automobiles, a variety of barriers have effectively closed the Korean automobile market to imports. These barriers include onerous standards and certification procedures, limits on consumer financing and advertising by foreign firms, and excise and registration taxes that fall disproportionately on the medium-sized and larger models that U.S. automakers produce. Until recently, Koreans were required to report the automobiles that they owned on their income tax returns, and owners of foreign cars feared tax audits. These barriers, which help explain why the foreign share of Korea's automobile market is only 0.3 percent, were serious enough to warrant active consideration as a "priority foreign country practice" in the U.S. Super 301 process this past year.

Negotiations led to the signing of a memorandum of understanding with Korea on September 27, 1995. The Korean Government agreed to reduce significantly the tax burden on larger automobiles and to affirm that foreign car ownership would not subject Koreans to tax audit or other harassment. In addition, Korea will substantially reduce the documentation required to secure safety approval and will allow testing for a new noise standard to be done outside Korea. Foreign firms will be able to establish or acquire automobile finance companies and will be given equal access to television advertising time.

Monitoring foreign practices. One of the principal objectives of U.S. trade policy has been the identification and elimination of unfair foreign trade barriers. The Administration has placed a high priority on enforcing U.S. trade agreements and on ensuring that other countries do not engage in practices that violate trade agreements they have signed with the United States. The U.S. Trade Representative, in close consultation with U.S. firms, its private sector advisory committees, and other interested parties, monitors the trade practices of other countries and their compliance with U.S. trade agreements and is responsible for addressing those practices identified as unfair.

MEASURING THE SUCCESS OF TRADE POLICY

The Administration's protrade policies have been associated with rapid export growth. Real exports of goods and services have grown by 20 percent since the first quarter of 1993 (Chart 8–2). Real export growth has risen: from 3.3 percent in 1993 to 8.3 percent in 1994 and 9.0 percent through the third quarter of 1995 (on a year-over-year basis). The United States is once again the largest merchandise exporter in the world, accounting for roughly 12 percent of global exports. Moreover, the U.S. share of industrial-country merchandise exports has grown to 18 percent, from 15 percent in 1986, and now exceeds the shares of Germany and Japan (at 15 and 14 percent, respectively).

Chart 8-2 **Export and Import Volumes**
Exports have grown vigorously in recent years, but, with imports also rising, the trade balance remains in deficit.

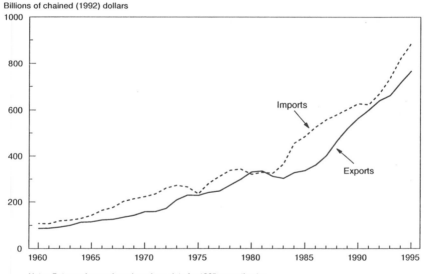

Billions of chained (1992) dollars

Note: Data are for goods and services; data for 1995 are estimates.
Sources: Department of Commerce and Council of Economic Advisers.

Although U.S. exporters are once again extremely competitive on world markets, the U.S. trade balance remains in deficit. The next section explains why the trade deficit is a misleading measure of the success of U.S. trade policies and the strength of the U.S. economy. Fundamentally, the trade deficit is caused by macroeconomic factors, not trade policy, which is capable of making only marginal changes in the overall deficit. Eliminating or substantially reducing the trade deficit will require macroeconomic policy measures, such as the elimination of the Federal budget deficit.

CAUSES AND CONSEQUENCES OF THE TRADE DEFICIT

International trade and competition make a vital contribution to the growth and well-being of the United States, and U.S. firms and workers have proved themselves successful in that competition. Yet despite the rapid growth of U.S. exports and export-related jobs, public commentary often focuses on the overall trade balance, which shows a large and seemingly intractable deficit. Many critics point to the trade deficit as evidence that the United States is not competing successfully and that international trade is detrimental to the health of the economy. Therefore, they argue, the United States should modify its longstanding policy of encouraging open markets and liberal trade.

This focus is unfortunate, because the trade balance is a deceptive indicator of the Nation's economic performance and of the benefit that the United States derives from trade. Trade policy is neither responsible for, nor capable of significantly changing, the overall trade balance. As noted above, trade policy can have a substantial impact on the sectoral and geographic composition of trade, but the aggregate trade balance is determined by larger macroeconomic factors. Persistent external deficits do entail costs, but effective policies to reduce these costs by narrowing the external deficit are beyond the realm of trade policy.

SOURCES OF THE U.S. TRADE DEFICIT

The trade balance is simply the difference between the value of goods and services sold by U.S. residents to foreigners and the value of goods and services that U.S. residents buy from foreigners. Most of what the United States produces (89 percent in 1995) is sold to residents of the United States; the rest is exported. And most of what the United States buys (88 percent in 1995) is produced here; the rest is imported. When we compare total production and total expenditure, those goods and services that we purchase from ourselves net out, and the difference is exports minus imports, or the trade balance. A trade deficit thus results when the Nation's expenditure exceeds its production.

Trade is by far the largest source of foreign income and foreign payments, but there are other external income flows: the main ones are interest and other investment earnings, aid grants, and transfers. Adding these other current flows to the trade balance produces the current account balance, which is the net income that the United States receives from the rest of the world. The current account balance thus represents the bottom line on the income statement of the United States. If it is positive, the United States is spending less than its total income and accumulating asset claims on the rest of the world. If it is negative, as it has been in most recent years, our expenditure exceeds our income, and we are borrowing from the rest of the world.

The net borrowing of the Nation can be expressed as the sum of the net borrowing by each of the principal sectors of the economy: government (Federal, State, and local), firms, and households. In other words, the current account deficit (CAD) is equal to the government's budget deficit (G − T, or net borrowing by the public sector) plus the difference between private sector investment and private sector saving (I − S, or net borrowing by the private sector):

$$(G - T) \quad + \quad (I \quad - \quad S) \quad = \quad CAD$$

(G − T)	+	(I	−	S)	=	CAD
Government deficit		Private investment		Private saving		Current account deficit

The crucial insight of this identity is that the current account deficit is a macroeconomic phenomenon: it reflects an imbalance between national saving and national investment. The fact that the relationship is an identity and always holds true also means that any effective policy to reduce the current account deficit must, in the end, narrow the gap between U.S. saving and U.S. investment.

Economic Performance and the Current Account

If the current account deficit has little to do with trade policy, neither does it necessarily indicate poor economic performance. In fact, in the short run it may indicate precisely the opposite. Consider two situations: one in which the economy is operating with fully employed resources, and one in which the economy is operating with excess capacity.

When resources are fully employed, a current account deficit does not constrain the level of economic activity and thus cannot represent "lost" production. The U.S. economy in the past 2 years provides a good example, since it has been very close to full employment and production capacity. During 1994 and the first three quarters of 1995, total U.S. production of goods and services (GDP) averaged $7.1 trillion per year. Total U.S. expenditure was $7.2 trillion. The difference, just over $100 billion worth of goods and services per year, came from overseas, as reflected in the trade deficit.

It would have been very difficult to have produced those extra goods and services ourselves and thus eliminated the trade deficit. The monthly unemployment rate in 1994 and 1995 averaged 5.8 percent and twice fell to 5.4 percent, very near the point at which economists believe inflation begins to accelerate. Both labor force participation and overtime in manufacturing were at postwar highs. In such a tight labor market, any attempt to close the trade deficit in 1994 or 1995 by producing more domestically would un-

251

doubtedly have been frustrated by rising prices, or by an increase in interest rates that would have reduced output in other sectors. In sum, when the economy is near full employment, the trade deficit does not affect the level of economic activity and therefore provides no insight into how well or poorly the economy is performing.

The second case to consider is an economy operating at less than full employment. Here trade outcomes can affect the level of economic activity. Rates of foreign economic growth and the exchange rate of the dollar have a strong influence on U.S. export sales, and therefore on the level of U.S. production. And unlike in the case of full employment, the expansionary impact from export sales in this situation is not necessarily fully offset. At the same time, the cyclical state of the U.S. economy exerts a strong influence on the demand for imports. In practice, this channel is so strong that the trade and current account deficits have tended to increase when the U.S. economy is growing rapidly, as it has in the last 3 years, and to diminish when the U.S. economy is weak. An increasing trade deficit is therefore usually the result of a strong economy, not the cause of a weak one. Over the past 15 years, U.S. employment growth has tended to be highest when the trade deficit was large, not when it was small (Chart 8–3).

Chart 8-3 **Employment Growth and the Trade Deficit**
The trade deficit tends to rise when employment growth is strong because of increased demand for imported goods and services.

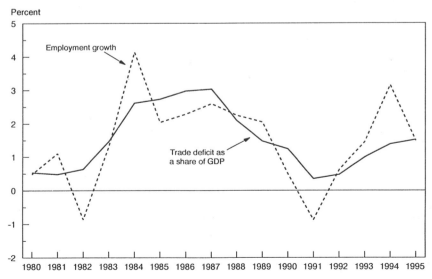

Note: Data for 1995 are estimates.
Sources: Departments of Commerce and Labor, and Council of Economic Advisers.

The same conclusion holds if we look across the other major industrial countries. In the 1990s trade balances have improved in those of the seven leading industrial market economies (the Group of Seven, or G–7) where economic growth and employment creation was weak (Chart 8–4).

Chart 8-4 **Economic Growth and Changes in Trade Balances in the G-7 Countries, 1990-94**
Across the major industrial countries, recent improvements in the trade balance have been associated with weak economic performance.

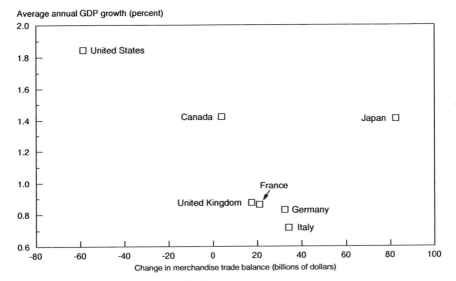

Note: Germany refers to unified Germany, 1991-94.
Sources: Department of Commerce, Organization for Economic Cooperation and Development, and Council of Economic Advisers.

Growth of the Current Account Deficit

From 1946 until 1982 the U.S. current account balance fluctuated around zero but was generally in surplus. Government deficits during recessions were balanced by weak domestic investment and an excess of private saving (Chart 8–5). The adoption, early in the 1980s, of tight monetary policy to combat inflation led to a sharp increase in U.S. interest rates, an inflow of foreign capital, and an appreciation of the dollar. At the same time, fiscal (tax and expenditure) policy led to large budget deficits that did not disappear when the economy was growing strongly and private investment was high. The so-called structural budget deficit, which is the actual deficit corrected for short-term fluctuations in GDP, increased by a full 2 percentage points of GDP between 1982 and 1984. Econometric simulations indicate that the shift in fiscal policies, coupled with a move toward more restrictive budget policies abroad, explains about two-thirds of the deterioration in the current account in the first half of the 1980s.

165-967 96 – 9

Chart 8-5   **Private Saving and Investment, the Fiscal Balance, and the Current Account**
The emergence of large fiscal deficits in the 1980s and a rebound in
investment in the 1990s led to increasing current account deficits.

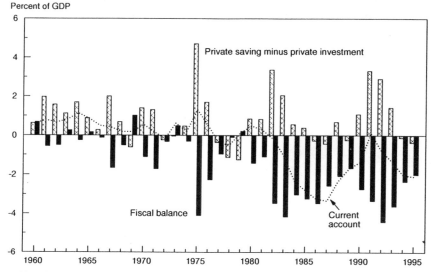

Note: The private saving and investment measures are gross private saving and gross private investment.
The fiscal balance is gross government saving less gross government investment.   The current account equals
net foreign investment plus capital grants received. Data for 1995 are estimates.
Sources: Department of Commerce and Council of Economic Advisers.

Fiscal policy changes in the middle of the 1980s partly reversed
the widening of the Federal budget deficit. But the slight reduction
in the budget deficit was more than offset by a fall in private saving: the U.S. gross private saving rate (the sum of the saving rates
of businesses and households), which averaged 18.3 percent of GDP
in the first half of the decade, fell to 16.0 percent in the second
half. In broad terms, then, the increase in the budget deficit and
the fall in the domestic saving rate were responsible for the chronically large U.S. current account deficit. Although the budget deficit
(both actual and structural) has fallen significantly during this Administration, a sharp increase in domestic investment during the
cyclical recovery has driven the current account further into deficit
over the past 3 years.

Current Account Developments in 1995

The current account deficit continued to increase in 1995, driven
largely by high U.S. economic growth relative to our major trading
partners. Although U.S. growth has been below the OECD average
for much of the postwar period, in the period since 1992, the U.S.
economy has grown faster than the economies of most other OECD
countries, including major trading partners such as Germany and
Japan (Chart 8-6). Although U.S. economic growth moderated in
1995, consistent with a desired "soft landing" of the economic expansion, it remained above the OECD average.

Chart 8-6 **Growth of Real GDP in the United States and Abroad**
Faster growth relative to other industrial countries since 1992 has contributed
to the rise in the current account deficit.

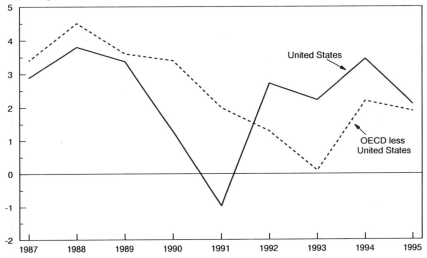

Note: Data for 1995 are estimates.
Sources: Department of Commerce, Organization for Economic Cooperation and Development, and
Council of Economic Advisers.

Along with relative economic growth rates, changes in relative prices (most often due to exchange-rate changes) have important short-run influences on both bilateral trade balances and the overall current account balance. Beginning in February 1995 the U.S. dollar depreciated against the currencies of our major trading partners, and most sharply against the Japanese yen (Chart 8–7). The depreciation of the dollar went beyond what many viewed as justified by economic fundamentals, and a statement by the G–7 finance ministers and central bank governors at the end of April called for an orderly reversal of the preceding exchange-rate movements. Interest rate reductions in Japan and Germany and concerted currency market intervention in July and August were followed by a recovery of the dollar. Between the end of April and the end of August, the dollar appreciated by 16 percent against the yen and by 6 percent against the deutsche mark. Although these bilateral moves are noteworthy and will have a significant effect on bilateral trade, the movement of the dollar against a weighted average of the currencies of U.S. trading partners was more modest, particularly when an index covering a broad range of trading partners is examined.

Relative price and income movements influence bilateral trade balances in the short run, and there were important developments along these lines with several U.S. trading partners in 1995. The

Chart 8-7   U.S. Dollar Exchange Rates
The dollar has fluctuated sharply against the currencies of Japan and other major trading partners, but less sharply against broader indexes of foreign currencies

Index, fourth quarter 1993=100

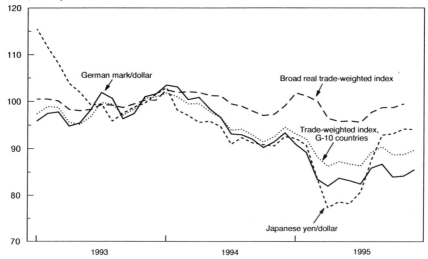

Note: The broad real trade-weighted index is relative to 101 trading partners, adjusted for domestic inflation. A rise in an index indicates an appreciation of the dollar.
Sources: Board of Governors of the Federal Reserve System, Federal Reserve Bank of Dallas, and Council of Economic Advisers.

most dramatic change was in the balance with Mexico, following a severe financial and exchange-rate crisis in that country beginning in December 1994 (Box 8–5). The dramatic nominal depreciation of the peso outstripped the sharp increase in Mexico's price level, and so the real (inflation-adjusted) value of the peso fell, encouraging exports and discouraging imports. In addition, the downturn in economic activity within Mexico greatly affected that country's demand for imports. Consequently, the U.S. bilateral balance with Mexico fell from a $1.4 billion surplus in the first 11 months of 1994 to a deficit of $14.4 billion for the first 11 months of 1995.

Even so, as was emphasized above, U.S. exports to Mexico have held up far better than those of Mexico's other trading partners, and the provisions of NAFTA spared U.S. exporters from the emergency measures that Mexico imposed on its trade with other countries. Despite the severity of the crisis, Mexico appears to be adjusting successfully, and its longer term prospects are encouraging. As Mexican economic growth resumes, imports from the United States should rebound strongly.

Trends in the U.S. trade balance with Japan over the past year are the result of income and relative price forces pulling in opposite directions. The Japanese economy has seen almost no growth in output since 1991, and the recovery that was expected to occur in 1995 failed to materialize; current estimates of Japanese economic growth for 1995 are about half a percent. Despite this stagnation in demand, imports by Japan have surged because of the appreciation of the yen over the past 3 years, coupled with some market-opening measures, and Japan's current account surplus has narrowed. U.S. exports to Japan have grown rapidly in the last 3 years, particularly in those sectors covered by Framework and other trade agreements. The U.S. bilateral deficit with Japan has declined since mid-1995 and for the first 11 months of the year it was down 7 percent relative to 1994. Should the long-awaited recovery in Japan begin this year, the deficit with Japan should decline further.

As the events of the past year illustrate, individual exchange-rate movements and shifts in economic growth rates have large influences on bilateral balances. Movements in the overall current account balance are generally less extreme, because of the averaging that takes place across various country markets. But the rate of U.S. growth relative to that of its trading partners, together with overall movements in the dollar's exchange rate, has a considerable influence on the U.S. external balance, particularly on a year-to-year basis. Over longer periods cyclical movements tend to average out, and real exchange rates are influenced more by the requirements of long-run current account positions and current account servicing requirements. Over this longer time frame it makes sense to think in terms of propensities rather than levels (in other words, the shares of national income devoted to private saving, to domestic investment, and to financing the government budget deficit). The emergence of the U.S. current account deficit over the past 15 years has been the result of a decline in national saving as a share of GDP (resulting from lower private saving and an increase in the Federal budget deficit, both as shares of GDP), which has more than offset a decline in the investment-GDP ratio since the early 1980s.

CONSEQUENCES OF THE CURRENT ACCOUNT DEFICIT

The current account deficits that arose in the 1980s are an indicator neither of the ability of the United States to compete in the world market, nor of the efficacy of U.S. trade policy. U.S. export growth, and more broadly the growth of the U.S. economy, are much more informative measures of our relative economic standing. The current account deficit has not prevented a rapid increase in employment, and the recent increase in the external deficit is primarily the result of rapid economic growth. Furthermore, given the fiscal policy adopted in the early 1980s and the subsequent decline in the U.S. saving rate, the ability to borrow overseas and run a current account deficit has been critical in maintaining domestic investment and growth over the last 15 years. Had the United States been forced to run a balanced current account, interest rates would have been higher, and investment and economic growth lower, than what we experienced.

If this is so, why should one care about the trade and current account deficits? As explained above, the current account deficit is the difference between our expenditure and our income, and represents our net borrowing from the rest of the world. By running a large and persistent current account deficit we have been borrowing against future income, building up liabilities to the rest of the world that will have to be serviced in the future. Estimates show the United States moving from a net creditor position of over $250 billion in the early 1980s to a net debtor position of over half a trillion dollars by 1994. The positive net international asset position that the United States had built up over 100 years was eliminated in the space of about 6 years during the 1980s.

The debt-servicing requirements of this buildup of external debt are already making their presence felt. Net income on U.S. external assets was over $30 billion per year in the early 1980s. This inflow declined over the 1980s and eventually turned negative: in 1995 our net overseas *payments* are likely to be over $11 billion. Although these numbers are still quite manageable in an economy that produces $7,000 billion in income each year, the current trend is for an increasing share of U.S. income to be paid out to foreigners, and thus to be unavailable to support U.S. consumption and investment. In a period in which the size of the retirement-aged population will increase sharply, servicing our net foreign debt will be a further drain on the future working population.

The extent to which we rely on foreign borrowing also influences the terms on which we can borrow. Modern portfolio theory emphasizes the importance of relative rates of return in determining asset holdings. To induce foreigners to hold a larger share of their assets as claims on the United States, we may have to offer a higher interest rate. Very rough estimates place the share of U.S. assets in foreign portfolios at about 9 percent, about 2 percentage points higher than in 1982. This does not appear to be unduly large given the low transactions costs, high liquidity, and strong investor protection that characterize U.S. financial markets. In addition, the ratio of U.S. external debt to GDP is still moderate, and well below the ratios of some other industrial countries. But as the stock of foreign claims on the United States increases, U.S. financial markets will inevitably be more sensitive to foreign perceptions and external considerations.

POLICY OPTIONS TO REDUCE THE CURRENT ACCOUNT DEFICIT

Given that a sustained current account deficit is costly to the Nation, what policy options are available to reduce it? As we have seen, trade policy has little impact on the overall current account balance. To shrink or eliminate the current account deficit, either the government budget deficit must be narrowed, or private saving must rise relative to investment, or both. Maintaining and if possible increasing the rate of investment in the United States is critical for the growth of American incomes and is a firmly held goal of the Administration. So the only desirable options are to raise the rate of saving and to reduce the government budget deficit. Unfortunately, the policy tools to raise private saving are inherently limited: anything that might strengthen incentives to save by raising the return to saving would also reduce the amount of saving required to meet a future wealth or consumption target. And if private saving incentives take the form of tax expenditures ("tax breaks"), the induced increase in private saving must be greater than the loss of tax revenue in order for national (public plus private) saving to increase. The budget deficit is under far more direct policy control. The Administration's budget, which would eliminate the Federal deficit by 2002, provides the most promising way of reducing the U.S. current account and trade deficits.

Reducing the U.S. current account deficit is primarily, but not entirely, in our own hands. Since global saving equals global investment, the sum of all countries' current account balances (when accurately measured) must equal zero. Thus a reduction in the U.S. current account deficit must go hand in hand with a decline in the current account surplus of the rest of the world. Complementary policy in foreign countries, particularly those with large current account surpluses, would assist in the transition. That is why an important component of the Framework negotiations with Japan focused on the promotion of macroeconomic policies in that country that would encourage strong domestic demand-led growth. But one should not exaggerate the foreign responsibility for reducing the U.S. deficit. A reduction in one country's surplus will not ensure a corresponding fall in the U.S. deficit. And even without any policy actions by foreign countries, changes in exchange rates and in world interest rates would accommodate the elimination of the U.S. current account deficit. Fundamentally, the U.S. current account balance will be determined by our own saving, investment, and budget policy, and continued reduction of the Federal budget deficit is the most effective tool for reducing our external deficit.

CONCLUSION

A system of liberal international trade and investment boosts overall living standards by allowing all participants to concentrate on what they do best, to learn from others, and to ensure competition. Consumers in open economies enjoy access to a wider variety of goods at lower prices than those living in economies that insulate domestic producers from foreign competition. Trade shifts jobs into sectors in which an economy is relatively efficient, and therefore boosts productivity and wages. In the United States, jobs supported by goods exports pay 13 percent more than the national average. Open trade and investment also have positive dynamic effects: exposure to the competitive pressures of the international marketplace spurs domestic firms to improve productivity and boost innovation. At the same time, exposure to international markets and foreign direct investment facilitates the flow of technology across borders, allowing producers to employ domestic resources more efficiently.

Abundant evidence testifies to the advantages of open markets over protectionism. Countries with outward-looking, liberal trade and investment policies grow faster, the data show, than countries with inward-looking, closed policies. The general consensus among economists is that open markets raise growth and productivity.

Achieving the benefits of trade requires continual change and adaptation. And even though most studies suggest that the effect has been small in the United States, trade can worsen wage inequality. The Administration therefore recognizes that, while outward-looking trade and foreign direct investment policies are critical to the future strength of the economy, we must help those injured by the lowering of trade barriers to make the requisite adjustments. In today's global economy, there is simply no alternative to competing.

This Administration has been remarkably successful in promoting competition around the world. A concerted set of multilateral, regional, and bilateral trade negotiations has produced the Uruguay Round agreement, NAFTA, and the Framework agreement with Japan. Ambitious plans have been laid for free trade across the Pacific and throughout the Americas. Partly reflecting this active trade policy, U.S. exports of goods and services have grown by 20 percent since this Administration took office.

The continuing external deficit remains a cause for concern, but it must be kept in mind that the deficit is caused by macroeconomic factors, not trade policy. It should not be used as a test of whether trade is beneficial or whether our trade policy is effective. The most effective policy option for reducing the trade deficit is the reduction or elimination of the Federal budget deficit.

Appendix A
REPORT TO THE PRESIDENT ON THE ACTIVITIES
OF THE
COUNCIL OF ECONOMIC ADVISERS DURING 1995

LETTER OF TRANSMITTAL

COUNCIL OF ECONOMIC ADVISERS
Washington, D.C., January 29, 1996

MR. PRESIDENT:

The Council of Economic Advisers submits this report on its activities during the calendar year 1995 in accordance with the requirements of the Congress, as set forth in section 10(d) of the Employment Act of 1946 as amended by the Full Employment and Balanced Growth Act of 1978.

Sincerely,

Joseph E. Stiglitz, *Chairman*
Martin N. Baily, *Member*
Alicia H. Munnell, *Member*

Council Members and their Dates of Service

Name	Position	Oath of office date	Separation date
Edwin G. Nourse	Chairman	August 9, 1946	November 1, 1949.
Leon H. Keyserling	Vice Chairman	August 9, 1946	
	Acting Chairman	November 2, 1949	
	Chairman	May 10, 1950	January 20, 1953.
John D. Clark	Member	August 9, 1946	
	Vice Chairman	May 10, 1950	February 11, 1953.
Roy Blough	Member	June 29, 1950	August 20, 1952.
Robert C. Turner	Member	September 8, 1952	January 20, 1953.
Arthur F. Burns	Chairman	March 19, 1953	December 1, 1956.
Neil H. Jacoby	Member	September 15, 1953	February 9, 1955.
Walter W. Stewart	Member	December 2, 1953	April 29, 1955.
Raymond J. Saulnier	Member	April 4, 1955	
	Chairman	December 3, 1956	January 20, 1961.
Joseph S. Davis	Member	May 2, 1955	October 31, 1958.
Paul W. McCracken	Member	December 3, 1956	January 31, 1959.
Karl Brandt	Member	November 1, 1958	January 20, 1961.
Henry C. Wallich	Member	May 7, 1959	January 20, 1961.
Walter W. Heller	Chairman	January 29, 1961	November 15, 1964.
James Tobin	Member	January 29, 1961	July 31, 1962.
Kermit Gordon	Member	January 29, 1961	December 27, 1962.
Gardner Ackley	Member	August 3, 1962	
	Chairman	November 16, 1964	February 15, 1968.
John P. Lewis	Member	May 17, 1963	August 31, 1964.
Otto Eckstein	Member	September 2, 1964	February 1, 1966.
Arthur M. Okun	Member	November 16, 1964	
	Chairman	February 15, 1968	January 20, 1969.
James S. Duesenberry	Member	February 2, 1966	June 30, 1968.
Merton J. Peck	Member	February 15, 1968	January 20, 1969.
Warren L. Smith	Member	July 1, 1968	January 20, 1969.
Paul W. McCracken	Chairman	February 4, 1969	December 31, 1971.
Hendrik S. Houthakker	Member	February 4, 1969	July 15, 1971.
Herbert Stein	Member	February 4, 1969	
	Chairman	January 1, 1972	August 31, 1974.
Ezra Solomon	Member	September 9, 1971	March 26, 1973.
Marina v.N. Whitman	Member	March 13, 1972	August 15, 1973.
Gary L. Seevers	Member	July 23, 1973	April 15, 1975.
William J. Fellner	Member	October 31, 1973	February 25, 1975.
Alan Greenspan	Chairman	September 4, 1974	January 20, 1977.
Paul W. MacAvoy	Member	June 13, 1975	November 15, 1976.
Burton G. Malkiel	Member	July 22, 1975	January 20, 1977.
Charles L. Schultze	Chairman	January 22, 1977	January 20, 1981.
William D. Nordhaus	Member	March 18, 1977	February 4, 1979.
Lyle E. Gramley	Member	March 18, 1977	May 27, 1980.
George C. Eads	Member	June 6, 1979	January 20, 1981.
Stephen M. Goldfeld	Member	August 20, 1980	January 20, 1981.
Murray L. Weidenbaum	Chairman	February 27, 1981	August 25, 1982.
William A. Niskanen	Member	June 12, 1981	March 30, 1985.
Jerry L. Jordan	Member	July 14, 1981	July 31, 1982.
Martin Feldstein	Chairman	October 14, 1982	July 10, 1984.
William Poole	Member	December 10, 1982	January 20, 1985.
Beryl W. Sprinkel	Chairman	April 18, 1985	January 20, 1989.
Thomas Gale Moore	Member	July 1, 1985	May 1, 1989.
Michael L. Mussa	Member	August 18, 1986	September 19, 1988.
Michael J. Boskin	Chairman	February 2, 1989	January 12, 1993.
John B. Taylor	Member	June 9, 1989	August 2, 1991.
Richard L. Schmalensee	Member	October 3, 1989	June 21, 1991.
David F. Bradford	Member	November 13, 1991	January 20, 1993.
Paul Wonnacott	Member	November 13, 1991	January 20, 1993.
Alan S. Blinder	Member	July 27, 1993	June 26, 1994.
Laura D'Andrea Tyson	Chair	February 5, 1993	April 22, 1995.
Joseph E. Stiglitz	Member	July 27, 1993	
	Chairman	June 28, 1995	
Martin N. Baily	Member	June 30, 1995	
Alicia H. Munnell	Member	January 29, 1996	

Report to the President on the Activities of the Council of Economic Advisers During 1995

The Council of Economic Advisers was established by the Employment Act of 1946 to provide the President with objective economic analysis and advice on the development and implementation of a wide range of domestic and international economic policy issues.

The Chairman of the Council

Joseph E. Stiglitz, who had been a Member of the Council since 1993, was appointed Chairman on June 28, 1995. Dr. Stiglitz replaced Laura D'Andrea Tyson who was appointed Assistant to the President for Economic Policy at the National Economic Council. Dr. Stiglitz is on leave from Stanford University, where he is the Joan Kenney Professor of Economics. Dr. Stiglitz is responsible for communicating the Council's views on macro and microeconomic issues directly to the President through both oral and written briefings and reports. Dr. Stiglitz represents the Council at meetings of the National Economic Council and the National Security Council and at daily White House senior staff meetings. He also participates in a range of other formal and informal meetings with the President, senior White House staff, and other senior government officials. Finally, Dr. Stiglitz is the Council's chief public spokesperson. He guides the work of the Council and exercises ultimate responsibility for the work of the professional staff.

The Members of the Council

Martin N. Baily is a Member of the Council of Economic Advisers. Dr. Baily is on leave from the University of Maryland where he is Professor of Economics.

Alicia H. Munnell is also a Member of the Council of Economic Advisers. Dr. Munnell had previously served in the Administration as Assistant Secretary for Economic Policy at the Department of the Treasury and had served as Senior Vice President and Director of Research at the Federal Reserve Bank of Boston.

The Chairman and Members work as a team on most economic policy issues. There is, however, an informal division of subject matter among the Members. Dr. Baily and Dr. Munnell share responsibility for domestic macroeconomic analysis, the Administration's economic forecast, and budget and tax issues. Dr. Baily is responsible for international economic issues and certain microeconomic issues, including technology and agriculture. Dr. Munnell has primary responsibility for health care, welfare reform, environmental, and labor issues. Finally, all three Council Members participate in the deliberations of the National Economic Council (NEC). Dr. Stiglitz is one of six members of the NEC Principals Committee.

WEEKLY ECONOMIC BRIEFING

Dr. Stiglitz continued to conduct a weekly briefing for the President, the Vice President, and the President's other senior economic and policy advisers. Dr. Baily and Dr. Munnell also were active participants. The Council, in cooperation with the Office of the Vice President, prepares a written *Weekly Economic Briefing of the President*, which serves as the basis for the oral briefing. The briefing includes analysis of current economic developments, more extended treatments of a wide range of economic issues and problems, and summaries of economic news on different regions and sectors of the economy.

MACROECONOMIC POLICIES

One of the primary functions of the Council is to advise the President on all major macroeconomic issues and developments. The Council prepares for the President, the Vice President, and the White House senior staff a comprehensive series of memoranda monitoring key economic indicators and analyzing current macroeconomic events.

The Council, the Department of the Treasury, and the Office of Management and Budget—the economic "Troika" —are responsible for producing the economic forecasts that underlie the Administration's budget proposals. The Council, under the leadership of Drs. Baily and Munnell, initiates the forecasting process twice each year. The first forecast is included in the Federal budget document published in February and the second forecast is published in the summer as part of the Administration's Mid-Session Review. In preparing these forecasts, the Council consults with a wide variety of outside sources, including leading private sector forecasters.

In 1995, the Council spent a substantial amount of time on budget and tax issues. The Council participated in the preparation of the President's balanced budget proposal. The Council also participated extensively in meetings on a range of budget issues, including Medicare and Medicaid, discretionary spending priorities, the Administration's tax proposals, and the elimination of corporate subsidies and loopholes. In addition, the Council participated in consultations with the Congressional Budget Office (CBO) on the economic assumptions that were developed for the 7-year balanced budget plan.

The Council prepared, with the Department of Labor, a report titled "Educating America: An Investment for Our Future," which presented the overwhelming evidence on the beneficial impact of education on our workers and on our economy. The Council also prepared a report titled "Supporting Research and Development to Promote Economic Growth: The Federal Government's Role," which describes the Federal role in research and development (R&D) and the importance of R&D investments to economic growth. These reports presented the case for protecting our Federal Government's investments in education and technology.

The Council continued its efforts to improve the American public's understanding of economic issues and the Administration's economic agenda through regular briefings with the economic and financial press corps, periodic discussions with outside economists and forecasters, and presentations to outside organizations.

INTERNATIONAL ECONOMIC POLICIES

Because international trade and financial developments are increasingly important to the U.S. economy, they have played an important role in the Administration's foreign policy and economic agenda. The Council has been an active participant in the National Economic Council/National Security Council international economic policy process, providing both technical and analytical support and policy guidance. In 1995, the Council's role included policy development and planning for the G-7 Economic Summit in Halifax, the APEC leaders meeting in Osaka, the Denver Ministerial for the Hemispheric Initiative and the U.S.–EU Summit in December. The Council also participated at the policy and analytical level in preparation for trade negotiations, including those with Japan on autos and auto parts, and with China on market access and intellectual property.

The Council has focused on the impacts of international trade and financial developments on overall U.S. economic performance and on U.S. financial markets. The Council has used its expertise on developments in other countries to identify lessons, successes as well as failures, to be gleaned from policy initiatives undertaken elsewhere. The *Weekly Economic Briefing of the President* regularly includes articles on international events and issues. In addition, the Council, along with the Department of the Treasury, issued a white paper in November titled "U.S. Trade Policy with Japan: Assessing the Record."

Because of the increasing importance of international economic issues to the U.S. economy, the Council has increasingly been called upon to represent the United States at international meetings and other forums. Dr. Stiglitz was asked to give the keynote address at the U.S.-R.O.C. Economic Conference in Anchorage in September and participated in meetings of the Joint Economic Development Group with Israel in September.

The Council plays a leading role in U.S. participation in the Organization for Economic Cooperation and Development (OECD). The Council heads the U.S. delegation to the semiannual Economic Policy Committee meetings, and Dr. Stiglitz is the Committee's Chairman. In that role, Dr. Stiglitz has led an effort to refocus the Economic Policy Committee meetings and the OECD's Economics Department's activity in order to make their work more timely and relevant to member country policy discussions. Dr. Baily was a member of the OECD's Working Party 3 on macroeconomic policy coordination, and Dr. Munnell led the U.S. delegation for Working Party 1 on microeconomic and structural issues.

MICROECONOMIC POLICIES

The Council was an active participant on microeconomic policy issues in 1995. Dr. Stiglitz is a member of the Regulatory Working Group, which addresses numerous policy issues related to regulatory reform. Dr. Stiglitz was deeply involved in preparation of the new "best practice" guidelines for economic assessments of regulatory impacts, issued by the Office of Management and Budget. The Council also participated in a range of other Administration efforts to reform regulation.

The Council was an active participant in the Administration's "Reinventing Government" effort, which has made government agencies more efficient and more performance oriented, and has revised and eliminated thousands of pages of regulations. The Council was active in efforts to restructure government agencies and programs, such as the Federal Aviation Administration and the housing programs of the Department of Housing and Urban Development. The Council was also deeply involved in developing the Administration's pension simplification proposal, which will make it easier and less costly for employers—especially small businesses—to set up retirement plans that deliver tax-favored retirement benefits to all employees.

The Council was heavily involved in efforts to implement comprehensive and procompetitive reform of telecommunications policy. These efforts are reflected in the sweeping new telecommunications legislation passed by the Congress in early 1996. The Council also played an important role in ongoing efforts to restructure INTELSAT, an international satellite consortium, to promote more competition in the market for satellite communications services while preserving universal access to such services.

The Council was active in various issues affecting natural resources and the environment. The Council assisted the Vice President in developing a program for reinventing environmental regulation. As part of that effort, the Council helped to develop options for expanding the use of market-based policies for air pollution control. The Council was involved in addressing administrative and legislative changes to the Nation's programs for managing hazardous wastes and cleaning up contaminated sites. The Council also participated in ongoing assessments of policies for addressing climate change. The Council was actively involved in the preparation of the Administration's positions on reauthorization of the Farm Bill, and Dr. Baily chaired an interagency group responsible for developing options to fund land acquisition and restoration projects in the Everglades.

Dr. Stiglitz and Dr. Munnell played key roles in assessing the implications of welfare reform policy, including the consequences of block grants. They also participated in the Administration's efforts to anticipate the impact of welfare reform on child poverty rates. In addition, Dr. Munnell participated in working groups on urban policy and initiatives for children.

Dr. Baily co-chaired a group studying the state of our Nation's economic statistics. This effort was designed to improve the quality and understanding of government economic statistics.

The Staff of the Council of Economic Advisers

The professional staff of the Council consists of the Chief of Staff, the Senior Statistician, thirteen senior economists, six staff economists, and two research assistants. The professional staff and their areas of concentration at the end of 1995 were:

Chief of Staff and General Counsel

Michele M. Jolin

Senior Economists

S. Lael Brainard	International Economics
Steven N. Braun	Macroeconomics and Forecasting
Robert S. Dohner	International Economics
George B. Frisvold	Agriculture
Thomas J. Kane	Labor, Welfare, and Education
Eileen Mauskopf	Macroeconomics and Finance
Mark J. Mazur	Public Finance
Robert G. Murphy	Macroeconomics and the *Weekly Economic Briefing of the President*
Peter R. Orszag	International Economics
Raymond Prince	Environment and Natural Resources
Marius Schwartz	Regulation, Industrial Organization, and Antitrust
Louise M. Sheiner	Public Finance
Michael A. Toman	Environment and Natural Resources

Senior Statistician

Catherine H. Furlong

Staff Economists

Michael A. Ash .... Labor, Education, and Public Sector
Carrie S. Cihak .... International Economics
Jonah B. Gelbach .... Public Finance and the *Weekly Economic Briefing of the President*
Valerie A. Mercer .... Macroeconomics
Andrea Richter .... International Economics and the *Weekly Economic Briefing of the President*
Scott J. Wallsten .... Industrial Organization, Science & Technology, and Regulation

Research Assistant

Ronald C. Chen .... Macroeconomics and the *Weekly Economic Briefing of the President*

Statistical Office

Mrs. Furlong directs the Statistical Office. The Statistical Office maintains and updates the Council's statistical information, oversees the publication of the *Economic Indicators* and the statistical appendix to the *Economic Report*, and verifies statistics in Presidential and Council memoranda, testimony, and speeches.

Susan P. Clements .... Statistician and Information Systems
Linda A. Reilly .... Statistical Assistant
Brian A. Amorosi .... Research Assistant
Margaret L. Snyder .... Statistical Aide

The Administrative Office

Elizabeth A. Kaminski .... Administrative Officer
Catherine Fibich .... Administrative Assistant

Office of the Chairman

Alice H. Williams .... Executive Assistant to the Chairman
Sandra F. Daigle .... Executive Assistant to the Chairman and Assistant to the Chief of Staff
Lisa D. Branch .... Executive Assistant to Dr. Baily
Francine P. Obermiller .... Executive Assistant to Dr. Munnell

Staff Secretaries

Mary E. Jones
Rosalind V. Rasin
Mary A. Thomas

Mrs. Thomas also served as executive assistant for the *Weekly Economic Briefing of the President.*

Michael Treadway provided editorial assistance in the preparation of the 1995 *Economic Report*. Robert E. Cumby, Georgetown University, and David M. Cutler, Harvard University, served as consultants during the year. Student assistants during the year were Matthew W. Alsdorf, Stacy M. Bondanella, Christopher L. Boyster, Loren A. Briggs, Michele M. Campbell, William P. Cowin, David B. Edelstein, William B. Ferretti, Amy C. Fisher, Barbara J. Hawkins, Michael G. Rand, Michael D. Rosenbaum, Toby Stickler, Megan R. Sweeney, Gregory P. Wolf, and Ari Zweiman. The following student assistants joined the Council in January to assist with the preparation of the Economic Report: Joseph W. Corrigan, Jason Imfeld, Samuel Krasnow, Mary Lesh, Robert P. Martin, and Michael Pond.

DEPARTURES

Thomas P. O'Donnell, who served as Chief of Staff, resigned in April 1995 to accept a position as Chief of Staff at the National Economic Council.

The Council's senior economists, in most cases, are on leave of absence from faculty positions at academic institutions or from other government agencies or research institutions. Their tenure with the Council is usually limited to 1 or 2 years. Most of the senior economists who resigned during the year returned to their previous affiliations. They are Michael R. Donihue (Colby College), Robert D. Innes (University of Arizona), Sally M. Kane (National Oceans and Atmospheric Administration, Department of Commerce), David I. Levine (University of California, Berkeley), Ellen E. Meade (Board of Governors of the Federal Reserve System), Jay S. Stowsky (University of California), and David W. Wilcox (Board of Governors of the Federal Reserve System). Jonathan B. Baker went on to a new position at the Federal Trade Commission.

Staff economists are generally graduate students who spend 1 year with the Council and then return to complete their dissertations. Those who returned to their graduate studies in 1995 are: Kimberly A. Clausing (Harvard University), Maya N. Federman (Harvard University), Carolyn Fischer (University of Michigan), Christopher L. Foote (University of Michigan), F. Halsey Rogers (University of California, Berkeley and The Brookings Institution) and Eric D. Wolff (Massachusetts Institute of Technology). Clark Dees served for 2 years as a Research Assistant at the Council. He is now at the University of Virginia.

Public Information

The Council's Annual Report is the principal medium through which the Council informs the public of its work and its views. It is an important vehicle for presenting the Administration's domestic and international economic policies. Annual distribution of the Report in recent years has averaged about 45,000 copies. The Council also has primary responsibility for compiling the monthly *Economic Indicators,* which is issued by the Joint Economic Committee of the Congress and has a distribution of approximately 10,000.

Appendix B
STATISTICAL TABLES RELATING TO INCOME,
EMPLOYMENT, AND PRODUCTION

CONTENTS

275

General Notes

Detail in these tables may not add to totals because of rounding.
Unless otherwise noted, all dollar figures are in current dollars.
Symbols used:

    ᵖ Preliminary.

    .... Not available (also, not applicable).

Data in these tables reflect revisions made by the source agencies from January 1995 through early February 1996.

In particular, tables containing national income and product accounts (NIPA) estimates reflect the comprehensive revisions released by the Department of Commerce in early 1996. For information on the revisions, see Box 2–2 in Chapter 2 of this *Report*. For further details, see the January/February 1996 issue of the *Survey of Current Business*.

TABLE B–1.—*Gross domestic product, 1959–95*

[Billions of dollars, except as noted; quarterly data at seasonally adjusted annual rates]

Year or quarter	Gross domestic product	Personal consumption expenditures				Gross private domestic investment						Change in business inventories
		Total	Durable goods	Non-durable goods	Services	Total	Fixed investment					
							Total	Nonresidential			Residential	
								Total	Structures	Producers' durable equipment		
1959	507.2	318.1	42.7	148.5	127.0	78.8	74.6	46.5	18.1	28.3	28.1	4.2
1960	526.6	332.2	43.3	152.9	136.0	78.8	75.5	49.2	19.6	29.7	26.3	3.2
1961	544.8	342.6	41.8	156.6	144.3	77.9	75.0	48.6	19.7	28.9	26.4	2.9
1962	585.2	363.4	46.9	162.8	153.7	87.9	81.8	52.8	20.8	32.1	29.0	6.1
1963	617.4	383.0	51.6	168.2	163.2	93.4	87.7	55.6	21.2	34.4	32.1	5.7
1964	663.0	411.4	56.7	178.7	176.1	101.7	96.7	62.4	23.7	38.7	34.3	5.0
1965	719.1	444.3	63.3	191.6	189.4	118.0	108.3	74.1	28.3	45.8	34.2	9.7
1966	787.8	481.9	68.3	208.8	204.8	130.4	116.7	84.4	31.3	53.0	32.3	13.8
1967	833.6	509.5	70.4	217.1	222.0	128.0	117.6	85.2	31.5	53.7	32.4	10.5
1968	910.6	559.8	80.8	235.7	243.4	139.9	130.8	92.1	33.6	58.5	38.7	9.1
1969	982.2	604.7	85.9	253.2	265.5	155.0	145.5	102.9	37.7	65.2	42.6	9.5
1970	1,035.6	648.1	85.0	272.0	291.1	150.2	148.1	106.7	40.3	66.4	41.4	2.2
1971	1,125.4	702.5	96.9	285.5	320.1	176.0	167.5	111.7	42.7	69.1	55.8	8.5
1972	1,237.3	770.7	110.4	308.0	352.3	205.6	195.7	126.1	47.2	78.9	69.7	9.9
1973	1,382.6	851.6	123.5	343.1	384.9	242.9	225.4	150.0	55.0	95.1	75.3	17.5
1974	1,496.9	931.2	122.3	384.5	424.4	245.6	231.5	165.6	61.2	104.3	66.0	14.1
1975	1,630.6	1,029.1	133.5	420.6	475.0	225.4	231.7	169.0	61.4	107.6	62.7	−6.3
1976	1,819.0	1,148.8	158.9	458.2	531.8	286.6	269.6	187.2	65.9	121.2	82.5	16.9
1977	2,026.9	1,277.1	181.1	496.9	599.0	356.6	333.5	223.2	74.6	148.7	110.3	23.1
1978	2,291.4	1,428.8	201.4	549.9	677.4	430.8	403.6	272.0	91.4	180.6	131.6	27.2
1979	2,557.5	1,593.5	213.9	624.0	755.6	480.9	464.0	323.0	114.9	208.1	141.0	16.9
1980	2,784.2	1,760.4	213.5	695.5	851.4	465.9	473.5	350.3	133.9	216.4	123.2	−7.6
1981	3,115.9	1,941.3	230.5	758.2	952.6	556.2	528.1	405.4	164.6	240.9	122.6	28.2
1982	3,242.1	2,076.8	239.3	786.8	1,050.7	501.1	515.6	409.9	175.0	234.9	105.7	−14.5
1983	3,514.5	2,283.4	279.8	830.3	1,173.3	547.1	552.0	399.4	152.7	246.7	152.5	−4.9
1984	3,902.4	2,492.3	325.1	883.6	1,283.6	715.6	648.1	468.3	176.0	292.3	179.8	67.5
1985	4,180.7	2,704.8	361.1	927.6	1,416.1	715.1	688.9	502.0	193.3	308.7	186.9	26.2
1986	4,422.2	2,892.7	398.7	957.2	1,536.8	722.5	712.9	494.8	175.8	319.0	218.1	9.6
1987	4,692.3	3,094.5	416.7	1,014.0	1,663.8	747.2	722.9	495.4	172.1	323.3	227.6	24.2
1988	5,049.6	3,349.7	451.0	1,081.1	1,817.6	773.9	763.1	530.6	181.3	349.3	232.5	10.9
1989	5,438.7	3,594.8	472.8	1,163.8	1,958.1	829.2	797.5	566.2	192.3	373.9	231.3	31.7
1990	5,743.8	3,839.3	476.5	1,245.3	2,117.5	799.7	791.6	575.9	200.8	375.1	215.7	8.0
1991	5,916.7	3,975.1	455.2	1,277.6	2,242.3	736.2	738.5	547.3	181.7	365.6	191.2	−2.3
1992	6,244.4	4,219.8	488.5	1,321.8	2,409.4	790.4	783.4	557.9	169.2	388.7	225.6	7.0
1993	6,550.2	4,454.1	530.7	1,368.9	2,554.6	871.1	850.5	598.8	171.8	427.0	251.7	20.6
1994	6,931.4	4,698.7	580.9	1,429.7	2,688.1	1,014.4	954.9	667.2	180.2	487.0	287.7	59.5
1990: I	5,660.4	3,759.2	493.3	1,220.7	2,045.3	822.5	813.9	581.2	201.9	379.3	232.7	8.6
II	5,751.0	3,811.8	477.6	1,230.2	2,104.1	835.2	794.0	571.6	202.4	369.2	222.4	41.2
III	5,782.4	3,879.2	473.2	1,256.2	2,149.8	804.9	791.2	580.3	203.5	376.7	210.9	13.8
IV	5,781.5	3,907.0	461.9	1,274.1	2,171.0	736.1	767.5	570.6	195.4	375.1	196.9	−31.4
1991: I	5,822.1	3,910.7	449.0	1,268.3	2,193.5	723.6	739.7	555.4	192.3	363.1	184.3	−16.1
II	5,892.3	3,961.0	452.7	1,279.7	2,228.6	716.2	736.2	550.2	187.6	362.6	185.9	−19.9
III	5,950.0	4,001.6	462.0	1,283.4	2,256.3	743.9	738.6	543.3	176.1	368.2	194.3	5.3
IV	6,002.3	4,027.1	457.3	1,279.0	2,290.7	760.9	739.5	539.2	170.8	368.4	200.3	21.4
1992: I	6,121.8	4,127.6	474.1	1,303.1	2,350.4	755.2	755.4	544.1	171.6	372.5	211.3	−0.3
II	6,201.2	4,183.0	481.3	1,308.4	2,393.3	790.8	780.5	556.8	170.4	386.3	223.7	10.2
III	6,271.7	4,238.9	492.5	1,326.3	2,420.1	799.7	788.1	561.0	167.6	393.4	227.1	11.6
IV	6,383.0	4,329.6	506.2	1,349.5	2,473.9	816.1	809.7	569.6	167.1	402.5	240.1	6.4
1993: I	6,442.8	4,367.8	508.3	1,354.1	2,505.3	843.6	823.8	580.3	170.2	410.1	243.5	19.9
II	6,503.2	4,424.7	525.2	1,364.2	2,535.4	855.9	834.3	591.1	169.7	421.3	243.2	21.6
III	6,571.3	4,481.0	536.7	1,371.4	2,572.9	873.8	851.8	599.2	171.4	427.7	252.6	22.0
IV	6,683.7	4,543.0	552.3	1,386.1	2,604.6	911.2	892.3	624.6	175.8	448.8	267.7	18.8
1994: I	6,772.8	4,599.2	562.6	1,399.7	2,636.8	957.6	917.4	638.8	171.8	467.0	278.5	40.2
II	6,885.0	4,665.1	573.1	1,416.6	2,675.4	1,016.5	942.0	653.5	179.1	474.4	288.5	74.5
III	6,987.6	4,734.4	585.3	1,443.5	2,705.6	1,033.6	968.9	678.5	181.0	497.5	290.4	64.7
IV	7,080.0	4,796.0	602.7	1,459.0	2,734.4	1,050.1	991.4	697.9	188.8	509.1	293.5	58.7
1995: I	7,147.8	4,836.3	593.0	1,471.6	2,771.7	1,072.0	1,013.9	723.6	194.5	529.0	290.4	58.1
II	7,196.5	4,908.7	604.0	1,486.9	2,817.9	1,050.3	1,016.3	734.4	197.6	536.8	281.9	34.0
III	7,297.2	4,965.1	616.0	1,491.3	2,857.8	1,067.1	1,036.5	746.3	202.3	544.0	290.2	30.6

See next page for continuation of table.

[Billions of dollars, except as noted; quarterly data at seasonally adjusted annual rates]

Year or quarter	Net exports of goods and services			Government consumption expenditures and gross investment					Final sales of domestic product	Gross domestic purchases [1]	Adden-dum: Gross national product [2]	Percent change from preceding period	
	Net exports	Exports	Imports	Total	Federal			State and local				Gross domestic product	Gross domestic purchases [1]
					Total	National defense	Non-defense						
1959	-1.7	20.6	22.3	112.0	67.2	55.7	11.5	44.8	503.0	508.9	510.1		
1960	2.4	25.3	22.8	113.2	65.6	54.9	10.8	47.6	523.3	524.1	529.8	3.8	3.0
1961	3.4	26.0	22.7	120.9	69.1	57.7	11.4	51.8	541.9	541.5	548.4	3.5	3.3
1962	2.4	27.4	25.0	131.4	76.5	62.3	14.2	55.0	579.1	582.8	589.4	7.4	7.6
1963	3.3	29.4	26.1	137.7	78.1	62.2	15.9	59.6	611.7	614.1	621.9	5.5	5.4
1964	5.5	33.6	28.1	144.4	79.4	61.3	18.1	65.0	658.0	657.6	668.0	7.4	7.1
1965	3.9	35.4	31.5	153.0	81.8	62.0	19.7	71.2	709.4	715.3	724.5	8.5	8.8
1966	1.9	38.9	37.1	173.6	94.1	73.4	20.7	79.5	774.0	785.9	793.0	9.5	9.9
1967	1.4	41.4	39.9	194.6	106.6	85.5	21.0	88.1	823.1	832.2	839.1	5.8	5.9
1968	-1.3	45.3	46.6	212.1	113.8	92.0	21.8	98.3	901.4	911.8	916.7	9.2	9.6
1969	-1.2	49.3	50.5	223.8	115.8	92.4	23.4	108.0	972.7	983.4	988.4	7.9	7.8
1970	1.2	57.0	55.8	236.1	115.9	90.6	25.3	120.2	1,033.4	1,034.4	1,042.0	5.4	5.2
1971	-3.0	59.3	62.3	249.9	117.1	88.7	28.3	132.8	1,116.9	1,128.4	1,133.1	8.7	9.1
1972	-8.0	66.2	74.2	268.9	125.1	93.2	31.9	143.8	1,227.4	1,245.3	1,246.0	9.9	10.4
1973	.6	91.8	91.2	287.6	128.2	94.7	33.5	159.4	1,365.2	1,382.0	1,395.4	11.7	11.0
1974	-3.1	124.3	127.5	323.2	139.9	101.9	38.0	183.3	1,482.8	1,500.0	1,512.6	8.3	8.5
1975	13.6	136.3	122.7	362.6	154.5	110.9	43.6	208.1	1,636.9	1,617.1	1,643.9	8.9	7.8
1976	-2.3	148.9	151.1	385.9	162.7	116.1	46.6	223.1	1,802.0	1,821.2	1,836.1	11.5	12.6
1977	-23.7	158.8	182.4	416.9	178.4	125.8	52.6	238.5	2,003.8	2,050.5	2,047.5	11.4	12.6
1978	-26.1	186.1	212.3	457.9	194.4	135.6	58.9	263.4	2,264.2	2,317.5	2,313.5	13.0	13.0
1979	-24.0	228.7	252.7	507.1	215.0	151.2	63.8	292.0	2,540.6	2,581.5	2,590.4	11.6	11.4
1980	-14.9	278.9	293.8	572.8	248.4	174.2	74.2	324.4	2,791.9	2,799.1	2,819.5	8.9	8.4
1981	-15.0	302.8	317.8	633.4	284.1	202.0	82.2	349.2	3,087.8	3,130.9	3,150.6	11.9	11.9
1982	-20.5	282.6	303.2	684.8	313.2	230.9	82.3	371.6	3,256.6	3,262.6	3,273.2	4.1	4.2
1983	-51.7	277.0	328.6	735.7	344.5	255.0	89.4	391.2	3,519.4	3,566.2	3,546.5	8.4	9.3
1984	-102.0	303.1	405.1	796.6	372.6	282.7	89.9	424.0	3,835.0	4,004.5	3,933.5	11.0	12.3
1985	-114.2	303.0	417.2	875.0	410.1	312.4	97.7	464.9	4,154.5	4,294.9	4,201.0	7.1	7.3
1986	-131.5	320.7	452.2	938.5	435.2	332.4	102.9	503.3	4,412.6	4,553.7	4,435.1	5.8	6.0
1987	-142.1	365.7	507.9	992.8	455.7	350.4	105.3	537.2	4,668.1	4,834.5	4,701.3	6.1	6.2
1988	-106.1	447.2	553.2	1,032.0	457.3	354.0	103.3	574.7	5,038.7	5,155.6	5,062.6	7.6	6.6
1989	-80.4	509.3	589.7	1,095.1	477.2	360.6	116.7	617.9	5,407.0	5,519.1	5,452.8	7.7	7.0
1990	-71.3	557.3	628.6	1,176.1	503.6	373.1	130.4	672.6	5,735.8	5,815.1	5,764.9	5.6	5.4
1991	-20.5	601.8	622.3	1,225.9	522.6	383.5	139.1	703.4	5,919.0	5,937.2	5,932.4	3.0	2.1
1992	-29.5	639.4	669.0	1,263.8	528.0	375.8	152.2	735.8	6,237.4	6,274.0	6,255.5	5.5	5.7
1993	-64.9	660.0	724.9	1,289.9	522.1	362.2	159.9	767.8	6,529.7	6,615.2	6,560.0	4.9	5.4
1994	-96.4	722.0	818.4	1,314.7	516.3	352.0	164.3	798.4	6,871.8	7,027.8	6,922.4	5.8	6.2
1990: I	-74.3	541.6	615.9	1,153.0	496.4	369.7	126.7	656.6	5,651.8	5,734.7	5,681.4	9.1	8.8
II	-60.3	554.8	615.1	1,164.3	500.1	370.6	129.5	664.2	5,709.8	5,811.3	5,767.8	6.6	5.5
III	-78.5	555.5	634.1	1,176.9	501.2	368.9	132.3	675.7	5,768.7	5,861.0	5,796.8	2.2	3.5
IV	-72.0	577.3	649.2	1,210.4	516.7	383.3	133.3	693.7	5,812.9	5,853.5	5,813.6	-.1	-.5
1991: I	-32.9	577.4	610.3	1,220.6	525.6	389.7	136.0	695.0	5,838.2	5,855.0	5,849.0	2.8	.1
II	-12.3	602.7	615.0	1,227.4	528.2	389.3	138.9	699.2	5,912.2	5,904.6	5,904.5	4.9	3.4
III	-22.0	602.6	624.5	1,226.5	520.9	382.1	138.8	705.5	5,944.7	5,972.0	5,959.4	4.0	4.6
IV	-14.8	624.4	639.3	1,229.2	515.5	373.0	142.6	713.6	5,980.9	6,017.1	6,016.6	3.6	3.1
1992: I	-8.9	632.4	641.3	1,247.9	521.8	372.8	149.0	726.1	6,122.1	6,130.7	6,138.3	8.2	7.8
II	-29.0	635.9	664.9	1,256.4	523.2	374.1	149.1	733.2	6,191.0	6,230.2	6,212.2	5.3	6.7
III	-37.6	640.2	677.8	1,270.7	532.0	380.9	151.1	738.7	6,260.1	6,309.3	6,281.1	4.6	5.2
IV	-42.7	649.1	691.8	1,280.0	535.0	375.3	159.7	745.1	6,376.6	6,425.7	6,390.5	7.3	7.6
1993: I	-47.4	649.4	696.8	1,278.8	525.0	365.2	159.8	753.8	6,422.9	6,490.1	6,458.4	3.8	4.1
II	-62.0	662.5	724.6	1,284.6	519.6	362.2	157.4	765.0	6,481.6	6,565.2	6,512.3	3.8	4.7
III	-77.1	648.5	725.6	1,293.6	520.8	360.7	160.1	772.7	6,549.3	6,648.4	6,584.8	4.3	5.2
IV	-73.2	679.4	752.6	1,302.7	522.9	360.8	162.2	779.7	6,664.9	6,756.9	6,684.5	7.0	6.7
1994: I	-80.3	681.5	761.7	1,296.4	511.3	346.7	164.6	785.0	6,732.6	6,853.1	6,773.6	5.4	5.8
II	-97.4	708.6	806.0	1,300.8	509.4	349.3	160.0	791.4	6,810.5	6,982.5	6,876.3	6.8	7.8
III	-108.4	734.2	842.6	1,328.0	523.6	362.1	161.5	804.4	6,922.9	7,096.0	6,977.6	6.1	6.7
IV	-99.7	763.6	863.3	1,333.5	520.9	349.6	171.2	812.6	7,021.3	7,179.6	7,062.2	5.4	4.8
1995: I	-106.6	778.6	885.1	1,346.0	519.9	347.7	172.1	826.1	7,089.7	7,254.5	7,140.5	3.9	4.2
II	-122.4	796.9	919.3	1,359.9	522.6	352.3	170.3	837.3	7,162.5	7,318.9	7,187.0	2.8	3.6
III	-100.6	813.2	913.7	1,365.5	517.3	346.2	171.1	848.2	7,266.6	7,397.7	7,281.3	5.7	4.4

[1] Gross domestic product (GDP) less exports of goods and services plus imports of goods and services.
[2] GDP plus net receipts of factor income from rest of the world.
Source: Department of Commerce, Bureau of Economic Analysis.

281

[Billions of chained (1992) dollars, except as noted; quarterly data at seasonally adjusted annual rates]

Year or quarter	Gross domestic product	Personal consumption expenditures				Gross private domestic investment							Change in business inventories
							Fixed investment						
		Total	Durable goods	Non-durable goods	Services	Total	Total	Nonresidential				Residential	
								Total	Total	Structures	Producers' durable equipment		
1959	2,212.3	1,394.6	103.1	606.3	687.4	274.2	267.1	147.7	85.8	71.4	131.1		13.5
1960	2,261.7	1,432.6	105.2	615.4	717.4	270.5	269.2	155.9	92.6	74.3	121.8		10.6
1961	2,309.8	1,461.5	101.2	626.7	746.5	265.2	267.9	154.5	93.9	72.5	122.2		8.9
1962	2,449.1	1,533.8	113.0	646.5	783.4	298.5	292.0	168.0	98.1	81.0	133.9		20.0
1963	2,554.0	1,596.6	124.0	660.0	818.7	318.1	313.7	176.4	99.2	87.1	149.6		18.1
1964	2,702.9	1,692.3	135.5	692.5	868.4	344.6	343.7	197.1	109.5	98.1	158.3		15.6
1965	2,874.8	1,799.1	152.6	729.3	914.6	392.5	378.5	231.3	126.9	115.9	153.7		30.2
1966	3,060.2	1,902.0	165.5	769.2	961.0	423.5	399.1	259.4	135.6	133.8	140.0		42.3
1967	3,140.2	1,958.6	168.1	781.4	1,007.6	406.9	391.0	255.3	132.2	132.5	135.6		32.1
1968	3,288.6	2,070.2	186.6	816.9	1,059.6	429.8	418.1	266.4	134.1	140.5	154.0		26.9
1969	3,388.0	2,147.5	193.3	838.6	1,110.8	454.4	442.9	285.6	141.3	152.2	158.6		27.2
1970	3,388.2	2,197.8	187.0	859.1	1,155.4	419.5	432.1	282.8	141.7	149.5	149.1		5.7
1971	3,500.1	2,279.5	205.7	874.5	1,197.9	467.4	464.9	282.4	139.4	150.7	190.0		22.7
1972	3,690.3	2,415.9	231.9	912.9	1,262.5	522.1	520.3	307.7	143.7	169.8	223.7		25.2
1973	3,902.3	2,532.6	255.8	942.9	1,319.4	583.5	567.5	352.5	155.4	201.2	222.3		39.0
1974	3,888.2	2,514.7	238.2	924.5	1,351.2	544.4	530.2	354.4	152.2	205.4	176.4		24.0
1975	3,865.1	2,570.0	238.1	938.3	1,398.3	440.5	471.0	317.3	136.2	183.9	153.5		−11.0
1976	4,081.1	2,714.3	268.5	984.8	1,457.1	536.6	517.6	332.6	139.6	195.2	189.7		29.0
1977	4,279.3	2,829.8	293.4	1,010.4	1,518.2	627.1	593.7	371.8	146.4	225.6	229.8		38.0
1978	4,493.7	2,951.6	308.8	1,045.7	1,589.3	686.0	660.8	422.6	162.3	259.6	245.0		42.3
1979	4,624.0	3,020.2	307.3	1,069.7	1,639.8	704.5	695.6	463.3	182.7	280.7	236.0		23.1
1980	4,611.9	3,009.7	282.6	1,065.1	1,670.7	626.2	648.4	461.1	195.0	268.2	186.1		−10.0
1981	4,724.9	3,046.4	285.8	1,074.3	1,696.1	689.7	660.6	485.7	210.4	278.2	171.2		33.1
1982	4,623.6	3,081.5	285.5	1,080.6	1,728.2	590.4	610.4	464.3	207.2	260.3	140.1		−15.6
1983	4,810.0	3,240.6	327.4	1,112.4	1,809.0	647.8	654.2	456.4	185.7	272.4	197.6		−5.9
1984	5,138.2	3,407.6	374.9	1,151.8	1,883.0	831.6	762.4	535.4	212.2	324.6	226.4		74.8
1985	5,329.5	3,566.5	411.4	1,178.3	1,977.3	829.2	799.3	568.4	227.8	342.4	229.5		29.8
1986	5,489.9	3,708.7	448.4	1,215.9	2,041.4	813.8	805.0	548.5	203.3	345.9	257.0		10.9
1987	5,648.4	3,822.3	454.9	1,239.3	2,126.9	820.5	799.4	542.4	195.9	346.9	257.6		26.2
1988	5,862.9	3,972.7	483.5	1,274.4	2,212.4	826.0	818.3	566.0	196.8	369.2	252.5		11.6
1989	6,060.4	4,064.6	496.2	1,303.5	2,262.3	861.9	832.0	588.8	201.2	387.6	243.2		33.3
1990	6,138.7	4,132.2	493.3	1,316.1	2,321.3	817.3	805.8	585.2	203.3	381.9	220.6		10.4
1991	6,079.0	4,105.8	462.0	1,302.9	2,341.0	737.7	741.3	547.7	181.6	366.2	193.4		−3.0
1992	6,244.4	4,219.8	488.5	1,321.8	2,409.4	790.4	783.4	557.9	169.2	388.7	225.6		7.3
1993	6,383.8	4,339.7	524.1	1,348.9	2,466.8	857.3	836.4	593.6	166.3	427.2	242.7		19.1
1994	6,604.2	4,471.1	562.0	1,390.5	2,519.4	979.6	921.1	652.1	168.8	484.1	268.9		58.9
1990: I	6,154.1	4,128.9	511.2	1,319.2	2,295.7	844.1	834.7	595.3	206.5	388.8	239.4		11.0
II	6,174.4	4,134.7	495.4	1,316.9	2,321.1	856.1	811.2	583.4	205.5	377.8	227.8		43.8
III	6,145.2	4,148.5	490.4	1,319.8	2,337.3	820.8	803.1	588.1	205.2	383.0	214.9		14.9
IV	6,081.0	4,116.4	476.3	1,308.4	2,331.2	748.1	774.4	573.9	196.0	377.9	200.3		−28.2
1991: I	6,047.9	4,084.5	458.6	1,300.6	2,325.3	725.5	742.6	555.1	192.2	362.9	187.4		−17.5
II	6,074.1	4,110.0	460.5	1,308.0	2,341.5	718.0	739.4	550.9	187.2	363.8	188.3		−20.8
III	6,089.3	4,119.5	467.3	1,307.1	2,345.0	744.9	741.0	545.3	175.5	369.8	195.6		4.9
IV	6,104.4	4,109.1	461.5	1,295.7	2,352.0	762.4	742.0	539.5	171.4	368.1	202.4		21.4
1992: I	6,175.3	4,173.8	476.1	1,314.4	2,383.2	757.9	758.3	544.4	172.7	371.7	213.9		−.1
II	6,214.2	4,196.4	481.1	1,312.0	2,403.2	792.8	782.4	557.5	171.0	386.4	224.9		11.3
III	6,260.9	4,226.7	491.9	1,321.1	2,413.6	798.6	787.3	560.6	167.4	393.1	226.7		12.1
IV	6,327.3	4,282.3	505.0	1,339.8	2,437.6	812.4	805.8	569.1	165.6	403.5	236.7		5.8
1993: I	6,327.0	4,290.0	506.0	1,336.9	2,447.0	834.8	815.4	577.5	167.0	410.5	237.9		18.5
II	6,353.7	4,319.0	519.6	1,344.7	2,454.9	843.2	821.1	586.4	164.8	421.7	234.8		20.8
III	6,390.4	4,359.7	528.9	1,354.2	2,476.7	857.6	835.4	593.1	165.1	428.2	242.2		19.5
IV	6,463.9	4,390.0	541.9	1,359.8	2,488.6	893.4	873.5	617.6	168.2	449.8	255.8		17.4
1994: I	6,504.6	4,418.8	549.6	1,372.7	2,497.0	933.5	892.4	628.6	163.0	466.5	263.6		40.1
II	6,581.5	4,457.7	555.4	1,383.7	2,519.0	984.6	911.4	639.5	169.0	471.2	271.6		74.1
III	6,639.5	4,485.8	563.0	1,397.2	2,526.3	994.1	930.8	660.4	169.1	492.4	270.3		64.0
IV	6,691.3	4,522.3	579.9	1,408.4	2,535.1	1,006.3	949.7	679.7	174.3	506.4	270.3		57.3
1995: I	6,701.6	4,530.9	566.9	1,416.8	2,548.1	1,024.2	969.6	704.4	178.5	527.1	265.9		54.5
II	6,709.4	4,568.8	576.6	1,423.5	2,569.6	998.3	966.1	710.6	180.0	531.9	256.6		30.6
III	6,763.2	4,601.1	589.8	1,425.3	2,586.9	1,008.9	980.6	719.8	182.4	538.6	261.8		27.1

See next page for continuation of table.

TABLE B-2.—*Real gross domestic product, 1959-95*—Continued

[Billions of chained (1992) dollars, except as noted; quarterly data at seasonally adjusted annual rates]

Year or quarter	Net exports of goods and services			Government consumption expenditures and gross investment						Final sales of domestic product	Gross domestic purchases [1]	Addendum: Gross national product [2]	Percent change from preceding period	
					Federal								Gross domestic product	Gross domestic purchases [1]
	Net exports	Exports	Imports	Total	Total	National defense	Non-defense	State and local						
1959	-34.8	71.9	106.6	618.5	360.5	307.6	58.8	256.8	2,206.9	2,270.4	2,224.3		
1960	-21.3	86.8	108.1	617.2	349.4	301.3	54.1	267.2	2,264.2	2.303.1	2,274.8	2.2	1.4
1961	-19.1	88.3	107.3	647.2	363.0	313.8	55.5	283.8	2,318.0	2,349.7	2,324.6	2.1	2.0
1962	-26.5	93.0	119.5	686.0	393.2	332.4	66.8	292.1	2,445.4	2,497.4	2,465.9	6.0	6.3
1963	-22.7	100.0	122.7	701.9	391.8	324.0	72.9	309.7	2,552.4	2,598.9	2,572.0	4.3	4.1
1964	-15.9	113.3	129.2	715.9	385.2	309.9	79.2	330.9	2,705.1	2,740.5	2,722.3	5.8	5.4
1965	-27.4	115.6	143.0	737.6	385.2	303.8	84.6	353.2	2,860.4	2,925.9	2,895.2	6.4	6.8
1966	-40.9	123.4	164.2	804.6	429.1	348.2	85.7	375.9	3,033.5	3,124.9	3,078.9	6.4	6.8
1967	-50.1	126.1	176.2	865.6	471.7	393.5	84.7	394.2	3,125.1	3,214.2	3,159.4	2.6	2.9
1968	-67.2	135.3	202.5	892.4	476.3	400.9	82.5	416.5	3,278.0	3,377.4	3,309.2	4.7	5.1
1969	-71.3	142.7	214.0	887.5	459.9	381.6	84.3	428.0	3,377.2	3,480.1	3,407.8	3.0	3.0
1970	-65.0	158.1	223.1	866.8	427.2	349.0	83.0	440.0	3,406.5	3,469.1	3,407.7	.0	-.3
1971	-75.8	159.2	235.0	851.0	397.0	313.7	86.3	454.4	3,499.8	3,592.5	3,522.2	3.3	3.6
1972	-88.9	172.0	261.0	854.1	390.2	300.3	91.9	464.5	3,689.5	3,794.0	3,714.3	5.4	5.6
1973	-63.0	209.6	272.6	848.4	371.1	281.2	91.5	478.5	3,883.9	3,975.2	3,936.0	5.7	4.8
1974	-35.6	229.8	265.3	862.9	368.8	273.5	96.4	495.6	3,873.4	3,925.7	3,927.1	-.4	-1.2
1975	-7.2	228.2	235.4	876.3	367.9	269.7	99.1	510.0	3,906.4	3,867.2	3,894.5	-.6	-1.5
1976	-39.9	241.6	281.5	876.8	364.3	264.7	100.4	514.3	4,061.7	4,122.9	4,116.9	5.6	6.6
1977	-64.2	247.4	311.6	884.7	370.1	266.4	104.3	516.4	4,240.8	4,351.5	4,320.2	4.9	5.5
1978	-65.6	273.1	338.6	910.6	377.7	266.7	111.4	534.7	4,464.4	4,565.7	4,534.4	5.0	4.9
1979	-45.3	299.0	344.3	924.9	383.3	271.0	112.7	543.5	4,614.4	4,668.2	4,680.8	2.9	2.2
1980	10.1	331.4	321.3	941.4	399.3	280.7	119.0	543.6	4,641.9	4,578.6	4,667.7	-.3	-1.9
1981	5.6	335.3	329.7	947.7	415.9	296.0	120.4	532.8	4,691.6	4,697.3	4,774.1	2.5	2.6
1982	-14.1	311.4	325.5	960.1	429.4	316.5	113.3	531.4	4,651.2	4,622.7	4,665.4	-2.1	-1.6
1983	-63.3	303.3	366.6	987.3	452.7	334.6	118.5	534.9	4,821.2	4,870.7	4,851.2	4.0	5.4
1984	-127.3	328.4	455.7	1,018.4	463.7	348.1	115.9	555.0	5,061.6	5,274.4	5,176.1	6.8	8.3
1985	-147.9	337.3	485.2	1,080.1	495.6	374.1	121.8	584.7	5,296.9	5,488.8	5,352.7	3.7	4.1
1986	-163.9	362.2	526.1	1,135.0	518.4	393.4	125.2	616.9	5,480.9	5,666.1	5,503.4	3.0	3.2
1987	-156.2	402.0	558.2	1,165.9	534.4	409.2	125.3	631.8	5,626.0	5,815.7	5,657.2	2.9	2.6
1988	-114.4	465.8	580.2	1,180.9	524.6	405.5	119.1	656.6	5,855.1	5,983.9	6,074.0	3.8	2.9
1989	-82.7	520.2	603.0	1,213.9	531.5	401.6	130.1	682.6	6,028.7	6,146.1	6,074.0	3.4	2.7
1990	-61.9	564.4	626.3	1,250.4	541.9	401.5	140.5	708.6	6,126.7	6,202.1	6,159.4	1.3	.9
1991	-22.3	599.9	622.2	1,258.0	539.4	397.5	142.0	718.7	6,082.6	6,101.1	6,094.4	-1.0	-1.6
1992	-29.5	639.4	669.0	1,263.8	528.0	375.8	152.2	735.8	6,237.4	6,274.0	6,255.5	2.7	2.8
1993	-74.4	660.6	735.0	1,260.5	508.7	354.9	153.8	751.8	6,362.9	6,457.3	6,393.7	2.2	2.9
1994	-108.1	715.1	823.3	1,259.9	489.7	336.9	152.6	770.5	6,546.3	6,709.7	6,596.6	3.5	3.9
1990: I	-67.1	555.2	622.3	1,246.5	542.9	404.1	138.9	703.8	6,144.6	6,222.9	6,174.3	4.1	3.2
II	-66.7	566.8	633.5	1,248.2	543.0	402.8	140.4	705.4	6,127.5	6,242.9	6,190.8	1.3	1.3
III	-71.2	561.8	633.0	1,246.8	538.2	396.1	142.2	708.7	6,126.6	6,218.4	6,158.8	-1.9	-1.6
IV	-42.5	573.9	616.4	1,259.9	543.5	403.1	140.5	716.5	6,108.1	6,124.3	6,113.4	-4.1	-5.9
1991: I	-24.3	572.3	596.6	1,262.6	547.3	408.4	139.0	715.5	6,065.4	6,072.2	6,074.8	-2.2	-3.4
II	-17.1	600.3	617.4	1,263.8	547.1	405.0	142.2	716.8	6,095.9	6,091.1	6,085.8	1.7	1.2
III	-29.8	603.6	633.4	1,255.1	536.3	395.0	141.4	718.8	6,085.4	6,119.1	6,098.3	1.0	1.9
IV	-17.9	623.5	641.4	1,250.7	526.9	381.7	145.3	723.8	6,083.8	6,122.3	6,118.7	1.0	.2
1992: I	-14.8	633.0	647.8	1,258.5	525.1	374.2	150.8	733.5	6,175.8	6,190.0	6,191.6	4.7	4.5
II	-32.5	635.8	668.3	1,257.5	523.3	373.3	150.0	734.2	6,203.8	6,246.8	6,225.1	2.5	3.7
III	-30.8	639.7	670.5	1,266.5	529.6	378.7	150.9	736.9	6,249.5	6,291.9	6,270.4	3.0	2.9
IV	-40.0	649.1	689.1	1,272.5	534.0	376.8	157.1	738.5	6,320.7	6,367.3	6,334.8	4.3	4.9
1993: I	-55.2	649.8	705.1	1,257.2	515.7	361.2	154.5	741.6	6,307.7	6,382.0	6,342.7	.0	.9
II	-67.0	662.3	729.4	1,257.9	509.2	356.4	152.7	748.8	6,331.6	6,420.2	6,362.9	1.7	2.4
III	-89.1	648.9	738.1	1,261.1	505.4	351.2	154.2	755.7	6,368.2	6,478.3	6,404.0	2.3	3.7
IV	-86.2	681.4	767.6	1,265.7	504.5	350.8	153.7	761.3	6,444.1	6,548.7	6,465.1	4.7	4.4
1994: I	-101.3	680.4	781.7	1,252.3	489.8	334.8	154.8	762.7	6,464.0	6,603.9	6,506.2	2.5	3.4
II	-112.2	704.3	816.5	1,249.7	483.3	335.5	147.7	766.8	6,509.0	6,691.0	6,573.9	4.8	5.4
III	-113.3	724.8	838.1	1,271.0	496.6	346.1	150.5	774.7	6,576.8	6,749.7	6,631.1	3.6	3.6
IV	-105.8	751.0	856.8	1,266.6	489.1	331.3	157.5	777.7	6,635.2	6,794.0	6,675.4	3.2	2.7
1995: I	-119.0	755.8	874.9	1,263.0	481.3	325.3	155.6	782.2	6,647.5	6,816.9	6,695.7	.6	1.4
II	-126.8	764.3	891.2	1,265.8	479.9	326.1	153.6	786.3	6,677.4	6,832.0	6,701.2	.5	.9
III	-114.1	779.7	893.9	1,264.4	473.2	319.8	153.1	791.7	6,735.0	6,873.6	6,749.5	3.2	2.5

[1] Gross domestic product (GDP) less exports of goods and services plus imports of goods and services.
[2] GDP plus net receipts of factor income from rest of the world.
Source: Department of Commerce, Bureau of Economic Analysis.

283

TABLE B–3.—*Chain-type price indexes for gross domestic product, 1959–95*

[Index numbers, 1992=100, except as noted; quarterly data seasonally adjusted]

Year or quarter	Gross domestic product	Personal consumption expenditures				Gross private domestic investment					
						Total	Fixed investment				
								Nonresidential			
		Total	Durable goods	Nondurable goods	Services		Total	Total	Structures	Producers' durable equipment	Residential
1959	23.0	22.8	41.4	24.5	18.5	29.6	27.9	31.5	21.2	39.7	21.4
1960	23.3	23.2	41.2	24.8	19.0	29.7	28.1	31.6	21.1	40.0	21.6
1961	23.6	23.4	41.3	25.0	19.3	29.7	28.0	31.5	21.0	39.9	21.6
1962	23.9	23.7	41.5	25.2	19.6	29.7	28.0	31.5	21.2	39.7	21.6
1963	24.2	24.0	41.6	25.5	19.9	29.6	28.0	31.5	21.4	39.5	21.5
1964	24.6	24.3	41.8	25.8	20.3	29.8	28.1	31.7	21.7	39.5	21.6
1965	25.0	24.7	41.4	26.3	20.7	30.2	28.6	32.1	22.3	39.6	22.3
1966	25.7	25.3	41.3	27.1	21.3	30.8	29.2	32.5	23.1	39.7	23.1
1967	26.6	26.0	41.9	27.8	22.0	31.6	30.1	33.4	23.8	40.6	23.9
1968	27.7	27.0	43.3	28.9	23.0	32.8	31.3	34.6	25.0	41.7	25.1
1969	29.0	28.2	44.5	30.2	23.9	34.4	32.9	36.0	26.7	42.9	26.9
1970	30.6	29.5	45.4	31.7	25.2	35.8	34.3	37.8	28.4	44.5	27.7
1971	32.1	30.8	47.1	32.6	26.7	37.6	36.0	39.6	30.6	45.9	29.4
1972	33.5	31.9	47.6	33.7	27.9	39.3	37.6	41.0	32.8	46.5	31.1
1973	35.4	33.6	48.3	36.4	29.2	41.3	39.7	42.6	35.4	47.3	33.9
1974	38.5	37.0	51.3	41.6	31.4	45.3	43.7	46.8	40.2	50.9	37.4
1975	42.2	40.0	56.0	44.8	34.0	51.0	49.2	53.3	45.0	58.6	40.9
1976	44.6	42.3	59.2	46.5	36.5	53.8	52.1	56.3	47.2	62.2	43.5
1977	47.5	45.1	61.7	49.2	39.5	57.5	56.2	60.0	50.9	65.9	48.0
1978	50.9	48.4	65.2	52.6	42.6	62.4	61.1	64.4	56.3	69.6	53.7
1979	55.3	52.8	69.6	58.3	46.1	68.0	66.7	69.7	62.9	74.1	59.7
1980	60.4	58.5	75.6	65.3	51.0	74.5	73.0	76.0	68.7	80.7	66.2
1981	66.1	63.7	80.6	70.6	56.2	81.4	79.9	83.5	78.2	86.6	71.6
1982	70.2	67.4	83.8	72.8	60.8	85.6	84.5	88.3	84.4	90.2	75.5
1983	73.2	70.5	85.5	74.6	64.9	85.4	84.4	87.5	82.2	90.6	77.2
1984	75.9	73.1	86.7	76.7	68.2	86.0	85.0	87.5	82.9	90.0	79.4
1985	78.6	75.8	87.8	78.7	71.6	87.0	86.2	88.3	84.9	90.1	81.5
1986	80.6	78.0	88.9	78.7	75.3	89.0	88.6	90.2	86.5	92.2	84.9
1987	83.1	81.0	91.6	81.8	78.2	91.0	90.4	91.3	87.9	93.2	88.3
1988	86.1	84.3	93.3	84.8	82.2	93.5	93.2	93.7	92.1	94.6	92.1
1989	89.7	88.4	95.3	89.3	86.6	96.1	95.9	96.2	95.6	96.4	95.1
1990	93.6	92.9	96.6	94.6	91.2	98.4	98.2	98.4	98.8	98.2	97.8
1991	97.3	96.8	98.5	98.1	95.8	99.7	99.6	99.9	100.1	99.8	98.8
1992	100.0	100.0	100.0	100.0	100.0	100.0	100.0	100.0	100.0	100.0	100.0
1993	102.6	102.6	101.3	101.5	103.6	101.7	101.7	100.9	103.3	99.9	103.7
1994	105.0	105.1	103.4	102.8	106.7	103.6	103.7	102.3	106.7	100.6	107.0
1990: I	92.0	91.0	96.5	92.6	89.1	97.6	97.5	97.6	97.8	97.5	97.2
II	93.2	92.2	96.4	93.4	90.7	98.0	97.9	98.0	98.5	97.7	97.6
III	94.2	93.5	96.5	95.2	92.0	98.6	98.5	98.7	99.2	98.4	98.1
IV	95.1	94.9	96.9	97.4	93.1	99.3	99.1	99.4	99.7	99.3	98.3
1991: I	96.3	95.7	97.9	97.5	94.3	99.7	99.6	100.1	100.1	100.1	98.4
II	97.0	96.4	98.4	97.8	95.2	99.7	99.6	99.9	100.2	99.8	98.7
III	97.7	97.1	98.8	98.2	96.2	99.7	99.7	99.8	100.4	99.5	99.3
IV	98.3	98.0	99.1	98.7	97.4	99.7	99.6	99.9	99.7	99.9	99.0
1992: I	99.1	98.9	99.6	99.2	98.6	99.6	99.6	99.9	99.3	100.2	98.8
II	99.8	99.7	100.1	99.7	99.6	99.8	99.8	99.9	99.7	100.0	99.5
III	100.2	100.3	100.1	100.4	100.3	100.1	100.1	100.1	100.1	100.1	100.2
IV	100.9	101.1	100.2	100.7	101.5	100.5	100.5	100.1	100.9	99.8	101.5
1993: I	101.8	101.8	100.5	101.3	102.4	101.0	101.0	100.5	101.9	99.9	102.3
II	102.4	102.5	101.1	101.5	103.3	101.6	101.6	100.8	103.0	99.9	103.6
III	102.8	102.8	101.5	101.3	103.9	101.9	102.0	101.0	103.8	99.9	104.3
IV	103.4	103.5	101.9	101.9	104.7	102.1	102.2	101.1	104.6	99.8	104.7
1994: I	104.1	104.1	102.4	102.0	105.6	102.8	102.8	101.6	105.5	100.1	105.7
II	104.6	104.7	103.2	102.4	106.2	103.3	103.4	102.2	106.0	100.7	106.2
III	105.2	105.5	104.0	103.3	107.1	104.0	104.1	102.8	107.1	101.1	107.4
IV	105.8	106.1	103.9	103.9	107.9	104.4	104.4	102.7	108.4	100.6	108.6
1995: I	106.7	106.8	104.7	103.9	108.8	104.6	104.6	102.8	109.0	100.4	109.2
II	107.3	107.5	104.9	104.5	109.7	105.4	105.3	103.5	109.8	101.1	109.9
III	108.0	108.0	104.8	104.7	110.5	106.1	106.0	104.0	110.8	101.4	110.9

See next page for continuation of table.

[Index numbers, 1992=100, except as noted; quarterly data seasonally adjusted]

Year or quarter	Exports and imports of goods and services		Government consumption expenditures and gross investment					Final sales of domestic product	Gross domestic purchases[1]		Gross national product	Percent change[2]		
				Federal									Gross domestic purchases	
	Exports	Imports	Total	Total	National defense	Nondefense	State and local		Total	Less food and energy		Gross domestic product	Total	Less food and energy
1959	28.7	20.9	18.1	18.6	18.1	19.5	17.4	22.8	22.5	....	23.0	....	....	....
1960	29.1	21.1	18.3	18.8	18.2	19.8	17.8	23.1	22.8		23.4	1.4	1.4	....
1961	29.5	21.1	18.7	19.0	18.4	20.5	18.2	23.4	23.1		23.6	1.2	1.1	....
1962	29.5	20.9	19.1	19.4	18.7	21.1	18.8	23.7	23.4		23.9	1.3	1.2	....
1963	29.4	21.3	19.6	19.9	19.2	21.7	19.3	24.0	23.7		24.2	1.2	1.3	....
1964	29.6	21.7	20.2	20.6	19.8	22.8	19.6	24.3	24.0		24.6	1.5	1.5	....
1965	30.6	22.1	20.7	21.2	20.4	23.2	20.2	24.8	24.5		25.0	1.9	1.8	....
1966	31.6	22.6	21.6	21.9	21.1	24.0	21.1	25.5	25.1		25.8	2.8	2.8	....
1967	32.8	22.7	22.5	22.6	21.7	24.7	22.3	26.3	25.9		26.6	3.2	3.0	....
1968	33.5	23.0	23.7	23.8	22.9	26.3	23.6	27.5	27.0		27.7	4.4	4.3	....
1969	34.5	23.6	25.2	25.1	24.2	27.7	25.2	28.8	28.3		29.0	4.7	4.7	....
1970	36.0	25.0	27.2	27.1	25.9	30.3	27.3	30.3	29.8		30.6	5.3	5.4	....
1971	37.3	26.5	29.3	29.4	28.2	32.7	29.2	31.9	31.4		32.2	5.2	5.3	....
1972	38.5	28.4	31.5	32.0	31.0	34.5	31.0	33.3	32.8		33.5	4.2	4.5	....
1973	43.8	33.4	33.9	34.5	33.7	36.5	33.3	35.1	34.7		35.4	5.6	5.8	....
1974	54.1	48.0	37.4	37.9	37.2	39.3	37.0	38.3	38.2		38.5	8.9	10.2	....
1975	59.7	52.1	41.4	41.9	41.1	43.8	40.8	41.9	41.8		42.2	9.4	9.3	....
1976	61.6	53.7	44.0	44.6	43.9	46.3	43.4	44.4	44.2		44.6	5.8	5.8	....
1977	64.2	58.5	47.1	48.2	47.2	50.3	46.2	47.2	47.2		47.5	6.4	6.8	....
1978	68.2	62.7	50.3	51.5	50.8	52.8	49.3	50.7	50.7		51.0	7.3	7.4	....
1979	76.5	73.4	54.8	56.1	55.8	56.6	53.7	55.1	55.3		55.3	8.5	9.0	....
1980	84.2	91.4	60.9	62.2	62.0	62.3	59.7	60.1	61.1		60.4	9.3	10.7	....
1981	90.3	96.4	66.8	68.3	68.2	68.3	65.6	65.8	66.8		66.1	9.4	9.2	....
1982	90.8	93.1	71.3	72.9	73.0	72.6	69.9	70.0	70.7	69.0	70.2	6.3	5.9	....
1983	91.3	89.6	74.5	76.1	76.2	75.4	73.2	73.0	73.3	72.0	73.2	4.2	3.8	4.3
1984	92.3	88.9	78.2	80.4	81.2	77.5	76.4	75.8	75.9	74.6	76.0	3.8	3.5	3.7
1985	89.8	86.0	81.0	82.7	83.5	80.2	79.5	78.4	78.4	77.3	78.6	3.4	3.2	3.5
1986	88.5	86.0	82.7	84.0	84.5	82.2	81.6	80.5	80.4	80.1	80.6	2.6	2.6	3.6
1987	91.0	91.0	85.2	85.3	85.6	84.0	85.0	83.0	83.1	82.9	83.1	3.1	3.4	3.5
1988	96.0	95.3	87.4	87.2	87.3	86.7	87.5	86.1	86.1	86.1	86.1	3.7	3.6	3.9
1989	97.9	97.8	90.2	89.8	89.8	89.7	90.5	89.7	89.8	89.6	89.8	4.2	4.2	4.0
1990	98.7	100.4	94.1	92.9	92.9	92.8	94.9	93.6	93.8	93.3	93.7	4.4	4.5	4.2
1991	100.3	100.0	97.4	96.9	96.5	97.9	97.9	97.3	97.3	97.0	97.3	3.9	3.7	3.9
1992	100.0	100.0	100.0	100.0	100.0	100.0	100.0	100.0	100.0	100.0	100.0	2.8	2.8	3.1
1993	99.9	98.6	102.3	102.6	102.1	104.0	102.1	102.6	102.5	102.6	102.6	2.6	2.5	2.6
1994	101.0	99.4	104.3	105.4	104.5	107.7	103.6	105.0	104.8	105.0	104.9	2.3	2.2	2.4
1990: I	97.5	98.8	92.5	91.4	91.5	91.2	93.3	92.0	92.2	91.8	92.1	4.9	5.4	4.4
II	97.9	97.1	93.3	92.1	92.1	92.3	94.2	93.2	93.1	92.9	93.2	5.2	4.2	4.9
III	98.9	100.0	94.4	93.1	93.1	93.0	95.3	94.2	94.3	93.9	94.2	4.3	5.2	4.3
IV	100.6	105.6	96.1	95.0	95.0	94.9	96.8	95.1	95.7	94.9	95.2	4.1	5.9	4.3
1991: I	100.9	102.2	96.6	95.9	95.4	97.5	97.1	96.2	96.4	95.9	96.3	4.8	3.1	4.4
II	100.5	99.7	97.2	96.6	96.1	97.9	97.6	97.0	97.0	96.6	97.0	3.2	2.2	3.0
III	99.8	98.5	97.7	97.1	96.7	98.3	98.2	97.7	97.6	97.4	97.7	2.8	2.6	3.2
IV	100.1	99.6	98.3	97.8	97.7	98.2	98.6	98.3	98.3	98.1	98.3	2.5	2.9	3.1
1992: I	99.9	99.0	99.2	99.4	99.6	98.8	99.0	99.1	99.0	99.0	99.1	3.4	3.2	3.8
II	100.1	99.6	99.9	100.0	100.2	99.5	99.9	99.8	99.8	99.8	99.8	2.8	2.9	2.9
III	100.1	101.0	100.3	100.4	100.6	100.1	100.2	100.2	100.3	100.3	100.2	1.5	2.1	2.0
IV	100.0	100.4	100.6	100.2	99.6	101.6	100.9	100.9	100.9	100.9	100.9	2.8	2.6	2.8
1993: I	99.9	98.8	101.7	101.8	101.1	103.4	101.7	101.8	101.7	101.8	101.8	3.8	3.1	3.5
II	100.1	99.4	102.1	102.0	101.6	103.1	101.3	102.2	102.4	102.3	102.4	2.2	2.4	2.4
III	99.9	98.3	102.6	103.0	102.7	103.8	102.3	102.8	102.6	102.9	102.8	1.8	1.3	1.8
IV	99.7	98.0	102.9	103.2	102.9	105.6	102.4	103.4	103.2	103.4	103.4	2.3	2.2	2.1
1994: I	100.1	97.4	103.5	104.4	103.5	106.3	102.9	104.2	103.8	104.1	104.1	2.8	2.3	2.7
II	100.6	98.7	104.1	105.4	104.1	108.3	103.2	104.6	104.4	104.7	104.6	1.9	2.3	2.5
III	101.3	100.6	104.5	105.4	104.7	107.4	103.8	105.3	105.1	105.4	105.2	2.4	3.0	2.5
IV	101.8	100.9	105.3	106.5	105.6	108.7	104.5	105.8	105.7	106.0	105.8	2.2	2.1	2.2
1995: I	103.2	101.4	106.6	108.2	107.1	110.7	105.6	106.7	106.5	106.8	106.7	3.3	2.9	3.1
II	104.6	103.6	107.5	109.0	108.2	110.9	106.5	107.3	107.2	107.5	107.3	2.5	2.9	2.8
III	104.8	103.0	108.1	109.5	108.5	111.8	107.1	108.0	107.8	108.2	108.0	2.4	2.0	2.4

[1] Gross domestic product (GDP) less exports of goods and services plus imports of goods and services.
[2] Percent change from preceding period; quarterly changes are at annual ratres.
Source: Department of Commerce, Bureau of Economic Analysis.

285

TABLE B-4.—*Quantity and price indexes for gross domestic product, and percent changes, 1959-95*

[Quarterly data are seasonally adjusted]

Year or quarter	Gross domestic product							
	Index numbers, 1992=100				Percent change from preceding period [1]			
	Current dollars	Chain-type quantity index	Chain-type price index	Implicit price deflator	Current dollars	Chain-type quantity index	Chain-type price index	Implicit price deflator
1959	8.1	35.4	23.0	22.9				
1960	8.4	36.2	23.3	23.3	3.8	2.2	1.4	1.5
1961	8.7	37.0	23.6	23.6	3.5	2.1	1.2	1.3
1962	9.4	39.2	23.9	23.9	7.4	6.0	1.3	1.3
1963	9.9	40.9	24.2	24.2	5.5	4.3	1.2	1.2
1964	10.6	43.3	24.6	24.5	7.4	5.8	1.5	1.5
1965	11.5	46.0	25.0	25.0	8.5	6.4	1.9	2.0
1966	12.6	49.0	25.7	25.7	9.5	6.4	2.8	2.9
1967	13.3	50.3	26.6	26.5	5.8	2.6	3.2	3.1
1968	14.6	52.7	27.7	27.7	9.2	4.7	4.4	4.3
1969	15.7	54.3	29.0	29.0	7.9	3.0	4.7	4.7
1970	16.6	54.3	30.6	30.6	5.4	.0	5.3	5.4
1971	18.0	56.1	32.1	32.2	8.7	3.3	5.2	5.2
1972	19.8	59.1	33.5	33.5	9.9	5.4	4.2	4.3
1973	22.1	62.5	35.4	35.4	11.7	5.7	5.6	5.7
1974	24.0	62.3	38.5	38.5	8.3	-.4	8.9	8.7
1975	26.1	61.9	42.2	42.2	8.9	-.6	9.4	9.6
1976	29.1	65.4	44.6	44.6	11.5	5.6	5.8	5.6
1977	32.5	68.5	47.5	47.4	11.4	4.9	6.4	6.3
1978	36.7	72.0	50.9	51.0	13.0	5.0	7.3	7.7
1979	41.0	74.1	55.3	55.3	11.6	2.9	8.5	8.5
1980	44.6	73.9	60.4	60.4	8.9	-.3	9.3	9.2
1981	49.9	75.7	66.1	65.9	11.9	2.5	9.4	9.2
1982	51.9	74.0	70.2	70.1	4.1	-2.1	6.3	6.3
1983	56.3	77.0	73.2	73.1	8.4	4.0	4.2	4.2
1984	62.5	82.3	75.9	75.9	11.0	6.8	3.8	3.9
1985	67.0	85.3	78.6	78.4	7.1	3.7	3.4	3.3
1986	70.8	87.9	80.6	80.6	5.8	3.0	2.6	2.7
1987	75.1	90.5	83.1	83.1	6.1	2.9	3.1	3.1
1988	80.9	93.9	86.1	86.1	7.6	3.8	3.7	3.7
1989	87.1	97.1	89.7	89.7	7.7	3.4	4.2	4.2
1990	92.0	98.3	93.6	93.6	5.6	1.3	4.4	4.3
1991	94.8	97.3	97.3	97.3	3.0	-1.0	3.9	4.0
1992	100.0	100.0	100.0	100.0	5.5	2.7	2.8	2.7
1993	104.9	102.2	102.6	102.6	4.9	2.2	2.6	2.6
1994	111.0	105.8	105.0	105.0	5.8	3.5	2.3	2.3
1990: I	90.6	98.6	92.0	92.0	9.1	4.1	4.9	4.9
II	92.1	98.9	93.2	93.1	6.6	1.3	5.2	5.2
III	92.6	98.4	94.2	94.1	2.2	-1.9	4.3	4.2
IV	92.6	97.4	95.1	95.1	-.1	-4.1	4.1	4.2
1991: I	93.2	96.9	96.3	96.3	2.8	-2.2	4.8	5.1
II	94.4	97.3	97.0	97.0	4.9	1.7	3.2	3.1
III	95.3	97.5	97.7	97.7	4.0	1.0	2.8	2.9
IV	96.1	97.8	98.3	98.3	3.6	1.0	2.5	2.5
1992: I	98.0	98.9	99.1	99.1	8.2	4.7	3.4	3.3
II	99.3	99.5	99.8	99.8	5.3	2.5	2.8	2.7
III	100.4	100.3	100.2	100.2	4.6	3.0	1.5	1.5
IV	102.2	101.3	100.9	100.9	7.3	4.3	2.8	2.9
1993: I	103.2	101.3	101.8	101.8	3.8	.0	3.8	3.8
II	104.1	101.7	102.4	102.4	3.8	1.7	2.2	2.1
III	105.2	102.3	102.8	102.8	4.3	2.3	1.8	1.9
IV	107.0	103.5	103.4	103.4	7.0	4.7	2.3	2.2
1994: I	108.5	104.2	104.1	104.1	5.4	2.5	2.8	2.8
II	110.3	105.4	104.6	104.6	6.8	4.8	1.9	1.9
III	111.9	106.3	105.2	105.2	6.1	3.6	2.4	2.4
IV	113.4	107.2	105.8	105.8	5.4	3.2	2.2	2.2
1995: I	114.5	107.3	106.7	106.7	3.9	.6	3.3	3.2
II	115.2	107.4	107.3	107.3	2.8	.5	2.5	2.3
III	116.9	108.3	108.0	107.9	5.7	3.2	2.4	2.4

[1] Percent changes shown here are calculated using unrounded data. Quarterly percent changes are at annual rates.

Source: Department of Commerce, Bureau of Economic Analysis.

286

TABLE B–5.—*Percent changes in real gross domestic product, 1960–95*

[Percent change from preceding period; quarterly data at seasonally adjusted annual rates]

Year or quarter	Gross domestic product	Personal consumption expenditures				Gross private domestic investment				Exports and imports of goods and services		Government consumption expenditures and gross investment		
						Nonresidential fixed								
		Total	Durable goods	Nondurable goods	Services	Total	Structures	Producers' durable equipment	Residential	Exports	Imports	Total	Federal	State and local
1960	2.2	2.7	2.0	1.5	4.4	5.6	7.9	4.1	-7.1	20.8	1.3	-0.2	-3.1	4.1
1961	2.1	2.0	-3.8	1.8	4.1	-.9	1.4	-2.4	.3	1.7	-.7	4.9	3.9	6.2
1962	6.0	4.9	11.7	3.1	4.9	8.7	4.5	11.6	9.6	5.4	11.3	6.0	8.3	2.9
1963	4.3	4.1	9.7	2.1	4.5	5.0	1.1	7.6	11.8	7.5	2.7	2.3	-.4	6.0
1964	5.8	6.0	9.2	4.9	6.1	11.8	10.4	12.6	5.8	13.3	5.3	2.0	-1.7	6.8
1965	6.4	6.3	12.7	5.3	5.3	17.3	15.9	18.2	-2.9	2.0	10.6	3.0	.0	6.7
1966	6.4	5.7	8.5	5.5	5.1	12.1	6.8	15.5	-8.9	6.7	14.9	9.1	11.4	6.4
1967	2.6	3.0	1.6	1.6	4.8	-1.6	-2.5	-1.0	-3.1	2.2	7.3	7.6	9.9	4.9
1968	4.7	5.7	11.0	4.5	5.2	4.3	1.4	6.1	13.6	7.3	14.9	3.1	1.0	5.7
1969	3.0	3.7	3.6	2.7	4.8	7.2	5.4	8.3	3.0	5.5	5.7	-.6	-3.4	2.8
1970	.0	2.3	-3.2	2.4	4.0	-1.0	.3	-1.8	-6.0	10.8	4.3	-2.3	-7.1	2.8
1971	3.3	3.7	10.0	1.8	3.7	-.1	-1.6	.8	27.4	.7	5.3	-1.8	-7.1	3.3
1972	5.4	6.0	12.7	4.4	5.4	9.0	3.1	12.7	17.8	8.1	11.0	.4	-1.7	2.2
1973	5.7	4.8	10.3	3.3	4.5	14.6	8.2	18.5	-.6	21.8	4.5	-.7	-4.9	3.0
1974	-.4	-.7	-6.9	-2.0	2.4	.5	-2.1	2.1	-20.6	9.6	-2.7	1.7	-.6	3.6
1975	-.6	2.2	.0	1.5	3.5	-10.5	-10.5	-10.5	-13.0	-.7	-11.3	1.5	-.2	2.9
1976	5.6	5.6	12.8	5.0	4.2	4.8	2.5	6.1	23.6	5.9	19.6	.1	-1.0	.8
1977	4.9	4.3	9.3	2.6	4.2	11.8	4.9	15.6	21.2	2.4	10.7	.9	1.6	.4
1978	5.0	4.3	5.3	3.5	4.7	13.7	10.9	15.1	6.6	10.4	8.7	2.9	2.1	3.6
1979	2.9	2.3	-.5	2.3	3.2	9.6	12.6	8.1	-3.7	9.5	1.7	1.6	1.5	1.6
1980	-.3	-.3	-8.0	-.4	1.9	-.5	6.7	-4.4	-21.1	10.8	-6.7	1.8	4.2	.0
1981	2.5	1.2	1.2	.9	1.5	5.3	7.9	3.7	-8.0	1.2	2.6	.7	4.2	-2.0
1982	-2.1	1.2	-.1	.6	1.9	-4.4	-1.5	-6.4	-18.2	-7.1	-1.3	1.3	3.2	-.3
1983	4.0	5.2	14.7	2.9	4.7	-1.7	-10.4	4.6	41.1	-2.6	12.6	2.8	5.4	.7
1984	6.8	5.2	14.5	3.5	4.1	17.3	14.3	19.2	14.6	8.3	24.3	3.1	2.4	3.8
1985	3.7	4.7	9.7	2.3	5.0	6.2	7.3	5.5	1.4	2.7	6.5	6.1	6.9	5.3
1986	3.0	4.0	9.0	3.2	3.2	-3.5	-10.8	1.0	12.0	7.4	8.4	5.1	4.6	5.5
1987	2.9	3.1	1.5	1.9	4.2	-1.1	-3.6	.3	.2	11.0	6.1	2.7	3.1	2.4
1988	3.8	3.9	6.3	2.8	4.0	4.4	.5	6.4	-2.0	15.9	3.9	1.3	-1.8	3.9
1989	3.4	2.3	2.6	2.3	2.3	4.0	2.2	5.0	-3.7	11.7	3.9	2.8	1.3	4.0
1990	1.3	1.7	-.6	1.0	2.6	-.6	1.1	-1.5	-9.3	8.5	3.9	3.0	2.0	3.8
1991	-1.0	-.6	-6.44	-1.0	.8	-6.4	-10.7	-4.1	-12.3	6.3	-.7	.6	-.5	1.4
1992	2.7	2.8	5.8	1.5	2.9	1.9	-6.8	6.2	16.6	6.6	7.5	.5	-2.1	2.4
1993	2.2	2.8	7.3	2.0	2.4	6.4	-1.7	10.0	7.6	3.3	9.9	-.3	-3.7	2.2
1994	3.5	3.0	7.2	3.1	2.1	9.8	1.5	13.2	10.8	8.3	12.0	.0	-3.7	2.5
1990: I	4.1	3.4	16.3	1.3	1.7	4.5	6.8	3.3	5.9	15.5	5.9	6.0	6.1	6.0
II	1.3	.6	-11.8	-.7	4.5	-7.8	-1.9	-10.8	-18.0	8.6	7.4	.5	.1	.9
III	-1.9	1.3	-4.0	.9	2.8	3.3	-.7	5.5	-20.8	-3.5	-.3	-.4	-3.5	1.9
IV	-4.1	-3.1	-11.0	-3.4	-1.0	-9.3	-16.6	-5.2	-24.5	8.9	-10.1	4.3	4.0	4.5
1991: I	-2.2	-3.1	-14.1	-2.4	-1.0	-12.5	-7.7	-14.9	-23.4	-1.1	-12.2	.9	2.8	-.6
II	1.7	2.5	1.7	2.3	2.8	-3.0	-10.0	.9	2.0	21.0	14.7	.4	-.1	.7
III	1.0	.9	6.1	-.3	.6	-4.0	-22.7	6.8	16.4	2.3	10.8	-2.7	-7.7	1.2
IV	1.0	-1.0	-4.9	-3.4	1.2	-4.1	-8.9	-1.8	14.7	13.8	5.1	-1.4	-6.8	2.8
1992: I	4.7	6.4	13.3	5.9	5.4	3.6	2.9	3.9	24.7	6.3	4.1	2.5	-1.4	5.4
II	2.5	2.2	4.3	-.7	3.4	10.0	-3.9	16.9	22.2	1.8	13.3	-.3	-1.4	.4
III	3.0	2.9	9.3	2.8	1.7	2.2	-8.1	7.1	3.3	2.5	1.3	2.9	4.9	1.4
IV	4.3	5.4	11.0	5.8	4.0	6.2	-4.3	11.0	18.7	6.0	11.6	1.9	3.4	.9
1993: I	.0	.7	.8	-.9	1.6	6.0	3.5	7.1	2.1	.4	9.6	-4.7	-13.1	1.7
II	1.7	2.7	11.2	2.3	1.3	6.3	-5.3	11.4	-5.1	7.9	14.5	.2	-4.9	3.9
III	2.3	3.8	7.3	2.9	3.6	4.7	.8	6.3	13.2	-7.9	4.9	1.0	-2.9	3.8
IV	4.7	2.8	10.2	1.7	1.9	17.5	7.5	21.7	24.3	21.5	17.0	1.5	-.7	3.0
1994: I	2.5	2.6	5.8	3.8	1.4	7.3	-11.8	15.6	12.8	-.6	7.5	-4.2	-11.1	.7
II	4.8	3.6	4.3	3.3	3.6	7.1	15.7	4.1	12.7	14.8	19.1	-.8	-5.3	2.2
III	3.6	2.5	5.6	4.0	1.2	13.7	-.2	19.3	-1.8	12.2	11.0	7.0	11.5	4.2
IV	3.2	3.3	12.6	3.2	1.4	12.2	13.0	11.9	-.1	15.3	9.3	-1.4	-5.9	1.6
1995: I	.6	.8	-8.7	2.4	2.1	15.3	9.9	17.4	-6.3	2.6	8.7	-1.1	-6.3	2.3
II	.5	3.4	7.0	1.9	3.4	3.6	3.4	3.7	-13.3	4.6	7.7	.9	-1.1	2.1
III	3.2	2.9	9.5	.5	2.7	5.3	5.6	5.2	8.4	8.3	1.2	-.4	-5.5	2.8

Source: Department of Commerce, Bureau of Economic Analysis.

287

TABLE B–6.—*Gross domestic product by major type of product, 1959–95*

[Billions of dollars; quarterly data at seasonally adjusted annual rates]

| Year or quarter | Gross domestic product | Final sales of domestic product | Change in business inventories | Goods [1] | | | | | | | Services [1] | Structures |
| | | | | Total | | | Durable goods | | Nondurable goods | | | |
				Total	Final sales	Change in business inventories	Final sales	Change in business inventories	Final sales	Change in business inventories		
1959	507.2	503.0	4.2	252.0	247.8	4.2	92.3	3.1	155.5	1.1	192.7	62.5
1960	526.6	523.3	3.2	257.8	254.6	3.2	95.1	1.7	159.5	1.6	206.8	61.9
1961	544.8	541.9	2.9	260.4	257.5	2.9	94.3	-.1	163.2	3.0	220.8	63.6
1962	585.2	579.1	6.1	281.2	275.1	6.1	104.5	3.4	170.7	2.7	236.1	67.8
1963	617.4	611.7	5.7	292.7	287.1	5.7	111.0	2.7	176.1	3.0	252.0	72.7
1964	663.0	658.0	5.0	313.2	308.1	5.0	120.5	4.0	187.6	1.0	271.4	78.4
1965	719.1	709.4	9.7	342.9	333.3	9.7	133.3	6.7	199.9	3.0	291.5	84.7
1966	787.8	774.0	13.8	380.6	366.8	13.8	149.0	10.2	217.8	3.6	319.2	88.0
1967	833.6	823.1	10.5	394.5	384.0	10.5	153.8	5.5	230.2	5.0	349.5	89.6
1968	910.6	901.4	9.1	426.7	417.6	9.1	167.8	4.6	249.8	4.5	383.9	100.0
1969	982.2	972.7	9.5	455.8	446.2	9.5	178.6	6.3	267.6	3.2	418.2	108.3
1970	1,035.6	1,033.4	2.2	467.5	465.3	2.2	180.2	.0	285.1	2.2	458.5	109.7
1971	1,125.4	1,116.9	8.5	493.2	484.7	8.5	187.0	3.2	297.7	5.3	503.8	128.4
1972	1,237.3	1,227.4	9.9	539.8	529.9	9.9	209.3	7.2	320.6	2.7	550.5	146.9
1973	1,382.6	1,365.2	17.5	619.2	601.8	17.5	241.4	14.6	360.3	2.9	600.5	162.9
1974	1,496.9	1,482.8	14.1	665.7	651.6	14.1	256.7	11.0	394.9	3.1	665.6	165.6
1975	1,630.6	1,636.9	-6.3	718.1	724.5	-6.3	288.1	-7.5	436.4	1.2	745.8	166.7
1976	1,819.0	1,802.0	16.9	804.0	787.1	16.9	322.5	10.6	464.6	6.3	823.8	191.2
1977	2,026.9	2,003.8	23.1	883.7	860.6	23.1	366.9	10.2	493.7	12.8	916.4	226.8
1978	2,291.4	2,264.2	27.2	996.5	969.3	27.2	416.9	20.3	552.5	6.9	1,023.1	271.8
1979	2,557.5	2,540.6	16.9	1,115.2	1,098.3	16.9	475.0	12.5	623.3	4.3	1,131.7	310.6
1980	2,784.2	2,791.9	-7.6	1,191.1	1,198.7	-7.6	502.9	-2.7	695.8	-4.9	1,274.1	319.1
1981	3,115.9	3,087.8	28.2	1,342.6	1,314.5	28.2	546.0	7.5	768.4	20.6	1,423.3	350.0
1982	3,242.1	3,256.6	-14.5	1,333.2	1,347.7	-14.5	544.4	-15.5	803.3	1.0	1,566.9	342.0
1983	3,514.5	3,519.4	-4.9	1,426.9	1,431.8	-4.9	586.1	4.0	845.7	-8.9	1,720.9	366.8
1984	3,902.4	3,835.0	67.5	1,607.0	1,539.6	67.5	655.1	43.6	884.5	23.9	1,871.8	423.6
1985	4,180.7	4,154.5	26.2	1,669.8	1,643.6	26.2	713.2	8.6	930.4	17.6	2,054.6	456.3
1986	4,422.2	4,412.6	9.6	1,720.6	1,711.0	9.6	741.3	.6	969.7	9.0	2,224.2	477.4
1987	4,692.3	4,668.1	24.2	1,804.8	1,780.6	24.2	764.7	21.5	1,015.9	2.8	2,398.1	489.3
1988	5,049.6	5,038.7	10.9	1,942.9	1,932.0	10.9	837.0	16.4	1,095.0	-5.5	2,600.0	506.7
1989	5,438.7	5,407.0	31.7	2,124.0	2,092.3	31.7	907.3	21.3	1,185.0	10.5	2,795.3	519.4
1990	5,743.8	5,735.8	8.0	2,203.8	2,195.8	8.0	935.7	2.5	1,260.1	5.6	3,016.9	523.1
1991	5,916.7	5,919.0	-2.3	2,234.0	2,236.3	-2.3	926.6	-16.6	1,309.7	14.3	3,201.3	481.4
1992	6,244.4	6,237.4	7.0	2,321.0	2,314.0	7.0	965.9	-10.9	1,348.1	17.9	3,411.1	512.3
1993	6,550.2	6,529.7	20.6	2,421.5	2,400.9	20.6	1,013.8	15.7	1,387.2	4.9	3,581.7	547.0
1994	6,931.4	6,871.8	59.5	2,593.8	2,534.2	59.5	1,085.9	31.9	1,448.3	27.6	3,742.3	595.3
1990: I	5,660.4	5,651.8	8.6	2,194.9	2,186.3	8.6	957.9	1.4	1,228.4	7.2	2,924.9	540.6
II	5,751.0	5,709.8	41.2	2,223.6	2,182.4	41.2	932.7	16.9	1,249.7	24.3	2,997.8	529.6
III	5,782.4	5,768.7	13.8	2,210.7	2,196.9	13.8	929.3	9.9	1,267.7	3.9	3,051.3	520.5
IV	5,781.5	5,812.9	-31.4	2,186.1	2,217.5	-31.4	922.9	-18.4	1,294.6	-13.1	3,093.7	501.7
1991: I	5,822.1	5,838.2	-16.1	2,207.9	2,224.0	-16.1	912.1	-38.7	1,311.8	22.6	3,131.6	482.6
II	5,892.3	5,912.2	-19.9	2,225.1	2,245.0	-19.9	936.0	-29.5	1,309.0	9.5	3,186.7	480.5
III	5,950.0	5,944.7	5.3	2,249.2	2,243.9	5.3	933.6	5.9	1,310.3	-.6	3,221.9	478.9
IV	6,002.3	5,980.9	21.4	2,253.8	2,232.4	21.4	924.8	-4.2	1,307.6	25.5	3,264.9	483.6
1992: I	6,121.8	6,122.1	-.3	2,281.1	2,281.4	-.3	944.6	-18.8	1,336.8	18.5	3,338.4	502.3
II	6,201.2	6,191.0	10.2	2,301.3	2,291.0	10.2	955.7	1.1	1,335.4	9.1	3,387.5	512.4
III	6,271.7	6,260.1	11.6	2,329.4	2,317.8	11.6	969.2	-11.1	1,348.6	22.7	3,432.1	510.1
IV	6,383.0	6,376.6	6.4	2,372.2	2,365.8	6.4	994.2	-14.9	1,371.6	21.3	3,486.4	524.4
1993: I	6,442.8	6,422.9	19.9	2,382.7	2,362.8	19.9	986.4	13.1	1,376.5	6.8	3,528.5	531.5
II	6,503.2	6,481.6	21.6	2,412.9	2,391.3	21.6	1,014.1	11.3	1,377.1	10.3	3,555.0	535.4
III	6,571.3	6,549.3	22.0	2,416.5	2,394.5	22.0	1,007.9	14.2	1,386.5	7.9	3,605.3	549.5
IV	6,683.7	6,664.9	18.8	2,474.0	2,455.1	18.8	1,046.6	24.3	1,408.5	-5.5	3,638.1	571.6
1994: I	6,772.8	6,732.6	40.2	2,524.4	2,484.2	40.2	1,062.6	25.1	1,421.6	15.1	3,673.8	574.7
II	6,885.0	6,810.5	74.5	2,572.9	2,498.3	74.5	1,067.9	35.1	1,430.4	39.5	3,720.3	591.9
III	6,987.6	6,922.9	64.7	2,618.2	2,553.5	64.7	1,099.9	34.2	1,453.6	30.5	3,769.0	600.5
IV	7,080.0	7,021.3	58.7	2,659.6	2,600.9	58.7	1,113.3	33.1	1,487.6	25.6	3,806.3	614.1
1995: I	7,147.8	7,089.7	58.1	2,675.4	2,617.3	58.1	1,118.6	54.4	1,498.7	3.7	3,852.6	619.8
II	7,196.5	7,162.5	34.0	2,676.3	2,642.3	34.0	1,134.0	28.5	1,508.3	5.4	3,904.5	615.7
III	7,297.2	7,266.6	30.6	2,715.6	2,685.0	30.6	1,162.6	25.5	1,522.5	5.1	3,949.1	632.4

[1] Exports and imports of certain goods, primarily military equipment purchased and sold by the Federal Government, are included in services.

Source: Department of Commerce, Bureau of Economic Analysis.

TABLE B–7.—*Real gross domestic product by major type of product, 1959–95*

[Billions of chained (1992) dollars; quarterly data at seasonally adjusted annual rates]

Year or quarter	Gross domestic product	Final sales of domestic product	Change in business inventories	Goods [1]							Services [1]	Structures
				Total			Durable goods		Nondurable goods			
				Total	Final sales	Change in business inventories	Final sales	Change in business inventories	Final sales	Change in business inventories		
1959	2,212.3	2,206.9	13.5	786.4	780.9	13.5	221.1	9.9	595.6	3.5	1,115.3	299.4
1960	2,261.7	2,264.2	10.6	795.6	795.6	10.6	227.3	5.2	602.6	5.3	1,167.1	296.5
1961	2,309.8	2,318.0	8.9	796.0	799.7	8.9	224.3	-.1	612.1	9.3	1,219.9	304.7
1962	2,449.1	2,445.4	20.0	853.5	848.6	20.0	247.7	10.7	634.7	9.1	1,277.5	322.2
1963	2,554.0	2,552.4	18.1	882.4	878.8	18.1	262.0	8.3	648.2	9.8	1,336.9	343.9
1964	2,702.9	2,705.1	15.6	936.7	935.8	15.6	283.8	12.1	682.7	3.0	1,406.3	367.0
1965	2,874.8	2,860.4	30.2	1,013.0	999.9	30.2	313.9	20.4	713.4	9.2	1,472.5	385.4
1966	3,060.2	3,033.5	42.3	1,099.9	1,077.9	42.3	350.0	30.9	751.8	10.9	1,557.8	385.9
1967	3,140.2	3,125.1	32.1	1,114.7	1,101.2	32.1	359.2	16.3	765.4	15.6	1,639.4	380.2
1968	3,288.6	3,278.0	26.9	1,166.6	1,156.5	26.9	378.7	13.2	801.8	13.6	1,712.0	403.6
1969	3,388.0	3,377.2	27.2	1,200.3	1,189.9	27.2	391.2	17.4	822.6	9.6	1,774.1	408.8
1970	3,388.2	3,406.5	5.7	1,181.6	1,193.4	5.7	383.2	-.1	837.8	5.9	1,824.0	391.1
1971	3,500.1	3,499.8	22.7	1,209.3	1,206.1	22.7	385.8	8.0	848.8	14.8	1,875.8	427.4
1972	3,690.3	3,689.5	25.2	1,296.5	1,293.2	25.2	431.8	18.0	885.4	7.2	1,936.1	459.0
1973	3,902.3	3,883.9	39.0	1,413.2	1,396.0	39.0	496.6	34.6	916.7	6.0	2,004.4	469.0
1974	3,888.2	3,873.4	24.0	1,400.9	1,386.5	24.0	496.9	20.6	905.9	4.5	2,063.3	420.5
1975	3,865.1	3,906.4	-11.0	1,373.4	1,404.4	-11.0	495.8	-13.9	926.7	2.3	2,123.5	382.3
1976	4,081.1	4,061.7	29.0	1,478.3	1,459.9	29.0	520.9	18.9	956.4	10.2	2,182.9	418.3
1977	4,279.3	4,240.8	38.0	1,560.0	1,525.7	38.0	567.0	17.2	970.8	20.8	2,250.5	458.7
1978	4,493.7	4,464.4	42.3	1,644.4	1,617.8	42.3	615.3	31.7	1,011.7	10.5	2,334.3	498.1
1979	4,624.0	4,614.4	23.1	1,700.6	1,690.7	23.1	654.6	18.4	1,042.9	5.1	2,391.3	511.7
1980	4,611.9	4,641.9	-10.0	1,687.4	1,711.2	-10.0	638.1	-3.6	1,085.6	-6.3	2,441.4	475.9
1981	4,724.9	4,691.6	33.1	1,765.7	1,735.1	33.1	638.8	9.1	1,111.0	23.6	2,475.8	468.8
1982	4,623.6	4,651.2	-15.6	1,684.1	1,706.7	-15.6	604.4	-17.8	1,122.6	2.0	2,518.7	428.5
1983	4,810.0	4,821.2	-5.9	1,754.8	1,762.6	-5.9	637.6	4.9	1,142.6	-10.4	2,598.4	460.7
1984	5,138.2	5,061.6	74.8	1,924.8	1,853.3	74.8	703.1	49.7	1,160.9	25.6	2,678.0	523.1
1985	5,329.5	5,296.9	29.8	1,971.7	1,940.6	29.8	758.2	10.0	1,189.0	19.7	2,797.8	550.3
1986	5,489.9	5,480.9	10.9	2,020.9	2,011.7	10.9	793.6	.9	1,223.5	10.2	2,903.2	558.4
1987	5,648.4	5,626.0	26.2	2,076.9	2,055.0	26.2	819.8	23.5	1,239.2	2.2	3,011.6	554.6
1988	5,862.9	5,855.1	11.6	2,178.9	2,171.0	11.6	897.0	17.6	1,274.8	-6.2	3,128.6	550.8
1989	6,060.4	6,028.7	33.3	2,300.2	2,269.2	33.3	951.9	22.4	1,317.2	11.0	3,208.5	546.0
1990	6,138.7	6,126.7	10.4	2,307.1	2,295.4	10.4	963.9	2.7	1,331.3	7.6	3,295.4	533.3
1991	6,079.0	6,082.6	-3.0	2,262.3	2,265.9	-3.0	934.2	-16.6	1,331.8	13.4	3,332.3	484.5
1992	6,244.4	6,237.4	7.3	2,321.0	2,314.0	7.3	965.9	-10.9	1,348.1	18.3	3,411.1	512.3
1993	6,383.8	6,362.9	19.1	2,389.6	2,368.7	19.1	1,006.9	15.4	1,361.8	3.7	3,464.9	529.4
1994	6,604.2	6,546.3	58.9	2,524.3	2,465.6	58.9	1,068.0	30.6	1,398.0	28.2	3,521.7	559.8
1990: I	6,154.1	6,144.6	11.0	2,328.3	2,318.8	11.0	991.4	1.9	1,326.5	9.1	3,264.8	555.9
II	6,174.4	6,127.5	43.8	2,335.6	2,289.5	43.8	963.8	17.3	1,325.5	26.3	3,293.9	541.4
III	6,145.2	6,126.6	14.9	2,304.6	2,286.4	14.9	955.6	10.2	1,330.8	4.7	3,310.1	528.2
IV	6,081.0	6,108.1	-28.2	2,260.1	2,286.8	-28.2	944.7	-18.4	1,342.2	-9.9	3,312.7	507.5
1991: I	6,047.9	6,065.4	-17.5	2,251.8	2,269.0	-17.5	926.0	-38.9	1,343.3	21.0	3,308.8	487.3
II	6,074.1	6,095.9	-20.8	2,256.1	2,277.7	-20.8	944.9	-29.5	1,332.8	8.4	3,335.0	483.4
III	6,089.3	6,085.4	4.9	2,271.1	2,267.2	4.9	938.2	6.1	1,329.0	-1.3	3,338.3	480.1
IV	6,104.4	6,083.8	21.4	2,270.1	2,249.6	21.4	927.5	-4.2	1,322.1	25.6	3,347.2	487.3
1992: I	6,175.3	6,175.8	-.1	2,288.9	2,289.3	-.1	945.2	-18.7	1,344.2	18.6	3,379.4	507.1
II	6,214.2	6,203.8	11.3	2,301.1	2,290.7	11.3	953.8	1.2	1,336.9	10.1	3,398.6	514.4
III	6,260.9	6,249.5	12.1	2,327.4	2,316.0	12.1	970.0	-11.4	1,346.0	23.7	3,424.2	509.4
IV	6,327.3	6,320.7	5.8	2,366.7	2,360.1	5.8	994.8	-14.8	1,365.3	20.8	3,442.3	518.5
1993: I	6,327.0	6,307.7	18.5	2,357.4	2,338.0	18.5	982.8	13.1	1,355.2	5.4	3,448.8	520.9
II	6,353.7	6,331.6	20.8	2,385.4	2,363.2	20.8	1,007.4	11.2	1,355.9	9.7	3,449.3	519.3
III	6,390.4	6,368.2	19.5	2,384.9	2,362.7	19.5	999.5	13.5	1,363.2	6.1	3,475.8	529.5
IV	6,463.9	6,444.1	17.4	2,430.7	2,410.7	17.4	1,038.0	23.6	1,373.0	-6.4	3,485.6	548.1
1994: I	6,504.6	6,464.0	40.1	2,467.9	2,426.8	40.1	1,048.7	24.3	1,378.4	15.8	3,491.1	546.6
II	6,581.5	6,509.0	74.1	2,508.8	2,435.3	74.1	1,048.4	33.9	1,387.1	40.4	3,513.4	560.6
III	6,639.5	6,576.8	64.0	2,541.9	2,478.5	64.0	1,077.3	32.7	1,401.6	31.2	3,536.4	562.8
IV	6,691.3	6,635.2	57.3	2,578.5	2,521.8	57.3	1,097.4	31.6	1,424.8	25.6	3,545.9	569.1
1995: I	6,701.6	6,647.5	54.5	2,580.3	2,525.6	54.5	1,097.9	51.6	1,428.2	2.2	3,552.6	570.8
II	6,709.4	6,677.4	30.6	2,573.2	2,541.1	30.6	1,112.2	26.7	1,429.4	3.6	3,574.7	563.3
III	6,763.2	6,735.0	27.1	2,602.6	2,574.3	27.1	1,140.0	23.6	1,435.2	3.2	3,589.7	573.0

[1] Exports and imports of certain goods, primarily military equipment purchased and sold by the Federal Government, are included in services.

Source: Department of Commerce, Bureau of Economic Analysis.

TABLE B-8.—*Gross domestic product by sector, 1959-95*

[Billions of dollars; quarterly data at seasonally adjusted annual rates]

Year or quarter	Gross domestic product	Business [1]			House-holds and institu-tions	General government [2]		
		Total [1]	Nonfarm [1]	Farm		Total	Federal	State and local
1959	507.2	436.9	418.0	18.9	12.4	57.9	31.8	26.1
1960	526.6	451.1	431.3	19.8	13.9	61.5	32.9	28.6
1961	544.8	464.9	444.8	20.1	14.5	65.5	34.2	31.3
1962	585.2	499.5	479.3	20.2	15.6	70.1	36.3	33.8
1963	617.4	525.9	505.5	20.4	16.7	74.8	38.1	36.7
1964	663.0	564.7	545.5	19.3	17.9	80.4	40.5	40.0
1965	719.1	613.8	591.9	21.9	19.3	86.0	42.3	43.7
1966	787.8	670.4	647.5	22.9	21.3	96.1	47.1	49.0
1967	833.6	703.7	681.5	22.2	23.4	106.5	51.6	54.9
1968	910.6	766.1	743.4	22.7	26.1	118.4	56.5	61.9
1969	982.2	823.3	798.1	25.2	29.5	129.5	60.2	69.3
1970	1,035.6	860.3	834.1	26.2	32.4	142.9	64.3	78.7
1971	1,125.4	933.9	905.8	28.1	35.6	155.9	68.2	87.7
1972	1,237.3	1,028.3	995.6	32.6	39.0	170.1	73.1	96.9
1973	1,382.6	1,154.6	1,104.9	49.8	43.0	185.0	76.9	108.1
1974	1,496.9	1,246.0	1,198.6	47.4	47.2	203.7	83.5	120.3
1975	1,630.6	1,351.5	1,302.7	48.8	52.0	227.1	91.7	135.4
1976	1,819.0	1,516.0	1,469.6	46.4	57.1	245.8	97.9	147.9
1977	2,026.9	1,697.5	1,650.3	47.2	62.4	266.9	106.1	160.9
1978	2,291.4	1,931.7	1,877.0	54.7	69.8	289.9	113.8	176.1
1979	2,557.5	2,164.3	2,099.8	64.5	77.3	315.9	122.3	193.6
1980	2,784.2	2,346.3	2,290.2	56.1	87.1	350.8	135.6	215.2
1981	3,115.9	2,631.8	2,561.9	69.9	97.6	386.4	151.0	235.4
1982	3,242.1	2,714.7	2,649.5	65.1	108.2	419.2	164.0	255.2
1983	3,514.5	2,950.0	2,900.8	49.2	119.2	445.3	173.5	271.8
1984	3,902.4	3,289.6	3,221.1	68.5	131.2	481.7	190.8	290.9
1985	4,180.7	3,520.2	3,453.1	67.1	140.9	519.6	203.6	316.0
1986	4,422.2	3,716.7	3,653.7	63.0	153.7	551.9	211.1	340.7
1987	4,692.3	3,933.1	3,868.0	65.1	173.3	586.0	221.3	364.7
1988	5,049.6	4,233.4	4,169.6	63.8	195.1	621.0	230.0	391.0
1989	5,438.7	4,563.7	4,487.5	76.2	214.6	660.3	240.5	419.8
1990	5,743.8	4,796.9	4,717.3	79.6	237.9	709.0	252.7	456.3
1991	5,916.7	4,908.5	4,835.6	72.9	257.4	750.7	268.1	482.6
1992	6,244.4	5,184.4	5,103.8	80.6	279.1	781.0	274.4	506.6
1993	6,550.2	5,448.9	5,376.7	72.1	294.9	806.5	276.6	529.9
1994	6,931.4	5,794.0	5,711.7	82.3	310.3	827.0	275.7	551.4
1990: I	5,660.4	4,739.6	4,660.9	78.7	228.6	692.3	248.7	443.5
II	5,751.0	4,812.7	4,730.1	82.6	235.5	702.8	250.4	452.4
III	5,782.4	4,825.7	4,746.1	79.6	242.8	713.9	253.1	460.8
IV	5,781.5	4,809.7	4,732.1	77.6	244.8	727.0	258.5	468.4
1991: I	5,822.1	4,830.5	4,759.9	70.6	249.2	742.4	267.9	474.5
II	5,892.3	4,887.5	4,810.5	77.0	255.7	749.1	268.5	480.6
III	5,950.0	4,937.6	4,866.8	70.7	259.7	752.8	268.1	484.7
IV	6.002.3	4,978.6	4,905.1	73.5	265.1	758.6	267.9	490.6
1992: I	6,121.8	5,080.1	5,000.9	79.1	270.1	771.7	274.4	497.3
II	6,201.2	5,143.0	5,062.7	80.3	278.3	780.0	275.8	504.2
III	6,271.7	5,205.2	5,121.0	84.2	281.7	784.8	275.2	509.6
IV	6,383.0	5,309.2	5,230.6	78.7	286.2	787.6	272.1	515.5
1993: I	6,442.8	5,351.5	5,279.8	71.7	290.5	800.7	278.8	522.0
II	6,503.2	5,408.8	5,333.7	75.1	290.8	803.6	275.9	527.7
III	6,571.3	5,462.9	5,397.7	65.1	298.7	809.7	276.9	532.9
IV	6,683.7	5,572.3	5,495.7	76.6	299.4	812.0	275.0	537.0
1994: I	6,772.8	5,646.3	5,559.2	87.1	306.0	820.5	277.1	543.4
II	6,885.0	5,750.0	5,667.6	82.4	309.5	825.5	277.2	548.3
III	6,987.6	5,847.1	5,767.5	79.6	312.3	828.2	274.0	554.2
IV	7,080.0	5,932.6	5,852.6	80.0	313.4	834.0	274.3	559.7
1995: I	7,147.8	5,986.0	5,909.3	76.6	316.7	845.1	278.6	566.5
II	7,196.5	6,024.7	5,947.9	76.8	321.3	850.4	278.9	571.6
III	7,297.2	6,117.0	6,039.2	77.8	324.3	855.9	278.8	577.1

[1] Includes compensation of employees in government enterprises.
[2] Compensation of government employees.

Source: Department of Commerce, Bureau of Economic Analysis.

290

TABLE B–9.—*Real gross domestic product by sector, 1959–95*

[Billions of chained (1992) dollars; quarterly data at seasonally adjusted annual rates]

Year or quarter	Gross domestic product	Business [1] Total [1]	Business [1] Nonfarm [1]	Business [1] Farm	Households and institutions	General government [2] Total	General government [2] Federal	General government [2] State and local
1959	2,212.3	1,723.6	1,677.8	34.0	105.0	415.1	232.1	186.4
1960	2,261.7	1,757.1	1,711.2	34.3	112.1	429.3	236.4	196.2
1961	2,309.8	1,791.7	1,748.7	33.5	113.1	444.6	241.5	206.4
1962	2,449.1	1,906.5	1,868.2	32.6	117.2	461.8	251.7	213.6
1963	2,554.0	1,992.8	1,953.3	33.9	120.1	475.7	254.3	224.6
1964	2,702.9	2,117.6	2,083.3	32.7	123.4	492.4	256.8	238.4
1965	2,874.8	2,263.0	2,227.6	34.5	127.9	509.3	258.8	253.0
1966	3,060.2	2,410.9	2,383.9	32.5	132.6	542.1	276.4	268.4
1967	3,140.2	2,463.9	2,430.1	35.8	136.9	571.1	295.1	279.2
1968	3,288.6	2,585.4	2,554.6	35.5	141.0	592.6	300.6	294.8
1969	3,388.0	2,665.6	2,634.4	36.4	145.5	607.3	301.7	307.8
1970	3,388.2	2,665.1	2,634.9	35.9	144.0	609.7	288.9	321.5
1971	3,500.1	2,768.0	2,736.2	37.5	147.2	611.3	276.1	334.9
1972	3,690.3	2,946.8	2,920.2	36.9	151.4	611.5	263.5	347.4
1973	3,902.3	3,145.7	3,126.9	36.3	154.9	614.8	253.8	360.2
1974	3,888.2	3,122.6	3,094.9	38.7	156.1	625.2	252.0	372.6
1975	3,865.1	3,091.8	3,049.7	43.4	161.2	631.1	249.0	381.7
1976	4,081.1	3,296.6	3,255.9	44.6	163.0	634.3	247.5	386.4
1977	4,279.3	3,481.4	3,431.3	50.2	167.5	639.1	246.3	392.6
1978	4,493.7	3,678.8	3,651.6	41.7	170.3	649.2	247.3	401.8
1979	4,624.0	3,798.4	3,762.6	46.3	173.7	654.2	245.1	409.3
1980	4,611.9	3,777.0	3,740.8	46.2	178.7	660.9	246.7	414.5
1981	4,724.9	3,882.5	3,816.0	63.3	182.7	662.3	248.3	414.2
1982	4,623.6	3,776.0	3,705.4	65.2	188.0	666.6	250.3	416.4
1983	4,810.0	3,952.8	3,915.7	45.0	192.3	668.7	254.2	414.4
1984	5,138.2	4,264.2	4,211.3	56.4	197.1	676.0	258.2	417.6
1985	5,329.5	4,431.3	4,357.5	71.9	203.4	693.2	263.9	429.2
1986	5,489.9	4,565.2	4,500.0	65.5	213.5	709.9	266.9	443.0
1987	5,648.4	4,698.8	4,636.1	63.7	224.1	724.2	272.3	452.0
1988	5,862.9	4,880.0	4,826.8	56.6	240.6	741.3	274.1	467.3
1989	6,060.4	5,047.8	4,984.8	64.8	253.4	758.1	276.2	481.9
1990	6,138.7	5,099.4	5,026.5	72.9	264.1	774.7	280.3	494.5
1991	6,079.0	5,025.9	4,954.9	71.2	272.1	781.1	281.0	500.1
1992	6,244.4	5,184.4	5,103.8	80.6	279.1	781.0	274.4	506.6
1993	6,383.8	5,313.0	5,242.0	71.0	287.9	782.9	267.3	515.6
1994	6,604.2	5,525.8	5,442.2	83.9	296.2	782.4	256.8	525.8
1990: I	6,154.1	5,123.5	5,055.1	69.4	259.3	770.3	279.8	490.5
II	6,174.4	5,137.7	5,063.4	74.1	262.7	773.3	280.0	493.4
III	6,145.2	5,101.6	5,028.8	72.7	266.5	776.7	280.9	495.9
IV	6,081.0	5,034.7	4,958.9	75.3	267.8	778.5	280.4	498.1
1991: I	6,047.9	4,995.5	4,924.8	70.9	269.0	783.7	284.9	498.9
II	6,074.1	5,020.2	4,947.2	73.1	271.6	782.5	282.3	500.2
III	6,089.3	5,037.2	4,968.1	69.3	272.8	779.3	279.4	499.9
IV	6,104.4	5,050.8	4,979.6	71.4	274.9	778.9	277.5	501.5
1992: I	6,175.3	5,118.7	5,039.7	79.0	277.3	779.3	275.8	503.5
II	6,214.2	5,156.7	5,075.3	81.4	277.2	780.3	275.0	505.3
III	6,260.9	5,198.8	5,115.8	83.0	279.8	782.3	274.0	508.4
IV	6,327.3	5,263.3	5,184.4	78.9	282.0	782.0	272.7	509.3
1993: I	6,327.0	5,260.4	5,184.8	75.6	283.5	783.2	271.5	511.7
II	6,353.7	5,283.3	5,209.7	73.7	287.1	783.2	269.0	514.3
III	6,390.4	5,317.2	5,256.0	60.8	289.6	783.6	266.4	517.3
IV	6,463.9	5,391.2	5,317.4	73.8	291.4	781.5	262.3	519.2
1994: I	6,504.6	5,428.2	5,344.1	84.6	293.4	783.1	261.1	522.2
II	6,581.5	5,503.1	5,418.9	84.8	295.9	782.7	258.1	524.7
III	6,639.5	5,559.7	5,475.7	84.3	296.8	783.2	255.9	527.5
IV	6,691.3	5,612.0	5,530.0	82.1	298.8	780.8	252.1	529.0
1995: I	6,701.6	5,621.6	5,542.4	79.1	300.1	780.1	250.2	530.2
II	6,709.4	5,628.4	5,551.2	76.9	301.7	779.7	249.1	530.9
III	6,763.2	5,680.5	5,607.0	72.9	303.1	779.9	247.7	532.5

[1] Includes compensation of employees in government enterprises.
[2] Compensation of government employees.

Source: Department of Commerce, Bureau of Economic Analysis.

291

TABLE B–10.—*Gross domestic product of nonfinancial corporate business, 1959–95*

[Billions of dollars; quarterly data at seasonally adjusted annual rates]

Year or quarter	Gross domestic product of non-financial corporate business	Consumption of fixed capital	Net domestic product — Total	Indirect business taxes¹	Domestic income — Total	Compensation of employees	Corporate profits — Total	Profits before tax	Profits tax liability	Profits after tax — Total	Dividends	Undistributed profits	Inventory valuation adjustment	Capital consumption adjustment	Net interest
1959	267.5	26.3	241.2	26.0	215.2	171.5	40.6	43.6	20.7	22.9	10.0	12.9	-0.3	-2.8	3.1
1960	278.1	27.2	250.9	28.3	222.6	181.2	38.0	40.3	19.2	21.1	10.6	10.6	-.2	-2.2	3.5
1961	285.5	27.8	257.8	29.5	228.2	185.3	38.9	40.1	19.5	20.7	10.6	10.1	.3	-1.5	4.0
1962	311.7	28.8	282.9	32.0	250.9	200.1	46.3	45.0	20.6	24.3	11.4	13.0	.0	1.3	4.5
1963	331.8	29.8	302.0	34.0	267.9	211.1	52.0	49.8	22.8	27.0	12.6	14.4	.1	2.2	4.8
1964	358.1	31.3	326.8	36.6	290.2	226.7	58.2	56.0	24.0	32.1	13.7	18.4	-.5	2.7	5.3
1965	393.5	33.5	360.0	39.2	320.8	246.5	68.2	66.2	27.2	39.0	15.6	23.4	-1.2	3.3	6.1
1966	431.0	36.7	394.3	40.5	353.8	274.0	72.5	71.4	29.5	41.9	16.8	25.1	-2.1	3.2	7.4
1967	453.4	40.1	413.4	43.1	370.3	292.3	69.2	67.5	27.8	39.7	17.5	22.2	-1.6	3.3	8.8
1968	500.5	43.8	456.7	49.7	407.0	323.2	73.6	74.0	33.6	40.4	19.1	21.3	-3.7	3.3	10.1
1969	543.3	47.5	495.8	54.7	441.1	358.8	69.1	70.8	33.3	37.5	19.1	18.4	-5.9	4.1	13.2
1970	561.4	51.6	509.8	58.8	451.0	378.7	55.2	58.1	27.2	31.0	18.5	12.5	-6.6	3.6	17.1
1971	606.4	56.3	550.1	64.5	485.6	402.0	65.5	67.1	29.9	37.1	18.5	18.7	-4.6	3.0	18.1
1972	673.3	62.1	611.2	69.2	542.1	447.1	75.8	78.6	33.8	44.8	20.1	24.7	-6.6	3.9	19.2
1973	754.5	67.6	686.8	76.3	610.5	505.9	82.1	98.6	40.2	58.4	21.1	37.3	-20.0	3.6	22.5
1974	814.6	78.7	736.0	81.4	654.6	556.8	69.5	109.2	42.2	67.0	21.7	45.2	-39.5	-.2	28.3
1975	881.2	94.4	786.8	87.4	699.5	580.3	90.4	109.9	41.5	68.4	24.8	43.6	-11.0	-8.5	28.7
1976	995.3	104.5	890.8	95.1	795.6	657.4	110.7	137.3	53.0	84.4	28.0	56.3	-14.9	-11.7	27.5
1977	1,125.4	125.8	999.7	104.1	895.6	742.6	122.4	158.6	59.9	98.7	31.5	67.2	-16.6	-19.5	30.6
1978	1,284.1	142.1	1,142.0	116.4	1,025.5	852.9	136.3	183.5	67.1	116.4	36.4	80.0	-25.0	-22.1	36.3
1979	1,429.7	163.7	1,266.0	125.4	1,140.6	968.1	127.4	195.5	69.6	125.9	38.1	87.9	-41.6	-26.6	45.1
1980	1,553.8	187.8	1,365.9	141.6	1,224.3	1,058.5	107.6	181.6	67.0	114.6	45.3	69.2	-43.0	-30.9	58.2
1981	1,767.3	218.3	1,549.1	170.4	1,378.7	1,171.5	135.3	181.4	63.9	117.5	53.3	64.2	-25.7	-20.4	71.9
1982	1,823.4	235.4	1,588.0	172.1	1,415.9	1,217.0	116.4	133.7	46.3	87.4	53.3	34.2	-9.9	-7.4	82.5
1983	1,950.3	248.9	1,701.4	189.0	1,512.4	1,280.5	155.3	157.4	59.4	97.9	64.2	33.8	-9.1	7.0	76.6
1984	2,187.5	255.1	1,932.4	210.2	1,722.2	1,421.7	212.7	191.0	73.7	117.3	67.8	49.5	-5.6	27.3	87.8
1985	2,319.3	266.5	2,052.8	224.4	1,828.4	1,521.9	215.9	167.6	69.9	97.6	72.3	25.4	.5	47.8	90.6
1986	2,416.3	283.7	2,132.6	235.8	1,896.8	1,603.2	195.5	151.5	75.6	75.9	73.9	2.1	11.4	32.6	98.1
1987	2,589.6	296.9	2,292.7	246.7	2,046.0	1,715.5	225.2	214.9	93.5	121.4	75.9	45.5	-20.7	31.0	105.3
1988	2,805.2	316.5	2,488.7	263.5	2,225.3	1,846.7	257.5	260.6	101.7	158.8	79.4	79.4	-29.3	26.3	121.0
1989	2,950.9	335.5	2,615.4	280.8	2,334.6	1,950.0	238.7	237.0	98.8	138.3	103.5	34.8	-17.5	19.1	145.9
1990	3,084.0	352.7	2,731.3	296.8	2,434.5	2,056.0	231.0	237.3	95.7	141.6	118.4	23.3	-13.5	7.2	147.5
1991	3,132.1	366.7	2,765.3	318.0	2,447.3	2,090.6	223.1	218.1	85.4	132.8	124.6	8.2	4.0	1.0	133.7
1992	3,262.6	376.1	2,886.5	337.0	2,549.5	2,195.3	250.0	257.8	91.1	166.7	133.6	33.1	-7.5	-.3	104.2
1993	3,437.5	390.1	3,047.4	356.2	2,691.2	2,294.3	297.3	303.7	103.5	200.3	152.6	47.6	-6.6	-.1	99.6
1994	3,688.4	412.8	3,275.5	379.6	2,895.9	2,433.8	364.6	372.5	129.9	242.7	161.8	80.9	-13.3	5.3	97.5
1990: I	3,042.8	346.4	2,696.4	290.5	2,405.9	2,022.0	237.5	227.9	90.5	137.3	119.5	17.8	-1.3	10.9	146.5
II	3,103.0	351.6	2,751.5	292.6	2,458.9	2,055.8	254.2	239.0	96.4	142.7	116.5	26.2	7.7	7.4	148.9
III	3,092.7	356.0	2,736.7	299.7	2,437.0	2,074.7	214.7	250.1	101.1	148.9	118.1	30.8	-40.0	4.7	147.6
IV	3,097.4	356.9	2,740.5	304.3	2,436.2	2,071.4	217.7	232.3	94.7	137.7	119.5	18.2	-20.3	5.6	147.1
1991: I	3,107.7	363.2	2,744.5	309.2	2,435.3	2,060.0	232.6	213.3	83.1	130.3	120.7	9.5	17.6	1.7	142.7
II	3,119.1	365.7	2,753.4	314.2	2,439.2	2,078.8	222.8	215.0	84.0	131.0	125.4	5.6	6.8	1.1	137.6
III	3,142.0	369.0	2,773.0	321.2	2,451.8	2,101.2	219.4	220.6	86.8	133.8	124.9	8.9	-.8	-.3	131.1
IV	3,159.5	369.1	2,790.4	327.3	2,463.1	2,122.2	217.5	223.7	87.5	136.2	127.5	8.7	-7.6	1.5	123.3
1992: I	3,202.2	368.6	2,833.6	330.4	2,503.1	2,152.8	240.2	236.3	82.4	153.9	124.0	29.9	.3	3.6	110.2
II	3,236.1	371.8	2,864.3	331.8	2,532.5	2,183.2	243.3	262.6	93.6	169.0	129.7	39.3	-21.9		106.0
III	3,270.5	387.9	2,882.7	337.8	2,544.9	2,209.3	234.8	254.4	89.9	164.5	134.3	30.2	-8.6	-11.0	100.8
IV	3,341.7	376.3	2,965.4	348.0	2,617.4	2,236.1	281.6	277.9	98.4	179.5	146.3	33.2	.2	3.5	99.7
1993: I	3,345.3	382.8	2,962.5	346.9	2,615.6	2,251.4	260.5	275.9	93.8	182.1	153.4	28.7	-14.6	-.7	103.6
II	3,407.8	387.5	3,020.4	352.9	2,667.4	2,279.8	286.9	303.2	103.9	199.3	150.1	49.2	-15.6	-.7	100.7
III	3,458.7	395.8	3,062.8	355.9	2,706.9	2,308.4	301.1	296.4	100.1	196.3	150.8	45.5	7.9	-3.3	97.5
IV	3,538.0	394.2	3,143.8	368.9	2,774.9	2,337.6	340.6	339.5	116.0	223.4	156.3	67.2	-4.0	5.1	96.7
1994: I	3,594.4	427.9	3,166.5	372.6	2,793.9	2,374.6	323.6	346.0	121.0	225.0	154.9	70.1	-3.9	-18.4	95.7
II	3,664.9	404.3	3,260.6	376.5	2,884.1	2,419.7	366.3	364.4	126.9	237.5	160.9	76.7	-9.8	11.7	98.1
III	3,707.2	408.7	3,298.5	382.1	2,916.4	2,443.8	374.2	378.0	130.9	247.1	161.0	86.1	-16.5	12.7	98.4
IV	3,786.9	410.4	3,376.6	387.2	2,989.4	2,497.1	394.3	401.8	140.6	261.1	170.1	91.0	-22.8	15.3	97.9
1995: I	3,796.4	415.0	3,381.4	394.1	2,987.3	2,521.8	364.6	405.1	142.2	262.9	172.1	90.8	-51.9	11.4	101.0
II	3,832.4	421.3	3,411.1	401.1	3,009.9	2,543.5	364.5	397.9	138.5	259.4	176.1	83.3	-42.3	8.9	101.9
III	3,916.2	426.4	3,489.8	401.7	3,088.1	2,581.7	404.7	406.0	141.3	264.7	174.9	89.7	-9.8	8.5	101.7

¹ Indirect business tax and nontax liability plus business transfer payments less subsidies.

Source: Department of Commerce, Bureau of Economic Analysis.

TABLE B–11.—*Output, costs, and profits of nonfinancial corporate business, 1959–95*

[Quarterly data at seasonally adjusted annual rates]

Year or quarter	Gross domestic product of nonfinancial corporate business (billions of dollars)		Current-dollar cost and profit per unit of real output (dollars)[1]							
	Current dollars	Chained (1992) dollars	Total cost and profit[2]	Consumption of fixed capital	Indirect business taxes[3]	Compensation of employees	Corporate profits with inventory valuation and capital consumption adjustments			Net interest
							Total	Profits tax liability	Profits after tax[4]	
1959	267.5	921.6	0.290	0.028	0.028	0.186	0.044	0.023	0.022	0.003
1960	278.1	947.5	.294	.029	.030	.191	.040	.020	.020	.004
1961	285.5	967.6	.295	.029	.031	.192	.040	.020	.020	.004
1962	311.7	1,046.8	.298	.027	.031	.191	.044	.020	.025	.004
1963	331.8	1,110.7	.299	.027	.031	.190	.047	.021	.026	.004
1964	358.1	1,189.4	.301	.026	.031	.191	.049	.020	.029	.004
1965	393.5	1,283.6	.307	.026	.031	.192	.053	.021	.032	.005
1966	431.0	1,363.1	.316	.027	.030	.201	.053	.022	.032	.005
1967	453.4	1,396.5	.325	.029	.031	.209	.050	.020	.030	.006
1968	500.5	1,488.1	.336	.029	.033	.217	.049	.023	.027	.007
1969	543.3	1,545.6	.351	.031	.035	.232	.045	.022	.023	.009
1970	561.4	1,525.5	.368	.034	.039	.248	.036	.018	.018	.011
1971	606.4	1,592.0	.381	.035	.041	.253	.041	.019	.022	.011
1972	673.3	1,717.2	.392	.036	.040	.260	.044	.020	.025	.011
1973	754.5	1,811.4	.416	.037	.042	.279	.045	.022	.023	.012
1974	814.6	1,780.6	.457	.044	.046	.313	.039	.024	.015	.016
1975	881.2	1,744.6	.505	.054	.050	.333	.052	.024	.028	.016
1976	995.3	1,892.2	.526	.055	.050	.347	.059	.028	.031	.015
1977	1,125.4	2,041.1	.551	.062	.051	.364	.060	.029	.031	.015
1978	1,284.1	2,165.7	.593	.066	.054	.394	.063	.031	.032	.017
1979	1,429.7	2,214.2	.646	.074	.057	.437	.058	.031	.026	.020
1980	1,553.8	2,222.2	.699	.085	.064	.476	.048	.030	.018	.026
1981	1,767.3	2,328.8	.759	.094	.073	.503	.058	.027	.031	.031
1982	1,823.4	2,298.8	.793	.102	.075	.529	.051	.020	.030	.036
1983	1,950.3	2,407.8	.810	.103	.078	.532	.064	.025	.040	.032
1984	2,187.5	2,634.6	.830	.097	.080	.540	.081	.028	.053	.033
1985	2,319.3	2,748.0	.844	.097	.082	.554	.079	.025	.053	.033
1986	2,416.3	2,832.4	.853	.100	.083	.566	.069	.027	.042	.035
1987	2,589.6	2,967.0	.873	.100	.083	.578	.076	.031	.044	.035
1988	2,805.2	3,122.1	.898	.101	.084	.591	.082	.033	.050	.039
1989	2,950.9	3,175.4	.929	.106	.088	.614	.075	.031	.044	.046
1990	3,084.0	3,212.5	.960	.110	.092	.640	.072	.030	.042	.046
1991	3,132.1	3,168.8	.988	.116	.100	.660	.070	.027	.043	.042
1992	3,262.6	3,262.6	1.000	.115	.103	.673	.077	.028	.049	.032
1993	3,437.5	3,380.0	1.017	.115	.105	.679	.088	.031	.057	.029
1994	3,688.4	3,567.1	1.034	.116	.106	.682	.102	.036	.066	.027
1990: I	3,042.8	3,208.3	.948	.108	.091	.630	.074	.028	.046	.046
II	3,103.0	3,243.0	.957	.108	.090	.634	.078	.030	.049	.046
III	3,092.7	3,208.5	.964	.111	.093	.647	.067	.032	.035	.046
IV	3,097.4	3,190.2	.971	.112	.095	.649	.068	.030	.039	.046
1991: I	3,107.7	3,164.3	.982	.115	.098	.651	.074	.026	.047	.045
II	3,119.1	3,158.4	.988	.116	.099	.658	.071	.027	.044	.044
III	3,142.0	3,170.1	.991	.116	.101	.663	.069	.027	.042	.041
IV	3,159.5	3,182.5	.993	.116	.103	.667	.068	.027	.041	.039
1992: I	3,202.2	3,216.6	.996	.115	.103	.669	.075	.026	.049	.034
II	3,236.1	3,238.1	.999	.115	.102	.674	.075	.029	.046	.033
III	3,270.5	3,267.3	1.001	.119	.103	.676	.072	.028	.044	.031
IV	3,341.7	3,328.5	1.004	.113	.105	.672	.085	.030	.055	.030
1993: I	3,345.3	3,304.0	1.012	.116	.105	.681	.079	.028	.050	.031
II	3,407.8	3,357.4	1.015	.115	.105	.679	.085	.031	.055	.030
III	3,458.7	3,398.4	1.018	.116	.105	.679	.089	.029	.059	.029
IV	3,538.0	3,460.1	1.023	.114	.107	.676	.098	.034	.065	.028
1994: I	3,594.4	3,496.2	1.028	.122	.107	.679	.093	.035	.058	.027
II	3,664.9	3,554.5	1.031	.114	.106	.681	.103	.036	.067	.028
III	3,707.2	3,576.2	1.037	.114	.107	.683	.105	.037	.068	.028
IV	3,786.9	3,641.5	1.040	.113	.106	.686	.108	.039	.070	.027
1995: I	3,796.4	3,631.6	1.045	.114	.109	.694	.100	.039	.061	.028
II	3,832.4	3,646.1	1.051	.116	.110	.698	.100	.038	.062	.028
III	3,916.2	3,715.2	1.054	.115	.108	.695	.109	.038	.071	.027

[1] Output is measured by gross domestic product of nonfinancial corporate business in chained (1992) dollars.
[2] This is equal to the deflator for gross domestic product of nonfinancial corporate business with the decimal point shifted two places to the left.
[3] Indirect business tax and nontax liability plus business transfer payments less subsidies.
[4] With inventory valuation and capital consumption adjustments.

Source: Department of Commerce, Bureau of Economic Analysis.

—*Personal consumption expenditures, 1959–95*

[Billions of dollars; quarterly data at seasonally adjusted annual rates]

Year or quarter	Personal consumption expenditures	Durable goods			Nondurable goods					Services					
		Total [1]	Motor vehicles and parts	Furniture and household equipment	Total [1]	Food	Clothing and shoes	Gasoline and oil	Fuel oil and coal	Total [1]	Housing [2]	Household operation		Transportation	Medical care
												Total [1]	Electricity and gas		
1959	318.1	42.7	18.9	18.1	148.5	80.7	26.4	11.3	4.0	127.0	45.0	18.7	7.6	10.5	16.4
1960	332.2	43.3	19.7	18.0	152.9	82.3	27.0	12.0	3.8	136.0	48.2	20.3	8.3	11.2	17.6
1961	342.6	41.8	17.8	18.3	156.6	84.0	27.6	12.0	3.8	144.3	51.2	21.2	8.8	11.7	18.7
1962	363.4	46.9	21.5	19.3	162.8	86.1	29.0	12.6	3.8	153.7	54.7	22.4	9.4	12.2	20.8
1963	383.0	51.6	24.4	20.7	168.2	88.3	29.8	13.0	4.0	163.2	58.0	23.6	9.9	12.7	22.6
1964	411.4	56.7	26.0	23.2	178.7	93.6	32.4	13.6	4.1	176.1	61.4	25.0	10.4	13.4	25.8
1965	444.3	63.3	29.9	25.1	191.6	100.7	34.1	14.8	4.4	189.4	65.4	26.5	10.9	14.5	28.0
1966	481.9	68.3	30.3	28.2	208.8	109.3	37.4	16.0	4.7	204.8	69.5	28.2	11.5	15.9	30.7
1967	509.5	70.4	30.0	30.0	217.1	112.5	39.2	17.1	4.8	222.0	74.1	30.2	12.2	17.3	33.9
1968	559.8	80.8	36.1	32.9	235.7	122.2	43.2	18.6	4.7	243.4	79.7	32.3	13.0	18.9	39.2
1969	604.7	85.9	38.4	34.7	253.2	131.5	46.5	20.5	4.6	265.5	86.8	35.1	14.0	20.9	44.7
1970	648.1	85.0	35.5	35.7	272.0	143.8	47.8	21.9	4.4	291.1	94.0	37.8	15.2	23.7	50.4
1971	702.5	96.9	44.5	37.8	285.5	149.7	51.7	23.2	4.6	320.1	102.7	41.0	16.6	27.1	56.9
1972	770.7	110.4	51.1	42.4	308.0	161.4	56.4	24.4	5.1	352.3	112.1	45.3	18.4	29.8	63.8
1973	851.6	123.5	56.1	47.9	343.1	179.6	62.5	28.1	6.3	384.9	122.7	49.8	20.0	31.2	71.6
1974	931.2	122.3	49.5	51.5	384.5	201.8	66.0	36.1	7.8	424.4	134.1	55.5	23.5	33.3	80.6
1975	1,029.1	133.5	54.8	54.5	420.6	223.1	70.8	39.7	8.4	475.0	147.0	63.7	28.5	35.7	93.5
1976	1,148.8	158.9	71.3	60.2	458.2	242.4	76.6	43.0	10.1	531.8	161.5	72.4	32.5	41.3	106.7
1977	1,277.1	181.1	83.5	67.1	496.9	262.4	84.1	46.9	11.1	599.0	179.5	81.9	37.6	49.2	123.0
1978	1,428.8	201.4	93.1	74.0	549.9	289.2	94.3	50.1	11.5	677.4	201.7	91.2	42.1	53.5	140.0
1979	1,593.5	213.9	93.5	82.3	624.0	324.2	101.2	66.2	14.4	755.6	226.6	100.0	46.8	59.1	158.0
1980	1,760.4	213.5	87.0	86.0	695.5	355.4	107.3	86.7	15.4	851.4	255.2	113.0	56.3	64.7	181.2
1981	1,941.3	230.5	95.8	91.3	758.2	382.8	117.2	97.9	15.8	952.6	287.9	126.0	63.4	68.7	213.0
1982	2,076.8	239.3	102.9	92.5	786.8	402.6	120.5	94.1	14.5	1,050.7	313.2	141.4	72.0	70.9	239.4
1983	2,283.4	279.8	126.9	105.3	830.3	422.9	130.9	93.1	13.6	1,173.3	339.0	155.9	80.7	79.4	267.8
1984	2,492.3	325.1	152.5	117.2	883.6	446.3	142.5	94.6	13.9	1,283.6	370.6	168.0	84.7	90.0	294.1
1985	2,704.8	361.1	175.7	126.3	927.6	466.5	152.1	97.2	13.6	1,416.1	407.1	180.3	88.8	100.0	321.8
1986	2,892.7	398.7	192.4	140.3	957.2	490.8	163.1	80.1	11.3	1,536.8	442.2	186.9	87.2	107.3	346.1
1987	3,094.5	416.7	193.1	150.4	1,014.0	513.9	174.4	85.4	11.2	1,663.8	476.6	194.9	88.9	118.2	381.1
1988	3,349.7	451.0	207.5	162.8	1,081.1	551.2	185.9	87.1	11.4	1,817.6	512.9	206.6	94.1	130.5	428.7
1989	3,594.8	472.8	214.4	173.3	1,163.8	588.4	199.9	96.6	11.4	1,958.1	547.4	219.8	98.8	137.8	477.1
1990	3,839.3	476.5	210.3	176.0	1,245.3	630.5	205.9	109.2	12.0	2,117.5	586.3	226.3	98.7	143.7	537.7
1991	3,975.1	455.2	187.6	178.5	1,277.6	650.0	211.3	103.9	11.3	2,242.3	616.5	237.6	104.9	145.3	586.5
1992	4,219.8	488.5	206.9	189.4	1,321.8	660.0	225.5	106.6	10.9	2,409.4	646.8	248.2	106.6	158.1	646.6
1993	4,454.1	530.7	226.1	205.5	1,368.9	685.7	235.7	108.1	10.6	2,554.6	673.2	268.5	115.9	169.6	697.4
1994	4,698.7	580.9	245.3	226.8	1,429.7	715.7	247.8	109.9	10.1	2,688.1	706.6	278.9	115.6	181.3	739.1
1990: I	3,759.2	493.3	223.4	178.9	1,220.7	617.6	205.8	102.8	11.5	2,045.3	571.1	219.1	93.5	141.5	514.2
II	3,811.8	477.6	211.5	176.4	1,230.2	627.5	205.6	100.4	11.3	2,104.1	581.5	227.0	99.5	143.2	530.6
III	3,879.2	473.2	208.5	175.0	1,256.2	637.1	206.8	109.6	12.7	2,149.8	593.5	229.6	101.0	144.2	547.2
IV	3,907.0	461.9	198.0	173.7	1,274.1	639.7	205.5	124.1	12.6	2,171.0	599.2	229.6	100.9	145.8	558.8
1991: I	3,910.7	449.0	183.6	175.2	1,268.3	644.0	207.2	108.4	11.9	2,193.5	605.8	230.7	101.6	143.0	568.2
II	3,961.0	452.7	183.3	179.7	1,279.7	652.9	212.7	103.6	10.8	2,228.6	612.9	239.9	108.1	143.9	578.6
III	4,001.6	462.0	192.5	180.6	1,283.4	653.2	214.1	102.1	11.3	2,256.3	619.7	240.5	106.1	145.9	591.3
IV	4,027.1	457.3	191.1	178.3	1,279.0	649.8	211.1	101.4	11.0	2,290.7	627.5	239.3	104.0	148.5	607.7
1992: I	4,127.6	474.1	199.1	184.8	1,303.1	657.3	219.6	102.3	10.4	2,350.4	636.6	241.5	102.1	154.9	624.2
II	4,183.0	481.3	204.0	186.5	1,308.4	652.3	222.3	105.8	11.8	2,393.3	643.4	248.8	106.2	156.9	640.6
III	4,238.9	492.5	208.3	190.6	1,326.3	657.9	228.1	109.4	10.6	2,420.1	649.9	243.6	106.6	156.0	655.0
IV	4,329.6	506.2	216.1	195.5	1,349.5	672.3	232.1	108.9	10.8	2,473.9	657.4	259.0	111.4	164.5	666.8
1993: I	4,367.8	508.3	214.2	198.3	1,354.1	676.5	230.6	110.6	10.9	2,505.3	663.7	260.8	113.2	166.7	681.9
II	4,424.7	525.2	225.4	202.1	1,364.2	683.0	234.0	108.0	10.6	2,535.4	670.1	264.2	113.3	168.4	691.9
III	4,481.0	536.7	228.3	207.7	1,371.4	687.9	236.7	106.6	10.6	2,572.9	675.9	273.6	118.6	170.0	702.9
IV	4,543.0	552.3	236.4	213.9	1,386.1	695.5	241.3	107.1	10.4	2,604.6	683.2	275.5	118.5	173.4	712.7
1994: I	4,599.2	562.6	243.3	216.0	1,399.7	701.4	242.8	105.9	11.3	2,636.8	693.2	270.4	117.3	176.5	722.4
II	4,665.1	573.1	242.4	223.4	1,416.6	710.7	245.4	106.4	9.8	2,675.4	701.6	282.5	119.2	180.6	732.9
III	4,734.4	585.3	245.0	230.2	1,443.5	721.1	249.4	113.4	9.9	2,705.6	711.3	281.6	114.4	183.2	743.6
IV	4,796.0	602.7	250.7	237.6	1,459.0	729.5	253.8	113.9	9.3	2,734.4	720.3	281.2	111.6	185.0	757.5
1995: I	4,836.3	593.0	240.6	237.1	1,471.6	738.4	252.8	116.2	9.5	2,771.7	729.8	286.3	113.6	187.1	771.0
II	4,908.7	604.0	248.3	239.2	1,486.9	744.6	254.3	118.3	10.4	2,817.9	739.0	293.7	118.2	191.6	779.5
III	4,965.1	616.0	254.0	244.3	1,491.3	750.9	255.5	113.1	9.8	2,857.8	747.7	300.0	123.4	194.2	787.9

[1] Includes other items not shown separately.
[2] Includes imputed rental value of owner-occupied housing.

Source: Department of Commerce, Bureau of Economic Analysis.

TABLE B–13.—*Real personal consumption expenditures, 1959–95*

[Billions of chained (1992) dollars; quarterly data at seasonally adjusted annual rates]

Year or quarter	Personal consumption expenditures	Durable goods Total¹	Motor vehicles and parts	Furniture and household equipment	Nondurable goods Total¹	Food	Clothing and shoes	Gasoline and oil	Fuel oil and coal	Services Total¹	Housing²	Household operation Total¹	Electricity and gas	Transportation	Medical care
1959	1,394.6	103.1	53.5	31.7	606.3	355.9	68.6	46.9	26.7	687.4	195.4	79.7	36.9	55.1	132.7
1960	1,432.6	105.2	56.8	31.3	615.4	358.7	69.3	48.5	25.6	717.4	205.6	83.5	38.9	56.9	136.7
1961	1,461.5	101.2	51.2	31.9	626.7	362.7	70.6	49.0	24.4	746.5	215.3	86.5	40.9	57.5	141.7
1962	1,533.8	113.0	60.8	33.9	646.5	367.3	73.7	51.1	24.3	783.4	227.4	90.7	43.7	59.7	153.3
1963	1,596.6	124.0	68.4	36.4	660.0	371.4	75.1	52.7	25.5	818.7	237.9	94.6	45.8	62.1	162.7
1964	1,692.3	135.5	72.4	41.1	692.5	386.3	81.0	55.5	26.5	868.4	249.0	99.2	48.3	65.4	180.5
1965	1,799.1	152.6	84.0	44.9	729.3	407.9	84.3	58.2	27.7	914.6	262.6	104.2	50.6	68.4	188.9
1966	1,902.0	165.5	85.5	50.7	769.2	424.7	90.0	61.8	28.5	961.0	274.6	109.8	53.4	72.7	197.6
1967	1,958.6	168.1	83.6	53.1	781.4	430.2	90.5	63.8	28.6	1,007.6	286.8	115.3	56.4	77.2	204.8
1968	2,070.2	186.6	97.2	56.5	816.9	450.9	94.3	68.2	27.0	1,059.6	300.9	119.9	59.4	81.9	220.8
1969	2,147.5	193.3	101.2	58.0	838.6	462.5	96.0	72.8	25.6	1,110.8	316.8	125.9	62.7	86.5	237.2
1970	2,197.8	187.0	91.2	58.6	859.1	477.2	94.8	77.3	23.8	1,155.4	329.3	130.2	65.4	89.1	250.8
1971	2,279.5	205.7	108.7	60.9	874.5	481.6	99.4	81.1	23.0	1,197.9	343.5	132.2	67.2	92.3	268.3
1972	2,415.9	231.9	124.3	67.5	912.9	496.8	106.1	84.4	25.3	1,262.5	361.5	138.9	70.8	98.1	286.4
1973	2,532.6	255.8	135.7	74.8	942.9	498.4	113.5	88.8	27.5	1,319.4	379.4	146.0	72.8	100.6	307.6
1974	2,514.7	238.2	112.5	75.6	924.5	490.6	111.9	84.4	21.7	1,351.2	399.1	147.5	73.7	101.1	320.2
1975	2,570.0	238.1	113.2	73.9	938.3	502.6	115.7	86.9	21.3	1,398.3	410.6	154.6	77.8	103.0	337.3
1976	2,714.3	268.5	136.8	78.8	984.8	529.4	121.2	90.4	23.9	1,457.1	422.9	161.4	80.5	107.3	353.5
1977	2,829.8	293.4	151.5	85.5	1,010.4	541.2	127.8	93.2	23.1	1,518.2	433.3	170.3	84.4	114.8	371.2
1978	2,951.6	308.8	158.0	90.5	1,045.7	545.7	139.9	95.3	23.0	1,589.3	454.5	178.6	87.6	118.0	385.7
1979	3,020.2	307.3	147.4	95.4	1,069.7	555.1	145.8	94.0	21.3	1,639.8	472.7	183.3	88.3	121.7	401.1
1980	3,009.7	282.6	127.5	93.5	1,065.1	558.7	148.1	88.6	16.5	1,670.7	486.6	187.4	90.7	115.6	415.5
1981	3,046.4	285.8	130.5	93.5	1,074.3	557.9	156.0	89.9	13.8	1,696.1	497.8	185.9	89.4	117.7	436.4
1982	3,081.5	285.5	133.9	91.3	1,080.6	565.1	157.1	91.0	12.8	1,728.2	500.9	187.0	90.3	109.9	442.2
1983	3,240.6	327.4	160.5	103.5	1,112.4	579.7	167.3	93.0	12.9	1,809.0	511.8	193.0	93.0	117.0	459.7
1984	3,407.6	374.9	187.7	115.5	1,151.8	589.9	179.9	95.9	12.8	1,883.0	531.8	197.7	93.6	128.6	472.4
1985	3,566.5	411.4	211.2	125.3	1,178.3	602.2	186.5	97.8	13.0	1,977.3	551.1	205.6	96.1	140.6	490.7
1986	3,708.7	448.4	224.8	140.6	1,215.9	614.0	199.9	102.5	13.4	2,041.4	565.5	209.8	95.1	145.7	510.3
1987	3,822.3	453.9	216.2	149.9	1,239.3	620.8	205.4	105.3	13.0	2,126.9	583.4	219.4	98.4	151.0	537.3
1988	3,972.7	485.5	229.4	160.8	1,274.4	641.6	210.0	106.5	13.2	2,212.4	600.9	229.2	103.4	159.0	561.3
1989	4,064.6	496.2	230.3	170.9	1,303.5	660.1	220.7	108.1	12.6	2,262.3	614.6	237.6	105.6	160.8	575.8
1990	4,132.2	493.3	224.3	173.5	1,316.1	662.9	217.9	107.3	11.2	2,321.3	627.2	240.1	103.7	159.9	602.8
1991	4,105.8	462.0	193.2	177.0	1,302.9	659.6	215.9	103.4	10.8	2,341.0	635.2	243.4	107.0	152.3	621.6
1992	4,219.8	488.5	206.9	189.4	1,321.8	660.0	225.5	106.6	10.9	2,409.4	646.8	248.2	106.6	158.1	646.6
1993	4,339.7	524.1	218.6	204.4	1,348.9	674.3	233.3	109.1	10.7	2,466.8	655.0	261.2	112.4	162.6	658.8
1994	4,471.1	562.0	228.2	230.1	1,390.5	689.1	247.2	110.4	10.3	2,519.4	668.2	266.0	111.5	171.3	668.8
1990:I	4,128.9	511.2	237.6	176.0	1,319.2	659.0	221.5	109.3	10.7	2,295.7	623.4	233.7	98.6	161.7	591.9
II	4,134.7	495.4	226.4	173.9	1,316.9	664.2	217.3	107.5	11.8	2,321.1	626.3	241.3	104.8	160.9	600.7
III	4,148.5	490.4	223.1	172.5	1,319.8	665.5	217.6	107.4	12.3	2,337.3	628.5	243.7	106.2	159.7	608.0
IV	4,116.4	476.3	210.0	171.5	1,308.4	662.9	215.1	104.9	9.9	2,331.2	630.6	241.9	105.3	157.3	610.6
1991:I	4,084.5	458.6	191.4	173.0	1,300.6	658.7	214.0	103.3	10.4	2,325.3	631.6	238.2	103.5	152.6	614.3
II	4,110.0	460.5	189.6	177.7	1,308.0	661.5	218.9	104.0	10.8	2,341.5	634.1	246.9	110.9	152.1	617.9
III	4,119.5	467.3	197.2	179.2	1,307.1	661.6	217.5	103.8	11.4	2,345.0	636.4	246.1	108.5	151.8	623.3
IV	4,109.1	461.5	194.6	178.0	1,295.7	656.5	213.1	102.5	10.6	2,352.0	638.6	242.5	105.1	152.6	630.8
1992:I	4,173.8	476.1	201.7	183.7	1,314.4	661.0	220.4	104.8	10.5	2,383.2	642.6	243.6	103.2	155.4	638.2
II	4,196.4	481.1	204.5	186.0	1,312.0	653.9	223.2	106.1	11.9	2,403.2	645.5	249.9	106.8	156.7	645.9
III	4,226.7	491.9	207.4	191.3	1,321.1	656.4	227.7	108.2	10.5	2,413.6	648.5	243.3	106.6	160.5	650.3
IV	4,282.3	505.0	213.9	196.4	1,339.8	668.6	230.9	107.3	10.7	2,437.6	650.6	256.1	109.7	159.6	652.2
1993:I	4,290.0	506.0	210.8	200.8	1,336.9	670.5	227.4	108.2	10.9	2,447.0	652.2	257.0	111.6	160.6	656.6
II	4,319.0	519.6	219.0	205.1	1,344.7	672.9	232.3	108.0	10.6	2,454.9	653.5	258.0	110.0	161.5	657.5
III	4,359.7	528.9	219.1	211.0	1,354.2	675.7	235.0	110.9	10.7	2,476.7	655.9	264.9	114.1	162.8	659.7
IV	4,390.0	541.9	225.4	216.8	1,359.8	677.9	238.6	109.3	10.6	2,488.6	658.5	265.0	113.7	165.7	661.4
1994:I	4,418.8	549.6	230.3	219.0	1,372.7	682.2	241.1	108.8	11.4	2,497.0	662.1	258.8	112.9	168.2	663.2
II	4,457.7	555.4	226.7	231.1	1,383.7	688.5	243.3	109.5	10.0	2,519.0	666.1	269.8	115.1	170.3	667.6
III	4,485.8	563.0	226.4	232.5	1,397.2	690.6	249.0	111.6	10.2	2,526.3	670.7	268.1	110.4	172.1	670.4
IV	4,522.3	579.9	229.4	242.7	1,408.4	695.1	255.5	111.6	9.6	2,535.1	674.1	267.1	107.6	174.5	674.2
1995:I	4,530.9	566.9	216.2	243.3	1,416.8	700.7	254.6	113.4	10.9	2,548.1	677.4	270.1	109.4	175.7	677.8
II	4,568.8	576.6	220.7	247.5	1,423.5	701.6	258.0	113.6	10.6	2,569.6	680.0	277.3	114.3	175.9	681.3
III	4,601.1	589.8	226.1	254.9	1,425.3	703.9	258.9	112.5	10.0	2,586.9	682.9	282.0	118.7	176.4	686.1

¹ Includes other items not shown separately.
² Includes imputed rental value of owner-occupied housing.

Source: Department of Commerce, Bureau of Economic Analysis.

TABLE B-14.—*Private gross fixed investment by type, 1959-95*

[Billions of dollars; quarterly data at seasonally adjusted annual rates]

Year or quarter	Private fixed invest-ment	Nonresidential											Resi-den-tial
		Total non-resi-dential	Structures				Producers' durable equipment						
			Total¹	Non-resi-dential buildings including farm	Utili-ties	Mining explo-ration, shafts, and wells	Total¹	Information processing and related equipment			Indus-trial equip-ment	Trans-porta-tion and related equip-ment	
								Total	Comput-ers and periph-eral equip-ment²	Other			
1959	74.6	46.5	18.1	10.6	4.9	2.5	28.3	4.0	0.0	4.0	8.4	8.3	28.1
1960	75.5	49.2	19.6	12.0	5.0	2.3	29.7	4.7	.2	4.5	9.3	8.5	26.3
1961	75.0	48.6	19.7	12.7	4.6	2.3	28.9	5.1	.3	4.8	8.7	8.0	26.4
1962	81.8	52.8	20.8	13.7	4.6	2.5	32.1	5.4	.3	5.1	9.2	9.8	29.0
1963	87.7	55.6	21.2	13.9	5.0	2.3	34.4	6.1	.7	5.3	10.0	9.4	32.1
1964	96.7	62.4	23.7	15.8	5.4	2.4	38.7	6.8	.9	5.8	11.4	10.6	34.3
1965	108.3	74.1	28.3	19.5	6.1	2.4	45.8	7.8	1.2	6.6	13.6	13.2	34.2
1966	116.7	84.4	31.3	21.3	7.1	2.5	53.0	9.6	1.7	7.9	16.1	14.5	32.3
1967	117.6	85.2	31.5	20.6	7.8	2.4	53.7	10.0	1.9	8.1	16.8	14.3	32.4
1968	130.8	92.1	33.6	21.1	9.2	2.6	58.5	10.6	1.9	8.6	17.2	17.6	38.7
1969	145.5	102.9	37.7	24.4	9.6	2.8	65.2	12.9	2.4	10.4	18.9	18.9	42.6
1970	148.1	106.7	40.3	25.4	11.1	2.8	66.4	14.3	2.7	11.6	20.2	16.2	41.4
1971	167.5	111.7	42.7	27.1	11.9	2.7	69.1	14.9	2.8	12.1	19.4	18.4	55.8
1972	195.7	126.1	47.2	30.1	13.1	3.1	78.9	16.5	3.5	13.1	21.3	21.8	69.7
1973	225.4	150.0	55.0	35.5	15.0	3.5	95.1	19.8	3.5	16.3	25.9	26.6	75.3
1974	231.5	165.6	61.2	38.3	16.5	5.2	104.3	22.9	3.9	19.0	30.5	26.3	66.0
1975	231.7	169.0	61.4	35.6	17.1	7.4	107.6	23.5	3.6	19.9	31.1	25.2	62.7
1976	269.6	187.2	65.9	35.9	20.0	8.6	121.2	27.2	4.4	22.8	33.9	30.0	82.5
1977	333.5	223.2	74.6	39.9	21.5	11.5	148.7	33.1	5.7	27.5	39.2	39.3	110.3
1978	403.6	272.0	91.4	49.7	24.1	15.4	180.6	41.8	7.6	34.2	47.4	47.3	131.6
1979	464.0	323.0	114.9	65.7	27.5	19.0	208.1	49.9	10.2	39.8	55.8	53.6	141.0
1980	473.5	350.3	133.9	73.7	30.2	27.4	216.4	58.9	12.5	46.4	60.4	48.4	123.2
1981	528.1	405.4	164.6	86.3	33.0	42.5	240.9	69.5	17.1	52.3	65.2	50.6	122.6
1982	515.6	409.9	175.0	94.5	32.5	44.8	234.9	72.7	18.9	53.9	62.2	46.8	105.7
1983	552.0	399.4	152.7	90.5	28.7	30.0	246.7	82.0	23.9	58.1	58.2	53.7	152.5
1984	648.1	468.3	176.0	110.0	30.0	31.3	292.3	98.6	31.6	67.0	67.4	64.8	179.8
1985	688.9	502.0	193.3	128.0	30.6	27.9	308.7	104.2	33.7	70.5	71.7	69.7	186.9
1986	712.9	494.8	175.8	123.3	31.2	15.7	319.0	108.8	33.4	75.4	74.6	71.8	218.1
1987	722.9	495.4	172.1	126.0	26.5	13.1	323.3	109.8	35.8	74.0	75.9	70.4	227.6
1988	763.1	530.6	181.3	133.3	27.1	15.7	349.3	118.2	38.1	80.1	82.9	76.0	232.5
1989	797.5	566.2	192.3	142.7	29.4	14.4	373.9	127.1	43.3	83.8	91.5	71.2	231.3
1990	791.6	575.9	200.8	148.9	27.5	17.5	375.1	124.2	38.9	85.2	89.8	75.5	215.7
1991	738.5	547.3	181.7	126.1	31.6	17.1	365.6	122.6	38.1	84.5	86.4	79.5	191.2
1992	783.4	557.9	169.2	113.2	34.5	13.3	388.7	134.2	43.9	90.2	89.3	86.2	225.6
1993	850.5	598.8	171.8	116.6	32.0	15.6	427.0	141.8	48.7	93.0	97.6	99.2	251.7
1994	954.9	667.2	180.2	126.2	33.7	13.5	487.0	160.4	54.5	106.0	109.7	117.1	287.7
1990:I	813.9	581.2	201.9	150.8	27.0	16.8	379.3	127.8	41.3	86.5	91.7	74.0	232.7
II ...	794.0	571.6	202.4	151.2	27.0	17.6	369.2	123.9	38.9	85.0	88.9	71.4	222.4
III ...	791.2	580.3	203.5	151.4	27.5	17.6	376.7	121.5	36.8	84.7	90.3	78.5	210.9
IV ...	767.5	570.6	195.4	142.1	28.4	18.1	375.1	123.4	38.6	84.7	88.1	78.3	196.9
1991:I	739.7	555.4	192.3	136.4	30.0	19.4	363.1	119.3	36.7	82.7	87.8	78.1	184.3
II ...	736.2	550.2	187.6	130.9	31.3	18.9	362.6	121.6	37.2	84.5	86.4	77.3	185.9
III ...	738.6	544.3	176.1	121.4	32.3	15.2	368.2	123.5	37.8	85.6	86.3	81.9	194.3
IV ...	739.5	539.2	170.8	115.7	33.0	15.0	368.4	125.9	40.7	85.2	85.2	80.6	200.3
1992:I	755.4	544.1	171.6	117.2	34.3	12.8	372.5	129.2	41.9	87.3	86.2	79.5	211.3
II ...	780.5	556.8	170.4	114.0	34.8	13.3	386.3	133.0	44.4	88.6	87.7	87.8	223.7
III ...	788.1	561.0	167.6	110.6	34.7	13.3	393.4	137.7	44.6	93.1	90.5	85.5	227.1
IV ..	809.7	569.6	167.1	111.0	34.2	13.8	402.5	136.8	44.9	91.9	92.8	91.9	240.1
1993:I	823.8	580.3	170.2	113.6	32.8	15.8	410.1	136.8	47.2	89.6	94.3	94.0	243.5
II ...	834.3	591.1	169.7	113.8	31.9	16.0	421.3	137.9	46.8	91.0	95.6	100.9	243.2
III ..	851.8	599.2	171.4	117.1	31.7	15.5	427.7	144.5	49.7	94.8	97.8	97.0	252.6
IV ..	892.3	624.6	175.8	121.8	31.7	15.1	448.8	148.0	51.2	96.8	102.8	105.1	267.7
1994:I	917.4	638.8	171.8	118.7	32.3	14.4	467.0	152.5	52.1	100.4	105.4	113.0	278.5
II ...	942.0	653.5	179.1	125.3	33.0	14.1	474.4	157.7	53.7	104.0	107.6	110.5	288.5
III ...	968.9	678.5	181.0	126.4	34.2	13.0	497.5	161.6	54.4	107.2	111.3	122.9	290.4
IV ..	991.4	697.9	188.8	134.4	35.2	12.4	509.1	169.9	57.7	112.2	114.6	122.1	293.5
1995:I	1,013.9	723.6	194.5	137.9	36.3	13.2	529.0	174.6	58.4	116.2	120.4	127.2	290.4
II ...	1,016.3	734.4	197.6	140.3	37.9	11.5	536.8	183.3	62.8	120.6	126.9	121.0	281.9
III ..	1,036.5	746.3	202.3	143.9	39.4	11.9	544.0	183.1	63.3	119.7	125.8	128.6	290.2

¹ Includes other items, not shown separately.
² Includes new computers and peripheral equipment only.
Source: Department of Commerce, Bureau of Economic Analysis.

TABLE B–15.—Real private gross fixed investment by type, 1959–95

[Billions of chained (1992) dollars; quarterly data at seasonally adjusted annual rates]

Year or quarter	Private fixed invest-ment	Nonresidential Total non-resi-dential	Structures Total¹	Non-resi-dential buildings including farm	Utili-ties	Mining explo-ration, shafts, and wells	Producers' durable equipment Total¹	Information processing and related equipment Total	Comput-ers and periph-eral equip-ment²	Other	Indus-trial equip-ment	Trans-portation and re-lated equip-ment	Resi-den-tial
1959	267.1	147.7	85.8	52.4	20.2	11.0	71.4	2.5	....	9.8	38.8	28.0	131.1
1960	269.2	155.9	92.6	59.9	20.4	10.3	74.3	3.0	....	11.1	41.9	28.8	121.8
1961	267.9	154.5	93.9	63.3	18.9	10.5	72.5	3.2	....	11.8	39.7	27.0	122.2
1962	292.0	168.0	98.1	67.4	19.0	11.0	81.0	3.6	....	12.5	41.8	33.4	133.9
1963	313.7	176.4	99.2	67.5	20.4	10.4	87.1	4.1	....	13.0	45.1	32.1	149.6
1964	343.7	197.1	109.5	75.0	22.2	11.1	98.1	4.6	....	14.1	51.0	36.3	158.3
1965	378.5	231.3	126.9	89.4	24.4	11.0	115.9	5.5	....	16.0	60.2	45.5	153.7
1966	399.1	259.4	135.6	94.2	27.8	10.4	133.8	7.1	....	18.9	69.2	50.1	140.0
1967	391.0	255.3	132.2	88.7	29.8	9.9	132.5	7.5	....	18.9	69.5	48.4	135.6
1968	418.1	266.4	134.1	86.2	33.3	10.0	140.5	8.0	....	19.5	68.1	58.2	154.0
1969	442.9	285.6	141.3	92.7	33.4	10.4	152.2	9.7	0.1	22.8	72.6	60.5	158.6
1970	432.1	282.8	141.7	91.1	35.7	9.8	149.5	10.7	.1	24.5	73.7	49.7	149.1
1971	464.9	282.4	139.4	89.4	36.1	9.1	150.7	11.4	.1	24.7	67.7	53.6	190.0
1972	520.3	307.7	143.7	91.8	37.6	9.7	169.8	12.9	.2	26.0	73.0	62.3	223.7
1973	567.5	352.5	155.4	100.3	40.0	10.4	201.2	15.4	.2	31.7	86.2	75.0	222.3
1974	530.2	344.4	152.2	97.6	37.6	12.3	205.4	17.5	.2	34.8	92.8	67.9	176.4
1975	471.0	317.3	136.2	82.5	34.4	14.4	183.9	16.9	.2	33.3	78.6	58.4	153.5
1976	517.6	332.6	139.6	80.6	38.0	15.6	195.2	19.4	.3	36.6	79.0	65.0	189.7
1977	593.7	371.8	146.4	83.6	38.2	18.0	225.6	24.1	.5	43.8	83.6	79.1	229.8
1978	660.8	422.6	162.3	95.3	40.0	20.0	259.6	31.7	1.0	52.4	93.0	87.3	245.0
1979	695.6	463.3	182.7	113.5	41.3	21.3	280.7	38.6	1.5	59.5	99.8	91.0	236.0
1980	648.4	461.1	195.0	114.4	41.2	30.0	268.2	45.4	2.4	64.9	95.5	74.2	186.1
1981	660.6	485.7	210.4	122.8	42.0	34.9	278.2	52.5	3.8	68.5	94.1	72.0	171.2
1982	610.4	464.3	207.2	126.6	39.5	32.2	260.3	54.5	4.7	67.0	85.5	63.7	140.1
1983	654.2	456.4	185.7	117.6	34.2	26.7	272.4	63.4	7.1	70.4	78.5	71.7	197.6
1984	762.4	535.4	212.2	137.6	35.4	30.3	324.6	79.8	11.6	79.0	89.9	85.1	226.4
1985	799.3	568.4	227.8	155.2	35.6	27.0	342.4	88.0	14.5	81.9	94.1	88.4	229.5
1986	805.0	548.5	203.3	144.5	36.5	15.8	345.9	94.1	16.7	84.6	93.5	85.6	257.0
1987	799.4	542.4	195.9	142.4	30.7	15.5	346.9	97.5	21.0	80.2	91.1	82.1	257.6
1988	818.3	566.0	196.8	145.3	30.0	15.8	369.2	106.6	24.0	85.7	95.3	87.1	252.5
1989	832.0	588.8	201.2	150.2	30.9	13.9	387.6	116.2	29.4	88.1	101.5	78.9	243.2
1990	805.8	585.2	203.3	152.0	28.1	16.1	381.9	116.2	29.4	88.2	95.0	81.2	220.6
1991	741.3	547.7	181.6	126.9	32.0	15.7	366.2	117.8	32.4	85.9	88.3	81.7	193.4
1992	783.4	557.9	169.2	113.2	34.5	13.3	388.7	134.2	43.9	90.2	89.3	86.2	225.6
1993	836.4	593.6	166.3	112.8	31.1	14.8	427.6	147.1	56.2	91.5	96.3	97.5	242.7
1994	921.1	652.1	168.8	117.7	31.7	12.6	484.1	170.4	69.3	102.6	105.9	111.7	268.9
1990:I	834.7	595.3	206.5	155.4	27.7	15.8	388.8	119.2	30.6	89.8	98.6	80.3	239.4
II	811.2	583.4	205.5	154.7	27.6	16.3	377.8	116.1	29.3	88.2	94.8	77.4	227.8
III	803.1	588.1	205.2	153.8	28.1	16.1	383.0	113.8	27.9	87.6	95.1	84.3	214.9
IV	774.4	573.9	196.0	143.8	28.9	16.3	377.9	115.7	29.9	87.1	91.4	82.8	200.3
1991:I	742.6	555.1	192.2	137.6	30.4	17.3	362.9	112.5	29.2	84.3	89.7	81.2	187.4
II	739.4	550.9	187.2	131.7	31.7	17.0	363.8	116.2	30.8	86.2	88.7	79.9	188.3
III	741.0	545.3	175.5	121.7	32.6	14.0	369.8	119.7	33.2	87.1	88.4	83.9	195.6
IV	742.0	539.5	171.4	116.4	33.3	14.4	368.1	122.5	36.6	86.2	86.4	81.6	202.4
1992:I	758.3	544.4	172.7	118.1	34.6	12.7	371.7	126.7	39.2	87.7	86.8	79.9	213.9
II	782.4	557.5	171.0	114.4	34.8	13.3	386.4	132.4	43.4	88.9	88.1	87.9	224.9
III	787.3	560.6	167.4	110.4	34.6	13.4	393.1	138.6	45.7	92.8	89.8	85.4	226.7
IV	805.8	569.1	165.6	109.8	33.9	13.7	403.5	138.9	47.5	91.5	92.6	91.5	236.7
1993:I	815.4	577.5	167.0	111.4	32.4	15.2	410.5	139.5	51.1	88.6	93.7	93.0	237.9
II	821.1	586.4	164.8	110.6	31.0	15.2	421.7	142.2	52.9	89.6	94.4	99.5	234.8
III	835.4	593.1	165.1	112.7	30.7	14.6	428.2	150.7	58.3	93.1	96.3	95.0	242.2
IV	873.5	617.6	168.2	116.3	30.5	14.2	449.8	156.0	62.5	94.6	100.7	102.7	255.8
1994:I	892.4	628.6	163.0	112.4	30.7	13.4	466.5	161.2	64.6	97.8	102.8	109.0	263.6
II	911.4	639.5	169.0	117.8	31.2	13.3	471.2	166.6	67.1	100.8	104.3	105.3	271.6
III	930.8	660.4	169.1	117.4	32.1	12.2	492.4	171.5	69.3	103.6	107.0	115.9	270.3
IV	949.7	679.7	174.3	123.3	32.7	11.5	506.4	182.5	76.3	108.3	109.4	116.5	270.3
1995:I	969.6	704.4	178.5	125.4	33.7	12.5	527.1	189.2	80.2	111.5	114.2	121.7	256.9
II	966.1	710.6	180.0	126.8	34.8	10.7	531.9	199.9	88.2	115.1	118.4	114.8	256.6
III	980.6	719.8	182.4	129.2	35.6	11.0	538.6	202.0	92.1	114.0	116.7	120.5	261.8

¹ Includes other items, not shown separately.
² Includes new computers and peripheral equipment only.

Source: Department of Commerce, Bureau of Economic Analysis.

TABLE B–16.—*Government consumption expenditures and gross investment by type, 1959–95*

[Billions of dollars; quarterly data at seasonally adjusted annual rates]

Year or quarter	Total	Federal Total	National defense Total	National defense Con-sumption ex-penditures	National defense Gross investment Struc-tures	National defense Gross investment Equip-ment	Nondefense Total	Nondefense Con-sumption ex-penditures	Nondefense Gross investment Struc-tures	Nondefense Gross investment Equip-ment	State and local Total	Con-sump-tion ex-pendi-tures	Gross investment Struc-tures	Gross investment Equip-ment
1959	112.0	67.2	55.7	42.0	2.5	11.2	11.5	9.9	1.5	0.2	44.8	30.9	12.8	1.1
1960	113.2	65.6	54.9	42.5	2.2	10.1	10.8	8.8	1.7	0.3	47.6	33.7	12.7	1.2
1961	120.9	69.1	57.7	43.9	2.4	11.5	11.4	9.0	1.9	0.5	51.8	36.7	13.8	1.2
1962	131.4	76.5	62.3	47.8	2.0	12.5	14.2	11.3	2.1	0.8	55.0	39.1	14.5	1.3
1963	137.7	78.1	62.2	49.6	1.6	11.0	15.9	12.4	2.3	1.1	59.6	42.2	16.0	1.5
1964	144.4	79.4	61.3	49.9	1.3	10.2	18.1	14.0	2.5	1.6	65.0	46.0	17.2	1.7
1965	153.0	81.8	62.0	52.0	1.1	8.9	19.7	15.1	2.8	1.8	71.2	50.5	19.0	1.8
1966	173.6	94.1	73.4	61.2	1.3	11.0	20.7	15.9	2.8	2.0	79.5	56.5	21.0	2.0
1967	194.6	106.6	85.5	71.3	1.2	13.0	21.0	17.0	2.2	1.8	88.1	62.9	23.0	2.2
1968	212.1	113.8	92.0	78.9	1.2	11.8	21.8	18.2	2.1	1.6	98.3	70.8	25.2	2.3
1969	223.8	115.8	92.4	80.0	1.5	10.9	23.4	20.0	1.9	1.5	108.0	79.8	25.6	2.6
1970	236.1	115.9	90.6	78.6	1.3	10.7	25.3	21.9	2.1	1.3	120.2	91.6	25.8	2.8
1971	249.9	117.1	88.7	79.2	1.8	7.7	28.3	24.6	2.5	1.3	132.8	102.9	27.0	2.9
1972	268.9	125.1	93.2	82.3	1.8	9.1	31.9	27.8	2.7	1.3	143.8	113.4	27.1	3.3
1973	287.6	128.2	94.7	83.7	2.1	8.9	33.5	29.2	3.1	1.2	159.4	126.4	29.1	3.8
1974	323.2	139.9	101.9	90.1	2.2	9.7	38.0	33.2	3.4	1.4	183.3	144.0	34.7	4.6
1975	362.6	154.5	110.9	97.0	2.3	11.6	43.6	38.0	4.1	1.4	208.1	164.9	38.1	5.1
1976	385.9	162.7	116.1	101.3	2.1	12.6	46.6	40.4	4.6	1.6	223.1	179.7	38.1	5.3
1977	416.9	178.4	125.8	109.6	2.4	13.8	52.6	45.7	5.0	1.9	238.5	196.1	36.9	5.4
1978	457.9	194.4	135.6	118.4	2.5	14.6	58.9	50.4	6.1	2.3	263.4	214.5	42.8	6.1
1979	507.1	215.0	151.2	130.7	2.5	18.0	63.8	55.2	6.3	2.4	292.0	235.9	49.0	7.1
1980	572.8	248.4	174.2	150.9	3.2	20.1	74.2	64.3	7.1	2.9	324.4	261.3	55.1	8.1
1981	633.4	284.1	202.0	174.3	3.2	24.5	82.2	71.7	7.7	2.8	349.2	285.3	55.4	8.5
1982	684.8	313.2	230.9	197.6	4.0	29.4	82.3	72.3	6.8	3.2	371.6	307.9	54.2	9.4
1983	735.7	344.5	255.0	214.9	4.8	35.4	89.4	78.2	6.7	4.5	391.2	326.2	54.2	10.8
1984	796.6	372.6	282.7	236.3	4.9	41.5	89.9	77.9	7.0	5.0	424.0	350.8	60.5	12.7
1985	875.0	410.1	312.4	257.6	6.2	48.5	97.7	84.9	7.3	5.4	464.9	382.6	67.6	14.8
1986	938.5	435.2	332.4	272.7	6.8	52.9	102.9	89.7	8.0	5.2	503.3	412.7	74.2	16.4
1987	992.8	455.7	350.4	287.6	7.7	55.1	105.3	90.7	9.0	5.6	537.2	441.1	78.8	17.2
1988	1,032.0	457.3	354.0	297.9	7.4	48.7	103.3	89.9	6.8	6.6	574.7	471.3	84.8	18.6
1989	1,095.1	477.2	360.6	303.3	6.4	51.0	116.7	101.9	6.9	7.9	617.9	507.2	88.7	21.9
1990	1,176.1	503.6	373.1	312.7	6.1	54.3	130.4	113.9	8.0	8.6	672.6	550.1	98.5	23.9
1991	1,225.9	522.6	383.5	325.4	4.6	53.5	139.1	120.6	9.2	9.3	703.4	579.4	100.5	23.4
1992	1,263.8	528.0	375.8	319.7	5.2	50.9	152.2	131.4	10.3	10.5	735.8	603.6	108.1	24.0
1993	1,289.9	522.1	362.2	313.0	4.8	44.4	159.9	138.4	11.2	10.3	767.8	627.9	113.9	25.9
1994	1,314.7	516.3	352.0	305.7	4.9	41.4	164.3	144.9	10.5	8.9	798.4	651.7	119.0	27.7
1990: I	1,153.0	496.4	369.7	311.7	6.3	51.7	126.7	110.0	8.2	8.5	656.6	535.3	97.7	23.6
II	1,164.3	500.1	370.6	310.8	6.3	53.5	129.5	112.9	8.1	8.4	664.2	543.9	96.5	23.9
III	1,176.9	501.2	368.9	307.3	6.4	55.2	132.3	115.9	8.1	8.3	675.7	554.0	97.6	24.1
IV	1,210.4	516.7	383.3	321.0	5.3	57.0	133.3	116.7	7.6	9.1	693.7	567.3	102.4	24.1
1991: I	1,220.6	525.6	389.7	331.3	4.8	53.6	136.0	119.3	7.7	9.0	695.0	572.1	99.3	23.7
II	1,227.4	528.2	389.3	328.6	4.8	55.9	138.9	120.5	9.1	9.3	699.2	576.9	99.0	23.3
III	1,226.5	520.9	382.1	323.1	4.5	54.5	138.8	120.6	9.1	9.1	705.5	581.5	100.8	23.2
IV	1,229.2	515.5	373.0	318.5	4.5	50.0	142.6	122.0	10.8	9.8	713.6	587.3	102.9	23.4
1992: I	1,247.9	521.8	372.8	317.2	5.2	50.4	149.0	128.5	10.3	10.1	726.1	592.6	109.9	23.6
II	1,256.4	523.2	374.1	317.3	5.5	51.4	149.1	129.1	10.2	9.9	733.2	600.8	108.6	23.8
III	1,270.7	532.0	380.9	323.5	4.8	52.7	151.1	130.9	9.6	10.5	738.7	607.4	107.1	24.2
IV	1,280.0	535.0	375.3	320.7	5.5	49.1	159.7	137.0	11.0	11.6	745.1	613.6	106.9	24.6
1993: I	1,278.8	525.0	365.2	313.9	4.7	46.6	159.8	136.9	11.7	11.2	753.8	620.8	107.7	25.3
II	1,284.6	519.6	362.2	312.1	4.7	45.5	157.4	135.9	10.8	10.7	765.0	626.0	113.3	25.7
III	1,293.6	520.8	360.7	314.6	4.9	41.1	160.1	138.4	11.3	10.5	772.7	630.8	115.7	26.2
IV	1,302.7	522.9	360.8	315.5	4.7	44.6	162.2	142.3	11.0	8.9	779.7	634.1	119.1	26.5
1994: I	1,296.4	511.3	346.7	301.3	4.8	40.7	164.6	145.4	10.6	8.5	785.0	642.4	115.5	27.1
II	1,300.8	509.4	349.3	303.4	4.7	41.3	160.0	141.7	9.9	8.4	791.4	647.3	116.7	27.5
III	1,328.0	523.6	362.1	313.3	5.1	43.8	161.5	142.2	10.0	9.4	804.4	655.4	121.1	27.9
IV	1,333.5	520.9	349.6	304.9	4.9	39.8	171.2	150.4	11.5	9.4	812.6	661.9	122.7	28.1
1995: I	1,346.0	519.9	347.7	303.0	5.7	39.1	172.1	151.8	11.0	9.3	826.1	672.1	125.5	28.5
II	1,359.9	522.6	352.3	305.3	4.9	42.1	170.3	150.8	10.2	9.3	837.3	680.1	128.3	28.9
III	1,365.5	517.3	346.2	301.9	5.5	38.8	171.1	152.2	9.3	9.6	848.2	686.5	132.4	29.3

Source: Department of Commerce, Bureau of Economic Analysis.

—*Real government consumption expenditures and gross investment by type, 1959–95*

[Billions of chained (1992) dollars; quarterly data at seasonally adjusted annual rates]

Year or quarter	Total	Federal Total	National defense Total	National defense Consumption expenditures	National defense Gross investment Structures	National defense Gross investment Equipment	Nondefense Total	Nondefense Consumption expenditures	Nondefense Gross investment Structures	Nondefense Gross investment Equipment	State and local Total	State and local Consumption expenditures	State and local Gross investment Structures	State and local Gross investment Equipment
1959	618.5	360.5	307.6	259.3	15.5	28.4	58.8	53.9	7.2	0.4	256.8	191.6	59.9	3.1
1960	617.2	349.4	301.3	260.8	13.7	25.6	54.1	47.1	8.1	.6	267.2	201.8	60.0	3.4
1961	647.2	363.0	313.8	265.8	14.6	29.0	55.5	46.5	9.0	1.0	283.8	213.0	65.0	3.5
1962	686.0	393.2	332.4	284.2	12.1	30.9	66.8	56.4	10.1	1.4	292.1	218.7	67.1	3.8
1963	701.9	391.8	324.0	287.9	9.9	26.4	72.9	60.4	10.9	1.9	309.7	229.5	72.7	4.3
1964	715.9	385.2	309.9	279.3	7.5	24.4	79.2	64.5	11.7	2.5	330.9	244.9	77.5	4.8
1965	737.6	385.2	303.8	281.1	6.7	21.0	84.6	67.7	12.4	3.2	353.2	261.1	83.0	5.1
1966	804.6	429.1	348.2	318.9	7.0	25.8	85.7	68.4	12.3	3.4	375.9	277.7	88.2	5.6
1967	865.6	471.7	393.5	360.2	6.4	29.9	84.7	71.5	9.3	3.0	394.2	289.8	93.9	5.8
1968	892.4	476.3	400.9	376.7	6.3	26.1	82.5	71.4	8.3	2.5	416.5	307.5	98.1	6.1
1969	887.5	459.9	381.6	361.6	6.8	23.1	84.3	75.1	7.1	2.2	428.0	324.4	92.9	6.5
1970	866.8	427.2	349.0	330.1	5.5	21.7	83.0	74.6	7.1	1.9	440.0	344.1	86.0	6.7
1971	851.0	397.0	313.7	304.6	7.0	14.6	86.3	77.5	7.9	1.8	454.4	362.1	83.1	6.8
1972	854.1	390.2	300.3	285.3	6.3	17.5	91.9	83.0	8.1	1.8	464.5	376.0	78.9	7.6
1973	848.4	371.1	281.2	265.5	6.4	17.1	91.5	82.3	8.7	1.6	478.5	389.9	78.3	8.5
1974	862.9	368.8	273.5	256.5	5.9	17.9	96.4	87.3	8.5	1.8	495.6	406.8	78.1	9.3
1975	876.3	367.9	269.7	248.9	5.7	20.4	99.1	89.9	8.9	1.7	510.0	423.1	77.4	9.0
1976	876.8	364.3	264.7	242.5	5.0	21.5	100.4	90.2	9.5	1.9	514.3	429.5	76.1	8.8
1977	884.7	370.1	266.4	243.7	5.1	22.0	104.3	93.5	9.8	2.1	516.4	437.6	71.3	8.6
1978	910.6	377.7	266.7	244.7	5.1	21.5	111.4	98.1	11.3	2.7	534.7	448.1	78.1	9.0
1979	924.9	383.3	271.0	245.9	4.3	24.5	112.7	100.4	10.6	2.6	543.5	452.3	81.4	9.7
1980	941.4	399.3	280.7	254.0	5.0	25.5	119.0	106.0	10.7	3.1	543.6	451.7	81.3	10.3
1981	947.7	415.9	296.0	266.4	4.8	28.3	120.4	107.9	10.5	2.9	532.8	450.3	73.3	10.1
1982	960.1	429.4	316.5	282.0	5.6	32.0	113.3	102.3	8.6	3.2	531.4	455.6	67.0	10.7
1983	987.3	452.7	334.6	293.3	6.6	37.0	118.5	105.9	8.4	4.7	534.9	458.2	66.3	12.1
1984	1,018.4	463.7	348.1	301.3	6.4	41.7	115.9	102.3	8.7	5.2	555.0	467.9	73.8	14.2
1985	1,080.1	495.6	374.1	318.2	7.9	48.6	121.8	107.4	8.9	5.7	584.7	487.8	80.9	16.4
1986	1,135.0	518.4	393.4	331.1	8.6	53.7	125.2	110.6	9.4	5.4	616.9	513.3	85.9	17.6
1987	1,165.9	534.4	409.2	341.1	9.2	58.4	125.3	109.2	10.3	5.9	631.8	525.5	87.8	18.8
1988	1,180.9	524.6	405.5	345.3	8.5	51.9	119.1	104.8	7.6	6.8	656.6	545.3	91.6	20.0
1989	1,213.9	531.5	401.6	340.9	6.9	53.8	130.1	114.8	7.4	7.9	682.6	566.3	93.5	23.0
1990	1,250.4	541.9	401.5	338.9	6.4	56.1	140.5	123.8	8.3	8.5	708.6	583.2	100.7	24.7
1991	1,258.0	539.4	397.5	338.7	4.7	54.1	142.0	123.6	9.3	9.2	718.7	593.8	101.3	23.6
1992	1,263.8	528.0	375.8	319.7	5.2	50.9	152.2	131.4	10.3	10.5	735.8	603.6	108.1	24.0
1993	1,260.5	508.7	354.9	306.9	4.4	43.6	153.8	132.4	11.0	10.4	751.8	614.6	111.5	25.7
1994	1,259.9	489.7	336.9	293.5	4.3	39.1	152.6	133.5	10.0	9.0	770.5	629.0	114.4	27.1
1990: I	1,246.5	542.9	404.1	343.6	6.7	53.9	138.9	122.0	8.5	8.5	703.8	578.1	101.0	24.6
II	1,248.2	543.0	402.8	340.0	6.7	56.0	140.4	123.7	8.4	8.3	705.4	581.6	99.0	24.8
III	1,246.8	538.2	396.1	332.4	6.7	56.9	142.2	125.7	8.4	8.2	708.7	585.0	99.0	24.8
IV	1,259.9	543.5	403.1	339.7	5.6	57.7	140.5	124.0	7.7	8.9	716.5	588.2	103.7	24.6
1991: I	1,262.6	547.3	408.4	348.9	4.9	54.6	139.0	122.4	7.9	8.8	715.5	590.9	100.6	23.9
II	1,263.8	547.1	405.0	343.8	4.9	56.3	142.2	123.8	9.2	9.2	716.8	593.5	99.7	23.7
III	1,255.1	536.3	395.0	335.2	4.5	55.3	141.4	123.2	9.1	9.0	718.8	594.2	101.2	23.5
IV	1,250.7	526.9	381.7	326.7	4.6	50.4	145.3	124.7	10.9	9.7	723.8	596.7	103.7	23.4
1992: I	1,258.5	525.1	374.2	318.3	5.2	50.7	150.8	130.4	10.4	10.1	733.5	599.0	110.8	23.6
II	1,257.5	522.3	373.3	316.5	5.5	51.3	150.0	129.9	10.2	9.8	734.2	601.7	108.8	23.8
III	1,266.5	529.6	378.7	321.2	4.8	52.7	150.9	130.7	9.6	10.5	736.9	605.9	106.8	24.2
IV	1,272.5	534.0	376.8	322.6	5.4	48.9	157.1	134.5	10.9	11.7	738.5	607.9	106.1	24.6
1993: I	1,257.2	515.7	361.2	310.4	4.5	46.2	154.5	131.7	11.5	11.3	741.6	610.3	106.2	25.1
II	1,257.9	509.2	356.4	307.1	4.4	44.9	152.7	131.4	10.6	10.8	748.8	612.4	110.9	25.5
III	1,261.1	505.4	351.2	306.6	4.4	40.2	154.2	132.6	11.0	10.6	755.7	616.6	113.2	26.0
IV	1,265.7	504.5	350.8	303.4	4.2	43.2	153.7	134.0	10.6	9.0	761.3	619.1	115.9	26.3
1994: I	1,252.3	489.8	334.8	291.6	4.2	39.0	154.8	135.8	10.3	8.6	762.7	624.0	112.0	26.7
II	1,249.7	483.3	335.5	292.7	4.1	38.7	147.7	129.6	9.5	8.5	766.8	626.9	113.0	26.9
III	1,271.0	496.6	346.1	300.2	4.4	41.4	150.5	131.5	9.5	9.4	774.7	631.2	116.2	27.2
IV	1,266.6	489.1	331.3	289.6	4.2	37.4	157.5	137.2	10.8	9.4	777.7	633.7	116.5	27.6
1995: I	1,263.0	481.3	325.3	283.8	4.9	36.6	155.6	135.9	10.3	9.4	782.2	636.1	118.2	27.9
II	1,265.8	479.9	326.1	283.2	4.2	38.7	153.6	134.7	9.4	9.4	786.3	637.9	120.2	28.2
III	1,264.4	473.2	319.8	279.3	4.7	35.8	153.1	134.8	8.5	9.7	791.7	640.6	122.7	28.5

Source: Department of Commerce, Bureau of Economic Analysis.

TABLE B–18.—*Inventories and final sales of domestic business, 1959–95*

[Billions of dollars, except as noted; seasonally adjusted]

Quarter	Inventories [1] Total[2]	Farm	Nonfarm Total[2]	Manu-facturing	Whole-sale trade	Retail trade	Other	Final sales of domestic busi-ness[3]	Ratio of inventories to final sales of domestic business Total	Nonfarm
Fourth quarter:										
1959	131.0	32.1	98.9	51.6	18.3	20.0	9.0	36.5	3.59	2.71
1960	134.7	32.9	101.8	52.8	18.6	21.4	8.9	37.7	3.57	2.70
1961	138.0	34.6	103.4	54.3	19.1	20.9	9.2	39.5	3.49	2.62
1962	145.8	36.8	109.0	57.6	19.9	22.3	9.2	41.8	3.48	2.61
1963	148.3	33.9	114.4	59.6	21.3	23.6	9.8	44.5	3.33	2.57
1964	154.0	32.5	121.4	63.2	22.7	24.9	10.6	47.4	3.25	2.56
1965	168.8	37.0	131.9	68.2	24.3	27.7	11.7	52.5	3.22	2.51
1966	186.2	37.5	148.6	78.3	27.7	30.1	12.5	55.6	3.35	2.67
1967	198.4	37.0	161.4	85.2	29.9	31.1	15.3	59.2	3.35	2.73
1968	214.1	40.3	173.8	91.4	31.7	34.4	16.3	65.1	3.29	2.67
1969	233.7	43.8	189.9	99.0	35.2	37.7	18.1	69.1	3.38	2.75
1970	242.0	42.3	199.7	102.8	39.0	38.7	19.3	72.9	3.32	2.74
1971	261.2	49.7	211.5	103.5	42.1	44.9	20.9	79.4	3.29	2.66
1972	289.7	60.9	228.8	109.4	46.0	50.0	23.4	88.5	3.28	2.59
1973	345.8	78.1	267.8	125.1	54.8	58.7	29.2	97.5	3.55	2.75
1974	398.6	68.4	330.3	158.2	69.8	64.2	38.0	105.4	3.78	3.13
1975	410.6	72.3	338.4	164.5	69.3	64.7	39.8	118.0	3.48	2.87
1976	443.4	68.3	375.1	181.1	77.2	73.3	43.5	129.7	3.42	2.89
1977	494.2	73.3	421.0	202.8	86.6	81.2	50.4	145.0	3.41	2.90
1978	581.9	97.9	484.0	228.4	101.9	94.5	59.1	167.6	3.47	2.89
1979	676.8	114.9	561.9	268.7	120.5	105.3	67.5	186.4	3.63	3.01
1980	737.5	114.7	622.8	296.5	138.5	113.7	74.0	204.8	3.60	3.04
1981	783.1	104.9	678.2	318.1	151.4	123.9	84.9	221.8	3.53	3.06
1982	768.4	110.4	658.0	299.5	150.3	123.5	84.6	232.8	3.30	2.83
1983	787.8	106.7	681.1	302.6	154.1	138.0	86.4	255.4	3.08	2.67
1984	860.7	109.2	751.5	333.4	169.0	157.3	91.8	276.7	3.11	2.72
1985	875.3	106.3	769.1	325.3	173.4	171.9	98.4	297.7	2.94	2.58
1986	862.7	94.5	768.2	314.6	177.2	176.8	99.5	315.7	2.73	2.43
1987	927.5	98.0	829.5	332.9	190.6	199.5	106.4	333.1	2.78	2.49
1988	992.8	102.0	890.8	358.8	208.5	213.8	109.6	362.8	2.74	2.46
1989	1,044.6	103.6	941.0	382.1	218.4	232.7	107.8	384.9	2.71	2.44
1990: I	1,051.9	106.2	945.7	385.9	221.6	229.8	108.4	394.2	2.67	2.40
II	1,062.7	107.2	955.5	387.5	226.3	234.1	107.6	397.6	2.67	2.40
III	1,087.1	109.1	977.9	401.0	230.9	237.3	108.7	401.0	2.71	2.44
IV	1,082.4	108.3	974.1	399.7	232.4	237.1	104.8	403.4	2.68	2.41
1991: I	1,072.3	111.2	961.1	393.7	233.7	232.7	101.0	403.9	2.65	2.38
II	1,056.5	105.5	951.0	385.5	230.3	233.6	101.7	409.0	2.58	2.33
III	1,053.0	99.0	954.1	383.5	231.3	237.5	101.7	411.0	2.56	2.32
IV	1,058.1	97.2	961.0	383.4	235.5	240.1	102.0	413.1	2.56	2.33
1992: I	1,065.6	105.0	960.6	379.2	236.9	240.1	104.4	423.4	2.52	2.27
II	1,070.8	104.1	966.8	378.1	240.5	244.1	104.1	427.7	2.50	2.26
III	1,076.3	104.8	971.5	380.1	242.0	246.4	103.0	432.8	2.49	2.24
IV	1,077.9	104.9	973.1	375.5	245.3	249.4	103.0	441.9	2.44	2.20
1993: I	1,097.3	109.9	987.4	378.0	248.0	259.0	102.5	444.3	2.47	2.22
II	1,101.3	105.5	995.8	380.5	249.6	261.7	104.0	448.9	2.45	2.22
III	1,103.4	101.7	1,001.7	380.1	252.8	263.3	105.5	453.4	2.43	2.21
IV	1,112.8	101.6	1,011.2	380.9	255.2	267.0	108.1	462.8	2.40	2.19
1994: I	1,130.2	107.2	1,023.0	385.5	257.3	270.2	110.1	467.2	2.42	2.19
II	1,147.0	103.3	1,043.8	390.3	263.3	278.1	111.9	473.0	2.43	2.21
III	1,167.4	102.5	1,064.9	397.7	270.7	283.4	113.1	481.9	2.42	2.21
IV	1,196.5	104.9	1,091.6	406.7	279.8	289.8	115.3	489.5	2.44	2.23
1995: I	1,235.4	105.8	1,129.6	421.0	291.9	296.1	120.6	494.0	2.50	2.29
II	1,246.0	101.2	1,144.8	426.5	297.8	298.0	122.5	499.2	2.50	2.29
III	1,250.6	99.3	1,151.4	429.3	299.7	299.9	122.4	507.2	2.47	2.27

[1] Inventories at end of quarter. Quarter-to-quarter change calculated from this table is not the current-dollar change in business inventories (CBI) component of GDP. The former is the difference between two inventory stocks, each valued at their respective end-of-quarter prices. The latter is the change in the physical volume of inventories valued at average prices of the quarter. In addition, changes calculated from this table are at quarterly rates, whereas CBI is stated at annual rates.
[2] Inventories of construction establishments are included in "other" nonfarm inventories.
[3] Quarterly totals at monthly rates. Final sales of domestic business equals final sales of domestic product less gross product of households and institutions and general government and includes a small amount of final sales by farms.

Note.—The industry classification of inventories is on an establishment basis. Estimates for nonfarm industries other than manufacturing and trade for 1986 and earlier periods are based on the 1972 Standard Industrial Classification (SIC). Manufacturing estimates for 1981 and earlier periods and trade estimates for 1966 and earlier periods are based on the 1972 SIC; later estimates for these industries are based on the 1987 SIC. The resulting discontinuities are small.

Source: Department of Commerce, Bureau of Economic Analysis.

300

[Billions of chained (1992) dollars, except as noted; seasonally adjusted]

Quarter	Inventories [1]							Final sales of domestic business [3]	Ratio of inventories to final sales of domestic business	
	Total [2]	Farm	Nonfarm						Total	Nonfarm
			Total [2]	Manu-facturing	Whole-sale trade	Retail trade	Other			
Fourth quarter:										
1959	401.4	89.8	303.6	148.2	56.5	59.4	37.6	144.3	2.78	2.10
1960	412.0	91.5	312.4	150.6	57.9	63.6	38.3	147.0	2.80	2.13
1961	420.9	93.9	318.6	155.1	59.3	62.3	40.1	153.5	2.74	2.08
1962	440.9	95.9	336.7	165.2	61.9	66.7	40.1	160.8	2.74	2.09
1963	459.0	97.5	353.1	171.5	66.3	70.3	42.2	169.5	2.71	2.08
1964	474.7	93.9	372.6	180.4	70.3	74.2	45.0	178.4	2.66	2.09
1965	504.8	96.3	400.3	192.6	74.7	81.7	48.4	194.2	2.60	2.06
1966	547.2	94.9	445.0	217.6	84.6	88.5	49.8	199.4	2.74	2.23
1967	579.2	97.4	474.5	234.4	91.0	88.4	56.9	206.4	2.81	2.30
1968	606.1	101.1	497.5	245.0	94.1	95.8	58.1	217.8	2.78	2.28
1969	633.3	101.4	524.8	256.0	100.6	102.3	61.4	221.7	2.86	2.37
1970	639.0	99.3	533.0	256.0	108.0	102.4	62.6	224.0	2.85	2.38
1971	661.7	103.6	551.1	253.1	113.8	116.1	64.9	234.4	2.82	2.35
1972	686.9	104.2	576.5	259.8	119.0	124.9	69.9	252.7	2.72	2.28
1973	725.9	106.5	615.0	277.7	122.4	134.8	77.4	261.1	2.78	2.36
1974	749.8	102.2	646.8	296.8	133.0	132.9	80.8	254.6	2.94	2.54
1975	738.8	107.6	628.3	289.7	127.5	126.3	81.5	265.6	2.78	2.37
1976	767.8	105.6	660.4	303.4	135.9	136.0	81.7	277.5	2.77	2.38
1977	805.8	111.7	692.1	311.8	146.5	143.7	87.1	291.7	2.76	2.37
1978	848.1	113.3	733.6	325.8	158.8	153.1	93.2	311.9	2.72	2.35
1979	871.2	117.0	752.8	338.5	166.3	153.1	91.5	319.3	2.73	2.36
1980	861.2	110.1	751.3	338.9	171.3	148.9	88.7	319.9	2.69	2.35
1981	894.3	119.6	774.1	343.5	176.0	157.2	94.4	318.9	2.80	2.43
1982	878.7	126.9	751.3	329.5	174.1	153.3	91.7	319.2	2.75	2.35
1983	872.8	109.8	763.4	329.5	173.5	166.2	92.4	338.2	2.58	2.26
1984	947.6	115.8	832.4	358.4	189.6	186.4	96.7	355.7	2.66	2.34
1985	977.4	122.2	855.8	353.9	194.8	201.3	105.1	370.8	2.64	2.31
1986	988.3	120.5	868.2	349.7	201.9	204.4	111.6	384.3	2.57	2.26
1987	1,014.5	111.5	902.5	354.8	208.5	223.9	115.1	393.8	2.58	2.29
1988	1,026.2	98.8	927.2	364.3	217.8	231.3	113.7	411.7	2.49	2.25
1989	1,059.5	98.9	960.7	383.5	223.3	245.0	108.9	420.7	2.52	2.28
1990: I	1,062.2	98.9	963.4	386.9	225.9	240.5	109.9	426.2	2.49	2.26
II	1,073.2	100.0	973.2	389.2	230.5	244.1	109.3	424.2	2.53	2.29
III	1,076.9	102.0	974.9	391.1	231.1	245.0	107.6	423.6	2.54	2.30
IV	1,069.9	101.4	968.4	390.1	231.3	243.5	103.4	421.8	2.54	2.30
1991: I	1,065.5	100.8	964.7	390.4	234.1	238.4	101.6	417.7	2.55	2.31
II	1,060.3	101.5	958.8	386.1	232.0	238.0	102.6	420.2	2.52	2.28
III	1,061.5	99.3	962.2	384.5	233.1	241.7	102.9	419.4	2.53	2.29
IV	1,066.9	99.7	967.2	384.0	236.9	243.3	103.0	419.2	2.55	2.31
1992: I	1,066.9	101.6	965.3	380.6	237.2	242.0	105.4	426.6	2.50	2.26
II	1,069.7	104.1	965.6	377.5	239.8	244.3	104.1	428.9	2.49	2.25
III	1,072.7	105.4	967.3	378.5	241.6	245.1	102.1	432.3	2.48	2.24
IV	1,074.2	105.1	969.1	374.7	244.7	247.2	102.6	438.1	2.45	2.21
1993: I	1,078.8	103.3	975.6	375.0	245.2	255.1	100.2	436.7	2.47	2.23
II	1,084.0	101.9	982.3	377.7	247.0	256.1	101.5	438.4	2.47	2.24
III	1,088.9	99.0	990.0	379.6	250.1	257.5	102.7	441.3	2.47	2.24
IV	1,093.2	97.9	995.5	380.2	250.6	259.6	105.1	447.6	2.44	2.22
1994: I	1,103.3	100.6	1,003.0	382.8	251.3	262.2	106.5	449.0	2.46	2.23
II	1,121.8	105.7	1,016.5	383.9	256.4	267.9	108.1	452.5	2.48	2.25
III	1,137.8	109.3	1,029.1	386.9	261.5	271.8	108.6	458.1	2.48	2.25
IV	1,152.1	110.1	1,042.4	388.5	267.2	276.1	110.4	463.0	2.49	2.25
1995: I	1,165.8	109.0	1,056.9	390.7	273.4	279.3	113.4	464.0	2.51	2.28
II	1,173.4	108.1	1,065.4	393.5	277.2	280.7	113.8	466.4	2.52	2.28
III	1,180.2	106.7	1,073.3	397.4	279.0	282.0	114.9	471.0	2.51	2.28

[1] Inventories at end of quarter. Quarter-to-quarter changes calculated from this table are at quarterly rates, whereas the real-dollar change in business inventories component of GDP is stated at annual rates.

[2] Inventories of construction establishments are included in "other" nonfarm inventories.

[3] Quarterly totals at monthly rates. Final sales of domestic business equals final sales of domestic product less gross product of households and institutions and general government and includes a small amount of final sales by farms.

Note.—The industry classification of inventories is on an establishment basis. Estimates for nonfarm industries other than manufacturing and trade for 1986 and earlier periods are based on the 1972 Standard Industrial Classification (SIC). Manufacturing estimates for 1981 and earlier periods and trade estimates for 1966 and earlier periods are based on the 1972 SIC; later estimates for these industries are based on the 1987 SIC. The resulting discontinuities are small.

Source: Department of Commerce, Bureau of Economic Analysis.

TABLE B–20.—*Foreign transactions in the national income and product accounts, 1959–95*

[Billions of dollars; quarterly data at seasonally adjusted annual rates]

Year or quarter	Receipts from rest of the world					Payments to rest of the world									
	Total¹	Exports of goods and services			Receipts of factor income³	Total	Imports of goods and services			Payments of factor income⁴	Transfer payments (net)				Net foreign investment
		Total	Goods²	Services²			Total	Goods²	Services²		Total	From persons (net)	From government (net)	From business	
1959	25.0	20.6	16.5	4.2	4.3	25.0	22.3	15.3	7.0	1.5	2.4	0.4	1.8	0.1	-1.2
1960	30.2	25.3	20.5	4.8	5.0	30.2	22.8	15.2	7.6	1.8	2.4	.5	1.9	.1	3.2
1961	31.4	26.0	20.9	5.1	5.4	31.4	22.7	15.1	7.6	1.8	2.7	.5	2.1	.1	4.3
1962	33.5	27.4	21.7	5.7	6.1	33.5	25.0	16.9	8.1	1.8	2.8	.5	2.1	.1	3.9
1963	36.1	29.4	23.3	6.1	6.6	36.1	26.1	17.7	8.4	2.1	2.8	.6	2.1	.1	5.0
1964	41.0	33.6	26.7	6.9	7.4	41.0	28.1	19.4	8.7	2.4	3.0	.7	2.1	.2	7.5
1965	43.5	35.4	27.8	7.6	8.1	43.5	31.5	22.2	9.3	2.7	3.0	.8	2.1	.2	6.2
1966	47.2	38.9	30.7	8.2	8.3	47.2	37.1	26.3	10.7	3.1	3.2	.8	2.2	.2	3.9
1967	50.2	41.4	32.2	9.2	8.9	50.2	39.9	27.8	12.2	3.4	3.4	1.0	2.1	.2	3.5
1968	55.6	45.3	35.3	10.0	10.3	55.6	46.6	33.9	12.6	4.1	3.2	1.0	1.9	.3	1.7
1969	61.2	49.3	38.3	11.0	11.9	61.2	50.5	36.8	13.7	5.8	3.2	1.1	1.8	.3	1.8
1970	70.8	57.0	44.5	12.4	13.0	70.8	55.8	40.9	14.9	6.6	3.6	1.2	2.0	.4	4.9
1971	74.2	59.3	45.6	13.8	14.1	74.2	62.3	46.6	15.8	6.4	4.1	1.3	2.4	.4	1.3
1972	83.4	66.2	51.8	14.4	16.4	83.4	74.2	56.9	17.3	7.7	4.3	1.3	2.5	.5	-2.9
1973	115.6	91.8	73.9	17.8	23.8	115.6	91.2	71.8	19.3	11.1	4.6	1.4	2.5	.7	8.7
1974	152.6	124.3	101.0	23.3	30.3	152.6	127.5	104.5	22.9	14.6	5.4	1.2	3.2	1.0	5.1
1975	164.4	136.3	109.6	26.7	28.2	164.4	122.7	99.0	23.7	14.9	5.4	1.2	3.5	.7	21.4
1976	181.7	148.9	117.8	31.1	32.9	181.7	151.1	124.6	26.5	15.7	6.0	1.2	3.7	1.1	8.9
1977	196.6	158.8	123.7	35.1	37.9	196.6	182.4	152.6	29.8	17.2	6.0	1.2	3.4	1.4	-9.0
1978	233.5	186.1	145.4	40.7	47.4	233.5	212.3	177.4	34.8	25.3	6.4	1.3	3.8	1.4	-10.4
1979	300.3	228.7	184.0	44.7	70.4	300.3	252.7	212.8	39.9	37.5	7.5	1.4	4.1	2.0	2.6
1980	361.9	278.9	225.8	53.2	81.8	361.9	293.8	248.6	45.3	46.5	9.0	1.6	5.0	2.4	12.5
1981	399.5	302.8	239.1	63.7	95.6	399.5	317.8	267.8	49.9	60.9	13.4	5.2	5.0	3.2	7.4
1982	379.5	282.6	215.0	67.6	96.9	379.5	303.2	250.5	52.6	65.8	16.7	6.2	7.0	3.4	-6.1
1983	374.6	277.0	207.3	69.7	97.6	374.6	328.6	272.7	56.0	65.6	17.7	6.5	7.8	3.4	-37.3
1984	421.8	303.1	225.6	77.5	118.7	421.8	405.1	336.3	68.8	87.6	20.6	7.4	9.7	3.5	-91.5
1985	411.1	303.0	222.2	80.8	108.1	411.1	417.2	343.3	73.9	87.7	23.1	7.8	12.2	3.1	-116.9
1986	427.1	320.7	226.0	94.7	106.5	427.1	452.2	370.0	82.2	93.6	24.3	8.1	12.9	3.3	-142.9
1987	481.8	365.7	257.5	108.2	116.0	481.8	507.9	414.8	93.1	107.1	23.3	8.7	11.2	3.3	-156.4
1988	591.9	447.2	325.8	121.4	144.7	591.9	553.2	452.1	101.1	131.7	25.1	9.1	11.4	4.6	-118.1
1989	678.3	509.3	371.7	137.6	169.0	678.3	589.7	484.5	105.3	154.8	26.1	9.6	11.4	5.1	-92.4
1990	734.8	557.3	398.5	158.8	177.5	734.8	628.6	508.0	120.6	156.4	28.4	9.9	13.3	5.2	-78.6
1991	757.9	601.8	426.4	175.4	156.2	757.9	622.3	500.7	121.6	140.5	-12.1	10.4	-27.9	5.4	7.3
1992	777.3	639.4	448.7	190.7	137.9	777.3	669.0	544.9	124.1	126.8	32.0	9.6	16.6	5.8	-50.5
1993	799.7	660.0	459.5	200.4	139.7	799.7	724.9	592.7	132.1	129.9	33.1	9.9	16.9	6.2	-88.2
1994	881.1	722.0	509.1	212.9	159.2	881.1	818.4	677.3	141.1	168.1	34.2	10.6	16.2	7.3	-139.6
1990:I	715.2	541.6	391.6	150.0	173.6	715.2	615.9	500.4	115.5	152.5	26.1	9.9	11.5	4.7	-79.4
II	728.1	554.8	399.8	155.1	173.3	728.1	615.1	497.4	117.8	156.4	30.3	9.5	15.5	5.3	-73.8
III	728.6	555.5	394.6	160.9	173.1	728.6	634.1	511.3	122.7	158.7	29.1	10.2	13.2	5.7	-93.3
IV	767.3	577.3	408.2	169.1	190.0	767.3	649.2	522.9	126.4	157.9	28.2	10.1	12.9	5.3	-68.1
1991:I	751.4	577.4	414.8	162.7	174.0	751.4	610.3	488.3	122.1	147.1	-61.3	10.4	-76.9	5.2	55.3
II	758.7	602.7	428.8	173.9	156.0	758.7	615.0	493.5	121.6	143.8	-16.1	10.3	-32.0	5.6	16.0
III	750.6	602.6	423.9	178.7	148.1	750.6	624.5	504.6	119.9	138.7	10.0	10.2	-5.4	5.2	-22.6
IV	771.0	624.4	438.1	186.3	146.6	771.0	639.3	516.5	122.7	132.2	18.9	10.6	2.6	5.7	-19.4
1992:I	773.1	632.4	442.1	190.3	140.7	773.1	641.3	516.8	124.5	124.2	27.5	9.4	12.4	5.7	-19.9
II	779.2	635.9	445.9	190.0	143.3	779.2	664.9	541.1	123.8	132.3	30.7	9.7	15.0	6.0	-48.7
III	774.0	640.2	447.7	192.5	133.8	774.0	677.8	557.2	120.6	124.3	27.8	9.2	12.9	5.8	-56.0
IV	783.0	649.1	459.0	190.1	133.9	783.0	691.8	564.4	127.4	126.4	42.0	9.9	26.1	5.9	-77.2
1993:I	784.8	649.4	451.2	198.3	135.3	784.8	696.8	569.7	127.1	119.7	27.7	9.9	12.3	5.5	-59.4
II	803.8	662.5	461.8	200.8	141.2	803.8	724.6	593.8	130.8	121.3	30.5	9.9	14.4	6.2	-83.4
III	788.6	648.5	448.3	200.2	140.1	788.6	725.6	593.7	131.9	126.6	31.1	9.8	15.1	6.2	-94.7
IV	821.6	679.4	477.0	202.4	142.1	821.6	752.6	613.8	138.8	141.3	42.9	10.1	25.8	6.9	-115.2
1994:I	825.8	681.5	476.0	205.5	144.4	825.8	761.7	622.4	139.3	143.6	29.5	10.8	11.5	7.2	-109.0
II	859.7	708.6	497.7	210.9	151.1	859.7	806.0	665.7	140.3	159.9	31.6	11.0	13.2	7.3	-137.7
III	899.7	734.2	517.2	216.9	165.6	899.7	842.6	699.9	142.6	175.6	31.2	10.3	13.7	7.3	-149.6
IV	939.3	763.6	545.4	218.2	175.7	939.3	863.3	720.9	142.3	193.4	44.5	10.5	26.5	7.6	-161.9
1995:I	975.5	778.6	558.9	219.7	196.9	975.5	885.1	740.3	144.8	204.1	30.6	10.5	12.3	7.8	-144.4
II	1,002.4	796.9	574.7	222.2	205.6	1,002.4	919.3	771.0	148.3	215.0	28.2	10.5	9.9	7.8	-160.1
III	1,017.1	813.2	588.3	224.9	203.9	1,017.1	913.7	765.4	148.3	219.8	32.2	10.6	13.8	7.9	-148.7

¹ Includes capital grants received by the United States (net), not shown separately. See Table B–28 for data.
² Certain goods, primarily military equipment purchased and sold by the Federal Government, are included in services.
³ Mainly receipts by U.S. residents of interest and dividends and reinvested earnings of foreign affiliates of U.S. corporations.
⁴ Mainly payments to foreign residents of interest and dividends and reinvested earnings of U.S. affiliates of foreign corporations.

Source: Department of Commerce, Bureau of Economic Analysis.

Table B-21.—*Real exports and imports of goods and services and receipts and payments of factor income, 1959–95*

[Billions of chained (1992) dollars; quarterly data at seasonally adjusted annual rates]

Year or quarter	Exports of goods and services					Receipts of factor income [2]	Imports of goods and services					Payments of factor income [3]
	Total	Goods [1]			Services [1]		Total	Goods [1]			Services [1]	
		Total	Durable goods	Nondurable goods				Total	Durable goods	Nondurable goods		
1959	71.9	51.7	23.7	30.4	18.6	20.8	106.6	71.1	23.7	49.5	34.9	7.5
1960	86.8	63.8	29.3	36.5	20.6	23.4	108.1	70.0	22.6	50.1	37.7	8.7
1961	88.3	64.2	29.5	36.8	22.0	25.2	107.3	69.9	21.8	51.8	37.0	8.8
1962	93.0	67.0	31.0	38.6	24.0	27.6	119.5	80.2	25.6	58.4	38.8	8.9
1963	100.0	72.3	32.7	42.2	25.5	29.8	122.7	83.5	27.0	60.1	38.7	9.9
1964	113.3	82.2	37.7	47.2	28.6	32.6	129.2	89.0	30.0	62.5	39.7	11.0
1965	115.6	82.6	39.3	45.9	30.8	34.6	143.0	101.6	37.1	67.2	40.9	12.0
1966	123.4	88.4	42.2	48.8	32.6	34.3	164.2	117.6	46.2	72.5	46.0	13.4
1967	126.1	88.8	48.8	40.4	35.5	35.7	176.2	123.8	49.5	74.7	51.7	14.3
1968	135.3	95.8	53.4	42.8	37.3	39.5	202.5	149.4	63.0	84.6	52.6	16.6
1969	142.7	100.8	57.7	43.2	39.6	43.7	214.0	157.5	67.3	87.8	55.9	21.9
1970	158.1	112.3	63.1	49.5	43.1	45.0	223.1	163.7	69.2	92.6	58.8	23.6
1971	159.2	111.9	62.7	49.6	45.0	46.4	235.0	177.4	76.1	98.3	57.2	22.0
1972	172.0	123.9	69.2	55.1	44.7	51.7	261.0	201.6	87.6	109.8	59.1	25.3
1973	209.6	152.4	86.3	66.5	52.6	70.4	272.6	215.8	93.2	118.4	56.7	34.1
1974	229.8	164.5	99.6	65.9	61.6	82.5	265.3	209.8	93.6	111.0	55.4	41.0
1975	228.2	160.7	97.5	64.2	65.6	70.2	235.4	183.4	76.5	103.0	52.5	38.7
1976	241.6	168.3	98.9	70.3	72.5	77.2	281.5	224.8	93.7	126.4	56.2	38.7
1977	247.4	170.5	98.7	72.8	77.2	83.4	311.6	252.2	106.0	140.7	58.4	39.5
1978	273.1	189.5	110.0	80.6	83.0	96.8	338.6	274.8	122.5	145.3	62.5	53.5
1979	299.0	211.9	125.2	87.9	83.9	132.4	344.3	279.5	125.4	147.0	63.4	73.0
1980	331.4	237.2	139.6	98.9	89.2	141.1	321.3	258.7	126.3	126.6	61.8	83.1
1981	335.3	234.7	134.7	101.4	98.5	150.1	329.7	264.0	136.8	122.8	65.4	99.4
1982	311.4	213.5	117.0	98.4	98.5	143.5	325.5	257.4	138.4	115.6	68.9	100.7
1983	303.3	207.3	114.6	94.4	96.8	138.2	366.6	292.4	166.8	123.1	74.4	95.9
1984	328.4	223.7	127.0	98.1	105.9	160.3	455.7	363.1	221.9	140.2	92.9	121.9
1985	337.3	231.7	137.3	95.3	106.1	140.5	485.2	385.9	244.1	142.0	99.7	116.8
1986	362.2	243.6	145.3	99.1	120.3	134.6	526.1	425.5	266.7	158.8	100.2	120.9
1987	402.0	270.5	165.7	105.0	133.4	141.9	558.2	445.2	278.5	166.8	113.1	133.0
1988	465.8	321.4	205.5	115.8	145.0	170.2	580.2	463.2	290.1	173.2	117.1	157.1
1989	520.2	361.7	236.7	124.9	158.7	189.9	603.0	482.7	302.6	180.1	120.2	176.7
1990	564.4	391.6	260.0	131.6	173.1	190.6	626.3	497.3	310.9	186.4	129.4	170.2
1991	599.9	419.2	279.6	139.6	180.8	161.1	622.2	497.1	312.7	184.4	125.3	145.7
1992	639.4	448.7	300.9	147.8	190.7	137.9	669.0	544.9	346.4	198.4	124.1	126.8
1993	660.6	464.5	318.3	146.2	196.2	136.5	735.0	602.5	389.9	212.5	132.5	126.6
1994	715.1	511.4	357.9	153.8	204.1	152.4	823.3	684.0	455.7	228.1	139.4	159.9
1990: I	555.2	386.8	256.1	130.6	168.6	189.5	622.3	494.2	303.1	191.1	128.5	169.5
II	566.8	394.8	264.2	130.6	172.2	187.1	633.5	504.0	313.3	190.7	129.8	171.0
III	561.8	388.0	258.6	129.4	174.3	185.1	633.0	503.2	315.4	187.7	130.2	171.7
IV	573.9	397.0	261.2	135.8	177.3	200.9	616.4	487.9	312.0	175.9	129.0	168.7
1991: I	572.3	403.3	263.1	140.1	168.9	181.4	596.6	472.2	298.9	173.3	124.8	154.7
II	600.3	419.8	282.8	137.1	180.6	161.5	617.4	490.8	304.8	186.0	126.8	149.9
III	603.6	420.0	281.9	138.1	183.8	152.0	633.4	509.4	320.2	189.2	124.1	143.0
IV	623.5	433.7	290.5	143.3	189.8	149.4	641.4	515.9	326.8	189.1	125.6	135.2
1992: I	633.0	440.3	294.5	145.8	192.8	141.9	647.8	521.2	331.2	190.0	126.7	125.6
II	635.8	445.1	298.4	146.6	190.7	143.5	668.3	543.6	344.6	199.0	124.7	132.6
III	639.7	448.3	299.5	148.8	191.3	133.4	670.5	552.8	351.0	201.8	117.7	123.9
IV	649.1	461.0	311.1	149.9	188.2	132.7	689.1	561.8	359.0	202.8	127.4	125.2
1993: I	649.8	454.3	308.5	145.8	195.5	133.0	705.1	577.3	371.9	205.3	127.8	117.3
II	662.3	465.8	319.0	146.8	196.5	138.2	729.4	598.6	384.2	214.4	130.8	128.9
III	648.9	453.3	310.6	142.7	195.6	136.7	738.1	605.1	391.4	213.7	133.0	123.1
IV	681.4	484.5	335.1	149.5	197.0	138.2	767.6	629.1	412.3	216.7	138.5	137.1
1994: I	680.4	481.5	336.8	144.9	199.0	139.5	781.7	643.0	422.9	219.8	138.8	138.0
II	704.3	501.8	352.9	149.3	202.7	145.0	816.5	676.4	449.0	227.2	140.2	152.6
III	724.8	518.3	361.7	156.7	206.8	158.0	838.1	698.1	463.9	233.9	140.2	166.3
IV	751.0	543.9	380.1	164.1	207.7	167.1	856.8	718.6	486.8	231.3	138.5	182.9
1995: I	755.8	548.9	386.1	163.2	207.6	186.3	874.9	732.8	497.9	234.4	142.4	191.9
II	764.3	557.8	396.7	161.8	207.4	193.6	891.2	750.5	511.3	238.6	141.1	201.5
III	779.7	571.1	406.3	165.5	209.6	191.7	893.9	752.4	512.1	239.7	141.8	205.1

[1] Certain goods, primarily military equipment purchased and sold by the Federal Government, are included in services.
[2] Mainly receipts by U.S. residents of interest and dividends and reinvested earnings of foreign affiliates of U.S. corporations.
[3] Mainly payments to foreign residents of interest and dividends and reinvested earnings of U.S. affiliates of foreign corporations.

Source: Department of Commerce, Bureau of Economic Analysis.

TABLE B–22.—*Relation of gross domestic product, gross national product, net national product, and national income, 1959–95*

[Billions of dollars; quarterly data at seasonally adjusted annual rates]

Year or quarter	Gross domestic product	Plus: Receipts of factor income from rest of the world [1]	Less: Payments of factor income to rest of the world [2]	Equals: Gross national product	Less: Consumption of fixed capital			Equals: Net national product	Less:			Plus: Subsidies less current surplus of government enterprises	Equals: National income
					Total	Private	Government		Indirect business tax and nontax liability	Business transfer payments	Statistical discrepancy		
1959	507.2	4.3	1.5	510.1	58.6	44.5	14.1	451.5	41.9	1.4	−2.1	0.1	410.4
1960	526.6	5.0	1.8	529.8	60.7	46.1	14.5	469.1	45.5	1.4	−3.7	.3	426.2
1961	544.8	5.4	1.8	548.4	62.2	47.2	15.0	486.2	48.1	1.5	−3.3	1.3	441.2
1962	585.2	6.1	1.8	589.4	64.7	48.9	15.8	524.8	51.7	1.6	−2.4	1.5	475.3
1963	617.4	6.6	2.1	621.9	67.2	50.5	16.7	554.7	54.7	1.8	−3.5	.9	502.6
1964	663.0	7.4	2.4	668.0	70.4	53.1	17.4	597.6	58.8	2.0	−2.1	1.4	540.2
1965	719.1	8.1	2.7	724.5	74.9	56.7	18.2	649.6	62.7	2.2	−1.4	1.7	587.8
1966	787.8	8.3	3.1	793.0	81.1	61.8	19.3	711.9	65.4	2.3	2.7	3.0	644.4
1967	833.6	8.9	3.4	839.1	87.8	67.0	20.8	751.3	70.4	2.5	.6	2.9	680.7
1968	910.6	10.3	4.1	916.7	95.4	73.0	22.4	821.3	79.0	2.8	.2	3.1	742.4
1969	982.2	11.9	5.8	988.4	103.6	79.5	24.1	884.8	86.6	3.1	−2.2	3.6	800.9
1970	1,035.6	13.0	6.6	1,042.0	111.9	86.1	25.8	930.1	94.3	3.2	1.0	4.9	836.6
1971	1,125.4	14.1	6.4	1,133.1	122.0	94.4	27.6	1,011.0	103.6	3.4	5.1	5.1	904.0
1972	1,237.3	16.4	7.7	1,246.0	134.8	104.9	29.9	1,111.2	111.4	3.9	3.2	6.4	999.2
1973	1,382.6	23.8	11.1	1,395.4	148.0	115.1	32.9	1,247.3	121.0	4.5	2.4	5.9	1,125.3
1974	1,496.9	30.3	14.6	1,512.6	171.7	133.7	38.0	1,340.9	129.3	5.0	4.5	4.5	1,206.7
1975	1,630.6	28.2	14.9	1,643.9	200.1	157.7	42.4	1,443.8	140.0	5.2	11.2	8.1	1,295.5
1976	1,819.0	32.9	15.7	1,836.1	218.9	174.1	44.7	1,617.2	151.6	6.5	18.9	7.4	1,447.5
1977	2,026.9	37.9	17.2	2,047.5	251.1	203.5	47.6	1,796.4	165.5	7.3	17.5	10.1	1,616.3
1978	2,291.4	47.4	25.3	2,313.5	281.8	230.4	51.5	2,031.6	177.8	8.2	17.6	11.1	1,839.2
1979	2,557.5	70.4	37.5	2,590.4	322.3	265.5	56.8	2,268.1	188.7	9.9	27.8	11.7	2,053.3
1980	2,784.2	81.8	46.5	2,819.5	368.0	304.6	63.4	2,451.5	212.0	11.2	27.4	15.2	2,216.1
1981	3,115.9	95.6	60.9	3,150.6	419.9	349.5	70.4	2,730.7	249.3	13.4	14.6	16.9	2,470.2
1982	3,242.1	96.9	65.8	3,273.2	456.3	378.3	78.1	2,816.9	256.4	15.2	−2.9	21.1	2,569.2
1983	3,514.5	97.6	65.6	3,546.5	477.9	397.8	80.1	3,068.7	280.1	16.2	36.5	25.6	2,761.4
1984	3,902.4	118.7	87.6	3,933.5	494.0	410.9	83.1	3,439.5	309.5	18.6	4.2	25.5	3,132.7
1985	4,180.7	108.1	87.7	4,201.0	519.5	432.4	87.1	3,681.5	329.6	20.9	1.4	21.9	3,351.5
1986	4,422.2	106.5	93.6	4,435.1	552.8	459.4	93.5	3,882.2	344.7	23.9	22.1	25.1	3,516.5
1987	4,692.3	116.0	107.1	4,701.3	581.9	483.2	98.7	4,119.4	364.8	24.2	−16.6	31.0	3,778.1
1988	5,049.6	144.7	131.7	5,062.6	620.2	516.0	104.2	4,442.5	385.5	25.4	−48.6	28.5	4,108.6
1989	5,438.7	169.0	154.8	5,452.8	662.2	551.9	110.3	4,790.6	414.7	26.3	11.4	24.0	4,362.1
1990	5,743.8	177.5	156.4	5,764.9	693.1	575.8	117.3	5,071.9	442.6	26.5	16.1	25.3	4,611.9
1991	5,916.7	156.2	140.5	5,932.4	723.1	599.6	123.5	5,209.3	478.1	26.3	8.7	23.6	4,719.7
1992	6,244.4	137.9	126.8	6,255.5	754.2	626.1	128.2	5,501.3	505.6	28.4	43.7	27.1	4,950.8
1993	6,550.2	139.7	129.9	6,560.0	773.8	640.0	133.8	5,786.2	540.0	28.3	55.1	31.7	5,194.4
1994	6,931.4	159.2	168.1	6,922.4	818.8	678.7	140.1	6,103.7	572.5	29.9	31.3	25.1	5,495.1
1990: I	5,660.4	173.6	152.5	5,681.4	680.1	565.6	114.5	5,001.3	432.1	26.1	43.0	23.8	4,523.9
II	5,751.0	173.3	156.4	5,767.8	689.0	573.2	115.8	5,078.9	436.1	26.8	17.4	24.5	4,623.1
III	5,782.4	173.1	158.7	5,796.8	698.6	580.6	118.0	5,098.2	447.3	26.9	16.3	25.7	4,633.4
IV	5,781.5	190.0	157.9	5,813.6	704.6	583.9	120.7	5,109.0	455.0	26.4	−12.3	27.3	4,667.2
1991: I	5,822.1	174.0	147.1	5,849.0	713.6	592.5	121.1	5,135.3	464.7	26.0	−6.5	24.4	4,675.6
II	5,892.3	156.0	143.8	5,904.5	719.6	596.4	123.2	5,184.9	472.9	26.3	5.6	22.7	4,702.8
III	5,950.0	148.1	138.7	5,959.4	725.7	601.4	124.3	5,233.7	483.7	26.0	17.2	23.5	4,730.4
IV	6,002.3	146.6	132.2	6,016.6	733.5	608.1	125.4	5,283.2	491.2	26.8	18.8	23.6	4,770.0
1992: I	6,121.8	140.7	124.2	6,138.3	727.6	601.3	126.3	5,410.7	495.7	27.6	23.3	24.6	4,888.7
II	6,201.2	143.3	132.3	6,212.2	734.1	606.4	127.7	5,478.1	497.9	28.5	36.2	25.4	4,941.0
III	6,271.7	133.8	124.3	6,281.1	809.2	680.5	128.6	5,471.9	507.1	28.6	51.6	26.9	4,911.6
IV	6,383.0	133.9	126.4	6,390.5	746.1	616.2	130.0	5,644.3	521.7	28.8	63.6	31.5	5,061.7
1993: I	6,442.8	135.3	119.7	6,458.4	765.6	633.8	131.7	5,692.9	524.7	27.8	80.7	35.2	5,094.9
II	6,503.2	141.2	132.1	6,512.3	767.6	634.6	133.0	5,744.7	535.1	28.3	55.0	33.7	5,159.9
III	6,571.3	140.1	126.6	6,584.8	783.1	648.4	134.6	5,801.7	541.7	28.3	48.6	29.9	5,213.0
IV	6,683.7	142.1	141.3	6,684.5	779.1	643.3	135.8	5,905.4	558.5	29.0	36.0	28.0	5,309.9
1994: I	6,772.8	144.4	143.6	6,773.6	887.4	748.7	138.7	5,886.1	562.1	29.6	21.1	27.2	5,300.5
II	6,885.0	151.1	159.9	6,876.3	791.2	652.7	138.5	6,085.1	568.0	29.9	17.5	24.0	5,493.7
III	6,987.6	165.6	175.6	6,977.6	796.7	656.7	140.0	6,180.8	576.4	29.9	46.7	23.4	5,551.2
IV	7,080.0	175.7	193.4	7,062.2	799.7	656.6	143.1	6,262.5	583.5	30.3	39.7	25.9	5,635.0
1995: I	7,147.8	196.9	204.1	7,140.5	809.5	664.6	144.9	6,331.1	586.0	30.3	36.2	19.2	5,697.7
II	7,196.5	205.6	215.0	7,187.0	820.1	673.6	146.5	6,366.9	594.8	30.4	21.6	18.7	5,738.9
III	7,297.2	203.9	219.8	7,281.3	829.0	681.8	147.2	6,452.3	596.8	30.5	−2.3	17.9	5,845.1

[1] Mainly receipts by U.S. residents of interest and dividends and reinvested earnings of foreign affiliates of U.S. corporations.
[2] Mainly payments to foreign residents of interest and dividends and reinvested earnings of U.S. affiliates of foreign corporations.

Source: Department of Commerce, Bureau of Economic Analysis.

TABLE B–23.—*Relation of national income and personal income, 1959–95*

[Billions of dollars; quarterly data at seasonally adjusted annual rates]

Year or quarter	National income	Less: Corporate profits with inventory valuation and capital consumption adjustments [1]	Less: Net interest	Less: Contributions for social insurance	Less: Wage accruals less disbursements	Plus: Personal interest income	Plus: Personal dividend income	Plus: Government transfer payments to persons	Plus: Business transfer payments to persons	Equals: Personal income
1959	410.4	50.2	10.2	18.8	0.0	22.7	12.7	25.7	1.3	393.5
1960	426.2	48.8	11.2	21.9	.0	25.0	13.4	27.5	1.3	411.7
1961	441.2	49.8	13.1	22.9	.0	26.9	14.0	31.5	1.4	429.1
1962	475.3	57.7	14.6	25.4	.0	29.3	15.0	32.6	1.5	456.1
1963	502.6	63.5	16.1	28.5	.0	32.4	16.1	34.5	1.7	479.1
1964	540.2	70.4	18.2	30.1	.0	36.1	18.0	36.0	1.8	513.5
1965	587.8	80.9	21.1	31.6	.0	40.3	20.2	39.1	2.0	555.8
1966	644.4	86.3	24.3	40.6	.0	44.9	20.9	43.6	2.1	604.7
1967	680.7	83.6	28.1	45.5	.0	49.5	22.1	52.3	2.3	649.7
1968	742.4	90.3	30.4	50.4	.0	54.6	24.5	60.6	2.5	713.5
1969	800.9	87.5	33.6	57.8	.0	60.8	25.1	67.5	2.8	778.2
1970	836.6	75.7	40.0	62.0	.0	69.2	23.5	81.8	2.8	836.1
1971	904.0	88.8	45.4	69.6	.6	75.7	23.5	97.0	3.0	898.9
1972	999.2	102.2	49.3	79.5	.0	81.8	25.5	108.4	3.4	987.3
1973	1,125.3	115.1	56.5	97.9	–.1	94.1	27.7	124.1	3.8	1,105.6
1974	1,206.7	103.7	71.8	111.7	–.5	112.4	29.6	147.4	4.0	1,213.3
1975	1,295.5	121.1	80.0	121.1	.1	123.0	29.2	185.7	4.5	1,315.6
1976	1,447.5	147.0	85.1	137.7	.1	134.6	35.0	202.8	5.5	1,455.4
1977	1,616.3	167.3	100.7	155.4	.1	155.7	39.5	217.5	5.9	1,611.4
1978	1,839.2	191.6	120.5	177.0	.3	184.5	44.3	234.8	6.8	1,820.2
1979	2,053.3	194.0	150.3	204.2	–.2	223.6	50.5	262.8	7.9	2,049.7
1980	2,216.1	167.1	191.9	225.0	.0	274.7	57.5	312.6	8.8	2,285.7
1981	2,470.2	183.9	234.5	261.6	.1	337.2	67.2	355.7	10.2	2,560.4
1982	2,569.2	159.2	264.9	280.6	.0	379.2	66.9	396.3	11.8	2,718.7
1983	2,761.4	212.3	275.9	301.9	–.4	403.2	77.4	426.6	12.8	2,891.7
1984	3,132.7	268.2	318.5	345.5	.2	472.3	79.4	438.5	15.1	3,205.5
1985	3,351.5	282.2	337.2	375.9	–.2	508.4	88.3	468.7	17.8	3,439.6
1986	3,516.5	271.0	363.1	402.0	.0	543.3	105.1	498.0	20.7	3,647.5
1987	3,778.1	309.7	372.2	423.3	.0	560.0	101.1	522.5	20.8	3,877.3
1988	4,108.6	357.2	398.9	462.8	.0	595.5	109.9	556.8	20.8	4,172.8
1989	4,362.1	356.4	456.6	491.2	.0	674.5	130.9	604.9	21.1	4,489.3
1990	4,611.9	369.5	467.3	518.5	.1	704.4	142.9	666.5	21.3	4,791.6
1991	4,719.7	382.5	448.0	543.5	–.1	699.2	153.6	749.1	20.8	4,968.5
1992	4,950.8	401.4	414.3	571.4	–15.8	667.2	159.4	835.7	22.5	5,264.2
1993	5,194.4	464.5	398.1	592.9	4.6	647.3	186.8	888.6	22.1	5,479.2
1994	5,495.1	526.5	392.8	628.3	14.8	661.6	199.6	933.8	22.6	5,750.2
1990: I	4,523.9	369.3	458.9	511.1	.0	690.6	142.0	649.2	21.3	4,687.8
II	4,623.1	392.8	465.0	516.2	.0	701.1	143.4	656.5	21.5	4,771.5
III	4,633.4	350.4	467.7	522.4	.0	711.6	143.3	669.3	21.3	4,838.4
IV	4,667.2	365.5	477.5	524.3	.2	714.2	142.7	691.0	21.1	4,868.6
1991: I	4,675.6	393.7	460.4	536.8	.2	705.4	149.3	725.6	20.8	4,885.6
II	4,702.8	380.0	450.6	540.9	–.4	702.2	153.1	742.5	20.7	4,950.2
III	4,730.4	376.8	446.6	546.0	.0	697.0	156.4	754.1	20.8	4,989.3
IV	4,770.0	379.6	434.3	550.3	.0	692.3	155.7	774.0	21.1	5,048.9
1992: I	4,888.7	417.3	419.2	565.1	.0	674.1	152.3	816.4	21.9	5,151.9
II	4,941.0	409.3	417.5	570.1	.0	673.0	154.5	831.0	22.5	5,225.1
III	4,911.6	351.3	408.1	574.8	.0	661.2	160.8	842.5	22.8	5,264.6
IV	5,061.7	427.7	412.4	575.7	–63.0	660.4	170.1	853.0	22.9	5,415.3
1993: I	5,094.9	426.4	412.6	578.3	64.0	659.0	180.0	873.6	22.3	5,348.7
II	5,159.9	449.0	402.6	592.8	1.0	651.6	185.4	884.8	22.1	5,458.4
III	5,213.0	469.6	390.4	597.5	1.0	640.0	189.7	894.3	22.0	5,500.5
IV	5,309.9	512.8	386.7	603.1	–47.4	638.6	192.1	901.6	22.1	5,609.1
1994: I	5,300.5	455.9	388.7	614.2	51.4	639.4	193.2	917.1	22.4	5,562.4
II	5,493.7	531.5	393.5	627.5	3.0	657.6	197.5	927.3	22.5	5,743.0
III	5,551.2	549.8	397.8	632.2	3.0	671.0	201.0	938.7	22.6	5,801.7
IV	5,635.0	568.9	391.1	639.3	1.6	678.4	206.7	952.0	22.7	5,893.9
1995: I	5,697.7	559.6	403.9	651.0	1.4	701.9	209.5	979.8	22.6	5,995.5
II	5,738.9	561.1	402.6	656.2	.0	713.9	212.2	994.2	22.6	6,061.9
III	5,845.1	614.4	399.8	664.0	.0	719.3	215.8	1,007.3	22.6	6,131.9

[1] Includes rest of world.

Source: Department of Commerce, Bureau of Economic Analysis.

TABLE B–24.—*National income by type of income, 1959–95*

[Billions of dollars; quarterly data at seasonally adjusted annual rates]

| Year or quarter | National income [1] | Compensation of employees | | | | | | | Proprietors' income with inventory valuation and capital consumption adjustments | | | | |
| | | Total | Wages and salaries | | | Supplements to wages and salaries | | | Total | Farm | | Nonfarm | |
			Total	Government	Other	Total	Employer contributions for social insurance	Other labor income		Total	Proprietors' income [2]	Total	Proprietors' income [3]
1959	410.4	281.2	259.8	46.0	213.8	21.4	10.9	10.6	50.5	10.9	11.8	39.6	40.2
1960	426.2	296.7	272.8	49.2	223.7	23.8	12.6	11.2	50.5	11.5	12.3	39.1	39.8
1961	441.2	305.6	280.5	52.4	228.0	25.1	13.3	11.8	53.0	12.1	12.9	40.9	41.8
1962	475.3	327.4	299.3	56.3	243.0	28.1	15.1	13.0	55.0	12.1	12.9	42.9	43.9
1963	502.6	345.5	314.8	60.0	254.8	30.7	16.7	14.0	56.3	12.0	12.7	44.3	45.2
1964	540.2	371.0	337.7	64.9	272.9	33.2	17.5	15.7	59.0	10.8	11.5	48.3	49.2
1965	587.8	399.8	363.7	69.9	293.8	36.1	18.3	17.8	63.5	13.0	13.8	50.4	51.9
1966	644.4	443.0	400.3	78.3	321.9	42.7	22.8	19.9	67.6	14.1	14.9	53.5	55.4
1967	680.7	475.5	428.9	86.4	342.5	46.6	24.9	21.7	69.1	12.7	13.7	56.4	58.3
1968	742.4	524.7	471.9	96.6	375.3	52.8	27.6	25.2	73.3	12.8	13.8	60.5	63.0
1969	800.9	578.3	518.3	105.5	412.7	60.0	31.5	28.5	77.1	14.6	15.8	62.5	65.0
1970	836.6	618.1	551.5	117.1	434.3	66.6	34.1	32.5	78.0	14.8	16.1	63.2	66.0
1971	904.0	660.1	584.5	126.7	457.8	75.6	38.9	36.7	83.9	15.5	16.9	68.3	72.0
1972	999.2	726.8	638.7	137.8	500.9	88.1	45.1	43.0	95.2	19.5	21.2	75.8	79.3
1973	1,125.3	813.1	708.6	148.7	560.0	104.4	55.3	49.2	113.3	32.6	34.6	80.7	85.9
1974	1,206.7	892.4	772.2	160.4	611.8	120.3	63.7	56.5	111.3	25.9	28.5	85.4	93.4
1975	1,295.5	951.3	814.7	176.1	638.6	136.6	70.6	65.9	116.5	24.2	27.7	92.3	99.2
1976	1,447.5	1,061.5	899.6	188.7	710.8	162.0	82.2	79.7	127.5	18.7	22.8	108.8	116.3
1977	1,616.3	1,182.9	994.0	202.4	791.6	188.9	94.1	94.7	140.8	17.9	22.3	122.9	131.0
1978	1,839.2	1,338.5	1,121.1	219.8	901.2	217.4	107.3	110.1	162.2	22.9	27.7	139.2	148.7
1979	2,053.3	1,503.3	1,255.7	236.9	1,018.8	247.5	123.2	124.3	177.3	26.6	32.2	150.8	160.9
1980	2,216.1	1,653.9	1,377.6	261.2	1,116.4	276.3	136.4	139.8	167.9	13.8	20.7	154.1	165.2
1981	2,470.2	1,827.8	1,517.6	285.6	1,232.0	310.2	157.1	153.0	178.3	23.7	31.6	154.6	160.7
1982	2,569.2	1,927.6	1,593.9	307.3	1,286.7	333.7	168.3	165.4	169.9	16.4	24.8	153.5	158.2
1983	2,761.4	2,044.2	1,684.8	324.5	1,360.3	359.4	182.2	177.2	181.7	6.0	14.1	175.8	172.2
1984	3,132.7	2,257.0	1,855.3	347.8	1,507.5	401.7	212.8	188.9	237.9	24.8	32.7	213.1	199.7
1985	3,351.5	2,425.7	1,995.7	373.5	1,622.1	430.0	226.9	203.1	257.4	24.9	32.4	232.5	210.5
1986	3,516.5	2,572.4	2,116.5	396.6	1,720.0	455.9	239.9	216.0	267.8	25.2	32.6	242.6	215.9
1987	3,778.1	2,757.7	2,272.7	423.1	1,849.5	485.0	249.7	235.4	292.9	32.3	39.6	260.6	238.2
1988	4,108.6	2,973.9	2,453.6	450.4	2,003.2	520.3	268.6	251.7	322.9	28.2	35.4	294.7	272.0
1989	4,362.1	3,151.6	2,598.1	479.4	2,118.7	553.5	280.4	273.1	345.0	36.8	44.3	308.2	284.8
1990	4,611.9	3,352.8	2,757.5	517.2	2,240.3	595.2	294.6	300.6	361.0	36.3	43.8	324.6	312.7
1991	4,719.7	3,457.9	2,827.6	546.0	2,281.5	630.4	307.7	322.7	362.9	30.2	37.7	332.7	325.0
1992	4,950.8	3,644.9	2,970.6	567.8	2,402.9	674.3	323.0	351.3	409.5	38.0	45.7	371.5	363.1
1993	5,194.4	3,804.8	3,095.2	584.2	2,511.0	714.2	333.3	380.9	420.0	32.0	39.5	388.1	381.0
1994	5,495.1	4,008.3	3,255.9	602.5	2,653.4	752.4	350.2	402.2	450.9	35.0	42.5	415.9	411.5
1990:I	4,523.9	3,285.5	2,704.0	504.3	2,199.6	581.5	290.1	291.4	354.7	36.1	43.5	318.6	302.2
II	4,623.1	3,344.7	2,753.0	514.3	2,238.6	591.7	294.0	297.8	362.7	39.4	46.7	323.3	309.4
III	4,633.4	3,384.9	2,784.5	520.8	2,263.6	600.5	296.4	304.0	365.6	36.0	43.5	329.6	319.7
IV	4,667.2	3,395.9	2,788.8	529.4	2,259.3	607.1	297.9	309.2	360.9	33.9	41.3	327.1	319.6
1991:I	4,675.6	3,405.7	2,789.5	541.5	2,248.0	616.2	303.8	312.4	349.2	27.6	35.1	321.6	313.0
II	4,702.8	3,440.7	2,814.7	544.9	2,269.8	626.0	306.3	319.7	365.1	34.2	41.6	331.0	323.3
III	4,730.4	3,474.2	2,838.8	546.9	2,292.0	635.4	309.1	326.3	365.2	28.0	35.5	337.1	329.9
IV	4,770.0	3,511.0	2,867.1	550.8	2,316.3	643.8	311.4	332.4	372.1	31.0	38.5	341.1	333.7
1992:I	4,888.7	3,577.1	2,916.5	561.4	2,355.1	660.7	319.9	340.8	396.5	36.7	44.2	359.8	350.8
II	4,941.0	3,626.5	2,956.2	567.2	2,389.0	670.3	322.7	347.6	406.9	37.9	45.4	368.9	360.7
III	4,911.6	3,669.2	2,988.2	569.8	2,418.3	681.0	325.1	355.9	412.1	39.9	48.3	372.3	364.4
IV	5,061.7	3,707.0	3,021.7	572.5	2,449.2	685.3	324.2	361.1	422.4	37.3	44.8	385.1	376.3
1993:I	5,094.9	3,744.1	3,045.9	580.9	2,465.0	698.2	325.9	372.2	413.5	31.5	39.0	382.0	375.5
II	5,159.9	3,787.8	3,075.1	581.4	2,493.8	712.6	333.5	379.1	417.6	35.8	43.3	381.8	375.7
III	5,213.0	3,834.8	3,114.9	586.3	2,528.6	719.9	335.6	384.3	414.2	26.1	33.8	388.1	380.0
IV	5,309.9	3,871.0	3,144.9	588.3	2,556.5	726.2	338.1	388.0	434.9	34.4	41.9	400.5	392.7
1994:I	5,300.5	3,933.6	3,195.2	596.5	2,598.7	738.5	342.9	395.6	421.1	40.8	48.2	380.3	399.3
II	5,493.7	3,993.3	3,242.8	601.7	2,641.1	750.5	350.0	400.5	454.4	35.1	42.5	419.3	409.1
III	5,551.2	4,022.7	3,265.5	603.7	2,661.7	757.2	352.3	404.9	458.7	31.9	39.4	426.8	415.1
IV	5,635.0	4,083.7	3,320.2	608.3	2,711.9	763.5	355.8	407.8	469.4	32.3	39.8	437.1	422.5
1995:I	5,697.7	4,141.6	3,363.0	616.3	2,746.6	778.6	360.8	417.7	472.0	28.5	36.1	443.5	429.6
II	5,738.9	4,198.9	3,393.3	619.6	2,773.6	785.6	363.6	422.0	474.7	27.6	35.1	447.1	433.1
III	5,845.1	4,232.9	3,439.3	624.1	2,815.2	793.7	367.8	425.9	479.7	27.4	34.9	452.3	436.4

[1] National income is the total net income earned in production. It differs from gross domestic product mainly in that it excludes depreciation charges and other allowances for business and institutional consumption of durable capital goods and indirect business taxes. See Table B–22.

See next page for continuation of table.

TABLE B–24.—*National income by type of income, 1959–95*—Continued

[Billions of dollars; quarterly data at seasonally adjusted annual rates]

Year or quarter	Rental income of persons with capital consumption adjustment			Corporate profits with inventory valuation and capital consumption adjustments										Net interest
	Total	Rental income of persons	Capital consumption adjustment	Total	Profits with inventory valuation adjustment and without capital consumption adjustment							Inventory valuation adjustment	Capital consumption adjustment	
					Total	Profits		Profits after tax						
						Profits before tax	Profits tax liability	Total	Dividends	Undistributed profits				
1959	18.2	19.7	-1.5	50.2	53.1	53.4	23.6	29.7	12.7	17.0	-0.3	-2.9	10.2
1960	19.1	20.6	-1.5	48.8	51.0	51.1	22.7	28.4	13.4	15.0	-.2	-2.2	11.2
1961	19.8	21.2	-1.4	49.8	51.3	51.0	22.8	28.2	14.0	14.3	.3	-1.5	13.1
1962	20.6	22.0	-1.4	57.7	56.4	56.4	24.0	32.4	15.0	17.4	.0	1.3	14.6
1963	21.3	22.6	-1.3	63.5	61.2	61.2	26.2	34.9	16.1	18.8	.1	2.3	16.1
1964	21.7	23.0	-1.3	70.4	67.5	68.0	28.0	40.0	18.0	22.0	-.5	2.8	18.2
1965	22.5	24.0	-1.5	80.9	77.6	78.8	30.9	47.9	20.2	27.8	-1.2	3.4	21.1
1966	23.2	24.9	-1.7	86.3	83.0	85.1	33.7	51.4	20.9	30.5	-2.1	3.3	24.3
1967	24.4	26.3	-1.9	83.6	80.3	81.8	32.7	49.2	22.1	27.1	-1.6	3.3	28.1
1968	23.7	26.0	-2.3	90.3	86.9	90.6	39.4	51.2	24.6	26.6	-3.7	3.4	30.4
1969	24.4	27.3	-2.8	87.5	83.2	89.0	39.7	49.4	25.2	24.1	-5.9	4.4	33.6
1970	24.7	27.8	-3.1	75.7	71.8	78.4	34.4	44.0	23.7	20.3	-6.6	3.9	40.0
1971	25.8	29.5	-3.7	88.8	85.5	90.1	37.7	52.4	23.7	28.6	-4.6	3.3	45.4
1972	25.7	30.3	-4.6	102.2	97.9	104.5	41.9	62.6	25.8	36.9	-6.6	4.3	49.3
1973	27.4	32.8	-5.4	115.1	110.9	130.9	49.3	81.6	28.1	53.5	-20.0	4.1	56.5
1974	27.5	34.4	-6.9	103.7	103.4	142.8	51.8	91.0	30.4	60.6	-39.5	.3	71.8
1975	26.6	34.9	-8.4	121.1	129.4	140.4	50.9	89.5	30.1	59.4	-11.0	-8.3	80.0
1976	26.3	35.7	-9.5	147.0	158.9	173.8	64.2	109.6	35.9	73.7	-14.9	-11.8	85.1
1977	24.7	36.4	-11.7	167.3	186.8	203.5	73.0	130.4	40.8	89.6	-16.6	-19.6	100.7
1978	26.5	41.2	-14.7	191.6	213.1	238.1	83.5	154.6	46.0	108.6	-25.0	-21.5	120.5
1979	28.4	46.7	-18.3	194.0	220.2	261.8	88.0	173.8	52.5	121.3	-41.6	-26.2	150.3
1980	35.3	57.3	-22.0	167.1	198.3	241.4	84.8	156.6	59.3	97.3	-43.0	-31.2	191.9
1981	45.7	70.7	-25.1	183.9	204.1	229.8	81.1	148.6	69.5	79.1	-25.7	-20.1	234.5
1982	47.6	74.7	-27.1	159.2	166.8	176.7	63.1	113.6	69.8	43.8	-9.9	-7.6	264.9
1983	47.2	74.8	-27.6	212.3	203.7	212.8	77.2	135.5	80.8	54.8	-9.1	8.6	275.9
1984	51.0	79.2	-28.2	268.2	238.5	244.2	94.0	150.1	83.2	66.9	-5.6	29.7	318.5
1985	49.1	79.0	-29.9	282.2	230.5	229.9	96.5	133.4	92.8	40.6	.5	51.8	337.2
1986	42.3	72.6	-30.4	271.0	234.0	222.6	106.5	116.1	110.2	5.8	11.4	37.0	363.1
1987	45.5	77.6	-32.1	309.7	272.9	293.6	127.1	166.5	107.0	59.5	-20.7	36.8	372.2
1988	55.7	89.7	-33.9	357.2	325.0	354.3	137.0	217.3	116.8	100.5	-29.3	32.2	398.9
1989	52.4	91.0	-38.5	356.4	330.6	348.1	141.3	206.8	138.9	67.9	-17.5	25.8	456.6
1990	61.4	98.6	-37.2	369.5	358.2	371.7	140.5	231.2	151.9	79.4	-13.5	11.3	467.3
1991	68.4	107.0	-38.6	382.5	378.2	374.2	133.4	240.8	163.1	77.7	4.0	4.3	448.0
1992	80.6	126.9	-46.2	401.4	398.9	406.4	143.0	263.4	169.5	93.9	-7.5	2.5	414.3
1993	102.5	144.3	-41.8	464.5	457.7	464.3	163.8	300.5	197.3	103.3	-6.6	6.7	398.1
1994	116.6	159.4	-42.8	526.5	514.9	528.2	195.3	332.9	211.0	121.9	-13.3	11.6	392.8
1990:I	55.5	92.3	-36.8	369.3	353.4	354.7	133.0	221.7	150.7	71.1	-1.3	15.9	458.9
II	57.9	94.9	-37.1	392.8	381.1	373.4	141.2	232.2	152.4	79.8	7.7	11.7	465.0
III	64.8	102.3	-37.5	350.4	341.9	381.9	148.0	233.9	152.4	81.6	-40.0	8.5	467.7
IV	67.3	104.9	-37.5	365.5	356.5	376.7	139.7	237.1	152.0	85.0	-20.3	9.0	477.5
1991:I	66.6	104.1	-37.5	393.7	388.3	370.7	130.1	240.7	158.6	82.0	17.6	5.4	460.4
II	66.3	103.9	-37.5	380.0	375.5	368.7	132.3	236.4	162.6	73.8	6.8	4.6	450.6
III	67.6	105.3	-37.7	376.8	373.8	374.6	136.0	238.6	165.9	72.7	-.8	3.0	446.6
IV	73.0	114.6	-41.6	379.6	375.2	382.8	135.2	247.6	165.3	82.2	-7.6	4.5	434.3
1992:I	78.6	114.8	-36.2	417.3	411.4	411.1	143.9	267.2	162.1	105.2	.3	5.9	419.2
II	80.9	117.5	-36.6	409.3	404.3	426.2	150.9	275.2	164.6	110.6	-21.9	5.0	417.5
III	70.8	144.8	-73.9	351.3	359.4	368.0	127.6	240.4	170.9	69.5	-8.6	-8.1	408.1
IV	92.3	130.4	-38.1	427.7	420.5	420.3	149.7	270.6	180.4	90.3	.2	7.2	412.4
1993:I	98.4	142.6	-44.2	426.4	421.4	436.0	151.5	284.6	190.2	94.4	-14.6	5.0	412.6
II	102.9	143.4	-40.5	449.0	443.2	458.8	162.6	296.2	195.8	100.4	-15.6	5.8	402.6
III	104.1	146.5	-42.5	469.6	465.9	458.0	159.3	298.6	200.2	98.4	7.9	3.8	390.4
IV	104.5	144.6	-40.1	512.8	500.4	504.5	181.7	322.7	202.9	119.8	-4.0	12.3	386.7
1994:I	101.1	162.2	-61.0	455.9	467.8	471.7	171.4	300.3	204.4	95.9	-3.9	-11.8	388.7
II	121.0	159.0	-37.9	531.5	513.4	523.2	192.8	330.4	208.8	121.7	-9.8	18.1	393.5
III	122.2	159.2	-37.0	549.8	531.0	547.5	203.4	344.1	212.5	131.6	-16.5	18.8	397.8
IV	121.9	157.2	-35.3	568.9	547.6	570.4	213.5	356.8	218.5	138.3	-22.8	21.3	391.1
1995:I	120.6	156.3	-35.7	559.6	542.2	594.1	217.3	376.8	221.7	155.1	-51.9	17.4	403.9
II	121.6	157.2	-35.6	561.1	546.1	588.4	214.2	374.1	224.6	149.6	-42.3	15.0	402.6
III	118.3	154.2	-35.8	614.4	599.8	609.6	224.5	385.1	228.5	156.6	-9.8	14.6	399.8

[2] Without capital consumption adjustment.
[3] Without inventory valuation and capital consumption adjustments.

Source: Department of Commerce, Bureau of Economic Analysis.

TABLE B-25.—Sources of personal income, 1959–95

[Billions of dollars; quarterly data at seasonally adjusted annual rates]

Year or quarter	Personal income	Wage and salary disbursements[1] Total	Private Industry Total	Commodity-producing industries Total	Manu-facturing	Distrib-utive indus-tries	Service indus-tries	Govern-ment	Other labor income[1]	Proprietors' income with inventory valuation and capital consumption adjustments Farm	Nonfarm
1959	393.5	259.8	213.8	109.9	86.9	65.1	38.8	46.0	10.6	10.9	39.6
1960	411.7	272.8	223.7	113.4	89.8	68.6	41.7	49.2	11.2	11.5	39.1
1961	429.1	280.5	228.0	114.0	89.9	69.6	44.4	52.4	11.8	12.1	40.9
1962	456.1	299.3	243.0	122.2	96.8	73.3	47.6	56.3	13.0	12.1	42.9
1963	479.1	314.8	254.8	127.4	100.7	76.8	50.7	60.0	14.0	12.0	44.3
1964	513.5	337.7	272.9	136.0	107.3	82.0	54.9	64.9	15.7	10.8	48.3
1965	555.8	363.7	293.8	146.6	115.7	87.9	59.4	69.9	17.8	13.0	50.4
1966	604.7	400.3	321.9	161.6	128.2	95.1	65.3	78.3	19.9	14.1	53.5
1967	649.7	428.9	342.5	169.0	134.3	101.6	72.0	86.4	21.7	12.7	56.4
1968	713.5	471.9	375.3	184.1	146.0	110.8	80.4	96.6	25.2	12.8	60.5
1969	778.2	518.3	412.7	200.4	157.7	121.7	90.6	105.5	28.5	14.6	62.5
1970	836.1	551.5	434.3	203.7	158.4	131.2	99.4	117.1	32.5	14.8	63.2
1971	898.9	583.9	457.4	209.1	160.5	140.4	107.9	126.5	36.7	15.5	68.3
1972	987.3	638.7	501.2	228.2	175.6	153.3	119.7	137.4	43.0	19.5	75.8
1973	1,105.6	708.7	560.0	255.9	196.6	170.3	133.9	148.7	49.2	32.6	80.7
1974	1,213.3	772.6	611.8	276.5	211.8	186.8	148.6	160.9	56.5	25.9	85.4
1975	1,315.6	814.6	638.6	277.1	211.6	198.1	163.4	176.0	65.9	24.2	92.3
1976	1,455.4	899.5	710.8	309.7	238.0	219.5	181.6	188.6	79.7	18.7	108.8
1977	1,611.4	993.9	791.6	346.1	266.7	242.7	202.8	202.3	94.7	17.9	122.9
1978	1,820.2	1,120.8	901.2	392.6	300.1	274.9	233.7	219.6	110.1	22.9	139.2
1979	2,049.7	1,255.9	1,018.8	442.5	335.3	308.5	267.8	237.1	124.3	26.6	150.8
1980	2,285.7	1,377.7	1,116.4	472.5	356.4	336.7	307.2	261.3	139.8	13.8	154.1
1981	2,560.4	1,517.6	1,232.0	514.9	388.0	368.5	348.6	285.6	153.0	23.7	154.6
1982	2,718.7	1,593.9	1,286.7	515.1	386.2	385.9	385.7	307.3	165.4	16.4	153.5
1983	2,891.7	1,685.3	1,360.3	528.2	401.2	405.7	426.4	325.0	177.2	6.0	175.8
1984	3,205.5	1,855.1	1,507.5	586.6	445.9	445.2	475.6	347.6	188.9	24.8	213.1
1985	3,439.6	1,995.9	1,622.1	620.7	468.9	476.5	525.0	373.8	203.1	24.9	232.5
1986	3,647.5	2,116.5	1,720.0	637.3	481.2	501.6	581.0	396.6	216.0	25.2	242.6
1987	3,877.3	2,272.7	1,849.5	660.4	497.2	535.4	653.7	423.1	235.4	32.3	260.6
1988	4,172.8	2,453.6	2,003.2	707.0	530.1	575.3	720.9	450.4	251.7	28.2	294.7
1989	4,489.3	2,598.1	2,118.7	732.4	548.1	606.8	779.5	479.4	273.1	36.8	308.2
1990	4,791.6	2,757.5	2,240.3	754.2	561.2	634.1	852.1	517.2	300.6	36.3	324.6
1991	4,968.5	2,827.6	2,281.5	746.3	562.5	646.6	888.6	546.1	322.7	30.2	332.7
1992	5,264.2	2,986.4	2,418.6	765.7	583.5	680.3	972.6	567.8	351.3	38.0	371.5
1993	5,479.2	3,090.6	2,506.3	781.3	593.1	698.4	1,026.6	584.2	380.9	32.0	388.1
1994	5,750.2	3,241.1	2,638.6	825.0	621.3	739.3	1,074.3	602.5	402.2	35.0	415.9
1990: I	4,687.8	2,704.0	2,199.6	748.7	554.8	624.4	826.5	504.3	291.4	36.1	318.6
II	4,771.5	2,753.0	2,238.6	757.7	563.9	633.9	847.1	514.3	297.8	39.4	323.3
III	4,838.4	2,784.4	2,263.6	758.5	564.9	638.9	866.2	520.8	304.0	36.0	329.6
IV	4,868.6	2,788.6	2,259.3	751.8	561.2	639.1	868.4	529.3	309.2	33.9	327.1
1991: I	4,885.6	2,789.3	2,248.0	742.5	555.5	636.7	868.8	541.3	312.4	27.6	321.6
II	4,950.2	2,815.1	2,269.8	742.8	558.4	644.6	882.5	545.3	319.7	34.2	331.0
III	4,983.3	2,838.8	2,292.0	749.4	566.3	649.7	892.8	546.9	326.3	28.0	337.1
IV	5,048.9	2,867.1	2,316.3	750.6	569.7	655.3	910.5	550.8	332.4	31.0	341.1
1992: I	5,151.9	2,916.5	2,355.1	752.7	571.5	666.2	936.2	561.4	340.8	36.7	359.8
II	5,225.1	2,956.2	2,389.0	761.9	579.6	673.6	953.4	567.2	347.6	37.9	368.9
III	5,264.6	2,988.2	2,418.3	764.6	583.0	681.5	972.2	569.8	355.9	39.9	372.3
IV	5,415.3	3,084.7	2,512.2	783.6	599.7	699.9	1,028.6	572.5	361.1	37.3	385.1
1993: I	5,348.7	2,981.9	2,401.0	757.1	573.8	674.7	969.2	580.9	372.2	31.5	382.0
II	5,458.4	3,074.2	2,492.8	778.5	591.5	696.2	1,018.1	581.4	379.1	35.8	381.8
III	5,500.5	3,113.9	2,527.6	785.5	596.0	704.0	1,038.1	586.3	384.3	26.1	388.1
IV	5,609.1	3,192.3	2,603.9	804.2	611.0	718.7	1,081.1	588.3	388.0	34.4	400.5
1994: I	5,562.4	3,143.7	2,547.3	801.2	604.3	714.5	1,031.6	596.5	395.6	40.8	380.3
II	5,743.0	3,239.8	2,638.1	820.7	618.8	738.8	1,078.6	601.7	400.5	35.1	419.3
III	5,801.7	3,262.4	2,658.7	832.0	626.1	741.5	1,085.2	603.7	404.9	31.9	426.8
IV	5,893.9	3,318.5	2,710.3	846.0	636.0	762.7	1,101.6	608.3	407.8	32.3	437.1
1995: I	5,995.5	3,361.6	2,745.2	856.2	643.4	768.8	1,120.2	616.3	417.7	28.5	443.5
II	6,061.9	3,393.3	2,773.6	855.0	640.5	778.6	1,140.0	619.6	422.0	27.6	447.1
III	6,131.9	3,439.3	2,815.2	859.9	642.9	792.4	1,162.8	624.1	425.9	27.4	452.3

[1] The total of wage and salary disbursements and other labor income differs from compensation of employees in Table B-24 in that it excludes employer contributions for social insurance and the excess of wage accruals over wage disbursements.

See next page for continuation of table.

[Billions of dollars; quarterly data at seasonally adjusted annual rates]

Year or quarter	Rental income of persons with capital consumption adjustment	Personal dividend income	Personal interest income	Transfer payments to persons							Less: Personal contributions for social insurance
				Total	Old-age, survivors, disability, and health insurance benefits	Government unemployment insurance benefits	Veterans benefits	Government employees retirement benefits	Aid to families with dependent children (AFDC)	Other	
1959	18.2	12.7	22.7	27.0	10.2	2.8	4.6	2.8	0.9	5.7	7.9
1960	19.1	13.4	25.0	28.8	11.1	3.0	4.6	3.1	1.0	6.1	9.3
1961	19.8	14.0	26.9	32.8	12.6	4.3	5.0	3.4	1.1	6.5	9.7
1962	20.6	15.0	29.3	34.1	14.3	3.1	4.7	3.7	1.3	7.0	10.3
1963	21.3	16.1	32.4	36.2	15.2	3.0	4.8	4.2	1.4	7.6	11.8
1964	21.7	18.0	36.1	37.9	16.0	2.7	4.7	4.7	1.5	8.2	12.6
1965	22.5	20.2	40.3	41.1	18.1	2.3	4.9	5.2	1.7	9.0	13.3
1966	23.2	20.9	44.9	45.7	20.8	1.9	4.9	6.1	1.9	10.3	17.8
1967	24.4	22.1	49.5	54.6	25.5	2.2	5.6	6.9	2.3	12.2	20.6
1968	23.7	24.5	54.6	63.2	30.2	2.1	5.9	7.6	2.8	14.5	22.9
1969	24.4	25.1	60.8	70.3	32.9	2.2	6.7	8.7	3.5	16.2	26.2
1970	24.7	23.5	69.2	84.6	38.5	4.0	7.7	10.2	4.8	19.4	27.9
1971	25.8	23.5	75.7	100.1	44.5	5.8	8.8	11.8	6.2	23.0	30.7
1972	25.7	25.5	81.8	111.8	49.6	5.7	9.7	13.8	6.9	26.1	34.5
1973	27.4	27.7	94.1	127.9	60.4	4.4	10.4	16.0	7.2	29.5	42.6
1974	27.5	29.6	112.4	151.3	70.1	6.8	11.8	19.0	7.9	35.7	47.9
1975	26.6	29.2	123.0	190.2	81.4	17.6	14.5	22.7	9.2	44.7	50.4
1976	26.3	35.0	134.6	208.3	92.9	15.8	14.4	26.1	10.1	49.1	55.5
1977	24.7	39.5	155.7	223.3	104.9	12.7	13.8	29.0	10.6	52.4	61.2
1978	26.5	44.3	184.5	241.6	116.2	9.7	13.9	32.7	10.7	58.4	69.8
1979	28.4	50.5	223.6	270.7	131.8	9.8	14.4	36.9	11.0	66.8	81.0
1980	35.3	57.5	274.7	321.5	154.2	16.1	15.0	43.0	12.4	80.8	88.6
1981	45.7	67.2	337.2	365.9	182.0	15.9	16.1	49.4	13.0	89.7	104.5
1982	47.6	66.9	379.2	408.1	204.5	25.2	16.4	54.6	13.3	94.1	112.3
1983	47.2	77.4	403.2	439.4	221.7	26.3	16.6	58.0	14.2	102.6	119.7
1984	51.0	79.4	472.3	453.6	235.7	15.9	16.4	60.9	14.8	109.9	132.7
1985	49.1	88.3	508.4	486.5	253.4	15.7	16.7	66.6	15.4	118.7	149.0
1986	42.3	105.1	543.3	518.6	269.2	16.3	16.7	70.7	16.4	129.3	162.1
1987	45.5	101.1	560.0	543.3	282.9	14.5	16.6	76.0	16.7	136.6	173.7
1988	55.7	109.9	595.5	577.6	300.4	13.3	16.9	82.2	17.3	147.6	194.2
1989	52.4	130.9	674.5	626.0	325.1	14.4	17.3	87.6	18.0	163.6	210.8
1990	61.4	142.9	704.4	687.8	352.0	18.1	17.8	94.5	19.8	185.6	223.9
1991	68.4	153.6	699.2	769.9	382.3	26.8	18.3	102.2	22.0	218.2	235.8
1992	80.6	159.4	667.2	858.2	414.0	38.9	19.3	109.0	23.3	253.8	248.4
1993	102.5	186.8	647.3	910.7	444.4	34.0	20.1	116.4	23.9	271.8	259.6
1994	116.6	199.6	661.6	956.3	472.9	23.7	20.2	125.8	24.2	289.5	278.1
1990: I	55.5	142.0	690.6	670.5	348.1	16.4	18.0	93.0	19.1	175.9	221.0
II	57.9	143.4	701.1	678.1	348.6	17.1	17.8	93.7	19.5	181.4	222.3
III	64.8	143.3	711.6	690.6	352.6	18.2	17.7	94.9	20.0	187.2	225.9
IV	67.3	142.7	714.2	712.0	358.7	20.9	17.8	96.4	20.5	197.6	226.4
1991: I	66.6	149.3	705.4	746.4	374.6	24.5	18.1	102.2	21.1	205.9	233.0
II	66.3	153.1	702.2	763.2	380.0	27.7	18.7	101.6	21.8	213.5	234.6
III	67.6	156.4	697.0	774.9	384.7	26.0	18.3	102.3	22.2	221.4	236.9
IV	73.0	155.7	692.3	795.1	389.9	29.2	18.2	102.9	22.7	232.2	238.9
1992: I	78.6	152.3	674.1	838.3	405.4	39.2	20.4	107.8	23.0	242.5	245.2
II	80.9	154.5	673.0	853.5	412.2	40.4	18.9	108.6	23.1	250.2	247.4
III	70.8	160.8	661.2	865.3	416.9	38.7	18.8	109.0	23.4	258.5	249.7
IV	92.3	170.1	660.4	875.8	421.5	37.1	19.1	110.5	23.5	264.2	251.4
1993: I	98.4	180.0	659.0	895.9	436.8	34.4	20.1	114.2	23.7	266.7	252.3
II	102.9	185.4	651.6	906.9	441.9	34.3	20.3	115.8	24.0	270.6	259.3
III	104.1	189.7	640.0	916.4	446.7	34.7	20.2	117.2	24.0	273.6	261.9
IV	104.5	192.1	638.6	923.6	452.1	32.6	20.0	118.5	24.1	276.3	265.0
1994: I	101.1	193.2	639.4	939.5	463.6	27.9	20.0	120.2	24.2	283.6	271.4
II	121.0	197.5	657.6	949.8	470.4	23.9	20.0	124.6	24.2	286.7	277.6
III	122.2	201.0	671.0	961.4	475.6	21.8	20.4	128.1	24.2	291.3	279.9
IV	121.9	206.7	678.4	974.7	482.1	21.2	20.3	130.4	24.1	295.5	283.5
1995: I	120.6	209.5	701.9	1,002.4	497.6	21.2	20.8	132.9	23.8	306.1	290.2
II	121.6	212.2	713.9	1,016.5	505.1	21.0	20.7	135.5	23.5	311.1	292.7
III	118.3	215.8	719.3	1,029.9	510.7	22.0	21.1	136.4	23.1	316.6	296.2

Note.—The industry classification of wage and salary disbursements and proprietors' income is on an establishment basis and is based on the 1987 Standard Industrial Classification (SIC) beginning 1987 and on the 1972 SIC for earlier years shown.

Source: Department of Commerce, Bureau of Economic Analysis.

TABLE B–26.—*Disposition of personal income, 1959–95*

[Billions of dollars, except as noted; quarterly data at seasonally adjusted annual rates]

Year or quarter	Personal income	Less: Personal tax and nontax payments	Equals: Disposable personal income	Less: Personal outlays				Equals: Personal saving	Percent of disposable personal income [1]		
				Total	Personal consumption expenditures	Interest paid by persons	Personal transfer payments to rest of the world (net)		Personal outlays		Personal saving
									Total	Personal consumption expenditures	
1959	393.5	44.5	349.0	324.7	318.1	6.1	0.4	24.3	93.0	91.1	7.0
1960	411.7	48.7	362.9	339.6	332.2	7.0	.5	23.3	93.6	91.5	6.4
1961	429.1	50.3	378.8	350.5	342.6	7.3	.5	28.3	92.5	90.5	7.5
1962	456.1	54.8	401.3	371.8	363.4	7.8	.5	29.5	92.6	90.6	7.4
1963	479.1	58.0	421.1	392.5	383.0	8.9	.6	28.6	93.2	90.9	6.8
1964	513.5	56.0	457.6	422.1	411.4	10.0	.7	35.5	92.2	89.9	7.7
1965	555.8	61.9	493.9	456.2	444.3	11.1	.8	37.8	92.4	89.9	7.6
1966	604.7	71.0	533.7	494.7	481.9	12.0	.8	39.1	92.7	90.3	7.3
1967	649.7	77.9	571.9	523.0	509.5	12.5	1.0	48.9	91.4	89.1	8.5
1968	713.5	92.1	621.4	574.6	559.8	13.8	1.0	46.8	92.5	90.1	7.5
1969	778.2	109.9	668.4	621.4	604.7	15.7	1.1	46.9	93.0	90.5	7.0
1970	836.1	109.0	727.1	666.1	648.1	16.8	1.2	61.0	91.6	89.1	8.4
1971	898.9	108.7	790.2	721.6	702.5	17.8	1.3	68.6	91.3	88.9	8.7
1972	987.3	132.0	855.3	791.6	770.7	19.6	1.3	63.6	92.6	90.1	7.4
1973	1,105.6	140.6	965.0	875.4	851.6	22.4	1.4	89.6	90.7	88.2	9.3
1974	1,213.3	159.1	1,054.2	956.6	931.2	24.2	1.2	97.6	90.7	88.3	9.3
1975	1,315.6	156.4	1,159.2	1,054.8	1,029.1	24.5	1.2	104.4	91.0	88.8	9.0
1976	1,455.4	182.3	1,273.0	1,176.7	1,148.8	26.7	1.2	96.4	92.4	90.2	7.6
1977	1,611.4	210.0	1,401.4	1,308.9	1,277.1	30.7	1.2	92.5	93.4	91.1	6.6
1978	1,820.2	240.1	1,580.1	1,467.6	1,428.8	37.5	1.3	112.6	92.9	90.4	7.1
1979	2,049.7	280.2	1,769.5	1,639.5	1,593.5	44.5	1.4	130.1	92.7	90.1	7.4
1980	2,285.7	312.4	1,973.3	1,811.5	1,760.4	49.4	1.6	161.8	91.8	89.2	8.2
1981	2,560.4	360.2	2,200.2	2,001.1	1,941.3	54.6	5.2	199.1	90.9	88.2	9.1
1982	2,718.7	371.4	2,347.3	2,141.8	2,076.8	58.8	6.2	205.5	91.2	88.5	8.8
1983	2,891.7	369.3	2,522.4	2,355.5	2,283.4	65.5	6.5	167.0	93.4	90.5	6.6
1984	3,205.5	395.5	2,810.0	2,574.4	2,492.3	74.7	7.4	235.7	91.6	88.7	8.4
1985	3,439.6	437.7	3,002.0	2,795.8	2,704.8	83.2	7.8	206.2	93.1	90.1	6.9
1986	3,647.5	459.9	3,187.6	2,991.1	2,892.7	90.3	8.1	196.5	93.8	90.7	6.2
1987	3,877.3	514.2	3,363.1	3,194.7	3,094.5	91.5	8.7	168.4	95.0	92.0	5.0
1988	4,172.8	532.0	3,640.8	3,451.7	3,349.7	92.9	9.1	189.1	94.8	92.0	5.2
1989	4,489.3	594.9	3,894.5	3,706.7	3,594.8	102.4	9.6	187.8	95.2	92.3	4.8
1990	4,791.6	624.8	4,166.8	3,958.1	3,839.3	108.9	9.9	208.7	95.0	92.1	5.0
1991	4,968.5	624.8	4,343.7	4,097.4	3,975.1	111.9	10.4	246.4	94.3	91.5	5.7
1992	5,264.2	650.5	4,613.7	4,341.0	4,219.8	111.7	9.6	272.6	94.1	91.5	5.9
1993	5,479.2	689.9	4,789.3	4,572.9	4,454.1	108.9	9.9	216.4	95.5	93.0	4.5
1994	5,750.2	731.4	5,018.8	4,826.5	4,698.7	117.2	10.6	192.3	96.2	93.6	3.8
1990: I	4,687.8	613.0	4,074.8	3,875.8	3,759.2	106.7	9.9	199.0	95.1	92.3	4.9
II	4,771.5	628.2	4,143.3	3,929.4	3,811.8	108.0	9.5	213.9	94.8	92.0	5.2
III	4,838.4	630.8	4,207.6	3,999.3	3,879.2	109.8	10.2	208.3	95.0	92.2	5.0
IV	4,868.6	627.1	4,241.5	4,027.9	3,907.0	110.9	10.1	213.5	95.0	92.1	5.0
1991: I	4,885.6	622.3	4,263.3	4,032.5	3,910.7	111.4	10.4	230.8	94.6	91.7	5.4
II	4,950.2	620.5	4,329.6	4,083.3	3,961.0	112.0	10.3	246.3	94.3	91.5	5.7
III	4,989.3	623.7	4,365.6	4,123.9	4,001.6	112.0	10.2	241.7	94.5	91.7	5.5
IV	5,048.9	632.5	4,416.4	4,149.8	4,027.1	112.1	10.6	266.6	94.0	91.2	6.0
1992: I	5,151.9	636.7	4,515.2	4,250.0	4,127.6	112.9	9.4	265.2	94.1	91.4	5.9
II	5,225.1	640.0	4,585.1	4,304.8	4,183.0	112.1	9.7	280.3	93.9	91.2	6.1
III	5,264.6	650.6	4,613.9	4,359.5	4,238.9	111.4	9.2	254.5	94.5	91.9	5.5
IV	5,415.3	674.8	4,740.5	4,450.0	4,329.6	110.4	9.9	290.5	93.9	91.3	6.1
1993: I	5,348.7	662.4	4,686.3	4,486.6	4,367.8	109.0	9.9	199.6	95.7	93.2	4.3
II	5,458.4	686.9	4,771.6	4,542.6	4,424.7	108.0	9.9	228.9	95.2	92.7	4.8
III	5,500.5	696.4	4,804.1	4,599.3	4,481.0	108.5	9.8	204.9	95.7	93.3	4.3
IV	5,609.1	713.8	4,895.3	4,663.2	4,543.0	110.0	10.1	232.1	95.3	92.8	4.7
1994: I	5,562.4	705.5	4,856.9	4,723.0	4,599.2	113.0	10.8	133.9	97.2	94.7	2.8
II	5,743.0	740.8	5,002.2	4,791.9	4,665.1	115.8	11.0	210.3	95.8	93.3	4.2
III	5,801.7	731.3	5,070.4	4,863.0	4,734.4	118.4	10.3	207.4	95.9	93.4	4.1
IV	5,893.9	748.1	5,145.7	4,927.9	4,796.0	121.5	10.5	217.8	95.8	93.2	4.2
1995: I	5,995.5	770.0	5,225.5	4,972.2	4,836.3	125.3	10.5	253.3	95.2	92.6	4.8
II	6,061.9	801.5	5,260.4	5,049.0	4,908.7	129.8	10.5	211.4	96.0	93.3	4.0
III	6,131.9	801.3	5,330.6	5,109.7	4,965.1	134.0	10.6	220.9	95.9	93.1	4.1

[1] Percents based on data in millions of dollars.

Source: Department of Commerce, Bureau of Economic Analysis.

—*Total and per capita disposable personal income and personal consumption expenditures in current and real dollars, 1959–95*

[Quarterly data at seasonally adjusted annual rates, except as noted]

Year or quarter	Disposable personal income				Personal consumption expenditures				Gross domestic product per capita (dollars)		Popula-tion (thou-sands) [1]
	Total (billions of dollars)		Per capita (dollars)		Total (billions of dollars)		Per capita (dollars)				
	Current dollars	Chained (1992) dollars	Current dollars	Chained (1992) dollars	Current dollars	Chained (1992) dollars	Current dollars	Chained (1992) dollars	Current dollars	Chained (1992) dollars	
1959	349.0	1,530.1	1,971	8,641	318.1	1,394.6	1,796	7,876	2,865	12,494	177,073
1960	362.9	1,565.4	2,008	8,660	332.2	1,432.6	1,838	7,926	2,913	12,512	180,760
1961	378.8	1,615.8	2,062	8,794	342.6	1,461.5	1,865	7,954	2,965	12,571	183,742
1962	401.3	1,693.7	2,151	9,077	363.4	1,533.8	1,948	8,220	3,136	13,125	186,590
1963	421.1	1,755.5	2,225	9,274	383.0	1,596.6	2,023	8,434	3,261	13,492	189,300
1964	457.6	1,881.9	2,384	9,805	411.4	1,692.3	2,144	8,817	3,455	14,083	191,927
1965	493.9	2,000.2	2,541	10,292	444.3	1,799.1	2,286	9,257	3,700	14,792	194,347
1966	533.7	2,106.6	2,715	10,715	481.9	1,902.0	2,451	9,674	4,007	15,565	196,599
1967	571.9	2,198.4	2,877	11,061	509.5	1,958.6	2,563	9,854	4,194	15,800	198,752
1968	621.4	2,298.2	3,096	11,448	559.8	2,070.2	2,789	10,313	4,536	16,382	200,745
1969	668.4	2,373.6	3,297	11,708	604.7	2,147.5	2,982	10,593	4,845	16,712	202,736
1970	727.1	2,465.6	3,545	12,022	648.1	2,197.8	3,160	10,717	5,050	16,520	205,089
1971	790.2	2,564.0	3,805	12,345	702.5	2,279.5	3,383	10,975	5,419	16,853	207,692
1972	855.3	2,680.8	4,074	12,770	770.7	2,415.9	3,671	11,508	5,894	17,579	209,924
1973	965.0	2,869.4	4,553	13,539	851.6	2,532.6	4,018	11,950	6,524	18,412	211,939
1974	1,054.2	2,847.0	4,928	13,310	931.2	2,514.7	4,353	11,756	6,998	18,178	213,898
1975	1,159.2	2,895.0	5,367	13,404	1,029.1	2,570.0	4,765	11,899	7,550	17,896	215,981
1976	1,273.0	3,008.0	5,837	13,793	1,148.8	2,714.3	5,268	12,446	8,341	18,713	218,086
1977	1,401.4	3,105.1	6,362	14,095	1,277.1	2,829.8	5,797	12,846	9,201	19,426	220,289
1978	1,580.1	3,264.2	7,097	14,662	1,428.8	2,951.6	6,418	13,258	10,292	20,185	222,629
1979	1,769.5	3,353.9	7,861	14,899	1,593.5	3,020.2	7,079	13,417	11,361	20,541	225,106
1980	1,973.3	3,373.3	8,665	14,813	1,760.4	3,009.7	7,730	13,216	12,226	20,252	227,726
1981	2,200.2	3,452.3	9,566	15,009	1,941.3	3,046.4	8,440	13,245	13,547	20,542	230,008
1982	2,347.3	3,483.0	10,108	14,999	2,076.8	3,081.5	8,943	13,270	13,961	19,911	232,218
1983	2,522.4	3,579.9	10,764	15,277	2,283.4	3,240.6	9,744	13,829	14,998	20,527	234,332
1984	2,810.0	3,841.9	11,887	16,252	2,492.3	3,407.6	10,543	14,415	16,508	21,736	236,394
1985	3,002.0	3,958.6	12,587	16,597	2,704.8	3,566.5	11,341	14,954	17,529	22,345	238,506
1986	3,187.6	4,087.0	13,244	16,981	2,892.7	3,708.7	12,019	15,409	18,374	22,810	240,682
1987	3,363.1	4,154.1	13,849	17,106	3,094.5	3,822.3	12,743	15,740	19,323	23,260	242,842
1988	3,640.8	4,318.1	14,857	17,621	3,349.7	3,972.7	13,669	16,211	20,605	23,924	245,061
1989	3,894.5	4,403.7	15,742	17,801	3,594.8	4,064.6	14,531	16,430	21,984	24,497	247,387
1990	4,166.8	4,484.6	16,670	17,942	3,839.3	4,132.2	15,360	16,532	22,979	24,559	249,956
1991	4,343.7	4,486.4	17,191	17,755	3,975.1	4,105.8	15,732	16,249	23,416	24,058	252,680
1992	4,613.7	4,613.7	18,062	18,062	4,219.8	4,219.8	16,520	16,520	24,447	24,447	255,432
1993	4,789.3	4,666.2	18,552	18,075	4,454.1	4,339.7	17,253	16,810	25,373	24,728	258,159
1994	5,018.8	4,775.6	19,253	18,320	4,698.7	4,471.1	18,025	17,152	26,589	25,335	260,681
1990:I	4,074.8	4,475.5	16,369	17,979	3,759.2	4,128.9	15,102	16,587	22,739	24,722	248,928
II	4,143.3	4,494.3	16,602	18,008	3,811.8	4,134.7	15,274	16,568	23,044	24,741	249,564
III	4,207.6	4,499.7	16,810	17,977	3,879.2	4,148.5	15,498	16,574	23,102	24,551	250,299
IV	4,241.5	4,468.8	16,896	17,802	3,907.0	4,116.4	15,564	16,398	23,031	24,224	251,031
1991:I	4,263.3	4,452.7	16,941	17,694	3,910.7	4,084.5	15,540	16,231	23,136	24,033	251,650
II	4,329.6	4,492.6	17,161	17,807	3,961.0	4,110.0	15,700	16,291	23,355	24,075	252,295
III	4,365.6	4,494.2	17,253	17,761	4,001.6	4,119.5	15,815	16,280	23,515	24,065	253,033
IV	4,416.4	4,506.3	17,405	17,759	4,027.1	4,109.1	15,871	16,194	23,655	24,058	253,743
1992:I	4,515.2	4,565.6	17,753	17,951	4,127.6	4,173.8	16,229	16,410	24,070	24,280	254,338
II	4,585.1	4,599.8	17,979	18,036	4,183.0	4,196.4	16,402	16,454	24,316	24,366	255,032
III	4,613.9	4,600.6	18,036	17,984	4,238.9	4,226.7	16,570	16,522	24,516	24,474	255,815
IV	4,740.5	4,688.7	18,478	18,277	4,329.6	4,282.3	16,877	16,692	24,881	24,664	256,543
1993:I	4,686.3	4,602.8	18,223	17,899	4,367.8	4,290.0	16,985	16,682	25,054	24,604	257,155
II	4,771.6	4,657.6	18,510	18,068	4,424.7	4,319.0	17,164	16,754	25,227	24,647	257,787
III	4,804.1	4,674.0	18,585	18,081	4,481.0	4,359.7	17,335	16,865	25,421	24,721	258,501
IV	4,895.3	4,730.4	18,887	18,251	4,543.0	4,390.0	17,528	16,937	25,787	24,939	259,192
1994:I	4,856.9	4,666.4	18,699	17,966	4,599.2	4,418.8	17,707	17,013	26,076	25,043	259,738
II	5,002.2	4,779.8	19,215	18,361	4,665.1	4,457.7	17,920	17,123	26,448	25,282	260,327
III	5,070.4	4,804.2	19,427	18,407	4,734.4	4,485.8	18,139	17,187	26,772	25,438	261,004
IV	5,145.7	4,852.0	19,666	18,544	4,796.0	4,522.3	18,330	17,283	27,059	25,573	261,653
1995:I	5,225.5	4,895.5	19,931	18,672	4,836.3	4,530.9	18,447	17,282	27,263	25,561	262,181
II	5,260.4	4,896.1	20,021	18,634	4,908.7	4,568.8	18,682	17,388	27,389	25,556	262,748
III	5,330.6	4,939.8	20,238	18,754	4,965.1	4,601.1	18,850	17,468	27,704	25,677	263,395

[1] Population of the United States including Armed Forces overseas; includes Alaska and Hawaii beginning 1960. Annual data are averages of quarterly data. Quarterly data are averages for the period.

Source: Department of Commerce (Bureau of Economic Analysis and Bureau of the Census).

TABLE B–28.—*Gross saving and investment, 1959–95*

[Billions of dollars, except as noted; quarterly data at seasonally adjusted annual rates]

Year or quarter	Gross saving													Capital grants received by the United States (net) [3]
	Gross private saving						Gross government saving							
				Gross business saving				Federal			State and local			
	Total	Total	Personal saving	Total [1]	Undistributed corporate profits [2]	Corporate and noncorporate consumption of fixed capital	Total	Total	Consumption of fixed capital	Current surplus or deficit (−) (NIPA)	Total	Consumption of fixed capital	Current surplus or deficit (−) (NIPA)	
1959	109.0	82.8	24.3	58.4	13.9	44.5	26.2	12.8	10.2	2.6	13.5	3.9	9.6	....
1960	113.9	82.1	23.3	58.8	12.7	46.1	31.8	17.8	10.5	7.4	14.0	4.0	9.9	....
1961	116.8	88.6	28.3	60.2	13.0	47.2	28.3	13.6	10.7	2.9	14.7	4.3	10.4	....
1962	127.4	97.1	29.5	67.6	18.7	48.9	30.3	14.0	11.2	2.8	16.3	4.6	11.7	....
1963	135.4	100.3	28.6	71.7	21.2	50.5	35.1	17.2	11.8	5.4	17.9	4.9	13.0	....
1964	145.8	112.9	35.5	77.4	24.4	53.1	32.9	13.0	12.1	.9	19.9	5.2	14.7	....
1965	161.0	124.4	37.8	86.6	29.9	56.7	36.6	15.9	12.5	3.4	20.8	5.7	15.1	....
1966	171.7	132.6	39.1	93.5	31.7	61.8	39.2	15.6	13.0	2.6	23.5	6.3	17.3	....
1967	174.4	144.7	48.9	95.9	28.9	67.0	29.7	5.6	13.9	−8.3	24.1	6.8	17.3	....
1968	185.8	146.1	46.8	99.3	26.3	73.0	39.7	12.0	14.9	−2.8	27.6	7.6	20.0	....
1969	202.9	149.0	46.9	102.1	22.6	79.5	53.9	24.3	15.6	8.7	29.6	8.5	21.1	....
1970	198.2	164.7	61.0	103.8	17.7	86.1	32.6	2.2	16.2	−14.1	30.4	9.6	20.8	0.9
1971	215.3	190.7	68.6	122.1	27.3	94.4	23.9	−8.5	16.9	−25.3	32.4	10.7	21.7	.7
1972	244.9	202.7	63.6	139.1	34.5	104.9	41.5	−2.4	18.2	−20.5	43.9	11.7	32.2	.7
1973	297.5	242.3	89.6	152.7	37.6	115.1	55.1	8.7	19.9	−11.1	46.4	13.0	33.4	0
1974	302.3	252.7	97.6	155.2	21.5	133.7	51.5	5.1	22.0	−16.9	46.5	16.0	30.5	6−2.0
1975	298.3	302.2	104.4	197.8	40.1	157.7	−3.9	−49.9	24.0	−73.9	46.0	18.4	27.6	0
1976	340.9	317.5	96.4	221.1	47.0	174.1	23.5	−31.9	25.4	−57.2	55.3	19.4	35.9	0
1977	395.5	349.4	92.5	256.9	53.4	203.5	46.1	−19.3	27.0	−46.3	65.4	20.7	44.7	0
1978	477.4	405.0	112.6	292.4	62.0	230.4	72.4	−2.8	28.9	−31.7	75.1	22.5	52.6	0
1979	540.9	449.1	130.1	319.0	53.5	265.5	90.7	13.0	31.5	−18.4	77.7	25.4	52.3	1.1
1980	547.4	489.5	161.8	327.6	23.0	304.6	56.8	−26.8	34.1	−61.0	83.6	29.2	54.4	1.2
1981	651.1	581.9	199.1	382.8	33.3	349.5	68.1	−20.6	37.1	−57.8	88.7	33.3	55.4	1.1
1982	604.7	610.1	205.5	404.6	26.3	378.3	−5.3	−92.8	41.9	−134.7	87.5	36.2	51.3	0
1983	589.6	619.1	167.0	452.1	54.3	397.8	−29.4	−131.8	42.6	−174.4	102.4	37.5	64.9	0
1984	751.5	737.5	235.7	501.9	91.0	410.9	14.0	−111.9	44.1	−156.0	125.9	39.0	86.9	0
1985	746.7	731.5	206.2	525.3	92.9	432.4	15.2	−116.9	46.1	−162.9	132.0	41.0	91.0	0
1986	721.0	710.1	195.5	513.6	54.2	459.4	10.8	−127.9	49.6	−177.5	138.8	43.9	94.9	0
1987	780.9	727.2	168.4	558.8	75.7	483.2	53.6	−77.2	51.7	−128.9	130.8	47.1	83.8	0
1988	877.2	808.4	189.1	619.3	103.3	516.0	68.8	−67.0	54.3	−121.3	135.8	49.9	85.9	0
1989	907.9	815.9	187.8	628.1	76.2	551.9	92.0	−56.4	57.0	−113.4	148.4	53.3	95.1	0
1990	904.4	861.7	208.7	653.0	77.2	575.8	42.7	−94.0	60.7	−154.7	136.7	56.6	80.1	0
1991	935.3	931.9	246.4	685.6	86.0	599.6	3.3	−132.2	63.9	−196.0	135.5	59.6	75.8	0
1992	905.4	971.9	272.6	699.2	88.9	626.1	−66.5	−215.0	65.9	−280.9	148.6	62.3	86.3	0
1993	938.4	964.5	216.4	748.1	103.4	640.0	−26.0	−186.5	68.2	−254.7	160.5	65.6	94.9	0
1994	1,055.9	1,006.0	192.4	813.7	120.2	678.7	49.9	−119.3	70.6	−189.9	169.2	69.4	99.7	0
1990:I	896.1	850.2	199.0	651.2	85.6	565.6	45.9	−94.8	59.3	−154.1	140.7	55.2	85.5	0
II ...	940.7	886.3	213.9	672.4	99.2	573.2	54.5	−84.4	59.7	−144.1	138.9	56.1	82.8	0
III ...	895.0	838.9	208.3	630.6	50.0	580.6	56.1	−81.9	60.8	−142.6	137.9	57.2	80.7	0
IV ...	885.7	871.2	213.5	657.7	73.8	583.9	14.5	−115.0	62.8	−177.7	129.4	57.9	71.5	0
1991:I	983.5	928.2	230.8	697.4	105.0	592.5	55.3	−72.0	62.6	−134.6	127.3	58.6	68.8	0
II ...	928.1	927.8	246.3	681.5	85.1	596.4	.2	−132.9	63.9	−196.7	133.1	59.4	73.7	0
III ...	905.4	918.0	241.7	676.3	74.9	601.4	−12.6	−149.7	64.3	−214.0	137.1	60.0	77.1	0
IV ...	924.0	953.7	266.6	687.2	79.1	608.1	−29.7	−174.0	64.8	−238.8	144.4	60.6	83.8	0
1992:I	921.5	977.8	265.2	712.6	111.3	601.3	−56.3	−202.2	65.2	−267.4	145.9	61.1	84.8	0
II ...	915.1	980.5	280.3	700.1	93.7	606.4	−65.3	−213.9	65.8	−279.6	148.5	62.0	86.6	0
III ...	901.0	987.8	254.5	733.4	52.9	680.5	−86.9	−231.5	66.0	−297.5	144.6	62.7	82.0	0
IV ...	884.0	941.3	290.5	650.8	97.7	616.2	−57.3	−212.5	66.5	−279.0	155.2	63.5	91.7	0
1993:I	910.7	982.2	199.6	782.5	84.7	633.8	−71.5	−216.4	67.3	−283.7	144.9	64.4	80.5	0
II ...	928.0	955.1	228.9	726.2	90.6	634.6	−27.1	−181.6	67.7	−249.2	154.5	65.3	89.1	0
III ...	940.4	964.3	204.9	759.5	110.1	648.4	−24.0	−184.8	68.6	−253.5	160.9	66.0	94.9	0
IV ...	974.6	956.2	232.1	724.1	128.1	643.3	18.4	−163.3	69.1	−232.4	181.7	66.7	115.0	0
1994:I	1,034.8	1,014.2	133.9	880.3	80.1	748.7	20.6	−143.4	69.5	−212.9	164.0	69.2	94.8	0
II ...	1,069.8	996.0	210.3	785.7	129.9	652.7	73.8	−99.9	70.0	−169.9	173.7	68.5	105.2	0
III ...	1,054.4	1,001.1	207.4	793.7	133.9	656.7	53.3	−115.9	70.4	−186.3	169.2	69.6	99.6	0
IV ...	1,064.9	1,012.8	217.8	795.0	136.8	656.6	52.0	−117.8	72.7	−190.4	169.8	70.5	99.3	0
1995:I	1,110.5	1,039.9	253.3	786.6	120.6	664.6	70.5	−99.9	73.5	−173.3	170.4	71.4	99.0	0
II ...	1,092.3	1,007.3	211.4	795.9	122.3	673.6	85.0	−86.3	74.2	−160.5	171.3	72.3	99.0	0
III ...	1,145.7	1,064.0	220.9	843.1	161.4	681.8	81.6	−84.6	73.8	−158.4	166.2	73.4	92.8	0

[1] Includes private wage accruals less disbursements not shown separately.
[2] With inventory valuation and capital consumption adjustments.
[3] Consists mainly of allocations of special drawing rights (SDRs).

See next page for continuation of table.

312

[Billions of dollars except as noted; quarterly data at seasonally adjusted annual rates]

Year or quarter	Gross investment				Statistical discrepancy	Addenda:	
	Total	Gross private domestic investment	Gross government investment[4]	Net foreign investment[5]		Gross saving as a percent of gross national product	Personal saving as a percent of disposable personal income
1959	106.9	78.8	29.3	-1.2	-2.1	21.4	7.0
1960	110.2	78.8	28.2	3.2	-3.7	21.5	6.4
1961	113.5	77.9	31.3	4.3	-3.3	21.3	7.5
1962	125.0	87.9	33.2	3.9	-2.4	21.6	7.4
1963	131.9	93.4	33.5	5.0	-3.5	21.8	6.8
1964	143.8	101.7	34.5	7.5	-2.1	21.8	7.7
1965	159.6	118.0	35.4	6.2	-1.4	22.2	7.6
1966	174.4	130.4	40.1	3.9	2.7	21.7	7.3
1967	175.1	128.0	43.5	3.5	.6	20.8	8.5
1968	186.0	139.9	44.3	1.7	.2	20.3	7.5
1969	200.7	155.0	43.9	1.8	-2.2	20.5	7.0
1970	199.1	150.2	44.0	4.9	1.0	19.0	8.4
1971	220.4	176.0	43.1	1.3	5.1	19.0	8.7
1972	248.1	205.6	45.4	-2.9	3.2	19.7	7.4
1973	299.9	242.9	48.3	8.7	2.4	21.3	9.3
1974	306.7	245.6	56.0	5.1	4.5	20.0	9.3
1975	309.5	225.4	62.7	21.4	11.2	18.1	9.0
1976	359.9	286.6	64.4	8.9	18.9	18.6	7.6
1977	413.0	356.6	65.4	-9.0	17.5	19.3	6.6
1978	494.9	430.8	74.6	-10.4	17.6	20.6	7.1
1979	568.7	480.9	85.3	2.6	27.8	20.9	7.4
1980	574.8	465.9	96.4	12.5	27.4	19.4	8.2
1981	665.7	556.2	102.1	7.4	14.6	20.7	9.1
1982	601.8	501.1	106.9	-6.1	-2.9	18.5	8.8
1983	626.2	547.1	116.5	-37.3	36.5	16.6	6.6
1984	755.7	715.6	131.7	-91.5	4.2	19.1	8.4
1985	748.0	715.1	149.9	-116.9	1.3	17.8	6.9
1986	743.1	722.5	163.5	-142.9	22.1	16.3	6.2
1987	764.2	747.2	173.5	-156.4	-16.6	16.6	5.0
1988	828.7	773.9	172.9	-118.1	-48.6	17.3	5.2
1989	919.5	829.2	182.7	-92.4	11.6	16.6	4.8
1990	920.5	799.7	199.4	-78.6	16.1	15.7	5.0
1991	944.0	736.2	200.5	7.3	8.8	15.8	5.7
1992	949.1	790.4	209.1	-50.5	43.7	14.5	5.9
1993	993.5	871.1	210.6	-88.2	55.1	14.3	4.5
1994	1,087.2	1,014.4	212.3	-139.6	31.3	15.3	3.8
1990: I	939.2	822.5	196.0	-79.4	43.0	15.8	4.9
II	958.1	835.2	196.7	-73.8	17.4	16.3	5.2
III	911.3	804.9	199.7	-93.3	16.3	15.4	5.0
IV	873.4	736.1	205.4	-68.1	-12.3	15.2	5.0
1991: I	977.0	723.6	198.1	55.3	-6.5	16.8	5.4
II	933.7	716.2	201.5	16.0	5.6	15.7	5.7
III	922.6	743.9	201.3	-22.6	17.2	15.2	5.5
IV	942.8	760.9	201.4	-19.4	18.8	15.4	6.0
1992: I	944.7	755.2	209.5	-19.9	23.3	15.0	5.9
II	951.4	790.8	209.3	-48.7	36.2	14.7	6.1
III	952.6	799.7	208.9	-56.0	51.6	14.3	5.5
IV	947.6	816.1	208.8	-77.2	63.6	13.8	6.1
1993: I	991.4	843.6	207.1	-59.4	80.7	14.1	4.3
II	983.1	855.9	210.6	-83.4	55.0	14.3	4.8
III	988.9	873.8	209.8	-94.7	48.6	14.3	4.3
IV	1,010.7	911.2	214.7	-115.2	36.0	14.6	4.7
1994: I	1,055.9	957.6	207.3	-109.0	21.1	15.3	2.8
II	1,087.3	1,016.5	208.5	-137.7	17.5	15.6	4.2
III	1,101.1	1,033.6	217.2	-149.6	46.7	15.1	4.1
IV	1,104.5	1,050.1	216.3	-161.9	39.7	15.1	4.2
1995: I	1,146.7	1,072.0	219.1	-144.4	36.2	15.6	4.8
II	1,113.9	1,050.3	223.7	-160.1	21.6	15.2	4.0
III	1,143.3	1,067.1	224.9	-148.7	-2.3	15.7	4.1

[4] For details on government investment, see Table B–16.
[5] Net exports of goods and services plus net receipts of factor income from rest of the world less net transfers plus net capital grants received by the United States. See also Table B–20.
[6] Consists of a U.S. payment to India under the Agricultural Trade Development and Assistance Act. This payment is included in capital grants received by the United States, net.

Source: Department of Commerce, Bureau of Economic Analysis.

TABLE B–29.—*Median money income (in 1994 dollars) and poverty status of families and persons, by race, selected years, 1976–94*

Year	Families [1]						Persons below poverty level		Median money income (in 1994 dollars) of persons 15 years old and over with income [2][3]			
	Number (millions)	Median money income (in 1994 dollars) [2]	Below poverty level						Males		Females	
			Total		Female householder							
			Number (millions)	Percent	Number (millions)	Percent	Number (millions)	Percent	All persons	Year-round full-time workers	All persons	Year-round full-time workers
ALL RACES												
1976	56.7	$37,319	5.3	9.4	2.5	33.0	25.0	11.8	$23,517	$34,577	$8,922	$20,738
1977	57.2	37,540	5.3	9.3	2.6	31.7	24.7	11.6	23,738	35,338	9,241	20,668
1978	57.8	38,730	5.3	9.1	2.7	31.4	24.5	11.4	24,008	35,265	8,932	21,167
1979[4]	59.6	39,227	5.5	9.2	2.6	30.4	26.1	11.7	23,590	35,005	8,716	21,090
1980	60.3	37,857	6.2	10.3	3.0	32.7	29.3	13.0	22,563	34,525	8,860	20,872
1981	61.0	36,825	6.9	11.2	3.3	34.6	31.8	14.0	22,161	34,035	8,978	20,490
1982	61.4	36,326	7.5	12.2	3.4	36.3	34.4	15.0	21,625	33,570	9,126	21,181
1983[5]	62.0	36,714	7.6	12.3	3.6	36.0	35.3	15.2	21,815	33,454	9,530	21,525
1984	62.7	37,703	7.3	11.6	3.5	34.5	33.7	14.4	22,251	34,239	9,796	21,998
1985	63.6	38,200	7.2	11.4	3.5	34.0	33.1	14.0	22,466	34,432	9,940	22,384
1986	64.5	39,833	7.0	10.9	3.6	34.6	32.4	13.6	23,141	35,014	10,290	22,775
1987[6]	65.2	40,403	7.0	10.7	3.7	34.2	32.2	13.4	23,203	34,807	10,821	22,914
1988	65.8	40,327	6.9	10.4	3.6	33.4	31.7	13.0	23,687	34,253	11,129	23,232
1989	66.1	40,890	6.8	10.3	3.5	32.2	31.5	12.8	23,775	33,965	11,502	23,471
1990	66.3	40,087	7.1	10.7	3.8	33.4	33.6	13.5	23,010	32,859	11,418	23,348
1991	67.2	39,105	7.7	11.5	4.2	35.6	35.7	14.2	22,272	33,003	11,399	23,117
1992[7]	68.2	38,632	8.1	11.9	4.3	35.4	38.0	14.8	21,607	32,568	11,317	23,337
1993	68.5	37,905	8.4	12.3	4.4	35.6	39.3	15.1	21,642	31,873	11,329	23,044
1994	69.3	38,782	8.1	11.6	4.2	34.6	38.1	14.5	21,720	31,612	11,466	23,265
WHITE												
1976	50.1	38,764	3.6	7.1	1.4	25.2	16.7	9.1	24,792	35,608	8,997	20,898
1977	50.5	39,254	3.5	7.0	1.4	24.0	16.4	8.9	24,863	36,060	9,382	20,800
1978	50.9	40,328	3.5	6.9	1.4	23.5	16.3	8.7	25,146	35,919	9,039	21,367
1979[4]	52.2	40,933	3.6	6.9	1.4	22.3	17.2	9.0	24,643	36,017	8,798	21,275
1980	52.7	39,443	4.2	8.0	1.6	25.7	19.7	10.2	24,000	35,510	8,908	21,074
1981	53.3	38,682	4.7	8.8	1.8	27.4	21.6	11.1	23,515	34,834	9,078	20,832
1982	53.4	38,140	5.1	9.6	1.8	27.9	23.5	12.0	22,862	34,464	9,250	21,466
1983[5]	53.9	38,444	5.2	9.7	1.9	28.3	24.0	12.1	22,950	34,343	9,697	21,812
1984	54.4	39,491	4.9	9.1	1.9	27.1	23.0	11.5	23,488	35,411	9,912	22,216
1985	55.0	40,152	5.0	9.1	2.0	27.4	22.9	11.4	23,567	35,388	10,133	22,701
1986	55.7	41,660	4.8	8.6	2.0	28.2	22.2	11.0	24,421	35,991	10,493	23,124
1987[6]	56.1	42,249	4.6	8.1	2.0	26.9	21.2	10.4	24,663	35,619	11,098	23,338
1988	56.5	42,487	4.5	7.9	1.9	26.5	20.7	10.1	25,004	35,405	11,404	23,580
1989	56.6	42,996	4.4	7.8	1.9	25.4	20.8	10.0	24,935	35,463	11,727	23,749
1990	56.8	41,858	4.6	8.1	2.0	26.8	22.3	10.7	24,005	34,109	11,698	23,629
1991	57.2	41,112	5.0	8.8	2.2	28.4	23.7	11.3	23,280	33,680	11,666	23,454
1992[7]	57.7	40,847	5.3	9.1	2.2	28.5	25.3	11.9	22,611	33,342	11,580	23,607
1993	57.9	40,306	5.5	9.4	2.4	29.2	26.2	12.2	22,544	32,647	11,554	23,567
1994	58.4	40,884	5.3	9.1	2.3	29.0	25.4	11.7	22,669	32,440	11,630	23,894
BLACK												
1976	5.8	23,058	1.6	27.9	1.1	52.2	7.6	31.1	14,927	25,503	8,478	19,538
1977	5.8	22,425	1.6	28.2	1.2	51.0	7.7	31.3	14,754	24,861	8,102	19,440
1978	5.9	23,885	1.6	27.5	1.2	50.6	7.6	30.6	15,064	27,510	8,139	19,804
1979[4]	6.2	23,179	1.7	27.8	1.2	49.4	8.1	31.0	15,255	25,957	8,007	19,494
1980	6.3	22,822	1.8	28.9	1.3	49.4	8.6	32.5	14,422	24,985	8,247	19,655
1981	6.4	21,820	2.0	30.8	1.4	52.9	9.2	34.2	13,983	24,646	8,065	18,814
1982	6.5	21,080	2.2	33.0	1.5	56.2	9.7	35.6	13,701	24,478	8,159	19,185
1983[5]	6.7	21,666	2.2	32.3	1.5	53.7	9.9	35.7	13,421	24,502	8,286	19,361
1984	6.8	22,010	2.1	30.9	1.5	51.7	9.5	33.8	13,476	24,167	8,792	20,021
1985	6.9	23,120	2.0	28.7	1.5	50.5	8.9	31.3	14,831	24,752	8,645	20,095
1986	7.1	23,804	2.0	28.0	1.5	50.1	9.0	31.1	14,633	25,375	8,878	20,234
1987[6]	7.2	24,012	2.1	29.4	1.6	51.1	9.5	32.4	14,631	25,468	9,066	20,845
1988	7.4	24,214	2.1	28.2	1.6	49.0	9.4	31.3	15,088	25,952	9,206	21,130
1989	7.5	24,153	2.1	27.8	1.5	46.5	9.3	30.7	15,070	24,745	9,412	21,359
1990	7.5	24,291	2.2	29.3	1.6	48.1	9.8	31.9	14,591	24,357	9,443	21,027
1991	7.7	23,447	2.3	30.4	1.8	51.2	10.2	32.7	14,104	24,622	9,593	20,820
1992[7]	8.0	22,291	2.5	31.1	1.9	50.2	10.8	33.4	13,800	24,286	9,387	21,399
1993	8.0	22,094	2.5	31.3	1.9	49.9	10.9	33.1	14,979	24,169	9,751	20,835
1994	8.1	24,698	2.2	27.3	1.7	46.2	10.2	30.6	14,982	24,405	10,544	20,628

[1] The term "family" refers to a group of two or more persons related by birth, marriage, or adoption and residing together. Every family must include a reference person. Beginning 1979, based on householder concept and restricted to primary families.

[2] Current dollar median money income deflated by CPI–U–X1.

[3] Prior to 1979, data are for persons 14 years and over.

[4] Based on 1980 census population controls; comparable with succeeding years.

[5] Reflects implementation of Hispanic population controls; comparable with succeeding years.

[6] Based on revised methodology; comparable with succeeding years.

[7] Based on 1990 census population controls; comparable with succeeding years.

Note.—Poverty rates (percent of persons below poverty level) for all races for years not shown above are: 1959, 22.4; 1960, 22.2; 1961, 21.9; 1962, 21.0; 1963, 19.5; 1964, 19.0; 1965, 17.3; 1966, 14.7; 1967, 14.2; 1968, 12.8; 1969, 12.1; 1970, 12.6; 1971, 12.5; 1972, 11.9; 1973, 11.1; 1974, 11.2; and 1975, 12.3.

Poverty thresholds are updated each year to reflect changes in the consumer price index (CPI–U).

For details see "Current Population Reports," Series P–60.

Source: Department of Commerce, Bureau of the Census.

POPULATION, EMPLOYMENT, WAGES, AND PRODUCTIVITY

TABLE B–30.—*Population by age group, 1929–95*
[Thousands of persons]

July 1	Total	Age (years)						
		Under 5	5–15	16–19	20–24	25–44	45–64	65 and over
1929	121,767	11,734	26,800	9,127	10,694	35,862	21,076	6,474
1933	125,579	10,612	26,897	9,302	11,152	37,319	22,933	7,363
1939	130,880	10,418	25,179	9,822	11,519	39,354	25,823	8,764
1940	132,122	10,579	24,811	9,895	11,690	39,868	26,249	9,031
1941	133,402	10,850	24,516	9,840	11,807	40,383	26,718	9,288
1942	134,860	11,301	24,231	9,730	11,955	40,861	27,196	9,584
1943	136,739	12,016	24,093	9,607	12,064	41,420	27,671	9,867
1944	138,397	12,524	23,949	9,561	12,062	42,016	28,138	10,147
1945	139,928	12,979	23,907	9,361	12,036	42,521	28,630	10,494
1946	141,389	13,244	24,103	9,119	12,004	43,027	29,064	10,828
1947	144,126	14,406	24,468	9,097	11,814	43,657	29,498	11,185
1948	146,631	14,919	25,209	8,952	11,794	44,288	29,931	11,538
1949	149,188	15,607	25,852	8,788	11,700	44,916	30,405	11,921
1950	152,271	16,410	26,721	8,542	11,680	45,672	30,849	12,397
1951	154,878	17,333	27,279	8,446	11,552	46,103	31,362	12,803
1952	157,553	17,312	28,894	8,414	11,350	46,495	31,884	13,203
1953	160,184	17,638	30,227	8,460	11,062	46,786	32,394	13,617
1954	163,026	18,057	31,480	8,637	10,832	47,001	32,942	14,076
1955	165,931	18,566	32,682	8,744	10,714	47,194	33,506	14,525
1956	168,903	19,003	33,994	8,916	10,616	47,379	34,057	14,938
1957	171,984	19,494	35,272	9,195	10,603	47,440	34,591	15,388
1958	174,882	19,887	36,445	9,543	10,756	47,337	35,109	15,806
1959	177,830	20,175	37,368	10,215	10,969	47,192	35,663	16,248
1960	180,671	20,341	38,494	10,683	11,134	47,140	36,203	16,675
1961	183,691	20,522	39,765	11,025	11,483	47,084	36,722	17,089
1962	186,538	20,469	41,205	11,180	11,959	47,013	37,255	17,457
1963	189,242	20,342	41,626	12,007	12,714	46,994	37,782	17,778
1964	191,889	20,165	42,297	12,736	13,269	46,958	38,338	18,127
1965	194,303	19,824	42,938	13,516	13,746	46,912	38,916	18,451
1966	196,560	19,208	43,702	14,311	14,050	47,001	39,534	18,755
1967	198,712	18,563	44,244	14,200	15,248	47,194	40,193	19,071
1968	200,706	17,913	44,622	14,452	15,786	47,721	40,846	19,365
1969	202,677	17,376	44,840	14,800	16,480	48,064	41,437	19,680
1970	205,052	17,166	44,816	15,289	17,202	48,473	41,999	20,107
1971	207,661	17,244	44,591	15,688	18,159	48,936	42,482	20,561
1972	209,896	17,101	44,203	16,039	18,153	50,482	42,898	21,020
1973	211,909	16,851	43,582	16,446	18,521	51,749	43,235	21,525
1974	213,854	16,487	42,989	16,769	18,975	53,051	43,522	22,061
1975	215,973	16,121	42,508	17,017	19,527	54,302	43,801	22,696
1976	218,035	15,617	42,099	17,194	19,986	55,852	44,008	23,278
1977	220,239	15,564	41,298	17,276	20,499	57,561	44,150	23,892
1978	222,585	15,735	40,428	17,288	20,946	59,400	44,286	24,502
1979	225,055	16,063	39,552	17,242	21,297	61,379	44,390	25,134
1980	227,726	16,451	38,838	17,167	21,590	63,470	44,504	25,707
1981	229,966	16,893	38,144	16,812	21,869	65,528	44,500	26,221
1982	232,188	17,228	37,784	16,332	21,902	67,692	44,462	26,787
1983	234,307	17,547	37,526	15,823	21,844	69,733	44,474	27,361
1984	236,348	17,695	37,461	15,295	21,737	71,735	44,547	27,878
1985	238,466	17,842	37,450	15,005	21,478	73,673	44,602	28,416
1986	240,651	17,963	37,404	15,024	20,942	75,651	44,660	29,008
1987	242,804	18,052	37,333	15,215	20,385	77,338	44,854	29,626
1988	245,021	18,195	37,593	15,198	19,846	78,595	45,471	30,124
1989	247,342	18,508	37,972	14,913	19,442	79,943	45,882	30,682
1990	249,913	18,849	38,588	14,449	19,307	81,196	46,288	31,235
1991	252,650	19,198	39,197	13,929	19,356	82,449	46,758	31,763
1992	255,419	19,506	39,905	13,671	19,192	82,530	48,345	32,270
1993	258,137	19,689	40,546	13,798	18,895	82,849	49,583	32,777
1994	260,660	19,734	41,223	14,032	18,451	83,180	50,887	33,152
1995	263,034	19,591	41,924	14,287	17,972	83,511	52,216	33,532

Note.—Includes Armed Forces overseas beginning 1940. Includes Alaska and Hawaii beginning 1950.
All estimates are consistent with decennial census enumerations.

Source: Department of Commerce, Bureau of the Census.

TABLE B–31.—*Civilian population and labor force, 1929–95*

[Monthly data seasonally adjusted, except as noted]

Year or month	Civilian noninstitutional population[1]	Civilian labor force					Not in labor force	Civilian labor force participation rate[2]	Civilian employment/population ratio[3]	Unemployment rate, civilian workers[4]
			Employment							
		Total	Total	Agricultural	Nonagricultural	Unemployment				
	Thousands of persons 14 years of age and over							Percent		
1929	....	49,180	47,630	10,450	37,180	1,550	....	....	....	3.2
1933	....	51,590	38,760	10,090	28,670	12,830	....	....	....	24.9
1939	....	55,230	45,750	9,610	36,140	9,480	....	....	....	17.2
1940	99,840	55,640	47,520	9,540	37,980	8,120	44,200	55.7	47.6	14.6
1941	99,900	55,910	50,350	9,100	41,250	5,560	43,990	56.0	50.4	9.9
1942	98,640	56,410	53,750	9,250	44,500	2,660	42,230	57.2	54.5	4.7
1943	94,640	55,540	54,470	9,080	45,390	1,070	39,100	58.7	57.6	1.9
1944	93,220	54,630	53,960	8,950	45,010	670	38,590	58.6	57.9	1.2
1945	94,090	53,860	52,820	8,580	44,240	1,040	40,230	57.2	56.1	1.9
1946	103,070	57,520	55,250	8,320	46,930	2,270	45,550	55.8	53.6	3.9
1947	106,018	60,168	57,812	8,256	49,557	2,356	45,850	56.8	54.5	3.9
	Thousands of persons 16 years of age and over									
1947	101,827	59,350	57,038	7,890	49,148	2,311	42,477	58.3	56.0	3.9
1948	103,068	60,621	58,343	7,629	50,714	2,276	42,447	58.8	56.6	3.8
1949	103,994	61,286	57,651	7,658	49,993	3,637	42,708	58.9	55.4	5.9
1950	104,995	62,208	58,918	7,160	51,758	3,288	42,787	59.2	56.1	5.3
1951	104,621	62,017	59,961	6,726	53,235	2,055	42,604	59.2	57.3	3.3
1952	105,231	62,138	60,250	6,500	53,749	1,883	43,093	59.0	57.3	3.0
1953[5]	107,056	63,015	61,179	6,260	54,919	1,834	44,041	58.9	57.1	2.9
1954	108,321	63,643	60,109	6,205	53,904	3,532	44,678	58.8	55.5	5.5
1955	109,683	65,023	62,170	6,450	55,722	2,852	44,660	59.3	56.7	4.4
1956	110,954	66,552	63,799	6,283	57,514	2,750	44,402	60.0	57.5	4.1
1957	112,265	66,929	64,071	5,947	58,123	2,859	45,336	59.6	57.1	4.3
1958	113,727	67,639	63,036	5,586	57,450	4,602	46,088	59.5	55.4	6.8
1959	115,329	68,369	64,630	5,565	59,065	3,740	46,960	59.3	56.0	5.5
1960[5]	117,245	69,628	65,778	5,458	60,318	3,852	47,617	59.4	56.1	5.5
1961	118,771	70,459	65,746	5,200	60,546	4,714	48,312	59.3	55.4	6.7
1962[5]	120,153	70,614	66,702	4,944	61,759	3,911	49,539	58.8	55.5	5.5
1963	122,416	71,833	67,762	4,687	63,076	4,070	50,583	58.7	55.4	5.7
1964	124,485	73,091	69,305	4,523	64,782	3,786	51,394	58.7	55.7	5.2
1965	126,513	74,455	71,088	4,361	66,726	3,366	52,058	58.9	56.2	4.5
1966	128,058	75,770	72,895	3,979	68,915	2,875	52,288	59.2	56.9	3.8
1967	129,874	77,347	74,372	3,844	70,527	2,975	52,527	59.6	57.3	3.8
1968	132,028	78,737	75,920	3,817	72,103	2,817	53,291	59.6	57.5	3.6
1969	134,335	80,734	77,902	3,606	74,296	2,832	53,602	60.1	58.0	3.5
1970	137,085	82,771	78,678	3,463	75,215	4,093	54,315	60.4	57.4	4.9
1971	140,216	84,382	79,367	3,394	75,972	5,016	55,834	60.2	56.6	5.9
1972[5]	144,126	87,034	82,153	3,484	78,669	4,882	57,091	60.4	57.0	5.6
1973[5]	147,096	89,429	85,064	3,470	81,594	4,365	57,667	60.8	57.8	4.9
1974	150,120	91,949	86,794	3,515	83,279	5,156	58,171	61.3	57.8	5.6
1975	153,153	93,775	85,846	3,408	82,438	7,929	59,377	61.2	56.1	8.5
1976	156,150	96,158	88,752	3,331	85,421	7,406	59,991	61.6	56.8	7.7
1977	159,033	99,009	92,017	3,283	88,734	6,991	60,025	62.3	57.9	7.1
1978[5]	161,910	102,251	96,048	3,387	92,661	6,202	59,659	63.2	59.3	6.1
1979	164,863	104,962	98,824	3,347	95,477	6,137	59,900	63.7	59.9	5.8
1980	167,745	106,940	99,303	3,364	95,938	7,637	60,806	63.8	59.2	7.1
1981	170,130	108,670	100,397	3,368	97,030	8,273	61,460	63.9	59.0	7.6
1982	172,271	110,204	99,526	3,401	96,125	10,678	62,067	64.0	57.8	9.7
1983	174,215	111,550	100,834	3,383	97,450	10,717	62,665	64.0	57.9	9.6
1984	176,383	113,544	105,005	3,321	101,685	8,539	62,839	64.4	59.5	7.5
1985	178,206	115,461	107,150	3,179	103,971	8,312	62,744	64.8	60.1	7.2
1986[5]	180,587	117,834	109,597	3,163	106,434	8,237	62,752	65.3	60.7	7.0
1987	182,753	119,865	112,440	3,208	109,232	7,425	62,888	65.6	61.5	6.2
1988	184,613	121,669	114,968	3,169	111,800	6,701	62,944	65.9	62.3	5.5
1989	186,393	123,869	117,342	3,199	114,142	6,528	62,523	66.5	63.0	5.3
1990	188,049	124,787	117,914	3,186	114,728	6,874	63,262	66.4	62.7	5.5
1991	189,765	125,303	116,877	3,233	113,644	8,426	64,462	66.0	61.6	6.7
1992	191,576	126,982	117,598	3,207	114,391	9,384	64,593	66.3	61.4	7.4
1993	193,550	128,040	119,306	3,074	116,232	8,734	65,509	66.2	61.6	6.8
1994[5]	196,814	131,056	123,060	3,409	119,651	7,996	65,758	66.6	62.5	6.1
1995	198,584	132,304	124,900	3,440	121,460	7,404	66,280	66.6	62.9	5.6

[1] Not seasonally adjusted.
[2] Civilian labor force as percent of civilian noninstitutional population.
[3] Civilian employment as percent of civilian noninstitutional population.
[4] Unemployed as percent of civilian labor force.

See next page for continuation of table.

316

[Monthly data seasonally adjusted, except as noted]

Year or month	Civilian noninstitutional population[1]	Civilian labor force Total	Employment Total	Employment Agricultural	Employment Nonagricultural	Unemployment	Not in labor force	Civilian labor force participation rate[2]	Civilian employment/population ratio[3]	Unemployment rate, civilian workers[4]
			Thousands of persons 16 years of age and over						Percent	
1992: Jan	190,759	126,149	117,130	3,136	113,994	9,019	64,610	66.1	61.4	7.1
Feb	190,884	126,209	116,919	3,218	113,701	9,290	64,675	66.1	61.3	7.4
Mar	191,022	126,545	117,255	3,208	114,047	9,290	64,477	66.2	61.4	7.3
Apr	191,168	126,917	117,670	3,220	114,450	9,247	64,251	66.4	61.6	7.3
May	191,307	127,036	117,534	3,192	114,342	9,502	64,271	66.4	61.4	7.5
June	191,455	127,269	117,498	3,248	114,250	9,771	64,186	66.5	61.4	7.7
July	191,622	127,358	117,763	3,217	114,546	9,595	64,264	66.5	61.5	7.5
Aug	191,790	127,339	117,749	3,237	114,512	9,590	64,451	66.4	61.4	7.5
Sept	191,947	127,306	117,772	3,211	114,561	9,534	64,641	66.3	61.4	7.5
Oct	192,131	126,933	117,723	3,188	114,535	9,210	65,198	66.1	61.3	7.3
Nov	192,316	127,287	117,974	3,170	114,804	9,313	65,029	66.2	61.3	7.3
Dec	192,509	127,469	118,155	3,222	114,933	9,314	65,040	66.2	61.4	7.3
1993: Jan	192,644	127,224	118,178	3,182	114,996	9,046	65,420	66.0	61.3	7.1
Feb	192,786	127,400	118,442	3,116	115,326	8,958	65,386	66.1	61.4	7.0
Mar	192,959	127,440	118,562	3,099	115,463	8,878	65,519	66.0	61.4	7.0
Apr	193,126	127,539	118,585	3,071	115,514	8,954	65,587	66.0	61.4	7.0
May	193,283	128,075	119,180	3,074	116,106	8,895	65,208	66.3	61.7	6.9
June	193,456	128,056	119,187	3,031	116,156	8,869	65,400	66.2	61.6	6.9
July	193,633	128,102	119,370	3,043	116,327	8,732	65,531	66.2	61.6	6.8
Aug	193,793	128,334	119,692	3,005	116,687	8,642	65,459	66.2	61.8	6.7
Sept	193,971	128,108	119,568	3,093	116,475	8,540	65,863	66.0	61.6	6.7
Oct	194,151	128,580	119,941	3,021	116,920	8,639	65,571	66.2	61.8	6.7
Nov	194,321	128,662	120,332	3,114	117,218	8,330	65,659	66.2	61.9	6.5
Dec	194,472	128,898	120,661	3,096	117,565	8,237	65,574	66.3	62.0	6.4
1994: Jan [5]	195,953	130,643	121,903	3,328	118,575	8,740	65,310	66.7	62.2	6.7
Feb	196,090	130,784	122,208	3,368	118,840	8,576	65,306	66.7	62.3	6.6
Mar	196,213	130,706	122,160	3,396	118,764	8,546	65,507	66.6	62.3	6.5
Apr	196,363	130,787	122,402	3,438	118,964	8,385	65,576	66.6	62.3	6.4
May	196,510	130,699	122,703	3,413	119,290	7,996	65,811	66.5	62.4	6.1
June	196,693	130,538	122,635	3,294	119,341	7,903	66,155	66.4	62.3	6.1
July	196,859	130,774	122,781	3,333	119,448	7,993	66,085	66.4	62.4	6.1
Aug	197,043	131,086	123,197	3,436	119,761	7,889	65,957	66.5	62.5	6.0
Sept	197,248	131,291	123,644	3,411	120,233	7,647	65,957	66.6	62.7	5.8
Oct	197,430	131,646	124,141	3,494	120,647	7,505	65,784	66.7	62.9	5.7
Nov	197,607	131,718	124,403	3,500	120,903	7,315	65,889	66.7	63.0	5.6
Dec	197,765	131,725	124,570	3,532	121,038	7,155	66,040	66.6	63.0	5.4
1995: Jan	197,753	132,136	124,639	3,575	121,064	7,498	65,617	66.8	63.0	5.7
Feb	197,886	132,308	125,125	3,656	121,469	7,183	65,578	66.9	63.2	5.4
Mar	198,007	132,511	125,274	3,698	121,576	7,237	65,496	66.9	63.3	5.5
Apr	198,148	132,737	125,072	3,594	121,478	7,665	65,412	67.0	63.1	5.8
May	198,286	131,811	124,319	3,357	120,962	7,492	66,476	66.5	62.7	5.7
June	198,453	131,869	124,485	3,451	121,034	7,384	66,583	66.4	62.7	5.6
July	198,615	132,519	124,959	3,409	121,550	7,559	66,096	66.7	62.9	5.7
Aug	198,801	132,211	124,779	3,362	121,417	7,431	66,590	66.5	62.8	5.6
Sept	199,005	132,591	125,140	3,273	121,867	7,451	66,414	66.6	62.9	5.6
Oct	199,192	132,648	125,399	3,455	121,944	7,249	66,544	66.6	63.0	5.5
Nov	199,355	132,442	125,010	3,276	121,734	7,432	66,913	66.4	62.7	5.6
Dec	199,508	132,284	124,904	3,306	121,598	7,380	67,224	66.3	62.6	5.6

[5] Not strictly comparable with earlier data due to population adjustments as follows: Beginning 1953, introduction of 1950 census data added about 600,000 to population and 350,000 to labor force, total employment, and agricultural employment. Beginning 1960, inclusion of Alaska and Hawaii added about 500,000 to population, 300,000 to labor force, and 240,000 to nonagricultural employment. Beginning 1962, introduction of 1960 census data reduced population by about 50,000 and labor force and employment by 200,000. Beginning 1972, introduction of 1970 census data added about 800,000 to civilian noninstitutional population and 333,000 to labor force and employment. A subsequent adjustment based on 1970 census in March 1973 added 60,000 to labor force and to employment. Beginning 1978, changes in sampling and estimation procedures introduced into the household survey added about 250,000 to labor force and to employment. Unemployment levels and rates were not significantly affected. Beginning 1986, the introduction of revised population controls added about 400,000 to the civilian population and labor force and 350,000 to civilian employment. Unemployment levels and rates were not significantly affected. Beginning 1994, introduction of adjusted 1990 census-based population controls added about 1.3 million to civilian population, 1.1 million to civilian labor force, 950,000 to civilian employment, and 200,000 to unemployment. Unemployment rates were not significantly affected.

Note.—Labor force data in Tables B–31 through B–40 are based on household interviews and relate to the calendar week including the 12th of the month. For definitions of terms, area samples used, historical comparability of the data, comparability with other series, etc., see "Employment and Earnings."

Source: Department of Labor, Bureau of Labor Statistics.

TABLE B–32.—*Civilian employment and unemployment by sex and age, 1947–95*

[Thousands of persons 16 years of age and over; monthly data seasonally adjusted]

Year or month	Civilian employment							Unemployment						
	Total	Males			Females			Total	Males			Females		
		Total	16–19 years	20 years and over	Total	16–19 years	20 years and over		Total	16–19 years	20 years and over	Total	16–19 years	20 years and over
1947	57,038	40,995	2,218	38,776	16,045	1,691	14,354	2,311	1,692	270	1,422	619	144	475
1948	58,343	41,725	2,344	39,382	16,617	1,682	14,936	2,276	1,559	256	1,305	717	153	564
1949	57,651	40,925	2,124	38,803	16,723	1,588	15,137	3,637	2,572	353	2,219	1,065	223	841
1950	58,918	41,578	2,186	39,394	17,340	1,517	15,824	3,288	2,239	318	1,922	1,049	195	854
1951	59,961	41,780	2,156	39,626	18,181	1,611	16,570	2,055	1,221	191	1,029	834	145	689
1952	60,250	41,682	2,107	39,578	18,568	1,612	16,958	1,883	1,185	205	980	698	140	559
1953	61,179	42,430	2,136	40,296	18,749	1,584	17,164	1,834	1,202	184	1,019	632	123	510
1954	60,109	41,619	1,985	39,634	18,490	1,490	17,000	3,532	2,344	310	2,035	1,188	191	997
1955	62,170	42,621	2,095	40,526	19,551	1,547	18,002	2,852	1,854	274	1,580	998	176	823
1956	63,799	43,379	2,164	41,216	20,419	1,654	18,767	2,750	1,711	269	1,442	1,039	209	832
1957	64,071	43,357	2,115	41,239	20,714	1,663	19,052	2,859	1,841	300	1,541	1,018	197	821
1958	63,036	42,423	2,012	40,411	20,613	1,570	19,043	4,602	3,098	416	2,681	1,504	262	1,242
1959	64,630	43,466	2,198	41,267	21,164	1,640	19,524	3,740	2,420	398	2,022	1,320	256	1,063
1960	65,778	43,904	2,361	41,543	21,874	1,768	20,105	3,852	2,486	426	2,060	1,366	286	1,080
1961	65,746	43,656	2,315	41,342	22,090	1,793	20,296	4,714	2,997	479	2,518	1,717	349	1,368
1962	66,702	44,177	2,362	41,815	22,525	1,833	20,693	3,911	2,423	408	2,016	1,488	313	1,175
1963	67,762	44,657	2,406	42,251	23,105	1,849	21,257	4,070	2,472	501	1,971	1,598	383	1,216
1964	69,305	45,474	2,587	42,886	23,831	1,929	21,903	3,786	2,205	487	1,718	1,581	385	1,195
1965	71,088	46,340	2,918	43,422	24,748	2,118	22,630	3,366	1,914	479	1,435	1,452	395	1,056
1966	72,895	46,919	3,253	43,668	25,976	2,468	23,510	2,875	1,551	432	1,120	1,324	405	921
1967	74,372	47,479	3,186	44,294	26,893	2,496	24,397	2,975	1,508	448	1,060	1,468	391	1,078
1968	75,920	48,114	3,255	44,859	27,807	2,526	25,281	2,817	1,419	426	993	1,397	412	985
1969	77,902	48,818	3,430	45,388	29,084	2,687	26,397	2,832	1,403	440	963	1,429	413	1,015
1970	78,678	48,990	3,409	45,581	29,688	2,735	26,952	4,093	2,238	599	1,638	1,855	506	1,349
1971	79,367	49,390	3,478	45,912	29,976	2,730	27,246	5,016	2,789	693	2,097	2,227	568	1,658
1972	82,153	50,896	3,765	47,130	31,257	2,980	28,276	4,882	2,659	711	1,948	2,222	598	1,625
1973	85,064	52,349	4,039	48,310	32,715	3,231	29,484	4,365	2,275	653	1,624	2,089	583	1,507
1974	86,794	53,024	4,103	48,922	33,769	3,345	30,424	5,156	2,714	757	1,957	2,441	665	1,777
1975	85,846	51,857	3,839	48,018	33,989	3,263	30,726	7,929	4,442	966	3,476	3,486	802	2,684
1976	88,752	53,138	3,947	49,190	35,615	3,389	32,226	7,406	4,036	939	3,098	3,369	780	2,588
1977	92,017	54,728	4,174	50,555	37,289	3,514	33,775	6,991	3,667	874	2,794	3,324	789	2,535
1978	96,048	56,479	4,336	52,143	39,569	3,734	35,836	6,202	3,142	813	2,328	3,061	769	2,292
1979	98,824	57,607	4,300	53,308	41,217	3,783	37,434	6,137	3,120	811	2,308	3,018	743	2,276
1980	99,303	57,186	4,085	53,101	42,117	3,625	38,492	7,637	4,267	913	3,353	3,370	755	2,615
1981	100,397	57,397	3,815	53,582	43,000	3,411	39,590	8,273	4,577	962	3,615	3,696	800	2,895
1982	99,526	56,271	3,379	52,891	43,256	3,170	40,086	10,678	6,179	1,090	5,089	4,499	886	3,613
1983	100,834	56,787	3,300	53,487	44,047	3,043	41,004	10,717	6,260	1,003	5,257	4,457	825	3,632
1984	105,005	59,091	3,322	55,769	45,915	3,122	42,793	8,539	4,744	812	3,932	3,794	687	3,107
1985	107,150	59,891	3,328	56,562	47,259	3,105	44,154	8,312	4,521	806	3,715	3,791	661	3,129
1986	109,597	60,892	3,323	57,569	48,706	3,149	45,556	8,237	4,530	779	3,751	3,707	675	3,032
1987	112,440	62,107	3,381	58,726	50,334	3,260	47,074	7,425	4,101	732	3,369	3,324	616	2,709
1988	114,968	63,273	3,492	59,781	51,696	3,313	48,383	6,701	3,655	667	2,987	3,046	558	2,487
1989	117,342	64,315	3,477	60,837	53,027	3,282	49,745	6,528	3,525	658	2,867	3,003	536	2,467
1990	117,914	64,435	3,237	61,198	53,479	3,024	50,455	6,874	3,799	629	3,170	3,075	519	2,555
1991	116,877	63,593	2,879	60,714	53,284	2,749	50,535	8,426	4,817	709	4,109	3,609	581	3,028
1992	117,598	63,805	2,786	61,019	53,793	2,613	51,181	9,384	5,380	761	4,619	4,005	591	3,413
1993	119,306	64,700	2,836	61,865	54,606	2,694	51,912	8,734	4,932	728	4,204	3,801	568	3,234
1994	123,060	66,450	3,156	63,294	56,610	3,005	53,606	7,996	4,367	740	3,627	3,629	580	3,049
1995	124,900	67,377	3,292	64,085	57,523	3,127	54,396	7,404	3,983	744	3,239	3,421	602	2,819
1994: Jan	121,903	65,846	3,101	62,745	56,057	2,990	53,067	8,740	4,863	808	4,055	3,877	571	3,306
Feb	122,208	65,887	3,120	62,767	56,321	2,966	53,355	8,576	4,752	766	3,986	3,824	587	3,237
Mar	122,160	65,981	3,104	62,877	56,179	3,003	53,176	8,546	4,626	755	3,871	3,920	585	3,335
Apr	122,402	66,058	3,099	62,959	56,344	3,026	53,318	8,385	4,567	785	3,782	3,818	670	3,148
May	122,703	66,197	3,117	63,080	56,506	3,025	53,481	7,996	4,348	776	3,572	3,648	584	3,064
June	122,635	66,255	3,212	63,043	56,380	3,052	53,328	7,903	4,266	707	3,559	3,637	581	3,056
July	122,781	66,226	3,150	63,076	56,555	3,014	53,541	7,993	4,429	758	3,671	3,564	569	2,995
Aug	123,197	66,458	3,187	63,271	56,739	3,017	53,722	7,889	4,283	737	3,546	3,606	581	3,025
Sept	123,644	66,682	3,165	63,517	56,962	2,918	54,044	7,647	4,109	717	3,392	3,538	551	2,987
Oct	124,141	67,059	3,239	63,820	57,082	2,992	54,090	7,505	4,074	717	3,357	3,431	570	2,861
Nov	124,403	67,244	3,193	64,051	57,159	3,030	54,129	7,315	3,924	630	3,294	3,391	536	2,855
Dec	124,570	67,483	3,202	64,281	57,087	3,050	54,037	7,155	3,896	727	3,169	3,259	571	2,688
1995: Jan	124,639	67,386	3,254	64,133	57,252	3,118	54,134	7,498	4,090	684	3,406	3,408	591	2,817
Feb	125,125	67,709	3,231	64,478	57,416	3,082	54,334	7,183	3,849	775	3,074	3,334	571	2,763
Mar	125,274	67,811	3,346	64,465	57,462	3,220	54,242	7,237	3,862	684	3,178	3,375	575	2,800
Apr	125,072	67,588	3,364	64,224	57,484	3,082	54,403	7,665	4,067	728	3,339	3,598	641	2,957
May	124,319	67,110	3,270	63,841	57,208	3,112	54,097	7,492	4,145	735	3,410	3,347	625	2,722
June	124,485	67,390	3,396	63,994	57,095	3,180	53,915	7,384	3,955	716	3,238	3,429	572	2,857
July	124,959	67,383	3,317	64,066	57,576	3,058	54,519	7,559	3,955	763	3,192	3,604	652	2,952
Aug	124,779	67,108	3,236	63,871	57,672	3,174	54,498	7,431	4,001	796	3,206	3,430	581	2,849
Sept	125,140	67,408	3,347	64,061	57,732	3,132	54,600	7,451	4,029	747	3,282	3,422	630	2,792
Oct	125,399	67,494	3,252	64,243	57,905	3,195	54,710	7,249	3,797	788	3,008	3,452	544	2,908
Nov	125,010	67,090	3,254	63,837	57,920	3,130	54,790	7,432	4,065	764	3,301	3,367	630	2,737
Dec	124,904	67,155	3,267	63,888	57,749	3,078	54,671	7,380	4,073	770	3,302	3,308	649	2,658

Note.—See footnote 5 and Note, Table B–31.

Source: Department of Labor, Bureau of Labor Statistics.

[Thousands of persons 16 years of age and over; monthly data seasonally adjusted]

Year or month	All civilian workers	White				Black and other				Black			
		Total	Males	Females	Both sexes 16–19	Total	Males	Females	Both sexes 16–19	Total	Males	Females	Both sexes 16–19
1954	60,109	53,957	37,846	16,111	3,078	6,152	3,773	2,379	396				
1955	62,170	55,833	38,719	17,114	3,225	6,341	3,904	2,437	418				
1956	63,799	57,269	39,368	17,901	3,389	6,534	4,013	2,521	430				
1957	64,071	57,465	39,349	18,116	3,374	6,604	4,006	2,598	407				
1958	63,036	56,613	38,591	18,022	3,216	6,423	3,833	2,590	365				
1959	64,630	58,006	39,494	18,512	3,475	6,623	3,971	2,652	362				
1960	65,778	58,850	39,755	19,095	3,700	6,928	4,149	2,779	430				
1961	65,746	58,913	39,588	19,325	3,693	6,833	4,068	2,765	414				
1962	66,702	59,698	40,016	19,682	3,774	7,003	4,160	2,843	420				
1963	67,762	60,622	40,428	20,194	3,851	7,140	4,229	2,911	404				
1964	69,305	61,922	41,115	20,807	4,076	7,383	4,359	3,024	440				
1965	71,088	63,446	41,844	21,602	4,562	7,643	4,496	3,147	474				
1966	72,895	65,021	42,331	22,690	5,176	7,877	4,588	3,289	545				
1967	74,372	66,361	42,833	23,528	5,114	8,011	4,646	3,365	568				
1968	75,920	67,750	43,411	24,339	5,195	8,169	4,702	3,467	584				
1969	77,902	69,518	44,048	25,470	5,508	8,384	4,770	3,614	609				
1970	78,678	70,217	44,178	26,039	5,571	8,464	4,813	3,650	574				
1971	79,367	70,878	44,595	26,283	5,670	8,488	4,796	3,692	538				
1972	82,153	73,370	45,944	27,426	6,173	8,783	4,952	3,832	573	7,802	4,368	3,433	509
1973	85,064	75,708	47,085	28,623	6,623	9,356	5,265	4,092	647	8,128	4,527	3,601	570
1974	86,794	77,184	47,674	29,511	6,796	9,610	5,352	4,258	652	8,203	4,527	3,677	554
1975	85,846	76,411	46,697	29,714	6,487	9,435	5,161	4,275	615	7,894	4,275	3,618	507
1976	88,752	78,853	47,775	31,078	6,724	9,899	5,363	4,536	611	8,227	4,404	3,823	508
1977	92,017	81,700	49,150	32,550	7,068	10,317	5,579	4,739	619	8,540	4,565	3,975	508
1978	96,048	84,936	50,544	34,392	7,367	11,112	5,936	5,177	703	9,102	4,796	4,307	571
1979	98,824	87,259	51,452	35,807	7,356	11,565	6,156	5,409	727	9,359	4,923	4,436	579
1980	99,303	87,715	51,127	36,587	7,021	11,588	6,059	5,529	689	9,313	4,798	4,515	547
1981	100,397	88,709	51,315	37,394	6,588	11,688	6,083	5,606	637	9,355	4,794	4,561	505
1982	99,526	87,903	50,287	37,615	5,984	11,624	5,983	5,641	565	9,189	4,637	4,552	428
1983	100,834	88,893	50,621	38,272	5,799	11,941	6,166	5,775	543	9,375	4,753	4,622	416
1984	105,005	92,120	52,462	39,659	5,836	12,885	6,629	6,256	607	10,119	5,124	4,995	474
1985	107,150	93,736	53,046	40,690	5,768	13,414	6,845	6,569	666	10,501	5,270	5,231	532
1986	109,597	95,660	53,785	41,876	5,792	13,937	7,107	6,830	681	10,814	5,428	5,386	536
1987	112,440	97,789	54,647	43,142	5,898	14,652	7,459	7,192	742	11,309	5,661	5,648	587
1988	114,968	99,812	55,550	44,262	6,030	15,156	7,722	7,434	774	11,658	5,824	5,834	601
1989	117,342	101,584	56,352	45,232	5,946	15,757	7,963	7,795	813	11,953	5,928	6,025	625
1990	117,914	102,087	56,432	45,654	5,518	15,827	8,003	7,825	743	11,966	5,915	6,051	573
1991	116,877	101,039	55,557	45,482	4,989	15,838	8,036	7,802	639	11,863	5,880	5,983	474
1992	117,598	101,479	55,709	45,771	4,761	16,119	8,096	8,023	637	11,933	5,846	6,087	474
1993	119,306	102,812	56,397	46,415	4,887	16,494	8,303	8,191	642	12,146	5,957	6,189	474
1994	123,060	105,190	57,452	47,738	5,398	17,870	8,998	8,872	763	12,835	6,241	6,595	552
1995	124,900	106,490	58,146	48,344	5,593	18,409	9,231	9,179	826	13,279	6,422	6,857	586
1994: Jan	121,903	104,268	57,043	47,225	5,305	17,603	8,818	8,785	809	12,544	6,044	6,500	597
Feb	122,208	104,612	57,053	47,559	5,336	17,637	8,881	8,756	747	12,624	6,124	6,500	537
Mar	122,160	104,412	57,042	47,370	5,355	17,689	8,921	8,768	740	12,718	6,186	6,532	547
Apr	122,402	104,591	57,113	47,478	5,398	17,778	8,948	8,830	742	12,775	6,199	6,576	546
May	122,703	104,978	57,213	47,765	5,427	17,811	9,009	8,802	718	12,810	6,271	6,539	497
June	122,635	104,687	57,273	47,414	5,477	17,850	8,944	8,906	774	12,838	6,214	6,624	552
July	122,781	105,006	57,352	47,654	5,424	17,731	8,856	8,875	759	12,767	6,150	6,617	542
Aug	123,197	105,401	57,558	47,843	5,463	17,826	8,911	8,915	757	12,795	6,168	6,627	541
Sept	123,644	105,740	57,650	48,090	5,254	17,997	9,053	8,944	801	12,927	6,286	6,641	570
Oct	124,141	106,010	57,877	48,133	5,414	18,131	9,167	8,964	778	13,022	6,369	6,653	569
Nov	124,403	106,242	58,028	48,214	5,431	18,161	9,192	8,969	778	13,054	6,393	6,661	579
Dec	124,570	106,352	58,185	48,167	5,493	18,202	9,260	8,942	744	13,119	6,458	6,661	534
1995: Jan	124,628	106,366	58,165	48,201	5,658	18,219	9,212	9,007	713	13,192	6,435	6,757	499
Feb	125,125	106,604	58,348	48,256	5,515	18,490	9,374	9,116	803	13,362	6,558	6,804	570
Mar	125,274	106,698	58,396	48,301	5,734	18,512	9,384	9,128	827	13,370	6,571	6,799	591
Apr	125,072	106,500	58,187	48,312	5,653	18,546	9,403	9,143	796	13,337	6,514	6,823	584
May	124,319	105,935	57,863	48,072	5,575	18,482	9,259	9,223	817	13,336	6,420	6,916	585
June	124,485	106,145	58,139	48,006	5,797	18,264	9,223	9,041	805	13,142	6,399	6,742	571
July	124,959	106,770	58,245	48,525	5,634	18,184	9,144	9,040	797	13,033	6,326	6,707	552
Aug	124,779	106,567	58,005	48,562	5,617	18,307	9,192	9,115	814	13,049	6,293	6,756	542
Sept	125,140	106,851	58,190	48,661	5,544	18,324	9,245	9,080	905	13,147	6,397	6,750	622
Oct	125,399	106,815	58,217	48,598	5,549	18,522	9,210	9,312	867	13,413	6,450	6,963	610
Nov	125,010	106,331	57,889	48,442	5,453	18,697	9,179	9,518	920	13,662	6,461	7,201	687
Dec	124,904	106,296	58,074	48,222	5,481	18,562	9,043	9,519	865	13,481	6,326	7,155	623

Note.—See footnote 5 and Note, Table B–31.
Source: Department of Labor, Bureau of Labor Statistics.

TABLE B–34.—*Unemployment by demographic characteristic, 1954–95*

[Thousands of persons 16 years of age and over; monthly data seasonally adjusted]

Year or month	All civilian workers	White				Black and other				Black			
		Total	Males	Fe-males	Both sexes 16–19	Total	Males	Fe-males	Both sexes 16–19	Total	Males	Fe-males	Both sexes 16–19
1954	3,532	2,859	1,913	946	423	673	431	242	79				
1955	2,852	2,252	1,478	774	373	601	376	225	77				
1956	2,750	2,159	1,366	793	382	591	345	246	95				
1957	2,859	2,289	1,477	812	401	570	364	206	96				
1958	4,602	3,680	2,489	1,191	541	923	610	313	138				
1959	3,740	2,946	1,903	1,043	525	793	517	276	128				
1960	3,852	3,065	1,988	1,077	575	788	498	290	138				
1961	4,714	3,743	2,398	1,345	669	971	599	372	159				
1962	3,911	3,052	1,915	1,137	580	861	509	352	142				
1963	4,070	3,208	1,976	1,232	708	863	496	367	176				
1964	3,786	2,999	1,779	1,220	708	787	426	361	165				
1965	3,366	2,691	1,556	1,135	705	678	360	318	171				
1966	2,875	2,255	1,241	1,014	651	622	310	312	186				
1967	2,975	2,338	1,208	1,130	635	638	300	338	203				
1968	2,817	2,226	1,142	1,084	644	590	277	313	194				
1969	2,832	2,260	1,137	1,123	660	571	267	304	193				
1970	4,093	3,339	1,857	1,482	871	754	380	374	235				
1971	5,016	4,085	2,309	1,777	1,011	930	481	450	249				
1972	4,882	3,906	2,173	1,733	1,021	977	486	491	288	906	448	458	279
1973	4,365	3,442	1,836	1,606	955	924	440	484	280	846	395	451	262
1974	5,156	4,097	2,169	1,927	1,104	1,058	544	514	318	965	494	470	297
1975	7,929	6,421	3,627	2,794	1,413	1,507	815	692	355	1,369	741	629	330
1976	7,406	5,914	3,258	2,656	1,364	1,492	779	713	355	1,334	698	637	330
1977	6,991	5,441	2,883	2,558	1,284	1,550	784	766	379	1,393	698	695	354
1978	6,202	4,698	2,411	2,287	1,189	1,505	731	774	394	1,330	641	690	360
1979	6,137	4,664	2,405	2,260	1,193	1,473	714	759	362	1,319	636	683	333
1980	7,637	5,884	3,345	2,540	1,291	1,752	922	830	377	1,553	815	738	343
1981	8,273	6,343	3,580	2,762	1,374	1,930	997	933	388	1,731	891	840	357
1982	10,678	8,241	4,846	3,395	1,534	2,437	1,334	1,104	443	2,142	1,167	975	396
1983	10,717	8,128	4,859	3,270	1,387	2,588	1,401	1,187	441	2,272	1,213	1,059	392
1984	8,539	6,372	3,600	2,772	1,116	2,167	1,144	1,022	384	1,914	1,003	911	353
1985	8,312	6,191	3,426	2,765	1,074	2,121	1,095	1,026	394	1,864	951	913	357
1986	8,237	6,140	3,433	2,708	1,070	2,097	1,097	999	383	1,840	946	894	347
1987	7,425	5,501	3,132	2,369	995	1,924	969	955	353	1,684	826	858	312
1988	6,701	4,944	2,766	2,177	910	1,757	888	869	316	1,547	771	776	288
1989	6,528	4,770	2,636	2,135	863	1,757	889	868	331	1,544	773	772	300
1990	6,874	5,091	2,866	2,225	856	1,783	933	850	292	1,527	793	734	258
1991	8,426	6,447	3,775	2,672	977	1,979	1,043	936	313	1,679	874	805	270
1992	9,384	7,047	4,121	2,926	983	2,337	1,259	1,079	369	1,958	1,046	912	313
1993	8,734	6,547	3,753	2,793	943	2,187	1,179	1,008	353	1,796	954	842	302
1994	7,996	5,892	3,275	2,617	960	2,104	1,092	1,011	360	1,666	848	818	300
1995	7,404	5,459	2,999	2,460	952	1,945	984	961	394	1,538	762	777	325
1994: Jan	8,740	6,401	3,607	2,794	1,023	2,274	1,207	1,067	338	1,879	976	903	292
Feb	8,576	6,284	3,540	2,744	996	2,250	1,183	1,067	342	1,838	954	884	291
Mar	8,546	6,229	3,479	2,750	986	2,258	1,116	1,142	347	1,807	856	951	289
Apr	8,385	6,218	3,489	2,729	1,116	2,159	1,086	1,073	361	1,732	868	864	300
May	7,996	5,851	3,244	2,607	992	2,113	1,075	1,038	362	1,700	868	832	307
June	7,903	5,836	3,191	2,645	917	2,063	1,074	989	372	1,643	839	804	312
July	7,993	5,905	3,295	2,610	934	2,044	1,120	924	385	1,613	872	741	323
Aug	7,889	5,785	3,168	2,617	933	2,107	1,119	988	378	1,634	851	783	306
Sept	7,647	5,641	3,077	2,564	912	2,034	1,053	981	342	1,550	780	770	269
Oct	7,505	5,545	3,059	2,486	912	2,095	1,070	1,025	404	1,627	805	822	341
Nov	7,315	5,395	2,950	2,445	849	1,967	1,007	960	339	1,524	762	762	285
Dec	7,155	5,363	2,987	2,376	946	1,846	953	893	349	1,422	710	712	283
1995: Jan	7,498	5,510	3,068	2,442	928	1,910	962	947	333	1,505	760	745	275
Feb	7,183	5,226	2,878	2,348	949	1,911	940	971	386	1,505	721	784	317
Mar	7,237	5,301	2,930	2,372	903	1,873	899	973	346	1,448	658	790	268
Apr	7,665	5,653	3,079	2,574	966	2,004	992	1,012	421	1,601	766	835	323
May	7,492	5,633	3,158	2,475	967	1,847	972	876	386	1,467	766	701	317
June	7,384	5,396	2,968	2,428	877	1,983	987	996	415	1,565	782	783	347
July	7,559	5,427	2,866	2,561	980	2,051	1,038	1,013	430	1,623	798	825	353
Aug	7,431	5,404	2,970	2,435	914	2,090	1,089	1,002	458	1,666	846	820	403
Sept	7,451	5,396	3,017	2,379	955	2,087	1,033	1,054	411	1,676	799	877	356
Oct	7,249	5,417	2,913	2,503	973	1,919	918	1,001	376	1,470	678	792	301
Nov	7,432	5,648	3,152	2,496	1,031	1,817	932	886	380	1,409	705	704	307
Dec	7,380	5,551	3,041	2,511	1,021	1,897	1,073	824	396	1,536	854	681	341

Note.—See footnote 5 and Note, Table B–31.

Source: Department of Labor, Bureau of Labor Statistics.

TABLE B–35.—*Civilian labor force participation rate and employment/population ratio, 1948–95*

[Percent;¹ monthly data seasonally adjusted]

Year or month	Labor force participation rate							Employment/population ratio						
	All civilian workers	Males	Females	Both sexes 16–19 years	White	Black and other	Black	All civilian workers	Males	Females	Both sexes 16–19 years	White	Black and other	Black
1948	58.8	86.6	32.7	52.5				56.6	83.5	31.3	47.7			
1949	58.9	86.4	33.1	52.2				55.4	81.3	31.2	45.2			
1950	59.2	86.4	33.9	51.8				56.1	82.0	32.0	45.5			
1951	59.2	86.3	34.6	52.2				57.3	84.0	33.1	47.9			
1952	59.0	86.3	34.7	51.3				57.3	83.9	33.4	46.9			
1953	58.9	86.0	34.4	50.2				57.1	83.6	33.3	46.4			
1954	58.8	85.5	34.6	48.3	58.2	64.0		55.5	81.0	32.5	42.3	55.2	58.0	
1955	59.3	85.4	35.7	48.9	58.7	64.2		56.7	81.8	34.0	43.5	56.5	58.7	
1956	60.0	85.5	36.9	50.9	59.4	64.9		57.5	82.3	35.1	45.3	57.3	59.5	
1957	59.6	84.8	36.9	49.6	59.1	64.4		57.1	81.3	35.1	43.9	56.8	59.3	
1958	59.5	84.2	37.1	47.4	58.9	64.8		55.4	78.5	34.5	39.9	55.3	56.7	
1959	59.3	83.7	37.1	46.7	58.7	64.3		56.0	79.3	35.0	39.9	55.9	57.5	
1960	59.4	83.3	37.7	47.5	58.8	64.5		56.1	78.9	35.5	40.5	55.9	57.9	
1961	59.3	82.9	38.1	46.9	58.8	64.1		55.4	77.6	35.4	39.1	55.3	56.2	
1962	58.8	82.0	37.9	46.1	58.3	63.2		55.5	77.7	35.6	39.4	55.4	56.3	
1963	58.7	81.4	38.3	45.2	58.2	63.0		55.4	77.1	35.8	37.4	55.3	56.2	
1964	58.7	81.0	38.7	44.5	58.2	63.1		55.7	77.3	36.3	37.3	55.5	57.0	
1965	58.9	80.7	39.3	45.7	58.4	62.9		56.2	77.5	37.1	38.9	56.0	57.8	
1966	59.2	80.4	40.3	48.2	58.7	63.0		56.9	77.9	38.3	42.1	56.8	58.4	
1967	59.6	80.4	41.1	48.4	59.2	62.8		57.3	78.0	39.0	42.2	57.2	58.2	
1968	59.6	80.1	41.6	48.3	59.3	62.2		57.5	77.8	39.6	42.2	57.4	58.0	
1969	60.1	79.8	42.7	49.4	59.9	62.1		58.0	77.6	40.7	43.4	58.0	58.1	
1970	60.4	79.7	43.3	49.9	60.2	61.8		57.4	76.2	40.8	42.3	57.5	56.8	
1971	60.2	79.1	43.4	49.7	60.1	60.9		56.6	74.9	40.4	41.3	56.8	54.9	
1972	60.4	78.9	43.9	51.9	60.4	60.2	59.9	57.0	75.0	41.0	43.5	57.4	54.1	53.7
1973	60.8	78.8	44.7	53.7	60.8	60.5	60.2	57.8	75.5	42.0	45.9	58.2	55.0	54.5
1974	61.3	78.7	45.7	54.8	61.4	60.3	59.8	57.8	74.9	42.6	46.0	58.3	54.3	53.5
1975	61.2	77.9	46.3	54.0	61.5	59.6	58.8	56.1	71.7	42.0	43.3	56.7	51.4	50.1
1976	61.6	77.5	47.3	54.5	61.8	59.8	59.0	56.8	72.0	43.2	44.2	57.5	52.0	50.8
1977	62.3	77.7	48.4	56.0	62.5	60.4	59.8	57.9	72.8	44.5	46.1	58.6	52.5	51.4
1978	63.2	77.9	50.0	57.8	63.3	62.2	61.5	59.3	73.8	46.4	48.3	60.0	54.7	53.6
1979	63.7	77.8	50.9	57.9	63.9	62.2	61.4	59.9	73.8	47.5	48.5	60.6	55.2	53.8
1980	63.8	77.4	51.5	56.7	64.1	61.7	61.0	59.2	72.0	47.7	46.6	60.0	53.6	52.3
1981	63.9	77.0	52.1	55.4	64.3	61.3	60.8	59.0	71.3	48.0	44.6	60.0	52.6	51.3
1982	64.0	76.6	52.6	54.1	64.3	61.6	61.0	57.8	69.0	47.7	41.5	58.8	50.9	49.4
1983	64.0	76.4	52.9	53.5	64.3	62.1	61.5	57.9	68.8	48.0	41.5	58.9	51.0	49.5
1984	64.4	76.4	53.6	53.9	64.6	62.6	62.2	59.5	70.7	49.5	43.7	60.5	53.6	52.3
1985	64.8	76.3	54.5	54.5	65.0	63.3	62.9	60.1	70.9	50.4	44.4	61.0	54.7	53.4
1986	65.3	76.3	55.3	54.7	65.5	63.7	63.3	60.7	71.0	51.4	44.6	61.5	55.4	54.1
1987	65.6	76.2	56.0	54.7	65.8	64.3	63.8	61.5	71.5	52.5	45.5	62.3	56.8	55.6
1988	65.9	76.2	56.6	55.3	66.2	64.0	63.8	62.3	72.0	53.4	46.8	63.1	57.4	56.3
1989	66.5	76.4	57.4	55.9	66.7	64.7	64.2	63.0	72.5	54.3	47.5	63.8	58.2	56.9
1990	66.4	76.1	57.5	53.7	66.8	63.7	63.3	62.7	71.9	54.3	45.4	63.6	57.3	56.2
1991	66.0	75.5	57.3	51.7	66.6	63.1	62.6	61.6	70.2	53.7	42.1	62.6	56.1	54.9
1992	66.3	75.6	57.8	51.3	66.7	63.8	63.3	61.4	69.7	53.8	41.0	62.4	55.7	54.3
1993	66.2	75.2	57.9	51.5	66.7	63.1	62.4	61.6	69.9	54.1	41.7	62.7	55.7	54.4
1994	66.6	75.1	58.8	52.7	67.1	63.9	63.4	62.5	70.4	55.3	43.4	63.5	57.2	56.1
1995	66.6	75.0	58.9	53.5	67.1	64.3	63.7	62.9	70.8	55.6	44.2	63.8	58.1	57.1
1994: Jan	66.7	75.3	58.7	53.1	67.1	64.2	63.5	62.2	70.1	54.9	43.3	63.2	56.9	55.2
Feb	66.7	75.2	58.9	52.7	67.2	64.2	63.6	62.3	70.1	55.2	43.1	63.4	56.9	55.5
Mar	66.6	75.1	58.8	52.9	67.0	64.3	63.8	62.3	70.2	55.0	43.4	63.2	57.0	55.8
Apr	66.6	75.0	58.8	53.6	67.1	64.1	63.6	62.3	70.2	55.1	43.3	63.3	57.2	56.0
May	66.5	74.9	58.8	52.9	67.0	63.9	63.6	62.4	70.3	55.2	43.3	63.5	57.2	56.1
June	66.4	74.8	58.6	53.2	66.8	63.8	63.4	62.3	70.3	55.1	44.1	63.3	57.2	56.2
July	66.4	74.9	58.7	52.5	67.0	63.2	62.8	62.4	70.2	55.2	43.2	63.4	56.7	55.8
Aug	66.5	74.9	58.8	52.8	67.1	63.6	63.0	62.5	70.3	55.3	43.5	63.6	56.9	55.8
Sept	66.6	74.9	58.9	51.5	67.2	63.8	63.1	62.7	70.5	55.5	42.6	63.8	57.3	56.3
Oct	66.7	75.1	58.9	52.7	67.2	64.3	63.7	62.9	70.8	55.5	43.7	63.9	57.6	56.6
Nov	66.7	75.1	58.9	51.8	67.2	63.8	63.3	63.0	71.0	55.6	43.6	64.0	57.6	56.7
Dec	66.6	75.3	58.6	52.9	67.2	63.5	63.1	63.0	71.1	55.6	43.8	64.0	57.6	56.9
1995: Jan	66.8	75.4	58.9	53.6	67.2	64.1	63.7	63.0	71.1	55.6	44.7	63.9	58.0	57.1
Feb	66.9	75.5	58.9	53.6	67.2	64.9	64.3	63.2	71.4	55.7	44.2	64.0	58.8	57.8
Mar	66.9	75.5	59.0	54.5	67.3	64.7	64.0	63.3	71.5	55.7	45.8	64.1	58.8	57.8
Apr	67.0	75.5	59.2	54.3	67.3	65.2	64.5	63.1	71.2	55.7	44.8	63.9	58.8	57.6
May	66.5	75.0	58.6	53.6	66.9	64.4	63.8	62.7	70.6	55.4	44.1	63.5	58.5	57.5
June	66.4	75.0	58.6	54.2	66.9	64.0	63.3	62.7	70.9	55.2	45.4	63.6	57.7	56.6
July	66.7	74.9	59.2	53.6	67.2	63.9	63.0	62.9	70.8	55.7	43.9	64.0	57.4	56.1
Aug	66.5	74.6	59.0	53.5	67.0	64.3	63.2	62.8	70.4	55.7	44.0	63.8	57.7	56.0
Sept	66.6	74.9	59.0	53.6	67.1	64.2	63.6	62.9	70.7	55.7	44.2	63.9	57.6	56.4
Oct	66.6	74.7	59.2	53.0	67.1	64.1	63.7	63.0	70.7	55.8	43.9	63.8	58.1	57.4
Nov	66.4	74.4	59.1	52.7	66.9	64.3	64.4	62.7	70.2	55.8	43.3	63.5	58.6	58.4
Dec	66.3	74.5	58.8	52.8	66.8	64.0	64.1	62.6	70.2	55.6	43.2	63.4	58.1	57.6

¹ Civilian labor force or civilian employment as percent of civilian noninstitutional population in group specified.

Note.—Data relate to persons 16 years of age and over.

See footnote 5 and Note, Table B–31.

Source: Department of Labor, Bureau of Labor Statistics.

TABLE B–36.—*Civilian labor force participation rate by demographic characteristic, 1954–95*

[Percent;[1] monthly data seasonally adjusted]

Year or month	All civilian workers	White Males Total	White Males 16–19 years	White Males 20 years and over	White Females Total	White Females 16–19 years	White Females 20 years and over	Black and other or black Males Total	Black and other or black Males 16–19 years	Black and other or black Males 20 years and over	Black and other or black Females Total	Black and other or black Females 16–19 years	Black and other or black Females 20 years and over
								Black and other					
1954	58.8	58.2	85.6	57.6	87.8	33.3	40.6	32.7	64.0	85.2	61.2	87.1	46.1	31.0	47.7
1955	59.3	58.7	85.4	58.6	87.5	34.5	40.7	34.0	64.2	85.1	60.8	87.8	46.1	32.7	47.5
1956	60.0	59.4	85.6	60.4	87.6	35.7	43.1	35.1	64.9	85.1	61.5	87.8	47.3	36.3	48.4
1957	59.6	59.1	84.8	59.2	86.9	35.7	42.2	35.2	64.4	84.2	58.8	87.0	47.1	33.2	48.6
1958	59.5	58.9	84.3	56.5	86.6	35.8	40.1	35.5	64.8	84.1	57.3	87.1	48.0	31.9	49.8
1959	59.3	58.7	83.8	55.9	86.3	36.0	39.6	35.6	64.3	83.4	55.5	86.7	47.7	28.2	49.8
1960	59.4	58.8	83.4	55.9	86.0	36.5	40.3	36.2	64.5	83.0	57.6	86.2	48.2	32.9	49.9
1961	59.3	58.8	83.0	54.5	85.7	36.9	40.6	36.6	64.1	82.2	55.8	85.5	48.3	32.8	50.1
1962	58.8	58.3	82.1	53.8	84.9	36.7	39.8	36.5	63.2	80.8	53.5	84.2	48.0	33.1	49.6
1963	58.7	58.2	81.5	53.1	84.4	37.2	38.7	37.0	63.0	80.2	51.5	83.9	48.1	32.6	49.9
1964	58.7	58.2	81.1	52.7	84.2	37.5	37.8	37.5	63.1	80.1	49.9	84.1	48.6	31.7	50.7
1965	58.9	58.4	80.8	54.1	83.9	38.1	39.2	38.0	62.9	79.6	51.3	83.7	48.6	29.5	51.1
1966	59.2	58.7	80.6	55.9	83.6	39.2	42.6	38.8	63.0	79.0	51.4	83.3	49.4	33.5	51.6
1967	59.6	59.2	80.6	56.3	83.5	40.1	42.5	39.8	62.8	78.5	51.1	82.9	49.5	35.2	51.6
1968	59.6	59.3	80.4	55.9	83.2	40.7	43.0	40.4	62.2	77.7	49.7	82.2	49.3	34.8	51.4
1969	60.1	59.9	80.2	56.8	83.0	41.8	44.6	41.5	62.1	76.9	49.6	81.4	49.8	34.6	52.0
1970	60.4	60.2	80.0	57.5	82.8	42.6	45.6	42.2	61.8	76.5	47.4	81.4	49.5	34.1	51.8
1971	60.2	60.1	79.6	57.9	82.3	42.6	45.4	42.3	60.9	74.9	44.7	80.0	49.2	31.2	51.8
1972	60.4	60.4	79.6	60.1	82.0	43.2	48.1	42.7	60.2	73.9	46.0	78.6	48.8	32.3	51.2
								Black					
1972	60.4	60.4	79.6	60.1	82.0	43.2	48.1	42.7	59.9	73.6	46.3	78.5	48.7	32.2	51.2
1973	60.8	60.8	79.4	62.0	81.6	44.1	50.1	43.5	60.2	73.4	45.7	78.4	49.3	34.2	51.6
1974	61.3	61.4	79.4	62.9	81.4	45.2	51.7	44.4	59.8	72.9	46.7	77.6	49.0	33.4	51.4
1975	61.2	61.5	78.7	61.9	80.7	45.9	51.5	45.3	58.8	70.9	42.6	76.0	48.8	34.2	51.1
1976	61.6	61.8	78.4	62.3	80.3	46.9	52.8	46.2	59.0	70.0	41.3	75.4	49.8	32.9	52.5
1977	62.3	62.5	78.5	64.0	80.2	48.0	54.5	47.3	59.8	70.6	43.2	75.6	50.8	32.9	53.6
1978	63.2	63.3	78.6	65.0	80.1	49.4	56.7	48.7	61.5	71.5	44.9	76.2	53.1	37.3	55.5
1979	63.7	63.9	78.6	64.8	80.1	50.5	57.4	49.8	61.4	71.3	43.6	76.3	53.1	36.8	55.4
1980	63.8	64.1	78.2	63.7	79.8	51.2	56.2	50.6	61.0	70.3	43.2	75.1	53.1	34.9	55.6
1981	63.9	64.3	77.9	62.4	79.5	51.9	55.4	51.5	60.8	70.0	41.6	74.5	53.5	34.0	56.0
1982	64.0	64.3	77.4	60.0	79.2	52.4	55.0	52.2	61.0	70.1	39.8	74.7	53.7	33.5	56.2
1983	64.0	64.3	77.1	59.4	78.9	52.7	54.5	52.5	61.5	70.6	39.9	75.2	54.2	33.0	56.8
1984	64.4	64.6	77.1	59.0	78.7	53.3	55.4	53.1	62.2	70.8	41.7	74.8	55.2	35.0	57.6
1985	64.8	65.0	77.0	59.7	78.5	54.1	55.2	54.0	62.9	70.8	44.6	74.4	56.5	37.9	58.6
1986	65.3	65.5	76.9	59.3	78.5	55.0	56.3	54.9	63.3	71.2	43.7	74.8	56.9	39.1	58.9
1987	65.6	65.8	76.8	59.0	78.4	55.7	56.5	55.6	63.8	71.1	43.6	74.7	58.0	39.6	60.0
1988	65.9	66.2	76.9	60.0	78.3	56.4	57.2	56.3	63.8	71.0	43.8	74.6	58.0	37.9	60.1
1989	66.5	66.7	77.1	61.0	78.5	57.2	57.1	57.2	64.2	71.0	44.6	74.4	58.7	40.4	60.6
1990	66.4	66.8	76.9	59.4	78.3	57.5	55.4	57.6	63.3	70.1	40.6	73.8	57.8	36.7	60.0
1991	66.0	66.6	76.4	57.2	77.8	57.4	54.3	57.7	62.6	69.5	37.4	73.4	57.0	33.5	59.3
1992	66.3	66.7	76.4	56.7	77.8	57.8	52.6	58.1	63.3	69.7	40.7	73.1	58.0	35.2	60.1
1993	66.2	66.7	76.1	56.5	77.5	58.0	53.7	58.3	62.4	68.6	39.5	72.0	57.4	34.5	59.5
1994	66.6	67.1	75.9	57.7	77.3	58.9	55.1	59.2	63.4	69.1	40.8	72.5	58.7	36.3	60.9
1995	66.6	67.1	75.7	58.5	77.1	59.0	55.5	59.2	63.7	69.0	40.1	72.5	59.5	39.8	61.4
1994: Jan	66.7	67.1	76.0	58.5	77.4	58.7	54.6	59.0	63.5	68.9	40.4	72.3	59.0	40.6	60.8
Feb	66.7	67.2	75.9	58.1	77.3	59.0	54.9	59.3	63.6	69.4	39.4	73.0	58.8	36.1	61.0
Mar	66.6	67.0	75.8	57.6	77.2	58.7	55.4	59.0	63.8	69.0	39.9	72.4	59.5	36.3	61.8
Apr	66.6	67.1	75.9	58.9	77.2	58.8	57.0	58.9	63.6	69.2	40.4	72.6	59.1	36.6	61.3
May	66.5	67.0	75.6	58.1	77.0	59.0	56.0	59.2	63.6	69.8	39.8	73.3	58.5	33.4	61.0
June	66.4	66.8	75.6	57.5	77.0	58.6	56.0	58.8	63.4	68.8	41.8	72.0	58.9	36.6	61.1
July	66.4	67.0	75.7	57.6	77.1	58.8	55.0	59.0	62.8	68.4	41.6	71.7	58.3	35.9	60.5
Aug	66.5	67.1	75.8	57.9	77.2	59.0	55.3	59.2	63.0	68.3	41.4	71.5	58.6	35.3	60.9
Sept	66.6	67.2	75.7	56.3	77.2	59.2	52.7	59.6	63.1	68.6	39.4	72.1	58.5	36.3	60.7
Oct	66.7	67.2	75.9	57.6	77.3	59.1	54.3	59.4	63.7	69.6	42.9	72.7	59.0	39.1	60.9
Nov	66.7	67.2	75.9	56.3	77.4	59.1	54.7	59.4	63.3	69.3	41.4	72.6	58.5	36.3	60.7
Dec	66.6	67.2	76.1	57.7	77.5	58.9	56.0	59.1	63.1	69.3	40.7	72.7	58.0	32.7	60.5
1995: Jan	66.8	67.2	76.1	58.5	77.5	58.9	57.6	59.0	63.7	69.6	36.3	73.6	58.8	32.9	61.4
Feb	66.9	67.2	76.1	58.4	77.5	58.9	55.3	59.1	64.3	70.3	42.4	73.7	59.4	36.7	61.7
Mar	66.9	67.3	76.2	59.5	77.5	58.9	57.0	59.1	64.0	69.8	36.3	73.8	59.4	40.0	61.3
Apr	67.0	67.3	76.0	60.0	77.3	59.1	55.9	59.4	64.5	70.2	41.0	73.7	59.8	39.4	61.9
May	66.5	66.9	75.7	58.7	77.0	58.7	55.7	58.9	63.8	69.2	38.4	73.0	59.5	40.4	61.4
June	66.4	66.9	75.7	60.1	77.0	58.6	56.3	58.7	63.3	69.1	41.0	72.5	58.7	39.8	60.6
July	66.7	67.2	75.7	59.6	76.9	59.3	55.6	59.5	63.0	68.4	40.9	71.7	58.7	38.7	60.6
Aug	66.5	67.0	75.5	58.2	76.8	59.1	55.4	59.4	63.2	68.5	42.2	71.6	58.9	40.8	60.7
Sept	66.6	67.1	75.7	58.1	77.0	59.1	54.6	59.4	63.6	68.9	40.6	72.4	59.2	44.1	60.7
Oct	66.6	67.1	75.5	58.1	76.9	59.2	54.8	59.5	63.7	68.1	38.3	71.8	60.1	40.5	62.1
Nov	66.4	66.9	75.3	57.0	76.8	58.9	55.0	59.2	64.4	68.4	41.9	71.8	61.2	42.1	63.1
Dec	66.3	66.8	75.4	57.8	76.8	58.7	54.2	59.0	64.1	68.4	40.4	71.9	60.6	42.8	62.4

[1] Civilian labor force as percent of civilian noninstitutional population in group specified.

Note.—Data relate to persons 16 years of age and over.

See footnote 5 and Note, Table B–31.

Source: Department of Labor, Bureau of Labor Statistics.

TABLE B–37.—*Civilian employment/population ratio by demographic characteristic, 1954–95*

[Percent;[1] monthly data seasonally adjusted]

Year or month	All civilian workers	White						Black and other or black					
		Total	Males			Females			Total	Males			Females	
			Total	16–19 years	20 years and over	Total	16–19 years	20 years and over	Total	Total	16–19 years	20 years and over	Total	16–19 years	20 years and over

(header note: Black and other)

Year or month	All civ.	Total	Males Total	16–19	20+	Females Total	16–19	20+	B&O Total	Males Total	16–19	20+	Females Total	16–19	20+
1954	55.5	55.2	81.5	49.9	84.0	31.4	36.4	31.1	58.0	76.5	52.4	79.2	41.9	24.7	43.7
1955	56.7	56.5	82.2	52.0	84.7	33.0	37.0	32.7	58.7	77.6	52.7	80.4	42.2	26.4	43.9
1956	57.5	57.3	82.7	54.1	85.0	34.2	38.9	33.8	59.5	78.4	52.2	81.3	43.0	28.0	44.7
1957	57.1	56.8	81.8	52.4	84.1	34.2	38.2	33.9	59.3	77.2	48.0	80.5	43.7	26.5	45.5
1958	55.4	55.3	79.2	47.6	81.8	33.6	35.0	33.5	56.7	72.5	42.0	76.0	42.8	22.8	45.0
1959	56.0	55.9	79.9	48.1	82.8	34.0	34.8	34.0	57.5	73.8	41.4	77.6	43.2	20.3	45.7
1960	56.1	55.9	79.4	48.1	82.4	34.6	35.1	34.5	57.9	74.1	43.8	77.9	43.6	24.8	45.8
1961	55.4	55.3	78.2	45.9	81.4	34.5	34.6	34.5	56.2	71.7	41.0	75.5	42.6	23.2	44.8
1962	55.5	55.4	78.4	46.4	81.5	34.7	34.8	34.7	56.3	72.0	41.7	75.7	42.7	23.1	44.9
1963	55.4	55.3	77.7	44.7	81.1	35.0	32.9	35.2	56.2	71.8	37.4	76.2	42.7	21.3	45.2
1964	55.7	55.5	77.8	45.0	81.3	35.5	32.2	35.8	57.0	72.9	37.8	77.7	43.4	21.8	46.1
1965	56.2	56.0	77.9	47.1	81.5	36.2	33.7	36.5	57.8	73.7	39.4	78.7	44.1	20.2	47.3
1966	56.9	56.8	78.3	50.1	81.7	37.5	37.5	37.5	58.4	74.0	40.5	79.2	45.1	23.1	48.2
1967	57.3	57.2	78.4	50.2	81.7	38.3	37.7	38.3	58.2	73.8	38.8	79.4	45.0	24.8	47.9
1968	57.5	57.4	78.3	50.3	81.6	38.9	37.8	39.1	58.0	73.3	38.7	78.9	45.2	24.7	48.2
1969	58.0	58.0	78.2	51.1	81.4	40.1	39.5	40.1	58.1	72.8	39.0	78.4	45.9	25.1	48.9
1970	57.4	57.5	76.8	49.6	80.1	40.3	39.5	40.4	56.8	70.9	35.5	76.8	44.9	22.4	48.2
1971	56.6	56.8	75.7	49.2	79.0	39.9	38.6	40.1	54.9	68.1	31.8	74.2	43.9	20.2	47.3
1972	57.0	57.4	76.0	51.5	79.0	40.7	41.3	40.6	54.1	67.3	32.4	73.2	43.3	19.9	46.7

(header note: Black)

Year or month	All civ.	Total	Males Total	16–19	20+	Females Total	16–19	20+	Black Total	Males Total	16–19	20+	Females Total	16–19	20+
1972	57.0	57.4	76.0	51.5	79.0	40.7	41.3	40.6	53.7	66.8	31.6	73.0	43.0	19.2	46.5
1973	57.8	58.2	76.5	54.3	79.2	41.8	43.6	41.6	54.5	67.5	32.8	73.7	43.8	22.0	47.2
1974	57.8	58.3	75.9	54.4	78.6	42.4	44.3	42.2	53.5	65.8	31.4	71.9	43.5	20.9	46.9
1975	56.1	56.7	73.0	50.6	75.7	42.0	42.5	41.9	50.1	60.6	26.3	66.5	41.6	20.2	44.9
1976	56.8	57.5	73.4	51.5	76.0	43.2	44.2	43.1	50.8	60.6	25.8	66.8	42.8	19.2	46.4
1977	57.9	58.6	74.1	54.4	76.5	44.5	45.9	44.4	51.4	61.4	26.4	67.5	43.3	18.5	47.0
1978	59.3	60.0	75.0	56.3	77.2	46.3	48.5	46.1	53.6	63.3	28.5	69.1	45.8	22.1	49.3
1979	59.9	60.6	75.1	55.7	77.3	47.5	49.4	47.3	53.8	63.4	28.7	69.1	46.0	22.4	49.3
1980	59.2	60.0	73.4	53.4	75.6	47.8	47.9	47.8	52.3	60.4	27.0	65.8	45.7	21.0	49.1
1981	59.0	60.0	72.8	51.3	75.1	48.3	46.2	48.5	51.3	59.1	24.6	64.5	45.1	19.7	48.5
1982	57.8	58.8	70.6	47.0	73.0	48.1	44.6	48.4	49.4	56.0	20.3	61.4	44.2	17.7	47.5
1983	57.9	58.9	70.4	47.4	72.6	48.5	44.5	48.9	49.5	56.3	20.4	61.6	44.1	17.0	47.4
1984	59.5	60.5	72.1	49.1	74.3	49.8	47.0	50.0	52.3	59.2	23.9	64.1	46.7	20.1	49.8
1985	60.1	61.0	72.3	49.9	74.3	50.7	47.1	51.0	53.4	60.0	26.3	64.6	48.1	23.1	50.9
1986	60.7	61.5	72.3	49.6	74.3	51.7	47.9	52.0	54.1	60.6	26.5	65.1	48.8	23.8	51.6
1987	61.5	62.3	72.7	49.9	74.7	52.8	49.0	53.1	55.6	62.0	28.5	66.4	50.3	25.8	53.0
1988	62.3	63.1	73.2	51.7	75.1	53.8	50.2	54.0	56.3	62.7	29.4	67.1	51.2	25.8	53.9
1989	63.0	63.8	73.7	52.6	75.4	54.6	50.5	54.9	56.9	62.8	30.4	67.0	52.0	27.1	54.6
1990	62.7	63.6	73.2	51.0	75.0	54.8	48.5	55.2	56.2	61.8	27.6	66.1	51.6	25.7	54.2
1991	61.6	62.6	71.5	47.2	73.3	54.3	46.1	54.8	54.9	60.5	23.8	64.9	50.3	21.4	53.1
1992	61.4	62.4	71.1	46.3	72.9	54.3	44.3	54.9	54.3	59.1	23.6	63.3	50.4	22.1	53.1
1993	61.6	62.7	71.3	46.6	73.1	54.7	45.8	55.3	54.4	59.1	23.6	63.2	50.5	21.6	53.2
1994	62.5	63.5	71.8	48.3	73.6	55.8	47.5	56.4	56.1	60.8	25.4	65.0	52.3	24.5	55.0
1995	62.9	63.8	72.0	49.4	73.8	56.1	48.1	56.7	57.1	61.7	25.2	66.1	53.4	26.1	56.1
1994:Jan	62.2	63.2	71.5	48.0	73.3	55.4	46.9	56.0	55.2	59.4	24.5	63.5	51.8	29.8	54.0
Feb	62.3	63.4	71.5	48.3	73.3	55.8	46.9	56.4	55.5	60.1	23.7	64.4	51.8	25.2	54.4
Mar	62.3	63.2	71.4	47.9	73.3	55.5	47.6	56.1	55.8	60.6	24.5	64.9	52.0	25.3	54.6
Apr	62.3	63.3	71.5	48.1	73.3	55.6	48.0	56.1	56.0	60.7	24.4	65.0	52.3	25.3	54.9
May	62.4	63.5	71.6	48.2	73.4	55.9	48.3	56.5	56.1	61.3	23.5	65.8	51.9	21.7	54.9
June	62.3	63.3	71.6	48.9	73.3	55.5	48.4	56.0	56.2	60.6	25.4	64.8	52.5	24.7	55.3
July	62.4	63.4	71.6	48.3	73.4	55.7	47.8	56.3	55.8	59.9	24.4	64.2	52.4	24.2	55.2
Aug	62.5	63.6	71.8	49.0	73.6	55.9	47.7	56.5	55.8	60.0	24.9	64.2	52.4	24.0	55.2
Sept	62.7	63.8	71.9	47.2	73.8	56.2	45.7	56.9	56.3	61.1	27.3	65.1	52.5	24.2	55.2
Oct	62.9	63.9	72.1	48.8	73.9	56.2	46.9	56.8	56.6	61.8	27.5	65.8	52.5	23.8	55.3
Nov	63.0	64.0	72.2	48.3	74.1	56.2	47.8	56.8	56.7	61.9	28.2	65.9	52.5	23.9	55.3
Dec	63.0	64.0	72.4	48.5	74.2	56.2	48.6	56.7	56.9	62.4	26.7	66.7	52.4	21.2	55.5
1995:Jan	63.0	63.9	72.3	49.7	74.1	56.1	50.1	56.5	57.1	62.3	23.9	66.8	53.0	20.7	56.2
Feb	63.2	64.0	72.5	49.0	74.3	56.1	48.1	56.7	57.8	63.4	26.0	67.8	53.3	24.8	56.1
Mar	63.3	64.1	72.5	50.7	74.2	56.2	50.0	56.6	57.8	63.4	24.8	68.0	53.2	27.7	55.7
Apr	63.1	63.9	72.2	50.9	73.9	56.1	48.1	56.7	57.6	62.8	26.5	67.1	53.3	25.3	56.1
May	62.7	63.5	71.8	49.8	73.5	55.8	47.7	56.4	57.5	61.8	23.0	66.6	54.0	28.1	56.6
June	62.7	63.6	72.1	51.4	73.7	55.7	49.8	56.1	56.6	61.5	25.1	66.0	52.6	25.1	55.3
July	62.9	64.0	72.1	50.9	73.8	56.3	47.2	56.9	56.1	60.8	23.9	65.2	52.2	24.7	55.0
Aug	62.8	63.8	71.8	49.0	73.6	56.3	48.6	56.8	56.0	60.3	22.7	64.9	52.6	24.9	55.3
Sept	62.9	63.9	71.9	48.8	73.8	56.4	47.4	57.0	56.4	61.2	27.3	65.4	52.4	26.6	55.0
Oct	63.0	63.8	71.9	47.9	73.8	56.3	48.2	56.8	57.4	61.6	25.5	66.1	54.0	27.3	56.6
Nov	62.7	63.5	71.4	47.5	73.3	56.1	46.8	56.7	58.4	61.7	28.5	66.0	55.8	29.6	58.4
Dec	62.6	63.4	71.6	48.5	73.4	55.8	45.9	56.5	57.6	60.3	24.0	64.7	55.4	29.7	57.9

[1] Civilian employment as percent of civilian noninstitutional population in group specified.

Note.—Data relate to persons 16 years of age and over.

See footnote 5 and Note, Table B–31.

Source: Department of Labor, Bureau of Labor Statistics.

TABLE B–38.—*Civilian unemployment rate, 1948–95*

[Percent;[1] monthly data seasonally adjusted]

Year or month	All civilian workers	Males Total	Males 16–19 years	Males 20 years and over	Females Total	Females 16–19 years	Females 20 years and over	Both sexes 16–19 years	White	Black and other	Black	Experienced wage and salary workers	Married men, spouse present[2]	Women who maintain families
1948	3.8	3.6	9.8	3.2	4.1	8.3	3.6	9.2	3.5	5.9		4.3		
1949	5.9	5.9	14.3	5.4	6.0	12.3	5.3	13.4	5.6	8.9		6.8	3.5	
1950	5.3	5.1	12.7	4.7	5.7	11.4	5.1	12.2	4.9	9.0		6.0	4.6	
1951	3.3	2.8	8.1	2.5	4.4	8.3	4.0	8.2	3.1	5.3		3.7	1.5	
1952	3.0	2.8	8.9	2.4	3.6	8.0	3.2	8.5	2.8	5.4		3.4	1.4	
1953	2.9	2.8	7.9	2.5	3.3	7.2	2.9	7.6	2.7	4.5		3.2	1.7	
1954	5.5	5.3	13.5	4.9	6.0	11.4	5.5	12.6	5.0	9.9		6.2	4.0	
1955	4.4	4.2	11.6	3.8	4.9	10.2	4.4	11.0	3.9	8.7		4.8	2.6	
1956	4.1	3.8	11.1	3.4	4.8	11.2	4.2	11.1	3.6	8.3		4.4	2.3	
1957	4.3	4.1	12.4	3.6	4.7	10.6	4.1	11.6	3.8	7.9		4.6	2.8	
1958	6.8	6.8	17.1	6.2	6.8	14.3	6.1	15.9	6.1	12.6		7.3	5.1	
1959	5.5	5.2	15.3	4.7	5.9	13.5	5.2	14.6	4.8	10.7		5.7	3.6	
1960	5.5	5.4	15.3	4.7	5.9	13.9	5.1	14.7	5.0	10.2		5.7	3.7	
1961	6.7	6.4	17.1	5.7	7.2	16.3	6.3	16.8	6.0	12.4		6.8	4.6	
1962	5.5	5.2	14.7	4.6	6.2	14.6	5.4	14.7	4.9	10.9		5.6	3.6	
1963	5.7	5.2	17.2	4.5	6.5	17.2	5.4	17.2	5.0	10.8		5.6	3.4	
1964	5.2	4.6	15.8	3.9	6.2	16.6	5.2	16.2	4.6	9.6		5.0	2.8	
1965	4.5	4.0	14.1	3.2	5.5	15.7	4.5	14.8	4.1	8.1		4.3	2.4	
1966	3.8	3.2	11.7	2.5	4.8	14.1	3.8	12.8	3.4	7.3		3.5	1.9	
1967	3.8	3.1	12.3	2.3	5.2	13.5	4.2	12.9	3.4	7.4		3.6	1.8	4.9
1968	3.6	2.9	11.6	2.2	4.8	14.0	3.8	12.7	3.2	6.7		3.4	1.6	4.4
1969	3.5	2.8	11.4	2.1	4.7	13.3	3.7	12.2	3.1	6.4		3.3	1.5	4.4
1970	4.9	4.4	15.0	3.5	5.9	15.6	4.8	15.3	4.5	8.2		4.8	2.6	5.4
1971	5.9	5.3	16.6	4.4	6.9	17.2	5.7	16.9	5.4	9.9		5.7	3.2	7.3
1972	5.6	5.0	15.9	4.0	6.6	16.7	5.4	16.2	5.1	10.0	10.4	5.3	2.8	7.2
1973	4.9	4.2	13.9	3.3	6.0	15.3	4.9	14.5	4.3	9.0	9.4	4.5	2.3	7.1
1974	5.6	4.9	15.6	3.8	6.7	16.6	5.5	16.0	5.0	9.9	10.5	5.3	2.7	7.0
1975	8.5	7.9	20.1	6.8	9.3	19.7	8.0	19.9	7.8	13.8	14.8	8.2	5.1	10.0
1976	7.7	7.1	19.2	5.9	8.6	18.7	7.4	19.0	7.0	13.1	14.0	7.3	4.2	10.1
1977	7.1	6.3	17.3	5.2	8.2	18.3	7.0	17.8	6.2	13.1	14.0	6.6	3.6	9.4
1978	6.1	5.3	15.8	4.3	7.2	17.1	6.0	16.4	5.2	11.9	12.8	5.6	2.8	8.5
1979	5.8	5.1	15.9	4.2	6.8	16.4	5.7	16.1	5.1	11.3	12.3	5.5	2.8	8.3
1980	7.1	6.9	18.3	5.9	7.4	17.2	6.4	17.8	6.3	13.1	14.3	6.9	4.2	9.2
1981	7.6	7.4	20.1	6.3	7.9	19.0	6.8	19.6	6.7	14.2	15.6	7.3	4.3	10.4
1982	9.7	9.9	24.4	8.8	9.4	21.9	8.3	23.2	8.6	17.3	18.9	9.3	6.5	11.7
1983	9.6	9.9	23.3	8.9	9.2	21.3	8.1	22.4	8.4	17.8	19.5	9.2	6.5	12.2
1984	7.5	7.4	19.6	6.6	7.6	18.0	6.8	18.9	6.5	14.4	15.9	7.1	4.6	10.3
1985	7.2	7.0	19.5	6.2	7.4	17.6	6.6	18.6	6.2	13.7	15.1	6.8	4.3	10.4
1986	7.0	6.9	19.0	6.1	7.1	17.6	6.2	18.3	6.0	13.1	14.5	6.6	4.4	9.8
1987	6.2	6.2	17.8	5.4	6.2	15.9	5.4	16.9	5.3	11.6	13.0	5.8	3.9	9.2
1988	5.5	5.5	16.0	4.8	5.6	14.4	4.9	15.3	4.7	10.4	11.7	5.2	3.3	8.1
1989	5.3	5.2	15.9	4.5	5.4	14.0	4.7	15.0	4.5	10.0	11.4	5.0	3.0	8.1
1990	5.5	5.6	16.3	4.9	5.4	14.7	4.8	15.5	4.7	10.1	11.3	5.3	3.4	8.2
1991	6.7	7.0	19.8	6.3	6.3	17.4	5.7	18.6	6.0	11.1	12.4	6.5	4.4	9.1
1992	7.4	7.8	21.5	7.0	6.9	18.5	6.3	20.0	6.5	12.7	14.1	7.1	5.0	9.9
1993	6.8	7.1	20.4	6.4	6.5	17.4	5.9	19.0	6.0	11.7	12.9	6.5	4.4	9.5
1994	6.1	6.2	19.0	5.4	6.0	16.2	5.4	17.6	5.3	10.5	11.5	5.9	3.7	8.9
1995	5.6	5.6	18.4	4.8	5.6	16.1	4.9	17.3	4.9	9.6	10.4	5.4	3.3	8.0
1994: Jan	6.7	6.9	20.7	6.1	6.5	16.0	5.9	18.5	5.8	11.4	13.0	6.6	4.2	9.3
Feb	6.6	6.7	19.7	6.0	6.4	16.5	5.7	18.2	5.7	11.3	12.7	6.4	4.3	9.5
Mar	6.5	6.6	19.6	5.8	6.5	16.3	5.9	18.0	5.6	11.3	12.4	6.4	4.1	9.4
Apr	6.4	6.5	20.2	5.7	6.3	18.1	5.6	19.2	5.6	10.8	11.9	6.2	3.9	9.1
May	6.1	6.2	19.9	5.4	6.1	16.2	5.4	18.1	5.3	10.6	11.7	5.9	3.7	8.9
June	6.1	6.0	18.0	5.3	6.1	16.0	5.4	17.1	5.3	10.4	11.3	5.9	3.6	8.8
July	6.1	6.3	19.4	5.5	5.9	15.8	5.3	17.7	5.3	10.3	11.2	6.0	3.6	7.9
Aug	6.0	6.1	18.8	5.3	6.0	16.1	5.3	17.5	5.2	10.6	11.3	5.8	3.5	8.8
Sept	5.8	5.8	18.5	5.1	5.8	15.9	5.2	17.2	5.1	10.2	10.7	5.7	3.4	8.9
Oct	5.7	5.7	18.1	5.0	5.7	16.0	5.0	17.1	5.0	10.4	11.1	5.5	3.3	8.9
Nov	5.6	5.5	16.5	4.9	5.6	15.0	5.0	15.8	4.8	9.8	10.5	5.4	3.2	8.7
Dec	5.4	5.5	18.5	4.7	5.4	15.8	4.7	17.2	4.8	9.2	9.8	5.3	3.2	8.8
1995: Jan	5.7	5.7	17.4	5.0	5.6	15.9	4.9	16.7	4.9	9.5	10.2	5.4	3.4	8.9
Feb	5.4	5.4	19.4	4.6	5.5	15.6	4.8	17.6	4.7	9.4	10.1	5.1	3.0	8.1
Mar	5.5	5.4	17.0	4.7	5.5	15.2	4.9	16.1	4.7	9.2	9.8	5.2	3.2	7.6
Apr	5.8	5.7	17.8	4.9	5.9	17.2	5.2	17.5	5.0	9.8	10.7	5.6	3.4	9.0
May	5.7	5.8	18.4	5.1	5.5	16.7	4.8	17.6	5.0	9.1	9.9	5.6	3.4	8.0
June	5.6	5.5	17.4	4.8	5.7	15.2	5.0	16.4	4.8	9.8	10.6	5.4	3.4	8.4
July	5.7	5.5	18.7	4.7	5.9	17.6	5.1	18.2	4.8	10.1	11.1	5.5	3.4	8.5
Aug	5.6	5.6	19.7	4.8	5.6	15.5	5.0	17.7	4.8	10.2	11.3	5.4	3.3	7.0
Sept	5.6	5.6	18.3	4.9	5.6	16.8	4.9	17.5	4.8	10.2	11.3	5.5	3.5	8.0
Oct	5.5	5.3	19.5	4.5	5.6	14.5	5.0	17.1	4.8	9.4	9.9	5.4	3.1	7.9
Nov	5.6	5.7	19.0	4.9	5.5	16.8	4.8	17.9	5.0	8.9	9.4	5.4	3.3	7.7
Dec	5.6	5.7	19.1	4.9	5.4	17.4	4.6	18.3	5.0	9.3	10.2	5.5	3.1	6.6

[1] Unemployed as percent of civilian labor force in group specified.
[2] Data for 1949 and 1951–54 are for April; 1950, for March.

Note.—Data relate to persons 16 years of age and over.

See footnote 5 and Note, Table B–31.

Source: Department of Labor, Bureau of Labor Statistics.

Table B-39.—*Civilian unemployment rate by demographic characteristic, 1954–95*

[Percent;[1] monthly data seasonally adjusted]

Year or month	All civilian workers	White							Black and other or black						
		Total	Males			Females			Males				Females		
			Total	16–19 years	20 years and over	Total	16–19 years	20 years and over	Total	16–19 years	20 years and over	Total	16–19 years	20 years and over	
									Black and other						
1954	5.5	5.0	4.8	13.4	4.4	5.5	10.4	5.1	9.9	10.3	14.4	9.9	9.2	20.6	8.4
1955	4.4	3.9	3.7	11.3	3.3	4.3	9.1	3.9	8.7	8.8	13.4	8.4	8.5	19.2	7.7
1956	4.1	3.6	3.4	10.5	3.0	4.2	9.7	3.7	8.3	7.9	15.0	7.4	8.9	22.8	7.8
1957	4.3	3.8	3.6	11.5	3.2	4.3	9.5	3.8	7.9	8.3	18.4	7.6	7.3	20.2	6.4
1958	6.8	6.1	6.1	15.7	5.5	6.2	12.7	5.6	12.6	13.7	26.8	12.7	10.8	28.4	9.5
1959	5.5	4.8	4.6	14.0	4.1	5.3	12.0	4.7	10.7	11.5	25.2	10.5	9.4	27.7	8.3
1960	5.5	5.0	4.8	14.0	4.2	5.3	12.7	4.6	10.2	10.7	24.0	9.6	9.4	24.8	8.3
1961	6.7	6.0	5.7	15.7	5.1	6.5	14.8	5.7	12.4	12.8	26.8	11.7	11.9	29.2	10.6
1962	5.5	4.9	4.6	13.7	4.0	5.5	12.8	4.7	10.9	10.9	22.0	10.0	11.0	30.2	9.6
1963	5.7	5.0	4.7	15.9	3.9	5.8	15.1	4.8	10.8	10.5	27.3	9.2	11.2	34.7	9.4
1964	5.2	4.6	4.1	14.7	3.4	5.5	14.9	4.6	9.6	8.9	24.3	7.7	10.7	31.6	9.0
1965	4.5	4.1	3.6	12.9	2.9	5.0	14.0	4.0	8.1	7.4	23.3	6.0	9.2	31.7	7.5
1966	3.8	3.4	2.8	10.5	2.2	4.3	12.1	3.3	7.3	6.3	21.3	4.9	8.7	31.3	6.6
1967	3.8	3.4	2.7	10.7	2.1	4.6	11.5	3.8	7.4	6.0	23.9	4.3	9.1	29.6	7.1
1968	3.6	3.2	2.6	10.1	2.0	4.3	12.1	3.4	6.7	5.6	22.1	3.9	8.3	28.7	6.3
1969	3.5	3.1	2.5	10.0	1.9	4.2	11.5	3.4	6.4	5.3	21.4	3.7	7.8	27.6	5.8
1970	4.9	4.5	4.0	13.7	3.2	5.4	13.4	4.4	8.2	7.3	25.0	5.6	9.3	34.5	6.9
1971	5.9	5.4	4.9	15.1	4.0	6.3	15.1	5.3	9.9	9.1	28.8	7.3	10.9	35.4	8.7
1972	5.6	5.1	4.5	14.2	3.6	5.9	14.2	4.9	10.0	8.9	29.7	6.9	11.4	38.4	8.8
									Black						
1972	5.6	5.1	4.5	14.2	3.6	5.9	14.2	4.9	10.4	9.3	31.7	7.0	11.8	40.5	9.0
1973	4.9	4.3	3.8	12.3	3.0	5.3	13.0	4.3	9.4	8.0	27.8	6.0	11.1	36.1	8.6
1974	5.6	5.0	4.4	13.5	3.5	6.1	14.5	5.1	10.5	9.8	33.1	7.4	11.3	37.4	8.8
1975	8.5	7.8	7.2	18.3	6.2	8.6	17.4	7.5	14.8	14.8	38.1	12.5	14.8	41.0	12.2
1976	7.7	7.0	6.4	17.3	5.4	7.9	16.4	6.8	14.0	13.7	37.5	11.4	14.3	41.6	11.7
1977	7.1	6.2	5.5	15.0	4.7	7.3	15.9	6.2	14.0	13.3	39.2	10.7	14.9	43.4	12.3
1978	6.1	5.2	4.6	13.5	3.7	6.2	14.4	5.2	12.8	11.8	36.7	9.3	13.8	40.8	11.2
1979	5.8	5.1	4.5	13.9	3.6	5.9	14.0	5.0	12.3	11.4	34.2	9.3	13.3	39.1	10.9
1980	7.1	6.3	6.1	16.2	5.3	6.5	14.8	5.6	14.3	14.5	37.5	12.4	14.0	39.8	11.9
1981	7.6	6.7	6.5	17.9	5.6	6.9	16.6	5.9	15.6	15.7	40.7	13.5	15.6	42.2	13.4
1982	9.7	8.6	8.8	21.7	7.8	8.3	19.0	7.3	18.9	20.1	48.9	17.8	17.6	47.1	15.4
1983	9.6	8.4	8.8	20.2	7.9	7.9	18.3	6.9	19.5	20.3	48.8	18.1	18.6	48.2	16.5
1984	7.5	6.5	6.4	16.8	5.7	6.5	15.2	5.8	15.9	16.4	42.7	14.3	15.4	42.6	13.5
1985	7.2	6.2	6.1	16.5	5.4	6.4	14.8	5.7	15.1	15.3	41.0	13.2	14.9	39.2	13.1
1986	7.0	6.0	6.0	16.3	5.3	6.1	14.9	5.4	14.5	14.8	39.3	12.9	14.2	39.2	12.4
1987	6.2	5.3	5.4	15.5	4.8	5.2	13.4	4.6	13.0	12.7	34.4	11.1	13.2	34.9	11.6
1988	5.5	4.7	4.7	13.9	4.1	4.7	12.3	4.1	11.7	11.7	32.7	10.1	11.7	32.0	10.4
1989	5.3	4.5	4.5	13.7	3.9	4.5	11.5	4.0	11.4	11.5	31.9	10.0	11.4	33.0	9.8
1990	5.5	4.7	4.8	14.2	4.3	4.6	12.6	4.1	11.3	11.8	32.1	10.4	10.8	30.0	9.6
1991	6.7	6.0	6.4	17.5	5.7	5.5	15.2	4.9	12.4	12.9	36.5	11.5	11.9	36.1	10.5
1992	7.4	6.5	6.9	18.4	6.3	6.0	15.7	5.4	14.1	15.2	42.0	13.4	13.0	37.2	11.7
1993	6.8	6.0	6.2	17.6	5.6	5.7	14.6	5.1	12.9	13.8	40.1	12.1	12.0	37.5	10.6
1994	6.1	5.3	5.4	16.3	4.8	5.2	13.8	4.6	11.5	12.0	37.6	10.3	11.0	32.6	9.8
1995	5.6	4.9	4.9	15.6	4.3	4.8	13.4	4.3	10.4	10.6	37.1	8.8	10.2	34.3	8.6
1994: Jan	6.7	5.8	5.9	18.0	5.2	5.6	14.1	5.0	13.0	13.9	39.3	12.2	12.2	26.7	11.3
Feb	6.6	5.7	5.8	16.9	5.2	5.5	14.4	4.9	12.7	13.5	39.9	11.8	12.0	30.3	10.9
Mar	6.5	5.6	5.7	16.8	5.1	5.5	14.2	4.9	12.4	12.2	38.6	10.4	12.7	30.3	11.7
Apr	6.4	5.6	5.8	18.3	5.0	5.4	15.9	4.7	11.9	12.3	39.7	10.5	11.6	31.0	10.5
May	6.1	5.3	5.4	17.0	4.7	5.2	13.7	4.6	11.7	12.2	40.9	10.3	11.3	35.0	10.0
June	6.1	5.3	5.3	15.1	4.7	5.3	13.6	4.7	11.3	11.9	39.3	10.0	10.8	32.6	9.5
July	6.1	5.3	5.4	16.1	4.8	5.2	13.1	4.7	11.2	12.4	41.4	10.4	10.1	32.7	8.8
Aug	6.0	5.2	5.2	15.4	4.6	5.2	13.7	4.6	11.3	12.1	39.9	10.2	10.6	31.9	9.4
Sept	5.8	5.1	5.1	16.2	4.4	5.1	13.3	4.6	10.7	11.0	30.8	9.8	10.4	33.4	9.0
Oct	5.7	5.0	5.0	15.2	4.4	4.9	13.5	4.4	11.1	11.2	35.9	9.5	11.0	39.1	9.2
Nov	5.6	4.8	4.8	14.3	4.3	4.8	12.6	4.3	10.5	10.6	32.0	9.2	10.3	34.1	8.9
Dec	5.4	4.8	4.9	16.0	4.2	4.7	13.2	4.1	9.8	9.9	34.3	8.3	9.7	35.0	8.3
1995: Jan	5.7	4.9	5.0	15.0	4.4	4.8	13.1	4.3	10.2	10.6	34.0	9.2	9.9	37.1	8.5
Feb	5.4	4.7	4.7	16.1	4.0	4.6	13.1	4.1	10.1	9.9	38.7	7.9	10.3	32.4	9.0
Mar	5.5	4.7	4.8	14.7	4.2	4.7	12.4	4.2	9.8	9.1	31.7	7.8	10.4	30.7	9.1
Apr	5.8	5.0	5.0	15.3	4.4	5.1	13.8	4.5	10.7	10.5	35.4	8.9	10.9	35.8	9.3
May	5.7	5.0	5.2	15.2	4.6	4.9	14.3	4.3	9.9	10.7	40.0	8.8	9.2	30.5	7.8
June	5.6	4.8	4.9	14.5	4.3	4.8	11.6	4.4	10.6	10.9	38.7	9.0	10.4	36.8	8.7
July	5.7	4.8	4.7	14.6	4.1	5.0	15.0	4.4	11.1	11.2	41.6	9.1	11.0	36.3	9.4
Aug	5.6	4.8	4.9	15.7	4.2	4.8	12.1	4.3	11.3	11.9	46.3	9.4	10.8	38.9	9.0
Sept	5.6	4.8	4.9	16.0	4.3	4.7	13.3	4.1	11.3	11.1	32.7	9.6	11.5	39.7	9.5
Oct	5.5	4.8	4.8	17.6	4.0	4.9	12.0	4.4	9.9	9.5	33.6	7.9	10.2	32.6	8.8
Nov	5.6	5.0	5.2	16.8	4.5	4.9	15.0	4.2	9.4	9.8	32.0	8.2	8.9	29.8	7.5
Dec	5.6	5.0	5.0	16.0	4.3	4.9	15.4	4.3	10.2	11.9	40.6	9.9	8.7	30.4	7.2

[1] Unemployed as percent of civilian labor force in group specified.

Note.—See Note, Table B–38.

Source: Department of Labor, Bureau of Labor Statistics.

TABLE B–40.—*Unemployment by duration and reason, 1950–95*

[Thousands of persons, except as noted; monthly data seasonally adjusted[1]]

Year or month	Unemployment	Duration of unemployment						Reason for unemployment				
		Less than 5 weeks	5–14 weeks	15–26 weeks	27 weeks and over	Average (mean) duration (weeks)	Median duration (weeks)	Job losers[3]			Job leavers	Reentrants	New entrants
								Total	On layoff	Other			
1950	3,288	1,450	1,055	425	357	12.1							
1951	2,055	1,177	574	166	137	9.7							
1952	1,883	1,135	516	148	84	8.4							
1953	1,834	1,142	482	132	78	8.0							
1954	3,532	1,605	1,116	495	317	11.8							
1955	2,852	1,335	815	366	336	13.0							
1956	2,750	1,412	805	301	232	11.3							
1957	2,859	1,408	891	321	239	10.5							
1958	4,602	1,753	1,396	785	667	13.9							
1959	3,740	1,585	1,114	469	571	14.4							
1960	3,852	1,719	1,176	503	454	12.8							
1961	4,714	1,806	1,376	728	804	15.6							
1962	3,911	1,663	1,134	534	585	14.7							
1963	4,070	1,751	1,231	535	553	14.0							
1964	3,786	1,697	1,117	491	482	13.3							
1965	3,366	1,628	983	404	351	11.8							
1966	2,875	1,573	779	287	239	10.4							
1967[2]	2,975	1,634	893	271	177	8.7	2.3	1,229	394	836	438	945	396
1968	2,817	1,594	810	256	156	8.4	4.5	1,070	334	736	431	909	407
1969	2,832	1,629	827	242	133	7.8	4.4	1,017	339	678	436	965	413
1970	4,093	2,139	1,290	428	235	8.6	4.9	1,811	675	1,137	550	1,228	504
1971	5,016	2,245	1,585	668	519	11.3	6.3	2,323	735	1,588	590	1,472	630
1972	4,882	2,242	1,472	601	566	12.0	6.2	2,108	582	1,526	641	1,456	677
1973	4,365	2,224	1,314	483	343	10.0	5.2	1,694	472	1,221	683	1,340	649
1974	5,156	2,604	1,597	574	381	9.8	5.2	2,242	746	1,495	768	1,463	681
1975	7,929	2,940	2,484	1,303	1,203	14.2	8.4	4,386	1,671	2,714	827	1,892	823
1976	7,406	2,844	2,196	1,018	1,348	15.8	8.2	3,679	1,050	2,628	903	1,928	895
1977	6,991	2,919	2,132	913	1,028	14.3	7.0	3,166	865	2,300	909	1,963	953
1978	6,202	2,865	1,923	766	648	11.9	5.9	2,585	712	1,873	874	1,857	885
1979	6,137	2,950	1,946	706	535	10.8	5.4	2,635	851	1,784	880	1,806	817
1980	7,637	3,295	2,470	1,052	820	11.9	6.5	3,947	1,488	2,459	891	1,927	872
1981	8,273	3,449	2,539	1,122	1,162	13.7	6.9	4,267	1,430	2,837	923	2,102	981
1982	10,678	3,883	3,311	1,708	1,776	15.6	8.7	6,268	2,127	4,141	840	2,384	1,185
1983	10,717	3,570	2,937	1,652	2,559	20.0	10.1	6,258	1,780	4,478	830	2,412	1,216
1984	8,539	3,350	2,451	1,104	1,634	18.2	7.9	4,421	1,171	3,250	823	2,184	1,110
1985	8,312	3,498	2,509	1,025	1,280	15.6	6.8	4,139	1,157	2,982	877	2,256	1,039
1986	8,237	3,448	2,557	1,045	1,187	15.0	6.9	4,033	1,090	2,943	1,015	2,160	1,029
1987	7,425	3,246	2,196	943	1,040	14.5	6.5	3,566	943	2,623	965	1,974	920
1988	6,701	3,084	2,007	801	809	13.5	5.9	3,092	851	2,241	983	1,809	816
1989	6,528	3,174	1,978	730	646	11.9	4.8	2,983	850	2,133	1,024	1,843	677
1990	6,874	3,169	2,201	809	695	12.1	5.4	3,322	1,018	2,305	1,014	1,883	654
1991	8,426	3,380	2,724	1,225	1,098	13.8	6.9	4,608	1,279	3,329	979	2,087	753
1992	9,384	3,270	2,760	1,424	1,930	17.9	8.8	5,291	1,246	4,045	975	2,228	890
1993	8,734	3,160	2,522	1,274	1,778	18.1	8.4	4,769	1,104	3,664	946	2,145	874
1994	7,996	2,728	2,408	1,237	1,623	18.8	9.2	3,815	977	2,838	791	2,786	604
1995	7,404	2,700	2,342	1,085	1,278	16.6	8.3	3,476	1,030	2,446	824	2,525	579
1994: Jan	8,740	3,319	2,351	1,308	1,738	18.4	8.5	4,395	1,149	3,246	817	2,824	644
Feb	8,576	2,677	2,670	1,318	1,748	18.8	8.9	4,163	1,091	3,072	852	2,936	636
Mar	8,546	2,749	2,574	1,264	1,792	19.2	9.1	4,068	1,011	3,057	823	2,989	630
Apr	8,385	2,772	2,482	1,237	1,735	19.1	9.2	3,880	979	2,901	810	3,164	679
May	7,996	2,651	2,461	1,160	1,693	19.4	9.2	3,640	811	2,829	796	2,863	611
June	7,903	2,754	2,452	1,193	1,547	18.4	9.1	3,734	931	2,803	788	2,785	498
July	7,993	2,768	2,365	1,234	1,589	19.0	9.2	3,863	1,031	2,832	770	2,766	594
Aug	7,889	2,655	2,572	1,198	1,575	18.9	9.2	3,706	1,012	2,694	786	2,758	621
Sept	7,647	2,675	2,294	1,213	1,555	18.8	9.5	3,574	824	2,750	874	2,620	600
Oct	7,505	2,434	2,256	1,344	1,590	19.3	10.1	3,513	848	2,665	755	2,626	614
Nov	7,315	2,599	2,163	1,187	1,474	18.2	9.1	3,495	881	2,614	710	2,575	578
Dec	7,155	2,587	2,149	1,088	1,368	17.8	8.7	3,442	930	2,512	704	2,525	555
1995: Jan	7,498	2,937	2,122	1,033	1,353	16.7	7.9	3,658	1,061	2,598	694	2,488	597
Feb	7,183	2,600	2,165	1,090	1,207	16.9	7.8	3,339	1,025	2,314	773	2,474	582
Mar	7,237	2,523	2,319	920	1,347	17.5	7.9	3,352	1,032	2,320	811	2,430	604
Apr	7,665	2,629	2,430	1,115	1,390	17.7	8.5	3,532	1,145	2,387	817	2,779	637
May	7,492	2,598	2,304	1,282	1,303	16.9	9.0	3,614	958	2,657	870	2,458	522
June	7,384	2,742	2,348	1,096	1,203	15.6	7.5	3,423	1,066	2,357	834	2,526	540
July	7,559	2,600	2,621	1,023	1,297	16.5	9.1	3,615	1,184	2,431	832	2,593	571
Aug	7,431	2,713	2,434	1,150	1,230	16.3	8.7	3,426	1,036	2,390	871	2,537	574
Sept	7,451	2,868	2,272	1,071	1,281	16.3	8.0	3,367	874	2,492	887	2,578	614
Oct	7,249	2,740	2,348	1,068	1,228	16.2	8.1	3,452	972	2,480	753	2,502	550
Nov	7,432	2,812	2,376	1,048	1,249	16.5	7.9	3,516	1,062	2,455	856	2,509	573
Dec	7,380	2,712	2,434	1,082	1,224	16.2	8.2	3,495	1,001	2,494	937	2,431	609

[1] Because of independent seasonal adjustment of the various series, detail will not add to totals.
[2] Data for 1967 by reason for unemployment are not equal to total unemployment.
[3] Beginning January 1994, job losers and persons who completed temporary jobs.

Note.—Data relate to persons 16 years of age and over.
See footnote 5 and Note, Table B–31.

Source: Department of Labor, Bureau of Labor Statistics.

TABLE B–41.—*Unemployment insurance programs, selected data, 1963–95*

Year or month	All programs			State programs					
	Covered employ-ment[1]	Insured unemploy-ment (weekly aver-age)[2][3]	Total benefits paid (millions of dollars)[2][4]	Insured unem-ployment	Initial claims	Exhaus-tions[5]	Insured unemploy-ment as percent of covered employ-ment	Benefits paid	
								Total (millions of dollars)[4]	Average weekly check (dollars)[6]
	Thousands			Weekly average; thousands					
1963	48,434	[7]1,973	3,026	[7]1,806	[7]298	30	4.3	2,775	35.27
1964	49,637	1,753	2,749	1,605	268	26	3.8	2,522	35.92
1965	51,580	1,450	2,360	1,328	232	21	3.0	2,166	37.19
1966	54,739	1,129	1,891	1,061	203	15	2.3	1,771	39.75
1967	56,342	1,270	2,222	1,205	226	17	2.5	2,092	41.25
1968	57,977	1,187	2,191	1,111	201	16	2.2	2,032	43.43
1969	59,999	1,177	2,299	1,101	200	16	2.1	2,128	46.17
1970	59,526	2,070	4,209	1,805	296	25	3.4	3,849	50.34
1971	59,375	2,608	6,154	2,150	295	39	4.1	4,957	54.02
1972	66,458	2,192	5,491	1,848	261	35	3.5	4,471	56.76
1973	69,897	1,793	4,517	1,632	247	29	2.7	4,008	59.00
1974	72,451	2,558	6,934	2,262	363	37	3.5	5,975	64.25
1975	71,037	4,937	16,802	3,986	478	81	6.0	11,755	70.23
1976	73,459	3,846	12,345	2,991	386	63	4.6	8,975	75.16
1977	76,419	3,308	10,999	2,655	375	55	3.9	8,357	78.79
1978	88,804	2,645	9,007	2,359	346	39	3.3	7,717	83.67
1979	92,062	2,592	9,401	2,434	388	39	2.9	8,613	89.67
1980	92,659	3,837	16,175	3,350	488	59	3.9	13,761	98.95
1981	93,300	3,410	15,287	3,047	460	57	3.5	13,262	106.70
1982	91,628	4,592	24,491	4,059	583	80	4.6	20,649	119.34
1983	91,898	3,774	21,000	3,395	438	80	3.9	17,787	123.59
1984	96,474	2,560	13,838	2,475	377	50	2.8	12,610	123.47
1985	99,186	2,699	15,283	2,617	397	49	2.9	14,131	128.14
1986	101,099	2,739	16,670	2,643	378	52	2.8	15,329	135.65
1987	103,936	2,369	14,929	2,300	328	46	2.4	13,607	140.55
1988	107,157	2,135	13,694	2,081	310	38	2.0	12,565	144.97
1989	109,925	2,205	14,948	2,158	330	37	2.1	13,760	151.73
1990	111,498	2,575	18,721	2,522	388	45	2.4	17,356	161.56
1991	109,613	3,406	26,717	3,342	447	67	3.2	24,526	169.88
1992	110,167	3,348	[9]26,460	3,245	408	74	3.1	23,869	173.64
1993	112,147	2,845	[9]22,950	2,751	341	62	2.6	20,539	179.62
1994	[8]115,255	2,746	22,844	2,670	340	57	2.5	20,401	182.16
1995[P]		2,641	21,909	2,575	356	51	2.3	19,700	187.30
				**	**		**		
1994: Jan		3,521	2,281.1	2,737	368	64	2.6	2,170.7	181.46
Feb		3,517	2,292.7	2,794	351	60	2.6	2,195.4	183.95
Mar		3,406	2,547.5	2,739	340	61	2.6	2,458.9	183.72
Apr		2,880	1,961.8	2,713	349	64	2.5	1,891.6	183.68
May		2,631	1,811.5	2,743	365	60	2.6	1,743.9	182.45
June		2,638	1,856.1	2,745	350	59	2.6	1,770.7	181.44
July		2,581	1,691.0	2,717	348	60	2.5	1,610.8	179.80
Aug		2,579	1,849.0	2,667	328	57	2.5	1,757.1	178.61
Sept		2,185	1,522.6	2,614	323	49	2.4	1,459.8	181.76
Oct		2,205	1,427.2	2,569	328	51	2.4	1,366.0	182.40
Nov		2,344	1,585.3	2,531	329	51	2.3	1,517.6	181.70
Dec		2,515	1,768.3	2,533	326	50	2.3	1,700.8	183.91
1995: Jan		3,283	2,220.9	2,515	335	57	2.3	2,146.9	186.19
Feb		3,182	2,098.0	2,518	338	52	2.3	2,030.4	189.50
Mar		2,957	2,317.2	2,498	342	52	2.3	2,244.1	189.92
Apr		2,728	1,788.4	2,488	352	57	2.3	1,730.0	188.46
May		2,481	1,815.7	2,552	374	52	2.3	1,753.0	187.64
June		2,402	1,718.3	2,633	377	49	2.4	1,660.4	186.74
July		2,638	1,723.0	2,685	375	54	2.4	1,668.0	184.92
Aug		2,465	1,807.5	2,626	342	50	2.4	1,745.9	183.31
Sept		2,201	1,483.5	2,613	351	45	2.4	1,430.5	186.58
Oct		2,297	1,567.1	2,658	362	48	2.4	1,508.1	187.48
Nov		2,427	1,670.6	2,634	374	48	2.4	1,604.3	187.07
Dec[P]		2,674	1,822.0	2,665	365	50	2.4	1,756.8	188.95

** Monthly data are seasonally adjusted.
[1] Includes persons under the State, UCFE (Federal employee, effective January 1955), RRB (Railroad Retirement Board) programs, and UCX (unemployment compensation for ex-servicemembers, effective October 1958) programs.
[2] Includes State, UCFE, RR, UCX, UCV (unemployment compensation for veterans, October 1952–January 1960), and SRA (Servicemen's Re-adjustment Act, September 1944–September 1951) programs. Also includes Federal and State extended benefit programs. Does not include FSB (Federal supplemental benefits), SUA (special unemployment assistance), Federal Supplemental Compensation, and Emergency Unemployment Compensation programs, except as noted in footnote 9.
[3] Covered workers who have completed at least 1 week of unemployment.
[4] Annual data are net amounts and monthly data are gross amounts.
[5] Individuals receiving final payments in benefit year.
[6] For total unemployment only.
[7] Programs include Puerto Rican sugarcane workers for initial claims and insured unemployment beginning July 1963.
[8] Latest data available for all programs combined. Workers covered by State programs account for about 97 percent of wage and salary earners.
[9] Including Emergency Unemployment Compensation and Federal Supplemental Compensation, total benefits paid for 1992 and 1993 would be approximately (in millions of dollars): for 1992, 39,990 and for 1993, 34,876.
Source: Department of Labor, Employment and Training Administration.

TABLE B–42.—*Employees on nonagricultural payrolls, by major industry, 1946–95*

[Thousands of persons; monthly data seasonally adjusted]

Year or month	Total	Goods-producing industries					
		Total	Mining	Construction	Manufacturing		
					Total	Durable goods	Nondurable goods
1946	41,652	17,248	862	1,683	14,703	7,785	6,918
1947	43,857	18,509	955	2,009	15,545	8,358	7,187
1948	44,866	18,774	994	2,198	15,582	8,298	7,285
1949	43,754	17,565	930	2,194	14,441	7,462	6,979
1950	45,197	18,506	901	2,364	15,241	8,066	7,175
1951	47,819	19,959	929	2,637	16,393	9,059	7,334
1952	48,793	20,198	898	2,668	16,632	9,320	7,313
1953	50,202	21,074	866	2,659	17,549	10,080	7,468
1954	48,990	19,751	791	2,646	16,314	9,101	7,213
1955	50,641	20,513	792	2,839	16,882	9,511	7,370
1956	52,369	21,104	822	3,039	17,243	9,802	7,442
1957	52,855	20,967	828	2,962	17,176	9,825	7,351
1958	51,322	19,513	751	2,817	15,945	8,801	7,144
1959	53,270	20,411	732	3,004	16,675	9,342	7,333
1960	54,189	20,434	712	2,926	16,796	9,429	7,367
1961	53,999	19,857	672	2,859	16,326	9,041	7,285
1962	55,549	20,451	650	2,948	16,853	9,450	7,403
1963	56,653	20,640	635	3,010	16,995	9,586	7,410
1964	58,283	21,005	634	3,097	17,274	9,785	7,489
1965	60,763	21,926	632	3,232	18,062	10,374	7,688
1966	63,901	23,158	627	3,317	19,214	11,250	7,963
1967	65,803	23,308	613	3,248	19,447	11,408	8,039
1968	67,897	23,737	606	3,350	19,781	11,594	8,187
1969	70,384	24,361	619	3,575	20,167	11,862	8,304
1970	70,880	23,578	623	3,588	19,367	11,176	8,190
1971	71,211	22,935	609	3,704	18,623	10,604	8,019
1972	73,675	23,668	628	3,889	19,151	11,022	8,129
1973	76,790	24,893	642	4,097	20,154	11,863	8,291
1974	78,265	24,794	697	4,020	20,077	11,897	8,181
1975	76,945	22,600	752	3,525	18,323	10,662	7,661
1976	79,382	23,352	779	3,576	18,997	11,051	7,946
1977	82,471	24,346	813	3,851	19,682	11,570	8,112
1978	86,697	25,585	851	4,229	20,505	12,245	8,259
1979	89,823	26,461	958	4,463	21,040	12,730	8,310
1980	90,406	25,658	1,027	4,346	20,285	12,159	8,127
1981	91,152	25,497	1,139	4,188	20,170	12,082	8,089
1982	89,544	23,812	1,128	3,904	18,780	11,014	7,766
1983	90,152	23,330	952	3,946	18,432	10,707	7,725
1984	94,408	24,718	966	4,380	19,372	11,476	7,896
1985	97,387	24,842	927	4,668	19,248	11,458	7,790
1986	99,344	24,533	777	4,810	18,947	11,195	7,752
1987	101,958	24,674	717	4,958	18,999	11,154	7,845
1988	105,210	25,125	713	5,098	19,314	11,363	7,951
1989	107,895	25,254	692	5,171	19,391	11,394	7,997
1990	109,419	24,905	709	5,120	19,076	11,109	7,968
1991	108,256	23,745	689	4,650	18,406	10,569	7,837
1992	108,604	23,231	635	4,492	18,104	10,277	7,827
1993	110,730	23,352	610	4,668	18,075	10,221	7,854
1994	114,034	23,913	600	5,010	18,303	10,431	7,872
1995ᵖ	116,609	24,228	579	5,246	18,404	10,595	7,809
1994: Jan	112,301	23,583	612	4,820	18,151	10,307	7,844
Feb	112,576	23,631	609	4,846	18,176	10,321	7,855
Mar	113,087	23,725	606	4,904	18,215	10,351	7,864
Apr	113,363	23,816	603	4,969	18,244	10,377	7,867
May	113,638	23,837	599	4,981	18,257	10,388	7,869
June	113,943	23,905	602	5,006	18,297	10,426	7,871
July	114,171	23,922	596	5,029	18,297	10,422	7,875
Aug	114,510	23,981	597	5,038	18,346	10,465	7,881
Sept	114,762	24,030	598	5,077	18,355	10,481	7,874
Oct	114,935	24,081	595	5,088	18,398	10,513	7,885
Nov	115,427	24,175	592	5,144	18,439	10,550	7,889
Dec	115,624	24,230	592	5,166	18,472	10,574	7,898
1995: Jan	115,810	24,293	590	5,201	18,502	10,596	7,906
Feb	116,123	24,324	588	5,213	18,523	10,622	7,901
Mar	116,302	24,370	589	5,256	18,525	10,633	7,892
Apr	116,310	24,331	583	5,242	18,506	10,632	7,874
May	116,248	24,228	582	5,190	18,456	10,611	7,845
June	116,547	24,240	582	5,230	18,428	10,597	7,831
July	116,575	24,156	577	5,226	18,353	10,569	7,784
Aug	116,838	24,165	575	5,233	18,357	10,587	7,770
Sept	116,932	24,157	573	5,262	18,322	10,572	7,750
Oct	117,000	24,159	571	5,287	18,301	10,565	7,736
Novᵖ	117,212	24,134	567	5,295	18,272	10,553	7,719
Decᵖ	117,373	24,184	566	5,302	18,316	10,613	7,703

Note.—Data in Tables B–42 and B–43 are based on reports from employing establishments and relate to full- and part-time wage and salary workers in nonagricultural establishments who received pay for any part of the pay period which includes the 12th of the month. Not comparable with labor force data (Tables B–31 through B–40), which include proprietors, self-employed persons, domestic servants,

See next page for continuation of table.

TABLE B–42.—*Employees on nonagricultural payrolls, by major industry, 1946–95*—Continued

[Thousands of persons; monthly data seasonally adjusted]

Year or month	Total	Service-producing industries							
		Transportation and public utilities	Wholesale trade	Retail trade	Finance, insurance, and real estate	Services	Government		
							Total	Federal	State and local
1946	24,404	4,061	2,298	6,077	1,675	4,697	5,595	2,254	3,341
1947	25,348	4,166	2,478	6,477	1,728	5,025	5,474	1,892	3,582
1948	26,092	4,189	2,612	6,659	1,800	5,181	5,650	1,863	3,787
1949	26,189	4,001	2,610	6,654	1,828	5,239	5,856	1,908	3,948
1950	26,691	4,034	2,643	6,743	1,888	5,356	6,026	1,928	4,098
1951	27,860	4,226	2,735	7,007	1,956	5,547	6,389	2,302	4,087
1952	28,595	4,248	2,821	7,184	2,035	5,699	6,609	2,420	4,188
1953	29,128	4,290	2,862	7,385	2,111	5,835	6,645	2,305	4,340
1954	29,239	4,084	2,875	7,360	2,200	5,969	6,751	2,188	4,563
1955	30,128	4,141	2,934	7,601	2,298	6,240	6,914	2,187	4,727
1956	31,264	4,244	3,027	7,831	2,389	6,497	7,278	2,209	5,069
1957	31,889	4,241	3,037	7,848	2,438	6,708	7,616	2,217	5,399
1958	31,811	3,976	2,989	7,761	2,481	6,765	7,839	2,191	5,648
1959	32,857	4,011	3,092	8,035	2,549	7,087	8,083	2,233	5,850
1960	33,755	4,004	3,153	8,238	2,628	7,378	8,353	2,270	6,083
1961	34,142	3,903	3,142	8,195	2,688	7,619	8,594	2,279	6,315
1962	35,098	3,906	3,207	8,359	2,754	7,982	8,890	2,340	6,550
1963	36,013	3,903	3,258	8,520	2,830	8,277	9,225	2,358	6,868
1964	37,278	3,951	3,347	8,812	2,911	8,660	9,596	2,348	7,248
1965	38,839	4,036	3,477	9,239	2,977	9,036	10,074	2,378	7,696
1966	40,743	4,158	3,608	9,637	3,058	9,498	10,784	2,564	8,220
1967	42,495	4,268	3,700	9,906	3,185	10,045	11,391	2,719	8,672
1968	44,158	4,318	3,791	10,308	3,337	10,567	11,839	2,737	9,102
1969	46,023	4,442	3,919	10,785	3,512	11,169	12,195	2,758	9,437
1970	47,302	4,515	4,006	11,034	3,645	11,548	12,554	2,731	9,823
1971	48,276	4,476	4,014	11,338	3,772	11,797	12,881	2,696	10,185
1972	50,007	4,541	4,127	11,822	3,908	12,276	13,334	2,684	10,649
1973	51,897	4,656	4,291	12,315	4,046	12,857	13,732	2,663	11,068
1974	53,471	4,725	4,447	12,539	4,148	13,441	14,170	2,724	11,446
1975	54,345	4,542	4,430	12,630	4,165	13,892	14,686	2,748	11,937
1976	56,030	4,582	4,562	13,193	4,271	14,551	14,871	2,733	12,138
1977	58,125	4,713	4,723	13,792	4,467	15,302	15,127	2,727	12,399
1978	61,113	4,923	4,985	14,556	4,724	16,252	15,672	2,753	12,919
1979	63,363	5,136	5,221	14,972	4,975	17,112	15,947	2,773	13,174
1980	64,748	5,146	5,292	15,018	5,160	17,890	16,241	2,866	13,375
1981	65,655	5,165	5,375	15,171	5,298	18,615	16,031	2,772	13,259
1982	65,732	5,081	5,295	15,158	5,340	19,021	15,837	2,739	13,098
1983	66,821	4,952	5,283	15,587	5,466	19,664	15,869	2,774	13,096
1984	69,690	5,156	5,568	16,512	5,684	20,746	16,024	2,807	13,216
1985	72,544	5,233	5,727	17,315	5,948	21,927	16,394	2,875	13,519
1986	74,811	5,247	5,761	17,880	6,273	22,957	16,693	2,899	13,794
1987	77,284	5,362	5,848	18,422	6,533	24,110	17,010	2,943	14,067
1988	80,086	5,514	6,030	19,023	6,630	25,504	17,386	2,971	14,415
1989	82,642	5,625	6,187	19,475	6,668	26,907	17,779	2,988	14,791
1990	84,514	5,793	6,173	19,601	6,709	27,934	18,304	3,085	15,219
1991	84,511	5,762	6,081	19,284	6,646	28,336	18,402	2,966	15,436
1992	85,373	5,721	5,997	19,356	6,602	29,052	18,645	2,969	15,676
1993	87,378	5,829	5,981	19,773	6,757	30,197	18,841	2,915	15,926
1994	90,121	6,006	6,140	20,437	6,933	31,488	19,118	2,870	16,247
1995ᴾ	92,381	6,194	6,323	20,840	6,949	32,796	19,279	2,821	16,457
1994: Jan	88,718	5,904	6,053	20,086	6,895	30,798	18,982	2,896	16,086
Feb	88,945	5,929	6,069	20,170	6,912	30,880	18,985	2,892	16,093
Mar	89,362	5,952	6,090	20,305	6,929	31,057	19,029	2,884	16,145
Apr	89,547	5,903	6,106	20,339	6,937	31,207	19,055	2,881	16,174
May	89,801	5,994	6,118	20,356	6,935	31,305	19,093	2,873	16,220
June	90,038	6,008	6,131	20,408	6,946	31,442	19,103	2,866	16,237
July	90,249	6,022	6,138	20,459	6,947	31,573	19,110	2,864	16,246
Aug	90,529	6,045	6,163	20,497	6,948	31,693	19,183	2,861	16,322
Sept	90,732	6,048	6,181	20,565	6,942	31,789	19,207	2,863	16,344
Oct	90,854	6,061	6,195	20,580	6,935	31,888	19,195	2,858	16,337
Nov	91,252	6,092	6,210	20,703	6,937	32,035	19,275	2,854	16,421
Dec	91,394	6,121	6,229	20,759	6,931	32,135	19,219	2,853	16,366
1995: Jan	91,517	6,129	6,251	20,760	6,927	32,228	19,222	2,838	16,384
Feb	91,799	6,156	6,275	20,794	6,929	32,404	19,241	2,831	16,410
Mar	91,932	6,175	6,287	20,760	6,938	32,524	19,248	2,828	16,420
Apr	91,979	6,184	6,300	20,762	6,924	32,548	19,261	2,826	16,435
May	92,020	6,177	6,298	20,747	6,925	32,630	19,243	2,831	16,412
June	92,307	6,192	6,320	20,798	6,930	32,784	19,283	2,838	16,445
July	92,419	6,195	6,333	20,851	6,938	32,820	19,282	2,834	16,448
Aug	92,673	6,217	6,340	20,837	6,947	32,986	19,346	2,825	16,521
Sept	92,775	6,206	6,346	20,899	6,957	33,047	19,320	2,812	16,508
Oct	92,841	6,217	6,359	20,897	6,977	33,076	19,315	2,801	16,514
Novᴾ	93,078	6,240	6,373	20,989	6,991	33,185	19,300	2,800	16,500
Decᴾ	93,189	6,251	6,393	20,969	7,001	33,250	19,325	2,794	16,531

Note (cont'd).—which count persons as employed when they are not at work because of industrial disputes, bad weather, etc., even if they are not paid for the time off; and which are based on a sample of the working-age population. For description and details of the various establishment data, see "Employment and Earnings."

Source: Department of Labor, Bureau of Labor Statistics.

329

TABLE B-43.—*Hours and earnings in private nonagricultural industries, 1959–95*[1]

[Monthly data seasonally adjusted, except as noted]

Year or month	Average weekly hours			Average hourly earnings			Average weekly earnings, total private			
	Total private	Manufacturing		Total private		Manufacturing (current dollars)	Level		Percent change from year earlier[3]	
		Total	Overtime	Current dollars	1982 dollars[2]		Current dollars	1982 dollars[2]	Current dollars	1982 dollars[2]
1959	39.0	40.3	2.7	$2.02	$6.69	$2.19	$78.78	$260.86	4.9	4.2
1960	38.6	39.7	2.5	2.09	6.79	2.26	80.67	261.92	2.4	.4
1961	38.6	39.8	2.4	2.14	6.88	2.32	82.60	265.59	2.4	1.4
1962	38.7	40.4	2.8	2.22	7.07	2.39	85.91	273.60	4.0	3.0
1963	38.8	40.5	2.8	2.28	7.17	2.45	88.46	278.18	3.0	1.7
1964	38.7	40.7	3.1	2.36	7.33	2.53	91.33	283.63	3.2	2.0
1965	38.8	41.2	3.6	2.46	7.52	2.61	95.45	291.90	4.5	2.9
1966	38.6	41.4	3.9	2.56	7.62	2.71	98.82	294.11	3.5	.8
1967	38.0	40.6	3.4	2.68	7.72	2.82	101.84	293.49	3.1	−.2
1968	37.8	40.7	3.6	2.85	7.89	3.01	107.73	298.42	5.8	1.7
1969	37.7	40.6	3.6	3.04	7.98	3.19	114.61	300.81	6.4	.8
1970	37.1	39.8	3.0	3.23	8.03	3.35	119.83	298.08	4.6	−.9
1971	36.9	39.9	2.9	3.45	8.21	3.57	127.31	303.12	6.2	1.7
1972	37.0	40.5	3.5	3.70	8.53	3.82	136.90	315.44	7.5	4.1
1973	36.9	40.7	3.8	3.94	8.55	4.09	145.39	315.38	6.2	−.0
1974	36.5	40.0	3.3	4.24	8.28	4.42	154.76	302.27	6.4	−4.2
1975	36.1	39.5	2.6	4.53	8.12	4.83	163.53	293.06	5.7	−3.0
1976	36.1	40.1	3.1	4.86	8.24	5.22	175.45	297.37	7.3	1.5
1977	36.0	40.3	3.5	5.25	8.36	5.68	189.00	300.96	7.7	1.2
1978	35.8	40.4	3.6	5.69	8.40	6.17	203.70	300.89	7.8	−.0
1979	35.7	40.2	3.3	6.16	8.17	6.70	219.91	291.66	8.0	−3.1
1980	35.3	39.7	2.8	6.66	7.78	7.27	235.10	274.65	6.9	−5.8
1981	35.2	39.8	2.8	7.25	7.69	7.99	255.20	270.63	8.5	−1.5
1982	34.8	38.9	2.3	7.68	7.68	8.49	267.26	267.26	4.7	−1.2
1983	35.0	40.1	3.0	8.02	7.79	8.83	280.70	272.52	5.0	2.0
1984	35.2	40.7	3.4	8.32	7.80	9.19	292.86	274.73	4.3	.8
1985	34.9	40.5	3.3	8.57	7.77	9.54	299.09	271.16	2.1	−1.3
1986	34.8	40.7	3.4	8.76	7.81	9.73	304.85	271.94	1.9	.3
1987	34.8	41.0	3.7	8.98	7.73	9.91	312.50	269.16	2.5	−1.0
1988	34.7	41.1	3.9	9.28	7.69	10.19	322.02	266.79	3.0	−.9
1989	34.6	41.0	3.8	9.66	7.64	10.48	334.24	264.22	3.8	−1.0
1990	34.5	40.8	3.6	10.01	7.52	10.83	345.35	259.47	3.3	−1.8
1991	34.3	40.7	3.6	10.32	7.45	11.18	353.98	255.40	2.5	−1.6
1992	34.4	41.0	3.8	10.57	7.41	11.46	363.61	254.99	2.7	−.2
1993	34.5	41.4	4.1	10.83	7.39	11.74	373.64	254.87	2.8	−.0
1994	34.7	42.0	4.7	11.13	7.41	12.06	386.21	256.96	3.4	.8
1995 *p*	34.5	41.5	4.4	11.46	7.42	12.35	395.37	255.90	2.4	−.4
1994: Jan	34.7	41.7	4.4	11.00	7.41	11.94	381.70	257.21	4.0	1.6
Feb	34.4	41.3	4.5	11.02	7.41	12.00	379.09	254.94	2.5	.1
Mar	34.7	42.2	4.7	11.03	7.40	11.99	382.74	256.87	3.5	1.2
Apr	34.7	42.1	4.7	11.05	7.40	12.00	383.44	256.83	3.5	1.3
May	34.7	42.0	4.6	11.08	7.41	12.00	384.48	257.18	2.8	.7
June	34.7	42.0	4.7	11.09	7.39	12.03	384.82	256.55	3.1	.6
July	34.7	42.0	4.7	11.13	7.39	12.06	386.21	256.45	3.3	.6
Aug	34.6	42.0	4.7	11.14	7.37	12.09	385.44	255.09	2.2	−.6
Sept	34.7	42.1	4.8	11.18	7.38	12.12	387.95	256.24	3.7	.7
Oct	34.9	42.1	4.7	11.25	7.42	12.14	392.63	258.99	4.3	1.7
Nov	34.6	42.1	4.8	11.24	7.40	12.17	388.90	256.02	3.1	.4
Dec	34.7	42.1	4.8	11.27	7.40	12.18	391.07	256.94	3.1	.4
1995: Jan	34.8	42.2	4.9	11.29	7.39	12.21	392.89	257.30	2.7	−.2
Feb	34.6	42.1	4.8	11.32	7.39	12.24	391.67	255.83	3.3	.3
Mar	34.6	42.0	4.7	11.34	7.38	12.25	392.36	255.44	2.6	−.4
Apr	34.6	41.5	4.5	11.40	7.40	12.28	394.44	255.96	2.5	−.7
May	34.2	41.4	4.4	11.37	7.36	12.28	388.85	251.85	1.1	−2.1
June	34.4	41.5	4.2	11.43	7.39	12.32	393.19	254.33	2.4	−.6
July	34.6	41.3	4.3	11.50	7.43	12.40	397.90	257.21	3.0	.2
Aug	34.4	41.5	4.3	11.48	7.41	12.41	394.91	254.95	2.5	−.0
Sept	34.5	41.7	4.5	11.54	7.44	12.43	398.13	256.53	2.5	.0
Oct	34.6	41.5	4.4	11.59	7.45	12.45	401.01	257.72	2.0	−.6
Nov *p*	34.4	41.5	4.4	11.58	7.44	12.47	398.35	256.01	2.3	−.1
Dec *p*	34.3	41.2	4.3	11.62	7.45	12.49	398.57	255.49	2.2	−.3

[1] For production or nonsupervisory workers; total includes private industry groups shown in Table B–42.
[2] Current dollars divided by the consumer price index for urban wage earners and clerical workers on a 1982=100 base.
[3] Percent changes are based on data that are not seasonally adjusted.

Note.—See Note, Table B–42.

Source: Department of Labor, Bureau of Labor Statistics.

TABLE B–44.—*Employment cost index, private industry, 1980–95*

Year and month	Total private: Total compensation	Wages and salaries	Benefits[1]	Goods-producing: Total compensation	Wages and salaries	Benefits[1]	Service-producing: Total compensation	Wages and salaries	Benefits[1]	Manufacturing: Total compensation	Wages and salaries	Benefits[1]	Nonmanufacturing: Total compensation	Wages and salaries	Benefits[1]
						Index, June 1989=100; not seasonally adjusted									
December:															
1980	64.8	67.1	59.4	66.7	69.7	60.5	63.3	65.3	58.4	66.0	68.9	59.9	64.2	66.2	59.1
1981	71.2	73.0	66.6	73.3	75.7	68.2	69.5	71.1	65.1	72.5	74.9	67.5	70.4	72.1	66.1
1982	75.8	77.6	71.4	77.8	80.0	73.2	74.1	75.9	69.6	76.9	79.1	72.4	75.1	76.8	70.6
1983	80.1	81.4	76.7	81.6	83.2	78.3	78.9	80.2	75.2	80.8	82.5	77.5	79.6	81.0	76.2
1984	84.0	84.8	81.7	85.4	86.4	83.2	82.9	83.7	80.4	85.0	86.1	82.7	83.4	84.2	81.1
1985	87.3	88.3	84.6	88.2	89.4	85.7	86.6	87.7	83.6	87.8	89.2	85.0	87.0	88.0	84.4
1986	90.1	91.1	87.5	91.0	92.3	88.3	89.3	90.3	86.8	90.7	92.1	87.5	89.7	90.6	87.5
1987	93.1	94.1	90.5	93.8	95.2	90.9	92.6	93.4	90.2	93.4	95.2	89.8	92.9	93.7	91.0
1988	97.6	98.0	96.7	97.9	98.2	97.3	97.3	97.8	96.1	97.6	98.1	96.6	97.5	97.8	96.8
1989	102.3	102.0	102.6	102.1	102.0	102.6	102.3	102.2	102.6	102.0	101.9	102.3	102.3	102.2	102.8
1990	107.0	106.1	109.4	107.0	105.8	109.9	107.0	106.3	109.0	107.2	106.2	109.5	106.9	106.1	109.3
1991	111.7	110.0	116.2	111.9	109.7	116.7	111.6	110.2	115.7	112.2	110.3	116.1	111.5	109.8	116.2
1992	115.6	112.9	122.2	116.1	112.8	123.4	115.2	113.0	121.2	116.5	113.7	122.6	115.1	112.6	122.0
1993	119.8	116.4	128.3	120.6	116.1	130.3	119.3	116.6	126.7	121.3	117.3	130.0	119.0	116.0	127.4
1994	123.5	119.7	133.0	124.3	119.6	134.8	122.8	119.7	131.5	125.1	120.8	134.3	122.6	119.1	132.3
1994: Mar	121.0	117.2	130.7	121.8	116.9	132.7	120.4	117.3	128.9	122.5	118.0	132.0	120.3	116.8	129.9
June	122.0	118.1	131.7	123.0	118.0	133.9	121.2	118.2	129.7	123.5	119.0	133.0	121.2	117.7	130.8
Sept	123.0	119.1	132.8	123.9	118.9	134.8	122.3	119.2	131.2	124.4	120.0	133.9	122.3	118.7	132.2
Dec	123.5	119.7	133.0	124.3	119.6	134.8	122.8	119.7	131.5	125.1	120.8	134.3	122.6	119.1	132.3
1995: Mar	124.5	120.6	134.5	125.3	120.4	135.9	123.9	120.7	133.2	126.2	121.9	135.4	123.7	120.0	133.9
June	125.4	121.5	135.1	125.9	121.4	135.9	124.9	121.6	134.1	126.9	122.9	135.2	124.6	120.9	134.7
Sept	126.2	122.4	135.6	126.5	122.1	136.2	125.8	122.6	134.8	127.3	123.5	135.5	125.5	121.9	135.4
						Index, June 1989=100; seasonally adjusted									
1994: Mar	120.8	117.3	130.2	121.5	116.9	132.2	120.2	117.4	128.5	122.3	118.0	131.3	120.2	116.8	129.5
June	121.8	118.3	131.5	122.7	118.0	133.5	121.1	118.2	129.6	123.4	119.0	132.7	121.2	117.7	130.7
Sept	122.8	119.1	132.8	123.7	118.9	134.7	122.1	119.1	131.2	124.5	120.0	133.9	122.2	118.6	132.2
Dec	123.6	119.8	133.8	124.5	119.6	135.8	122.9	119.7	132.0	125.4	120.8	135.3	122.8	119.2	132.9
1995: Mar	124.3	120.6	134.0	125.1	120.4	135.4	123.8	120.8	132.8	126.0	121.9	134.7	123.6	120.0	133.5
June	125.2	121.5	134.7	125.8	121.4	135.5	124.8	121.6	134.1	126.9	122.9	134.9	124.6	120.9	134.6
Sept	125.9	122.3	135.4	126.5	122.1	136.1	125.6	122.4	134.7	127.4	123.5	135.5	125.3	121.8	135.4
						Percent change from 12 months earlier, not seasonally adjusted									
December:															
1980	9.6	9.1	11.7	9.9	9.4	10.8	9.7	8.8	12.5	9.8	9.4	10.5	9.7	8.9	12.6
1981	9.9	8.8	12.1	9.9	8.6	12.7	9.8	8.9	11.5	9.8	8.7	12.7	9.7	8.9	11.8
1982	6.5	6.3	7.2	6.1	5.7	7.3	6.6	6.8	6.9	6.1	5.6	7.3	6.7	6.5	6.8
1983	5.7	4.9	7.4	4.9	4.0	7.0	6.5	5.7	8.0	5.1	4.3	7.0	6.0	5.5	7.9
1984	4.9	4.2	6.5	4.7	3.8	6.3	5.1	4.4	6.9	5.2	4.4	6.7	4.8	4.0	6.4
1985	3.9	4.1	3.5	3.3	3.5	3.0	4.5	4.8	4.0	3.3	3.6	2.8	4.3	4.5	4.1
1986	3.2	3.2	3.4	3.2	3.2	3.0	3.1	3.0	3.8	3.3	3.3	2.9	3.1	3.0	3.7
1987	3.3	3.3	3.4	3.1	3.1	2.9	3.7	3.4	3.9	3.0	3.4	2.6	3.6	3.4	4.0
1988	4.8	4.1	6.9	4.4	3.2	7.0	5.1	4.7	6.5	4.5	3.0	7.6	5.0	4.4	6.4
1989	4.8	4.1	6.1	4.3	3.9	5.4	5.1	4.5	6.8	4.5	3.9	5.9	4.9	4.5	6.2
1990	4.6	4.0	6.6	4.8	3.7	7.1	4.6	4.0	6.2	5.1	4.2	7.0	4.5	3.8	6.3
1991	4.4	3.7	6.2	4.6	3.7	6.2	4.3	3.7	6.1	4.7	3.9	6.0	4.3	3.5	6.3
1992	3.5	2.6	5.2	3.8	2.8	5.7	3.2	2.5	4.8	3.8	3.1	5.6	3.2	2.6	5.0
1993	3.6	3.1	5.0	3.9	2.9	5.6	3.6	3.2	4.5	4.1	3.2	6.0	3.4	3.0	4.4
1994	3.1	2.8	3.7	3.1	3.0	3.5	2.9	2.7	2.7	3.8	3.1	3.0	3.0	2.7	3.8
1994: Mar	3.3	2.9	4.4	3.2	2.7	4.2	3.4	3.0	4.5	3.3	2.9	4.1	3.4	3.0	4.6
June	3.4	3.1	3.9	3.3	3.1	3.8	3.3	3.1	4.1	3.2	3.0	3.4	3.4	3.1	4.2
Sept	3.3	2.9	4.0	3.3	3.1	3.7	3.2	2.8	4.4	3.2	3.2	3.3	3.3	2.9	4.5
Dec	3.1	2.8	3.7	3.1	3.0	3.5	2.9	2.7	2.7	3.8	3.1	3.0	3.0	2.7	3.8
1995: Mar	2.9	2.9	2.9	2.9	3.0	2.4	2.9	2.9	3.3	3.0	3.3	2.6	2.8	2.7	3.1
June	2.8	2.9	2.6	2.4	2.9	1.5	3.1	2.9	3.4	2.8	3.3	1.7	2.8	2.7	3.0
Sept	2.6	2.8	2.1	2.1	2.7	1.0	2.9	2.7	2.4	2.3	2.9	1.2	2.6	2.7	2.4
						Percent change from 3 months earlier, seasonally adjusted									
1994: Mar	0.8	0.8	0.9	0.7	0.7	0.8	0.7	0.6	1.0	0.6	0.6	0.2	0.8	0.6	1.3
June	.8	.9	1.0	1.0	.9	1.0	.7	.7	.9	.9	.8	1.1	.8	.8	.9
Sept	.8	.7	1.0	.8	.8	.9	.8	.8	1.2	.9	.8	.9	.8	.8	1.1
Dec	.7	.6	.8	.6	.6	.8	.7	.5	.6	.7	.7	1.0	.5	.5	.5
1995: Mar	.6	.7	.1	.5	.7	-.3	.7	.9	.6	.5	.9	-.4	.7	.7	.5
June	.7	.7	.5	.6	.8	.1	.8	.7	1.0	.7	.8	.1	.8	.8	.8
Sept	.6	.7	.5	.6	.6	.4	.6	.7	.4	.4	.5	.4	.6	.7	.6

[1] Employer costs for employee benefits.

Note.—The employment cost index is a measure of the change in the cost of labor, free from the influence of employment shifts among occupations and industries.

Data exclude farm and household workers.

Through December 1981, percent changes are based on unrounded data; thereafter changes are based on indexes as published.

Source: Department of Labor, Bureau of Labor Statistics.

TABLE B-45.—*Productivity and related data, business sector, 1959-95*

[Index numbers, 1992=100; quarterly data seasonally adjusted]

Year or quarter	Output per hour of all persons		Output[1]		Hours of all persons[2]		Compensation per hour[3]		Real compensation per hour[4]		Unit labor costs		Implicit price deflator[5]	
	Business sector	Nonfarm business sector	Business sector	Nonfarm business sector	Business sector	Nonfarm business sector	Business sector	Nonfarm business sector	Business sector	Nonfarm business sector	Business sector	Nonfarm business sector	Business sector	Nonfarm business sector
1959	49.8	54.1	33.8	33.5	67.8	61.9	12.9	13.7	62.1	65.8	25.9	25.3	25.5	25.0
1960	50.5	54.7	34.3	34.0	67.9	62.3	13.4	14.3	63.7	67.6	26.6	26.1	25.8	25.3
1961	52.2	56.4	34.9	347	66.8	61.5	14.0	14.7	65.5	69.2	26.7	26.2	26.1	25.5
1962	54.8	59.0	37.1	37.1	67.8	62.8	14.6	15.3	67.9	71.3	26.7	26.0	26.4	25.8
1963	56.9	61.0	38.8	38.7	68.2	63.5	15.2	15.9	69.6	72.9	26.7	26.1	26.5	26.0
1964	59.6	63.7	41.3	41.4	69.2	65.0	16.0	16.6	72.3	75.3	26.8	26.1	26.8	26.3
1965	61.8	65.7	44.2	44.3	71.4	67.4	16.6	17.2	73.9	76.5	26.8	26.2	27.3	26.7
1966	64.4	68.0	47.1	47.4	73.1	69.7	17.7	18.2	76.8	78.7	27.5	26.7	28.0	27.3
1967	65.9	69.2	48.0	48.2	72.9	69.7	18.7	19.2	78.7	80.8	28.4	27.8	28.8	28.2
1968	68.2	71.6	50.4	50.8	73.9	70.9	20.3	20.8	81.7	83.7	29.7	29.0	29.9	29.3
1969	68.7	71.7	52.0	52.3	75.7	72.9	21.7	22.2	83.1	84.8	31.7	30.9	31.1	30.5
1970	69.8	72.6	51.8	52.2	74.3	71.8	23.4	23.8	84.6	86.0	33.5	32.7	32.6	31.9
1971	72.7	75.6	53.8	54.1	74.0	71.6	24.9	25.3	86.2	87.7	34.2	33.5	34.9	33.3
1972	75.2	78.2	57.4	57.9	76.3	74.0	26.5	27.0	88.9	90.5	35.2	34.5	35.2	34.3
1973	77.6	80.7	61.3	62.1	79.0	76.9	28.8	29.2	90.9	92.2	37.1	36.1	37.0	35.5
1974	76.6	79.4	60.6	61.1	79.1	77.0	31.6	32.1	89.9	91.2	41.2	40.4	40.4	39.1
1975	79.0	81.5	59.9	60.1	75.8	73.7	34.8	35.3	90.7	92.1	44.1	43.3	44.3	43.2
1976	82.2	84.5	64.0	64.3	77.9	76.1	38.0	38.4	93.6	94.6	46.2	45.4	46.6	45.6
1977	83.8	85.8	67.8	68.0	80.9	79.2	41.0	41.4	95.0	95.9	48.9	48.3	49.3	48.6
1978	84.5	87.0	71.6	72.3	84.8	83.2	44.7	45.2	96.3	97.3	53.0	52.0	53.1	51.9
1979	84.3	86.4	73.8	74.3	87.5	86.1	49.1	49.5	94.9	95.7	58.3	57.3	57.7	56.4
1980	84.1	86.0	72.9	73.5	86.8	85.4	54.4	54.8	92.7	93.4	64.7	63.8	62.9	61.9
1981	85.8	87.0	74.9	74.8	87.3	86.0	59.6	60.2	92.0	92.9	69.5	69.1	68.6	67.9
1982	85.2	86.3	72.6	72.4	85.2	83.9	64.1	64.6	93.1	93.9	75.2	74.9	72.6	72.2
1983	88.0	89.9	76.2	76.8	86.6	85.4	66.7	67.3	93.9	94.9	75.7	74.9	75.3	74.7
1984	90.2	91.5	82.5	82.8	91.5	90.5	69.6	70.2	94.0	94.8	77.2	76.8	77.7	77.0
1985	91.9	92.4	85.9	85.8	93.4	92.8	73.1	73.5	95.3	95.8	79.5	79.5	79.9	79.7
1986	94.2	94.9	88.6	88.7	94.0	93.5	76.9	77.3	98.4	98.9	81.6	81.4	81.6	81.4
1987	94.1	94.7	91.1	91.4	96.8	96.5	79.9	80.2	98.6	99.0	84.9	84.7	83.8	83.5
1988	94.6	95.3	94.6	95.1	100.0	99.8	83.5	83.6	99.0	99.2	88.2	87.8	86.8	86.4
1989	95.4	95.8	97.8	98.1	102.5	102.4	85.8	85.8	97.1	97.1	89.9	89.6	90.5	90.0
1990	96.2	96.3	98.7	98.8	102.6	102.7	90.8	90.6	97.4	97.3	94.3	94.1	94.0	93.8
1991	96.7	96.9	96.9	97.1	100.3	100.2	95.1	95.1	97.9	97.9	98.3	98.1	97.7	97.6
1992	100.0	100.0	100.0	100.0	100.0	100.0	100.0	100.0	100.0	100.0	100.0	100.0	100.0	100.0
1993	100.2	100.2	102.6	102.9	102.4	102.7	102.6	102.3	99.6	99.3	102.4	102.1	102.5	102.5
1994	101.0	100.7	106.9	106.9	105.9	106.2	104.8	104.5	99.2	98.9	103.8	103.8	104.8	104.9
1990:I	96.3	96.4	99.3	99.6	103.2	103.2	88.6	88.5	97.1	96.9	92.1	91.8	92.5	92.2
II	96.7	96.7	99.5	99.7	102.9	103.1	90.4	90.1	98.0	97.7	93.5	93.2	93.7	93.4
III	96.3	96.3	98.7	98.8	102.4	102.6	91.5	91.3	97.6	97.4	95.0	94.8	94.5	94.3
IV	95.5	95.5	97.2	97.2	101.8	101.8	92.4	92.3	96.9	96.8	96.8	96.7	95.5	95.4
1991:I	95.8	96.0	96.3	96.5	100.5	100.5	93.3	93.3	97.1	97.1	97.4	97.2	96.7	96.7
II	96.6	96.8	96.9	97.0	100.2	100.2	94.7	94.7	97.9	97.9	98.0	97.8	97.4	97.3
III	97.0	97.3	97.2	97.4	100.2	100.1	95.7	95.7	98.2	98.2	98.6	98.4	98.1	98.0
IV	97.4	97.5	97.3	97.5	99.9	100.0	96.8	96.7	98.5	98.5	99.4	99.2	98.6	98.5
1992:I	99.3	99.3	98.8	98.8	99.5	99.6	98.6	98.5	99.7	99.6	99.3	99.3	99.3	99.2
II	99.9	100.0	99.6	99.6	99.7	99.6	99.5	99.6	99.8	99.9	99.9	99.6	99.7	99.8
III	99.7	99.6	99.8	99.8	100.1	100.1	100.7	100.7	100.3	100.2	101.0	101.0	100.1	100.1
IV	101.1	101.1	101.7	101.8	100.6	100.7	101.2	101.2	99.9	99.9	100.1	100.1	100.9	100.9
1993:I	100.2	100.1	101.4	101.6	101.3	101.5	101.6	101.4	99.6	99.4	101.4	101.3	101.7	101.8
II	99.8	99.7	102.0	102.2	102.2	102.5	102.5	102.1	99.7	99.3	102.6	102.4	102.3	102.4
III	100.1	100.2	102.8	103.2	102.6	103.0	103.0	102.6	99.8	99.4	102.9	102.9	102.7	102.7
IV	100.8	100.6	104.3	104.6	103.5	103.9	103.3	102.9	99.2	98.9	102.5	102.3	103.3	103.3
1994:I	100.3	100.0	104.8	104.8	104.5	104.8	104.2	103.7	99.6	99.1	103.8	103.7	103.9	103.9
II	100.7	100.4	106.5	106.6	105.8	106.1	104.5	104.3	99.3	99.0	103.9	103.8	104.4	104.5
III	101.4	101.1	107.6	107.7	106.2	106.5	104.9	104.6	98.8	98.5	103.5	103.4	105.1	105.3
IV	101.5	101.3	108.7	108.8	107.1	107.4	105.7	105.4	99.0	98.7	104.1	104.1	105.6	105.7
1995:I	101.1	101.0	108.8	109.0	107.6	107.9	106.6	106.4	99.0	98.9	105.4	105.3	106.3	106.5
II	101.9	101.8	108.9	109.1	106.9	107.2	108.0	107.8	99.6	99.3	106.0	105.9	106.9	107.0
III	102.2	102.1	110.1	110.3	107.7	108.0	109.1	108.8	100.0	99.8	106.8	106.5	107.6	107.6

[1] Output refers to real gross domestic product originating in the sector.

[2] Hours at work of all persons engaged in the sector, including hours of proprietors and unpaid family workers. Estimates based primarily on establishment data.

[3] Wages and salaries of employees plus employers' contributions for social insurance and private benefit plans. Also includes an estimate of wages, salaries, and supplemental payments for the self-employed.

[4] Hourly compensation divided by the consumer price index for all urban consumers.

[5] Current dollar output divided by the output index.

Note.—Data shown in this table reflect the January 1996 comprehensive revisions of the national income and product accounts released by the Department of Commerce and are computed using chain-type output indexes. The data also reflect the incorporation of the 1994 Hours at Work Survey.

Source: Department of Labor, Bureau of Labor Statistics.

TABLE B–46.—*Changes in productivity and related data, business sector, 1960–95*

[Percent change from preceding period; quarterly data at seasonally adjusted annual rates]

Year or quarter	Output per hour of all persons		Output[1]		Hours of all persons[2]		Compensation per hour[3]		Real compensation per hour[4]		Unit labor costs		Implicit price deflator[5]	
	Business sector	Nonfarm business sector	Business sector	Nonfarm business sector	Business sector	Nonfarm business sector	Business sector	Nonfarm business sector	Business sector	Nonfarm business sector	Business sector	Nonfarm business sector	Business sector	Nonfarm business sector
1960	1.5	1.1	1.6	1.6	0.1	0.6	4.4	4.4	2.6	2.7	2.8	3.3	1.3	1.1
1961	3.4	3.1	1.7	1.9	-1.7	-1.2	4.0	3.4	2.9	2.3	.5	.2	1.0	.9
1962	4.8	4.7	6.4	6.9	1.6	2.1	4.7	4.1	3.6	3.1	-.1	-.5	.9	.8
1963	4.0	3.4	4.5	4.5	.5	1.0	3.8	3.6	2.5	2.2	-.2	.1	.7	.9
1964	4.8	4.4	6.4	6.8	1.6	2.3	5.2	4.6	3.9	3.3	.5	.2	1.0	1.2
1965	3.7	3.1	7.0	7.0	3.2	3.8	3.8	3.3	2.2	1.7	.2	.2	1.7	1.5
1966	4.2	3.5	6.6	7.1	2.4	3.5	6.9	5.8	3.9	2.9	2.6	2.2	2.6	2.3
1967	2.4	1.8	2.0	1.7	-.3	-.1	5.7	5.9	2.6	2.7	3.3	4.0	2.8	3.3
1968	3.6	3.5	5.0	5.2	1.4	1.7	8.2	7.9	3.8	3.5	4.4	4.3	3.8	3.9
1969	.6	.1	3.0	3.0	2.4	2.9	7.3	6.8	1.7	1.3	6.6	6.7	4.3	4.2
1970	1.6	1.4	-.3	-.2	-1.8	-1.6	7.5	7.2	1.7	1.4	5.8	5.8	4.6	4.5
1971	4.3	4.0	3.8	3.8	-.4	-.3	6.5	6.5	2.0	2.0	2.1	2.3	4.5	4.6
1972	3.4	3.5	6.6	6.9	3.2	3.3	6.3	6.5	3.0	3.2	2.9	2.9	3.4	2.9
1973	3.2	3.2	6.9	7.3	3.6	3.9	8.6	8.2	2.3	1.9	5.2	4.9	5.2	3.6
1974	-1.3	-1.6	-1.2	-1.5	.1	.1	9.9	9.9	-1.1	-1.0	11.3	11.7	9.0	10.0
1975	3.1	2.7	-1.2	-1.7	-4.2	-4.3	10.2	10.1	.9	.9	6.8	7.3	9.8	10.6
1976	4.0	3.7	6.9	7.1	2.8	3.2	9.1	8.7	3.2	2.7	4.9	4.7	5.1	5.6
1977	2.0	1.5	5.9	5.7	3.8	4.1	8.1	8.0	1.5	1.4	5.9	6.4	5.9	6.4
1978	.7	1.3	5.6	6.4	4.8	5.0	9.1	9.1	1.4	1.4	8.2	7.7	7.8	6.9
1979	-.2	-.7	3.0	2.8	3.2	3.5	9.8	9.5	-1.4	-1.7	10.0	10.3	8.6	8.6
1980	-.3	-.4	-1.1	-1.2	-.9	-.8	10.8	10.8	-2.4	-2.4	11.1	11.2	9.0	9.8
1981	2.0	1.2	2.7	1.9	.6	.7	9.5	9.7	-.7	-.6	7.3	8.4	9.0	9.6
1982	-.7	-.9	-3.1	-3.3	-2.4	-2.4	7.5	7.4	1.2	1.2	8.2	8.3	5.9	6.4
1983	3.3	4.2	5.0	6.1	1.7	1.8	4.1	4.2	.8	1.0	.8	0	3.7	3.4
1984	2.5	1.8	8.2	7.9	5.6	5.9	4.5	4.3	.2	-.0	2.0	2.4	3.2	3.1
1985	1.9	1.0	4.1	3.6	2.1	2.5	4.9	4.6	1.3	1.0	3.0	3.6	2.8	3.4
1986	2.6	2.7	3.2	3.4	.6	.7	5.2	5.2	3.3	3.3	2.6	2.5	2.2	2.2
1987	-.1	-.2	2.9	3.0	3.0	3.2	3.9	3.7	.2	.1	4.0	4.0	2.7	2.6
1988	.5	.6	3.8	4.1	3.3	3.5	4.5	4.3	.4	.1	4.0	3.7	3.5	3.4
1989	.8	.5	3.4	3.2	2.5	2.6	2.8	2.7	-1.9	-2.1	1.9	2.1	4.2	4.2
1990	.8	.5	.9	.7	.1	.2	5.8	5.5	.4	.1	4.9	5.0	4.0	4.2
1991	.5	.7	-1.8	-1.8	-2.3	-2.4	4.8	4.9	.5	.7	4.2	4.3	3.9	4.1
1992	3.4	3.2	3.2	3.0	-.3	-.2	5.2	5.2	2.1	2.1	1.7	1.9	2.4	2.4
1993	.2	.2	2.6	2.9	2.4	2.7	2.6	2.3	-.4	-.7	2.4	2.1	2.5	2.5
1994	.7	.5	4.2	4.0	3.4	3.4	2.2	2.2	-.4	-.4	1.4	1.6	2.2	2.3
1990: I	2.4	1.4	4.5	4.2	2.1	2.7	7.0	6.1	0	-.9	4.6	4.6	4.3	4.6
II	1.7	1.1	.9	.4	-.8	-.6	8.0	7.6	3.7	3.4	6.2	6.5	5.1	5.3
III	-1.5	-1.6	-3.4	-3.4	-2.0	-1.8	5.3	5.4	-1.7	-1.6	6.9	7.1	3.7	3.9
IV	-3.5	-3.2	-6.0	-6.3	-2.5	-3.2	4.0	4.4	-2.8	-2.4	7.8	7.9	4.3	4.8
1991: I	1.5	2.0	-3.4	-3.0	-4.8	-5.0	4.0	4.2	.9	1.1	2.4	2.1	5.2	5.5
II	3.5	3.4	2.3	2.1	-1.2	-1.3	5.8	6.0	3.3	3.5	2.2	2.5	2.8	2.5
III	1.5	1.9	1.3	1.7	-.2	-.2	4.4	4.5	1.2	1.4	2.8	2.6	2.8	3.0
IV	1.7	1.2	.7	.5	-.9	-.6	4.7	4.4	1.3	1.0	3.0	3.2	2.1	2.1
1992: I	8.1	7.3	6.2	5.6	-1.7	-1.5	7.8	7.7	4.9	4.8	-.3	.4	2.8	3.0
II	2.5	2.8	3.2	3.1	.7	.3	3.7	4.2	.5	1.1	1.2	1.4	1.9	2.1
III	-.7	-1.2	.8	.7	1.6	2.0	4.8	4.4	1.7	1.3	5.6	5.7	1.5	1.4
IV	5.6	6.1	7.9	8.4	2.2	2.2	2.1	2.1	-1.3	-1.3	-3.3	-3.7	3.0	3.2
1993: I	-3.7	-3.9	-1.1	-.9	2.6	3.1	1.6	1.0	-1.4	-2.0	5.4	5.1	3.4	3.8
II	-1.3	-1.7	2.2	2.4	3.6	4.2	3.4	2.7	.3	-.3	4.8	4.5	2.5	2.1
III	1.3	2.1	3.0	4.1	1.7	2.0	2.2	2.0	.5	.3	.9	-.1	1.4	1.2
IV	2.7	1.6	6.3	5.3	3.5	3.6	1.1	1.1	-2.1	-2.1	-1.6	-.5	2.4	2.6
1994: I	-1.9	-2.5	1.8	.9	3.7	3.5	3.4	3.3	1.3	1.1	5.4	5.9	2.4	2.5
II	1.4	1.9	6.7	6.8	5.3	4.8	1.5	2.1	-1.0	-.4	.1	.2	1.8	2.2
III	2.8	2.6	4.1	4.2	1.3	1.6	1.5	1.2	-2.0	-2.3	-1.3	-1.4	2.6	2.9
IV	.7	.9	4.0	4.2	3.3	3.3	2.9	3.3	.7	1.0	2.3	2.4	2.0	1.8
1995: I	-1.6	-1.1	.6	.8	2.2	1.9	3.4	3.7	.3	.6	5.0	4.9	2.8	2.9
II	3.0	3.0	.3	.5	-2.5	-2.4	5.6	5.4	2.1	2.0	2.5	2.3	2.1	1.9
III	1.2	1.4	4.1	4.4	2.8	2.9	3.9	3.9	1.9	1.8	2.7	2.4	2.6	2.3

[1] Output refers to real gross domestic product originating in the sector.
[2] Hours at work of all persons engaged in the sector, including hours of proprietors and unpaid family workers. Estimates based primarily on establishment data.
[3] Wages and salaries of employees plus employers' contributions for social insurance and private benefit plans. Also includes an estimate of wages, salaries, and supplemental payments for the self-employed.
[4] Hourly compensation divided by the consumer price index for all urban consumers.
[5] Current dollar output divided by the output index.

Note.—Percent changes are based on original data and may differ slightly from percent changes based on indexes in Table B–45. See Note, Table B–45.

Source: Department of Labor, Bureau of Labor Statistics.

PRODUCTION AND BUSINESS ACTIVITY

TABLE B–47.—*Industrial production indexes, major industry divisions, 1947–95*

[1987=100; monthly data seasonally adjusted]

Year or month	Total industrial production	Manufacturing Total	Manufacturing Durable	Manufacturing Nondurable	Mining	Utilities
1947	22.7	21.2	19.9	22.6	55.5	11.7
1948	23.6	22.0	20.8	23.4	58.3	13.0
1949	22.3	20.8	18.9	23.0	51.7	13.9
1950	25.8	24.2	23.0	25.6	57.7	15.8
1951	28.0	26.1	25.9	26.4	63.4	18.1
1952	29.1	27.2	27.5	26.9	62.8	19.6
1953	31.6	29.6	31.1	28.0	64.5	21.3
1954	29.9	27.7	27.4	28.2	63.2	22.9
1955	33.7	31.3	31.3	31.3	70.5	25.6
1956	35.1	32.5	32.4	32.9	74.2	28.1
1957	35.6	32.9	32.6	33.5	74.3	30.0
1958	33.3	30.6	28.5	33.7	68.1	31.4
1959	37.3	34.5	32.8	37.1	71.3	34.5
1960	38.1	35.2	33.3	38.0	72.7	36.9
1961	38.4	35.3	32.7	39.1	73.1	39.0
1962	41.6	38.4	36.3	41.5	75.2	41.9
1963	44.0	40.7	38.7	43.8	78.2	44.8
1964	47.0	43.5	41.4	46.6	81.4	48.7
1965	51.7	48.2	47.1	49.8	84.4	51.7
1966	56.3	52.6	52.3	52.9	88.9	55.6
1967	57.5	53.6	52.9	54.6	90.6	58.4
1968	60.7	56.6	55.5	58.1	94.1	63.1
1969	63.5	59.1	57.7	61.1	97.8	68.7
1970	61.4	56.4	53.3	61.1	100.4	72.9
1971	62.2	57.3	53.1	63.6	97.8	76.4
1972	68.3	63.3	59.3	69.3	99.9	81.3
1973	73.8	68.9	66.2	72.7	100.8	84.5
1974	72.7	67.9	64.8	72.3	100.3	83.5
1975	66.3	61.1	56.7	67.7	98.0	84.3
1976	72.4	67.4	62.6	74.6	98.9	87.6
1977	78.2	73.3	68.7	80.1	101.5	89.9
1978	82.6	77.8	73.9	83.5	104.6	92.7
1979	85.7	80.9	78.3	84.6	106.6	95.3
1980	84.1	78.8	75.7	83.1	110.0	95.9
1981	85.7	80.3	77.4	84.5	114.3	94.3
1982	81.9	76.6	72.7	82.5	109.3	91.8
1983	84.9	80.9	76.8	87.0	104.8	93.6
1984	92.8	89.3	88.4	90.8	111.9	97.0
1985	94.4	91.6	91.8	91.5	109.0	99.5
1986	95.3	94.3	93.9	94.9	101.0	96.3
1987	100.0	100.0	100.0	100.0	100.0	100.0
1988	104.4	104.7	106.6	102.3	101.3	105.0
1989	106.0	106.4	108.6	103.7	100.0	108.7
1990	106.0	106.1	107.4	104.4	102.0	109.9
1991	104.2	103.8	104.1	103.4	100.2	112.3
1992	107.7	108.2	109.3	106.7	98.9	111.9
1993	111.5	112.3	115.6	108.6	98.0	116.3
1994	118.1	119.7	125.8	113.0	100.3	117.9
1995ᴾ	121.9	123.9	132.5	114.4	99.8	122.1
1994: Jan	114.6	115.5	120.8	109.7	98.2	120.4
Feb	115.5	116.6	122.0	110.5	99.6	118.9
Mar	116.4	117.8	122.9	112.1	100.9	117.1
Apr	116.8	118.5	123.9	112.3	100.7	115.2
May	117.5	119.1	124.4	113.2	100.9	115.3
June	118.1	119.5	125.0	113.3	101.1	120.0
July	118.4	120.0	125.7	113.5	101.0	118.1
Aug	118.9	120.7	127.1	113.6	100.5	117.9
Sept	119.1	120.9	127.6	113.4	100.6	116.9
Oct	119.9	122.0	128.8	114.4	99.5	117.2
Nov	120.5	122.7	129.5	115.1	99.9	116.7
Dec	121.5	123.8	131.2	115.5	100.7	116.5
1995: Jan	121.8	124.1	131.8	115.6	100.6	117.3
Feb	121.7	123.9	132.1	114.8	100.8	118.5
Mar	121.9	124.0	132.2	115.1	100.3	119.2
Apr	121.4	123.5	131.6	114.6	100.6	118.8
May	121.3	123.2	131.1	114.4	100.5	122.1
June	121.4	123.3	131.5	114.3	101.0	121.0
July	121.5	123.3	131.5	114.3	100.7	122.7
Aug	122.7	124.2	133.2	114.3	100.0	128.8
Sept	122.8	124.9	134.4	114.4	100.0	122.7
Oct ᴾ	122.3	124.4	133.4	114.5	98.0	123.3
Nov ᴾ	122.7	124.7	134.5	113.8	97.7	125.1
Dec ᴾ	122.8	124.8	134.9	113.6	97.6	125.6

Source: Board of Governors of the Federal Reserve System.

334

TABLE B-48.—*Industrial production indexes, market groupings, 1947-95*

[1987=100; monthly data seasonally adjusted]

Year or month	Total industrial production	Final products Total	Consumer goods Total	Automotive products	Other durable goods	Nondurable goods	Equipment Total¹	Business	Defense and space	Intermediate products	Materials Total	Durable	Nondurable	Energy
1947	22.7	20.8	25.4	21.7	22.8	27.0	15.0	14.7	7.5	22.4	25.1	21.5	....	....
1948	23.6	21.5	26.2	22.6	23.8	27.7	15.8	15.3	8.8	23.6	26.2	22.1	....	....
1949	22.3	20.9	26.1	22.5	22.0	27.9	14.1	13.4	9.2	22.4	23.9	19.8	....	....
1950	25.8	23.5	29.7	28.3	30.4	30.3	15.3	14.3	10.8	26.1	28.6	24.9	....	....
1951	28.0	25.4	29.4	25.0	26.2	31.3	21.2	17.5	26.5	27.4	31.6	28.3	....	....
1952	29.1	27.3	30.1	22.5	26.2	32.6	25.5	19.8	37.2	27.2	32.1	28.9	....	....
1953	31.6	29.1	31.9	28.4	29.6	33.5	27.6	20.6	44.6	29.1	35.6	33.8	....	....
1954	29.9	27.6	31.7	26.5	27.3	33.9	24.2	18.1	39.3	29.0	32.9	29.2	25.2	52.7
1955	33.7	29.8	35.4	35.2	32.2	36.5	24.7	19.6	35.9	32.9	38.9	35.7	28.9	59.3
1956	35.1	31.6	36.7	28.9	33.9	38.8	27.1	22.7	35.1	34.4	39.9	35.8	30.2	62.7
1957	35.6	32.5	37.6	30.3	33.2	40.1	28.2	23.6	36.7	34.4	39.9	35.8	30.1	63.4
1958	33.3	31.0	37.2	24.1	31.3	41.3	25.2	19.9	36.8	33.6	35.9	30.1	29.9	58.8
1959	37.3	34.0	40.9	30.2	36.0	44.1	27.7	22.4	38.8	37.1	41.4	35.9	34.2	62.3
1960	38.1	35.1	42.4	34.6	36.2	45.5	28.5	23.0	39.9	37.4	42.0	36.3	34.8	63.1
1961	38.4	35.4	43.3	31.6	37.3	47.0	28.1	22.3	40.6	38.1	42.0	35.5	36.2	63.6
1962	41.6	38.4	46.2	38.3	40.5	49.2	31.3	24.3	46.9	40.4	45.8	39.4	39.2	65.8
1963	44.0	40.6	48.8	41.9	43.7	51.4	33.1	25.5	50.6	42.7	48.7	42.1	41.6	69.7
1964	47.0	42.9	51.5	43.9	47.7	54.0	35.0	28.5	49.0	45.5	52.6	45.9	45.2	72.5
1965	51.7	47.1	55.5	54.1	54.1	56.3	39.6	32.6	54.3	48.4	58.7	52.6	49.6	75.8
1966	56.3	51.6	58.4	53.9	59.6	59.0	46.1	37.8	63.7	51.4	63.9	57.9	53.6	80.6
1967	57.5	53.7	59.8	47.4	60.4	62.0	49.0	38.6	72.7	53.5	63.3	55.9	54.5	83.4
1968	60.7	56.3	63.4	56.4	64.7	64.5	50.4	40.3	72.9	56.6	67.5	59.2	59.9	87.2
1969	63.5	58.1	65.8	56.7	69.0	66.7	51.8	42.9	69.4	59.6	71.5	62.3	64.9	91.7
1970	61.4	56.0	65.0	47.7	66.9	67.8	48.1	41.3	58.7	58.7	69.0	66.5	65.2	96.2
1971	62.2	56.5	68.8	60.8	70.8	69.7	45.0	39.3	52.8	60.5	70.0	56.8	68.0	97.1
1972	68.3	61.3	74.3	65.6	81.0	74.2	49.3	44.8	51.3	67.6	77.2	64.2	74.9	100.8
1973	73.8	65.9	77.6	72.4	85.7	76.5	55.0	52.4	50.1	71.9	84.5	73.3	80.4	101.5
1974	72.7	65.7	75.2	62.6	79.3	76.5	56.8	54.7	49.4	69.4	82.8	71.2	80.8	98.8
1975	66.3	61.8	72.3	59.0	69.8	74.9	52.0	48.8	48.5	62.6	72.6	59.3	71.9	96.7
1976	72.4	66.2	79.4	73.2	78.2	80.4	53.8	50.6	49.2	69.0	81.2	68.4	81.4	99.0
1977	78.2	71.6	85.1	84.0	87.4	84.4	58.8	56.7	49.2	74.9	87.3	75.3	86.7	101.1
1978	82.6	76.1	88.4	86.3	91.2	87.8	64.2	63.1	49.5	79.1	91.8	81.4	89.7	102.2
1979	85.7	79.0	87.3	78.5	89.8	87.7	71.0	71.5	51.5	81.2	95.4	85.3	92.9	105.0
1980	84.1	80.0	85.3	59.5	85.1	89.1	74.6	73.5	57.4	77.0	91.3	79.3	88.7	106.2
1981	85.7	82.1	85.8	59.2	86.3	89.6	78.2	76.1	58.5	77.0	92.8	82.1	90.5	104.3
1982	81.9	80.8	84.5	57.5	78.1	89.7	77.0	72.9	65.7	75.1	85.1	73.4	82.1	100.7
1983	84.9	83.0	88.8	71.9	86.2	91.9	76.8	71.9	71.8	80.3	88.3	79.2	89.2	98.9
1984	92.8	91.0	92.8	86.6	94.6	93.4	89.2	85.4	78.9	86.2	96.6	92.1	93.0	103.8
1985	94.4	94.2	93.7	92.7	90.6	94.4	94.8	91.1	89.4	88.3	96.6	92.9	91.7	103.4
1986	95.3	95.7	96.8	95.3	93.9	97.6	94.5	93.1	96.0	91.9	95.9	93.7	94.4	99.5
1987	100.0	100.0	100.0	100.0	100.0	100.0	100.0	100.0	100.0	100.0	100.0	100.0	100.0	100.0
1988	104.4	104.8	102.9	106.4	103.0	102.4	107.5	110.0	99.7	101.8	105.0	106.8	104.4	102.3
1989	106.0	106.8	104.0	108.2	105.2	103.2	110.9	115.5	100.1	102.0	106.7	108.4	107.1	103.1
1990	106.0	107.0	103.4	100.7	103.6	103.8	112.1	116.9	98.8	101.2	106.8	107.6	108.0	104.2
1991	104.2	105.4	103.0	91.1	100.3	105.0	108.8	115.9	90.8	96.8	105.5	105.6	106.4	104.3
1992	107.7	108.7	106.0	100.9	104.9	106.9	112.5	123.4	84.8	99.3	109.7	112.8	110.1	103.7
1993	111.5	112.7	109.5	115.1	111.8	108.6	117.5	131.8	79.3	101.8	113.8	120.1	111.6	103.5
1994	118.1	118.3	113.7	130.8	118.5	111.2	125.3	144.9	71.9	107.3	120.0	132.3	118.0	105.3
1995ᴾ	121.9	121.4	115.0	130.6	118.7	112.8	131.5	155.8	66.0	109.0	127.5	141.5	119.9	106.7
1994:Jan	114.6	115.6	111.8	129.3	114.7	109.5	121.5	138.2	75.8	104.1	117.3	126.0	112.8	104.1
Feb	115.5	116.6	112.6	133.7	115.4	109.9	122.6	140.1	74.9	104.7	118.3	127.1	114.5	104.3
Mar	116.4	117.1	113.1	130.0	116.3	110.8	123.2	140.8	74.9	105.4	119.8	129.2	116.1	104.9
Apr	116.8	117.3	113.1	130.1	117.9	110.6	123.7	141.6	74.7	106.1	120.3	130.1	116.2	104.8
May	117.5	117.7	113.5	127.9	117.6	111.4	124.0	142.4	73.3	106.8	121.2	131.2	117.9	104.8
June	118.1	118.2	114.1	128.9	119.1	111.4	124.5	143.4	72.1	107.4	122.0	131.5	118.6	106.6
July	118.4	118.4	114.1	127.1	121.8	111.7	124.9	144.7	70.5	108.1	122.2	132.4	118.8	105.3
Aug	118.9	118.8	114.2	131.1	120.4	111.5	126.0	146.8	69.6	107.7	123.3	133.7	120.1	105.9
Sept	119.1	118.6	113.4	130.1	119.9	110.7	126.7	147.6	69.5	108.1	123.7	134.7	119.8	105.9
Oct	119.9	119.6	114.4	130.9	120.3	111.8	127.9	149.5	69.6	109.5	124.1	135.8	119.6	105.2
Nov	120.5	120.1	114.8	131.5	120.0	112.3	128.3	150.2	69.4	109.6	125.2	137.3	120.6	105.6
Dec	121.5	120.9	115.5	133.9	121.8	112.6	129.3	151.5	69.2	110.9	126.6	139.2	122.1	106.0
1995:Jan	121.8	121.3	115.5	134.4	120.8	112.7	130.4	153.2	68.9	109.5	127.1	140.0	122.2	106.2
Feb	121.7	121.1	114.9	135.3	120.4	111.9	131.0	154.3	68.2	109.5	127.1	140.2	121.5	106.4
Mar	121.9	121.5	115.3	134.4	118.6	112.7	131.4	155.1	67.8	109.2	127.2	140.3	121.5	106.4
Apr	121.4	120.9	114.4	131.7	119.0	111.8	131.3	155.0	67.1	108.2	127.0	139.8	121.7	106.6
May	121.3	120.6	114.1	127.1	116.7	112.4	130.8	154.3	66.8	108.2	127.2	139.8	122.2	107.2
June	121.4	121.1	114.8	129.1	116.3	113.1	131.2	155.1	66.8	108.2	126.8	139.7	120.4	107.2
July	121.5	121.2	114.6	125.3	118.1	113.0	131.6	155.7	66.5	108.5	126.8	140.2	118.9	107.5
Aug	122.7	122.4	115.9	130.7	118.1	113.9	132.9	157.5	66.1	109.4	128.1	142.3	118.8	108.5
Sept	122.8	122.6	116.0	132.9	119.6	113.7	133.1	158.2	65.2	109.5	128.1	144.1	117.8	105.8
Octᴾ	122.3	121.5	115.2	128.5	118.9	113.2	131.5	156.5	64.3	109.4	128.2	143.9	119.0	105.6
Novᴾ	122.7	121.8	115.5	130.3	120.3	113.3	131.8	157.4	63.1	109.3	128.7	145.4	117.4	106.0
Decᴾ	122.8	122.1	115.4	132.5	121.2	112.7	132.7	158.8	62.5	109.6	128.6	145.0	117.7	106.2

¹ Two components—oil and gas well drilling and manufactured homes—are included in total equipment, but not in detail shown.

Source: Board of Governors of the Federal Reserve System.

TABLE B–49.—*Industrial production indexes, selected manufactures, 1947–95*

[1987=100; monthly data seasonally adjusted]

Year or month	Durable manufactures							Nondurable manufactures				
	Primary metals		Fabri-cated metal prod-ucts	Indus-trial ma-chin-ery and equip-ment	Electri-cal machin-ery	Transportation equipment		Lum-ber and prod-ucts	Apparel prod-ucts	Textile mill prod-ucts	Printing and publish-ing	Chem-icals and prod-ucts	Foods
	Total	Iron and steel				Total	Motor vehicles and parts						
1947	70.2	102.1	37.5	12.0	8.5	19.6	27.3	38.8	43.1	35.2	22.1	8.7	33.1
1948	73.0	106.8	38.2	12.1	8.8	21.4	29.6	40.4	45.0	37.7	23.2	9.4	32.8
1949	61.4	91.2	34.4	10.3	8.3	21.5	30.4	35.7	44.5	34.8	23.8	9.3	33.1
1950	77.3	112.4	42.2	11.6	11.3	25.7	39.0	43.4	47.9	39.6	24.9	11.6	34.3
1951	84.1	125.7	45.1	14.7	11.4	28.7	35.8	43.2	47.0	39.2	25.4	13.1	35.0
1952	76.8	110.6	44.0	16.0	13.0	33.3	30.7	42.7	49.5	38.9	25.3	13.7	35.7
1953	87.0	127.5	49.6	16.7	14.9	41.8	38.7	45.1	50.1	39.9	26.5	14.8	36.4
1954	70.4	99.1	44.7	14.2	13.3	36.4	33.3	44.8	49.5	37.3	27.6	15.0	37.2
1955	91.5	131.8	51.0	15.6	15.3	41.9	44.6	50.1	54.7	42.5	30.3	17.6	39.3
1956	90.9	129.3	51.8	17.9	16.5	40.6	36.2	49.5	56.0	43.7	32.3	18.9	41.5
1957	87.1	124.6	53.1	17.9	16.4	43.5	38.0	45.4	55.8	41.6	33.4	19.9	42.2
1958	69.0	93.9	47.6	15.0	15.0	34.3	28.0	46.1	54.3	41.1	32.6	20.6	43.2
1959	80.7	108.1	53.4	17.5	18.2	38.9	36.4	52.3	59.7	46.4	34.8	24.0	45.4
1960	80.4	109.9	53.4	17.6	19.8	40.3	41.1	49.3	60.9	45.6	36.2	24.9	46.6
1961	78.9	104.9	52.1	17.1	21.0	37.8	36.0	51.6	61.3	46.9	36.4	26.1	47.9
1962	84.6	109.3	56.7	19.2	24.1	43.7	43.9	54.4	63.8	50.1	37.7	29.0	49.5
1963	91.2	119.1	58.5	20.5	24.8	48.0	48.6	56.9	66.4	51.9	39.7	31.7	51.2
1964	102.9	135.5	62.1	23.3	26.2	49.2	49.9	61.1	68.7	56.0	42.1	34.8	53.6
1965	113.2	148.7	68.3	26.2	31.3	58.5	63.7	63.5	72.6	61.0	44.8	38.7	54.8
1966	120.2	153.1	73.1	30.5	37.5	62.7	62.6	65.9	74.5	64.7	48.3	42.2	56.9
1967	111.1	141.5	76.5	31.1	37.7	61.3	55.1	65.3	74.1	64.8	50.9	44.2	59.4
1968	115.1	146.1	80.6	31.3	39.8	66.6	66.0	67.2	76.0	72.3	51.7	49.6	61.0
1969	123.8	159.2	81.9	33.9	42.3	66.1	66.3	67.1	78.4	76.0	54.2	53.7	63.0
1970	115.2	148.2	75.9	32.8	40.5	55.5	53.3	66.7	75.3	74.4	52.7	55.9	64.0
1971	109.2	135.5	75.6	30.5	40.7	60.1	66.9	68.5	76.2	78.5	53.2	59.5	66.0
1972	122.4	150.6	82.9	35.4	46.5	64.1	73.0	78.4	80.9	86.0	56.7	66.9	69.5
1973	138.9	171.5	92.1	41.4	53.0	73.0	85.0	78.7	81.5	89.6	58.3	73.1	70.9
1974	134.5	166.1	88.4	44.1	52.4	66.4	73.4	71.4	77.9	81.5	57.4	75.8	71.9
1975	107.2	133.5	76.7	38.1	45.1	59.7	62.2	66.5	71.1	77.7	53.7	69.1	71.4
1976	119.9	147.1	84.9	40.0	50.7	68.0	81.9	75.6	83.9	86.3	58.7	77.3	75.5
1977	121.5	145.1	92.7	45.1	58.4	73.7	94.7	82.3	91.6	91.6	64.3	83.3	79.0
1978	130.7	155.3	96.2	50.2	64.0	79.5	99.2	83.6	93.9	92.0	68.1	88.0	81.8
1979	133.0	156.5	99.5	56.9	71.3	81.0	91.0	82.4	89.0	95.0	69.9	91.3	82.6
1980	110.8	126.0	92.5	60.6	73.3	72.3	67.0	76.9	89.2	92.1	70.3	87.8	84.6
1981	117.5	135.1	91.1	65.9	75.4	68.7	64.4	74.7	91.0	89.4	72.1	89.2	86.5
1982	83.2	86.2	83.2	63.9	75.9	64.8	58.8	67.3	90.1	83.0	75.2	81.8	87.7
1983	91.0	96.1	85.5	64.3	80.3	72.7	74.5	79.9	93.8	93.2	79.0	87.5	90.1
1984	102.4	105.9	93.3	80.8	94.1	83.1	90.6	86.0	95.7	93.7	84.5	91.4	92.1
1985	101.8	104.5	94.5	86.8	93.1	91.8	99.0	88.0	92.6	89.7	87.6	91.4	94.9
1986	93.7	90.8	93.8	90.3	94.3	96.9	98.5	95.1	96.3	93.9	90.6	94.6	97.4
1987	100.0	100.0	100.0	100.0	100.0	100.0	100.0	100.0	100.0	100.0	100.0	100.0	100.0
1988	108.7	112.7	104.2	113.0	108.5	105.2	105.7	100.1	98.1	98.6	100.9	106.0	101.5
1989	107.2	111.2	102.8	117.3	111.0	109.6	106.9	99.4	95.0	100.3	101.1	109.2	102.5
1990	106.5	111.5	99.5	117.6	111.4	107.0	101.0	97.1	92.2	97.1	100.8	111.8	103.7
1991	98.6	100.5	94.5	114.7	113.9	101.1	94.4	90.2	92.7	96.5	97.0	110.5	105.3
1992	101.9	104.7	99.0	124.0	123.5	104.8	107.4	95.2	95.0	104.0	98.1	114.4	106.9
1993	107.7	111.9	103.1	138.1	134.1	109.2	122.9	97.1	97.1	109.9	98.8	115.4	109.5
1994 *P*	116.4	119.3	110.5	157.7	154.3	115.3	141.2	104.0	100.1	113.5	100.1	121.3	113.2
1995 *P*	119.3	122.2	114.0	177.6	175.0	113.3	141.9	104.5	95.8	112.7	99.4	125.0	115.2
1994: Jan	110.1	110.9	106.4	148.3	142.1	114.8	138.9	101.8	97.0	110.9	98.1	116.4	111.3
Feb	113.3	117.0	106.6	149.3	144.5	116.3	143.0	101.2	97.7	110.5	99.1	118.7	110.3
Mar	113.4	116.8	108.3	151.8	147.3	115.0	139.8	101.6	98.9	111.7	100.3	119.9	113.2
Apr	116.8	122.3	109.0	152.9	149.7	115.0	139.6	102.4	99.6	113.7	100.0	120.1	113.1
May	117.8	123.3	109.5	154.8	151.2	114.1	137.3	104.1	100.1	112.3	100.0	122.5	113.0
June	115.6	118.3	110.2	155.8	153.3	114.2	138.0	104.6	100.7	113.0	100.5	122.6	112.9
July	116.7	119.6	111.3	158.2	156.2	112.1	134.8	105.4	101.0	116.1	100.5	122.0	113.8
Aug	113.6	112.4	111.7	161.2	158.1	115.6	142.5	104.2	100.8	113.3	99.7	122.3	113.5
Sept	118.1	120.3	111.9	162.7	159.0	114.8	141.5	105.7	101.1	114.1	100.2	120.6	113.7
Oct	119.7	122.9	112.3	164.7	161.1	115.7	142.9	105.1	101.9	115.5	100.9	122.1	113.8
Nov	120.0	122.6	113.3	165.9	162.8	116.3	144.1	104.3	101.0	115.9	101.3	123.2	114.8
Dec	122.8	127.4	114.8	167.5	166.3	117.3	145.9	108.6	101.6	116.6	100.7	124.7	114.9
1995: Jan	121.5	125.5	114.3	171.4	166.7	117.8	147.3	107.1	100.6	117.2	100.1	126.2	115.9
Feb	120.8	124.9	115.0	171.8	167.7	118.5	148.4	105.0	99.8	115.9	100.3	124.7	114.2
Mar	121.3	125.8	114.3	172.4	169.4	118.0	147.6	103.9	99.3	116.2	99.3	125.0	115.0
Apr	120.2	123.5	112.3	174.3	169.6	115.7	143.0	103.9	97.4	117.2	99.2	123.5	115.1
May	119.5	123.0	113.7	174.6	171.1	113.2	138.8	101.7	97.5	113.6	99.0	124.0	115.9
June	117.5	119.2	113.7	174.4	173.0	113.4	139.7	103.0	95.5	110.4	98.6	124.4	116.1
July	118.3	119.3	112.4	176.0	175.7	111.6	136.7	103.7	94.8	109.9	99.0	124.0	115.3
Aug	115.4	117.7	114.3	179.5	178.7	114.1	142.1	103.7	94.5	112.4	100.5	124.4	115.5
Sept	121.0	127.0	115.1	181.3	180.8	114.1	143.3	106.2	94.5	110.5	99.8	125.3	115.5
Oct *P*	115.8	115.5	114.1	183.9	182.3	109.3	139.7	105.5	93.0	111.2	99.2	126.9	115.3
Nov *P*	121.8	125.0	114.8	186.3	183.8	108.4	140.6	105.2	92.6	110.1	99.5	125.8	114.8
Dec *P*	119.8	121.7	114.9	187.7	183.7	109.5	141.0	105.6	92.9	109.2	98.7	125.9	114.4

Source: Board of Governors of the Federal Reserve System.

336

TABLE B–50.—*Capacity utilization rates, 1948–95*

[Percent;[1] monthly data seasonally adjusted]

Year or month	Total industry	Manufacturing					Mining	Utilities
		Total	Durable goods	Non-durable goods	Primary processing	Advanced processing		
1948		82.5			87.3	80.0		
1949		74.2			76.2	73.2		
1950		82.8			88.5	79.8		
1951		85.8			90.2	83.4		
1952		85.4			84.9	85.9		
1953		89.3			89.4	89.3		
1954		80.1			80.6	80.0		
1955		87.0			92.0	84.2		
1956		86.1			89.4	84.4		
1957		83.6			84.7	83.1		
1958		75.0			75.4	74.9		
1959		81.6			83.0	81.1		
1960		80.1			79.8	80.5		
1961		77.3			77.9	77.2		
1962		81.4			81.5	81.6		
1963		83.5			83.8	83.4		
1964		85.6			87.8	84.6		
1965		89.5			91.0	88.8		
1966		91.1			91.4	91.1		
1967	86.4	87.2	87.1	86.3	85.4	88.0	81.2	93.4
1968	86.8	87.2	86.8	86.6	86.3	87.4	83.5	94.1
1969	86.9	86.8	86.3	86.6	86.9	86.5	86.6	95.8
1970	80.8	79.7	76.7	82.9	80.4	79.1	88.9	95.4
1971	79.2	78.2	74.3	82.8	79.3	77.4	87.4	93.9
1972	84.3	83.7	80.9	86.6	86.4	82.5	90.4	94.6
1973	88.4	88.1	87.5	87.5	91.5	86.5	92.5	92.9
1974	84.2	83.8	82.7	84.0	86.0	82.8	92.5	86.8
1975	74.6	73.2	70.2	76.4	72.9	73.5	89.9	84.0
1976	79.3	78.5	75.4	81.8	80.1	77.8	90.0	84.8
1977	83.3	82.8	80.3	85.2	84.0	81.9	90.9	84.6
1978	85.5	85.1	83.5	86.2	86.3	84.3	91.3	84.8
1979	86.2	85.4	84.9	85.1	86.4	84.8	91.9	85.9
1980	82.1	80.2	78.6	81.4	78.0	81.3	94.0	85.5
1981	80.9	78.8	76.6	81.0	78.0	79.1	94.6	82.8
1982	75.0	72.8	69.0	78.0	69.0	74.6	86.5	79.5
1983	75.8	74.9	70.5	81.1	74.8	74.9	79.9	80.3
1984	81.1	80.4	78.3	83.1	80.4	80.3	84.4	82.5
1985	80.3	79.5	77.8	81.9	79.8	79.4	82.9	83.5
1986	79.2	79.1	76.2	83.0	80.9	78.3	78.2	80.2
1987	81.5	81.6	78.6	85.6	84.9	80.1	79.9	82.0
1988	83.7	83.6	81.9	85.9	86.9	82.2	84.1	84.2
1989	83.7	83.2	81.6	85.3	86.2	82.0	85.4	86.0
1990	82.1	81.3	79.1	84.0	84.1	80.1	88.4	85.7
1991	79.2	78.0	75.0	81.6	79.8	77.2	87.4	85.8
1992	80.3	79.5	76.9	82.5	82.4	78.2	86.9	84.7
1993	81.4	80.6	79.1	82.3	84.1	79.0	87.0	87.0
1994	83.9	83.3	82.6	84.0	87.9	81.3	89.6	87.7
1995 ᴾ	83.7	83.0	82.9	83.0	87.4	81.1	89.1	90.4
1994: Jan	82.6	81.7	81.1	82.3	85.6	80.0	87.7	90.1
Feb	83.0	82.2	81.7	82.7	86.0	80.5	88.9	89.0
Mar	83.5	82.8	81.9	83.8	86.8	81.0	90.1	87.5
Apr	83.6	83.0	82.3	83.8	87.4	81.1	89.9	86.1
May	83.8	83.2	82.3	84.3	88.1	81.1	90.1	86.1
June	84.0	83.2	82.3	84.2	87.9	81.2	90.3	89.6
July	84.0	83.3	82.5	84.2	88.3	81.2	90.2	88.1
Aug	84.2	83.6	83.0	84.1	88.2	81.6	89.8	88.0
Sept	84.0	83.5	83.1	83.9	88.5	81.4	89.8	87.2
Oct	84.4	83.9	83.5	84.4	88.6	82.0	88.9	87.4
Nov	84.6	84.2	83.7	84.8	89.1	82.1	89.2	87.0
Dec	85.1	84.7	84.4	85.0	90.2	82.4	89.9	86.8
1995: Jan	85.1	84.6	84.4	84.9	89.7	82.5	89.8	87.3
Feb	84.7	84.2	84.2	84.1	89.3	82.0	90.0	88.2
Mar	84.6	84.0	83.9	84.1	88.9	81.9	89.6	88.6
Apr	84.0	83.3	83.2	83.5	88.2	81.3	89.8	88.2
May	83.7	82.8	82.5	83.2	87.7	80.8	89.7	90.6
June	83.5	82.6	82.3	83.0	86.9	80.8	90.1	89.7
July	83.3	82.3	82.0	82.7	86.6	80.5	89.9	90.8
Aug	83.8	82.6	82.6	82.6	86.1	81.2	89.2	95.3
Sept	83.6	82.8	83.0	82.4	86.8	81.1	89.2	90.7
Oct ᴾ	83.0	82.2	82.0	82.3	86.1	80.5	87.5	91.0
Nov ᴾ	83.0	82.1	82.3	81.7	86.3	80.3	87.2	92.3
Dec ᴾ	82.8	81.8	82.2	81.3	86.0	80.1	87.0	92.5

[1] Output as percent of capacity.

Source: Board of Governors of the Federal Reserve System.

TABLE B-51.—*New construction activity, 1959–95*

[Value put in place, billions of dollars; monthly data at seasonally adjusted annual rates]

Year or month	Total new construction	Private construction							Public construction		
		Total	Residential buildings[1]		Nonresidential buildings and other construction[1]				Total	Federal	State and local[5]
			Total[2]	New housing units	Total	Commercial[3]	Industrial	Other[4]			
1959	55.4	39.3	24.3	19.2	15.1	3.9	2.1	9.0	16.1	3.7	12.3
1960	54.7	38.9	23.0	17.3	15.9	4.2	2.9	8.9	15.9	3.6	12.2
1961	56.4	39.3	23.1	17.1	16.2	4.7	2.8	8.7	17.1	3.9	13.3
1962	60.2	42.3	25.2	19.4	17.2	5.1	2.8	9.2	17.9	3.9	14.0
1963	64.8	45.5	27.9	21.7	17.6	5.0	2.9	9.7	19.4	4.0	15.4
New series											
1964	72.1	51.9	30.5	24.1	21.4	6.8	3.6	11.0	20.2	3.7	16.5
1965	78.0	56.1	30.2	23.8	25.8	8.1	5.1	12.6	21.9	3.9	18.0
1966	81.2	57.4	28.6	21.8	28.8	8.1	6.6	14.1	23.8	3.8	20.0
1967	83.0	57.6	28.7	21.5	28.8	8.0	6.0	14.9	25.4	3.3	22.1
1968	92.4	65.0	34.2	26.7	30.8	9.0	6.0	15.8	27.4	3.2	24.2
1969	99.8	72.0	37.2	29.2	34.8	10.8	6.8	17.2	27.8	3.2	24.6
1970	100.7	72.8	35.9	27.1	37.0	11.2	6.6	19.2	27.9	3.1	24.8
1971	117.3	87.6	48.5	38.7	39.1	13.1	5.5	20.5	29.7	3.8	25.9
1972	133.3	103.3	60.7	50.1	42.6	15.7	4.8	22.1	30.0	4.2	25.8
1973	146.8	114.5	65.1	54.6	49.4	18.1	6.4	24.9	32.3	4.7	27.6
1974	147.5	109.3	56.0	43.4	53.4	18.1	8.1	27.2	38.1	5.1	33.0
1975	145.6	102.3	51.6	36.3	50.7	14.3	8.3	28.2	43.3	6.1	37.2
1976	165.4	121.5	68.3	50.8	53.2	14.1	7.4	31.6	44.0	6.8	37.2
1977	193.1	150.0	92.0	72.2	58.0	16.4	8.0	33.7	43.1	7.1	36.0
1978	230.2	180.0	109.8	85.6	70.2	20.6	11.5	38.2	50.1	8.1	42.0
1979	259.8	203.2	116.4	89.3	86.8	28.3	15.6	42.8	56.6	8.6	48.1
1980	259.7	196.1	100.4	69.6	95.7	34.6	14.6	46.6	63.6	9.6	54.0
1981	272.0	207.3	99.2	69.4	108.0	40.2	18.0	49.8	64.7	10.4	54.3
1982	260.6	197.5	84.7	57.0	112.9	44.1	18.5	50.2	63.1	10.0	53.1
1983	294.9	231.5	125.5	94.6	106.0	43.9	13.8	48.2	63.5	10.6	52.9
1984	348.8	278.6	153.8	113.8	124.8	59.1	14.8	50.8	70.2	11.2	59.0
1985	377.4	299.5	158.5	114.7	141.1	72.6	17.1	51.3	77.8	12.0	65.8
1986	407.7	323.1	187.1	133.2	136.0	69.5	14.9	51.6	84.6	12.4	72.2
1987	419.4	328.7	194.7	139.9	134.1	68.9	15.0	50.1	90.6	14.1	76.6
1988	432.3	337.5	198.1	138.9	139.4	71.5	16.5	51.5	94.7	12.3	82.5
1989	443.7	345.5	196.6	139.2	148.9	73.9	20.4	54.6	98.2	12.2	86.0
1990	442.2	334.7	182.9	128.0	151.8	72.5	23.8	55.4	107.5	12.1	95.4
1991	403.4	293.3	157.8	110.6	135.5	54.8	22.3	58.4	110.1	12.8	97.3
1992	435.0	315.7	187.9	129.6	127.8	45.0	20.7	62.1	119.3	14.4	104.9
1993	464.5	339.2	210.5	144.1	128.7	46.9	19.5	62.3	125.3	14.4	110.9
1994	506.9	376.6	238.9	167.9	137.7	52.7	21.1	63.9	130.3	14.4	116.0
1994: Jan	487.2	360.2	228.7	159.8	131.5	48.2	19.2	64.1	127.0	14.1	112.9
Feb	488.9	363.0	232.5	163.4	130.5	46.6	19.7	64.2	125.9	15.0	110.9
Mar	493.9	369.5	235.4	165.7	134.1	50.4	20.1	63.6	124.4	12.5	111.9
Apr	495.6	371.1	237.5	167.9	133.6	52.0	20.5	61.0	124.5	13.0	111.5
May	501.2	374.8	239.9	169.7	135.0	53.0	20.4	61.5	126.3	13.3	113.0
June	505.8	377.0	239.8	169.1	137.2	52.6	20.1	64.5	128.8	14.0	114.8
July	509.6	378.4	240.5	170.0	137.9	52.0	20.2	65.7	131.2	13.6	117.6
Aug	509.9	379.7	240.1	169.3	139.6	52.1	21.3	66.2	130.2	14.0	116.2
Sept	518.3	384.5	242.2	170.6	142.2	54.5	21.9	65.9	133.9	14.5	119.4
Oct	521.3	382.9	240.5	168.3	142.5	55.0	21.9	65.6	138.3	16.4	121.9
Nov	520.2	387.1	242.4	169.3	144.6	56.3	25.1	63.2	133.1	15.4	117.7
Dec	521.8	386.1	243.6	169.7	142.5	58.1	22.8	61.7	135.7	16.9	118.8
1995: Jan	521.1	384.8	241.9	168.6	142.9	58.6	22.7	61.5	136.2	16.0	120.3
Feb	521.4	383.7	240.2	167.2	143.4	59.3	23.4	60.7	137.8	16.0	121.8
Mar	523.5	383.3	237.9	163.9	145.4	60.8	23.9	60.7	140.2	16.5	123.6
Apr	522.1	382.2	234.1	159.8	148.1	60.3	24.7	63.1	139.9	14.8	125.1
May	514.5	376.1	231.3	156.4	144.8	57.1	24.8	62.9	138.4	15.5	122.9
June	518.9	377.5	228.4	153.2	149.1	61.5	24.4	63.2	141.4	14.7	126.8
July	528.2	385.2	232.4	157.6	152.8	63.5	24.4	64.9	143.0	14.6	128.3
Aug	526.5	383.6	232.3	161.0	151.3	63.0	24.2	64.1	143.0	16.0	127.0
Sept ᵖ	532.3	384.9	235.6	163.9	149.3	61.5	24.1	63.7	147.4	15.8	131.5
Oct ᵖ	546.9	390.9	237.4	166.3	153.5	64.9	25.3	63.3	155.9	18.2	137.7

[1] Beginning 1960, farm residential buildings included in residential buildings; prior to 1960, included in nonresidential buildings and other construction.

[2] Includes residential improvements, not shown separately. Prior to 1964, also includes nonhousekeeping units (hotels, motels, etc.).

[3] Office buildings, warehouses, stores, restaurants, garages, etc., and, beginning 1964, hotels and motels; prior to 1964 hotels and motels are included in total residential.

[4] Religious, educational, hospital and institutional, miscellaneous nonresidential, farm (see also footnote 1), public utilities (telecommunications, gas, electric, railroad, and petroleum pipelines), and all other private.

[5] Includes Federal grants-in-aid for State and local projects.

Source: Department of Commerce, Bureau of the Census.

TABLE B-52.—New housing units started and authorized, 1959-95

[Thousands of units]

Year or month	New housing units started						New private housing units authorized[2]			
	Private and public[1]		Private (farm and nonfarm)[1]					Type of structure		
	Total (farm and nonfarm)	Nonfarm	Total	Type of structure			Total	1 unit	2 to 4 units	5 units or more
				1 unit	2 to 4 units	5 units or more				
1959	1,553.7	1,531.3	1,517.0	1,234.0	282.9		1,208.3	938.3	77.1	192.9
1960	1,296.1	1,274.0	1,252.2	994.7	257.5		998.0	746.1	64.6	187.4
1961	1,365.0	1,336.8	1,313.0	974.3	338.7		1,064.2	722.8	67.6	273.8
1962	1,492.5	1,468.7	1,462.9	991.4	471.5		1,186.6	716.2	87.1	383.3
1963	1,634.9	1,614.8	1,603.2	1,012.4	590.7		1,334.7	750.2	118.9	465.6
1964	1,561.0	1,534.0	1,528.8	970.5	108.4	450.0	1,285.8	720.1	100.8	464.9
1965	1,509.7	1,487.5	1,472.8	963.7	86.6	422.5	1,239.8	709.9	84.8	445.1
1966	1,195.8	1,172.8	1,164.9	778.6	61.1	325.1	971.9	563.2	61.0	347.7
1967	1,321.9	1,298.8	1,291.6	843.9	71.6	376.1	1,141.0	650.6	73.0	417.5
1968	1,545.4	1,521.4	1,507.6	899.4	80.9	527.3	1,353.4	694.7	84.3	574.4
1969	1,499.5	1,482.3	1,466.8	810.6	85.0	571.2	1,323.7	625.9	85.2	612.7
1970	1,469.0	(3)	1,433.6	812.9	84.8	535.9	1,351.5	646.8	88.1	616.7
1971	2,084.5	(3)	2,052.2	1,151.0	120.3	780.9	1,924.6	906.1	132.9	885.7
1972	2,378.5	(3)	2,356.6	1,309.2	141.3	906.2	2,218.9	1,033.1	148.6	1,037.2
1973	2,057.5	(3)	2,045.3	1,132.0	118.3	795.0	1,819.5	882.1	117.0	820.5
1974	1,352.5	(3)	1,337.7	888.1	68.1	381.6	1,074.4	643.8	64.3	366.2
1975	1,171.4	(3)	1,160.4	892.2	64.0	204.3	939.2	675.5	63.9	199.8
1976	1,547.6	(3)	1,537.5	1,162.4	85.9	289.2	1,296.2	893.6	93.1	309.5
1977	2,001.7	(3)	1,987.1	1,450.9	121.7	414.4	1,690.0	1,126.1	121.3	442.7
1978	2,036.1	(3)	2,020.3	1,433.3	125.0	462.0	1,800.5	1,182.6	130.6	487.3
1979	1,760.0	(3)	1,745.1	1,194.1	122.0	429.0	1,551.8	981.5	125.4	444.8
1980	1,312.6	(3)	1,292.2	852.2	109.5	330.5	1,190.6	710.4	114.5	365.7
1981	1,100.3	(3)	1,084.2	705.4	91.1	287.7	985.5	564.3	101.8	319.4
1982	1,072.1	(3)	1,062.2	662.6	80.0	319.6	1,000.5	546.4	88.3	365.8
1983	1,712.5	(3)	1,703.0	1,067.6	113.5	522.0	1,605.2	901.5	133.6	570.1
1984	1,755.8	(3)	1,749.5	1,084.2	121.4	544.0	1,681.8	922.4	142.6	616.8
1985	1,745.0	(3)	1,741.8	1,072.4	93.4	576.1	1,733.3	956.6	120.1	656.6
1986	1,807.1	(3)	1,805.4	1,179.4	84.0	542.0	1,769.4	1,077.6	108.4	583.5
1987	1,622.7	(3)	1,620.5	1,146.4	65.3	408.7	1,534.8	1,024.4	89.3	421.1
1988	(4)	(3)	1,488.1	1,081.3	58.8	348.0	1,455.6	993.8	75.7	386.1
1989	(4)	(3)	1,376.1	1,003.3	55.2	317.6	1,338.4	931.7	67.0	339.8
1990	(4)	(3)	1,192.7	894.8	37.5	260.4	1,110.8	793.9	54.3	262.6
1991	(4)	(3)	1,013.9	840.4	35.6	137.9	948.8	753.5	43.1	152.1
1992	(4)	(3)	1,199.7	1,029.9	30.7	139.0	1,094.9	910.7	45.8	138.4
1993	(4)	(3)	1,287.6	1,125.7	29.4	132.6	1,199.1	986.5	52.3	160.2
1994	(4)	(3)	1,457.0	1,198.4	35.0	223.5	1,371.6	1,068.5	62.2	241.0
Seasonally adjusted annual rates										
1994:Jan	(4)	(3)	1,266	1,122	23	121	1,386	1,113	68	205
Feb	(4)	(3)	1,318	1,112	32	174	1,271	1,063	56	152
Mar	(4)	(3)	1,499	1,259	30	210	1,335	1,074	61	200
Apr	(4)	(3)	1,463	1,209	31	223	1,375	1,067	61	247
May	(4)	(3)	1,489	1,197	36	256	1,377	1,101	65	211
June	(4)	(3)	1,370	1,174	18	178	1,350	1,062	60	228
July	(4)	(3)	1,440	1,219	32	189	1,347	1,049	61	237
Aug	(4)	(3)	1,463	1,174	40	249	1,386	1,063	59	264
Sept	(4)	(3)	1,511	1,235	42	234	1,426	1,066	61	299
Oct	(4)	(3)	1,451	1,164	39	248	1,401	1,046	69	286
Nov	(4)	(3)	1,536	1,186	62	288	1,358	1,025	68	265
Dec	(4)	(3)	1,545	1,250	33	262	1,420	1,105	61	254
1995:Jan	(4)	(3)	1,366	1,055	38	273	1,293	990	66	237
Feb	(4)	(3)	1,319	1,048	42	229	1,282	931	54	297
Mar	(4)	(3)	1,238	987	35	216	1,235	911	67	257
Apr	(4)	(3)	1,269	1,009	26	234	1,243	905	61	277
May	(4)	(3)	1,282	988	36	258	1,243	930	63	250
June	(4)	(3)	1,298	1,034	33	231	1,275	958	65	252
July	(4)	(3)	1,432	1,107	40	285	1,355	1,011	61	283
Aug	(4)	(3)	1,392	1,126	28	238	1,368	1,044	63	261
Sept	(4)	(3)	1,410	1,139	40	231	1,405	1,073	72	260
Oct p	(4)	(3)	1,343	1,102	33	208	1,384	1,051	68	265
Nov p	(4)	(3)	1,420	1,102	36	282	1,448	1,069	73	306

[1] Units in structures built by private developers for sale upon completion to local public housing authorities under the Department of Housing and Urban Development "Turnkey" program are classified as private housing. Military housing starts, including those financed with mortgages insured by FHA under Section 803 of the National Housing Act, are included in publicly owned starts and excluded from total private starts.

[2] Authorized by issuance of local building permit: in 19,000 permit-issuing places beginning 1994; in 17,000 places for 1984-93; in 16,000 places for 1978-83; in 14,000 places for 1972-77; in 13,000 places for 1967-71; in 12,000 places for 1963-66; and in 10,000 places prior to 1963.

[3] Not available separately beginning January 1970.

[4] Series discontinued December 1988.

Source: Department of Commerce, Bureau of the Census.

339

TABLE B-53.—*Manufacturing and trade sales and inventories, 1954–95*

[Amounts in millions of dollars; monthly data seasonally adjusted]

Year or month	Total manufacturing and trade			Manufacturing			Merchant wholesalers			Retail trade		
	Sales¹	Inventories²	Ratio³	Sales¹	Inventories²	Ratio³	Sales¹	Inventories²	Ratio³	Sales¹	Inventories²	Ratio³
1954	46,443	73,175	1.60	23,355	41,612	1.81	8,993	10,637	1.18	14,095	20,926	1.51
1955	51,694	79,516	1.47	26,480	45,069	1.62	9,893	11,678	1.13	15,321	22,769	1.43
1956	54,063	87,304	1.55	27,740	50,642	1.73	10,513	13,260	1.19	15,811	23,402	1.47
1957	55,879	89,052	1.59	28,736	51,871	1.80	10,475	12,730	1.23	16,667	24,451	1.44
1958	54,201	87,055	1.61	27,248	50,203	1.84	10,257	12,739	1.24	16,696	24,113	1.44
1959	59,729	92,097	1.54	30,286	52,913	1.75	11,491	13,879	1.21	17,951	25,305	1.41
1960	60,827	94,719	1.56	30,878	53,786	1.74	11,656	14,120	1.21	18,294	26,813	1.47
1961	61,159	95,580	1.56	30,922	54,871	1.77	11,988	14,488	1.21	18,249	26,221	1.44
1962	65,662	101,049	1.54	33,358	58,172	1.74	12,674	14,936	1.18	19,630	27,941	1.42
1963	68,995	105,463	1.53	35,058	60,029	1.71	13,382	16,048	1.20	20,556	29,386	1.43
1964	73,682	111,504	1.51	37,331	63,410	1.70	14,529	17,000	1.17	21,823	31,094	1.42
1965	80,283	120,929	1.51	40,995	68,207	1.66	15,611	18,317	1.17	23,677	34,405	1.45
1966	87,187	136,824	1.57	44,870	77,986	1.74	16,987	20,765	1.22	25,330	38,073	1.50
1967	90,820	145,681	1.60	46,486	84,646	1.82	19,576	25,786	1.32	24,757	35,249	1.42
1968	98,685	156,611	1.59	50,229	90,560	1.80	21,012	27,166	1.29	27,445	38,885	1.42
1969	105,690	170,400	1.61	53,501	98,145	1.83	22,818	29,800	1.31	29,371	42,455	1.45
1970	108,221	178,594	1.65	52,805	101,599	1.92	24,167	33,354	1.38	31,249	43,641	1.40
1971	116,895	188,991	1.62	55,906	102,567	1.83	26,492	36,568	1.38	34,497	49,856	1.45
1972	131,081	203,227	1.55	63,027	108,121	1.72	29,866	40,297	1.35	38,189	54,809	1.44
1973	153,677	234,406	1.53	72,931	124,499	1.71	38,115	46,918	1.23	42,631	62,989	1.48
1974	177,912	287,144	1.61	84,790	157,625	1.86	47,982	58,667	1.22	45,141	70,852	1.57
1975	182,198	288,992	1.59	86,589	159,708	1.84	46,634	57,774	1.24	48,975	71,510	1.46
1976	204,150	318,345	1.56	98,797	174,636	1.77	50,698	64,622	1.27	54,655	79,087	1.45
1977	229,513	350,706	1.53	113,201	188,378	1.66	56,136	73,179	1.30	60,176	89,149	1.48
1978	260,320	400,931	1.54	126,905	211,691	1.67	66,413	86,934	1.31	67,002	102,306	1.53
1979	297,701	452,640	1.52	143,936	242,157	1.68	79,051	99,679	1.26	74,713	110,804	1.48
1980	327,233	508,924	1.56	154,391	265,215	1.72	93,099	122,631	1.32	79,743	121,078	1.52
1981	355,822	545,786	1.53	168,129	283,413	1.69	101,180	129,654	1.28	86,514	132,719	1.53
1982	347,625	573,908	1.67	163,351	311,852	1.95	95,211	127,428	1.36	89,062	134,628	1.49
1983	369,286	590,287	1.56	172,547	312,379	1.78	99,225	130,075	1.28	97,514	147,833	1.44
1984	410,124	649,780	1.53	190,682	339,516	1.73	112,199	142,452	1.23	107,243	167,812	1.49
1985	422,583	664,089	1.56	194,538	334,799	1.73	113,459	147,409	1.28	114,586	181,881	1.52
1986	430,419	662,753	1.55	194,657	322,669	1.68	114,960	153,574	1.32	120,803	186,510	1.56
1987	457,735	709,814	1.50	206,326	338,075	1.59	122,968	163,903	1.29	128,442	207,836	1.55
1988	496,079	765,270	1.49	223,541	367,422	1.58	134,521	178,801	1.30	138,017	219,047	1.54
1989	523,065	811,154	1.52	232,724	386,911	1.64	143,760	187,009	1.28	146,581	237,234	1.58
1990	542,682	834,391	1.52	239,459	399,068	1.65	149,506	195,550	1.29	153,718	239,773	1.55
1991	538,485	829,685	1.54	235,518	386,348	1.67	148,306	200,062	1.33	154,661	243,275	1.54
1992	561,293	838,895	1.49	244,511	379,238	1.57	154,150	207,663	1.32	162,632	251,994	1.52
1993	593,076	860,979	1.44	258,520	377,425	1.47	161,681	215,878	1.31	172,875	267,676	1.51
1994	639,770	916,550	1.39	280,835	391,810	1.37	172,521	234,722	1.30	186,414	290,018	1.50
1994: Jan	611,246	862,844	1.41	268,330	378,908	1.41	164,963	216,890	1.31	177,953	267,046	1.50
Feb	619,760	867,093	1.40	271,815	380,068	1.40	166,382	218,326	1.31	181,563	268,699	1.48
Mar	627,790	866,214	1.38	274,497	379,772	1.38	169,411	217,295	1.28	183,882	269,147	1.46
Apr	626,577	870,731	1.39	274,243	380,645	1.39	168,757	219,270	1.30	183,577	270,816	1.48
May	628,646	880,441	1.40	276,232	382,382	1.38	169,257	223,145	1.32	183,157	274,914	1.50
June	634,614	885,082	1.39	278,566	383,106	1.38	170,884	222,970	1.30	185,164	279,006	1.51
July	632,993	890,318	1.41	275,485	386,645	1.40	172,073	225,908	1.31	185,435	277,765	1.50
Aug	652,773	896,946	1.37	288,080	387,012	1.34	176,743	226,815	1.28	187,950	283,119	1.51
Sept	650,790	902,022	1.39	286,134	386,531	1.35	175,759	228,619	1.30	188,897	286,872	1.52
Oct	653,389	908,519	1.39	283,975	388,063	1.37	177,903	231,982	1.30	191,511	288,474	1.51
Nov	661,571	913,799	1.38	291,191	389,988	1.34	178,711	233,824	1.31	191,669	289,987	1.51
Dec	670,968	916,550	1.37	296,053	391,810	1.32	182,830	234,772	1.28	192,085	290,018	1.51
1995: Jan	673,918	928,672	1.38	297,790	396,104	1.33	182,829	238,272	1.30	193,299	294,296	1.52
Feb	675,480	936,091	1.39	298,556	399,726	1.34	185,056	240,365	1.30	191,868	296,000	1.54
Mar	674,797	942,743	1.40	298,437	402,081	1.35	183,207	243,462	1.33	193,153	297,200	1.54
Apr	672,912	952,235	1.42	295,293	405,678	1.37	184,597	246,867	1.34	193,022	299,690	1.55
May	678,444	956,516	1.41	297,093	408,289	1.37	186,244	247,702	1.33	195,107	300,525	1.54
June	682,958	960,157	1.41	298,712	410,011	1.37	187,472	249,813	1.33	196,774	300,333	1.53
July	675,776	964,894	1.43	293,474	412,423	1.41	186,232	253,060	1.36	196,070	299,411	1.53
Aug	687,610	968,658	1.41	303,021	413,146	1.36	187,203	253,017	1.35	197,386	302,495	1.53
Sept	689,804	973,482	1.41	304,280	416,177	1.37	188,303	254,063	1.35	197,221	303,242	1.54
Oct	688,407	979,840	1.42	303,155	417,816	1.38	188,517	256,134	1.36	196,735	305,890	1.55
Novᴾ										189,353	255,146	1.35	198,019		

¹ Annual data are averages of monthly not seasonally adjusted figures.
² Seasonally adjusted, end of period. Inventories beginning January 1982 for manufacturing and December 1980 for wholesale and retail trade are not comparable with earlier periods.
³ Inventory/sales ratio. Annual data are: beginning 1982, averages of monthly ratios; for 1958–81, ratio of December inventories to monthly average sales for the year; and for earlier years, weighted averages. Monthly data are ratio of inventories at end of month to sales for month.

Note.—Earlier data are not strictly comparable with data beginning 1958 for manufacturing and beginning 1967 for wholesale and retail trade.

Source: Department of Commerce, Bureau of the Census.

TABLE B-54.—Manufacturers' shipments and inventories, 1954-95

[Millions of dollars; monthly data seasonally adjusted]

| Year or month | Shipments[1] | | | Inventories[2] | | | | | | | | |
| | Total | Durable goods industries | Nondurable goods industries | Total | Durable goods industries | | | | Nondurable goods industries | | | |
					Total	Materials and supplies	Work in process	Finished goods	Total	Materials and supplies	Work in process	Finished goods
1954	23,355	11,828	11,527	41,612	23,710	7,894	9,721	6,040	17,902	8,167	2,440	7,415
1955	26,480	14,071	12,409	45,069	26,405	9,194	10,756	6,348	18,664	8,556	2,571	7,666
1956	27,740	14,715	13,025	50,642	30,447	10,417	12,317	7,565	20,195	8,971	2,721	8,622
1957	28,736	15,237	13,499	51,871	31,728	10,608	12,837	8,125	20,143	8,775	2,864	8,624
1958	27,248	13,553	13,695	50,203	30,194	9,970	12,408	7,816	20,009	8,676	2,827	8,506
1959	30,286	15,597	14,689	52,913	32,012	10,709	13,086	8,217	20,901	9,094	2,942	8,865
1960	30,878	15,870	15,008	53,786	32,337	10,306	12,809	9,222	21,449	9,097	2,947	9,405
1961	30,922	15,601	15,321	54,871	32,496	10,246	13,211	9,039	22,375	9,505	3,108	9,762
1962	33,358	17,247	16,111	58,172	34,565	10,794	14,124	9,647	23,607	9,836	3,304	10,467
1963	35,058	18,255	16,803	60,029	35,776	11,053	14,835	9,888	24,253	10,009	3,420	10,824
1964	37,331	19,611	17,720	63,410	38,421	11,946	16,158	10,317	24,989	10,167	3,531	11,291
1965	40,995	22,193	18,802	68,207	42,189	13,298	18,055	10,836	26,018	10,487	3,825	11,706
1966	44,870	24,617	20,253	77,986	49,852	15,464	21,908	12,480	28,134	11,197	4,226	12,711
1967	46,486	25,233	21,253	84,646	54,896	16,423	24,933	13,540	29,750	11,760	4,431	13,559
1968	50,229	27,624	22,605	90,560	58,732	17,344	27,213	14,175	31,828	12,328	4,852	14,648
1969	53,501	29,403	24,098	98,145	64,598	18,636	30,282	15,680	33,547	12,753	5,120	15,674
1970	52,805	28,156	24,649	101,599	66,651	19,149	29,745	17,757	34,948	13,168	5,271	16,509
1971	55,906	29,924	25,982	102,567	66,136	19,679	28,550	17,907	36,431	13,686	5,678	17,067
1972	63,027	33,987	29,040	108,121	70,067	20,807	30,713	18,547	38,054	14,677	5,998	17,379
1973	72,931	39,635	33,296	124,499	81,192	25,944	35,490	19,758	43,307	18,147	6,729	18,431
1974	84,790	44,173	40,617	157,625	101,493	35,070	42,530	23,893	56,132	23,744	8,189	24,199
1975	86,589	43,598	42,991	159,708	102,590	33,903	43,227	25,460	57,118	23,565	8,834	24,719
1976	98,797	50,623	48,174	174,636	111,988	37,457	46,074	28,457	62,648	25,847	9,929	26,872
1977	113,201	59,168	54,033	188,378	120,877	40,186	50,226	30,465	67,501	27,387	10,961	29,153
1978	126,905	67,731	59,174	211,691	138,181	45,198	58,848	34,135	73,510	29,619	12,085	31,806
1979	143,936	75,927	68,009	242,157	160,734	52,670	69,325	38,739	81,423	32,814	13,910	34,699
1980	154,391	77,419	76,972	265,215	174,788	55,173	76,945	42,670	90,427	36,606	15,884	37,937
1981	168,129	83,727	84,402	283,413	186,443	57,998	80,998	47,447	96,970	38,165	16,194	42,611
1982	163,351	79,212	84,139	311,852	200,444	59,136	86,707	54,601	111,408	44,039	18,612	48,757
1983	172,547	85,481	87,066	312,379	199,854	60,325	86,899	52,630	112,525	44,816	18,691	49,018
1984	190,682	97,940	92,742	339,516	221,330	66,031	98,251	57,048	118,186	45,692	19,328	53,166
1985	194,538	101,279	93,259	334,799	218,212	64,005	98,085	56,122	116,587	44,087	19,445	53,055
1986	194,657	103,238	91,419	322,669	212,006	61,409	96,926	53,671	110,663	42,309	18,124	50,230
1987	206,326	108,128	98,198	338,075	220,776	63,614	102,328	54,834	117,299	45,287	19,279	52,733
1988	223,541	117,993	105,549	367,422	241,402	69,388	112,380	59,634	126,020	49,030	20,446	56,544
1989	232,724	121,703	111,022	386,911	256,065	71,942	121,919	62,204	130,846	49,632	21,261	59,953
1990	239,459	122,387	117,072	399,068	259,988	72,788	122,520	64,680	139,080	51,606	22,447	65,027
1991	235,518	119,151	116,367	386,348	249,117	69,987	115,107	64,023	137,231	51,556	21,886	63,789
1992	244,511	125,553	118,958	379,238	237,717	68,165	107,140	62,412	141,521	52,194	22,887	66,440
1993	258,520	135,981	122,539	377,425	236,303	68,434	105,358	62,511	141,122	51,866	23,347	65,909
1994	280,835	151,060	129,775	391,810	247,644	74,965	105,136	67,543	144,166	52,987	23,869	67,310
1994: Jan	268,330	144,709	123,621	378,908	238,172	68,157	105,770	64,245	140,736	51,434	23,349	65,953
Feb	271,815	146,260	125,555	380,068	238,832	68,803	105,305	64,724	141,236	51,485	23,278	66,473
Mar	274,497	147,388	127,109	379,772	238,195	68,780	105,075	64,340	141,577	51,785	23,417	66,375
Apr	274,243	146,932	127,311	380,645	239,164	69,576	104,959	64,629	141,481	51,705	23,205	66,571
May	276,232	148,510	127,722	382,382	240,539	70,231	105,506	64,802	141,843	51,953	23,403	66,487
June	278,566	150,010	128,556	383,106	241,039	70,763	106,108	64,168	142,067	52,001	23,652	66,414
July	275,485	146,472	129,013	386,645	243,392	71,732	106,531	65,129	143,253	52,044	23,888	67,321
Aug	288,080	155,619	132,461	387,012	244,116	72,238	106,207	65,671	142,896	52,093	23,752	67,051
Sept	286,134	154,350	131,784	386,531	243,814	72,713	105,458	65,643	142,717	52,571	23,905	66,241
Oct	283,975	152,586	131,389	388,063	244,925	73,367	105,215	66,343	143,138	52,536	24,026	66,576
Nov	291,191	157,292	133,899	389,988	246,374	74,404	104,954	67,016	143,614	52,600	24,198	66,816
Dec	296,053	159,299	136,754	391,810	247,644	74,965	105,136	67,543	144,166	52,987	23,869	67,310
1995: Jan	297,790	161,079	136,711	396,104	250,251	75,524	106,765	67,962	145,853	53,554	24,014	68,285
Feb	298,556	161,206	137,350	399,726	252,124	76,486	107,115	68,523	147,602	54,315	24,223	69,064
Mar	298,437	161,571	136,866	402,081	253,237	76,627	106,903	69,707	148,844	55,255	24,183	69,406
Apr	295,293	157,970	137,323	405,678	255,334	77,494	107,840	70,000	150,344	55,714	24,283	70,347
May	297,093	159,612	137,481	408,289	256,717	77,927	108,408	70,452	151,502	56,220	24,499	70,784
June	298,712	160,828	137,884	410,011	257,442	78,441	107,902	71,099	152,569	56,727	24,708	71,134
July	293,474	155,919	137,555	412,423	259,532	79,171	108,897	71,464	152,891	56,852	24,790	71,249
Aug	303,021	164,196	138,825	413,146	260,091	79,903	108,762	71,426	153,055	57,007	24,737	71,311
Sept p	304,280	165,939	138,341	416,177	261,706	80,231	109,370	72,105	154,471	57,381	24,924	72,166
Oct p	303,155	164,629	138,526	417,816	263,508	81,459	109,490	72,559	154,308	57,124	24,836	72,348

[1] Annual data are averages of monthly not seasonally adjusted figures.
[2] Seasonally adjusted, end of period. Data beginning 1982 are not comparable with data for prior periods.

Note.—Data beginning 1958 are not strictly comparable with earlier data.

Source: Department of Commerce, Bureau of the Census.

[Amounts in millions of dollars; monthly data seasonally adjusted]

Year or month	New orders[1]				Unfilled orders[2]			Unfilled orders—shipments ratio[3]		
	Total	Durable goods industries		Non-durable goods industries	Total	Durable goods industries	Non-durable goods industries	Total	Durable goods industries	Non-durable goods industries
		Total	Capital goods industries, non-defense							
1954	22,335	10,768		11,566	48,266	45,250	3,016	3.42	4.12	0.96
1955	27,465	14,996		12,469	60,004	56,241	3,763	3.63	4.27	1.12
1956	28,368	15,365		13,003	67,375	63,880	3,495	3.87	4.55	1.04
1957	27,559	14,111		13,448	53,183	50,352	2,831	3.35	4.00	.85
1958	27,193	13,387		13,805	46,609	43,807	2,802	3.02	3.62	.85
1959	30,711	15,979		14,732	51,717	48,369	3,348	2.94	3.47	.92
1960	30,232	15,288		14,944	44,213	41,650	2,563	2.71	3.29	.71
1961	31,112	15,753		15,359	46,624	43,582	3,042	2.58	3.08	.78
1962	33,440	17,363		16,078	47,798	45,170	2,628	2.64	3.18	.68
1963	35,511	18,671		16,840	53,417	50,346	3,071	2.74	3.31	.72
1964	38,240	20,507		17,732	64,518	61,315	3,203	2.99	3.59	.71
1965	42,137	23,286		18,851	78,249	74,459	3,790	3.25	3.86	.79
1966	46,420	26,163		20,258	96,846	93,002	3,844	3.74	4.48	.75
1967	47,067	25,803		21,265	103,711	99,735	3,976	3.66	4.37	.73
1968	50,657	28,051	6,314	22,606	108,377	104,393	3,984	3.79	4.58	.69
1969	53,990	29,876	7,046	24,114	114,341	110,161	4,180	3.71	4.45	.69
1970	52,022	27,340	6,072	24,682	105,008	100,412	4,596	3.61	4.36	.76
1971	55,921	29,905	6,682	26,016	105,247	100,225	5,022	3.32	4.00	.76
1972	64,182	35,038	7,745	29,144	119,349	113,034	6,315	3.26	3.85	.86
1973	76,003	42,627	9,926	33,376	156,561	149,204	7,357	3.80	4.51	.91
1974	87,327	46,862	11,594	40,465	187,043	181,519	5,524	4.09	4.93	.62
1975	85,139	41,957	9,886	43,181	169,546	161,664	7,882	3.69	4.45	.82
1976	99,513	51,307	11,490	48,206	178,128	169,857	8,271	3.24	3.88	.74
1977	115,109	61,035	13,681	54,073	202,024	193,323	8,701	3.24	3.85	.71
1978	131,629	72,278	17,588	59,351	259,169	248,281	10,888	3.57	4.20	.81
1979	147,604	79,483	21,154	68,121	303,593	291,321	12,272	3.89	4.62	.82
1980	156,359	79,392	21,135	76,967	327,416	315,202	12,214	3.85	4.58	.75
1981	168,025	83,654	21,806	84,371	326,547	314,707	11,840	3.87	4.68	.69
1982	162,140	78,064	19,213	84,077	311,887	300,798	11,089	3.84	4.74	.62
1983	175,451	88,140	19,624	87,311	347,273	333,114	14,159	3.53	4.29	.69
1984	192,879	100,164	23,669	92,715	373,529	359,651	13,878	3.60	4.37	.64
1985	195,706	102,356	24,545	93,351	387,095	372,027	15,068	3.67	4.46	.68
1986	195,204	103,647	23,983	91,557	393,412	376,622	16,790	3.59	4.40	.70
1987	209,389	110,809	26,095	98,579	430,288	408,602	21,686	3.63	4.42	.83
1988	227,026	121,445	30,729	105,581	471,951	450,002	21,949	3.64	4.45	.76
1989	235,932	124,933	32,725	110,999	510,459	488,780	21,679	4.00	4.91	.78
1990	240,646	123,556	32,254	117,090	524,846	502,914	21,932	4.14	5.13	.76
1991	234,354	117,878	29,468	116,476	511,122	487,892	23,230	4.08	5.06	.81
1992	241,545	122,614	29,653	118,932	475,304	452,383	22,921	3.46	4.21	.77
1993	255,701	133,273	31,889	122,428	441,947	420,288	21,659	3.04	3.65	.72
1994	281,953	151,878	37,530	130,074	456,838	431,305	25,533	2.87	3.43	.76
1994: Jan	272,616	148,549	36,630	124,067	446,233	424,128	22,105	3.11	3.73	.74
Feb	271,786	145,882	36,382	125,904	446,204	423,750	22,454	3.07	3.69	.74
Mar	274,691	146,906	36,127	127,785	446,398	423,268	23,130	3.03	3.63	.76
Apr	275,182	147,345	35,815	127,837	447,337	423,681	23,656	3.04	3.64	.77
May	277,441	149,412	35,498	128,029	448,546	424,583	23,963	3.01	3.60	.76
June	279,788	151,212	38,055	128,576	449,767	425,784	23,983	2.98	3.58	.76
July	274,305	145,251	36,310	129,054	448,587	424,563	24,024	2.99	3.60	.75
Aug	287,222	154,675	37,595	132,547	447,729	423,619	24,110	2.89	3.47	.73
Sept	287,248	155,433	39,056	131,815	448,843	424,702	24,141	2.90	3.48	.74
Oct	285,985	154,150	38,276	131,835	450,853	426,266	24,587	2.94	3.52	.76
Nov	293,716	159,321	40,781	134,395	453,378	428,295	25,083	2.88	3.45	.76
Dec	299,514	162,310	37,759	137,204	456,838	431,305	25,533	2.87	3.43	.76
1995: Jan	301,724	164,507	41,785	137,217	460,772	434,733	26,039	2.85	3.41	.76
Feb	300,804	163,338	42,055	137,466	463,020	436,865	26,155	2.86	3.42	.76
Mar	299,625	163,042	42,628	136,583	464,208	438,336	25,872	2.85	3.41	.75
Apr	293,069	155,553	40,072	137,516	461,984	435,919	26,065	2.86	3.44	.75
May	297,046	159,502	43,115	137,544	461,937	435,809	26,128	2.82	3.38	.75
June	296,754	159,031	42,964	137,723	459,979	434,012	25,967	2.78	3.34	.72
July	293,863	156,130	40,233	137,733	460,368	434,223	26,145	2.84	3.42	.74
Aug	301,903	164,082	41,676	137,821	459,250	434,109	25,141	2.74	3.30	.70
Sept *p*	306,123	168,951	46,941	137,172	461,093	437,121	23,972	2.74	3.30	.67
Oct *p*	305,143	167,068	43,488	138,075	463,081	439,560	23,521	2.77	3.34	.66

[1] Annual data are averages of monthly not seasonally adjusted figures.
[2] Seasonally adjusted, end of period.
[3] Ratio of unfilled orders at end of period to shipments for period; excludes industries with no unfilled orders. Annual figures relate to seasonally adjusted data for December.

Note.—Data beginning 1958 are not strictly comparable with earlier data.

Source: Department of Commerce, Bureau of the Census.

PRICES

TABLE B-56.—*Consumer price indexes for major expenditure classes, 1950-95*

[For all urban consumers; 1982-84=100]

| Year or month | All items (CPI-U) | Food and beverages | | Housing | | | | Apparel and upkeep | Transportation | Medical care | Entertainment | Other goods and services | Energy² |
		Total¹	Food	Total	Shelter	Fuel and other utilities	Household furnishings and operation						
1950	24.1		25.4					40.3	22.7	15.1			
1951	26.0		28.2					43.9	24.1	15.9			
1952	26.5		28.7					43.5	25.7	16.7			
1953	26.7		28.3		22.0	22.5		43.1	26.5	17.3			
1954	26.9		28.2		22.5	22.6		43.1	26.1	17.8			
1955	26.8		27.8		22.7	23.0		42.9	25.8	18.2			
1956	27.2		28.0		23.1	23.6		43.7	26.2	18.9			
1957	28.1		28.9		24.0	24.3		44.5	27.7	19.7			21.5
1958	28.9		30.2		24.5	24.8		44.6	28.6	20.6			21.5
1959	29.1		29.7		24.7	25.4		45.0	29.8	21.5			21.9
1960	29.6		30.0		25.2	26.0		45.7	29.8	22.3			22.4
1961	29.9		30.4		25.4	26.3		46.1	30.1	22.9			22.5
1962	30.2		30.6		25.8	26.3		46.3	30.8	23.5			22.6
1963	30.6		31.1		26.1	26.6		46.9	30.9	24.1			22.6
1964	31.0		31.5		26.5	26.6		47.3	31.4	24.6			22.5
1965	31.5		32.2		27.0	26.6		47.8	31.9	25.2			22.9
1966	32.4		33.8		27.8	26.7		49.0	32.3	26.3			23.3
1967	33.4	35.0	34.1	30.8	28.8	27.1	42.0	51.0	33.3	28.2	40.7	35.1	23.8
1968	34.8	36.2	35.3	32.0	30.1	27.4	43.6	53.7	34.3	29.9	43.0	36.9	24.2
1969	36.7	38.1	37.1	34.0	32.6	28.0	45.2	56.8	35.7	31.9	45.2	38.7	24.8
1970	38.8	40.1	39.2	36.4	35.5	29.1	46.8	59.2	37.5	34.0	47.5	40.9	25.5
1971	40.5	41.4	40.4	38.0	37.0	31.1	48.6	61.1	39.5	36.1	50.0	42.9	26.5
1972	41.8	43.1	42.1	39.4	38.7	32.5	49.7	62.3	39.9	37.3	51.5	44.7	27.2
1973	44.4	48.8	48.2	41.2	40.5	34.3	51.1	64.6	41.2	38.8	52.9	46.4	29.4
1974	49.3	55.5	55.1	45.8	44.4	40.7	56.8	69.4	45.8	42.4	56.9	49.8	38.1
1975	53.8	60.2	59.8	50.7	48.8	45.4	63.4	72.5	50.1	47.5	62.0	53.9	42.1
1976	56.9	62.1	61.6	53.8	51.5	49.4	67.3	75.2	55.1	52.0	65.1	57.0	45.1
1977	60.6	65.8	65.5	57.4	54.9	54.7	70.4	78.6	59.0	57.0	68.3	60.4	49.4
1978	65.2	72.2	72.0	62.4	60.5	58.5	74.7	81.4	61.7	61.8	71.9	64.3	52.5
1979	72.6	79.9	79.9	70.1	68.9	64.8	79.9	84.9	70.5	67.5	76.7	68.9	65.7
1980	82.4	86.7	86.8	81.1	81.0	75.4	86.3	90.9	83.1	74.9	83.6	75.2	86.0
1981	90.9	93.5	93.6	90.4	90.5	86.4	93.0	95.3	93.2	82.9	90.1	82.6	97.7
1982	96.5	97.3	97.4	96.9	96.9	94.9	98.0	97.8	97.0	92.5	96.0	91.1	99.2
1983	99.6	99.5	99.4	99.5	99.1	100.2	100.2	100.2	99.3	100.6	100.1	101.1	99.9
1984	103.9	103.2	103.2	103.6	104.0	104.8	101.9	102.1	103.7	106.8	103.8	107.9	100.9
1985	107.6	105.6	105.6	107.7	109.8	106.5	103.8	105.0	106.4	113.5	107.9	114.5	101.6
1986	109.6	109.1	109.0	110.9	115.8	104.1	105.2	105.9	102.3	122.0	111.6	121.4	88.2
1987	113.6	113.5	113.5	114.2	121.3	103.0	107.1	110.6	105.4	130.1	115.3	128.5	88.6
1988	118.3	118.2	118.2	118.5	127.1	104.4	109.4	115.4	108.7	138.6	120.3	137.0	89.3
1989	124.0	124.9	125.1	123.0	132.8	107.8	111.2	118.6	114.1	149.3	126.5	147.7	94.3
1990	130.7	132.1	132.4	128.5	140.0	111.6	113.3	124.1	120.5	162.8	132.4	159.0	102.1
1991	136.2	136.8	136.3	133.6	146.3	115.3	116.0	128.7	123.8	177.0	138.4	171.6	102.5
1992	140.3	138.7	137.9	137.5	151.2	117.8	118.0	131.9	126.5	190.1	142.3	183.3	103.0
1993	144.5	141.6	140.9	141.2	155.7	121.3	119.3	133.7	130.4	201.4	145.8	192.9	104.2
1994	148.2	144.9	144.3	144.8	160.5	122.8	121.0	133.4	134.3	211.0	150.1	198.5	104.6
1995	152.4	148.9	148.4	148.5	165.7	123.7	123.0	132.0	139.1	220.5	153.9	206.9	105.2
1994:Jan	146.2	144.3	143.7	142.9	158.1	121.6	120.5	130.4	131.6	206.4	148.5	195.1	101.3
Feb	146.7	143.6	142.9	143.7	159.1	122.4	120.4	132.4	131.9	207.7	149.1	195.2	102.0
Mar	147.2	143.9	143.2	144.1	159.8	122.4	120.6	136.1	132.2	208.3	149.6	195.5	101.9
Apr	147.4	144.0	143.4	143.9	159.6	121.6	120.6	136.3	132.6	209.2	149.7	196.4	102.0
May	147.5	144.1	143.5	144.1	159.6	122.2	121.1	135.6	132.8	209.7	149.9	197.1	102.9
June	148.0	144.2	143.5	144.9	160.1	124.2	121.4	133.8	133.8	210.4	149.8	197.6	105.7
July	148.4	144.8	144.2	145.4	160.8	124.3	121.5	130.9	134.6	211.5	150.2	198.0	106.8
Aug	149.0	145.3	144.8	145.9	161.7	124.3	121.4	131.1	135.9	212.2	150.2	199.4	108.5
Sept	149.4	145.6	145.0	145.8	161.6	124.2	121.4	134.2	135.9	212.8	150.7	201.4	108.2
Oct	149.5	145.6	145.0	145.7	162.0	122.4	121.4	135.2	136.1	214.0	151.0	201.9	105.8
Nov	149.7	145.9	145.3	145.5	162.1	121.8	121.1	134.2	137.1	214.7	151.6	202.3	105.7
Dec	149.7	147.2	146.8	145.4	161.8	122.0	120.8	130.5	137.1	215.3	151.2	202.4	104.7
1995:Jan	150.3	147.9	147.5	146.4	162.9	122.9	121.8	129.4	137.3	216.6	152.1	203.0	104.2
Feb	150.9	147.8	147.4	147.0	163.8	122.6	122.4	131.1	137.5	217.9	152.5	204.1	103.7
Mar	151.4	147.9	147.4	147.4	164.5	122.3	122.6	134.4	138.0	218.4	152.6	204.0	103.2
Apr	151.9	148.9	148.4	147.4	164.7	122.1	122.6	134.8	139.1	218.9	153.3	204.3	103.9
May	152.2	148.7	148.3	147.6	164.8	122.5	122.7	133.4	140.3	219.3	153.6	204.9	106.3
June	152.5	148.4	147.9	148.5	165.5	125.0	122.5	130.5	141.1	219.8	153.2	205.3	109.3
July	152.5	148.6	148.1	149.2	166.4	125.1	123.0	128.3	140.1	220.8	153.6	205.7	108.1
Aug	152.9	148.9	148.4	149.6	166.8	125.7	123.4	130.1	139.2	221.6	154.1	207.7	107.4
Sept	153.2	149.4	148.9	149.5	166.8	124.9	123.8	132.7	138.8	222.1	154.9	210.2	106.2
Oct	153.7	149.8	149.4	149.7	167.3	123.9	123.9	134.5	139.4	222.9	155.2	210.7	104.5
Nov	153.6	149.8	149.4	149.4	167.3	123.1	123.6	133.7	139.4	223.5	156.0	211.2	102.8
Dec	153.5	150.3	149.9	149.7	167.4	123.7	123.8	130.6	139.1	223.8	156.2	211.4	103.3

¹ Includes alcoholic beverages, not shown separately.
² Household fuels—gas (piped), electricity, fuel oil, etc.—and motor fuel. Motor oil, coolant, etc. also included through 1982.

Note.—Data beginning 1983 incorporate a rental equivalence measure for homeowners' costs.

Source: Department of Labor, Bureau of Labor Statistics.

[For all urban consumers; 1982–84=100, except as noted]

Year or month	Food and beverages Total¹	Food Total	Food At home	Food Away from home	Shelter Total	Renters' costs Total²	Rent, residential	Homeowners' costs²	Maintenance and repairs	Fuel and other utilities Total	Fuels Total	Fuel oil and other household fuel commodities	Gas (piped) and electricity (energy services)	Other utilities and public services
1950	25.4	27.3					29.7					11.3	19.2	
1951	28.2	30.3					30.9					11.8	19.3	
1952	28.7	30.8					32.2					12.1	19.5	
1953	28.3	30.3	21.5	22.0			33.9		20.5	22.5		12.6	19.9	
1954	28.2	30.1	21.9	22.5			35.1		20.9	22.6		12.6	20.2	
1955	27.8	29.5	22.1	22.7			35.6		21.4	23.0		12.7	20.7	
1956	28.0	29.6	22.6	23.1			36.3		22.3	23.6		13.3	20.9	
1957	28.9	30.6	23.4	24.0			37.0		23.2	24.3		14.0	21.1	
1958	30.2	32.0	24.1	24.5			37.6		23.6	24.8		13.7	21.9	
1959	29.7	31.2	24.8	24.7			38.2		24.0	25.4		13.9	22.4	
1960	30.0	31.5	25.4	25.2			38.7		24.4	26.0		13.8	23.3	
1961	30.4	31.8	26.0	25.4			39.2		24.8	26.3		14.1	23.5	
1962	30.6	32.0	26.7	25.8			39.7		25.0	26.3		14.2	23.5	
1963	31.1	32.4	27.3	26.1			40.1		25.3	26.6		14.4	23.5	
1964	31.5	32.7	27.8	26.5			40.5		25.8	26.6		14.4	23.5	
1965	32.2	33.5	28.4	27.0			40.9		26.3	26.6		14.6	23.5	
1966	33.8	35.2	29.7	27.8			41.5		27.5	26.7		15.0	23.6	
1967	35.0	34.1	35.1	31.3	28.8		42.2		28.9	27.1	21.4	15.5	23.7	46.6
1968	36.2	35.3	36.3	32.9	30.1		43.3		30.6	27.4	21.7	16.0	23.9	47.1
1969	38.1	37.1	38.0	34.9	32.6		44.7		33.2	28.0	22.1	16.3	24.3	48.4
1970	40.1	39.2	39.9	37.5	35.5		46.5		35.8	29.1	23.1	17.0	25.4	50.0
1971	41.4	40.4	40.9	39.4	37.0		48.7		38.6	31.1	24.7	18.2	27.1	53.4
1972	43.1	42.1	42.7	41.0	38.7		50.4		40.6	32.5	25.7	18.3	28.5	56.2
1973	48.8	48.2	49.7	44.2	40.5		52.5		43.6	34.3	27.5	21.1	29.9	57.8
1974	55.5	55.1	57.1	49.8	44.4		55.2		49.5	40.7	34.4	33.2	34.5	60.7
1975	60.2	59.8	61.8	54.5	48.8		58.0		54.1	45.4	39.4	36.4	40.1	63.9
1976	62.1	61.6	63.1	58.2	51.5		61.1		57.6	49.4	43.3	38.8	44.7	67.7
1977	65.8	65.5	66.8	62.6	54.9		64.8		62.0	54.7	49.0	43.9	50.5	70.8
1978	72.2	72.0	73.8	68.3	60.5		69.3		67.2	58.5	53.0	46.2	55.0	73.7
1979	79.9	79.9	81.8	75.9	68.9		74.3		74.0	64.8	61.3	62.4	61.0	74.3
1980	86.7	86.8	88.4	83.4	81.0		80.9		82.4	75.4	74.8	86.1	71.4	77.0
1981	93.5	93.6	94.8	90.9	90.5		87.9		90.7	86.4	87.2	104.6	81.9	84.3
1982	97.3	97.4	98.1	95.8	96.9		94.6		96.4	94.9	95.6	103.4	93.2	93.3
1983	99.5	99.4	99.1	100.0	99.1	103.0	100.1	102.5	99.9	100.2	100.5	97.2	101.5	99.5
1984	103.2	103.2	102.8	104.2	104.0	108.6	105.3	107.3	103.7	104.8	104.0	99.4	105.4	107.2
1985	105.6	105.6	104.3	108.3	109.8	115.4	111.8	113.1	106.5	106.5	104.5	95.9	107.1	112.1
1986	109.1	109.0	107.3	112.5	115.8	121.9	118.3	119.4	107.9	104.1	99.2	77.6	105.7	117.9
1987	113.5	113.5	111.9	117.0	121.3	128.1	123.1	124.8	111.8	103.0	97.3	77.9	103.8	120.1
1988	118.2	118.2	116.6	121.8	127.1	133.6	127.8	131.1	114.7	104.4	98.0	78.1	104.6	122.9
1989	124.9	125.1	124.2	127.4	132.8	138.9	132.8	137.3	118.0	107.8	100.9	81.7	107.5	127.1
1990	132.1	132.4	132.3	133.4	140.0	146.7	138.4	144.6	122.2	111.6	104.5	99.3	109.3	131.7
1991	136.8	136.3	135.8	137.9	146.3	155.6	143.3	150.2	126.3	115.3	106.7	94.6	112.6	137.9
1992	138.7	137.9	136.8	140.7	151.2	160.9	146.9	155.3	128.6	117.8	108.1	90.7	114.8	142.5
1993	141.6	140.9	140.1	143.2	155.7	165.0	150.3	160.2	130.6	121.3	111.2	90.3	118.5	147.0
1994	144.9	144.3	144.1	145.7	160.5	169.4	154.0	165.5	130.8	122.8	111.7	88.8	119.2	150.2
1995	148.9	148.4	148.8	149.0	165.7	174.3	157.8	171.0	135.0	123.7	115.5	88.1	119.2	152.8
1994: Jan	144.3	143.7	143.8	144.5	158.1	166.8	152.2	162.9	128.9	121.6	110.6	88.9	118.0	148.9
Feb	143.6	142.9	142.6	144.6	159.1	168.9	152.8	163.7	129.4	122.4	111.1	93.6	117.9	150.0
Mar	143.9	143.2	142.8	144.8	159.8	170.1	153.2	164.1	129.3	122.4	111.1	92.5	118.1	150.1
Apr	144.0	143.4	143.0	145.1	159.6	169.1	153.3	164.2	130.2	121.6	109.8	90.2	116.9	150.0
May	144.1	143.5	143.0	145.3	159.6	168.5	153.3	164.5	131.0	122.2	110.6	88.7	118.0	150.4
June	144.2	143.5	142.9	145.5	160.1	169.6	153.4	164.8	131.5	124.2	113.9	87.7	122.1	150.4
July	144.8	144.2	144.0	145.6	160.8	171.0	153.9	165.3	131.3	124.3	114.1	87.1	122.3	150.4
Aug	145.3	144.8	144.7	145.9	161.7	172.1	154.5	166.1	131.2	124.3	114.0	86.8	122.2	150.6
Sept	145.6	145.0	145.0	146.2	161.6	169.4	155.0	167.1	131.6	124.2	113.8	86.8	122.1	150.3
Oct	145.6	145.0	144.8	146.4	162.0	169.8	155.2	167.5	130.8	122.4	110.8	87.0	118.5	150.4
Nov	145.9	145.3	145.1	146.8	162.1	168.9	155.6	167.9	131.2	121.8	109.9	87.7	117.3	150.5
Dec	147.2	146.8	147.3	147.1	161.8	168.2	155.7	167.8	132.7	122.0	110.1	88.4	117.4	150.6
1995: Jan	147.9	147.5	148.2	147.4	162.9	170.7	156.1	168.4	133.1	122.9	110.7	89.4	118.0	152.1
Feb	147.8	147.4	147.7	147.6	163.8	172.9	156.4	168.9	133.8	122.6	110.4	89.6	117.6	151.8
Mar	147.9	147.4	147.6	148.1	164.5	174.6	156.7	169.2	134.2	122.3	109.8	89.0	117.1	151.9
Apr	148.9	148.4	149.2	148.3	164.7	174.1	157.0	169.6	134.2	122.1	109.3	88.4	116.6	152.2
May	148.7	148.3	148.7	148.6	164.8	173.7	157.2	170.0	134.6	122.5	109.8	88.3	117.2	152.3
June	148.4	147.9	148.1	148.8	165.5	174.7	157.5	170.6	135.0	125.0	113.8	87.9	121.9	152.7
July	148.6	148.1	148.2	149.1	166.4	176.7	157.9	171.2	135.1	125.1	113.7	87.1	121.9	153.0
Aug	148.9	148.4	148.4	149.4	166.8	176.9	158.2	171.6	135.4	125.7	114.6	86.6	123.0	153.1
Sept	149.4	148.9	149.2	149.6	166.8	175.1	158.5	172.4	135.4	124.9	113.4	86.6	121.6	153.2
Oct	149.8	149.4	149.7	150.0	167.3	175.3	158.9	173.0	136.3	123.9	111.5	86.9	119.3	153.5
Nov	149.8	149.4	149.5	150.2	167.3	173.8	159.3	173.5	136.2	123.1	110.1	87.7	117.6	153.6
Dec	150.3	149.9	150.3	150.4	167.4	173.2	159.6	174.0	136.6	123.7	110.9	89.6	118.3	153.9

¹ Includes alcoholic beverages, not shown separately.
² December 1982=100.

See next page for continuation of table.

[For all urban consumers; 1982–84=100, except as noted]

Year or month	Transportation	Private transportation						Public transportation	Medical care		
	Total	Total[3]	New cars	Used cars	Motor fuel[4]	Automobile maintenance and repair	Other		Total	Medical care commodities	Medical care services
1950	22.7	24.5	41.1		19.0	18.9		13.4	15.1	39.7	12.8
1951	24.1	25.6	43.1		19.5	20.4		14.8	15.9	40.8	13.4
1952	25.7	27.3	46.8		20.0	20.8		15.8	16.7	41.2	14.3
1953	26.5	27.8	47.2	26.7	21.2	22.0		16.8	17.3	41.5	14.8
1954	26.1	27.1	46.5	22.7	21.8	22.7		18.0	17.8	42.0	15.3
1955	25.8	26.7	44.8	21.5	22.1	23.2		18.5	18.2	42.5	15.7
1956	26.2	27.1	46.1	20.7	22.8	24.2		19.2	18.9	43.4	16.3
1957	27.7	28.6	48.5	23.2	23.8	25.0		19.9	19.7	44.6	17.0
1958	28.6	29.5	50.0	24.0	23.4	25.4		20.9	20.6	46.1	17.9
1959	29.8	30.8	52.2	26.8	23.7	26.0		21.5	21.5	46.8	18.7
1960	29.8	30.6	51.5	25.0	24.4	26.5		22.2	22.3	46.9	19.5
1961	30.1	30.8	51.5	26.0	24.1	27.1		23.2	22.9	46.3	20.2
1962	30.8	31.4	51.3	28.4	24.3	27.5		24.0	23.5	45.6	20.9
1963	30.9	31.6	51.0	28.7	24.2	27.8		24.3	24.1	45.2	21.5
1964	31.4	32.0	50.9	30.0	24.1	28.2		24.7	24.6	45.1	22.0
1965	31.9	32.5	49.7	29.8	25.1	28.7		25.2	25.2	45.0	22.7
1966	32.3	32.9	48.8	29.0	25.6	29.2		26.1	26.3	45.1	23.9
1967	33.3	33.8	49.3	29.9	26.4	30.4	37.9	27.4	28.2	44.9	26.0
1968	34.3	34.8	50.7		26.8	32.1	39.2	28.7	29.9	45.0	27.9
1969	35.7	36.0	51.5	30.9	27.6	34.1	41.6	30.9	31.9	45.4	30.2
1970	37.5	37.5	53.0	31.2	27.9	36.6	45.2	35.2	34.0	46.5	32.3
1971	39.5	39.4	55.2	33.0	28.1	39.3	48.6	37.8	36.1	47.3	34.7
1972	39.9	39.7	54.7	33.1	28.4	41.1	48.9	39.3	37.3	47.4	35.9
1973	41.2	41.0	54.8	35.2	31.2	43.2	48.4	39.7	38.8	47.5	37.5
1974	45.8	46.2	57.9	36.7	42.2	47.6	50.2	40.6	42.4	49.2	41.4
1975	50.1	50.6	62.9	43.8	45.1	53.7	53.5	43.5	47.5	53.3	46.6
1976	55.1	55.6	66.9	50.3	47.0	57.6	61.8	47.8	52.0	56.5	51.3
1977	59.0	59.7	70.4	54.7	49.7	61.9	67.2	50.0	57.0	60.2	56.4
1978	61.7	62.5	75.8	55.8	51.8	67.0	69.9	51.5	61.8	64.4	61.2
1979	70.5	71.7	81.8	60.2	70.1	73.7	75.2	54.9	67.5	69.0	67.2
1980	83.1	84.2	88.4	62.3	97.4	81.5	84.3	69.0	74.9	75.4	74.8
1981	93.2	93.8	93.7	76.9	108.5	89.2	91.4	85.6	82.9	83.7	82.8
1982	97.0	97.1	97.4	88.8	102.8	96.0	97.7	94.9	92.5	92.3	92.6
1983	99.3	99.3	99.9	98.7	99.4	100.3	98.8	99.5	100.6	100.2	100.7
1984	103.7	103.6	102.8	112.5	97.9	103.8	103.5	105.7	106.8	107.5	106.7
1985	106.4	106.2	106.1	113.7	98.7	106.8	109.0	110.5	113.5	115.2	113.2
1986	102.3	101.2	110.6	108.8	77.1	110.3	115.1	117.0	122.0	122.8	121.9
1987	105.4	104.2	114.6	113.1	80.2	114.8	120.8	121.1	130.1	131.0	130.0
1988	108.7	107.6	116.9	118.0	80.9	119.7	127.9	123.3	138.6	139.9	138.3
1989	114.1	112.9	119.2	120.4	88.5	124.9	135.8	129.5	149.3	150.8	148.9
1990	120.5	118.8	121.0	117.6	101.2	130.1	142.5	142.6	162.8	163.4	162.7
1991	123.8	121.9	125.3	118.1	99.4	136.0	149.1	148.9	177.0	176.8	177.1
1992	126.5	124.6	128.4	123.2	99.0	141.3	153.2	151.4	190.1	188.1	190.5
1993	130.4	127.5	131.5	133.9	98.0	145.9	156.8	167.0	201.4	195.0	202.9
1994	134.3	131.4	136.0	141.7	98.5	150.2	162.1	172.0	211.0	200.7	213.4
1995	139.1	136.3	139.0	156.5	100.0	154.0	170.6	175.9	220.5	204.5	224.2
1994: Jan	131.6	128.2	134.7	136.8	92.6	148.1	159.5	175.3	206.4	197.8	208.4
Feb	131.9	128.5	135.0	134.1	93.6	148.6	159.7	175.9	207.7	198.7	209.8
Mar	132.2	128.6	135.3	133.6	93.3	149.0	160.2	178.5	208.3	199.1	210.4
Apr	132.6	129.2	135.4	135.3	94.8	149.4	160.4	176.5	209.2	199.7	211.4
May	132.8	130.0	135.7	137.9	96.0	149.7	160.8	169.9	209.7	200.1	212.0
June	133.8	131.0	135.8	140.9	98.2	149.8	161.3	169.9	210.4	200.5	212.6
July	134.6	131.8	135.8	142.6	100.5	150.0	161.5	171.4	211.5	201.3	213.8
Aug	135.9	133.0	135.6	144.0	104.1	150.7	162.0	173.2	212.2	201.7	214.7
Sept	135.9	133.1	135.7	145.4	103.7	151.2	162.1	171.7	212.8	201.7	215.4
Oct	136.1	133.6	136.6	147.7	101.8	151.7	164.1	168.4	214.0	202.2	216.8
Nov	137.1	134.8	137.7	150.1	102.7	151.8	166.2	167.2	214.7	202.7	217.5
Dec	137.1	134.9	138.5	151.5	100.4	151.9	167.6	165.6	215.3	202.9	218.2
1995: Jan	137.3	134.9	139.0	152.4	98.7	152.0	168.8	168.4	216.6	203.1	219.8
Feb	137.5	135.0	139.1	153.3	98.0	152.5	169.4	169.9	217.9	203.5	221.3
Mar	138.0	135.2	139.0	154.8	97.5	152.7	170.2	174.5	218.4	203.7	221.8
Apr	139.1	136.2	139.3	156.7	99.5	153.2	170.9	176.7	218.9	203.6	222.4
May	140.3	137.5	139.3	157.7	104.2	153.8	170.5	176.7	219.3	203.4	223.0
June	141.1	137.9	139.1	158.3	106.1	153.6	169.9	182.5	219.8	203.8	223.5
July	140.1	136.9	138.3	157.5	103.6	154.0	169.6	181.8	220.8	204.4	224.6
Aug	139.2	136.3	137.9	157.0	101.1	154.5	170.3	177.1	221.6	204.7	225.6
Sept	138.8	135.9	137.8	156.5	99.8	155.1	170.1	176.1	222.1	204.8	226.1
Oct	139.4	136.3	138.6	157.2	98.3	155.4	172.0	178.7	222.9	205.7	226.9
Nov	139.4	136.5	140.1	157.8	96.4	155.7	172.7	177.5	223.5	206.3	227.4
Dec	139.1	136.6	140.7	158.2	96.4	155.7	172.4	170.7	223.8	206.6	227.8

[3] Includes other new vehicles, not shown separately. Includes direct pricing of new trucks and motorcycles beginning 1982.
[4] Includes direct pricing of diesel fuel and gasohol beginning 1981.

Note.—See Note, Table B–56.

Source: Department of Labor, Bureau of Labor Statistics.

[For all urban consumers; 1982–84=100, except as noted]

Year or month	All items (CPI–U)	Commodities			Services			Special indexes				
		All com-modities	Food	Com-modities less food	All services	Medi-cal care serv-ices	Services less medical care services	All items less food	All items less energy	All items less food and energy	All items less medi-cal care	CPI–U–X1 (all items) (Dec. 1982 =97.6)[1]
1950	24.1	29.0	25.4	31.4	16.9	12.8	....	23.8	....	....	....	26.2
1951	26.0	31.6	28.2	33.8	17.8	13.4	....	25.3	....	....	....	28.3
1952	26.5	32.0	28.7	34.1	18.6	14.3	....	25.9	....	....	....	28.8
1953	26.7	31.9	28.3	34.2	19.4	14.8	....	26.4	....	....	....	29.0
1954	26.9	31.6	28.2	33.8	20.0	15.3	....	26.6	....	....	....	29.2
1955	26.8	31.3	27.8	33.6	20.4	15.7	....	26.6	....	....	....	29.1
1956	27.2	31.6	28.0	33.9	20.9	16.3	....	27.1	....	....	....	29.6
1957	28.1	32.6	28.9	34.9	21.8	17.0	22.8	28.0	28.9	28.9	28.7	30.5
1958	28.9	33.3	30.2	35.3	22.6	17.9	23.6	28.6	29.7	29.6	29.5	31.4
1959	29.1	33.3	29.7	35.8	23.3	18.7	24.2	29.2	29.9	30.2	29.8	31.6
1960	29.6	33.6	30.0	36.0	24.1	19.5	25.0	29.7	30.4	30.6	30.2	32.2
1961	29.9	33.8	30.4	36.1	24.5	20.2	25.4	30.0	30.7	31.0	30.5	32.5
1962	30.2	34.1	30.6	36.3	25.0	20.9	25.9	30.3	31.1	31.4	30.8	32.8
1963	30.6	34.4	31.1	36.6	25.5	21.5	26.3	30.7	31.5	31.8	31.1	33.3
1964	31.0	34.8	31.5	36.9	26.0	22.0	26.8	31.1	32.0	32.3	31.5	33.7
1965	31.5	35.2	32.2	37.2	26.6	22.7	27.4	31.6	32.5	32.7	32.0	34.2
1966	32.4	36.1	33.8	37.7	27.6	23.9	28.3	32.3	33.5	33.5	33.0	35.2
1967	33.4	36.8	34.1	38.6	28.8	26.0	29.3	33.4	34.4	34.7	33.7	36.3
1968	34.8	38.1	35.3	40.0	30.3	27.9	30.8	34.9	35.9	36.3	35.1	37.7
1969	36.7	39.9	37.1	41.7	32.4	30.2	32.9	36.8	38.0	38.4	37.0	39.4
1970	38.8	41.7	39.2	43.4	35.0	32.3	35.6	39.0	40.3	40.8	39.2	41.3
1971	40.5	43.2	40.4	45.1	37.0	34.7	37.5	40.8	42.0	42.7	40.8	43.1
1972	41.8	44.5	42.1	46.1	38.4	35.9	38.9	42.0	43.4	44.0	42.1	44.4
1973	44.4	47.8	48.2	47.7	40.1	37.5	40.6	43.7	46.1	45.6	44.8	47.2
1974	49.3	53.5	55.1	52.8	43.8	41.4	44.3	48.0	50.6	49.4	49.8	51.9
1975	53.8	58.2	59.8	57.6	48.0	46.6	48.3	52.5	55.1	53.9	54.3	56.2
1976	56.9	60.7	61.6	60.5	52.0	51.3	52.2	56.0	58.2	57.4	57.2	59.4
1977	60.6	64.2	65.5	63.8	56.0	56.4	55.9	59.6	61.9	61.0	60.8	63.2
1978	65.2	68.8	72.0	67.5	60.8	61.2	60.7	63.9	66.7	65.5	65.4	67.5
1979	72.6	76.6	79.9	75.3	67.5	67.2	67.5	71.2	73.4	71.9	72.9	74.0
1980	82.4	86.0	86.8	85.7	77.9	74.8	78.2	81.5	81.9	80.8	82.8	82.3
1981	90.9	93.2	93.6	93.1	88.1	82.8	88.7	90.4	90.1	89.2	91.4	90.1
1982	96.5	97.0	97.4	96.9	96.0	92.6	96.4	96.3	96.1	95.8	96.8	95.6
1983	99.6	99.8	99.4	100.0	99.4	100.7	99.2	99.7	99.6	99.6	99.6	99.6
1984	103.9	103.2	103.2	103.1	104.6	106.7	104.4	104.0	104.3	104.6	103.7	103.9
1985	107.5	105.4	105.6	105.2	109.9	113.2	109.6	108.0	108.4	109.1	107.2	107.6
1986	109.6	104.4	109.0	101.7	115.4	121.9	114.6	109.8	112.6	113.5	108.8	109.6
1987	113.6	107.7	113.5	104.3	120.2	130.0	119.1	113.6	117.2	118.2	112.6	113.6
1988	118.3	111.5	118.2	107.7	125.7	138.3	124.3	118.3	122.3	123.4	117.0	118.3
1989	124.0	116.7	125.1	112.0	131.9	148.9	130.1	123.7	128.1	129.0	122.4	124.0
1990	130.7	122.8	132.4	117.4	139.2	162.7	136.8	130.3	134.7	135.5	128.8	130.7
1991	136.2	126.6	136.3	121.3	146.3	177.1	143.3	136.1	140.9	142.1	133.8	136.2
1992	140.3	129.1	137.9	124.2	152.0	190.5	148.4	140.8	145.4	147.3	137.5	140.3
1993	144.5	131.5	140.9	126.3	157.9	202.9	153.6	145.1	150.0	152.2	141.2	144.5
1994	148.2	133.8	144.3	127.9	163.1	213.4	158.4	149.0	154.1	156.5	144.7	148.2
1995	152.4	136.4	148.4	129.8	168.7	224.2	163.5	153.1	158.7	161.2	148.6	152.4
1994: Jan	146.2	132.0	143.7	125.6	160.7	208.4	156.2	146.6	152.2	154.3	142.8	146.2
Feb	146.7	132.2	142.9	126.2	161.5	209.8	157.0	147.3	152.6	155.0	143.2	146.7
Mar	147.2	132.8	143.2	127.0	162.1	210.4	157.5	148.0	153.3	155.8	143.8	147.2
Apr	147.4	133.1	143.4	127.4	162.0	211.4	157.4	148.1	153.4	155.9	143.9	147.4
May	147.5	133.4	143.5	127.8	162.0	212.0	157.4	148.3	153.5	156.0	144.0	147.5
June	148.0	133.5	143.5	127.9	162.8	212.6	158.2	148.8	153.7	156.2	144.5	148.0
July	148.4	133.7	144.2	127.8	163.4	213.8	158.7	149.1	154.0	156.4	144.8	148.4
Aug	149.0	134.3	144.8	128.4	164.2	214.7	159.4	149.8	154.6	157.0	145.5	149.0
Sept	149.4	134.8	145.0	129.0	164.4	215.4	159.6	150.2	155.0	157.5	145.8	149.4
Oct	149.5	134.9	145.0	129.3	164.6	216.8	159.7	150.4	155.5	158.0	145.9	149.5
Nov	149.7	135.2	145.3	129.5	164.7	217.5	159.8	150.6	155.7	158.2	146.1	149.7
Dec	149.7	135.1	146.8	128.5	164.7	218.2	159.7	150.2	155.7	157.9	146.0	149.7
1995: Jan	150.3	135.1	147.5	128.3	165.9	219.8	160.9	150.8	156.5	158.7	146.6	150.3
Feb	150.9	135.4	147.4	128.8	166.7	221.3	161.6	151.5	157.2	159.6	147.1	150.9
Mar	151.4	135.9	147.4	129.5	167.3	221.8	162.2	152.1	157.8	160.4	147.6	151.4
Apr	151.9	136.6	148.4	130.1	167.5	222.4	162.4	152.5	158.3	160.7	148.1	151.9
May	152.2	136.9	148.3	130.6	167.7	223.0	162.6	152.9	158.3	160.8	148.4	152.2
June	152.5	136.6	147.9	130.4	168.6	223.5	163.5	153.3	158.3	160.9	148.7	152.5
July	152.5	136.2	148.1	129.5	169.2	224.6	164.1	153.4	158.5	161.1	148.7	152.5
Aug	152.9	136.3	148.4	129.7	169.8	225.6	164.6	153.7	159.0	161.6	149.0	152.9
Sept	153.2	136.8	148.9	130.1	170.0	226.1	164.7	154.0	159.5	162.1	149.4	153.2
Oct	153.7	137.2	149.4	130.5	170.4	226.9	165.1	154.4	160.2	162.8	149.8	153.7
Nov	153.6	137.2	149.4	130.4	170.3	227.4	165.0	154.4	160.3	163.0	149.7	153.6
Dec	153.5	137.0	149.9	129.9	170.4	227.8	165.0	154.2	160.2	162.7	149.6	153.5

[1] CPI–U–X1 is a rental equivalence approach to homeowners' costs for the consumer price index for years prior to 1983, the first year for which the official index (CPI–U) incorporates such a measure. CPI–U–X1 is rebased to the December 1982 value of the CPI–U (1982–84=100); thus it is identical with CPI–U data for December 1982 and all subsequent periods. Data prior to 1967 estimated by moving the se-ries at the same rate as the CPI–U for each year.

Note.—See Note, Table B–56.

Source: Department of Labor, Bureau of Labor Statistics.

[For all urban consumers; percent change]

Year or month	All items (CPI–U)		All items less food		All items less energy		All items less food and energy		All items less medical care	
	Dec. to Dec.[1]	Year to year	Dec. to Dec.[1]	Year to year	Dec. to Dec.[1]	Year to year	Dec. to Dec.[1]	Year to year	Dec. to Dec.[1]	Year to year
1958	1.8	2.8	1.8	2.1	2.1	2.8	1.7	2.4	1.7	2.8
1959	1.7	.7	2.1	2.1	1.3	.7	2.0	2.0	1.4	1.0
1960	1.4	1.7	1.0	1.7	1.3	1.7	1.0	1.3	1.3	1.3
1961	.7	1.0	1.3	1.0	.7	1.0	1.3	1.3	.3	1.0
1962	1.3	1.0	1.0	1.0	1.3	1.3	1.3	1.3	1.3	1.0
1963	1.6	1.3	1.6	1.3	1.9	1.3	1.6	1.3	1.6	1.0
1964	1.0	1.3	1.0	1.3	1.3	1.6	1.2	1.6	1.0	1.3
1965	1.9	1.6	1.6	1.6	1.9	1.6	1.5	1.2	1.9	1.6
1966	3.5	2.9	3.5	2.2	3.4	3.1	3.3	2.4	3.4	3.1
1967	3.0	3.1	3.3	3.4	3.2	2.7	3.8	3.6	2.7	2.1
1968	4.7	4.2	5.0	4.5	4.9	4.4	5.1	4.6	4.7	4.2
1969	6.2	5.5	5.6	5.4	6.5	5.8	6.2	5.8	6.1	5.4
1970	5.6	5.7	6.6	6.0	5.4	6.1	6.6	6.3	5.2	5.9
1971	3.3	4.4	3.0	4.6	3.4	4.2	3.1	4.7	3.2	4.1
1972	3.4	3.2	2.9	2.9	3.5	3.3	3.0	3.0	3.4	3.2
1973	8.7	6.2	5.6	4.0	8.2	6.2	4.7	3.6	9.1	6.4
1974	12.3	11.0	12.2	9.8	11.7	9.8	11.1	8.3	12.2	11.2
1975	6.9	9.1	7.3	9.4	6.6	8.9	6.7	9.1	6.7	9.0
1976	4.9	5.8	6.1	6.7	4.8	5.6	6.1	6.5	4.5	5.3
1977	6.7	6.5	6.4	6.4	6.7	6.4	6.5	6.3	6.7	6.3
1978	9.0	7.6	8.3	7.2	9.1	7.8	8.5	7.4	9.1	7.6
1979	13.3	11.3	14.0	11.4	11.1	10.0	11.3	9.8	13.4	11.5
1980	12.5	13.5	13.0	14.5	11.7	11.6	12.2	12.4	12.5	13.6
1981	8.9	10.3	9.8	10.9	8.5	10.0	9.5	10.4	8.8	10.4
1982	3.8	6.2	4.1	6.5	4.2	6.7	4.5	7.4	3.6	5.9
1983	3.8	3.2	4.1	3.5	4.5	3.6	4.8	4.0	3.6	2.9
1984	3.9	4.3	3.9	4.3	4.4	4.7	4.7	5.0	3.9	4.1
1985	3.8	3.6	4.1	3.8	4.0	3.9	4.3	4.3	3.5	3.4
1986	1.1	1.9	.5	1.7	3.8	3.9	3.8	4.0	.7	1.5
1987	4.4	3.6	4.6	3.5	4.1	4.1	4.2	4.1	4.3	3.5
1988	4.4	4.1	4.2	4.1	4.7	4.4	4.7	4.4	4.2	3.9
1989	4.6	4.8	4.5	4.6	4.6	4.7	4.4	4.5	4.5	4.6
1990	6.1	5.4	6.3	5.3	5.2	5.2	5.2	5.0	5.9	5.2
1991	3.1	4.2	3.3	4.5	3.9	4.6	4.4	4.9	2.7	3.9
1992	2.9	3.0	3.2	3.5	3.0	3.2	3.3	3.7	2.7	2.8
1993	2.7	3.0	2.7	3.1	3.1	3.2	3.2	3.3	2.6	2.7
1994	2.7	2.6	2.6	2.7	2.6	2.7	2.6	2.8	2.5	2.5
1995	2.5	2.8	2.7	2.8	2.9	3.0	3.0	3.0	2.5	2.7

	Percent change from preceding period									
	Unadjusted	Seasonally adjusted	Unadjusted	Seasonally adjusted	Unadjusted	Seasonally adjusted	Unadjusted	Seasonally adjusted	Unadjusted	Seasonally adjusted
1994: Jan	0.3	0.1	0.1	0.1	0.3	0.1	0.3	0.2	0.2	0.1
Feb	.3	.3	.5	.3	.3	.2	.5	.2	.3	.2
Mar	.3	.2	.5	.3	.5	.3	.5	.3	.4	.3
Apr	.1	.2	.1	.1	.1	.2	.1	.2	.1	.1
May	.1	.1	.1	.2	.1	.3	.1	.3	.1	.1
June	.3	.3	.3	.3	.1	.3	.1	.3	.3	.3
July	.3	.3	.2	.3	.2	.3	.1	.2	.2	.3
Aug	.4	.4	.5	.3	.4	.3	.4	.3	.5	.3
Sept	.3	.2	.3	.2	.3	.2	.3	.2	.2	.1
Oct	.1	.1	.1	.1	.3	.2	.3	.2	.1	.1
Nov	.1	.1	.1	.2	.1	.1	.1	.2	.1	.1
Dec	0	.2	-.3	.1	0	.3	-.2	.1	-.1	.2
1995: Jan	.4	.3	.4	.4	.5	.3	.5	.4	.4	.3
Feb	.4	.3	.5	.3	.4	.3	.6	.3	.3	.3
Mar	.3	.2	.4	.3	.4	.3	.5	.3	.3	.2
Apr	.3	.4	.3	.3	.3	.4	.2	.4	.3	.4
May	.2	.3	.3	.3	0	.2	.1	.2	.2	.2
June	.2	.1	.3	.2	0	.2	.1	.2	.2	.2
July	0	.2	.1	.1	.1	.2	.1	.2	0	.1
Aug	.3	.1	.2	.1	.3	.2	.3	.2	.2	.1
Sept	.2	.1	.2	.1	.3	.3	.3	.2	.3	.1
Oct	.3	.3	.3	.3	.4	.3	.4	.3	.3	.3
Nov	-.1	0	0	0	.1	.1	.1	.1	-.1	0
Dec	-.1	.2	-.1	.3	-.1	.1	-.2	.1	-.1	.2

[1] Changes from December to December are based on unadjusted indexes.

Note.—See Note, Table B–56.

Source: Department of Labor, Bureau of Labor Statistics.

TABLE B-60.—*Changes in consumer price indexes for commodities and services, 1929–95*

[For all urban consumers; percent change]

Year	All items (CPI–U)		Commod- ities				Serv- ices				Medical care[2]		Energy[3]	
			Total		Food		Total		Medical care					
	Dec. to Dec.[1]	Year to year	Dec. to Dec.[1]	Year to year	Dec. to Dec.[1]	Year to year	Dec. to Dec.[1]	Year to year	Dec. to Dec.[1]	Year to year	Dec. to Dec.[1]	Year to year	Dec. to Dec.[1]	Year to year
1929	0.6	0	....	....	2.5	1.2	....	....	....	....	....	....	....	....
1933	.8	-5.1	....	....	6.9	-2.8	....	....	....	....	....	....	....	....
1939	0	-1.4	-0.7	-2.0	-2.5	-2.5	0	0	1.2	1.2	1.0	0	....	....
1940	.7	.7	1.4	.7	2.5	1.7	.8	.8	0	0	0	1.0	....	....
1941	9.9	5.0	13.3	6.7	15.7	9.2	2.4	.8	1.2	0	1.0	0	....	....
1942	9.0	10.9	12.9	14.5	17.9	17.6	2.3	3.1	3.5	3.5	3.8	2.9	....	....
1943	3.0	6.1	4.2	9.3	3.0	11.0	2.3	2.3	5.6	4.5	4.6	4.7	....	....
1944	2.3	1.7	2.0	1.0	0	-1.2	2.2	2.2	3.2	4.3	2.6	3.6	....	....
1945	2.2	2.3	2.9	3.0	3.5	2.4	.7	1.5	3.1	3.1	2.6	2.6	....	....
1946	18.1	8.3	24.8	10.6	31.3	14.5	3.6	1.4	9.0	5.1	8.3	5.0	....	....
1947	8.8	14.4	10.3	20.5	11.3	21.7	5.6	4.3	6.4	8.7	6.9	8.0	....	....
1948	3.0	8.1	1.7	7.2	-.8	8.3	5.9	6.1	6.9	7.1	5.8	6.7	....	....
1949	-2.1	-1.2	-4.1	-2.7	-3.9	-4.2	3.7	5.1	1.6	3.3	1.4	2.8	....	....
1950	5.9	1.3	7.8	.7	9.8	1.6	3.6	3.0	4.0	2.4	3.4	2.0	....	....
1951	6.0	7.9	5.9	9.0	7.1	11.0	5.2	5.3	5.3	4.7	5.8	5.3	....	....
1952	.8	1.9	-.9	1.3	-1.0	1.8	4.4	4.5	5.8	6.7	4.3	5.0	....	....
1953	.7	.8	-.3	-.3	-1.1	-1.4	4.2	4.3	3.4	3.5	3.5	3.6	....	....
1954	-.7	.7	-1.6	-.9	-1.8	-.4	2.0	3.1	2.6	3.4	2.3	2.9	....	....
1955	.4	-.4	-.3	-.9	-.7	-1.4	2.0	2.0	3.2	2.6	3.3	2.2	....	....
1956	3.0	1.5	2.6	1.0	2.9	.7	3.4	2.5	3.8	3.8	3.2	3.8	....	....
1957	2.9	3.3	2.8	3.2	2.8	3.2	4.2	4.3	4.8	4.3	4.7	4.2	....	....
1958	1.8	2.8	1.2	2.1	2.4	4.5	2.7	3.7	4.6	5.3	4.5	4.6	-0.9	0
1959	1.7	.7	.6	0	-1.0	-1.7	3.9	3.1	4.9	4.5	3.8	4.4	4.7	1.9
1960	1.4	1.7	1.2	.9	3.1	1.0	2.5	3.4	3.7	4.3	3.2	3.7	1.3	2.3
1961	.7	1.0	0	.6	-.7	1.3	2.1	1.7	3.5	3.6	3.1	2.7	-1.3	.4
1962	1.3	1.0	.9	.9	1.3	.7	1.6	2.0	2.9	3.5	2.2	2.6	2.2	.4
1963	1.6	1.3	1.5	.9	2.0	1.6	2.4	2.0	2.8	2.9	2.5	2.6	-.9	0
1964	1.0	1.3	.9	1.2	1.3	1.3	1.6	2.0	2.3	2.3	2.1	2.1	0	-.4
1965	1.9	1.6	1.4	1.1	3.5	2.2	2.7	2.3	3.6	3.2	2.8	2.4	1.8	1.8
1966	3.5	2.9	2.5	2.6	4.0	5.0	4.8	3.8	8.3	5.3	6.7	4.4	1.7	1.7
1967	3.0	3.1	2.5	1.9	1.2	.9	4.3	4.3	8.0	8.8	6.3	7.2	1.7	2.1
1968	4.7	4.2	4.0	3.5	4.4	3.5	5.8	5.2	7.1	7.3	6.2	6.0	1.7	1.7
1969	6.2	5.5	5.4	4.7	7.0	5.1	7.7	6.9	7.3	8.2	6.2	6.7	2.9	2.5
1970	5.6	5.7	3.9	4.5	2.3	5.7	8.1	8.0	8.1	7.0	7.4	6.6	4.8	2.8
1971	3.3	4.4	2.8	3.6	4.3	3.1	4.1	5.7	5.4	7.4	4.6	6.2	3.1	3.9
1972	3.4	3.2	3.4	3.0	4.6	4.2	3.4	3.8	3.7	3.5	3.3	3.3	2.6	2.6
1973	8.7	6.2	10.4	7.4	20.3	14.5	6.2	4.4	6.0	4.5	5.3	4.0	17.0	8.1
1974	12.3	11.0	12.8	11.9	12.0	14.3	11.4	9.2	13.2	10.4	12.6	9.3	21.6	29.6
1975	6.9	9.1	6.2	8.8	6.6	8.5	8.2	9.6	10.3	12.6	9.8	12.0	11.4	10.5
1976	4.9	5.8	3.3	4.3	.5	3.0	7.2	8.3	10.8	10.1	10.0	9.5	7.1	7.1
1977	6.7	6.5	6.1	5.8	8.1	6.3	8.0	7.7	9.0	9.9	8.9	9.6	7.2	9.5
1978	9.0	7.6	8.8	7.2	11.8	9.9	9.3	8.6	9.3	8.5	8.8	8.4	7.9	6.3
1979	13.3	11.3	13.0	11.3	10.2	11.0	13.6	11.0	10.5	9.8	10.1	9.2	37.5	25.1
1980	12.5	13.5	11.0	12.3	10.2	8.6	14.2	15.4	10.1	11.3	9.9	11.0	18.0	30.9
1981	8.9	10.3	6.0	8.4	4.3	7.8	13.0	13.1	12.6	10.7	12.5	10.7	11.9	13.6
1982	3.8	6.2	3.6	4.1	3.1	4.1	4.3	9.0	11.2	11.8	11.0	11.6	1.3	1.5
1983	3.8	3.2	2.9	2.9	2.7	2.1	4.8	3.5	6.2	8.7	6.4	8.8	-.5	.7
1984	3.9	4.3	2.7	3.4	3.8	3.8	5.4	5.2	5.8	6.0	6.1	6.2	.2	1.0
1985	3.8	3.6	2.5	2.1	2.6	2.3	5.1	5.1	6.8	6.1	6.8	6.3	1.8	.7
1986	1.1	1.9	-2.0	-.9	3.8	3.2	4.5	5.0	7.9	7.7	7.7	7.5	-19.7	-13.2
1987	4.4	3.6	4.6	3.2	3.5	4.1	4.3	4.2	5.6	6.6	5.8	6.6	8.2	.5
1988	4.4	4.1	3.8	3.5	5.2	4.1	4.8	4.6	6.9	6.4	6.9	6.5	.5	.8
1989	4.6	4.8	4.1	4.7	5.6	5.8	5.1	4.9	8.6	7.7	8.5	7.7	5.1	5.6
1990	6.1	5.4	6.6	5.2	5.3	5.8	5.7	5.5	9.9	9.3	9.6	9.0	18.1	8.3
1991	3.1	4.2	1.2	3.1	1.9	2.9	4.6	5.1	8.0	8.9	7.9	8.7	-7.4	.4
1992	2.9	3.0	2.0	2.0	1.5	1.2	3.6	3.9	7.0	7.6	6.6	7.4	2.0	.5
1993	2.7	3.0	1.5	1.9	2.9	2.2	3.8	3.9	5.9	6.5	5.4	5.9	-1.4	1.2
1994	2.7	2.6	2.3	1.7	2.9	2.4	2.9	3.3	5.4	5.2	4.9	4.8	2.2	.4
1995	2.5	2.8	1.4	1.9	2.1	2.8	3.5	3.4	4.4	5.1	3.9	4.5	-1.3	.6

[1] Changes from December to December are based on unadjusted indexes.

[2] Commodities and services.

[3] Household fuels—gas (piped), electricity, fuel oil, etc.—and motor fuel. Motor oil, coolant, etc. also included through 1982.

Note.—See Note, Table B-56.

Source: Department of Labor, Bureau of Labor Statistics.

TABLE B-61.—*Producer price indexes by stage of processing, 1950-95*

[1982=100]

Year or month	Total finished goods	Finished goods								
		Consumer foods			Finished goods excluding consumer foods					Total finished consumer goods
		Total	Crude	Proc-essed	Total	Consumer goods			Capital equipment	
						Total	Durable	Non-durable		
1950	28.2	32.7	36.5	32.4	....	29.0	36.5	25.1	23.2	29.9
1951	30.8	36.7	41.9	36.2	....	31.1	38.9	27.0	25.5	32.7
1952	30.6	36.4	44.6	35.4	....	30.7	39.2	26.3	25.9	32.3
1953	30.3	34.5	41.6	33.6	....	31.0	39.5	26.6	26.3	31.7
1954	30.4	34.2	37.5	34.0	....	31.1	39.8	26.7	26.7	31.7
1955	30.5	33.4	39.1	32.7	....	31.3	40.2	26.8	27.4	31.5
1956	31.3	33.3	39.1	32.7	....	32.1	41.6	27.3	29.5	32.0
1957	32.5	34.4	38.5	34.1	....	32.9	42.8	27.9	31.3	32.9
1958	33.2	36.5	41.0	36.1	....	32.9	43.4	27.8	32.1	33.6
1959	33.1	34.8	37.3	34.7	....	33.3	43.9	28.2	32.7	33.3
1960	33.4	35.5	39.8	35.2	....	33.5	43.8	28.4	32.8	33.6
1961	33.4	35.4	38.0	35.3	....	33.4	43.6	28.4	32.9	33.6
1962	33.5	35.7	38.4	35.6	....	33.4	43.4	28.4	33.0	33.7
1963	33.4	35.3	37.8	35.2	....	33.4	43.1	28.5	33.1	33.5
1964	33.5	35.4	38.9	35.2	....	33.3	43.3	28.4	33.4	33.6
1965	34.1	36.8	39.0	36.8	....	33.6	43.2	28.8	33.8	34.2
1966	35.2	39.2	41.5	39.2	....	34.1	43.4	29.3	34.6	35.4
1967	35.6	38.5	39.6	38.8	35.0	34.7	44.1	30.0	35.8	35.6
1968	36.6	40.0	42.5	40.0	35.9	35.5	45.1	30.6	37.0	36.5
1969	38.0	42.4	45.9	42.3	36.9	36.3	45.9	31.5	38.3	37.9
1970	39.3	43.8	46.0	43.9	38.2	37.4	47.2	32.5	40.1	39.1
1971	40.5	44.5	45.8	44.7	39.6	38.7	48.9	33.5	41.7	40.2
1972	41.8	46.9	48.0	47.2	40.4	39.4	50.0	34.1	42.8	41.5
1973	45.6	56.5	63.6	55.8	42.0	41.2	50.9	36.1	44.2	46.0
1974	52.6	64.4	71.6	63.9	48.8	48.2	55.5	44.0	50.5	53.1
1975	58.2	69.8	71.7	70.3	54.7	53.2	61.0	48.9	58.2	58.2
1976	60.8	69.6	76.7	69.0	58.1	56.5	63.7	52.4	62.1	60.4
1977	64.7	73.3	79.5	72.7	62.2	60.6	67.4	56.8	66.1	64.3
1978	69.8	79.9	85.8	79.4	66.7	64.9	73.6	60.0	71.3	69.4
1979	77.6	87.3	92.3	86.8	74.6	73.5	80.8	69.3	77.5	77.5
1980	88.0	92.4	93.9	92.3	86.7	87.1	91.0	85.1	85.8	88.6
1981	96.1	97.8	104.4	97.2	95.6	96.1	96.4	95.8	94.6	96.6
1982	100.0	100.0	100.0	100.0	100.0	100.0	100.0	100.0	100.0	100.0
1983	101.6	101.0	102.4	100.9	101.8	101.2	102.8	100.5	102.8	101.3
1984	103.7	105.4	111.4	104.9	103.2	102.2	104.5	101.1	105.2	103.3
1985	104.7	104.6	102.9	104.8	104.6	103.3	106.5	101.7	107.5	103.8
1986	103.2	107.3	105.6	107.4	101.9	98.5	108.9	93.3	109.7	101.4
1987	105.4	109.5	107.1	109.6	104.0	100.7	111.5	94.9	111.7	103.6
1988	108.0	112.6	109.8	112.7	106.5	103.1	113.8	97.3	114.3	106.2
1989	113.6	118.7	119.6	118.6	111.8	108.9	117.6	103.8	118.8	112.1
1990	119.2	124.4	123.0	124.4	117.4	115.3	120.4	111.5	122.9	118.2
1991	121.7	124.1	119.3	124.4	120.9	118.7	123.9	115.0	126.7	120.5
1992	123.2	123.3	107.6	124.4	123.1	120.8	125.7	117.3	129.1	121.7
1993	124.7	125.7	114.4	126.5	124.4	121.7	128.0	117.6	131.4	123.0
1994	125.5	126.8	111.3	127.9	125.1	121.6	130.9	116.2	134.1	123.3
1995	127.9	129.0	118.7	129.7	127.5	123.9	132.6	118.8	136.7	125.6
1994: Jan	124.5	127.0	124.2	127.2	123.7	119.9	130.5	114.0	133.3	122.2
Feb	124.8	126.7	109.4	128.0	124.1	120.5	130.5	114.9	133.5	122.5
Mar	124.9	127.5	112.2	128.7	124.1	120.4	130.5	114.7	133.6	122.6
Apr	125.0	127.1	105.3	128.7	124.3	120.7	130.4	115.1	133.8	122.7
May	125.3	126.6	103.1	128.3	124.8	121.2	130.9	115.6	134.1	122.9
June	125.6	125.9	103.5	127.6	125.4	122.0	130.8	116.9	134.2	123.3
July	126.0	126.2	106.3	127.7	125.8	122.5	130.9	117.5	134.2	123.8
Aug	126.5	126.6	104.7	128.2	126.4	123.4	131.0	118.7	134.3	124.5
Sept	125.6	126.3	106.6	127.8	125.3	122.2	129.2	117.8	133.5	123.5
Oct	125.8	126.1	104.3	127.7	125.6	122.0	132.1	116.3	134.8	123.4
Nov	126.1	126.9	114.3	127.8	125.8	122.3	132.1	116.7	134.8	123.8
Dec	126.2	128.6	142.3	127.5	125.5	121.8	132.2	115.9	135.1	123.9
1995: Jan	126.6	127.9	120.1	128.5	126.2	122.4	132.6	116.7	135.9	124.2
Feb	126.9	128.4	117.2	129.2	126.4	122.6	132.7	116.9	136.1	124.5
Mar	127.1	128.7	118.6	129.4	126.6	122.9	132.4	117.3	136.2	124.7
Apr	127.6	128.7	130.8	128.5	127.2	123.6	132.4	118.4	136.4	125.2
May	128.1	128.0	122.7	128.4	128.0	124.7	132.3	120.1	136.5	125.9
June	128.2	127.4	111.0	128.6	128.3	125.1	132.0	120.8	136.4	126.0
July	128.2	128.5	110.2	129.8	128.0	124.7	132.1	120.1	136.6	126.0
Aug[1]	128.1	128.8	108.2	130.3	127.8	124.4	131.9	119.8	136.6	125.9
Sept	127.9	129.9	123.1	130.4	127.2	123.9	130.2	119.9	135.7	125.9
Oct	128.5	129.7	112.1	131.0	128.0	124.3	133.9	118.7	137.7	126.0
Nov	128.6	130.9	125.9	131.3	127.8	123.9	134.5	117.8	138.0	126.1
Dec	129.0	131.0	124.0	131.4	128.3	124.5	134.5	118.8	138.1	126.6

[1] Data have been revised through August 1995 to reflect the availability of late reports and corrections by respondents. All data are subject to revision 4 months after original publication.

See next page for continuation of table.

165-967 96 - 12

TABLE B–61.—*Producer price indexes by stage of processing, 1950–95*—Continued

[1982=100]

Year or month	Intermediate materials, supplies, and components								Crude materials for further processing				
	Total	Foods and feeds[2]	Other	Materials and components		Processed fuels and lubricants	Containers	Supplies	Total	Foodstuffs and feedstuffs	Other		
				For manufacturing	For construction						Total	Fuel	Other
1950	25.3	....	24.6	26.9	26.2	15.2	25.2	29.0	32.7	43.4	....	8.8	27.8
1951	28.4	....	27.6	30.5	28.7	15.9	29.6	32.6	37.6	50.2	....	9.0	32.0
1952	27.5	....	26.7	29.3	28.5	15.7	28.0	32.6	34.5	47.3	....	9.0	27.8
1953	27.7	....	27.0	29.7	29.0	15.8	28.0	31.0	31.9	42.3	....	9.3	26.6
1954	27.9	....	27.2	29.8	29.1	15.8	28.5	31.7	31.6	42.3	....	8.9	26.1
1955	28.4	....	28.0	30.5	30.3	15.8	28.9	31.2	30.4	38.4	....	8.9	27.5
1956	29.6	....	29.3	32.0	31.8	16.3	31.0	32.0	30.6	37.6	....	9.5	28.6
1957	30.3	....	30.1	32.7	32.0	17.2	32.4	32.3	31.2	39.2	....	10.1	28.2
1958	30.4	....	30.1	32.8	32.0	16.2	33.2	33.1	31.9	41.6	....	10.2	27.1
1959	30.8	....	30.5	33.3	32.9	16.2	33.0	33.5	31.1	38.8	....	10.4	28.1
1960	30.8	....	30.7	33.3	32.7	16.6	33.4	33.3	30.4	38.4	....	10.5	26.9
1961	30.6	....	30.3	32.9	32.2	16.8	33.2	33.7	30.2	37.9	....	10.5	27.2
1962	30.6	....	30.2	32.7	32.1	16.7	33.6	34.5	30.5	38.6	....	10.4	27.1
1963	30.7	....	30.1	32.7	32.2	16.6	33.2	35.0	29.9	37.5	....	10.5	26.7
1964	30.8	....	30.3	33.1	32.5	16.2	32.9	34.7	29.6	36.6	....	10.5	27.2
1965	31.2	....	30.7	33.6	32.8	16.5	33.5	35.0	31.1	39.2	....	10.6	27.7
1966	32.0	....	31.3	34.3	33.6	16.8	34.5	36.5	33.1	42.7	....	10.9	28.3
1967	32.2	41.8	31.7	34.5	34.0	16.9	35.0	36.8	31.3	40.3	21.1	11.3	26.5
1968	33.0	41.5	32.5	35.3	35.7	16.5	35.9	37.1	31.8	40.9	21.6	11.5	27.1
1969	34.1	42.9	33.6	36.5	37.7	16.6	37.2	37.8	33.9	44.1	22.5	12.0	28.4
1970	35.4	45.6	34.8	38.0	38.3	17.7	39.0	39.7	35.2	45.2	23.8	13.8	29.1
1971	36.8	46.7	36.2	38.9	40.8	19.5	40.8	40.8	36.0	46.1	24.7	15.7	29.4
1972	38.2	49.5	37.7	40.4	43.0	20.1	42.7	42.5	39.9	51.5	27.0	16.8	32.3
1973	42.4	70.3	40.6	44.1	46.5	22.2	45.2	51.7	54.5	72.6	34.3	18.6	42.9
1974	52.5	83.6	50.5	56.0	55.0	33.6	53.3	56.8	61.4	76.4	44.1	24.8	54.5
1975	58.0	81.6	56.6	61.7	60.1	39.4	60.0	61.8	61.6	77.4	43.7	30.6	50.0
1976	60.9	77.4	60.0	64.0	64.1	42.3	63.1	65.8	63.4	76.8	48.2	34.5	54.9
1977	64.9	79.6	64.1	67.4	69.3	47.7	65.9	69.3	65.5	77.5	51.7	42.0	56.3
1978	69.5	84.8	68.6	72.0	76.5	49.9	71.0	72.9	73.4	87.3	57.5	48.2	61.9
1979	78.4	94.5	77.4	80.9	84.2	61.6	79.4	80.2	85.9	100.0	69.6	57.3	75.5
1980	90.3	105.5	89.4	91.7	91.3	85.0	89.1	89.9	95.3	104.6	84.6	69.4	91.8
1981	98.6	104.6	98.2	98.7	97.9	100.6	96.7	96.9	103.0	103.9	101.8	84.8	109.8
1982	100.0	100.0	100.0	100.0	100.0	100.0	100.0	100.0	100.0	100.0	100.0	100.0	100.0
1983	100.6	103.6	100.5	101.2	102.8	95.4	100.4	101.8	101.3	101.8	100.7	105.1	98.8
1984	103.1	105.7	103.0	104.1	105.6	95.7	105.9	104.1	103.5	104.7	102.2	105.1	101.0
1985	102.7	97.3	103.0	103.3	107.3	92.8	109.0	104.4	95.8	94.8	96.9	102.7	94.3
1986	99.1	96.2	99.3	102.2	108.1	72.7	110.3	105.6	87.7	93.2	81.6	92.2	76.0
1987	101.5	99.2	101.7	105.3	109.8	73.3	114.5	107.7	93.7	96.2	87.9	84.1	88.5
1988	107.1	109.5	106.9	113.2	116.1	71.2	120.1	113.7	96.0	106.1	85.5	82.1	85.9
1989	112.0	113.8	111.9	118.1	121.3	76.4	125.4	118.1	103.1	111.2	93.4	85.3	95.8
1990	114.5	113.3	114.5	118.7	122.9	85.9	127.7	119.4	108.9	113.1	101.5	84.8	107.3
1991	114.4	111.1	114.6	118.1	124.5	85.3	128.1	121.4	101.2	105.5	94.6	82.9	97.5
1992	114.7	110.7	114.9	117.9	126.5	84.5	127.7	122.7	100.4	105.1	93.5	84.0	94.2
1993	116.2	112.7	116.4	118.9	132.0	84.7	126.4	125.0	102.4	108.4	94.7	87.1	94.1
1994	118.5	114.8	118.7	122.1	136.6	83.1	129.7	127.0	101.8	106.5	94.8	82.4	97.0
1995	124.9	114.8	125.5	130.5	142.2	84.1	148.9	132.1	102.6	105.8	96.6	71.7	105.7
1994:Jan	116.2	116.8	116.2	119.5	135.0	79.5	126.2	126.4	103.2	112.2	93.5	93.8	88.6
Feb	116.6	117.2	116.6	119.7	135.1	81.3	126.1	126.6	101.8	113.1	90.7	86.1	88.7
Mar	116.8	117.4	116.8	120.0	135.5	81.0	126.0	126.6	104.1	114.2	93.7	91.0	90.5
Apr	116.9	117.1	116.9	120.4	135.1	80.7	126.3	126.5	104.1	113.1	94.4	88.7	92.8
May	117.2	116.5	117.3	120.7	135.3	81.3	127.5	126.6	103.0	109.7	94.7	83.0	96.5
June	118.2	115.5	118.3	121.2	136.2	84.4	127.9	126.9	103.2	107.8	96.4	82.1	99.5
July	118.7	113.4	119.0	121.7	136.3	85.9	128.2	126.9	102.2	103.6	97.3	78.3	103.0
Aug	119.5	113.6	119.8	122.5	136.8	87.5	129.4	126.9	101.9	101.8	98.0	80.7	102.7
Sept	120.1	113.9	120.4	123.7	137.5	86.6	131.6	127.2	99.7	101.3	94.8	78.6	99.1
Oct	120.0	112.2	120.4	124.5	138.0	83.0	133.9	127.5	98.2	98.9	94.0	74.8	100.0
Nov	120.9	112.1	121.3	125.5	139.1	83.5	136.2	127.9	99.1	100.4	94.5	73.2	101.6
Dec	121.1	111.5	121.6	126.2	139.4	82.3	137.4	128.4	100.5	101.6	95.9	77.8	101.3
1995:Jan	122.5	111.8	123.0	128.1	140.5	82.3	139.9	129.5	101.5	102.2	97.2	77.1	103.6
Feb	123.4	111.8	124.0	129.3	141.0	82.5	144.6	130.0	102.6	104.1	97.7	72.3	107.0
Mar	124.0	112.6	124.5	129.9	141.7	82.7	145.9	130.6	102.3	103.2	97.8	71.0	107.9
Apr	124.7	111.7	125.4	130.7	142.2	83.5	146.9	131.2	103.6	101.8	100.7	71.9	111.8
May	125.3	110.7	126.0	130.9	142.2	85.4	149.0	131.4	102.8	99.6	100.9	72.6	111.6
June	125.8	111.6	126.6	131.0	142.0	87.4	151.4	131.9	103.4	102.1	100.1	74.1	109.7
July	126.0	113.6	126.6	131.3	142.6	86.3	152.0	132.4	102.1	104.6	96.6	72.9	105.1
Aug[1]	126.0	114.8	126.6	131.3	142.9	86.0	152.0	132.7	100.5	104.8	93.8	66.5	104.4
Sept	126.0	115.9	126.6	131.4	143.3	85.4	151.9	133.1	102.4	108.7	94.4	67.4	104.8
Oct	125.3	118.7	125.7	131.0	142.9	82.6	151.4	133.5	101.6	109.3	92.9	69.9	101.1
Nov	125.1	121.4	125.3	130.6	142.5	82.2	151.2	134.3	103.6	113.9	93.1	72.6	99.9
Dec	125.1	123.0	125.2	129.9	142.1	83.2	150.6	134.7	104.6	114.7	94.1	72.1	101.7

[2] Intermediate materials for food manufacturing and feeds.

Source: Department of Labor, Bureau of Labor Statistics.

TABLE B–62.—*Producer price indexes by stage of processing, special groups, 1974–95*

[1982=100]

Year or month	Finished goods						Intermediate materials, supplies, and components				Crude materials for further processing			
	Total	Foods	Energy	Excluding foods and energy			Total	Foods and feeds¹	Energy	Other	Total	Foodstuffs and feedstuffs	Energy	Other
				Total	Capital equipment	Consumer goods excluding foods and energy								
1974	52.6	64.4	26.2	53.6	50.5	55.5	52.5	83.6	33.1	54.0	61.4	76.4	27.8	83.3
1975	58.2	69.8	30.7	59.7	58.2	60.6	58.0	81.6	38.7	60.2	61.6	77.4	33.3	69.3
1976	60.8	69.6	34.3	63.1	62.1	63.7	60.9	77.4	41.5	63.8	63.4	76.8	35.3	80.2
1977	64.7	73.3	39.7	66.9	66.1	67.3	64.9	79.6	46.8	67.6	65.5	77.5	40.4	79.8
1978	69.8	79.9	42.3	71.9	71.3	72.2	69.5	84.8	49.1	72.5	73.4	87.3	45.2	87.8
1979	77.6	87.3	57.1	78.3	77.5	78.8	78.4	94.5	61.1	80.7	85.9	100.0	54.9	106.2
1980	88.0	92.4	85.2	87.1	85.8	87.8	90.3	105.5	84.9	90.3	95.3	104.6	73.1	113.1
1981	96.1	97.8	101.5	94.6	94.6	94.6	98.6	104.6	100.5	97.7	103.0	103.9	97.7	111.7
1982	100.0	100.0	100.0	100.0	100.0	100.0	100.0	100.0	100.0	100.0	100.0	100.0	100.0	100.0
1983	101.6	101.0	95.2	103.0	102.8	103.1	100.6	103.6	95.3	101.6	101.3	101.8	98.7	105.3
1984	103.7	105.4	91.2	105.5	105.2	105.7	103.1	105.7	95.5	104.7	103.5	104.7	98.0	111.7
1985	104.7	104.6	87.6	108.1	107.5	108.4	102.7	97.3	92.6	105.2	95.8	94.8	93.3	104.9
1986	103.2	107.3	63.0	110.6	109.7	111.1	99.1	96.2	72.6	104.9	87.7	93.2	71.8	103.1
1987	105.4	109.5	61.8	113.3	111.7	114.2	101.5	99.2	73.0	107.8	93.7	96.2	75.0	115.7
1988	108.0	112.6	59.8	117.0	114.3	118.5	107.1	109.5	70.9	115.2	96.0	106.1	67.7	133.0
1989	113.6	118.7	65.7	122.1	118.8	124.0	112.0	113.8	76.1	120.2	103.1	111.2	75.9	137.9
1990	119.2	124.4	75.0	126.6	122.9	128.8	114.5	113.3	85.5	120.9	108.9	113.1	85.9	136.3
1991	121.7	124.1	78.1	131.1	126.7	133.7	114.4	111.1	85.1	121.4	101.2	105.5	80.4	128.2
1992	123.2	123.3	77.8	134.2	129.1	137.3	114.7	110.7	84.3	122.0	100.4	105.1	78.8	128.4
1993	124.7	125.7	78.0	135.8	131.4	138.5	116.2	112.7	84.6	123.8	102.4	108.4	76.7	140.2
1994	125.5	126.8	77.0	137.1	134.1	139.0	118.5	114.8	83.0	127.1	101.8	106.5	72.1	156.2
1995	127.9	129.0	78.1	139.9	136.7	141.9	124.9	114.8	84.0	135.2	102.6	105.8	69.2	173.6
1994:Jan	124.5	127.0	73.6	136.6	133.3	138.6	116.2	116.8	79.5	124.8	103.2	112.2	72.9	147.9
Feb	124.8	126.7	74.9	136.7	133.5	138.7	116.6	117.2	81.1	124.9	101.8	113.1	68.3	152.0
Mar	124.9	127.5	74.7	136.7	133.6	138.6	116.8	117.4	80.9	125.2	104.1	114.2	71.7	153.1
Apr	125.0	127.1	75.5	136.7	133.8	138.5	116.9	117.1	80.6	125.4	104.1	113.1	72.5	153.3
May	125.3	126.6	76.2	137.0	134.1	138.8	117.2	116.5	81.2	125.7	103.0	109.7	73.4	151.4
June	125.6	125.9	78.3	137.1	134.2	138.9	118.2	115.5	84.2	126.3	103.2	107.8	75.2	152.4
July	126.0	126.2	79.6	137.1	134.2	138.9	118.7	113.4	85.8	126.7	102.2	103.6	75.3	155.6
Aug	126.5	126.6	81.4	137.2	134.3	139.0	119.5	113.6	87.3	127.3	101.9	101.8	75.6	157.9
Sept	126.5	126.3	79.6	136.4	133.5	138.2	120.1	113.9	86.5	128.3	99.7	101.3	71.3	159.2
Oct	125.8	126.1	77.1	137.8	134.8	139.6	120.0	112.2	83.0	129.2	98.2	98.9	70.2	159.3
Nov	126.1	126.9	77.7	137.8	134.8	139.7	120.9	112.1	83.4	130.2	99.1	100.4	69.3	164.1
Dec	126.2	128.6	75.9	138.1	135.1	140.0	121.1	111.5	82.2	130.9	100.5	101.6	69.9	168.4
1995:Jan	126.6	127.9	76.6	138.7	135.9	140.5	122.5	111.8	82.2	132.6	101.5	102.2	69.8	174.1
Feb	126.9	128.4	76.6	139.0	136.1	140.8	123.4	111.8	82.4	133.8	102.6	104.1	69.6	177.0
Mar	127.1	128.7	76.8	139.2	136.2	141.1	124.0	112.6	82.6	134.4	102.3	103.2	69.1	179.1
Apr	127.6	128.7	78.2	139.4	136.4	141.3	124.7	111.7	83.5	135.2	103.6	101.8	72.0	181.4
May	128.1	128.0	80.4	139.7	136.5	141.7	125.3	110.7	85.2	135.6	102.8	99.6	72.4	180.5
June	128.2	127.4	81.4	139.7	136.4	141.7	125.8	111.6	87.3	135.7	103.4	102.1	71.5	180.6
July	128.2	128.5	79.9	139.9	136.6	142.0	126.0	113.6	86.2	136.1	102.1	104.6	68.2	177.0
Aug²	128.1	128.8	79.4	139.8	136.6	141.9	126.0	114.8	85.9	136.1	100.5	104.8	65.6	174.0
Sept	127.9	129.9	79.0	139.2	135.7	141.3	126.0	115.9	85.3	136.2	102.4	108.7	67.2	171.1
Oct	128.5	129.7	76.8	141.1	137.7	143.2	125.3	118.7	82.5	135.8	101.6	109.3	66.9	165.6
Nov	128.6	130.9	75.2	141.2	138.0	143.6	125.1	121.4	82.0	135.5	103.6	113.9	68.3	161.7
Dec	129.0	131.0	76.6	141.6	138.1	143.8	125.1	123.0	83.1	135.0	104.6	114.7	69.9	160.7

¹ Intermediate materials for food manufacturing and feeds.
² Data have been revised through August 1995 to reflect the availability of late reports and corrections by respondents. All data are subject to revision 4 months after original publication.

Source: Department of Labor, Bureau of Labor Statistics.

TABLE B–63.—*Producer price indexes for major commodity groups, 1950–95*

[1982=100]

Year or month	Farm products and processed foods and feeds			Industrial commodities				
	Total	Farm products	Processed foods and feeds	Total	Textile products and apparel	Hides, skins, leather, and related products	Fuels and related products and power[1]	Chemicals and allied products[1]
1950	37.7	44.0	33.2	25.0	50.2	32.9	12.6	30.4
1951	43.0	51.2	36.9	27.6	56.0	37.7	13.0	34.8
1952	41.3	48.4	36.4	26.9	50.5	30.5	13.0	33.0
1953	38.6	43.8	34.8	27.2	49.3	31.0	13.4	33.4
1954	38.5	43.2	35.4	27.2	48.2	29.5	13.2	33.8
1955	36.6	40.5	33.8	27.8	48.2	29.4	13.2	33.7
1956	36.4	40.0	33.8	29.1	48.2	31.2	13.6	33.9
1957	37.7	41.1	34.8	29.9	48.3	31.2	14.3	34.6
1958	39.4	42.9	36.5	30.0	47.4	31.6	13.7	34.9
1959	37.6	40.2	35.6	30.5	48.1	35.9	13.7	34.8
1960	37.7	40.1	35.6	30.5	48.6	34.6	13.9	34.8
1961	37.7	39.7	36.2	30.4	47.8	34.9	14.0	34.5
1962	38.1	40.4	36.5	30.4	48.2	35.3	14.0	33.9
1963	37.7	39.6	36.8	30.3	48.2	34.3	13.9	33.5
1964	37.5	39.0	36.7	30.5	48.5	34.4	13.5	33.6
1965	39.0	40.7	38.0	30.9	48.8	35.9	13.8	33.9
1966	41.6	43.7	40.2	31.5	48.9	39.4	14.1	34.0
1967	40.2	41.3	39.8	32.0	48.9	38.1	14.4	34.2
1968	41.1	42.3	40.6	32.8	50.7	39.3	14.3	34.1
1969	43.4	45.0	42.7	33.9	51.8	41.5	14.6	34.2
1970	44.9	45.8	44.6	35.2	52.4	42.0	15.3	35.0
1971	45.8	46.6	45.5	36.5	53.3	43.4	16.6	35.6
1972	49.2	51.6	48.0	37.8	55.5	50.0	17.1	35.6
1973	63.9	72.7	58.9	40.3	60.5	54.5	19.4	37.6
1974	71.3	77.4	68.0	49.2	68.0	55.2	30.1	50.2
1975	74.0	77.0	72.6	54.9	67.4	56.5	35.4	62.0
1976	73.6	78.8	70.8	58.4	72.4	63.9	38.3	64.0
1977	75.9	79.4	74.0	62.5	75.3	68.3	43.6	65.9
1978	83.0	87.7	80.6	67.0	78.1	76.1	46.5	68.0
1979	92.3	99.6	88.5	75.7	82.5	96.1	58.9	76.0
1980	98.3	102.9	95.9	88.0	89.7	94.7	82.8	89.0
1981	101.1	105.2	98.9	97.4	97.6	99.3	100.2	98.4
1982	100.0	100.0	100.0	100.0	100.0	100.0	100.0	100.0
1983	102.0	102.4	101.8	101.1	100.3	103.2	95.9	100.3
1984	105.5	105.5	105.4	103.3	102.7	109.0	94.8	102.9
1985	100.7	95.1	103.5	103.7	102.9	108.9	91.4	103.7
1986	101.2	92.9	105.4	100.0	103.2	113.0	69.8	102.6
1987	103.7	95.5	107.9	102.6	105.1	120.4	70.2	106.4
1988	110.0	104.9	112.7	106.3	109.2	131.4	66.7	116.3
1989	115.4	110.9	117.8	111.6	112.3	136.3	72.9	123.0
1990	118.6	112.2	121.9	115.8	115.0	141.7	82.3	123.6
1991	116.4	105.7	121.9	116.5	116.3	138.9	81.2	125.6
1992	115.9	103.6	122.1	117.4	117.8	140.4	80.4	125.9
1993	118.4	107.1	124.0	119.0	118.0	143.7	80.0	128.2
1994	119.1	106.3	125.5	120.7	118.3	148.5	77.8	132.1
1995	120.5	107.4	127.0	125.5	120.8	153.6	77.9	142.6
1994: Jan	121.4	112.0	126.0	118.7	117.9	145.1	75.4	128.3
Feb	121.6	112.3	126.2	118.8	117.9	143.8	75.4	128.2
Mar	122.2	112.8	126.8	119.2	117.9	144.6	76.0	128.3
Apr	121.6	111.5	126.6	119.4	117.9	146.1	76.4	129.3
May	120.3	108.7	126.1	119.8	118.0	146.7	77.2	130.2
June	119.3	107.2	125.4	120.7	118.1	147.2	79.5	130.7
July	117.5	102.8	124.9	121.2	118.4	148.7	80.6	131.2
Aug	117.1	101.0	125.2	121.9	118.5	149.0	82.0	132.6
Sept	117.1	101.3	125.0	121.7	118.7	150.8	79.9	134.8
Oct	115.9	98.8	124.5	121.8	118.6	153.2	77.4	136.4
Nov	116.9	101.4	124.7	122.4	118.6	153.7	77.5	137.2
Dec	118.1	105.5	124.3	122.6	118.8	153.5	76.6	138.4
1995: Jan	118.0	103.6	125.2	123.7	119.4	154.1	76.8	140.4
Feb	118.9	104.9	125.9	124.4	119.9	155.2	76.8	141.8
Mar	119.2	105.1	126.2	124.7	120.1	156.2	76.8	142.5
Apr	118.7	104.8	125.6	125.6	120.4	156.1	78.5	144.1
May	117.5	102.6	125.0	126.3	120.8	157.8	80.0	144.4
June	118.3	104.2	125.3	126.6	120.8	155.0	81.0	143.8
July	119.9	106.2	126.7	126.2	121.0	154.9	79.2	143.6
Aug[2]	120.0	105.1	127.5	126.0	121.1	153.2	78.3	142.9
Sept	122.0	110.6	127.6	125.8	121.3	151.7	78.3	143.4
Oct	122.6	109.9	128.9	125.5	121.6	150.5	76.3	142.1
Nov	125.0	115.1	130.0	125.3	121.3	149.2	75.9	141.6
Dec	125.6	116.4	130.1	125.5	121.5	149.4	77.2	140.4

[1] Prices for some items in this grouping are lagged and refer to 1 month earlier than the index month.
[2] Data have been revised through August 1995 to reflect the availability of late reports and corrections by respondents. All data are subject to revision 4 months after original publication.

See next page for continuation of table.

[1982=100]

Year or month	Rubber and plastic products	Lumber and wood products	Pulp, paper, and allied products	Metals and metal products	Machinery and equipment	Furniture and household durables	Non-metallic mineral products	Transportation equipment		Miscella-neous products
								Total	Motor vehicles and equipment	
1950	35.6	31.4	25.7	22.0	22.6	40.9	23.5	....	30.0	28.6
1951	43.7	34.1	30.5	24.5	25.3	44.4	25.0	....	31.6	30.3
1952	39.6	33.2	29.7	24.5	25.3	43.5	25.0	....	33.4	30.2
1953	36.9	33.1	29.6	25.3	25.9	44.4	26.0	....	33.3	31.0
1954	37.5	32.5	29.6	25.5	26.3	44.9	26.6	....	33.4	31.3
1955	42.4	34.1	30.4	27.2	27.2	45.1	27.3	....	34.3	31.3
1956	43.0	34.6	32.4	29.6	29.3	46.3	28.5	....	36.3	31.7
1957	42.8	32.8	33.0	30.2	31.4	47.5	29.6	....	37.9	32.6
1958	42.8	32.5	33.4	30.0	32.1	47.9	29.9	....	39.0	33.3
1959	42.6	34.7	33.7	30.6	32.8	48.0	30.3	....	39.9	33.4
1960	42.7	33.5	34.0	30.6	33.0	47.8	30.4	....	39.3	33.6
1961	41.1	32.0	33.0	30.5	33.0	47.5	30.5	....	39.2	33.7
1962	39.9	32.2	33.4	30.2	33.0	47.2	30.5	....	39.2	33.9
1963	40.1	32.8	33.1	30.3	33.1	46.9	30.3	....	38.9	34.2
1964	39.6	33.5	33.0	31.1	33.3	47.1	30.4	....	39.1	34.4
1965	39.7	33.7	33.3	32.0	33.7	46.8	30.4	....	39.2	34.7
1966	40.5	35.2	34.2	32.8	34.7	47.4	30.7	....	39.2	35.3
1967	41.4	35.1	34.6	33.2	35.9	48.3	31.2	....	39.8	36.2
1968	42.8	39.8	35.0	34.0	37.0	49.7	32.4	....	40.9	37.0
1969	43.6	44.0	36.0	36.0	38.2	50.7	33.6	40.4	41.7	38.1
1970	44.9	39.9	37.5	38.7	40.0	51.9	35.3	41.9	43.3	39.8
1971	45.2	44.7	38.1	39.4	41.4	53.1	38.2	44.2	45.7	40.8
1972	45.3	50.7	39.3	40.9	42.3	53.8	39.4	45.5	47.0	41.5
1973	46.6	62.2	42.3	44.0	43.7	55.7	40.7	46.1	47.4	43.3
1974	56.4	64.5	52.5	57.0	50.0	61.8	47.8	50.3	51.4	48.1
1975	62.2	62.1	59.0	61.5	57.9	67.5	54.4	56.7	57.6	53.4
1976	66.0	72.2	62.1	65.0	61.3	70.3	58.2	60.5	61.2	55.6
1977	69.4	83.0	64.6	69.3	65.2	73.2	62.6	64.6	65.2	59.4
1978	72.4	96.9	67.7	75.3	70.3	77.5	69.6	69.5	70.0	66.7
1979	80.5	105.5	75.9	86.0	76.7	82.8	77.6	75.3	75.8	75.5
1980	90.1	101.5	86.3	95.0	86.0	90.7	88.4	82.9	83.1	93.6
1981	96.4	102.8	94.8	99.6	94.4	95.9	96.7	94.3	94.6	96.1
1982	100.0	100.0	100.0	100.0	100.0	100.0	100.0	100.0	100.0	100.0
1983	100.8	107.9	103.3	101.8	102.7	103.4	101.6	102.8	102.2	104.8
1984	102.3	108.0	110.3	104.8	105.1	105.7	105.4	105.2	104.1	107.0
1985	101.9	106.6	113.3	104.4	107.2	107.1	108.6	107.9	106.4	109.4
1986	101.9	107.2	116.1	103.2	108.8	108.2	110.0	110.5	109.1	111.6
1987	103.0	112.8	121.8	107.1	110.4	109.9	110.0	112.5	111.7	114.9
1988	109.3	118.9	130.4	118.7	113.2	113.1	111.2	114.3	113.1	120.2
1989	112.6	126.7	137.8	124.1	117.4	116.9	112.6	117.7	116.2	126.5
1990	113.6	129.7	141.2	122.9	120.7	119.2	114.7	121.5	118.2	134.2
1991	115.1	132.1	142.9	120.2	123.0	121.2	117.2	126.4	122.1	140.8
1992	115.1	146.6	145.2	119.2	123.4	122.2	117.3	130.4	124.9	145.3
1993	116.0	174.0	147.3	119.2	124.0	123.7	120.0	133.7	128.0	145.4
1994	117.6	180.0	152.5	124.8	125.1	126.1	124.2	137.2	131.4	141.9
1995	124.3	178.2	172.2	134.5	126.5	128.1	129.0	139.6	133.0	145.1
1994: Jan	116.2	184.6	148.6	120.7	124.6	125.2	121.8	136.5	130.7	141.9
Feb	116.2	183.3	148.8	121.7	124.7	125.4	122.2	136.6	130.9	141.8
Mar	116.2	184.2	149.2	122.3	124.9	125.5	122.9	136.6	130.8	141.6
Apr	116.2	180.3	149.4	122.5	125.1	125.8	123.4	136.7	130.8	141.7
May	116.5	178.2	150.1	122.7	125.2	126.1	123.7	137.1	131.4	141.5
June	116.7	179.4	151.0	123.5	125.2	126.2	124.3	137.0	131.3	141.6
July	117.1	177.4	152.0	124.7	125.3	126.4	124.5	137.2	131.5	141.8
Aug	117.4	177.7	153.1	125.5	125.2	126.3	124.8	137.2	131.6	141.8
Sept	118.5	178.3	154.5	126.5	125.2	126.2	125.1	135.6	129.0	141.8
Oct	119.6	177.8	156.2	127.3	125.2	126.4	125.5	138.5	132.8	142.0
Nov	120.3	179.4	158.0	129.4	125.3	126.7	125.8	138.3	132.5	142.4
Dec	120.9	179.2	159.5	130.6	125.4	126.7	126.0	138.7	133.0	142.4
1995: Jan	122.1	179.6	163.2	133.4	125.9	127.2	126.9	139.6	133.4	143.0
Feb	122.7	179.5	165.9	134.6	126.2	127.5	127.5	139.6	133.3	143.6
Mar	123.4	180.6	168.1	134.7	126.2	127.5	128.2	139.4	133.1	143.8
Apr	124.1	180.4	170.6	135.2	126.4	127.8	129.3	139.3	132.9	144.3
May	124.7	179.7	172.7	134.7	126.5	128.0	129.4	139.3	132.7	145.2
June	125.1	178.0	174.5	134.8	126.5	128.1	129.3	139.0	132.2	145.3
July	125.2	178.2	175.4	135.2	126.6	128.2	129.3	139.0	132.2	145.7
Aug [2]	125.3	177.8	175.6	135.5	126.5	128.4	129.4	138.9	131.9	146.6
Sept	125.2	179.3	175.6	135.0	126.7	128.4	129.6	137.0	129.0	145.8
Oct	124.9	177.6	175.0	134.1	126.8	128.5	129.6	140.9	134.6	145.6
Nov	124.7	174.5	175.1	133.7	127.0	128.9	129.7	141.5	135.5	145.5
Dec	124.5	173.6	174.5	133.3	127.0	128.9	129.7	141.5	135.4	146.8

Source: Department of Labor, Bureau of Labor Statistics.

TABLE B-64.—Changes in producer price indexes for finished goods, 1958–95

[Percent change]

Year or month	Total finished goods Dec. to Dec.¹	Total finished goods Year to year	Finished consumer foods Dec. to Dec.¹	Finished consumer foods Year to year	Excl. consumer foods Total Dec. to Dec.¹	Excl. consumer foods Total Year to year	Consumer goods Dec. to Dec.¹	Consumer goods Year to year	Capital equipment Dec. to Dec.¹	Capital equipment Year to year	Finished energy goods Dec. to Dec.¹	Finished energy goods Year to year	Excl. foods and energy Dec. to Dec.¹	Excl. foods and energy Year to year
1958	0.3	2.2	0.6	6.1			0.3	0	1.2	2.6				
1959	-.3	-.3	-3.7	-4.7			.9	1.2	.9	1.9				
1960	1.8	.9	5.3	2.0			.3	.6	.3	.3				
1961	-.6	0	-1.9	-.3			-.3	-.3	0	.3				
1962	.3	.3	.6	.8			0	0	.3	.3				
1963	-.3	-.3	-1.4	-1.1			0	0	.6	.3				
1964	.6	.3	.6	.3			.3	-.3	.9	.9				
1965	3.3	1.8	9.1	4.0			.9	.9	1.5	1.2				
1966	2.0	3.2	1.3	6.5			1.8	1.5	3.8	2.4				
1967	1.7	1.1	-.3	-1.8			2.0	1.8	3.1	3.5				
1968	3.1	2.8	4.6	3.9	2.5	2.6	2.0	2.3	3.0	3.4				
1969	4.9	3.8	8.1	6.0	3.3	2.8	2.8	2.3	4.8	3.5				
1970	2.1	3.4	-2.3	3.3	4.3	3.5	3.8	3.0	4.8	4.7				
1971	3.3	3.1	5.8	1.6	2.0	3.7	2.1	3.5	2.4	4.0				
1972	3.9	3.2	7.9	5.4	2.3	2.0	2.1	1.8	2.1	2.6				
1973	11.7	9.1	22.7	20.5	6.6	4.0	7.5	4.6	5.1	3.3				
1974	18.3	15.4	12.8	14.0	21.1	16.2	20.3	17.0	22.7	14.3			17.7	11.4
1975	6.6	10.6	5.6	8.4	7.2	12.1	6.8	10.4	8.1	15.2	16.3	17.2	6.0	11.4
1976	3.8	4.5	-2.5	-.3	6.2	6.2	6.0	6.2	6.5	6.7	11.6	11.7	5.7	5.7
1977	6.7	6.4	6.9	5.3	6.8	7.1	6.7	7.3	7.2	6.4	12.0	15.7	6.2	6.0
1978	9.3	7.9	11.7	9.0	8.3	7.2	8.5	7.1	8.0	7.9	8.5	6.5	8.4	7.5
1979	12.8	11.2	7.4	9.3	14.8	11.8	17.6	13.3	8.8	8.7	58.1	35.0	9.4	8.9
1980	11.8	13.4	7.5	5.8	13.4	16.2	14.1	18.5	11.4	10.7	27.9	49.2	10.8	11.2
1981	7.1	9.2	1.5	5.8	8.7	10.3	8.6	10.3	9.2	10.3	14.1	19.1	7.7	8.6
1982	3.6	4.1	2.0	2.2	4.2	4.6	4.2	4.1	3.9	5.7	-.1	-1.5	4.9	5.7
1983	.6	1.6	2.3	1.0	0	1.8	-.9	1.2	2.0	2.8	-9.2	-4.8	1.9	3.0
1984	1.7	2.1	3.5	4.4	1.1	1.4	.8	1.0	1.8	2.3	-4.2	-4.2	2.0	2.4
1985	1.8	1.0	.6	-.8	2.2	1.4	2.1	1.1	2.7	2.2	-.2	-3.9	2.7	2.5
1986	-2.3	-1.4	2.8	2.6	-4.0	-2.6	-6.6	-4.6	2.1	2.0	-38.1	-28.1	2.7	2.3
1987	2.2	2.1	-.2	2.1	3.2	2.1	4.1	2.2	1.3	1.8	11.2	-1.9	2.1	2.4
1988	4.0	2.5	5.7	2.8	3.2	2.4	3.1	2.4	3.6	2.3	-3.6	-3.2	4.3	3.3
1989	4.9	5.2	5.2	5.4	4.8	5.0	5.3	5.6	3.8	3.9	9.5	9.9	4.2	4.4
1990	5.7	4.9	2.6	4.8	6.9	5.0	8.7	5.9	3.4	3.5	30.7	14.2	3.5	3.7
1991	-.1	2.1	-1.5	-.2	.3	3.0	-.7	2.9	2.5	3.1	-9.6	4.1	3.1	3.6
1992	1.6	1.2	1.6	-.6	1.6	1.8	1.6	1.8	1.7	1.9	-.3	-.4	2.0	2.4
1993	.2	1.2	2.4	1.9	-.4	1.1	-1.4	.7	1.8	1.8	-4.1	.3	.4	1.2
1994	1.7	.6	1.1	.9	1.9	.6	2.0	-.1	2.0	2.1	3.5	-1.3	1.6	1.0
1995	2.2	1.9	1.9	1.7	2.2	1.9	2.2	1.9	2.2	1.9	.9	1.4	2.5	2.0

Percent change from preceding month

Year or month	Total finished goods Unadjusted	Total finished goods Seasonally adjusted	Finished consumer foods Unadjusted	Finished consumer foods Seasonally adjusted	Excl. consumer foods Total Unadjusted	Excl. consumer foods Total Seasonally adjusted	Consumer goods Unadjusted	Consumer goods Seasonally adjusted	Capital equipment Unadjusted	Capital equipment Seasonally adjusted	Finished energy goods Unadjusted	Finished energy goods Seasonally adjusted	Excl. foods and energy Unadjusted	Excl. foods and energy Seasonally adjusted
1994:Jan	0.3	0.5	-0.2	-0.2	0.5	0.6	0.4	0.7	0.6	0.4	0.4	1.9	0.5	0.4
Feb	.2	.2	-.2	-.3	.3	.5	.5	.6	.2	.2	1.8	2.1	.1	.1
Mar	.1	0	.6	.3	0	-.1	-.1	-.2	.1	.2	-.3	-.5	0	.1
Apr	.1	0	-.3	-.5	.2	.2	.2	.1	.1	.3	1.1	.1	0	.1
May	.2	-.1	-.4	-.6	.4	.1	.4	0	.1	.3	.9	-1.0	.2	.3
June	.2	.1	-.6	-.4	.5	.2	.7	.2	.1	.1	2.8	.3	.1	.1
July	.3	.2	.2	.4	.3	.2	.4	.2	0	.1	1.7	.9	0	.1
Aug	.4	.6	.3	.2	.5	.6	.6	.7	.1	.2	2.3	2.3	.1	.2
Sept	-.7	-.3	-.2	-.2	-.9	-.3	-1.0	-.6	-.6	.2	-2.2	-2.4	-.6	.1
Oct	.2	-.4	-.2	-.1	.2	-.5	-.2	-.5	1.0	.1	-3.1	-1.3	1.0	-.4
Nov	.2	.6	.6	1.0	.2	.5	.2	.7	0	.1	.8	2.2	0	.2
Dec	.1	.3	1.3	1.3	-.2	.1	-.4	0	.2	.3	-2.3	-.9	.2	.2
1995:Jan	.3	.5	-.5	-.5	.6	.7	.5	.8	.4	.4	.9	2.5	.4	.4
Feb	.2	.2	.4	.3	.2	.2	.2	.2	.1	.1	0	.3	.2	.1
Mar	.2	.2	.2	-.1	.2	.2	.2	.2	.1	.1	.3	0	.1	.2
Apr	.4	.2	0	-.2	.5	.3	.6	.5	.1	.2	1.8	.9	.1	.3
May	.4	.2	-.5	-.7	.6	.4	.9	.4	.1	.2	2.8	.6	.2	.3
June	.1	-.2	-.5	-.3	.2	-.2	.3	-.2	-.1	0	1.2	-1.1	0	.1
July	0	.1	.9	1.0	-.2	-.2	-.3	-.5	.1	.2	-1.8	-2.5	.1	.2
Aug²	-.1	0	.2	.2	-.2	0	-.2	-.1	0	.1	-.6	-.5	-.1	.1
Sept	-.2	.2	.9	.9	-.5	0	-.4	0	-.7	.1	-.5	-.8	-.4	.2
Oct	.5	-.1	-.2	0	.6	-.1	.3	-.2	1.5	-.1	-2.8	-.9	1.4	0
Nov	.1	.5	.9	1.2	-.2	.2	-.3	.2	.2	.4	-2.1	-.5	.3	.4
Dec	.3	.5	.1	.1	.4	.8	.5	.9	.1	.1	1.9	3.3	.1	.1

¹ Changes from December to December are based on unadjusted indexes.
² Data have been revised through August 1995 to reflect the availability of late reports and corrections by respondents. All data are subject to revision 4 months after original publication.

Source: Department of Labor, Bureau of Labor Statistics.

MONEY STOCK, CREDIT, AND FINANCE

TABLE B-65.—*Money stock, liquid assets, and debt measures, 1959-95*

[Averages of daily figures, except debt; billions of dollars, seasonally adjusted]

Year and month	M1 — Sum of currency, demand deposits, travelers checks, and other checkable deposits (OCDs)	M2 — M1 plus overnight RPs and Eurodollars, MMMF balances (general purpose and broker/dealer), MMDAs, and savings and small time deposits	M3 — M2 plus large time deposits, term RPs, term Eurodollars, and institution-only MMMF balances	L — M3 plus other liquid assets	Debt[1] — Debt of domestic nonfinancial sectors (monthly average of adjacent month-end levels)	Percent change from year or 6 months earlier[2] M1	M2	M3	Debt
December:									
1959	140.0	297.8	299.8	388.6	687.6	....	....	....	7.6
1960	140.7	312.3	315.3	403.6	723.0	0.5	4.9	5.2	5.1
1961	145.2	335.5	341.0	430.8	765.7	3.2	7.4	8.2	5.9
1962	147.8	362.7	371.4	466.1	818.4	1.8	8.1	8.9	6.9
1963	153.3	393.2	406.0	503.8	873.4	3.7	8.4	9.3	6.7
1964	160.3	424.8	442.5	540.4	936.9	4.6	8.0	9.0	7.3
1965	167.9	459.3	482.2	584.4	1,003.7	4.7	8.1	9.0	7.1
1966	172.0	480.0	505.1	614.7	1,070.9	2.4	4.5	4.7	6.7
1967	183.3	524.3	557.1	666.5	1,145.2	6.6	9.2	10.3	6.9
1968	197.4	566.3	606.2	728.9	1,236.8	7.7	8.0	8.8	8.0
1969	203.9	589.5	615.0	763.5	1,326.7	3.3	4.1	1.5	7.3
1970	214.4	628.1	677.4	816.2	1,416.2	5.1	6.5	10.1	6.7
1971	228.3	712.7	776.1	902.9	1,549.8	6.5	13.5	14.6	9.4
1972	249.2	805.2	886.0	1,022.9	1,705.4	9.2	13.0	14.2	10.0
1973	262.8	861.0	984.9	1,142.4	1,890.7	5.5	6.9	11.2	10.9
1974	274.3	908.5	1,070.3	1,250.2	2,063.8	4.4	5.5	8.7	9.2
1975	287.4	1,023.2	1,172.2	1,366.9	2,251.8	4.8	12.6	9.5	9.1
1976	306.3	1,163.7	1,311.7	1,516.6	2,497.0	6.6	13.7	11.9	10.9
1977	331.1	1,286.5	1,472.5	1,705.3	2,816.6	8.1	10.6	12.3	12.8
1978	358.1	1,388.6	1,646.3	1,910.6	3,208.7	8.2	7.9	11.8	13.9
1979	382.4	1,496.9	1,803.7	2,116.9	3,596.2	6.8	7.8	9.6	12.1
1980	408.5	1,629.3	1,988.5	2,325.6	3,943.2	6.8	8.8	10.2	9.6
1981	436.3	1,793.3	2,236.6	2,599.0	4,343.6	6.8	10.1	12.5	10.2
1982	474.3	1,953.2	2,440.6	2,849.7	4,760.0	8.7	8.9	9.1	9.6
1983	521.0	2,187.7	2,684.8	3,147.6	5,327.6	9.8	12.0	10.0	11.9
1984	552.1	2,378.4	2,981.5	3,524.3	6,114.9	6.0	8.7	11.1	14.8
1985	619.8	2,576.0	3,200.2	3,827.9	7,036.3	12.3	8.3	7.3	15.1
1986	724.4	2,820.3	3,488.7	4,125.1	7,924.6	16.9	9.5	9.0	12.6
1987	749.8	2,922.3	3,675.8	4,331.1	8,671.2	3.5	3.6	5.4	9.4
1988	786.9	3,083.5	3,915.6	4,667.1	9,446.4	4.9	5.5	6.5	8.9
1989	794.2	3,243.0	4,066.0	4,893.9	10,173.5	.9	5.2	3.8	7.7
1990	825.8	3,356.0	4,123.2	4,973.6	10,854.0	4.0	3.5	1.4	6.7
1991	897.3	3,457.9	4,176.0	5,000.5	11,338.6	8.7	3.0	1.3	4.5
1992	1,024.4	3,515.3	4,182.9	5,069.2	11,881.7	14.2	1.7	.2	4.8
1993	1,128.6	3,583.6	4,242.3	5,154.4	12,516.4	10.2	1.9	1.4	5.3
1994	1,148.0	3,617.0	4,303.9	5,283.9	13,153.2	1.7	.9	1.5	5.1
1995	1,123.0	3,780.7	4,563.5	....	....	-2.2	4.5	6.0	....
1994: Jan	1,132.5	3,589.1	4,245.7	5,166.3	12,555.6	8.7	2.6	2.1	5.0
Feb	1,137.0	3,586.2	4,231.7	5,169.9	12,605.3	7.7	2.1	1.2	4.9
Mar	1,141.1	3,597.5	4,240.3	5,181.4	12,674.7	6.6	2.2	1.2	5.1
Apr	1,142.8	3,605.2	4,250.2	5,190.5	12,737.0	5.3	2.3	1.3	5.5
May	1,143.5	3,607.8	4,250.3	5,205.9	12,801.3	3.8	1.7	.8	5.6
June	1,147.0	3,604.3	4,255.1	5,202.2	12,843.7	3.3	1.2	.6	5.2
July	1,152.2	3,616.8	4,274.2	5,228.9	12,864.3	3.5	1.5	1.3	4.9
Aug	1,150.8	3,615.0	4,273.7	5,238.8	12,926.3	2.4	1.6	2.0	5.1
Sept	1,151.0	3,614.2	4,279.9	5,237.8	12,986.6	1.7	.9	1.9	4.9
Oct	1,148.2	3,610.2	4,286.3	5,251.2	13,036.8	.9	.3	1.7	4.7
Nov	1,147.6	3,611.9	4,291.9	5,262.4	13,111.3	.7	.2	2.0	4.8
Dec	1,148.0	3,617.0	4,303.9	5,283.9	13,153.2	.2	.7	2.3	4.8
1995: Jan	1,149.0	3,628.9	4,326.9	5,309.6	13,201.9	-.6	.7	2.5	5.2
Feb	1,147.3	3,624.6	4,336.7	5,349.6	13,279.8	-.6	.5	2.9	5.5
Mar	1,147.9	3,632.2	4,359.9	5,392.5	13,342.3	-.5	1.0	3.7	5.5
Apr	1,149.7	3,645.4	4,382.0	5,421.1	13,419.3	.3	2.0	4.5	5.9
May	1,143.0	3,661.9	4,409.7	5,451.8	13,519.6	-.8	2.8	5.5	6.2
June	1,143.9	3,698.1	4,455.2	5,491.8	13,578.3	-.7	4.5	7.0	6.5
July	1,145.0	3,717.3	4,486.3	5,546.8	13,613.6	-.7	4.9	7.4	6.2
Aug	1,143.4	3,743.1	4,516.9	5,584.2	13,665.5	-.7	6.5	8.3	5.8
Sept	1,139.8	3,756.8	4,534.0	5,624.6	13,704.1	-1.4	6.9	8.0	5.4
Oct	1,129.9	3,753.8	4,546.6	5,645.6	13,744.3	-3.4	5.9	7.5	4.8
Nov	1,126.5	3,761.7	4,550.0	5,648.4	13,804.2	-2.9	5.5	6.4	4.2
Dec	1,123.0	3,780.7	4,563.5	....	....	-3.7	4.5	4.9	....

[1] Consists of outstanding credit market debt of the U.S. Government, State and local governments, and private nonfinancial sectors; data derived from flow of funds accounts.

[2] Annual changes are from December to December; monthly changes are from 6 months earlier at a simple annual rate.

Note.—See Table B-66 for components.

Data do not reflect revisions released on February 8, 1996.

Source: Board of Governors of the Federal Reserve System.

TABLE B–66.—*Components of money stock measures and liquid assets, 1959–95*

[Averages of daily figures; billions of dollars, seasonally adjusted, except as noted]

Year and month	Currency	Travelers checks	Demand deposits	Other checkable deposits (OCDs)	Overnight repurchase agreements (RPs) net, plus overnight Eurodollars [1] NSA	Money market mutual fund (MMMF) balances — General purpose and broker/ dealer [2]	Money market mutual fund (MMMF) balances — Institution only [2]	Savings deposits, including money market deposit accounts (MMDAs) [3]
December:								
1959	28.8	0.3	110.8	0.0	0.0	0.0	0.0	146.5
1960	28.7	.3	111.6	.0	.0	.0	.0	159.1
1961	29.3	.4	115.5	.0	.0	.0	.0	175.5
1962	30.3	.4	117.1	.0	.0	.0	.0	194.7
1963	32.2	.4	120.6	.1	.0	.0	.0	214.4
1964	33.9	.5	125.8	.1	.0	.0	.0	235.3
1965	36.0	.5	131.3	.1	.0	.0	.0	256.9
1966	38.0	.6	133.4	.1	.0	.0	.0	253.2
1967	40.0	.6	142.5	.1	.0	.0	.0	263.7
1968	43.0	.7	153.6	.1	.0	.0	.0	268.9
1969	45.7	.8	157.3	.2	2.2	.0	.0	263.6
1970	48.6	.9	164.8	.1	1.3	.0	.0	260.9
1971	52.0	1.0	175.1	.2	2.3	.0	.0	292.2
1972	56.2	1.2	191.6	.2	2.8	.0	.0	321.4
1973	60.8	1.4	200.3	.3	5.3	.0	.0	326.7
1974	67.0	1.7	205.1	.4	5.7	1.7	.2	338.6
1975	72.8	2.1	211.6	.9	6.0	2.7	.4	388.9
1976	79.5	2.6	221.5	2.7	10.8	2.4	.6	453.3
1977	87.4	2.9	236.6	4.2	15.0	2.4	.9	492.4
1978	96.0	3.3	250.4	8.4	20.8	6.4	3.1	482.2
1979	104.8	3.5	257.3	16.8	22.4	33.4	9.5	424.1
1980	115.4	3.9	261.1	28.0	29.3	61.6	15.2	400.6
1981	122.6	4.1	231.1	78.4	37.6	150.6	38.0	344.2
1982	132.5	4.1	233.8	103.9	40.8	185.6	50.0	400.4
1983	146.2	4.7	238.2	131.9	57.3	139.2	41.4	685.1
1984	156.1	5.0	243.7	147.4	63.2	168.4	62.1	704.8
1985	167.9	5.6	266.6	179.8	76.3	178.0	64.1	815.4
1986	180.7	6.1	302.1	235.6	84.9	210.6	84.5	941.0
1987	196.8	6.6	286.8	259.5	87.3	224.5	91.1	937.7
1988	212.2	7.0	286.8	280.9	85.1	245.9	90.5	926.7
1989	222.6	6.9	279.3	285.4	81.5	322.4	107.2	891.0
1990	246.8	7.8	277.4	293.9	77.7	358.2	134.0	920.5
1991	267.4	7.7	289.5	332.7	79.9	374.2	180.0	1,041.2
1992	292.8	8.1	338.9	384.6	83.1	356.9	200.2	1,183.6
1993	322.1	7.9	383.9	414.7	96.5	360.1	198.1	1,215.7
1994	354.5	8.4	382.2	402.9	117.2	389.0	180.8	1,144.2
1995	372.5	8.9	389.1	352.5	119.0	476.9	216.6	1,131.3
1994: Jan	325.4	8.0	386.9	412.3	98.0	361.2	194.6	1,221.1
Feb	328.9	8.0	388.6	411.6	94.9	359.5	182.1	1,221.9
Mar	332.0	8.0	388.6	412.5	100.1	361.9	183.8	1,222.0
Apr	334.5	8.1	388.1	412.0	98.9	370.5	183.1	1,220.0
May	337.3	8.1	385.6	412.4	102.5	373.5	177.5	1,214.8
June	340.0	8.2	386.3	412.5	106.9	370.7	177.9	1,206.8
July	342.8	8.3	388.1	413.1	109.6	376.1	178.7	1,201.2
Aug	345.1	8.3	386.6	410.8	111.1	377.0	177.4	1,192.6
Sept	347.2	8.4	386.5	408.9	112.1	377.4	176.3	1,183.7
Oct	350.0	8.3	384.5	405.4	114.1	379.5	180.8	1,171.0
Nov	353.0	8.4	382.5	403.8	113.5	383.3	180.5	1,157.8
Dec	354.5	8.4	382.2	402.9	117.2	389.0	180.8	1,144.2
1995: Jan	357.7	8.4	383.6	399.3	123.9	392.1	186.3	1,129.8
Feb	358.8	8.4	384.1	395.9	118.4	391.5	180.4	1,111.9
Mar	362.5	8.8	383.3	393.3	118.3	390.9	189.0	1,094.9
Apr	365.7	9.2	381.2	393.6	115.9	396.0	192.9	1,082.4
May	368.1	9.2	380.6	385.0	116.7	405.4	194.8	1,081.4
June	367.4	9.0	386.8	380.7	117.6	426.2	205.6	1,091.1
July	367.1	8.9	389.5	379.4	114.4	442.0	212.4	1,091.4
Aug	368.3	8.9	390.1	376.2	118.2	455.9	210.8	1,098.1
Sept	369.1	8.8	389.8	372.0	120.9	462.6	213.5	1,105.2
Oct	370.5	8.8	387.3	363.4	118.5	466.4	215.8	1,112.2
Nov	371.0	8.8	387.0	359.7	116.3	471.3	214.8	1,117.0
Dec	372.5	8.9	389.1	352.5	119.0	476.9	216.6	1,131.3

[1] Includes continuing contract RPs.
[2] Data prior to 1983 are not seasonally adjusted.
[3] Data prior to 1982 are savings deposits only; MMDA data begin December 1982.

See next page for continuation of table.

[Averages of daily figures; billions of dollars, seasonally adjusted, except as noted]

Year and month	Small denomination time deposits [4]	Large denomination time deposits [4]	Term repurchase agreements (RPs) NSA	Term Euro-dollars NSA	Savings bonds	Short-term Treasury securities	Bankers acceptances	Commercial paper
December:								
1959	11.4	1.2	0.0	0.7	46.1	38.6	0.6	3.6
1960	12.5	2.0	.0	.8	45.7	36.7	.9	5.1
1961	14.8	3.9	.0	1.5	46.5	37.0	1.1	5.2
1962	20.1	7.0	.0	1.6	46.9	39.8	1.1	6.8
1963	25.6	10.8	.0	1.9	48.1	40.7	1.2	7.7
1964	29.2	15.2	.0	2.4	49.0	38.5	1.3	9.1
1965	34.5	21.2	.0	1.8	49.6	40.7	1.6	10.2
1966	55.0	23.1	.0	2.2	50.2	43.2	1.8	14.4
1967	77.8	30.9	.0	2.2	51.2	38.7	1.8	17.8
1968	100.6	37.4	.0	2.9	51.8	46.1	2.3	22.5
1969	120.4	20.4	2.7	2.7	51.7	59.5	3.3	34.0
1970	151.2	45.1	1.6	2.2	52.0	48.8	3.5	34.5
1971	189.8	57.6	2.7	2.7	54.3	36.0	3.8	32.7
1972	231.7	73.3	3.5	3.6	57.6	40.7	3.5	35.2
1973	265.8	111.0	6.7	5.5	60.4	49.3	5.0	42.8
1974	287.9	144.7	7.8	8.1	63.3	52.8	12.6	51.2
1975	337.8	129.7	8.1	9.8	67.2	68.4	10.7	48.5
1976	390.7	118.1	13.9	14.8	71.8	69.8	10.8	52.5
1977	445.4	145.2	18.9	20.2	76.4	78.3	14.1	64.0
1978	520.9	195.6	26.2	31.8	80.3	81.3	22.0	80.7
1979	634.2	223.2	29.1	44.7	79.5	108.2	27.1	98.3
1980	728.5	260.2	33.5	50.3	72.3	133.9	32.0	98.8
1981	823.1	303.8	35.3	67.5	67.8	149.4	39.9	105.3
1982	850.9	324.8	33.4	81.7	68.0	183.0	44.5	113.6
1983	784.1	316.4	49.9	91.5	71.1	213.6	45.0	133.2
1984	888.8	403.2	57.6	83.4	74.2	262.5	45.4	160.7
1985	885.7	422.4	62.5	76.9	79.5	298.7	42.1	207.5
1986	859.0	420.2	81.1	85.1	91.8	276.1	37.1	231.3
1987	922.7	467.0	107.3	91.6	100.6	249.5	44.5	260.6
1988	1,038.6	518.3	123.2	106.3	109.4	266.6	40.2	335.4
1989	1,153.7	541.5	100.4	83.8	117.5	323.5	40.6	346.4
1990	1,174.0	480.9	90.9	71.6	126.0	333.3	35.9	355.2
1991	1,066.6	416.6	73.3	59.4	137.9	328.1	23.8	334.8
1992	869.2	353.8	82.0	45.9	156.6	344.3	20.8	364.5
1993	785.1	332.7	97.6	46.5	171.5	341.6	14.9	384.7
1994	821.0	361.4	105.6	52.2	180.3	384.3	14.0	401.3
1995	933.2	418.9	105.4	57.1	....	....	....	....
1994: Jan	779.5	335.1	93.5	45.5	172.5	349.7	14.8	391.4
Feb	775.0	331.8	92.1	47.9	173.2	350.9	14.9	401.2
Mar	772.0	330.3	95.1	46.2	173.9	362.2	15.7	390.3
Apr	770.2	329.8	98.6	46.5	174.8	365.2	15.9	384.5
May	770.8	332.4	97.6	47.7	175.7	372.0	15.6	392.2
June	772.9	335.0	102.1	50.3	176.7	368.5	14.9	387.0
July	776.5	338.4	102.8	50.9	177.7	372.7	13.2	391.1
Aug	782.8	342.0	101.0	51.1	178.5	377.4	13.8	395.4
Sept	789.6	348.2	101.7	51.9	179.1	373.8	14.8	390.2
Oct	799.7	353.6	101.9	52.6	179.5	372.4	13.1	399.9
Nov	810.8	357.4	103.1	54.3	179.9	375.7	13.5	401.4
Dec	821.0	361.4	105.6	52.2	180.3	384.3	14.0	401.3
1995: Jan	836.5	361.9	109.4	52.9	180.5	385.9	13.4	402.8
Feb	856.4	371.3	113.4	56.1	180.4	404.4	13.4	414.7
Mar	879.3	378.8	113.4	58.2	180.5	416.4	14.1	421.7
Apr	898.2	379.6	116.5	59.7	180.9	413.5	13.9	430.8
May	912.3	383.4	121.7	60.8	181.6	404.4	12.3	443.8
June	919.3	385.6	119.9	62.0	182.3	415.5	11.3	427.5
July	924.0	392.2	115.5	63.2	183.0	437.6	11.8	428.0
Aug	927.2	395.3	118.3	62.9	183.7	436.5	12.2	435.0
Sept	928.8	398.8	116.4	62.4	184.1	455.6	12.9	438.0
Oct	930.3	411.4	116.3	61.9	184.4	460.4	13.0	441.2
Nov	932.6	416.8	111.6	61.1	184.6	465.0	13.1	435.6
Dec	933.2	418.9	105.4	57.1	....	....	....	....

[4] Small denomination and large denomination deposits are those issued in amounts of less than $100,000 and more than $100,000, respectively.

Note.—NSA indicates data are not seasonally adjusted.
See also Table B-65.
Data do not reflect revisions released on February 8, 1996.

Source: Board of Governors of the Federal Reserve System.

TABLE B-67.—*Aggregate reserves of depository institutions and monetary base, 1959–95*

[Averages of daily figures [1]; millions of dollars; seasonally adjusted, except as noted]

| Year and month | Adjusted for changes in reserve requirements [2] | | | | | Borrowings of depository institutions from the Federal Reserve, NSA | | |
| | Reserves of depository institutions | | | | Monetary base | | | |
	Total	Nonborrowed	Nonborrowed plus extended credit	Required	Monetary base	Total	Seasonal	Extended credit
December:								
1959	11,109	10,168	10,168	10,603	40,880	941		
1960	11,247	11,172	11,172	10,503	40,977	74		
1961	11,499	11,366	11,366	10,915	41,853	133		
1962	11,604	11,344	11,344	11,033	42,957	260		
1963	11,730	11,397	11,397	11,239	45,003	332		
1964	12,011	11,747	11,747	11,605	47,161	264		
1965	12,316	11,872	11,872	11,892	49,620	444		
1966	12,223	11,690	11,690	11,884	51,565	532		
1967	13,180	12,952	12,952	12,805	54,579	228		
1968	13,767	13,021	13,021	13,341	58,357	746		
1969	14,168	13,049	13,049	13,882	61,569	1,119		
1970	14,558	14,225	14,225	14,309	65,013	332		
1971	15,230	15,104	15,104	15,049	69,108	126		
1972	16,645	15,595	15,595	16,361	75,167	1,050		
1973	17,021	15,723	15,723	16,717	81,073	1,298	41	
1974	17,550	16,823	16,970	17,292	87,535	727	32	147
1975	17,822	17,692	17,704	17,556	93,887	130	14	12
1976	18,388	18,335	18,335	18,115	101,515	53	13	
1977	18,990	18,420	18,420	18,800	110,323	569	55	
1978	19,753	18,885	18,885	19,521	120,445	868	135	
1979	20,720	19,248	19,248	20,279	131,143	1,473	82	
1980	22,015	20,325	20,328	21,501	142,004	1,690	116	3
1981	22,443	21,807	21,956	22,124	149,021	636	54	148
1982	23,600	22,966	23,152	23,100	160,127	634	33	186
1983	25,367	24,593	24,595	24,806	175,467	774	96	2
1984	26,847	23,661	26,265	25,993	187,224	3,186	113	2,604
1985	31,452	30,133	30,633	30,415	203,539	1,318	56	499
1986	38,940	38,113	38,416	37,570	223,574	827	38	303
1987	38,856	38,078	38,562	37,809	239,775	777	93	483
1988	40,399	38,683	39,927	39,352	256,897	1,716	130	1,244
1989	40,498	40,232	40,252	39,575	267,713	265	84	20
1990	41,771	41,445	41,468	40,106	293,275	326	76	23
1991	45,536	45,343	45,344	44,557	317,432	192	38	1
1992	54,354	54,230	54,231	53,199	351,116	124	18	1
1993	60,502	60,420	60,420	59,440	386,602	82	31	0
1994	59,342	59,133	59,133	58,174	418,223	209	100	0
1995	56,334	56,077	56,077	55,056	434,438	257	40	0
1994: Jan	60,645	60,571	60,571	59,197	389,945	73	15	0
Feb	60,775	60,705	60,705	59,635	393,771	70	15	0
Mar	60,587	60,532	60,532	59,620	396,668	55	24	0
Apr	60,480	60,356	60,356	59,329	399,229	124	57	0
May	60,105	59,905	59,905	59,190	401,680	200	134	0
June	59,989	59,656	59,656	58,885	404,213	333	226	0
July	60,105	59,647	59,647	58,998	407,175	458	364	0
Aug	59,839	59,370	59,370	58,835	409,244	469	445	0
Sept	59,794	59,307	59,307	58,734	411,338	487	444	0
Oct	59,496	59,116	59,116	58,693	413,854	380	339	0
Nov	59,401	59,152	59,152	58,394	416,788	249	164	0
Dec	59,342	59,133	59,133	58,174	418,223	209	100	0
1995: Jan	59,124	58,988	58,992	57,785	421,054	136	46	4
Feb	58,919	58,860	58,860	57,973	422,312	59	33	0
Mar	58,552	58,483	58,483	57,757	425,350	69	51	0
Apr	57,957	57,847	57,847	57,204	428,127	111	82	0
May	57,761	57,611	57,611	56,881	430,687	150	137	0
June	57,352	57,080	57,080	56,388	429,755	272	172	0
July	57,655	57,284	57,284	56,565	429,659	371	231	0
Aug	57,515	57,233	57,233	56,527	430,858	282	258	0
Sept	57,368	57,091	57,091	56,418	431,249	278	252	0
Oct	56,821	56,575	56,575	55,739	432,437	245	199	0
Nov	56,269	56,065	56,065	55,326	432,705	204	73	0
Dec	56,334	56,077	56,077	55,056	434,438	257	40	0

[1] Data are prorated averages of biweekly (maintenance period) averages of daily figures.
[2] Aggregate reserves incorporate adjustments for discontinuities associated with regulatory changes to reserve requirements. For details on aggregate reserves series see *Federal Reserve Bulletin.*

Note.—NSA indicates data are not seasonally adjusted.
Monetary base data do not reflect revisions released on February 8, 1996.

Source: Board of Governors of the Federal Reserve System.

TABLE B–68.—*Bank credit at all commercial banks, 1972–95*

[Monthly average; billions of dollars, seasonally adjusted [1]]

Year and month	Total bank credit	Securities in bank credit			Loans and leases in bank credit							
		Total securities	U.S. Government securities	Other securities	Total loans and leases [2]	Commercial and industrial	Real estate			Consumer	Security	Other
							Total	Revolving home equity	Other			
December:												
1972	572.5	182.4	89.0	93.4	390.1	137.1	98.1			86.3	15.6	53.0
1973	647.8	187.6	88.2	99.4	460.2	165.0	117.3			98.6	12.9	66.4
1974	713.7	193.8	86.3	107.5	519.9	196.6	130.1			102.4	12.7	78.1
1975	745.1	227.9	116.7	111.2	517.2	189.3	134.4			104.9	13.5	75.1
1976	804.6	249.8	136.3	113.5	554.8	190.9	148.8			116.3	17.7	81.1
1977	891.5	259.3	136.6	122.7	632.3	211.0	175.2			138.3	21.0	86.8
1978	1,013.9	266.8	137.6	129.2	747.1	246.2	210.5			164.7	19.7	106.0
1979	1,135.6	286.2	144.3	141.9	849.4	291.4	241.9			184.5	18.7	112.9
1980	1,238.6	325.0	170.6	154.4	913.5	325.7	262.6			179.2	18.0	128.0
1981	1,307.0	339.8	179.3	160.5	967.3	355.4	284.1			182.5	21.4	123.9
1982	1,400.4	366.5	201.7	164.8	1,033.9	392.5	299.9			188.2	25.3	128.0
1983	1,552.2	428.3	259.2	169.1	1,123.9	414.2	331.0			212.9	28.0	137.8
1984	1,722.9	400.7	259.8	140.9	1,322.2	473.2	376.3			254.2	35.0	183.5
1985	1,910.4	449.8	270.8	179.0	1,460.6	500.2	425.9			295.0	43.3	196.2
1986	2,093.7	504.0	310.1	193.9	1,589.7	536.7	494.1			315.4	40.3	203.2
1987	2,241.2	531.6	335.8	195.8	1,709.6	566.4	587.2			328.2	34.5	193.3
New series												
1988	2,436.1	562.0	366.8	195.2	1,874.1	608.0	675.1	40.1	635.0	357.8	40.7	192.5
1989	2,609.1	584.5	400.0	184.5	2,024.7	639.3	770.2	50.3	719.9	378.3	41.4	195.5
1990	2,751.6	633.7	455.6	178.2	2,117.8	640.8	855.3	62.3	793.0	383.4	45.0	193.2
1991	2,856.4	745.0	565.2	179.8	2,111.4	619.5	880.0	69.6	810.3	366.6	54.4	190.9
1992	2,957.0	843.4	666.8	176.7	2,113.6	596.2	901.3	73.5	827.7	358.9	64.1	193.0
1993	3,113.7	918.7	733.9	184.8	2,195.0	585.9	940.5	73.0	867.5	397.5	87.5	190.6
1994	3,362.2	952.3	732.0	220.2	2,374.0	645.2	1,001.7	75.3	926.4	451.3	76.2	199.6
1995	3,594.3	990.5	714.1	276.4	2,603.9	718.0	1,077.2	79.3	998.0	493.5	81.5	233.6
1994: Jan	3,154.9	951.3	742.9	208.3	2,203.6	590.6	942.4	73.0	869.4	394.7	85.5	190.4
Feb	3,159.2	947.8	744.3	203.5	2,211.4	592.1	941.9	73.1	868.8	398.6	88.5	190.3
Mar	3,181.2	959.5	755.2	204.3	2,221.7	595.6	944.1	73.0	871.1	402.5	89.0	190.5
Apr	3,202.9	972.4	763.8	208.6	2,230.5	601.1	947.8	73.0	874.7	407.6	82.2	191.8
May	3,206.5	966.8	757.3	209.4	2,239.7	605.5	952.0	73.2	878.8	412.1	80.4	189.8
June	3,219.9	969.9	758.7	211.1	2,250.0	609.5	957.9	73.5	884.4	416.5	78.5	187.7
July	3,253.1	977.4	757.3	220.0	2,275.8	616.3	965.1	73.5	891.6	422.9	80.5	190.9
Aug	3,264.1	967.7	752.2	215.5	2,296.4	621.9	972.8	73.8	899.0	428.4	80.2	193.2
Sept	3,277.8	966.6	750.3	216.3	2,311.2	626.9	980.4	74.1	906.3	433.8	75.0	195.1
Oct	3,292.2	961.6	740.9	220.7	2,330.6	633.7	985.7	74.5	911.2	440.6	75.0	195.6
Nov	3,302.2	955.4	734.8	220.6	2,346.8	639.6	990.9	74.9	916.0	444.6	74.2	197.5
Dec	3,326.2	952.3	732.0	220.2	2,374.0	645.2	1,001.7	75.3	926.4	451.3	76.2	199.6
1995: Jan	3,354.9	950.2	729.3	220.8	2,404.7	656.7	1,013.8	75.7	938.0	457.5	73.3	203.4
Feb	3,367.5	939.3	724.8	214.5	2,428.3	670.2	1,021.8	76.0	945.9	459.7	73.4	203.1
Mar	3,393.0	942.0	712.0	230.0	2,451.0	673.9	1,029.0	76.1	952.9	464.6	76.0	207.5
Apr	3,470.5	996.2	708.8	287.4	2,474.3	680.8	1,036.6	76.6	960.0	470.6	77.8	208.5
May	3,491.8	986.4	711.0	275.4	2,505.4	687.8	1,043.9	77.2	966.7	473.2	88.1	212.4
June	3,512.6	985.9	710.3	275.6	2,526.7	692.0	1,053.1	77.8	975.3	479.0	87.6	215.0
July	3,525.7	976.4	704.3	272.1	2,549.3	697.7	1,062.4	78.0	984.4	481.4	86.6	221.2
Aug	3,540.7	978.8	709.1	269.7	2,561.9	701.8	1,068.2	78.2	989.9	486.1	83.6	222.2
Sept	3,563.3	983.0	709.1	273.9	2,580.3	708.4	1,072.2	78.4	993.8	489.8	85.9	224.0
Oct	3,575.1	986.1	714.7	271.4	2,589.1	710.6	1,075.6	78.5	997.1	489.5	85.7	227.6
Nov	3,585.0	987.8	716.7	271.2	2,597.2	714.9	1,076.9	79.0	998.0	491.5	85.1	228.8
Dec	3,594.3	990.5	714.1	276.4	2,603.9	718.0	1,077.2	79.3	998.0	493.5	81.5	233.6

[1] Data are Wednesday values or prorated averages of Wednesday values for domestically chartered commercial banks, branches and agencies of foreign banks, New York State investment companies, and foreign-related institutions. Beginning 1988, data are adjusted for breaks caused by reclassifications of assets and liabilities.

[2] Excludes Federal funds sold to, reverse repurchase agreements (RPs) with, and loans to commercial banks in the United States.

Note.—Data are not strictly comparable because of breaks in the series.

Source: Board of Governors of the Federal Reserve System.

Year and month	U.S. Treasury securities					Corporate bonds (Moody's)		High-grade municipal bonds (Standard & Poor's) [3]	New-home mortgage yields [3]	Commercial paper 6 months [4]	Prime rate charged by banks [5]	Discount rate, Federal Reserve Bank of New York [5]	Federal funds rate [6]
	Bills (new issues) [1]		Constant maturities [2]										
	3-month	6-month	3-year	10-year	30-year	Aaa	Baa						
1929						4.73	5.90	4.27		5.85	5.50-6.00	5.16	
1933	0.515					4.49	7.76	4.71		1.73	1.50-4.00	2.56	
1939	.023					3.01	4.96	2.76		.59	1.50	1.00	
1940	.014					2.84	4.75	2.50		.56	1.50	1.00	
1941	.103					2.77	4.33	2.10		.53	1.50	1.00	
1942	.326					2.83	4.28	2.36		.66	1.50	7 1.00	
1943	.373					2.73	3.91	2.06		.69	1.50	7 1.00	
1944	.375					2.72	3.61	1.86		.73	1.50	7 1.00	
1945	.375					2.62	3.29	1.67		.75	1.50	7 1.00	
1946	.375					2.53	3.05	1.64		.81	1.50	7 1.00	
1947	.594					2.61	3.24	2.01		1.03	1.50-1.75	1.00	
1948	1.040					2.82	3.47	2.40		1.44	1.75-2.00	1.34	
1949	1.102					2.66	3.42	2.21		1.49	2.00	1.50	
1950	1.218					2.62	3.24	1.98		1.45	2.07	1.59	
1951	1.552					2.86	3.41	2.00		2.16	2.56	1.75	
1952	1.766					2.96	3.52	2.19		2.33	3.00	1.75	
1953	1.931		2.47	2.85		3.20	3.74	2.72		2.52	3.17	1.99	
1954	.953		1.63	2.40		2.90	3.51	2.37		1.58	3.05	1.60	
1955	1.753		2.47	2.82		3.06	3.53	2.53		2.18	3.16	1.89	1.78
1956	2.658		3.19	3.18		3.36	3.88	2.93		3.31	3.77	2.77	2.73
1957	3.267		3.98	3.65		3.89	4.71	3.60		3.81	4.20	3.12	3.11
1958	1.839		2.84	3.32		3.79	4.73	3.56		2.46	3.83	2.15	1.57
1959	3.405	3.832	4.46	4.33		4.38	5.05	3.95		3.97	4.48	3.36	3.30
1960	2.928	3.247	3.98	4.12		4.41	5.19	3.73		3.85	4.82	3.53	3.22
1961	2.378	2.605	3.54	3.88		4.35	5.08	3.46		2.97	4.50	3.00	1.96
1962	2.778	2.908	3.47	3.95		4.33	5.02	3.18		3.26	4.50	3.00	2.68
1963	3.157	3.253	3.67	4.00		4.26	4.86	3.23	5.89	3.55	4.50	3.23	3.18
1964	3.549	3.686	4.03	4.19		4.40	4.83	3.22	5.83	3.97	4.50	3.55	3.50
1965	3.954	4.055	4.22	4.28		4.49	4.87	3.27	5.81	4.38	4.54	4.04	4.07
1966	4.881	5.082	5.23	4.92		5.13	5.67	3.82	6.25	5.55	5.63	4.50	5.11
1967	4.321	4.630	5.03	5.07		5.51	6.23	3.98	6.46	5.10	5.61	4.19	4.22
1968	5.339	5.470	5.68	5.65		6.18	6.94	4.51	6.97	5.90	6.30	5.16	5.66
1969	6.677	6.853	7.02	6.67		7.03	7.81	5.81	7.81	7.83	7.96	5.87	8.20
1970	6.458	6.562	7.29	7.35		8.04	9.11	6.51	8.45	7.71	7.91	5.95	7.18
1971	4.348	4.511	5.65	6.16		7.39	8.56	5.70	7.74	5.11	5.72	4.88	4.66
1972	4.071	4.466	5.72	6.21		7.21	8.16	5.27	7.60	4.73	5.25	4.50	4.43
1973	7.041	7.178	6.95	6.84		7.44	8.24	5.18	7.96	8.15	8.03	6.44	8.73
1974	7.886	7.926	7.82	7.56		8.57	9.50	6.09	8.92	9.84	10.81	7.83	10.50
1975	5.838	6.122	7.49	7.99		8.83	10.61	6.89	9.00	6.32	7.86	6.25	5.82
1976	4.989	5.266	6.77	7.61		8.43	9.75	6.49	9.00	5.34	6.84	5.50	5.04
1977	5.265	5.510	6.69	7.42	7.75	8.02	8.97	5.56	9.02	5.61	6.83	5.46	5.54
1978	7.221	7.572	8.29	8.41	8.49	8.73	9.49	5.90	9.56	7.99	9.06	7.46	7.93
1979	10.041	10.017	9.71	9.44	9.28	9.63	10.69	6.39	10.78	10.91	12.67	10.28	11.19
1980	11.506	11.374	11.55	11.46	11.27	11.94	13.67	8.51	12.66	12.29	15.27	11.77	13.36
1981	14.029	13.776	14.44	13.91	13.45	14.17	16.04	11.23	14.70	14.76	18.87	13.42	16.38
1982	10.686	11.084	12.92	13.00	12.76	13.79	16.11	11.57	15.14	11.89	14.86	11.02	12.26
1983	8.63	8.75	10.45	11.10	11.18	12.04	13.55	9.47	12.57	8.89	10.79	8.50	9.09
1984	9.58	9.80	11.89	12.44	12.41	12.71	14.19	10.15	12.38	10.16	12.04	8.80	10.23
1985	7.48	7.66	9.64	10.62	10.79	11.37	12.72	9.18	11.55	8.01	9.93	7.69	8.10
1986	5.98	6.03	7.06	7.68	7.78	9.02	10.39	7.38	10.17	6.39	8.33	6.33	6.81
1987	5.82	6.05	7.68	8.39	8.59	9.38	10.58	7.73	9.31	6.85	8.21	5.66	6.66
1988	6.69	6.92	8.26	8.85	8.96	9.71	10.83	7.76	9.19	7.68	9.32	6.20	7.57
1989	8.12	8.04	8.55	8.49	8.45	9.26	10.18	7.24	10.13	8.80	10.87	6.93	9.21
1990	7.51	7.47	8.26	8.55	8.61	9.32	10.36	7.25	10.05	7.95	10.01	6.98	8.10
1991	5.42	5.49	6.82	7.86	8.14	8.77	9.80	6.89	9.32	5.85	8.46	5.45	5.69
1992	3.45	3.57	5.30	7.01	7.67	8.14	8.98	6.41	8.24	3.80	6.25	3.25	3.52
1993	3.02	3.14	4.44	5.87	6.59	7.22	7.93	5.63	7.20	3.30	6.00	3.00	3.02
1994	4.29	4.66	6.27	7.09	7.37	7.97	8.63	6.19	7.49	4.93	7.15	3.60	4.21
1995	5.51	5.59	6.25	6.57	6.88	7.59	8.20	5.95	7.87	5.93	8.83	5.21	5.83

[1] Rate on new issues within period; bank-discount basis.
[2] Yields on the more actively traded issues adjusted to constant maturities by the Treasury Department.
[3] Effective rate (in the primary market) on conventional mortgages, reflecting fees and charges as well as contract rate and assuming, on the average, repayment at end of 10 years. Rates beginning January 1973 not strictly comparable with prior rates.
[4] Bank-discount basis; prior to November 1979, data are for 4–6 months paper.
[5] For monthly data, high and low for the period. Prime rate for 1929–33 and 1947–48 are ranges of the rate in effect during the period.
[6] Since July 19, 1975, the daily effective rate is an average of the rates on a given day weighted by the volume of transactions at these rates. Prior to that date, the daily effective rate was the rate considered most representative of the day's transactions, usually the one at which most transactions occurred.
[7] From October 30, 1942, to April 24, 1946, a preferential rate of 0.50 percent was in effect for advances secured by Government securities maturing in 1 year or less.

See next page for continuation of table.

[Percent per annum]

Year and month	U.S. Treasury securities					Corporate bonds (Moody's)		High-grade munici-pal bonds (Stand-ard & Poor's)	New-home mort-gage yields[3]	Com-mer-cial paper, 6 months[4]	Prime rate charged by banks[5]	Discount rate, Federal Reserve Bank of New York[5]	Federal funds rate[6]
	Bills (new issues)[1]		Constant maturities[2]										
	3-month	6-month	3-year	10-year	30-year	Aaa	Baa						
											High-low	High-low	
1991:													
Jan	6.30	6.34	7.38	8.09	8.27	9.04	10.45	7.05	9.65	7.02	10.00– 9.50	6.50–6.50	6.91
Feb	5.95	5.93	7.08	7.85	8.03	8.83	10.07	6.90	9.57	6.41	9.50– 9.00	6.50–6.00	6.25
Mar	5.91	5.91	7.35	8.11	8.29	8.93	10.09	7.07	9.43	6.36	9.00– 9.00	6.00–6.00	6.12
Apr	5.67	5.73	7.23	8.04	8.21	8.86	9.94	7.05	9.60	6.07	9.00– 9.00	6.00–5.50	5.91
May	5.51	5.65	7.12	8.07	8.27	8.86	9.86	7.05	9.60	6.07	9.00– 9.00	6.00–5.50	5.78
June	5.60	5.76	7.39	8.28	8.47	9.01	9.96	7.09	9.52	5.94	9.00– 8.50	5.50–5.50	5.90
July	5.58	5.71	7.38	8.27	8.45	9.00	9.89	7.03	9.46	6.16	8.50– 8.50	5.50–5.50	5.82
Aug	5.39	5.47	6.80	7.90	8.14	8.75	9.65	6.89	9.43	6.14	8.50– 8.50	5.50–5.50	5.66
Sept	5.25	5.29	6.50	7.65	7.95	8.61	9.51	6.80	9.48	5.76	8.50– 8.50	5.50–5.00	5.45
Oct	5.03	5.08	6.23	7.53	7.93	8.55	9.49	6.59	9.30	5.59	8.50– 8.00	5.50–5.00	5.21
Nov	4.60	4.66	5.90	7.42	7.92	8.48	9.45	6.64	9.04	5.33	8.00– 8.00	5.00–5.00	4.81
Dec	4.12	4.16	5.39	7.09	7.70	8.31	9.26	6.63	8.64	4.93	8.00– 7.50	5.00–4.50	4.43
										8.53	7.50– 6.50	4.50–3.50	
1992:													
Jan	3.84	3.88	5.40	7.03	7.58	8.20	9.13	6.41	8.49	4.06	6.50–6.50	3.50–3.50	4.03
Feb	3.84	3.94	5.72	7.34	7.85	8.29	9.23	6.67	8.65	4.13	6.50–6.50	3.50–3.50	4.06
Mar	4.05	4.19	6.18	7.54	7.97	8.35	9.25	6.69	8.51	4.38	6.50–6.50	3.50–3.50	3.98
Apr	3.81	3.93	5.93	7.48	7.96	8.33	9.21	6.64	8.58	4.13	6.50–6.50	3.50–3.50	3.73
May	3.66	3.78	5.81	7.39	7.89	8.28	9.13	6.57	8.59	3.97	6.50–6.50	3.50–3.50	3.82
June	3.70	3.81	5.60	7.26	7.84	8.22	9.05	6.50	8.43	3.99	6.50–6.50	3.50–3.50	3.76
July	3.28	3.36	4.91	6.84	7.60	8.07	8.84	6.12	8.00	3.53	6.50–6.00	3.50–3.00	3.25
Aug	3.14	3.23	4.72	6.59	7.39	7.95	8.65	6.08	8.00	3.44	6.00–6.00	3.00–3.00	3.30
Sept	2.97	3.01	4.42	6.42	7.34	7.92	8.62	6.24	7.93	3.26	6.00–6.00	3.00–3.00	3.22
Oct	2.84	2.98	4.64	6.59	7.53	7.99	8.84	6.43	7.90	3.33	6.00–6.00	3.00–3.00	3.10
Nov	3.14	3.35	5.14	6.87	7.61	8.10	8.96	6.35	8.07	3.67	6.00–6.00	3.00–3.00	3.09
Dec	3.25	3.39	5.21	6.77	7.44	7.98	8.81	6.24	7.88	3.70	6.00–6.00	3.00–3.00	2.92
1993:													
Jan	3.06	3.17	4.93	6.60	7.34	7.91	8.67	6.18	7.82	3.35	6.00–6.00	3.00–3.00	3.02
Feb	2.95	3.08	4.58	6.26	7.09	7.71	8.39	5.87	7.77	3.27	6.00–6.00	3.00–3.00	3.03
Mar	2.97	3.08	4.40	5.98	6.82	7.58	8.15	5.65	7.46	3.24	6.00–6.00	3.00–3.00	3.07
Apr	2.89	3.00	4.30	5.97	6.85	7.46	8.14	5.78	7.46	3.19	6.00–6.00	3.00–3.00	2.96
May	2.96	3.07	4.40	6.04	6.92	7.43	8.21	5.73	7.37	3.20	6.00–6.00	3.00–3.00	3.00
June	3.10	3.23	4.53	5.96	6.81	7.33	8.07	5.73	7.23	3.38	6.00–6.00	3.00–3.00	3.04
July	3.05	3.15	4.43	5.81	6.63	7.17	7.93	5.60	7.20	3.35	6.00–6.00	3.00–3.00	3.06
Aug	3.05	3.17	4.36	5.68	6.32	6.85	7.60	5.50	7.05	3.33	6.00–6.00	3.00–3.00	3.03
Sept	2.96	3.06	4.17	5.36	6.00	6.66	7.34	5.31	6.95	3.25	6.00–6.00	3.00–3.00	3.09
Oct	3.04	3.13	4.18	5.33	5.94	6.67	7.31	5.29	6.80	3.27	6.00–6.00	3.00–3.00	2.99
Nov	3.12	3.27	4.50	5.72	6.21	6.93	7.66	5.47	6.80	3.43	6.00–6.00	3.00–3.00	3.02
Dec	3.08	3.25	4.54	5.77	6.25	6.93	7.69	5.35	6.92	3.40	6.00–6.00	3.00–3.00	2.96
1994:													
Jan	3.02	3.19	4.48	5.75	6.29	6.92	7.65	5.30	6.95	3.30	6.00–6.00	3.00–3.00	3.05
Feb	3.21	3.38	4.83	5.97	6.49	7.08	7.76	5.44	6.85	3.62	6.00–6.00	3.00–3.00	3.25
Mar	3.52	3.79	5.40	6.48	6.91	7.48	8.13	5.93	6.99	4.08	6.00–6.25	3.00–3.00	3.34
Apr	3.74	4.13	5.99	6.97	7.27	7.88	8.52	6.28	7.31	4.40	6.25–6.75	3.00–3.00	3.56
May	4.19	4.64	6.34	7.18	7.41	7.99	8.62	6.26	7.43	4.92	6.75–7.25	3.00–3.50	4.01
June	4.18	4.58	6.27	7.10	7.40	7.97	8.65	6.14	7.62	4.86	7.25–7.25	3.50–3.50	4.25
July	4.39	4.81	6.48	7.30	7.58	8.11	8.80	6.19	7.71	5.13	7.25–7.25	3.50–3.50	4.26
Aug	4.50	4.91	6.50	7.24	7.49	8.07	8.74	6.19	7.67	5.19	7.25–7.75	3.50–4.00	4.47
Sept	4.64	5.02	6.69	7.46	7.71	8.34	8.98	6.33	7.70	5.32	7.75–7.75	4.00–4.00	4.73
Oct	4.96	5.39	7.04	7.74	7.94	8.57	9.20	6.50	7.76	5.70	7.75–7.75	4.00–4.00	4.76
Nov	5.25	5.69	7.44	7.96	8.08	8.68	9.32	6.96	7.81	6.01	7.75–8.50	4.00–4.75	5.29
Dec	5.64	6.21	7.71	7.81	7.87	8.46	9.10	6.76	7.83	6.62	8.50–8.50	4.75–4.75	5.45
1995:													
Jan	5.81	6.31	7.66	7.78	7.85	8.46	9.08	6.53	8.18	6.63	8.50–8.50	4.75–4.75	5.53
Feb	5.80	6.10	7.25	7.47	7.61	8.26	8.85	6.24	8.28	6.38	8.50–9.00	4.75–5.25	5.92
Mar	5.73	5.91	6.89	7.20	7.45	8.12	8.70	6.10	8.21	6.30	9.00–9.00	5.25–5.25	5.98
Apr	5.67	5.80	6.68	7.06	7.36	8.03	8.60	6.01	8.15	6.19	9.00–9.00	5.25–5.25	6.05
May	5.70	5.73	6.27	6.63	6.95	7.65	8.20	5.90	7.99	6.07	9.00–9.00	5.25–5.25	6.01
June	5.50	5.46	5.80	6.17	6.57	7.30	7.90	5.83	7.73	5.79	9.00–9.00	5.25–5.25	6.00
July	5.47	5.41	5.89	6.28	6.72	7.41	8.04	5.98	7.78	5.68	9.00–8.75	5.25–5.25	5.85
Aug	5.41	5.40	6.10	6.49	6.86	7.57	8.19	6.07	7.75	5.75	8.75–8.75	5.25–5.25	5.74
Sept	5.26	5.28	5.89	6.20	6.55	7.32	7.93	5.88	7.69	5.66	8.75–8.75	5.25–5.25	5.80
Oct	5.30	5.34	5.77	6.04	6.37	7.12	7.75	5.77	7.58	5.71	8.75–8.75	5.25–5.25	5.76
Nov	5.35	5.29	5.57	5.93	6.26	7.02	7.68	5.61	7.46	5.59	8.75–8.75	5.25–5.25	5.80
Dec	5.16	5.15	5.39	5.71	6.06	6.82	7.49	5.42	7.40	5.43	8.75–8.50	5.25–5.25	5.60

Sources: Department of the Treasury, Board of Governors of the Federal Reserve System, Federal Housing Finance Board, Moody's Investors Service, and Standard & Poor's Corporation.

TABLE B–70.—*Total funds raised in credit markets, 1986–95*

[Billions of dollars; quarterly data at seasonally adjusted annual rates]

Item	1986	1987	1988	1989	1990	1991	1992	1993	1994
NONFINANCIAL:									
Total net borrowing by domestic.									
nonfinancial sectors	863.6	733.7	767.7	720.3	669.4	480.6	545.3	625.9	617.0
U.S. Government	216.0	143.9	155.1	146.4	246.9	278.2	304.0	256.1	155.9
Treasury securities	215.6	142.4	137.7	144.7	238.7	292.0	303.8	248.3	155.7
Agency issues and mortgages	.4	1.5	17.4	1.6	8.2	–13.8	.2	7.8	.2
Private domestic nonfinancial sectors	647.6	589.8	612.6	574.0	422.5	202.4	241.3	369.8	461.1
Tax-exempt securities	59.9	91.6	59.3	52.9	49.3	87.8	30.5	74.8	–29.3
Corporate bonds	127.1	78.8	103.1	73.8	47.1	78.8	67.6	75.2	23.3
Mortgages	300.6	330.3	298.8	293.7	232.4	158.4	130.9	157.2	196.5
Home mortgages	206.0	247.6	229.3	235.2	226.3	173.6	187.6	187.9	204.5
Multifamily residential	33.2	16.9	17.7	10.6	1.5	–5.5	–10.4	–6.0	1.3
Commercial	72.2	73.3	56.5	50.3	6.1	–10.0	–47.8	–25.0	–11.1
Farm	–10.7	–7.4	–4.8	–2.5	–1.6	.4	1.4	.5	1.8
Consumer credit	57.5	32.9	50.1	45.8	15.6	–14.8	7.3	58.9	121.2
Bank loans n.e.c	55.5	10.8	33.9	27.8	.4	–40.9	–13.7	3.8	72.7
Commercial paper	–9.3	1.6	11.9	21.4	9.7	–18.4	8.6	10.0	21.4
Other	56.3	43.8	55.5	58.5	68.1	–48.5	10.1	–10.2	55.4
By borrowing sector:	647.6	589.8	612.6	574.0	422.5	202.4	241.3	369.8	461.1
Households	261.1	306.5	259.1	269.5	263.7	182.7	200.7	246.5	360.3
Nonfinancial domestic business	313.1	192.2	299.0	253.4	112.2	–61.9	19.5	61.0	144.3
Farm	–17.4	–11.6	–10.2	.6	1.0	2.1	1.3	2.0	2.8
Nonfarm noncorporate	94.3	55.2	84.2	69.6	1.1	–11.0	–16.0	7.0	12.1
Corporate	236.3	148.7	225.0	183.2	110.0	–53.0	34.1	52.0	129.3
State and local governments	73.4	91.1	54.5	51.1	46.6	81.6	21.1	62.3	–43.4
Foreign net borrowing in United States	9.7	6.2	6.4	10.2	23.9	14.8	22.6	68.8	–20.3
Bonds	3.1	7.4	6.9	4.9	21.4	15.0	15.7	81.3	7.1
Bank loans n.e.c	–1.0	–3.6	–1.8	–.1	–2.9	3.1	2.3	.7	1.4
Commercial paper	11.5	3.8	8.7	13.1	12.3	6.4	5.2	–9.0	–27.3
U.S. Government and other loans	–3.9	–1.4	–7.5	–7.6	–7.0	–9.8	–.6	–4.2	–1.6
Total domestic plus foreign	873.3	739.9	774.1	730.5	693.2	495.4	568.0	694.7	596.6
FINANCIAL:									
Total net borrowing by domestic financial sectors	327.8	291.6	249.2	226.4	210.9	154.5	240.1	290.8	459.4
U.S. Government related	178.1	168.3	119.8	149.5	167.4	145.7	155.8	164.2	284.3
Private domestic financial sectors	149.7	123.3	129.5	76.9	43.6	8.7	84.3	126.6	175.2
By borrowing sector:	327.8	291.6	249.2	226.4	210.9	154.5	240.1	290.8	459.4
Government-sponsored enterprises	14.9	29.5	44.9	25.2	17.0	9.1	40.2	80.6	172.1
Federally related mortgage pools	163.3	138.8	74.9	124.3	150.3	136.6	115.6	83.6	112.1
Private domestic financial sectors	149.7	123.3	129.5	76.9	43.6	8.7	84.3	126.6	175.2
Commercial banks	–3.1	7.2	–3.2	–1.0	.9	–10.7	7.7	4.6	9.9
Bank holding companies	10.7	14.3	5.2	6.2	–27.7	–2.5	2.3	8.8	10.3
Savings institutions	24.3	28.7	21.6	–15.0	–30.9	–44.7	–7.0	11.3	12.8
Funding corporations	12.0	9.7	38.0	12.5	15.4	–6.5	13.2	2.9	24.2
Finance companies	51.5	23.2	23.9	27.4	23.8	17.7	–1.6	.2	50.2
Asset-backed securities issuers	42.0	49.9	37.6	29.1	59.8	52.9	58.6	83.0	64.5
Other	12.3	–9.6	6.3	17.8	2.3	2.5	11.0	15.8	3.2
ALL SECTORS, BY TRANSACTION:	1,201.1	1,031.5	1,023.3	956.9	904.1	649.9	808.0	985.5	1,056.0
U.S. Government securities	394.5	312.9	274.9	295.8	414.4	424.0	459.8	420.3	444.9
Tax-exempt securities	59.9	91.6	59.3	52.9	49.3	87.8	30.5	74.8	–29.3
Corporate and foreign bonds	222.5	164.7	162.2	120.9	122.0	162.5	166.1	276.3	143.8
Mortgages	300.9	330.6	299.1	294.0	233.0	158.9	131.5	160.8	206.3
Consumer credit	57.5	32.9	50.1	45.8	15.6	–14.8	7.3	58.9	121.2
Bank loans n.e.c	66.8	–1.1	34.8	41.2	2.2	–29.1	–9.3	–8.5	61.8
Open-market paper	26.4	32.3	75.4	65.9	30.7	–44.0	13.1	–5.1	35.7
Other loans	72.7	67.5	67.5	40.5	37.1	–95.6	8.9	8.0	71.7

See next page for continuation of table.

TABLE B-70.—*Total funds raised in credit markets, 1986-95*—Continued

[Billions of dollars; quarterly data at seasonally adjusted annual rates]

Item	1993				1994				1995		
	I	II	III	IV	I	II	III	IV	I	II	III
NONFINANCIAL:											
Total net borrowing by domestic											
nonfinancial sectors	449.7	792.7	598.0	663.2	652.5	581.2	580.0	654.3	831.0	877.5	513.1
U.S. Government	238.6	346.3	172.9	266.7	206.4	131.3	135.6	150.1	266.8	202.8	65.8
Treasury securities	235.4	342.2	156.6	259.0	207.7	126.6	132.8	155.7	268.0	201.2	65.4
Agency issues and mortgages	3.2	4.1	16.2	7.7	-1.3	4.7	2.9	-5.7	-1.2	1.6	.4
Private domestic nonfinancial											
sectors	211.1	446.4	425.2	396.4	446.1	449.9	444.3	504.2	564.2	674.8	447.3
Tax-exempt securities	89.9	134.5	54.7	20.1	15.7	-20.7	-58.4	-53.8	-53.3	-10.6	-115.8
Corporate bonds	85.7	75.7	72.0	67.4	34.2	37.4	15.4	6.2	55.3	99.0	60.7
Mortgages	92.2	169.4	210.2	157.0	174.2	194.2	203.9	213.5	219.6	238.8	251.9
Home mortgages	115.9	212.0	227.5	196.0	203.3	186.2	208.8	219.8	192.5	204.2	215.3
Multifamily residential	-6.1	-10.8	-5.0	-2.3	-.3	4.0	5.6	-4.2	2.9	15.0	11.9
Commercial	-17.7	-32.9	-12.7	-36.9	-29.4	1.1	-12.7	-3.4	22.5	17.8	22.4
Farm	.2	1.0	.4	.2	.6	2.9	2.2	1.4	1.7	1.8	2.3
Consumer credit	13.1	45.4	64.4	112.8	65.0	129.8	124.8	165.2	93.8	158.1	109.6
Bank loans n.e.c	-30.0	5.1	16.9	23.2	57.7	58.7	97.1	77.1	143.5	94.4	99.4
Commercial paper	-1.0	29.1	10.9	1.0	26.1	9.7	26.4	23.5	23.1	37.5	16.0
Other	-38.9	-12.7	-3.9	14.9	73.2	40.8	35.1	72.4	82.2	57.7	25.6
By borrowing sector:	211.1	446.4	425.2	396.4	446.1	449.9	444.3	504.2	564.2	674.8	447.3
Households	111.6	246.7	312.9	314.9	292.3	349.9	379.7	419.1	301.8	388.9	380.3
Nonfinancial domestic business	13.3	82.3	76.6	71.8	154.1	139.4	130.0	153.6	314.5	302.8	187.0
Farm	-2.0	1.9	4.1	4.2	3.1	7.8	2.4	-2.0	.9	3.6	4.3
Nonfarm noncorporate	2.5	11.0	5.1	9.4	13.2	10.0	8.8	16.5	51.3	43.5	21.5
Corporate	12.9	69.5	67.4	58.3	137.7	121.7	118.8	139.1	262.3	255.7	161.1
State and local governments	86.2	117.4	35.8	9.8	-.3	-39.5	-65.4	-68.5	-52.1	-16.9	-119.9
Foreign net borrowing in United											
States	48.8	63.2	121.1	42.1	-100.3	-34.2	19.6	33.5	61.4	40.4	97.5
Bonds	78.1	63.2	123.7	60.1	-2.6	-17.4	20.8	27.7	13.5	49.9	55.0
Bank loans n.e.c	1.5	6.6	1.0	-6.3	6.0	-4.5	4.7	-.5	8.1	5.6	8.2
Commercial paper	-21.7	-.6	-1.6	-12.0	-101.8	-5.2	-8.1	5.9	37.9	-11.1	30.9
U.S. Government and other loans	-9.1	-5.9	-2.1	.3	-1.8	-7.1	2.2	.4	1.9	-4.0	3.4
Total domestic plus foreign	498.6	855.9	719.1	705.3	552.2	547.0	599.5	687.8	892.4	918.0	610.6
FINANCIAL:											
Total net borrowing by domestic											
financial sectors	156.7	186.0	435.0	385.4	493.1	380.1	419.7	544.8	268.7	432.0	407.7
U.S. Government related	145.8	63.6	290.3	156.9	309.4	264.5	245.7	317.5	93.0	197.7	230.1
Private domestic financial sectors	10.9	122.4	144.7	228.5	183.8	115.5	174.0	227.3	175.7	234.4	177.6
By borrowing sector:	156.7	186.0	435.0	385.4	493.1	380.1	419.7	544.8	268.7	432.0	407.7
Government-sponsored enter-											
prises	32.2	68.8	167.8	53.4	140.8	146.6	152.1	249.0	62.9	127.2	101.5
Federally related mortgage											
pools	113.6	-5.2	122.5	103.5	168.5	117.9	93.6	68.5	30.0	70.5	128.6
Private domestic financial sec-											
tors	10.9	122.4	144.7	228.5	183.8	115.5	174.0	227.3	175.7	234.4	177.6
Commercial banks	2.1	10.9	5.0	.4	.9	10.6	23.9	4.1	6.3	18.2	9.6
Bank holding companies	21.1	1.3	.5	12.2	3.5	10.1	11.5	16.0	13.3	23.8	25.2
Savings institutions	9.9	12.5	12.3	10.3	-5.5	5.8	14.8	36.1	-18.9	-6.8	4.9
Funding corporations	-31.8	3.9	8.7	30.9	48.8	-10.5	47.3	11.1	61.6	21.4	41.9
Finance companies	-18.8	-16.2	16.2	19.4	63.7	63.6	16.3	57.3	83.1	57.2	6.5
Asset-backed securities is-											
suers	62.4	61.5	82.0	126.1	89.4	38.5	55.4	74.5	60.8	99.4	97.1
Other	-34.1	48.4	20.1	29.2	-17.1	-2.4	4.7	28.2	-30.3	21.1	-7.7
ALL SECTORS, BY TRANSACTION:	655.2	1,041.9	1,154.2	1,090.7	1,045.3	927.0	1,019.2	1,232.6	1,161.1	1,350.0	1,018.3
U.S. Government securities	384.4	409.9	463.2	423.6	534.9	395.8	381.3	467.5	359.8	400.5	295.9
Tax-exempt securities	89.9	134.5	54.7	20.1	15.7	-20.7	-58.4	-53.8	-53.3	-10.6	-115.8
Corporate and foreign bonds	265.2	235.1	334.8	269.9	192.7	116.4	135.7	130.4	225.3	319.1	248.7
Mortgages	93.6	170.7	216.4	162.5	184.0	206.6	215.9	218.4	224.7	243.6	254.2
Consumer credit	13.1	45.4	64.4	112.8	65.0	129.8	124.8	165.2	93.8	158.1	109.6
Bank loans, n.e.c	-64.5	24.6	2.0	4.0	51.8	26.8	90.1	78.5	151.7	124.1	100.7
Open-market paper	-98.8	12.9	-1.0	66.5	-40.7	8.8	59.6	115.3	99.5	60.4	90.2
Other loans	-27.7	8.9	19.7	31.2	41.9	63.5	70.2	111.0	59.6	55.0	34.8

Source: Board of Governors of the Federal Reserve System.

363

TABLE B–71.—*Mortgage debt outstanding by type of property and of financing, 1940–95*

[Billions of dollars]

End of year or quarter	All properties	Farm properties	Nonfarm properties				Nonfarm properties by type of mortgage					
							Government underwritten				Conventional[2]	
			Total	1-to 4-family houses	Multifamily properties	Commercial properties	Total[1]	1- to 4-family houses			Total	1-to 4-family houses
								Total	FHA insured	VA guaranteed		
1940	36.5	6.5	30.0	17.4	5.7	6.9	2.3	2.3	2.3		27.7	15.1
1941	37.6	6.4	31.2	18.4	5.9	7.0	3.0	3.0	3.0		28.2	15.4
1942	36.7	6.0	30.8	18.2	5.8	6.7	3.7	3.7	3.7		27.1	14.5
1943	35.3	5.4	29.9	17.8	5.8	6.3	4.1	4.1	4.1		25.8	13.7
1944	34.7	4.9	29.7	17.9	5.6	6.2	4.2	4.2	4.2		25.5	13.7
1945	35.5	4.8	30.8	18.6	5.7	6.4	4.3	4.3	4.1	0.2	26.5	14.3
1946	41.8	4.9	36.9	23.0	6.1	7.7	6.3	6.1	3.7	2.4	30.6	16.9
1947	48.9	5.1	43.9	28.2	6.6	9.1	9.8	9.3	3.8	5.5	34.1	18.9
1948	56.2	5.3	50.9	33.3	7.5	10.2	13.6	12.5	5.3	7.2	37.3	20.8
1949	62.7	5.6	57.1	37.6	8.6	10.8	17.1	15.0	6.9	8.1	40.0	22.6
1950	72.8	6.1	66.7	45.2	10.1	11.5	22.1	18.8	8.5	10.3	44.7	26.3
1951	82.3	6.7	75.6	51.7	11.5	12.5	26.6	22.9	9.7	13.2	49.1	28.9
1952	91.4	7.2	84.2	58.5	12.3	13.4	29.3	25.4	10.8	14.6	54.9	33.2
1953	101.3	7.7	93.6	66.1	12.9	14.5	32.1	28.1	12.0	16.1	61.5	38.0
1954	113.7	8.2	105.4	75.7	13.5	16.3	36.2	32.1	12.8	19.3	69.3	43.6
1955	129.9	9.0	120.9	88.2	14.3	18.3	42.9	38.9	14.3	24.6	78.0	49.3
1956	144.5	9.8	134.6	99.0	14.9	20.7	47.8	43.9	15.5	28.4	86.8	55.1
1957	156.5	10.4	146.1	107.6	15.3	23.2	51.6	47.2	16.5	30.7	94.6	60.4
1958	171.8	11.1	160.7	117.7	16.8	26.1	55.2	50.1	19.7	30.4	105.5	67.6
1959	190.8	12.1	178.7	130.9	18.7	29.2	59.3	53.8	23.8	30.0	119.4	77.0
1960	207.5	12.8	194.7	141.9	20.3	32.4	62.3	56.4	26.7	29.7	132.3	85.5
1961	228.0	13.9	214.1	154.6	23.0	36.5	65.6	59.1	29.5	29.6	148.5	95.5
1962	251.4	15.2	236.2	169.3	25.8	41.1	69.4	62.2	32.3	29.9	166.9	107.1
1963	278.5	16.8	261.7	186.4	29.0	46.2	73.4	65.9	35.0	30.9	188.2	120.5
1964	305.9	18.9	287.0	203.4	33.6	50.0	77.2	69.2	38.3	30.9	209.8	134.1
1965	333.3	21.2	312.1	220.5	37.2	54.5	81.2	73.1	42.0	31.1	231.0	147.4
1966	356.5	23.1	333.4	232.9	40.3	60.1	84.1	76.1	44.8	31.3	249.3	156.9
1967	381.2	25.1	356.1	247.3	43.9	64.8	88.2	79.9	47.4	32.5	267.9	167.4
1968	411.1	27.5	383.5	264.8	47.3	71.4	93.4	84.4	50.6	33.8	290.1	180.4
1969	441.6	29.4	412.2	283.2	52.2	76.9	100.2	90.2	54.5	35.7	312.0	193.0
1970	473.7	30.5	443.2	297.4	60.1	85.6	109.2	97.3	59.9	37.3	333.9	200.2
1971	524.2	32.4	491.8	325.9	70.1	95.9	120.7	105.2	65.7	39.5	371.1	220.7
1972	597.4	35.4	562.0	366.5	82.8	112.7	131.1	113.0	68.2	44.7	430.9	253.5
1973	672.6	39.8	632.8	407.9	93.1	131.7	135.0	116.2	66.2	50.0	497.7	291.7
1974	732.5	44.9	687.5	440.7	100.0	146.9	140.2	121.3	65.1	56.2	547.3	319.4
1975	791.9	49.9	742.0	482.1	100.6	159.3	147.0	127.7	66.1	61.6	595.0	354.3
1976	878.6	55.4	823.2	546.3	105.7	171.2	154.1	133.5	66.5	67.0	669.0	412.8
1977	1,010.3	63.9	946.4	642.7	114.0	189.7	161.7	141.6	68.0	73.6	784.6	501.0
1978	1,163.0	72.8	1,090.2	753.5	124.9	211.8	176.4	153.4	71.4	82.0	913.9	600.2
1979	1,328.4	86.8	1,241.7	870.5	134.9	236.3	199.0	172.9	81.0	92.0	1,042.7	697.6
1980	1,463.0	97.5	1,365.5	969.0	141.0	255.5	225.1	195.2	93.6	101.6	1,140.4	773.9
1981	1,572.8	107.2	1,465.5	1,049.1	138.9	277.5	238.9	207.6	101.3	106.2	1,226.7	841.5
1982	1,650.7	111.3	1,539.3	1,096.4	140.8	302.2	248.9	217.9	108.0	109.9	1,290.5	878.5
1983	1,841.9	113.7	1,728.2	1,219.4	154.0	354.8	279.8	248.8	127.4	121.4	1,448.4	970.5
1984	2,071.1	112.4	1,958.7	1,360.4	177.0	421.4	294.8	265.9	136.7	129.1	1,663.9	1,094.5
1985	2,334.2	105.9	2,228.3	1,535.7	205.3	487.3	328.3	288.8	153.0	135.8	1,900.0	1,246.9
1986	2,635.1	95.2	2,539.9	1,741.7	238.5	559.7	370.5	328.6	185.5	143.1	2,169.4	1,413.1
1987	2,985.3	87.7	2,897.6	1,976.5	260.9	660.2	431.4	387.9	235.5	152.4	2,466.1	1,588.6
1988	3,280.3	83.0	3,197.3	2,217.4	277.5	702.4	459.7	414.2	258.8	155.4	2,737.7	1,803.3
1989	3,582.1	80.5	3,501.7	2,459.5	288.5	753.7	486.8	440.1	282.8	157.3	3,014.8	2,019.4
1990	3,803.7	78.9	3,724.8	2,676.2	289.8	758.8	517.9	470.9	310.9	160.0	3,206.9	2,205.3
1991	3,962.6	79.3	3,883.3	2,849.8	284.4	749.1	537.2	493.3	330.6	162.7	3,346.1	2,356.5
1992	4,094.1	80.7	4,013.3	3,037.4	274.2	701.7	533.3	489.8	326.0	163.8	3,480.0	2,547.7
1993	4,269.0	81.2	4,187.8	3,227.6	270.8	689.4	513.4	469.5	303.2	166.2	3,674.4	2,758.2
1994	4,475.2	83.0	4,392.3	3,432.2	275.3	684.8	559.3	514.2	336.8	177.3	3,833.0	2,918.0
1993: I	4,104.1	80.8	4,023.3	3,053.0	272.8	697.5	530.5	487.0	323.4	163.6	3,492.8	2,566.1
II	4,154.2	81.0	4,073.1	3,113.4	270.2	689.5	522.6	479.0	315.2	163.8	3,550.5	2,634.4
III	4,212.9	81.1	4,131.8	3,174.9	269.5	687.4	520.1	476.2	312.5	163.7	3,611.7	2,698.7
IV	4,269.0	81.2	4,187.8	3,227.6	270.8	689.4	513.4	469.5	303.2	166.2	3,674.4	2,758.2
1994: I	4,301.1	81.3	4,219.8	3,264.6	271.5	683.7	521.2	476.7	309.7	167.0	3,698.6	2,787.9
II	4,360.3	82.1	4,278.2	3,318.7	273.6	686.0	533.5	488.8	318.8	170.0	3,744.7	2,829.9
III	4,419.4	82.6	4,336.7	3,376.0	276.0	684.8	551.1	506.2	331.9	174.3	3,785.7	2,869.7
IV	4,475.2	83.0	4,392.3	3,432.2	275.3	684.8	559.3	514.2	336.8	177.3	3,833.0	2,918.0
1995: I	4,517.2	83.4	4,433.8	3,466.1	276.4	691.3	565.4	520.3	341.7	178.6	3,868.4	2,945.8
II	4,585.6	83.9	4,501.8	3,524.7	280.6	696.5	571.3	525.8	345.5	180.3	3,930.5	2,998.9
III p	4,654.6	84.4	4,570.2	3,583.9	283.8	702.5	578.4	531.0	348.5	182.5	3,991.8	3,052.9

[1] Includes FHA insured multifamily properties, not shown separately.
[2] Derived figures. Total includes multifamily and commercial properties, not shown separately.

Source: Board of Governors of the Federal Reserve System, based on data from various Government and private organizations.

TABLE B–72.—*Mortgage debt outstanding by holder, 1940–95*

[Billions of dollars]

End of year or quarter	Total	Major financial institutions				Other holders	
		Total	Savings institutions[1]	Commercial banks[2]	Life insurance companies	Federal and related agencies[3]	Individuals and others[4]
1940	36.5	19.5	9.0	4.6	6.0	4.9	12.0
1941	37.6	20.7	9.4	4.9	6.4	4.7	12.2
1942	36.7	20.7	9.2	4.7	6.7	4.3	11.7
1943	35.3	20.2	9.0	4.5	6.7	3.6	11.5
1944	34.7	20.2	9.1	4.4	6.7	3.0	11.5
1945	35.5	21.0	9.6	4.8	6.6	2.4	12.1
1946	41.8	26.0	11.5	7.2	7.2	2.0	13.8
1947	48.9	31.8	13.8	9.4	8.7	1.8	15.3
1948	56.2	37.8	16.1	10.9	10.8	1.8	16.6
1949	62.7	42.9	18.3	11.6	12.9	2.3	17.5
1950	72.8	51.7	21.9	13.7	16.1	2.8	18.4
1951	82.3	59.5	25.5	14.7	19.3	3.5	19.3
1952	91.4	66.9	29.8	15.9	21.3	4.1	20.4
1953	101.3	75.1	34.9	16.9	23.3	4.6	21.7
1954	113.7	85.7	41.1	18.6	26.0	4.8	23.2
1955	129.9	99.3	48.9	21.0	29.4	5.3	25.3
1956	144.5	111.2	55.5	22.7	33.0	6.2	27.1
1957	156.5	119.7	61.2	23.3	35.2	7.7	29.1
1958	171.8	131.5	68.9	25.5	37.1	8.0	32.3
1959	190.8	145.5	78.1	28.1	39.2	10.2	35.1
1960	207.5	157.6	87.0	28.8	41.8	11.5	38.4
1961	228.0	172.6	98.0	30.4	44.2	12.2	43.1
1962	251.4	192.5	111.1	34.5	46.9	12.6	46.3
1963	278.5	217.1	127.2	39.4	50.5	11.8	49.5
1964	305.9	241.0	141.9	44.0	55.2	12.2	52.7
1965	333.3	264.6	154.9	49.7	60.0	13.5	55.2
1966	356.5	280.8	161.8	54.4	64.6	17.5	58.2
1967	381.2	298.8	172.3	59.0	67.5	20.9	61.4
1968	411.1	319.9	184.3	65.7	70.0	25.1	66.1
1969	441.6	339.1	196.4	70.7	72.0	31.1	71.4
1970	473.7	355.9	208.3	73.3	74.4	38.3	79.4
1971	524.2	394.2	236.2	82.5	75.5	46.4	83.6
1972	597.4	450.0	273.7	99.3	76.9	54.6	92.8
1973	672.6	505.4	305.0	119.1	81.4	64.8	102.4
1974	732.5	542.6	324.2	132.1	86.2	82.2	107.7
1975	791.9	581.2	355.8	136.2	89.2	101.1	109.6
1976	878.6	647.5	404.6	151.3	91.6	116.7	114.4
1977	1,010.3	745.2	469.4	179.0	96.8	140.5	124.6
1978	1,163.0	848.2	528.0	214.0	106.2	170.6	144.3
1979	1,328.4	938.2	574.6	245.2	118.4	216.0	174.3
1980	1,463.0	996.8	603.1	262.7	131.1	256.8	209.4
1981	1,572.8	1,040.5	618.5	284.2	137.7	289.4	242.9
1982	1,650.7	1,021.3	578.1	301.3	142.0	355.4	273.9
1983	1,841.9	1,108.2	626.7	330.5	151.0	433.4	300.3
1984	2,071.1	1,245.9	709.7	379.5	156.7	490.6	334.6
1985	2,334.2	1,361.5	760.5	429.2	171.8	581.9	390.8
1986	2,635.1	1,474.3	778.0	502.5	193.8	733.7	427.0
1987	2,985.3	1,665.3	860.5	592.4	212.4	858.9	461.1
1988	3,280.3	1,831.5	924.6	674.0	232.9	937.8	511.1
1989	3,582.1	1,931.5	910.3	767.1	254.2	1,067.3	583.3
1990	3,803.7	1,914.3	801.6	844.8	267.9	1,258.9	630.5
1991	3,962.6	1,846.7	705.4	876.1	265.3	1,422.6	693.2
1992	4,094.1	1,769.2	628.0	894.5	246.7	1,558.3	766.6
1993	4,269.0	1,767.8	598.3	940.4	229.1	1,684.2	816.9
1994	4,475.2	1,815.8	596.2	1,004.3	215.3	1,791.3	868.2
1993: I	4,104.1	1,753.3	617.2	891.8	244.4	1,586.9	763.9
II	4,154.2	1,765.7	612.4	911.0	242.2	1,600.3	788.2
III	4,212.9	1,770.0	609.7	922.7	237.6	1,636.7	806.3
IV	4,269.0	1,767.8	598.3	940.4	229.1	1,684.2	816.9
1994: I	4,301.1	1,746.4	584.5	937.9	224.0	1,727.0	827.7
II	4,360.3	1,763.2	585.7	956.8	220.7	1,759.9	837.2
III	4,419.4	1,786.1	587.5	981.4	217.2	1,780.8	852.5
IV	4,475.2	1,815.8	596.2	1,004.3	215.3	1,791.3	868.2
1995: I	4,517.2	1,841.8	601.8	1,024.9	215.2	1,796.2	879.3
II	4,585.6	1,868.2	599.7	1,053.0	215.4	1,812.1	905.3
III ᵖ	4,654.6	1,895.3	604.6	1,072.8	217.9	1,841.1	918.2

[1] Includes savings banks and savings and loan associations. Data reported by Federal Savings and Loan Insurance Corporation-insured institutions include loans in process for 1987 and exclude loans in process beginning 1988.

[2] Includes loans held by nondeposit trust companies, but not by bank trust departments.

[3] Includes Government National Mortgage Association (GNMA), Federal Housing Administration, Veterans Administration, Farmers Home Administration (FmHA), and in earlier years Reconstruction Finance Corporation, Homeowners Loan Corporation, Federal Farm Mortgage Corporation, and Public Housing Administration. Also includes U.S.-sponsored agencies such as Federal National Mortgage Association (FNMA), Federal Land Banks, Federal Home Loan Mortgage Corporation (FHLMC), and mortgage pass-through securities issued or guaranteed by GNMA, FHLMC, FNMA or FmHA. Other U.S. agencies (amounts small or current separate data not readily available) included with "individuals and others."

[4] Includes private mortgage pools.

Source: Board of Governors of the Federal Reserve System, based on data from various Government and private organizations.

TABLE B–73.—*Consumer credit outstanding, 1955–95*

[Amount outstanding (end of month); billions of dollars, seasonally adjusted]

Year and month	Total consumer credit	Installment credit [1]				Noninstallment credit [4]
		Total	Automobile	Revolving [2]	Other [3]	
December:						
1955	41.9	29.8	13.5		16.3	12.1
1956	45.5	32.7	14.5		18.2	12.8
1957	48.1	34.9	15.5		19.4	13.2
1958	48.4	34.7	14.3		20.5	13.6
1959	55.9	40.4	16.6		23.8	15.5
1960	60.0	44.3	18.1		26.2	15.7
1961	62.3	45.4	17.7		27.8	16.9
1962	68.2	50.4	20.0		30.4	17.9
1963	76.6	57.1	22.9		34.2	19.6
1964	86.0	64.7	25.9		38.8	21.3
1965	95.9	72.8	29.4		43.4	23.1
1966	101.8	78.2	31.0		47.1	23.7
1967	106.7	81.8	31.1		50.6	24.9
1968	117.2	90.1	34.4	2.0	53.7	27.1
1969	126.9	99.4	36.9	3.6	58.9	27.5
1970	131.6	103.9	36.3	4.9	62.7	27.7
1971	147.1	116.4	40.5	8.3	67.7	30.6
1972	166.0	131.3	47.8	9.4	74.0	34.8
1973	190.6	152.9	53.7	11.3	87.9	37.7
1974	199.4	162.2	54.2	13.2	94.7	37.2
1975	205.0	167.0	57.0	14.5	95.5	37.9
1976	228.2	187.8	66.8	16.6	104.4	40.4
1977	263.8	221.5	80.9	36.7	103.8	42.3
1978	308.3	262.0	98.7	45.2	118.0	46.3
1979	347.5	296.5	112.5	53.4	130.7	51.0
1980	350.3	298.2	112.0	55.1	131.1	52.1
1981	366.9	311.3	119.0	61.1	131.2	55.6
1982	383.1	325.8	125.9	66.5	133.4	57.3
1983	431.2	369.0	143.6	79.1	146.3	62.2
1984	511.3	442.6	173.6	100.3	168.8	68.7
1985	591.3	517.7	210.2	121.8	185.7	73.6
1986	648.0	572.0	247.8	135.8	188.4	76.0
1987	680.0	608.7	266.3	153.1	189.3	71.4
1988 [5]	729.1	662.6	285.4	174.3	202.9	66.6
1989	782.1	717.2	291.5	199.2	226.5	64.9
1990	797.3	734.9	283.1	223.5	228.3	62.4
1991	781.0	728.4	259.6	245.3	223.5	52.6
1992	786.4	730.8	257.4	258.1	215.3	55.6
1993	843.3	790.4	280.6	286.6	223.2	53.0
1994	961.1	902.9	317.2	334.5	251.1	58.3
1995 ᴾ	1,087.8	1,022.9	353.1	394.8	275.1	64.9
1994: Jan	848.9	795.9	282.7	288.5	224.7	53.0
Feb	854.7	800.3	283.2	291.4	225.7	54.4
Mar	865.4	811.1	287.1	295.8	228.2	54.3
Apr	876.0	821.2	290.8	300.4	230.0	54.8
May	886.4	832.2	294.9	304.5	232.8	54.3
June	896.5	842.3	298.9	308.3	235.1	54.2
July	904.1	849.9	300.6	312.7	236.6	54.2
Aug	917.1	863.5	304.3	319.7	239.5	53.6
Sept	928.2	873.6	308.7	322.0	242.9	54.6
Oct	941.7	882.2	311.2	324.7	246.4	59.5
Nov	952.3	895.6	315.2	332.4	248.0	56.7
Dec	961.1	902.9	317.2	334.5	251.1	58.3
1995: Jan	973.1	914.4	319.3	340.2	254.9	58.7
Feb	979.0	918.9	321.0	345.1	252.8	60.1
Mar	994.6	933.0	323.3	351.5	258.2	61.6
Apr	1,007.3	946.3	326.2	358.7	261.4	61.0
May	1,020.3	959.1	328.0	366.1	265.0	61.2
June	1,032.3	970.6	330.7	372.3	267.5	61.7
July	1,042.8	979.4	337.1	375.3	267.0	63.4
Aug	1,052.9	989.7	339.8	379.7	270.3	63.2
Sept	1,059.6	993.8	341.2	382.1	270.6	65.8
Oct	1,068.7	1,005.2	344.7	387.2	273.3	63.5
Nov	1,077.9	1,015.0	349.1	390.1	275.8	62.9
Dec ᴾ	1,087.8	1,022.9	353.1	394.8	275.1	64.9

[1] Installment credit covers most short- and intermediate-term credit extended to individuals through regular business channels, usually to finance the purchase of consumer goods and services or to refinance debts incurred for such purposes, and scheduled to be repaid (or with the option of repayment) in two or more installments. Credit secured by real estate is excluded.

[2] Consists of credit cards at retailers, gasoline companies, and commercial banks, and check credit at commercial banks. Excludes 30-day charge credit held by travel and entertainment companies. Prior to 1968, included in "other," except gasoline companies included in noninstallment credit prior to 1971. Beginning 1977, includes open-end credit at retailers, previously included in "other." Also beginning 1977, some retail credit was reclassified from commercial into consumer credit.

[3] Includes mobile home loans and all other installment loans not included in automobile or revolving credit, such as loans for education, boats, trailers, or vacations. These loans may be secured or unsecured.

[4] Noninstallment credit is credit scheduled to be repaid in a lump sum, including single-payment loans, charge accounts, and service credit. Because of inconsistencies in the data and infrequent benchmarking, series is no longer published by the Federal Reserve Board on a regular basis. Data are shown here as a general indication of trends.

[5] Data newly available in January 1989 result in breaks in many series between December 1988 and subsequent months.

Source: Board of Governors of the Federal Reserve System.

GOVERNMENT FINANCE

TABLE B–74.—*Federal receipts, outlays, surplus or deficit, and debt, selected fiscal years, 1929–95*

[Billions of dollars; fiscal years]

Fiscal year or period	Total			On-budget			Off-budget			Gross Federal debt (end of period)		Adden-dum: Gross domestic product
	Receipts	Outlays	Surplus or deficit (–)	Receipts	Outlays	Surplus or deficit (–)	Receipts	Outlays	Surplus or deficit (–)	Total	Held by the public	
1929	3.9	3.1	0.7	3.9	3.1	0.7				[1] 16.9		
1933	2.0	4.6	–2.6	2.0	4.6	–2.6				[1] 22.5		56.8
1939	6.3	9.1	–2.8	5.8	9.2	–3.4	0.5	–0.0	0.5	48.2	41.4	87.8
1940	6.5	9.5	–2.9	6.0	9.5	–3.5	.6	–.0	.6	50.7	42.8	95.4
1941	8.7	13.7	–4.9	8.0	13.6	–5.6	.7	.0	.7	57.5	48.2	112.5
1942	14.6	35.1	–20.5	13.7	35.1	–21.3	.9	.1	.8	79.2	67.8	141.8
1943	24.0	78.6	–54.6	22.9	78.5	–55.6	1.1	.1	1.0	142.6	127.8	175.4
1944	43.7	91.3	–47.6	42.5	91.2	–48.7	1.3	.1	1.2	204.1	184.8	201.7
1945	45.2	92.7	–47.6	43.8	92.6	–48.7	1.3	.1	1.2	260.1	235.2	212.0
1946	39.3	55.2	–15.9	38.1	55.0	–17.0	1.2	.2	1.0	271.0	241.9	212.5
1947	38.5	34.5	4.0	37.1	34.2	2.9	1.5	.3	1.2	257.1	224.3	222.9
1948	41.6	29.8	11.8	39.9	29.4	10.5	1.6	.4	1.2	252.0	216.3	246.7
1949	39.4	38.8	.6	37.7	38.4	–.7	1.7	.4	1.3	252.6	214.3	262.7
1950	39.4	42.6	–3.1	37.3	42.0	–4.7	2.1	.5	1.6	256.9	219.0	265.8
1951	51.6	45.5	6.1	48.5	44.2	4.3	3.1	1.3	1.8	255.3	214.3	313.5
1952	66.2	67.7	–1.5	62.6	66.0	–3.4	3.6	1.7	1.9	259.1	214.8	340.5
1953	69.6	76.1	–6.5	65.5	73.8	–8.3	4.1	2.3	1.8	266.0	218.4	363.8
1954	69.7	70.9	–1.2	65.1	67.9	–2.8	4.6	2.9	1.7	270.8	224.5	368.0
1955	65.5	68.4	–3.0	60.4	64.5	–4.1	5.1	4.0	1.1	274.4	226.6	384.7
1956	74.6	70.6	3.9	68.2	65.7	2.5	6.4	5.0	1.5	272.7	222.2	416.3
1957	80.0	76.6	3.4	73.2	70.6	2.6	6.8	6.0	.8	272.3	219.3	438.3
1958	79.6	82.4	–2.8	71.6	74.9	–3.3	8.0	7.5	.5	279.7	226.3	448.1
1959	79.2	92.1	–12.8	71.0	83.1	–12.1	8.3	9.0	–.7	287.5	234.7	480.2
1960	92.5	92.2	.3	81.9	81.3	.5	10.6	10.9	–.2	290.5	236.8	504.6
1961	94.4	97.7	–3.3	82.3	86.0	–3.8	12.1	11.7	.4	292.6	238.4	517.0
1962	99.7	106.8	–7.1	87.4	93.3	–5.9	12.3	13.5	–1.3	302.9	248.0	555.2
1963	106.6	111.3	–4.8	92.4	96.4	–4.0	14.2	15.0	–.8	310.3	254.0	584.5
1964	112.6	118.5	–5.9	96.2	102.8	–6.5	16.4	15.7	.6	316.1	256.8	625.3
1965	116.8	118.2	–1.4	100.1	101.7	–1.6	16.7	16.5	.2	322.3	260.8	671.0
1966	130.8	134.5	–3.7	111.7	114.8	–3.1	19.1	19.7	–.6	328.5	263.7	735.4
1967	148.8	157.5	–8.6	124.4	137.0	–12.6	24.4	20.4	4.0	340.4	266.6	793.3
1968	153.0	178.1	–25.2	128.1	155.8	–27.7	24.9	22.3	2.6	368.7	289.5	847.2
1969	186.9	183.6	3.2	157.9	158.4	–.5	29.0	25.2	3.7	365.8	278.1	925.7
1970	192.8	195.6	–2.8	159.3	168.0	–8.7	33.5	27.6	5.9	380.9	283.2	985.4
1971	187.1	210.2	–23.0	151.3	177.3	–26.1	35.8	32.8	3.0	408.2	303.0	1,050.9
1972	207.3	230.7	–23.4	167.4	193.8	–26.4	39.9	36.9	3.1	435.9	322.4	1,147.8
1973	230.8	245.7	–14.9	184.7	200.1	–15.4	46.1	45.6	.5	466.3	340.9	1,274.0
1974	263.2	269.4	–6.1	209.3	217.3	–8.0	53.9	52.1	1.8	483.9	343.7	1,403.6
1975	279.1	332.3	–53.2	216.6	271.9	–55.3	62.5	60.4	2.0	541.9	394.7	1,509.8
1976	298.1	371.8	–73.7	231.7	302.2	–70.5	66.4	69.6	–3.2	629.0	477.4	1,684.2
Transition quarter	81.2	96.0	–14.7	63.2	76.6	–13.3	18.0	19.4	–1.4	643.6	495.5	445.0
1977	355.6	409.2	–53.7	278.7	328.5	–49.8	76.8	80.7	–3.9	706.4	549.1	1,917.2
1978	399.6	458.7	–59.2	314.2	369.1	–54.9	85.4	89.7	–4.3	776.6	607.1	2,155.0
1979	463.3	504.0	–40.7	365.3	404.1	–38.7	98.0	100.0	–2.0	829.5	640.3	2,429.5
1980	517.1	590.9	–73.8	403.9	476.6	–72.7	113.2	114.3	–1.1	909.1	709.8	2,644.1
1981	599.3	678.2	–79.0	469.1	543.1	–74.0	130.2	135.2	–5.0	994.8	785.3	2,964.4
1982	617.8	745.8	–128.0	474.3	594.4	–120.1	143.5	151.4	–7.9	1,137.3	919.8	3,122.2
1983	600.6	808.4	–207.8	453.2	661.3	–208.0	147.3	147.1	.2	1,371.7	1,131.6	3,316.5
1984	666.5	851.8	–185.4	500.4	686.0	–185.7	166.1	165.8	.3	1,564.7	1,300.5	3,695.0
1985	734.1	946.4	–212.3	547.9	769.6	–221.7	186.2	176.8	9.4	1,817.5	1,499.9	3,967.7
1986	769.1	990.3	–221.2	568.9	806.8	–238.0	200.2	183.5	16.7	2,120.6	1,736.7	4,219.0
1987	854.1	1,003.9	–149.8	640.7	810.1	–169.3	213.4	193.8	19.6	2,346.1	1,888.7	4,452.4
1988	909.0	1,064.1	–155.2	667.5	861.4	–194.0	241.5	202.7	38.8	2,601.3	2,050.8	4,808.4
1989	990.7	1,143.2	–152.5	727.0	932.3	–205.2	263.7	210.9	52.8	2,868.0	2,189.9	5,173.3
1990	1,031.3	1,252.7	–221.4	749.7	1,027.6	–278.0	281.7	225.1	56.6	3,206.6	2,410.7	5,481.5
1991	1,054.3	1,323.4	–269.2	760.4	1,081.8	–321.4	293.9	241.7	52.2	3,598.5	2,688.1	5,676.4
1992	1,090.5	1,380.9	–290.4	788.0	1,128.5	–340.5	302.4	252.3	50.1	4,002.1	2,998.8	5,921.5
1993	1,153.5	1,408.7	–255.1	841.6	1,142.1	–300.5	311.9	266.6	45.3	4,351.4	3,247.5	6,258.6
1994	1,257.7	1,460.9	–203.2	922.7	1,181.5	–258.8	335.0	279.4	55.7	4,643.7	3,432.2	6,633.6
1995 [2]	1,350.6	1,514.4	–163.8	999.5	1,225.7	–226.2	351.1	288.7	62.4	4,921.0	3,603.3	7,004.5

[1] Not strictly comparable with later data.
[2] Estimates for 1995 from *Final Monthly Treasury Statement*, October 1995, except GDP calculated using quarterly seasonally adjusted data.

Note.—Through fiscal year 1976, the fiscal year was on a July 1–June 30 basis; beginning October 1976 (fiscal year 1977), the fiscal year is on an October 1–September 30 basis. The 3-month period from July 1, 1976 through September 30, 1976 is a separate fiscal period known as the transition quarter.

Refunds of receipts are excluded from receipts and outlays.

Data shown in this table are from *Budget of the United States Government, Fiscal Year 1996*, February 1995 (except as noted); all GDP data shown are pre-1996 benchmark.

Sources: Department of Commerce (Bureau of Economic Analysis), Department of the Treasury, and Office of Management and Budget.

TABLE B-75.—*Federal budget receipts, outlays, surplus or deficit, and debt, as percent of gross domestic product, 1934–95*

[Percent; fiscal years]

Fiscal year or period	Receipts	Outlays		Surplus or deficit (-)	Gross Federal debt (end of period)	
		Total	National defense		Total	Held by public
1934	4.9	10.8		-5.9		
1935	5.3	9.3		-4.1		
1936	5.1	10.6		-5.6		
1937	6.2	8.7		-2.5		
1938	7.7	7.8		-.1		
1939	7.2	10.4		-3.2	54.9	47.2
1940	6.9	9.9	1.7	-3.1	53.1	44.8
1941	7.7	12.1	5.7	-4.4	51.1	42.9
1942	10.3	24.8	18.1	-14.5	55.9	47.8
1943	13.7	44.8	38.0	-31.1	81.3	72.8
1944	21.7	45.3	39.2	-23.6	101.2	91.6
1945	21.3	43.7	39.1	-22.4	122.7	110.9
1946	18.5	26.0	20.1	-7.5	127.5	113.8
1947	17.3	15.5	5.7	1.8	115.4	100.6
1948	16.8	12.1	3.7	4.8	102.2	87.7
1949	15.0	14.8	5.0	.2	96.2	81.6
1950	14.8	16.0	5.2	-1.2	96.6	82.4
1951	16.5	14.5	7.5	1.9	81.4	68.4
1952	19.4	19.9	13.5	-.4	76.1	63.1
1953	19.1	20.9	14.5	-1.8	73.1	60.0
1954	18.9	19.3	13.4	-.3	73.6	61.0
1955	17.0	17.8	11.1	-.8	71.3	58.9
1956	17.9	17.0	10.2	.9	65.5	53.4
1957	18.3	17.5	10.4	.8	62.1	50.0
1958	17.8	18.4	10.4	-.6	62.4	50.5
1959	16.5	19.2	10.2	-2.7	59.9	48.9
1960	18.3	18.3	9.5	.1	57.6	46.9
1961	18.3	18.9	9.6	-.6	56.6	46.1
1962	18.0	19.2	9.4	-1.3	54.6	44.7
1963	18.2	19.0	9.1	-.8	53.1	43.5
1964	18.0	19.0	8.8	-.9	50.5	41.1
1965	17.4	17.6	7.5	-.2	48.0	38.9
1966	17.8	18.3	7.9	-.5	44.7	35.9
1967	18.8	19.8	9.0	-1.1	42.9	33.6
1968	18.1	21.0	9.7	-3.0	43.5	34.2
1969	20.2	19.8	8.9	.4	39.5	30.0
1970	19.6	19.9	8.3	-.3	38.7	28.7
1971	17.8	20.0	7.5	-2.2	38.8	28.8
1972	18.1	20.1	6.9	-2.0	38.0	28.1
1973	18.1	19.3	6.0	-1.2	36.6	26.8
1974	18.8	19.2	5.7	-.4	34.5	24.5
1975	18.5	22.0	5.7	-3.5	35.9	26.1
1976	17.7	22.1	5.3	-4.4	37.3	28.3
Transition quarter	18.3	21.6	5.0	-3.3	36.2	27.8
1977	18.5	21.3	5.1	-2.8	36.8	28.6
1978	18.5	21.3	4.8	-2.7	36.0	28.2
1979	19.1	20.7	4.8	-1.7	34.1	26.4
1980	19.6	22.3	5.1	-2.8	34.4	26.8
1981	20.2	22.9	5.3	-2.7	33.6	26.5
1982	19.8	23.9	5.9	-4.1	36.4	29.5
1983	18.1	24.4	6.3	-6.3	41.4	34.1
1984	18.0	23.1	6.2	-5.0	42.3	35.2
1985	18.5	23.9	6.4	-5.4	45.8	37.8
1986	18.2	23.5	6.5	-5.2	50.3	41.2
1987	19.2	22.5	6.3	-3.4	52.7	42.4
1988	18.9	22.1	6.0	-3.2	54.1	42.7
1989	19.2	22.1	5.9	-2.9	55.4	42.3
1990	18.8	22.9	5.5	-4.0	58.5	44.0
1991	18.6	23.3	4.8	-4.7	63.4	47.4
1992	18.4	23.3	5.0	-4.9	67.6	50.6
1993	18.4	22.5	4.7	-4.1	69.5	51.9
1994	19.0	22.0	4.2	-3.1	70.0	51.7
1995 [1]	19.3	21.6	3.9	-2.3	70.3	51.4

[1] Estimates.

Note.—Data shown in this table are from *Budget of the United States Government, Fiscal Year 1996*, February 1995, except as noted in footnote 2, Table B-74.

See also Note, Table B-74.

Sources: Department of the Treasury and Office of Management and Budget.

—*Federal receipts and outlays, by major category, and surplus or deficit, 1940-95*

[Billions of dollars; fiscal years]

Fiscal year or period	Receipts (on-budget and off-budget)					Outlays (on-budget and off-budget)											Surplus or deficit (−) (on-budget and off-budget)
	Total	Individual income taxes	Corporation income taxes	Social insurance taxes and contributions	Other	Total	National defense Total	National defense Department of Defense, military	International affairs	Health	Medicare	Income security	Social security	Net interest	Other	
1940	6.5	0.9	1.2	1.8	2.7	9.5	1.7		0.1	0.1		1.5	0.0	0.9	5.3	−2.9
1941	8.7	1.3	2.1	1.9	3.3	13.7	6.4		.1	.1		1.9	.1	.9	4.1	−4.9
1942	14.6	3.3	4.7	2.5	4.2	35.1	25.7		1.0	.1		1.8	.1	1.1	5.4	−20.5
1943	24.0	6.5	9.6	3.0	4.9	78.6	66.7		1.3	.1		1.7	.2	1.5	7.0	−54.6
1944	43.7	19.7	14.8	3.5	5.7	91.3	79.1		1.4	.2		1.5	.2	2.2	6.6	−47.6
1945	45.2	18.4	16.0	3.5	7.3	92.7	83.0		1.9	.2		1.1	.3	3.1	3.1	−47.6
1946	39.3	16.1	11.9	3.1	8.2	55.2	42.7		1.9	.2		2.4	.4	4.1	3.6	−15.9
1947	38.5	17.9	8.6	3.4	8.5	34.5	12.8		5.8	.2		2.8	.5	4.2	8.2	4.0
1948	41.6	19.3	9.7	3.8	8.8	29.8	9.1		4.6	.2		2.5	.6	4.3	8.5	11.8
1949	39.4	15.6	11.2	3.8	8.9	38.8	13.2		6.1	.2		3.2	.7	4.5	11.1	.6
1950	39.4	15.8	10.4	4.3	8.9	42.6	13.7		4.7	.3		4.1	.8	4.8	14.2	−3.1
1951	51.6	21.6	14.1	5.7	10.2	45.5	23.6		3.6	.3		3.4	1.6	4.7	8.4	6.1
1952	66.2	27.9	21.2	6.4	10.6	67.7	46.1		2.7	.3		3.7	2.1	4.7	8.1	−1.5
1953	69.6	29.8	21.2	6.8	11.7	76.1	52.8		2.1	.3		3.8	2.7	5.2	9.1	−6.5
1954	69.7	29.5	21.1	7.2	11.9	70.9	49.3		1.6	.3		4.4	3.4	4.8	7.1	−1.2
1955	65.5	28.7	17.9	7.9	11.0	68.4	42.7		2.2	.3		5.1	4.4	4.9	8.9	−3.0
1956	74.6	32.2	20.9	9.3	12.2	70.6	42.5		2.4	.4		4.7	5.5	5.1	10.1	3.9
1957	80.0	35.6	21.2	10.0	13.2	76.6	45.4		3.1	.5		5.4	6.7	5.4	10.1	3.4
1958	79.6	34.7	20.1	11.2	13.6	82.4	46.8		3.4	.5		7.5	8.2	5.6	10.3	−2.8
1959	79.2	36.7	17.3	11.7	13.5	92.1	49.0		3.1	.7		8.2	9.7	5.8	15.5	−12.8
1960	92.5	40.7	21.5	14.7	15.6	92.2	48.1		3.0	.8		7.4	11.6	6.9	14.4	.3
1961	94.4	41.3	21.0	16.4	15.7	97.7	49.6		3.2	.9		9.7	12.5	6.7	15.2	−3.3
1962	99.7	45.6	20.5	17.0	16.5	106.8	52.3	50.1	5.6	1.2		9.2	14.4	6.9	17.2	−7.1
1963	106.6	47.6	21.6	19.8	17.6	111.3	53.4	51.1	5.3	1.5		9.3	15.8	7.7	18.3	−4.8
1964	112.6	48.7	23.5	22.0	18.5	118.5	54.8	52.6	4.9	1.8		9.7	16.6	8.2	22.6	−5.9
1965	116.8	48.8	25.5	22.2	20.3	118.2	50.6	48.8	5.3	1.8		9.5	17.5	8.6	25.0	−1.4
1966	130.8	55.4	30.1	25.5	19.8	134.5	58.1	56.6	5.6	2.5	0.1	9.7	20.7	9.4	28.5	−3.7
1967	148.8	61.5	34.0	32.6	20.7	157.5	71.4	70.1	5.6	3.4	2.7	10.3	21.7	10.3	32.1	−8.6
1968	153.0	68.7	28.7	33.9	21.7	178.1	81.9	80.4	5.3	4.4	4.6	11.8	23.9	11.1	35.1	−25.2
1969	186.9	87.2	36.7	39.0	23.9	183.6	82.5	80.8	4.6	5.2	5.7	13.1	27.3	12.7	32.6	3.2
1970	192.8	90.4	32.8	44.4	25.2	195.6	81.7	80.1	4.3	5.9	6.2	15.6	30.3	14.4	37.2	−2.8
1971	187.1	86.2	26.8	47.3	26.8	210.2	78.9	77.5	4.2	6.8	6.6	22.9	35.9	14.8	40.0	−23.0
1972	207.3	94.7	32.2	52.6	27.8	230.7	79.2	77.6	4.8	8.7	7.5	27.6	40.2	15.5	47.3	−23.4
1973	230.8	103.2	36.2	63.1	28.3	245.7	76.7	75.0	4.1	9.4	8.1	28.3	49.1	17.3	52.8	−14.9
1974	263.2	119.0	38.6	75.1	30.6	269.4	79.3	77.9	5.7	10.7	9.6	33.7	55.9	21.4	52.9	−6.1
1975	279.1	122.4	40.6	84.5	31.5	332.3	86.5	84.9	7.1	12.9	12.9	50.2	64.7	23.2	74.9	−53.2
1976	298.1	131.6	41.4	90.8	34.3	371.8	89.6	87.9	6.4	15.7	15.8	60.8	73.9	26.7	82.8	−73.7
Transition quarter	81.2	38.8	8.5	25.2	8.8	96.0	22.3	21.8	2.5	3.9	4.3	15.0	19.8	6.9	21.4	−14.7
1977	355.6	157.6	54.9	106.5	36.6	409.2	97.2	95.1	6.4	17.3	19.3	61.0	85.1	29.9	93.0	−53.7
1978	399.6	181.0	60.0	121.0	37.7	458.7	104.5	102.3	7.5	18.5	22.8	61.5	93.9	35.5	114.7	−59.2
1979	463.3	217.8	65.7	138.9	40.8	504.0	116.3	113.6	7.5	20.5	26.5	66.4	104.1	42.6	120.2	−40.7
1980	517.1	244.1	64.6	157.8	50.6	590.9	134.0	130.9	12.7	23.2	32.1	86.5	118.5	52.5	131.4	−73.8
1981	599.3	285.9	61.1	182.7	69.5	678.2	157.5	153.9	13.1	26.9	39.1	99.7	139.6	68.8	133.5	−79.0
1982	617.8	297.7	49.2	201.5	69.3	745.8	185.3	180.7	12.3	27.4	46.6	107.7	156.0	85.0	125.4	−128.0
1983	600.6	288.9	37.0	209.0	65.6	808.4	209.9	204.4	11.8	28.6	52.6	122.6	170.7	89.8	122.3	−207.8
1984	666.5	298.4	56.9	239.4	71.8	851.8	227.4	220.9	15.9	30.4	57.5	112.7	178.2	111.1	118.6	−185.4
1985	734.1	334.5	61.3	265.2	73.0	946.4	252.7	245.2	16.2	33.5	65.8	128.2	188.6	129.5	131.8	−212.3
1986	769.1	349.0	63.1	283.9	73.1	990.3	273.4	265.5	14.2	35.9	70.2	119.8	198.8	136.0	142.1	−221.2
1987	854.1	392.6	83.9	303.3	74.3	1,003.9	282.0	274.0	11.6	40.0	75.1	123.3	207.4	138.7	125.9	−149.8
1988	909.0	401.2	94.5	334.3	78.9	1,064.1	290.4	281.9	10.5	44.5	78.9	129.3	219.3	151.8	139.4	−155.2
1989	990.7	445.7	103.3	359.4	82.3	1,143.2	303.6	294.9	9.6	48.4	85.0	136.0	232.5	169.3	158.8	−152.5
1990	1,031.3	466.9	93.5	380.0	90.9	1,252.7	299.3	289.8	13.8	57.7	98.1	147.0	248.6	184.2	203.9	−221.4
1991	1,054.3	467.8	98.1	396.0	92.3	1,323.4	273.3	262.4	15.9	71.2	104.5	170.3	269.0	194.5	224.8	−269.2
1992	1,090.5	476.0	100.3	413.7	100.5	1,380.9	298.4	286.9	16.1	89.5	119.0	196.9	287.6	199.4	173.9	−290.4
1993	1,153.5	509.7	117.5	428.3	98.0	1,408.7	291.1	278.6	17.2	99.4	130.6	207.3	304.6	198.8	159.7	−255.1
1994	1,257.7	543.1	140.4	461.5	112.8	1,460.9	281.6	268.6	17.1	107.1	144.7	214.0	319.6	203.0	173.8	−203.2
1995 [1]	1,350.6	590.2	157.1	484.5	118.9	1,514.4	272.2	259.6	16.4	114.8	159.9	220.2	335.8	232.2	162.9	−163.8

[1] Estimates.

Note.—Through fiscal year 1976, the fiscal year was on a July 1-June 30 basis; beginning October 1976 (fiscal year 1977), the fiscal year is on an October 1-September 30 basis. The 3-month period from July 1, 1976 through September 30, 1976 is a separate fiscal period known as the transition quarter.

Refunds of receipts are excluded from receipts and outlays.

Data shown in this table are from *Budget of the United States Government, Fiscal Year 1996*, February 1995, except 1995 data are from *Final Monthly Treasury Statement*, October 1995.

Sources: Department of the Treasury and Office of Management and Budget.

TABLE B–77.—*Federal receipts, outlays, and debt, fiscal years 1989–95*

[Millions of dollars; fiscal years]

Description	Actual						Estimates
	1989	1990	1991	1992	1993	1994	1995
RECEIPTS AND OUTLAYS:							
Total receipts	990,691	1,031,321	1,054,272	1,090,453	1,153,535	1,257,745	1,350,576
Total outlays	1,143,172	1,252,705	1,323,441	1,380,856	1,408,675	1,460,914	1,514,389
Total surplus or deficit (–)	–152,481	–221,384	–269,169	–290,403	–255,140	–203,169	–163,813
On-budget receipts	727,026	749,666	760,388	788,027	841,601	922,719	999,496
On-budget outlays	932,261	1,027,640	1,081,754	1,128,518	1,142,088	1,181,542	1,225,724
On-budget surplus or deficit (–)	–205,235	–277,974	–321,367	–340,490	–300,487	–258,823	–226,228
Off-budget receipts	263,666	281,656	293,885	302,426	311,934	335,026	351,080
Off-budget outlays	210,911	225,065	241,687	252,339	266,587	279,372	288,665
Off-budget surplus or deficit (–)	52,754	56,590	52,198	50,087	45,347	55,654	62,415
OUTSTANDING DEBT, END OF PERIOD:							
Gross Federal debt	2,868,039	3,206,564	3,598,498	4,002,136	4,351,416	4,643,711	4,920,950
Held by Government accounts	678,157	795,841	910,362	1,003,302	1,103,945	1,211,498	1,317,612
Held by the public	2,189,882	2,410,722	2,688,137	2,998,834	3,247,471	3,432,213	3,603,338
Federal Reserve System	220,088	234,410	258,591	296,397	325,653	355,150	....
Other	1,969,795	2,176,312	2,429,546	2,702,437	2,921,818	3,077,063	....
RECEIPTS: ON-BUDGET AND OFF-BUDGET	990,691	1,031,321	1,054,272	1,090,453	1,153,535	1,257,745	1,350,576
Individual income taxes	445,690	466,884	467,827	475,964	509,680	543,055	590,157
Corporation income taxes	103,291	93,507	98,086	100,270	117,520	140,385	157,088
Social insurance taxes and contributions	359,416	380,047	396,016	413,689	428,300	461,475	484,474
On-budget	95,751	98,392	102,131	111,263	116,366	126,450	....
Off-budget	263,666	281,656	293,885	302,426	311,934	335,026	....
Excise taxes	34,386	35,345	42,402	45,569	48,057	55,225	57,485
Estate and gift taxes	8,745	11,500	11,138	11,143	12,577	15,225	14,764
Customs duties and fees	16,334	16,707	15,949	17,359	18,802	20,099	19,300
Miscellaneous receipts	22,829	27,330	22,854	26,458	18,599	22,282	27,306
Deposits of earnings by Federal Reserve System	19,604	24,319	19,158	22,920	14,908	18,023	....
All other	3,225	3,011	3,696	3,538	3,691	4,259	....
OUTLAYS: ON-BUDGET AND OFF-BUDGET	1,143,172	1,252,705	1,323,441	1,380,856	1,408,675	1,460,914	1,514,389
National defense	303,559	299,331	273,292	˙298,350	291,086	281,563	272,179
International affairs	9,573	13,764	15,851	16,107	17,248	17,083	16,448
General science, space, and technology	12,838	14,444	16,111	16,409	17,030	16,227	17,563
Energy	2,706	3,341	2,436	4,500	4,319	5,219	5,146
Natural resources and environment	16,182	17,080	18,559	20,025	20,239	21,064	23,328
Agriculture	16,919	11,958	15,183	15,205	20,490	15,121	9,763
Commerce and housing credit	29,211	67,142	75,312	10,093	–22,719	–5,122	–18,740
On-budget	29,520	65,516	73,994	9,434	–24,160	–6,225	....
Off-budget	–310	1,626	1,317	659	1,441	1,103	....
Transportation	27,608	29,485	31,099	33,333	35,004	38,134	38,555
Community and regional development	5,362	8,498	6,811	6,838	9,052	10,454	11,000
Education, training, employment, and social services	36,674	38,755	43,354	45,248	50,012	46,307	52,706
Health	48,390	57,716	71,183	89,497	99,415	107,122	114,760
Medicare	84,964	98,102	104,489	119,024	130,552	144,747	159,854
Income security	136,031	147,022	170,276	196,948	207,250	214,036	220,214
Social security	232,542	248,623	269,015	287,585	304,585	319,565	335,847
On-budget	5,069	3,625	2,619	6,166	6,236	5,683	....
Off-budget	227,473	244,998	266,395	281,418	298,349	313,881	....
Veterans benefits and services	30,066	29,112	31,349	34,138	35,720	37,642	37,935
Administration of justice	9,474	9,993	12,276	14,426	14,955	15,256	16,255
General government	9,017	10,734	11,661	12,990	13,009	11,312	13,856
Net interest	169,266	184,221	194,541	199,421	198,811	202,957	232,175
On-budget	180,661	200,212	214,763	223,059	225,599	232,160	....
Off-budget	–11,395	–15,991	–20,222	–23,637	–26,788	–29,203	....
Undistributed offsetting receipts	–37,212	–36,615	–39,356	–39,280	–37,386	–37,772	–44,455
On-budget	–32,354	–31,048	–33,553	–33,179	–30,970	–31,362	....
Off-budget	–4,858	–5,567	–5,804	–6,101	–6,416	–6,409	....

Note.—Through fiscal year 1976, the fiscal year was on a July 1–June 30 basis; beginning October 1976 (fiscal year 1977), the fiscal year is on an October 1–September 30 basis. The 3-month period from July 1, 1976 through September 30, 1976 is a separate fiscal period known as the transition quarter.

Refunds of receipts are excluded from receipts and outlays.

Data shown in this table are from *Budget of the United States Government, Fiscal Year 1996,* February 1995, except 1995 data are from *Final Monthly Treasury Statement,* October 1995.

Sources: Department of the Treasury and Office of Management and Budget.

370

[Billions of dollars; quarterly data at seasonally adjusted annual rates]

Year or quarter	Total government			Federal Government			State and local government			Addendum: Grants-in-aid to State and local governments
	Receipts	Current expenditures	Current surplus or deficit (−) (NIPA)	Receipts	Current expenditures	Current surplus or deficit (−) (NIPA)	Receipts	Current expenditures	Current surplus or deficit (−) (NIPA)	
1959	128.8	116.6	12.2	90.6	88.0	2.6	45.0	35.4	9.6	6.8
1960	138.8	121.5	17.3	97.0	89.6	7.4	48.3	38.4	9.9	6.5
1961	144.1	130.8	13.3	99.0	96.1	2.9	52.4	42.0	10.4	7.2
1962	155.8	141.3	14.5	107.2	104.4	2.8	56.6	44.8	11.7	8.0
1963	167.5	149.1	18.4	115.5	110.2	5.4	61.1	48.1	13.0	9.1
1964	172.9	157.3	15.6	116.2	115.4	.9	67.1	52.4	14.7	10.4
1965	187.0	168.6	18.5	125.8	122.4	3.4	72.3	57.2	15.1	11.1
1966	210.7	190.8	19.9	143.5	140.9	2.6	81.5	64.3	17.3	14.4
1967	226.4	217.5	8.9	152.6	160.9	-8.3	89.8	72.5	17.3	15.9
1968	260.9	243.7	17.2	176.8	179.7	-2.8	102.7	82.6	20.0	18.6
1969	293.9	264.1	29.8	199.5	190.8	8.7	114.8	93.7	21.1	20.3
1970	299.6	292.9	6.7	195.1	209.1	-14.1	129.0	108.2	20.8	24.4
1971	319.6	323.2	-3.7	203.3	228.6	-25.3	145.3	123.7	21.7	29.0
1972	364.8	353.1	11.6	232.6	253.1	-20.5	169.7	137.5	32.2	37.5
1973	408.8	386.5	22.2	264.0	275.1	-11.1	185.3	152.0	33.4	40.6
1974	451.8	438.3	13.6	295.1	312.0	-16.9	200.6	170.2	30.5	43.9
1975	468.4	514.7	-46.3	297.4	371.3	-73.9	225.6	198.0	27.6	54.6
1976	535.9	557.1	-21.3	343.1	400.3	-57.2	253.9	217.9	35.9	61.1
1977	603.9	605.5	-1.5	389.6	435.9	-46.3	281.9	237.1	44.7	67.5
1978	678.5	657.5	20.9	446.5	478.1	-31.7	309.3	256.7	52.6	77.3
1979	761.1	727.3	33.8	511.1	529.5	-18.4	330.6	278.3	52.3	80.5
1980	834.2	840.8	-6.6	561.5	622.5	-61.0	361.4	307.0	54.4	88.7
1981	952.2	954.6	-2.4	649.3	707.1	-57.8	390.8	335.4	55.4	87.9
1982	971.5	1,054.9	-83.4	646.4	781.0	-134.7	409.0	357.7	51.3	83.9
1983	1,028.6	1,138.1	-109.5	671.9	846.3	-174.4	443.6	378.8	64.9	87.0
1984	1,144.5	1,213.7	-69.1	746.9	902.9	-156.0	492.0	405.1	86.9	94.4
1985	1,239.7	1,311.7	-71.9	811.3	974.2	-162.9	528.7	437.8	91.0	100.3
1986	1,313.1	1,395.7	-82.6	850.1	1,027.6	-177.5	570.6	475.7	94.9	107.6
1987	1,429.4	1,474.5	-45.1	937.4	1,066.3	-128.9	594.9	511.1	83.8	102.9
1988	1,517.3	1,552.7	-35.4	997.2	1,118.5	-121.3	631.4	545.5	85.9	111.2
1989	1,642.1	1,660.2	-18.1	1,079.3	1,192.7	-113.4	681.0	585.7	95.3	118.2
1990	1,726.4	1,800.9	-74.5	1,129.8	1,284.5	-154.7	728.9	648.8	80.1	132.4
1991	1,779.8	1,900.0	-120.2	1,149.0	1,345.0	-196.0	784.2	708.3	75.8	153.4
1992	1,870.6	2,065.2	-194.6	1,198.5	1,479.4	-280.9	844.3	758.0	86.3	172.2
1993	1,986.6	2,146.4	-159.8	1,275.3	1,530.0	-254.7	897.1	802.2	94.9	185.7
1994	2,127.5	2,217.7	-90.2	1,377.0	1,566.9	-189.9	946.4	846.6	99.7	195.9
1990: I	1,689.2	1,757.8	-68.6	1,107.3	1,261.5	-154.1	710.3	624.8	85.5	128.4
II	1,721.8	1,783.1	-61.4	1,132.7	1,276.9	-144.1	721.3	638.5	82.8	132.2
III	1,748.5	1,810.4	-61.9	1,144.1	1,286.7	-142.6	736.2	655.5	80.7	131.8
IV	1,746.1	1,852.4	-106.2	1,135.2	1,313.0	-177.7	748.0	676.5	71.5	137.1
1991: I	1,753.9	1,819.7	-65.9	1,140.1	1,274.7	-134.6	758.5	689.8	68.8	144.8
II	1,766.6	1,889.6	-123.0	1,142.6	1,339.3	-196.7	775.8	702.1	73.7	151.8
III	1,789.4	1,926.3	-136.9	1,152.3	1,366.3	-214.0	791.4	714.3	77.1	154.4
IV	1,809.3	1,964.3	-155.1	1,160.9	1,399.8	-238.8	811.0	727.2	83.8	162.7
1992: I	1,841.4	2,024.0	-182.6	1,183.4	1,450.7	-267.4	823.4	738.6	84.8	165.4
II	1,858.9	2,051.9	-193.0	1,193.1	1,472.8	-279.6	838.8	752.2	86.6	173.0
III	1,860.1	2,075.7	-215.5	1,187.0	1,484.5	-297.5	847.3	765.4	82.0	174.2
IV	1,921.8	2,109.1	-187.3	1,230.5	1,509.5	-279.0	867.7	775.9	91.7	176.3
1993: I	1,916.8	2,120.0	-203.2	1,225.2	1,508.9	-283.7	869.0	788.5	80.5	177.3
II	1,977.4	2,137.5	-160.1	1,271.3	1,520.5	-249.2	887.6	798.5	89.1	181.5
III	1,995.0	2,153.6	-158.6	1,280.3	1,533.8	-253.5	901.9	807.0	94.9	187.2
IV	2,057.1	2,174.5	-117.4	1,324.4	1,556.8	-232.4	929.7	814.7	115.0	197.0
1994: I	2,053.3	2,171.4	-118.1	1,321.9	1,534.7	-212.9	923.6	828.8	94.8	192.2
II	2,129.1	2,193.8	-64.7	1,382.8	1,552.7	-169.9	943.8	838.6	105.2	197.5
III	2,143.3	2,230.0	-86.7	1,387.1	1,573.5	-186.3	953.1	853.5	99.6	196.9
IV	2,184.4	2,275.6	-91.1	1,416.3	1,606.8	-190.4	965.0	865.6	99.3	196.9
1995: I	2,224.4	2,298.7	-74.4	1,449.3	1,622.6	-173.3	980.9	882.0	99.0	205.8
II	2,266.2	2,328.2	-61.5	1,483.2	1,643.8	-160.5	994.8	895.8	99.0	211.3
III	2,286.6	2,352.2	-65.6	1,489.9	1,648.4	-158.4	1,000.5	907.6	92.8	203.8

Note.—Federal grants-in-aid to State and local governments are reflected in Federal expenditures and State and local receipts. Total government receipts and expenditures have been adjusted to eliminate this duplication.

Source: Department of Commerce, Bureau of Economic Analysis.

TABLE B–79.—*Federal and State and local government receipts and current expenditures, national income and product accounts (NIPA), by major type, 1959–95*

[Billions of dollars; quarterly data at seasonally adjusted annual rates]

Year or quarter	Receipts					Current expenditures			Net interest paid			Less: Dividends received by government [2]	Subsidies less current surplus of government enterprises	Current surplus or deficit (–) (NIPA)	Addendum: Grants-in-aid to State and local governments
	Total	Personal tax and nontax receipts	Corporate profits tax accruals	Indirect business tax and nontax accruals	Contributions for social insurance	Total [1]	Consumption expenditures	Transfer payments	Total	Interest paid	Less: Interest received by government [2]				
1959	128.8	44.5	23.6	41.9	18.8	116.6	82.7	27.5	6.3				0.1	12.2	6.8
1960	138.8	48.7	22.7	45.5	21.9	121.5	85.0	29.3	6.9	10.1	3.3		.3	17.3	6.5
1961	144.1	50.3	22.8	48.1	22.9	130.8	89.6	33.6	6.4	9.9	3.5		1.3	13.3	7.2
1962	155.8	54.8	24.0	51.7	25.4	141.3	98.2	34.7	6.9	10.8	3.9		1.5	14.5	8.0
1963	167.5	58.0	26.2	54.7	28.5	149.1	104.2	36.6	7.4	11.6	4.2		.9	18.4	9.1
1964	172.9	56.0	28.0	58.8	30.1	157.3	109.9	38.1	7.9	12.5	4.6		1.4	15.6	10.4
1965	187.0	61.9	30.9	62.7	31.6	168.6	117.6	41.1	8.1	13.2	5.1		1.7	18.5	11.1
1966	210.7	71.0	33.7	65.4	40.6	190.8	133.5	45.8	8.5	14.5	6.0		3.0	19.9	14.4
1967	226.4	77.9	32.7	70.4	45.5	217.5	151.2	54.5	8.9	15.7	6.8		2.9	8.9	15.9
1968	260.9	92.1	39.4	79.0	50.4	243.7	167.8	62.6	10.3	18.1	7.7	0.1	3.1	17.2	18.6
1969	293.9	109.9	39.7	86.6	57.8	264.1	179.9	69.3	11.5	19.8	8.3	.2	3.6	29.8	20.3
1970	299.6	109.0	34.4	94.3	62.0	292.9	192.1	83.8	12.4	22.3	9.9	.2	4.9	6.7	24.4
1971	319.6	108.7	37.7	103.6	69.6	323.2	206.7	99.4	12.5	23.1	10.6	.3	5.1	–3.7	29.0
1972	364.8	132.0	41.9	111.4	79.5	353.1	223.6	110.9	12.9	24.8	11.9	.3	6.4	11.6	37.5
1973	408.8	140.6	49.3	121.0	97.9	386.5	239.4	126.6	15.2	29.6	14.4	.5	5.9	22.2	40.6
1974	451.8	159.1	51.8	129.3	111.7	438.3	267.2	150.5	16.3	33.6	17.3	.9	4.5	13.6	43.9
1975	468.4	156.4	50.9	140.0	121.1	514.7	299.9	189.2	18.5	37.7	19.2	.9	8.1	–46.3	54.6
1976	535.9	182.3	64.2	151.6	137.7	557.1	321.4	206.5	22.8	43.6	20.9	.9	7.4	–21.3	61.1
1977	603.9	210.0	73.0	165.5	155.4	605.5	351.5	220.9	24.4	47.9	23.5	1.3	10.1	–1.5	67.5
1978	678.5	240.1	83.5	177.8	177.0	657.5	383.3	238.6	26.5	56.8	30.3	1.7	11.1	20.9	77.3
1979	761.1	280.2	88.0	188.7	204.2	727.3	421.8	266.9	28.7	68.6	39.9	2.0	11.7	33.8	80.5
1980	834.2	312.4	84.8	212.0	225.0	840.8	476.4	317.6	33.4	83.9	50.5	1.9	15.2	–6.6	88.7
1981	952.2	360.2	81.1	249.3	261.6	954.6	531.3	360.7	48.1	110.2	62.1	2.3	16.9	–2.4	87.9
1982	971.5	371.4	63.1	256.4	280.6	1,054.9	577.9	403.3	55.5	130.6	75.0	2.9	21.1	–83.4	83.9
1983	1,028.6	369.3	77.2	280.1	301.9	1,138.1	619.2	434.4	61.8	146.7	84.9	3.4	25.6	–109.5	87.0
1984	1,144.5	395.5	94.0	309.5	345.5	1,213.7	664.9	448.2	79.1	174.7	95.6	3.9	25.5	–69.1	94.4
1985	1,239.7	437.7	96.5	329.6	375.9	1,311.7	725.1	480.9	88.0	195.9	107.9	4.5	21.9	–71.9	100.3
1986	1,313.1	459.9	106.5	344.7	402.0	1,395.7	775.0	510.9	89.8	208.0	118.2	5.1	25.1	–82.6	107.6
1987	1,429.4	514.2	127.1	364.8	423.3	1,474.5	819.3	533.7	96.3	216.0	119.7	5.9	31.0	–45.1	102.9
1988	1,517.3	532.0	137.0	385.5	462.8	1,552.7	859.1	568.3	103.7	229.7	125.9	6.9	28.5	–35.4	111.2
1989	1,642.1	594.9	141.3	414.7	491.2	1,660.2	912.4	616.3	115.5	251.0	135.5	8.1	24.0	–18.1	118.2
1990	1,726.4	624.8	140.5	442.6	518.5	1,800.9	976.7	678.8	128.2	268.6	140.4	9.0	25.3	–74.5	132.4
1991	1,779.8	624.8	133.4	478.1	543.5	1,900.0	1,025.4	721.1	139.4	282.8	143.5	9.5	23.6	–120.2	153.4
1992	1,870.6	650.5	143.0	505.6	571.4	2,065.2	1,054.7	852.3	141.2	282.7	141.5	10.1	27.1	–194.6	172.2
1993	1,986.6	689.9	163.8	540.0	592.9	2,146.4	1,079.3	905.5	140.4	278.8	138.4	10.5	31.7	–159.8	185.7
1994	2,127.5	731.4	195.3	572.5	628.3	2,217.7	1,102.3	950.0	151.7	288.3	136.6	11.4	25.1	–90.2	195.9
1990: I	1,689.2	613.0	133.0	432.1	511.1	1,757.8	957.0	660.7	125.0	260.6	135.6	8.7	23.8	–68.6	128.4
II	1,721.8	628.2	141.2	436.1	516.2	1,783.1	967.6	672.0	128.0	264.6	136.6	9.0	24.5	–61.4	132.2
III	1,748.5	630.8	148.0	447.3	522.4	1,810.4	977.2	682.5	134.1	271.9	137.8	9.0	25.7	–61.9	131.8
IV	1,746.1	627.1	139.7	455.0	524.3	1,852.4	1,005.0	703.8	125.8	277.2	151.5	9.3	27.3	–106.2	137.1
1991: I	1,753.9	622.3	130.1	464.7	536.8	1,819.7	1,022.6	648.7	133.7	279.2	145.5	9.4	24.4	–65.9	144.8
II	1,766.6	620.5	132.3	472.9	540.9	1,889.6	1,025.9	710.5	139.6	282.7	143.2	9.5	22.7	–123.0	151.8
III	1,789.4	623.7	136.0	483.7	546.0	1,926.3	1,025.2	748.7	138.3	282.4	144.1	9.5	23.5	–136.9	154.4
IV	1,809.3	632.5	135.2	491.2	550.3	1,964.3	1,027.8	776.6	145.9	286.9	141.0	9.6	23.6	–155.1	162.7
1992: I	1,841.4	636.7	143.9	495.7	565.1	2,024.0	1,038.4	828.8	142.0	283.2	141.2	9.8	24.6	–182.6	165.4
II	1,858.9	640.0	150.9	497.9	570.1	2,051.9	1,047.1	846.0	143.5	285.1	141.6	10.1	25.4	–193.0	173.0
III	1,860.1	650.6	127.6	507.1	574.8	2,075.7	1,061.8	855.4	141.7	282.9	141.3	10.1	26.9	–215.5	174.2
IV	1,921.8	674.8	149.7	521.7	575.7	2,109.1	1,071.3	879.1	137.6	279.4	141.9	10.3	31.5	–187.3	176.3
1993: I	1,916.8	662.4	151.5	524.7	578.3	2,120.0	1,071.6	885.9	137.5	276.7	139.2	10.2	35.2	–203.2	177.3
II	1,977.4	686.9	162.6	535.1	592.8	2,137.5	1,074.0	899.3	141.0	279.8	138.9	10.4	33.7	–160.1	181.5
III	1,995.0	696.4	159.3	547.1	597.5	2,153.6	1,083.7	909.4	141.1	279.8	138.5	10.5	29.9	–158.6	187.2
IV	2,057.1	713.8	181.7	558.5	603.1	2,174.5	1,087.9	927.4	142.0	279.0	137.1	10.8	28.0	–117.4	197.0
1994: I	2,053.3	705.5	171.4	562.1	614.2	2,171.4	1,089.0	926.8	137.7	274.6	136.9	11.1	27.2	–118.1	192.2
II	2,129.1	740.8	192.8	568.0	627.5	2,193.8	1,092.3	940.5	148.3	284.7	136.4	11.3	24.0	–64.7	197.5
III	2,143.3	731.3	203.4	576.4	632.2	2,230.0	1,110.9	952.4	154.8	291.2	136.4	11.5	23.4	–86.7	196.9
IV	2,184.4	748.1	213.5	583.5	639.3	2,275.6	1,117.2	978.4	165.8	302.6	136.8	11.8	25.9	–91.1	196.9
1995: I	2,224.4	770.0	217.3	586.0	651.0	2,298.7	1,126.9	992.1	172.7	309.6	136.9	12.2	19.2	–74.4	205.8
II	2,266.7	801.5	214.2	594.8	656.2	2,328.2	1,136.2	1,004.1	181.5	318.9	137.4	12.4	18.7	–61.5	211.3
III	2,286.6	801.3	224.5	596.8	664.0	2,352.2	1,140.6	1,021.0	185.5	320.7	135.2	12.7	17.9	–65.6	203.8

[1] Includes an item for the difference between wage accruals and disbursements, not shown separately.
[2] Prior to 1968, dividends received is included in interest received.

Source: Department of Commerce, Bureau of Economic Analysis.

372

TABLE B–80.—*Federal Government receipts and current expenditures, national income and product accounts (NIPA), 1959–95*

[Billions of dollars; quarterly data at seasonally adjusted annual rates]

Year or quarter	Total	Receipts — Personal tax and nontax receipts	Corporate profits tax accruals	Indirect business tax and nontax accruals	Contributions for social insurance	Current expenditures — Total[1]	Consumption expenditures Total	National defense	Transfer payments To persons	To rest of the world (net)	Grants-in-aid to State and local governments (net)	Net interest paid	Subsidies less current government enterprises	Current surplus or deficit (–) (NIPA)
1959	90.6	39.8	22.5	12.6	15.7	88.0	51.8	42.0	20.1	1.8	6.8	6.2	1.3	2.6
1960	97.0	43.5	21.4	13.5	18.5	89.6	51.3	42.5	21.6	1.9	6.5	6.8	1.6	7.4
1961	99.0	44.6	21.5	13.7	19.2	96.1	52.9	43.9	25.0	2.1	7.2	6.3	2.6	2.9
1962	107.2	48.5	22.5	14.7	21.5	104.4	59.1	47.8	25.6	2.1	8.0	6.8	2.9	2.8
1963	115.5	51.3	24.6	15.4	24.3	110.2	62.0	49.6	27.0	2.1	9.1	7.3	2.6	5.4
1964	116.2	48.4	26.1	16.3	25.4	115.4	63.9	49.9	27.9	2.1	10.4	8.0	3.1	.9
1965	125.8	53.7	28.9	16.6	26.6	122.4	67.2	52.0	30.3	2.1	11.1	8.4	3.4	3.4
1966	143.5	61.5	31.4	15.7	34.9	140.9	77.0	61.2	33.5	2.2	14.4	9.2	4.6	2.6
1967	152.6	67.2	30.0	16.5	38.9	160.9	88.3	71.3	40.2	2.1	15.9	9.8	4.5	–8.3
1968	176.8	79.3	36.1	18.2	43.2	179.7	97.0	78.9	46.2	1.9	18.6	11.3	4.6	–2.8
1969	199.5	94.7	36.1	19.2	49.5	190.8	100.1	80.0	50.8	1.8	20.3	12.7	5.1	8.7
1970	195.1	92.2	30.6	19.5	52.8	209.1	100.5	78.6	61.6	2.0	24.4	14.1	6.5	–14.1
1971	203.3	89.9	33.5	20.5	59.4	228.6	103.8	79.2	73.0	2.4	29.0	13.8	6.6	–25.3
1972	232.6	107.8	36.6	20.1	68.1	253.1	110.1	82.3	80.9	2.5	37.5	14.4	8.0	–20.5
1973	264.0	114.3	43.3	21.5	84.9	275.1	112.9	83.7	93.7	2.5	40.6	18.0	7.4	–11.1
1974	295.1	130.9	45.1	22.1	97.1	312.0	123.3	90.1	115.0	3.2	43.9	20.7	5.5	–16.9
1975	297.4	125.4	43.6	24.2	104.2	371.3	135.0	97.0	146.8	3.5	54.6	23.0	8.6	–73.9
1976	343.1	146.6	54.6	23.8	118.2	400.3	141.7	101.3	159.3	3.7	61.1	26.8	7.8	–57.2
1977	389.6	169.1	61.6	25.6	133.3	435.9	155.4	109.6	170.1	3.4	67.5	29.1	10.4	–46.3
1978	446.5	193.8	71.4	28.9	152.4	478.1	168.8	118.4	182.4	3.8	77.3	34.6	11.4	–31.7
1979	511.1	229.7	74.4	30.1	176.8	529.5	185.9	130.7	205.7	4.1	80.5	42.1	11.3	–18.4
1980	561.5	256.2	70.3	39.7	195.3	622.5	215.2	150.9	247.0	5.0	88.7	52.7	13.9	–61.0
1981	649.3	297.2	65.7	57.3	229.1	707.1	246.0	174.3	282.1	5.0	87.9	71.7	14.4	–57.8
1982	646.4	302.9	49.0	49.7	244.8	781.0	270.0	197.6	316.4	7.0	83.9	84.4	19.4	–134.7
1983	671.9	293.0	61.3	53.3	264.2	846.3	293.0	214.9	340.0	7.8	87.0	92.8	25.4	–174.4
1984	746.9	308.3	75.2	57.9	305.3	902.9	314.1	236.3	344.6	9.7	94.4	113.3	27.1	–156.0
1985	811.3	343.7	76.3	58.2	333.1	974.2	342.5	257.6	366.9	12.2	100.3	126.9	25.2	–162.9
1986	850.1	358.3	83.8	53.2	354.7	1,027.6	362.3	272.7	386.2	12.9	107.6	130.5	28.0	–177.5
1987	937.4	402.4	103.2	57.8	374.1	1,066.3	378.2	287.6	401.8	11.2	102.9	137.8	34.4	–128.9
1988	997.2	414.4	111.0	60.9	410.9	1,118.5	387.8	297.9	425.8	11.4	111.2	148.4	33.8	–121.3
1989	1,079.3	463.4	117.1	61.7	437.1	1,192.7	405.2	303.3	460.3	11.4	118.2	166.7	30.8	–113.4
1990	1,129.8	485.7	118.0	65.1	461.1	1,284.5	426.6	312.7	500.0	13.3	132.4	179.9	32.4	–154.7
1991	1,149.0	476.9	109.8	79.7	482.6	1,345.0	445.9	325.4	550.1	–27.9	153.4	192.7	30.8	–196.0
1992	1,198.5	490.8	118.6	81.9	507.1	1,479.4	451.0	319.7	608.5	16.6	172.2	195.8	35.1	–280.9
1993	1,275.3	523.6	137.5	88.2	526.0	1,530.0	451.4	313.0	641.8	16.9	185.7	192.3	41.8	–254.7
1994	1,377.0	561.4	164.4	92.6	558.6	1,566.9	450.6	305.7	666.4	16.2	195.9	201.4	36.4	–189.9
1990: I	1,107.3	477.4	111.6	63.2	455.1	1,261.5	421.7	311.7	492.7	11.5	128.4	176.2	30.9	–154.1
II	1,132.7	490.7	118.5	64.2	459.3	1,276.9	423.7	310.8	494.1	15.5	132.2	179.7	31.7	–144.1
III	1,144.1	489.7	124.3	65.5	464.5	1,286.7	423.2	307.3	500.0	13.2	131.8	185.8	32.7	–142.6
IV	1,135.2	484.9	117.4	67.4	465.6	1,313.0	437.7	321.0	513.3	12.9	137.1	177.8	34.4	–177.7
1991: I	1,140.1	478.4	107.3	77.2	477.2	1,274.7	450.5	331.3	538.6	–76.9	144.8	186.3	31.6	–134.6
II	1,142.6	474.3	108.9	79.1	480.3	1,339.3	449.1	328.6	547.5	–32.0	151.8	192.6	30.0	–196.7
III	1,152.3	476.0	111.8	79.9	484.7	1,366.3	443.7	323.1	551.0	–5.4	154.4	191.9	30.7	–214.0
IV	1,160.9	479.0	111.1	82.8	488.1	1,399.8	440.5	318.5	563.2	2.6	162.7	200.0	30.9	–238.8
1992: I	1,183.4	481.0	119.6	80.8	502.0	1,450.7	445.8	317.2	598.7	12.4	165.4	196.8	31.8	–267.4
II	1,193.1	481.6	125.3	80.2	506.1	1,472.8	446.3	317.3	606.9	15.0	173.0	198.4	33.1	–279.6
III	1,187.0	490.7	106.0	80.2	510.1	1,484.5	454.4	323.5	611.3	12.9	174.2	196.4	35.3	–297.5
IV	1,230.5	510.0	123.7	86.5	510.3	1,509.5	457.7	320.7	617.2	26.1	176.3	191.8	40.3	–279.0
1993: I	1,225.2	501.0	127.5	84.3	512.4	1,508.9	450.8	313.9	633.4	12.3	177.3	190.4	44.7	–283.7
II	1,271.3	521.0	136.5	87.5	526.2	1,520.5	447.9	312.1	639.8	14.4	181.5	193.2	43.6	–249.2
III	1,280.3	529.1	133.7	87.2	530.3	1,533.8	453.0	314.6	645.3	15.1	187.2	192.7	40.5	–253.5
IV	1,324.4	543.4	152.2	93.7	535.1	1,556.8	453.8	311.5	648.7	25.8	197.0	192.9	38.6	–232.4
1994: I	1,321.9	539.3	144.3	92.8	545.5	1,534.7	446.7	301.3	659.7	11.5	192.2	188.2	36.5	–212.9
II	1,382.8	571.3	162.2	91.3	558.1	1,552.7	445.1	303.4	663.4	13.2	197.5	198.2	35.3	–169.9
III	1,387.1	560.4	171.3	93.3	562.1	1,573.5	455.5	313.3	667.8	13.7	196.9	204.4	35.2	–186.3
IV	1,416.3	574.5	180.0	93.2	568.6	1,606.8	455.3	304.9	674.7	26.5	196.9	214.9	38.5	–190.4
1995: I	1,449.3	594.6	183.1	91.7	579.9	1,622.6	454.8	303.0	696.2	12.3	205.8	221.2	32.3	–173.3
II	1,483.2	624.4	180.7	93.5	584.6	1,643.8	456.1	305.3	705.2	9.9	211.3	229.2	32.0	–160.5
III	1,489.9	620.3	189.1	88.8	591.8	1,648.4	454.1	301.9	713.0	13.8	203.8	232.7	31.1	–158.4

[1] Includes an item for the difference between wage accruals and disbursements, not shown separately.

Source: Department of Commerce, Bureau of Economic Analysis.

165-967 96 – 13

TABLE B–81.—*State and local government receipts and current expenditures, national income and product accounts (NIPA), 1959–95*

[Billions of dollars; quarterly data at seasonally adjusted annual rates]

Year or quarter	Receipts						Current expenditures					Current surplus or deficit (−) (NIPA)
	Total	Personal tax and nontax receipts	Corporate profits tax accruals	Indirect business tax and nontax accruals	Contributions for social insurance	Federal grants-in-aid	Total[1]	Consumption expenditures	Transfer payments to persons	Net interest paid less dividends received	Subsidies less current surplus of government enterprises	
1959	45.0	4.6	1.2	29.3	3.1	6.8	35.4	30.9	5.6	0.1	−1.2	9.6
1960	48.3	5.2	1.2	32.0	3.4	6.5	38.4	33.7	5.9	.1	−1.3	9.9
1961	52.4	5.7	1.3	34.4	3.7	7.2	42.0	36.7	6.5	.1	−1.4	10.4
1962	56.6	6.3	1.5	37.0	3.9	8.0	44.8	39.1	7.0	.2	−1.4	11.7
1963	61.1	6.7	1.7	39.4	4.2	9.1	48.1	42.2	7.5	.1	−1.7	13.0
1964	67.1	7.5	1.8	42.6	4.7	10.4	52.4	46.0	8.2	−.1	−1.7	14.7
1965	72.3	8.1	2.0	46.1	5.0	11.1	57.2	50.5	8.8	−.3	−1.7	15.1
1966	81.5	9.5	2.2	49.7	5.7	14.4	64.3	56.5	10.1	−.6	−1.7	17.3
1967	89.8	10.6	2.6	53.9	6.7	15.9	72.5	62.9	12.1	−.9	−1.6	17.3
1968	102.7	12.7	3.3	60.8	7.2	18.6	82.6	70.8	14.5	−1.1	−1.6	20.0
1969	114.8	15.2	3.6	67.4	8.3	20.3	93.7	79.8	16.7	−1.4	−1.5	21.1
1970	129.0	16.7	3.7	74.8	9.2	24.4	108.2	91.6	20.1	−2.0	−1.6	20.8
1971	145.3	18.7	4.3	83.1	10.2	29.0	123.7	102.9	24.0	−1.7	−1.4	21.7
1972	169.7	24.2	5.3	91.2	11.5	37.5	137.5	113.4	27.5	−1.8	−1.6	32.2
1973	185.3	26.3	6.0	99.5	13.0	40.6	152.0	126.4	30.4	−3.4	−1.5	33.4
1974	200.6	28.2	6.7	107.2	14.6	43.9	170.2	144.0	32.3	−5.3	−.9	30.5
1975	225.6	31.0	7.3	115.8	16.8	54.6	198.0	164.9	38.9	−5.4	−.4	27.6
1976	253.9	35.8	9.6	127.8	19.5	61.1	217.9	179.7	43.6	−5.0	−.4	35.9
1977	281.9	41.0	11.4	139.9	22.1	67.5	237.1	196.1	47.4	−6.0	−.3	44.7
1978	309.3	46.3	12.1	148.9	24.7	77.3	256.7	214.5	52.4	−9.8	−.3	52.6
1979	330.6	50.5	13.6	158.6	27.4	80.5	278.3	235.9	57.2	−15.3	.4	52.3
1980	361.4	56.2	14.5	172.3	29.7	88.7	307.0	261.3	65.7	−21.2	1.2	54.4
1981	390.8	63.0	15.4	192.0	32.5	87.9	335.4	285.3	73.6	−25.9	2.4	55.4
1982	409.0	68.5	14.0	206.8	35.8	83.9	357.7	307.9	79.9	−31.8	1.7	51.3
1983	443.6	76.2	15.9	226.8	37.7	87.0	378.8	326.2	86.6	−34.4	.2	64.9
1984	492.0	87.1	18.8	251.5	40.2	94.4	405.1	350.8	93.9	−38.0	−1.6	86.9
1985	528.7	94.0	20.2	271.4	42.8	100.3	437.8	382.6	101.9	−43.4	−3.3	91.0
1986	570.6	101.6	22.7	291.5	47.3	107.6	475.7	412.7	111.8	−45.8	−3.0	94.9
1987	594.9	111.8	23.9	307.1	49.2	102.9	511.1	441.1	120.7	−47.4	−3.4	83.8
1988	631.4	117.6	26.0	324.6	51.9	111.2	545.5	471.3	131.0	−51.5	−5.3	85.9
1989	681.0	131.4	24.2	353.0	54.1	118.2	585.7	507.2	144.5	−59.3	−6.8	95.3
1990	728.9	139.1	22.5	377.6	57.4	132.4	648.8	550.1	166.5	−60.7	−7.1	80.1
1991	784.2	147.8	23.6	398.4	60.9	153.4	708.3	579.4	199.0	−62.8	−7.2	75.8
1992	844.3	159.7	24.4	423.7	64.3	172.2	758.0	603.6	227.2	−64.8	−8.0	86.3
1993	897.1	166.2	26.3	451.8	66.9	185.7	802.2	627.9	246.8	−62.4	−10.1	94.9
1994	946.4	170.0	30.9	479.9	69.7	195.9	846.6	651.7	267.4	−61.2	−11.2	99.7
1990:I	710.3	135.6	21.4	368.9	56.0	128.4	624.8	535.3	156.5	−59.9	−7.1	85.5
II	721.3	137.5	22.7	371.9	56.9	132.2	638.5	543.9	162.4	−60.7	−7.1	82.8
III	736.2	141.2	23.7	381.8	57.9	131.8	655.5	554.0	169.3	−60.8	−7.0	80.7
IV	748.0	142.3	22.2	387.7	58.7	137.1	676.5	567.3	177.7	−61.3	−7.1	71.5
1991:I	758.5	143.9	22.8	387.5	59.6	144.8	689.8	572.1	186.9	−62.0	−7.2	68.8
II	775.8	146.3	23.4	393.8	60.5	151.8	702.1	576.9	195.0	−62.5	−7.2	73.7
III	791.4	147.7	24.3	403.8	61.3	154.4	714.3	581.5	203.1	−63.1	−7.2	77.1
IV	811.0	153.5	24.2	408.4	62.2	162.7	727.2	587.3	210.8	−63.6	−7.2	83.8
1992:I	823.4	155.7	24.3	414.9	63.1	165.4	738.6	592.6	217.7	−64.5	−7.2	84.8
II	838.8	158.4	25.7	417.7	64.0	173.0	752.2	600.8	224.1	−65.0	−7.7	86.6
III	847.3	159.9	21.6	427.0	64.7	174.2	765.4	607.4	231.2	−64.9	−8.3	82.0
IV	867.7	164.9	25.9	435.2	65.4	176.3	775.9	613.6	235.8	−64.5	−8.9	91.7
1993:I	869.0	161.4	24.0	440.4	65.9	177.3	788.5	620.8	240.3	−63.1	−9.5	80.5
II	887.6	165.9	26.1	447.6	66.6	181.5	798.5	626.0	245.0	−62.7	−9.9	89.1
III	901.9	167.3	25.7	454.5	67.2	187.2	807.0	630.8	249.0	−62.1	−10.6	94.9
IV	929.7	170.4	29.5	464.9	67.9	197.0	814.7	634.1	252.8	−61.7	−10.6	115.0
1994:I	923.6	166.2	27.1	469.3	68.8	192.2	828.8	642.4	257.4	−61.6	−9.3	94.8
II	943.8	169.5	30.6	476.7	69.4	197.5	838.6	647.3	263.8	−61.2	−11.3	105.2
III	953.1	170.8	32.2	483.1	70.1	196.9	853.5	655.4	270.9	−61.1	−11.8	99.6
IV	965.0	173.6	33.6	490.3	70.6	196.9	865.6	661.9	277.2	−60.9	−12.6	99.3
1995:I	980.9	175.5	34.2	494.3	71.1	205.8	882.0	672.1	283.6	−60.7	−13.1	99.0
II	994.8	177.0	33.5	501.3	71.6	211.3	895.8	680.1	289.0	−60.1	−13.3	99.0
III	1,000.5	181.0	35.4	508.1	72.2	203.8	907.6	686.5	294.3	−59.9	−13.2	92.8

[1] Includes an item for the difference between wage accruals and disbursements, not shown separately.

Source: Department of Commerce, Bureau of Economic Analysis.

TABLE B–82.—State and local government revenues and expenditures, selected fiscal years, 1927–92

[Millions of dollars]

Fiscal year [1]	General revenues by source [2]							General expenditures by function [2]				
	Total	Property taxes	Sales and gross receipts taxes	Individual income taxes	Corporation net income taxes	Revenue from Federal Government	All other [3]	Total	Education	Highways	Public welfare	All other [4]
1927	7,271	4,730	470	70	92	116	1,793	7,210	2,235	1,809	151	3,015
1932	7,267	4,487	752	74	79	232	1,643	7,765	2,311	1,741	444	3,269
1934	7,678	4,076	1,008	80	49	1,016	1,449	7,181	1,831	1,509	889	2,952
1936	8,395	4,093	1,484	153	113	948	1,604	7,644	2,177	1,425	827	3,215
1938	9,228	4,440	1,794	218	165	800	1,811	8,757	2,491	1,650	1,069	3,547
1940	9,609	4,430	1,982	224	156	945	1,872	9,229	2,638	1,573	1,156	3,862
1942	10,418	4,537	2,351	276	272	858	2,123	9,190	2,586	1,490	1,225	3,889
1944	10,908	4,604	2,289	342	451	954	2,269	8,863	2,793	1,200	1,133	3,737
1946	12,356	4,986	2,986	422	447	855	2,661	11,028	3,356	1,672	1,409	4,591
1948	17,250	6,126	4,442	543	592	1,861	3,685	17,684	5,379	3,036	2,099	7,170
1950	20,911	7,349	5,154	788	593	2,486	4,541	22,787	7,177	3,803	2,940	8,867
1952	25,181	8,652	6,357	998	846	2,566	5,763	26,098	8,318	4,650	2,788	10,342
1953	27,307	9,375	6,927	1,065	817	2,870	6,252	27,910	9,390	4,987	2,914	10,619
1954	29,012	9,967	7,276	1,127	778	2,966	6,897	30,701	10,557	5,527	3,060	11,557
1955	31,073	10,735	7,643	1,237	744	3,131	7,584	33,724	11,907	6,452	3,168	12,197
1956	34,667	11,749	8,691	1,538	890	3,335	8,465	36,711	13,220	6,953	3,139	13,399
1957	38,164	12,864	9,467	1,754	984	3,843	9,252	40,375	14,134	7,816	3,485	14,940
1958	41,219	14,047	9,829	1,759	1,018	4,865	9,699	44,851	15,919	8,567	3,818	16,547
1959	45,306	14,983	10,437	1,994	1,001	6,377	10,516	48,887	17,283	9,592	4,136	17,876
1960	50,505	16,405	11,849	2,463	1,180	6,974	11,634	51,876	18,719	9,428	4,404	19,325
1961	54,037	18,002	12,463	2,613	1,266	7,131	12,563	56,201	20,574	9,844	4,720	21,063
1962	58,252	19,054	13,494	3,037	1,308	7,871	13,489	60,206	22,216	10,357	5,084	22,549
1963	62,890	20,089	14,456	3,269	1,505	8,722	14,850	64,816	23,776	11,136	5,481	24,423
1962–63	62,269	19,833	14,446	3,267	1,505	8,663	14,556	63,977	23,729	11,150	5,420	23,678
1963–64	68,443	21,241	15,762	3,791	1,695	10,002	15,951	69,302	26,286	11,664	5,766	25,586
1964–65	74,000	22,583	17,118	4,090	1,929	11,029	17,250	74,678	28,563	12,221	6,315	27,579
1965–66	83,036	24,670	19,085	4,760	2,038	13,214	19,269	82,843	33,287	12,770	6,757	30,029
1966–67	91,197	26,047	20,530	5,825	2,227	15,370	21,197	93,350	37,919	13,932	8,218	33,281
1967–68	101,264	27,747	22,911	7,308	2,518	17,181	23,598	102,411	41,158	14,481	9,857	36,915
1968–69	114,550	30,673	26,519	8,908	3,180	19,153	26,118	116,728	47,238	15,417	12,110	41,963
1969–70	130,756	34,054	30,322	10,812	3,738	21,857	29,971	131,332	52,718	16,427	14,679	47,508
1970–71	144,927	37,852	33,233	11,900	3,424	26,146	32,374	150,674	59,413	18,095	18,226	54,940
1971–72	167,541	42,877	37,518	15,227	4,416	31,342	36,162	168,549	65,814	19,021	21,117	62,597
1972–73	190,222	45,283	42,047	17,994	5,425	39,264	40,210	181,357	69,714	18,615	23,582	69,446
1973–74	207,670	47,705	46,098	19,491	6,015	41,820	46,541	198,959	75,833	19,946	25,085	78,096
1974–75	228,171	51,491	49,815	21,454	6,642	47,034	51,735	230,722	87,858	22,528	28,156	92,180
1975–76	256,176	57,001	54,547	24,575	7,273	55,589	57,191	256,731	97,216	23,907	32,604	103,004
1976–77	285,157	62,527	60,641	29,246	9,174	62,444	61,124	274,215	102,780	23,058	35,906	112,472
1977–78	315,960	66,422	67,596	33,176	10,738	69,592	68,436	296,984	110,758	24,609	39,140	122,477
1978–79	343,236	64,944	74,247	36,932	12,128	75,164	79,821	327,517	119,448	28,440	41,898	137,731
1979–80	382,322	68,499	79,927	42,080	13,321	83,029	95,466	369,086	133,211	33,311	47,288	155,277
1980–81	423,404	74,969	85,971	46,426	14,143	90,294	111,599	407,449	145,784	34,603	54,105	172,957
1981–82	457,654	82,067	93,613	50,738	15,028	87,282	128,926	436,733	154,282	34,520	57,996	189,935
1982–83	486,753	89,105	100,247	55,129	14,258	90,007	138,008	466,516	163,876	36,655	60,906	205,079
1983–84	542,730	96,457	114,097	64,529	17,141	96,935	153,570	505,008	176,108	39,419	66,414	223,068
1984–85	598,121	103,757	126,376	70,361	19,152	106,158	172,317	553,899	192,686	44,989	71,479	244,745
1985–86	641,486	111,709	135,005	74,365	19,994	113,099	187,314	605,623	210,819	49,368	75,868	269,568
1986–87	686,860	121,203	144,091	83,935	22,425	114,857	200,350	657,134	226,619	52,355	82,650	295,510
1987–88	726,762	132,212	156,452	88,350	23,663	117,602	208,482	704,921	242,683	55,621	89,090	317,528
1988–89	786,129	142,400	166,336	97,806	25,926	125,824	227,838	762,360	263,898	58,105	97,879	342,479
1989–90	849,502	155,613	177,885	105,640	23,566	136,802	249,996	834,818	288,148	61,057	110,518	375,095
1990–91	902,207	167,999	185,570	109,341	22,242	154,099	262,955	908,108	309,302	64,937	130,402	403,467
1991–92	973,326	178,412	196,417	115,556	23,833	179,209	279,898	975,848	326,275	66,689	158,212	424,672

[1] Fiscal years not the same for all governments. See Note.
[2] Excludes revenues or expenditures of publicly owned utilities and liquor stores, and of insurance-trust activities. Intergovernmental receipts and payments between State and local governments are also excluded.
[3] Includes other taxes and charges and miscellaneous revenues.
[4] Includes expenditures for libraries, hospitals, health, employment security administration, veterans' services, air transportation, water transport and terminals, parking facilities, and transit subsidies, police protection, fire protection, correction, protective inspection and regulation, sewerage, natural resources, parks and recreation, housing and community development, solid waste management, financial administration, judicial and legal, general public buildings, other government administration, interest on general debt, and general expenditures, n.e.c.

Note.—Data for fiscal years listed from 1962–63 to 1991–92 are the aggregations of data for government fiscal years that ended in the 12-month period from July 1 to June 30 of those years. Data for 1963 and earlier years include data for government fiscal years ending during that particular calendar year.

Data are not available for intervening years.

Source: Department of Commerce, Bureau of the Census.

[Millions of dollars]

End of year or month	Total interest-bearing public debt securities	Marketable				Nonmarketable				
		Total ¹	Treasury bills	Treasury notes	Treasury bonds	Total	U.S. savings bonds	Foreign government and public series ²	Government account series	Other ³
Fiscal year:										
1967	322,286	⁴210,672	58,535	49,108	97,418	111,614	51,213	1,514	56,155	2,732
1968	344,401	226,592	64,440	71,073	91,079	117,808	51,712	3,741	59,526	2,829
1969	351,729	226,107	68,356	78,946	78,805	125,623	51,711	4,070	66,790	3,052
1970	369,026	232,599	76,154	93,489	62,956	136,426	51,281	4,755	76,323	4,067
1971	396,289	245,473	86,677	104,807	53,989	150,816	53,003	9,270	82,784	5,759
1972	425,360	257,202	94,648	113,419	49,135	168,158	55,921	18,985	89,598	3,654
1973	456,353	262,971	100,061	117,840	45,071	193,382	59,418	28,524	101,738	3,702
1974	473,238	266,575	105,019	128,419	33,137	206,663	61,921	25,011	115,442	4,289
1975	532,122	315,606	128,569	150,257	36,779	216,516	65,482	23,216	124,173	3,645
1976	619,254	392,581	161,198	191,758	39,626	226,673	69,733	21,500	130,557	4,883
1977	697,629	443,508	156,091	241,692	45,724	254,121	75,411	21,799	140,113	16,798
1978	766,971	485,155	160,936	267,865	56,355	281,816	79,798	21,680	153,271	27,067
1979	819,007	506,693	161,378	274,242	71,073	312,314	80,440	28,115	176,360	27,399
1980	906,402	594,506	199,832	310,903	83,772	311,896	72,727	25,158	189,848	24,163
1981	996,495	683,209	223,388	363,643	96,178	313,286	68,017	20,499	201,052	23,718
1982	1,140,883	824,422	277,900	442,890	103,631	316,461	67,274	14,641	210,462	24,084
1983	1,375,751	1,024,000	340,733	557,525	125,742	351,751	70,024	11,450	234,684	35,593
1984	1,559,570	1,176,556	356,798	661,687	158,070	383,015	72,832	8,806	259,534	41,843
1985	1,821,010	1,360,179	384,220	776,449	199,510	460,831	77,011	6,638	313,928	63,254
1986	2,122,684	¹1,564,329	410,730	896,884	241,716	558,355	85,551	4,128	365,872	102,804
1987	2,347,750	¹1,675,980	378,263	1,005,127	277,590	671,769	97,004	4,350	440,658	129,757
1988	2,599,877	¹1,802,905	398,451	1,089,578	299,875	796,972	106,176	6,320	536,455	148,021
1989	2,836,309	¹1,892,763	406,597	1,133,193	337,974	943,546	114,025	6,818	663,677	159,026
1990	3,210,943	¹2,092,759	482,454	1,218,081	377,224	1,118,184	122,152	36,041	779,412	180,579
1991	3,662,759	¹2,390,660	564,589	1,387,717	423,354	1,272,099	133,512	41,639	908,406	188,542
1992	4,061,801	¹2,677,476	634,287	1,566,349	461,840	1,384,325	148,266	37,039	1,011,020	188,000
1993	4,408,567	¹2,904,910	658,381	1,734,161	497,367	1,503,657	167,024	42,459	1,114,289	179,885
1994	4,689,524	¹3,091,602	697,295	1,867,507	511,800	1,597,922	176,413	41,996	1,211,689	167,824
1995	4,950,644	¹3,260,447	742,462	1,980,343	522,643	1,690,197	181,181	40,950	1,324,270	143,796
1994:Jan	4,523,027	¹2,986,024	702,292	1,772,877	495,855	1,537,002	170,736	43,222	1,147,831	175,213
Feb	4,556,241	¹3,017,122	700,686	1,797,213	504,223	1,539,120	171,750	42,724	1,148,964	175,682
Mar	4,572,619	¹3,042,902	721,146	1,802,537	504,219	1,529,717	172,632	42,724	1,138,405	175,956
Apr	4,548,547	¹3,003,364	705,340	1,778,805	504,219	1,545,183	173,533	42,708	1,152,758	176,184
May	4,605,977	¹3,046,277	700,228	1,829,211	501,838	1,559,700	174,237	42,517	1,167,948	174,998
June	4,642,523	¹3,050,989	698,446	1,835,705	501,837	1,591,534	174,859	42,229	1,200,606	173,840
July	4,616,171	¹3,034,469	706,064	1,811,569	501,837	1,581,702	175,460	41,924	1,194,806	169,512
Aug	4,688,745	¹3,103,702	716,177	1,860,724	511,800	1,585,043	175,915	41,788	1,198,058	169,282
Sept	4,689,524	¹3,091,602	697,295	1,867,507	511,800	1,597,922	176,413	41,996	1,211,689	167,824
Oct	4,730,969	¹3,123,224	721,146	1,875,275	511,799	1,607,746	177,187	42,880	1,221,401	166,278
Nov	4,775,318	¹3,164,390	745,294	1,893,798	510,297	1,610,928	177,755	42,683	1,225,944	164,546
Dec	4,769,171	¹3,126,035	733,753	1,866,986	510,296	1,643,137	177,786	42,471	1,259,827	163,053
1995:Jan	4,812,208	¹3,173,398	741,771	1,906,332	510,294	1,638,810	178,041	42,536	1,262,642	155,591
Feb	4,850,521	¹3,211,929	756,351	1,922,913	517,665	1,638,593	178,465	42,979	1,262,711	154,438
Mar	4,860,502	¹3,227,333	756,447	1,938,223	517,664	1,633,169	178,839	41,797	1,259,184	153,349
Apr	4,831,533	¹3,182,253	735,178	1,914,413	517,662	1,649,279	179,458	41,662	1,275,568	152,591
May	4,900,346	¹3,241,464	750,702	1,961,107	514,655	1,658,881	179,824	41,614	1,283,765	153,678
June	4,947,814	¹3,252,620	748,240	1,974,663	514,654	1,695,194	180,136	41,442	1,322,041	151,575
July	4,956,625	¹3,270,977	759,354	1,981,968	514,654	1,685,648	180,547	41,237	1,320,685	143,179
Aug	4,967,192	¹3,286,057	750,167	1,998,247	522,643	1,681,135	180,785	41,261	1,314,973	144,116
Sept	4,950,644	¹3,260,447	742,462	1,980,343	522,643	1,690,197	181,181	40,950	1,324,270	143,796
Oct	4,981,739	¹3,293,172	738,605	2,016,925	522,642	1,688,567	181,819	40,800	1,325,155	140,793
Nov	4,985,790	¹3,351,483	785,682	2,029,642	521,159	1,634,308	182,203	40,800	1,273,059	138,246
Dec	4,964,371	¹3,307,179	760,680	2,010,340	521,158	1,657,191	181,918	40,805	1,299,585	134,883

¹ Includes Federal Financing Bank securities, not shown separately, in the amount of 15,000 million dollars.
² Nonmarketable certificates of indebtedness, notes, bonds, and bills in the Treasury foreign series of dollar-denominated and foreign-currency denominated issues.
³ Includes depository bonds, retirement plan bonds, Rural Electrification Administration bonds, State and local bonds, and special issues held only by U.S. Government agencies and trust funds and the Federal home loan banks.
⁴ Includes $5,610 million in certificates not shown separately.

Note.—Through fiscal year 1976, the fiscal year was on a July 1–June 30 basis; beginning October 1976 (fiscal year 1977), the fiscal year is on an October 1–September 30 basis.

Source: Department of the Treasury.

TABLE B–84.—*Maturity distribution and average length of marketable interest-bearing public debt securities held by private investors, 1967–95*

End of year or month	Amount outstanding, privately held	Within 1 year	1 to 5 years	5 to 10 years	10 to 20 years	20 years and over	Average length Years	Average length Months
			Maturity class					
			Millions of dollars				Years	Months
Fiscal year:								
1967	150,321	56,561	53,584	21,057	6,153	12,968	5	1
1968	159,671	66,746	52,295	21,850	6,110	12,670	4	5
1969	156,008	69,311	50,182	18,078	6,097	12,337	4	2
1970	157,910	76,443	57,035	8,286	7,876	8,272	3	8
1971	161,863	74,803	58,557	14,503	6,357	7,645	3	6
1972	165,978	79,509	57,157	16,033	6,358	6,922	3	3
1973	167,869	84,041	54,139	16,385	8,741	4,564	3	1
1974	164,862	87,150	50,103	14,197	9,930	3,481	2	11
1975	210,382	115,677	65,852	15,385	8,857	4,611	2	8
1976	279,782	150,296	90,578	24,169	8,087	6,652	2	7
1977	326,674	161,329	113,319	33,067	8,428	10,531	2	11
1978	356,501	163,819	132,993	33,500	11,383	14,805	3	3
1979	380,530	181,883	127,574	32,279	18,489	20,304	3	7
1980	463,717	220,084	156,244	38,809	25,901	22,679	3	9
1981	549,863	256,187	182,237	48,743	32,569	30,127	4	0
1982	682,043	314,436	221,783	75,749	33,017	37,058	3	11
1983	862,631	379,579	294,955	99,174	40,826	48,097	4	1
1984	1,017,488	437,941	332,808	130,417	49,664	66,658	4	6
1985	1,185,675	472,661	402,766	159,383	62,853	88,012	4	11
1986	1,354,275	506,903	467,348	189,995	70,664	119,365	5	3
1987	1,445,366	483,582	526,746	209,160	72,862	153,016	5	9
1988	1,555,208	524,201	552,993	232,453	74,186	171,375	5	9
1989	1,654,660	546,751	578,333	247,428	80,616	201,532	6	0
1990	1,841,903	626,297	630,144	267,573	82,713	235,176	6	1
1991	2,113,799	713,778	761,243	280,574	84,900	273,304	6	0
1992	2,363,802	808,705	866,329	295,921	84,706	308,141	5	11
1993	2,562,336	858,135	978,714	306,663	94,345	324,479	5	10
1994	2,719,861	877,932	1,128,322	289,998	88,208	335,401	5	8
1995	2,870,781	1,002,875	1,157,492	290,111	87,297	333,006	5	4
1994: Jan	2,628,451	894,898	1,029,878	296,604	86,408	320,663	5	7
Feb	2,661,872	899,813	1,041,195	300,082	86,573	334,208	5	9
Mar	2,683,420	908,889	1,054,336	299,433	86,355	334,407	5	8
Apr	2,639,251	887,454	1,041,071	289,963	86,355	334,407	5	8
May	2,680,916	893,359	1,076,198	295,356	87,866	328,138	5	8
June	2,676,695	878,396	1,087,030	295,184	87,702	328,383	5	7
July	2,667,897	888,349	1,076,723	286,051	87,621	329,153	5	7
Aug	2,731,481	899,256	1,116,418	292,971	88,235	334,601	5	8
Sept	2,719,861	877,932	1,128,322	289,998	88,208	335,401	5	8
Oct	2,750,705	904,001	1,144,298	279,896	88,058	334,451	5	7
Nov	2,782,099	926,834	1,149,907	290,468	84,856	330,035	5	6
Dec	2,737,789	906,618	1,130,084	288,781	84,157	328,150	5	6
1995: Jan	2,791,905	927,146	1,169,586	280,372	84,832	329,970	5	5
Feb	2,829,671	950,006	1,170,648	283,190	96,284	329,543	5	6
Mar	2,841,506	963,767	1,171,125	280,798	96,284	329,533	5	5
Apr	2,795,125	952,570	1,148,083	269,784	95,990	328,699	5	5
May	2,851,360	980,967	1,173,686	278,581	89,857	328,269	5	5
June	2,847,129	980,975	1,170,628	277,926	89,447	328,153	5	4
July	2,878,926	1,007,159	1,174,571	278,600	89,897	328,699	5	3
Aug	2,896,671	999,545	1,187,061	290,211	86,847	333,006	5	5
Sept	2,870,781	1,002,875	1,157,492	290,111	87,297	333,006	5	4
Oct	2,901,629	1,007,132	1,182,933	290,311	87,397	333,856	5	4
Nov	2,954,168	1,065,179	1,176,195	292,576	93,490	326,727	5	3
Dec	2,901,387	1,049,518	1,142,392	291,881	92,636	324,959	5	3

Note.—All issues classified to final maturity.
Through fiscal year 1976, the fiscal year was on a July 1–June 30 basis; beginning October 1976 (fiscal year 1977), the fiscal year is on an October 1–September 30 basis.

Source: Department of the Treasury.

TABLE B–85.—*Estimated ownership of public debt securities by private investors, 1976–95*

[Par values;[1] billions of dollars]

End of month	Total	Commercial banks[2]	Held by private investors — Nonbank investors — Total	Individuals[3] Total	Savings bonds[4]	Other securities	Insurance companies	Money market funds	Corporations[5]	State and local governments[6]	Foreign and international[7]	Other investors[8]
1976: June	376.4	92.5	283.9	96.1	69.6	26.5	10.7	0.8	23.3	32.7	69.8	50.5
Dec	409.5	103.8	305.7	101.6	72.0	29.6	12.7	1.1	23.5	39.3	78.1	49.4
1977: June	421.0	102.9	318.1	104.9	74.4	30.5	13.0	.8	22.1	49.6	87.9	39.8
Dec	461.3	102.0	359.3	107.8	76.7	31.1	15.1	.9	18.2	59.1	109.6	48.6
1978: June	477.8	99.6	378.2	109.0	79.1	29.9	14.2	1.3	17.3	69.6	119.5	47.3
Dec	508.6	95.3	413.3	114.0	80.7	33.3	15.3	1.5	17.3	81.1	133.1	51.0
1979: June	516.6	94.6	422.0	115.5	80.6	34.9	16.0	3.8	18.6	102.7	114.9	50.5
Dec	540.5	95.6	444.9	118.0	79.9	38.1	15.6	5.6	17.0	100.2	119.0	69.5
1980: June	558.2	98.5	459.7	116.5	73.4	43.1	15.3	5.3	14.0	100.1	118.2	90.3
Dec	616.4	111.5	504.9	117.1	72.5	44.6	18.1	3.5	19.3	114.2	129.7	103.0
1981: June	651.2	115.0	536.2	107.4	69.2	38.2	19.9	9.0	19.9	125.6	136.6	117.8
Dec	694.5	113.8	580.7	110.8	68.1	42.7	21.6	21.5	17.9	133.4	136.6	138.9
1982: June	740.9	114.7	626.2	114.1	67.4	46.7	24.4	22.4	17.6	155.4	137.2	155.1
Dec	848.4	134.0	714.4	116.5	68.3	48.2	30.6	42.6	24.5	160.7	149.5	190.0
1983: June	948.6	167.4	781.2	121.3	69.7	51.6	37.8	28.3	32.8	181.8	160.1	219.1
Dec	1,022.6	179.5	843.1	133.4	71.5	61.9	46.0	22.8	39.7	196.6	166.3	238.3
1984: June	1,102.2	180.6	921.6	142.2	72.9	69.3	51.2	14.9	45.3	219.7	171.6	276.6
Dec	1,212.5	181.5	1,031.0	143.8	74.5	69.3	64.5	25.9	50.1	239.9	205.9	300.9
1985: June	1,292.0	195.6	1,096.4	148.7	76.7	72.0	69.1	24.8	54.9	272.9	213.8	312.2
Dec	1,417.2	189.4	1,227.8	154.8	79.8	75.0	80.5	25.1	59.0	354.1	224.8	329.6
1986: June	1,502.7	194.4	1,308.3	159.5	83.8	75.7	87.9	22.8	61.2	397.7	250.9	328.2
Dec	1,602.0	197.7	1,404.3	162.7	92.3	70.4	101.6	28.6	68.8	436.6	263.4	342.6
1987: June	1,658.1	192.5	1,465.6	165.6	96.8	68.8	104.7	20.6	79.7	482.7	281.1	331.2
Dec	1,731.4	194.4	1,537.0	172.4	101.1	71.3	108.1	14.6	84.6	490.3	299.7	367.3
1988: June	1,786.7	190.8	1,595.9	182.0	106.2	75.8	113.5	13.4	87.6	493.0	345.4	360.9
Dec	1,858.5	185.3	1,673.2	190.4	109.6	80.8	118.6	11.8	86.0	493.1	362.2	411.1
1989: June	1,909.1	178.4	1,730.7	211.7	114.0	97.7	120.6	11.3	91.0	459.9	369.1	467.1
Dec	2,015.8	165.3	1,850.5	216.4	117.7	98.7	123.9	14.9	93.4	473.5	429.6	498.8
1990: June	2,141.8	177.3	1,964.5	229.6	121.9	107.7	133.7	28.0	96.9	525.2	427.3	523.8
Dec	2,288.3	172.1	2,116.2	233.8	126.2	107.6	138.2	45.5	108.9	531.5	458.4	599.9
1991: Mar	2,360.6	187.5	2,173.1	238.3	129.7	108.6	147.2	65.4	114.9	548.7	464.3	594.3
June	2,397.9	196.2	2,201.7	243.5	133.2	110.3	156.8	55.4	130.8	550.8	473.6	590.8
Sept	2,489.4	217.5	2,271.9	257.5	135.4	122.1	171.4	64.5	142.0	561.0	477.3	598.3
Dec	2,563.2	232.5	2,330.7	263.9	138.1	125.8	181.8	80.0	150.8	568.2	491.7	594.3
1992: Mar	2,664.0	255.9	2,408.1	268.1	142.0	126.1	188.4	84.8	166.0	587.8	507.9	605.1
June	2,712.4	267.0	2,445.4	275.1	145.4	129.7	192.8	79.4	175.0	588.8	529.6	604.7
Sept	2,765.5	287.5	2,478.0	281.2	150.3	130.9	194.8	79.4	180.8	586.9	535.2	619.7
Dec	2,839.9	294.4	2,545.5	289.2	157.3	131.9	197.5	79.7	192.5	579.3	549.7	657.5
1993: Mar	2,895.0	310.2	2,584.8	297.7	163.6	134.1	208.0	77.9	199.3	596.9	564.2	640.9
June	2,938.4	307.2	2,631.2	303.0	166.5	136.4	217.8	76.2	206.1	620.9	567.7	639.5
Sept	2,983.0	313.9	2,669.1	305.8	169.1	136.7	229.4	74.8	215.6	627.5	591.3	624.6
Dec	3,047.4	322.2	2,725.2	309.9	171.9	137.9	234.5	80.8	213.0	631.9	622.9	632.3
1994: Mar	3,094.6	344.9	2,749.7	315.1	175.0	140.1	234.5	69.3	216.3	626.9	633.3	654.3
June	3,088.2	330.8	2,757.4	321.1	177.1	144.0	239.9	59.9	226.3	614.1	633.1	663.0
Sept	3,127.8	313.9	2,813.9	327.2	178.6	148.6	246.2	59.9	229.3	568.8	655.6	726.9
Dec	3,168.0	290.6	2,877.4	331.2	180.5	150.7	242.8	67.6	226.5	521.4	688.6	799.3
1995: Mar	3,239.2	307.5	2,931.7	342.8	181.4	161.4	249.2	67.7	230.3	503.1	729.0	809.5
June	3,245.0	297.7	2,947.3	344.2	182.6	161.6	253.5	58.7	227.7	470.9	784.1	808.2
Sept	3,290.5	295.0	2,984.5	345.9	183.5	162.4	255.0	64.2	224.1	422.9	848.1	824.3

[1] U.S. savings bonds, series A–F and J, are included at current redemption value.

[2] Includes domestically chartered banks, U.S. branches and agencies of foreign banks, New York investment companies majority owned by foreign banks, and Edge Act corporations owned by domestically chartered and foreign banks.

[3] Includes partnerships and personal trust accounts.

[4] Includes U.S. savings notes. Sales began May 1, 1967, and were discontinued June 30, 1970.

[5] Exclusive of banks and insurance companies.

[6] State and local government holdings have been redefined (beginning 1979) to include their fully defeased debt that is backed by nonmarketable Federal securities. Includes State and local pension funds.

[7] Consists of the investments of foreign and international accounts (both official and private) in U.S. public debt issues. Reflects 1978 benchmark through December 1984; December 1984 benchmark through 1989; and December 1989 benchmark thereafter.

[8] Includes savings and loan associations, credit unions, nonprofit institutions, mutual savings banks, corporate pension trust funds, dealers and brokers, certain Government deposit accounts, and Government-sponsored enterprises.

Source: Department of the Treasury.

CORPORATE PROFITS AND FINANCE

TABLE B–86.—*Corporate profits with inventory valuation and capital consumption adjustments,*
1959–95

[Billions of dollars; quarterly data at seasonally adjusted annual rates]

Year or quarter	Corporate profits with inventory valuation and capital consumption adjustments	Corporate profits tax liability	Corporate profits after tax with inventory valuation and capital consumption adjustments		
			Total	Dividends	Undistributed profits with inventory valuation and capital consumption adjustments
1959	50.2	23.6	26.6	12.7	13.9
1960	48.8	22.7	26.1	13.4	12.7
1961	49.8	22.8	27.0	14.0	13.0
1962	57.7	24.0	33.7	15.0	18.7
1963	63.5	26.2	37.3	16.1	21.2
1964	70.4	28.0	42.4	18.0	24.4
1965	80.9	30.9	50.1	20.2	29.9
1966	86.3	33.7	52.6	20.9	31.7
1967	83.6	32.7	50.9	22.1	28.9
1968	90.3	39.4	51.0	24.6	26.3
1969	87.5	39.7	47.9	25.2	22.6
1970	75.7	34.4	41.4	23.7	17.7
1971	88.8	37.7	51.0	23.7	27.3
1972	102.2	41.9	60.3	25.8	34.5
1973	115.1	49.3	65.8	28.1	37.6
1974	103.7	51.8	51.9	30.4	21.5
1975	121.1	50.9	70.2	30.1	40.1
1976	147.0	64.2	82.8	35.9	47.0
1977	167.3	73.0	94.2	40.8	53.4
1978	191.6	83.5	108.1	46.0	62.0
1979	194.0	88.0	106.0	52.5	53.5
1980	167.1	84.8	82.3	59.3	23.0
1981	183.9	81.1	102.8	69.5	33.3
1982	159.2	63.1	96.1	69.8	26.3
1983	212.3	77.2	135.1	80.8	54.3
1984	268.2	94.0	174.2	83.2	91.0
1985	282.2	96.5	185.7	92.8	92.9
1986	271.0	106.5	164.5	110.2	54.2
1987	309.7	127.1	182.6	107.0	75.7
1988	357.2	137.0	220.2	116.8	103.3
1989	356.4	141.3	215.1	138.9	76.2
1990	369.5	140.5	229.0	151.9	77.2
1991	382.5	133.4	249.1	163.1	86.0
1992	401.4	143.0	258.4	169.5	88.9
1993	464.5	163.8	300.7	197.3	103.4
1994	526.5	195.3	331.2	211.0	120.2
1990: I	369.3	133.0	236.3	150.7	85.6
II	392.8	141.2	251.6	152.4	99.2
III	350.4	148.0	202.4	152.4	50.0
IV	365.5	139.7	225.9	152.0	73.8
1991: I	393.7	130.1	263.6	158.6	105.0
II	380.0	132.3	247.7	162.6	85.1
III	376.8	136.0	240.7	165.9	74.9
IV	379.6	135.2	244.4	165.3	79.1
1992: I	417.3	143.9	273.4	162.1	111.3
II	409.3	150.9	258.3	164.6	93.7
III	351.3	127.6	223.8	170.9	52.9
IV	427.7	149.7	278.0	180.4	97.7
1993: I	426.4	151.5	274.9	190.2	84.7
II	449.0	162.6	286.4	195.8	90.6
III	469.6	159.3	310.3	200.2	110.1
IV	512.8	181.7	331.1	202.9	128.1
1994: I	455.9	171.4	284.5	204.4	80.1
II	531.5	192.8	338.7	208.8	129.9
III	549.8	203.4	346.4	212.5	133.9
IV	568.9	213.5	355.3	218.5	136.8
1995: I	559.6	217.3	342.3	221.7	120.6
II	561.1	214.2	346.8	224.6	122.3
III	614.4	224.5	389.9	228.5	161.4

Source: Department of Commerce, Bureau of Economic Analysis.

379

TABLE B–87.—*Corporate profits by industry, 1959–95*

[Billions of dollars; quarterly data at seasonally adjusted annual rates]

Year or quarter	Total	Corporate profits with inventory valuation adjustment and without capital consumption adjustment										Rest of the world
		Domestic industries										
		Total	Financial[1]			Nonfinancial						
			Total	Federal Reserve banks	Other	Total	Manufacturing[2]	Transportation and public utilities	Wholesale trade	Retail trade	Other	
1959	53.1	50.4	7.0	0.7	6.3	43.4	26.5	7.1	2.8	3.3	3.6	2.7
1960	51.0	47.8	7.7	.9	6.7	40.2	23.8	7.5	2.5	2.8	3.6	3.1
1961	51.3	48.0	7.5	.8	6.8	40.4	23.4	7.9	2.5	3.0	3.6	3.3
1962	56.4	52.6	7.6	.9	6.8	45.0	26.3	8.5	2.8	3.4	3.9	3.8
1963	61.2	57.1	7.3	1.0	6.4	49.8	29.6	9.5	2.8	3.6	4.4	4.1
1964	67.5	63.0	7.5	1.1	6.4	55.5	32.4	10.2	3.4	4.5	5.1	4.5
1965	77.6	72.9	7.9	1.3	6.5	65.0	39.7	11.0	3.8	4.9	5.6	4.7
1966	83.0	78.5	9.2	1.7	7.5	69.3	42.4	11.9	3.9	4.8	6.2	4.5
1967	80.3	75.5	9.5	2.0	7.6	66.0	39.0	10.9	4.0	5.6	6.4	4.8
1968	86.9	81.3	10.9	2.5	8.4	70.4	41.7	11.0	4.5	6.4	6.8	5.6
1969	83.2	76.6	11.6	3.1	8.5	65.0	37.0	10.6	4.8	6.4	6.2	6.6
1970	71.8	64.7	13.1	3.5	9.6	51.6	27.1	8.2	4.3	6.0	5.9	7.1
1971	85.5	77.7	15.2	3.3	11.9	62.5	34.8	8.9	5.1	7.2	6.6	7.9
1972	97.9	88.4	16.4	3.3	13.1	72.0	41.4	9.4	6.8	7.4	7.1	9.5
1973	110.9	96.0	17.5	4.5	13.0	78.5	46.7	9.0	8.0	6.6	8.2	14.9
1974	103.4	85.9	16.2	5.7	10.5	69.7	40.7	7.6	11.3	2.3	7.7	17.5
1975	129.4	114.8	15.9	5.6	10.3	98.9	54.5	10.9	13.6	8.2	11.6	14.6
1976	158.9	142.3	19.9	5.9	14.0	122.4	70.7	15.3	12.7	10.5	13.3	16.5
1977	186.8	167.7	25.7	6.1	19.6	142.0	78.5	18.5	15.4	12.4	17.1	19.1
1978	213.1	190.2	31.8	7.6	24.1	158.4	89.6	21.7	15.4	12.3	19.4	22.9
1979	220.2	185.6	31.6	9.4	22.2	153.9	88.3	16.9	18.5	9.8	20.5	34.6
1980	198.3	162.9	24.3	11.8	12.6	138.5	75.8	18.3	16.7	6.1	21.6	35.5
1981	204.1	174.4	18.7	14.4	4.3	155.7	87.5	20.1	21.9	9.8	16.3	29.7
1982	166.8	139.4	15.6	15.2	.4	123.8	63.4	20.9	19.0	13.1	7.4	27.4
1983	203.7	173.1	24.8	14.6	10.2	148.3	72.8	29.7	18.7	18.7	8.4	30.6
1984	238.5	205.8	20.5	16.4	4.1	185.3	86.6	39.7	27.8	21.5	9.8	32.7
1985	230.5	197.1	29.0	16.3	12.6	168.1	81.6	34.3	20.6	22.5	9.1	33.4
1986	234.0	199.3	36.4	15.5	20.9	162.9	60.2	38.1	22.9	23.7	18.0	34.6
1987	272.9	231.3	37.1	15.7	21.4	194.2	85.0	41.7	16.7	23.9	26.9	41.6
1988	325.0	274.3	43.0	17.6	25.4	231.2	115.1	48.7	19.3	19.6	28.5	50.7
1989	330.6	272.6	53.1	20.2	32.9	219.6	109.3	42.6	20.4	20.7	26.6	58.0
1990	358.2	292.5	68.6	21.4	47.2	223.8	112.3	43.2	17.2	20.6	30.6	65.7
1991	378.2	309.5	87.4	20.3	67.1	222.1	92.7	53.9	20.6	26.1	28.9	68.7
1992	398.9	334.0	83.7	17.8	65.9	250.3	96.3	57.8	23.0	32.2	41.0	64.9
1993	457.7	388.1	91.0	16.1	74.9	297.2	109.7	70.6	25.5	39.2	52.1	69.6
1994	514.9	453.7	94.4	17.8	76.6	359.3	142.7	81.3	34.5	42.2	58.6	61.3
1990: I	353.4	289.7	63.1	20.6	42.5	226.5	115.9	42.1	18.9	19.9	29.8	63.7
II	381.1	316.2	69.4	21.2	48.2	246.7	125.1	48.7	19.0	22.7	31.3	64.9
III	341.9	281.5	71.5	22.2	49.2	210.0	99.8	46.8	13.9	17.0	32.5	60.4
IV	356.5	282.5	70.5	21.4	49.0	212.1	108.4	35.3	16.9	22.8	28.6	73.9
1991: I	388.3	313.2	82.2	21.0	61.2	230.9	104.3	52.3	21.0	25.3	28.1	75.2
II	375.5	309.2	87.5	20.2	67.3	221.7	91.7	55.6	22.9	23.8	27.8	66.2
III	373.8	311.9	92.2	20.1	72.0	219.8	90.8	53.5	21.4	26.5	27.5	61.9
IV	375.2	303.6	87.6	19.7	67.9	216.1	83.8	54.5	17.0	28.6	32.2	71.5
1992: I	411.4	341.7	105.1	18.8	86.3	236.6	92.0	61.2	14.6	32.0	36.8	69.7
II	404.3	337.6	96.9	18.4	78.5	240.7	89.6	57.4	21.8	34.3	37.5	66.7
III	359.4	295.6	49.7	17.3	32.4	245.9	98.4	54.3	27.4	25.2	40.6	63.9
IV	420.5	361.2	83.1	16.7	66.4	278.1	105.1	58.3	28.3	37.3	49.3	59.3
1993: I	421.4	347.0	85.7	16.5	69.2	261.2	90.4	68.5	17.9	36.3	48.2	74.5
II	443.2	375.7	88.1	16.1	72.0	287.6	108.4	66.4	28.6	38.1	46.2	67.5
III	465.9	393.1	88.8	15.9	72.9	304.3	106.0	73.6	27.0	42.4	55.2	72.8
IV	500.4	436.8	101.3	15.9	85.5	335.4	134.0	74.0	28.7	39.8	59.0	63.7
1994: I	467.8	407.0	64.9	16.1	48.8	342.1	145.3	73.3	28.8	38.3	56.3	60.8
II	513.4	452.4	97.8	16.9	80.9	354.6	134.2	81.3	39.5	43.2	56.5	61.0
III	531.0	469.9	108.4	18.1	90.3	361.5	142.8	81.6	34.3	43.7	59.0	61.1
IV	547.6	485.5	106.4	19.8	86.6	379.0	148.4	89.0	35.4	43.6	62.5	62.2
1995: I	542.2	467.5	114.3	21.5	92.7	353.2	134.7	88.5	29.7	36.0	64.3	74.8
II	546.1	468.2	112.6	22.3	90.3	355.6	137.8	92.5	26.4	36.6	62.3	77.8
III	599.8	526.6	130.4	21.9	108.5	396.2	153.0	102.4	31.0	42.4	67.4	73.2

[1] Consists of the following industries: Depository institutions; nondepository credit institutions; security and commodity brokers; insurance carriers; regulated investment companies; small business investment companies; and real estate investment trusts.
[2] See Table B–88 for industry detail.

Note.—The industry classification is on a company basis and is based on the 1987 Standard Industrial Classification (SIC) beginning 1987, and on the 1972 SIC for earlier years shown.

Source: Department of Commerce, Bureau of Economic Analysis.

[Billions of dollars; quarterly data at seasonally adjusted annual rates]

Year or quarter	Total manufac-turing	Corporate profits with inventory valuation adjustment and without capital consumption adjustment											
		Durable goods							Nondurable goods				
		Total	Primary metal indus-tries	Fabri-cated metal prod-ucts	Indus-trial machin-ery and equip-ment	Elec-tronic and other electric equip-ment	Motor vehicles and equip-ment	Other	Total	Food and kindred prod-ucts	Chem-icals and al-lied prod-ucts	Petro-leum and coal prod-ucts	Other
1959	26.5	13.7	2.3	1.1	2.2	1.7	3.0	3.5	12.8	2.5	3.5	2.6	4.3
1960	23.8	11.7	2.0	.8	1.8	1.3	3.0	2.8	12.1	2.2	3.1	2.6	4.2
1961	23.4	11.4	1.6	1.0	1.9	1.3	2.5	3.1	12.0	2.4	3.3	2.2	4.2
1962	26.3	14.1	1.6	1.2	2.4	1.5	4.0	3.5	12.2	2.4	3.2	2.2	4.4
1963	29.6	16.4	2.0	1.3	2.5	1.6	4.9	4.0	13.2	2.7	3.7	2.2	4.7
1964	32.4	18.0	2.5	1.4	3.3	1.7	4.6	4.5	14.4	2.7	4.1	2.3	5.3
1965	39.7	23.2	3.1	2.1	4.0	2.7	6.2	5.2	16.4	2.8	4.6	2.9	6.1
1966	42.4	23.9	3.6	2.4	4.5	3.0	5.1	5.3	18.4	3.3	4.9	3.4	6.8
1967	39.0	21.2	2.7	2.5	4.1	3.0	4.0	5.0	17.8	3.2	4.3	3.9	6.4
1968	41.7	22.4	1.9	2.3	4.1	2.9	5.5	5.7	19.2	3.2	5.2	3.7	7.0
1969	37.0	19.0	1.4	2.0	3.7	2.3	4.8	4.9	18.0	3.0	4.6	3.3	7.0
1970	27.1	10.4	.8	1.1	3.0	1.3	1.3	3.0	16.8	3.2	3.9	3.6	6.1
1971	34.8	16.6	.8	1.5	3.0	1.9	5.1	4.2	18.2	3.5	4.5	3.7	6.5
1972	41.4	22.6	1.6	2.2	4.3	2.8	5.9	5.7	18.8	2.9	5.2	3.2	7.5
1973	46.7	25.0	2.3	2.6	4.7	3.2	5.9	6.3	21.7	2.5	6.1	5.2	7.9
1974	40.7	15.1	5.0	1.8	3.1	.5	.7	4.1	25.7	2.6	5.2	10.7	7.2
1975	54.5	20.3	2.7	3.2	4.8	2.6	2.2	4.8	34.1	8.6	6.3	9.8	9.4
1976	70.7	31.2	2.1	3.9	6.7	3.8	7.4	7.4	39.5	7.1	8.2	13.3	11.0
1977	78.5	37.6	1.0	4.5	8.3	5.8	9.3	8.6	41.0	6.8	7.7	12.9	13.6
1978	89.6	45.0	3.6	5.0	10.4	6.6	8.9	10.5	44.6	6.1	8.2	15.5	14.8
1979	88.3	36.5	3.5	5.2	9.1	5.4	4.6	8.6	51.8	5.8	7.1	24.5	14.6
1980	75.8	17.9	2.6	4.3	7.5	5.0	-4.3	2.8	57.8	6.0	5.5	33.6	12.9
1981	87.5	18.1	3.0	4.4	8.2	4.9	.2	-2.7	69.4	9.0	7.6	38.6	14.2
1982	63.4	4.9	-4.7	2.6	3.4	1.3	-.3	2.7	58.5	7.3	4.7	31.6	14.9
1983	72.8	18.6	-5.0	3.0	3.7	3.4	5.2	8.3	54.2	6.1	6.9	22.5	18.6
1984	86.6	36.7	-.5	4.6	5.5	5.1	8.9	13.0	49.9	6.5	7.7	16.1	19.6
1985	81.6	30.1	-.8	4.7	5.5	2.5	7.3	10.8	51.6	8.6	6.1	17.3	19.6
1986	60.2	28.6	.9	5.2	2.7	2.7	4.4	12.7	31.7	7.3	8.0	-5.8	22.1
1987	85.0	40.1	2.7	5.4	4.7	6.5	3.8	17.0	45.0	11.3	15.1	-3.8	22.4
1988	115.1	49.2	5.9	6.3	9.4	5.7	5.7	16.2	65.9	11.9	19.3	10.4	24.3
1989	109.3	49.3	6.0	6.5	11.1	9.5	2.2	13.9	60.0	11.0	19.0	5.0	25.0
1990	112.3	40.9	3.3	6.2	10.2	8.4	-2.2	15.0	71.4	14.5	17.0	17.0	22.9
1991	92.7	30.5	1.3	5.4	4.3	8.9	-5.4	16.0	62.1	18.2	15.7	5.9	22.3
1992	96.3	37.1	-.1	6.5	5.6	10.0	-1.1	16.2	59.1	18.3	16.5	-1.6	26.0
1993	109.7	54.2	.2	7.7	7.0	14.8	4.2	20.3	55.5	16.2	16.4	-2.2	25.1
1994	142.7	77.2	.7	10.7	9.0	22.5	10.2	24.1	65.5	19.1	18.0	-.1	28.4
1990: I	115.9	48.9	5.6	7.6	12.4	10.3	-4.0	17.0	67.0	9.5	18.1	15.7	23.7
II	125.1	44.6	3.7	6.5	10.4	9.5	.0	14.6	80.5	14.9	20.2	21.3	24.2
III	99.8	42.3	1.5	5.6	10.0	8.5	1.9	14.8	57.5	16.1	17.0	-.3	24.7
IV	108.4	27.9	2.6	5.0	7.9	5.4	-6.6	13.7	80.5	17.5	12.6	31.4	19.0
1991: I	104.3	22.6	1.7	3.6	5.4	7.4	-9.6	14.1	81.7	17.7	12.9	32.4	18.7
II	91.7	35.3	1.5	6.2	5.0	9.9	-5.2	18.0	56.3	17.6	14.5	1.7	22.5
III	90.8	32.2	1.1	5.6	2.0	8.6	-2.3	17.1	58.6	21.5	17.0	-6.1	26.3
IV	83.8	31.9	1.0	6.1	5.0	9.7	-4.7	14.8	51.9	16.1	18.5	-4.5	21.9
1992: I	92.0	33.4	.5	6.2	4.7	9.8	-2.0	14.2	58.6	15.9	17.1	1.8	23.8
II	89.6	35.3	.3	6.4	5.4	8.5	-.2	14.8	54.3	20.2	15.2	-6.9	25.8
III	98.4	37.2	-.5	7.2	6.0	9.7	-2.8	17.6	61.2	20.0	16.2	-1.8	26.8
IV	105.1	42.6	-.8	6.4	6.4	11.8	.4	18.4	62.4	17.2	17.3	.4	27.6
1993: I	90.4	36.9	-1.2	5.3	3.8	12.6	-.4	16.9	53.5	18.8	17.5	-8.7	25.9
II	108.4	52.4	1.4	7.8	7.1	11.9	4.2	20.1	56.0	15.2	15.3	-1.6	27.1
III	106.0	55.4	-.5	8.1	9.1	15.9	2.3	20.5	50.7	16.0	15.3	-2.6	21.9
IV	134.0	72.1	1.3	9.5	7.9	18.8	10.7	23.8	61.9	14.6	17.5	4.2	25.6
1994: I	145.3	76.0	.6	10.9	8.7	18.9	14.2	22.7	69.3	19.5	17.6	.5	31.7
II	134.2	75.1	.9	10.6	9.1	21.2	9.5	23.8	59.1	18.0	18.5	-8.2	30.8
III	142.8	75.6	.8	10.2	8.0	23.8	8.5	24.3	67.1	19.7	17.0	3.3	27.1
IV	148.4	81.8	.4	11.1	10.1	26.1	8.6	25.5	66.7	19.4	19.0	4.2	24.2
1995: I	134.7	75.8	2.2	10.2	12.5	23.2	6.7	21.0	58.8	18.3	16.8	-2.3	26.0
II	137.8	74.0	4.7	11.5	12.1	22.4	3.0	20.4	63.8	18.4	21.3	-.2	24.3
III	153.0	78.1	3.2	11.8	12.6	27.5	4.4	20.2	74.9	16.7	23.5	5.3	29.3

Note.—The industry classification is on a company basis and is based on the 1987 Standard Industrial Classification (SIC) beginning 1987 and on the 1972 SIC for earlier years shown. In the 1972 SIC, the categories shown here as "industrial machinery and equipment" and "electronic and other electric equipment" were identified as "machinery, except electrical" and "electric and electronic equipment," respectively.

Source: Department of Commerce, Bureau of Economic Analysis.

TABLE B–89.—*Sales, profits, and stockholders' equity, all manufacturing corporations, 1952–95*

[Billions of dollars]

Year or quarter	All manufacturing corporations				Durable goods industries				Nondurable goods industries			
	Sales (net)	Profits Before income taxes[1]	Profits After income taxes	Stock-holders' equity[2]	Sales (net)	Profits Before income taxes[1]	After income taxes	Stock-holders' equity[2]	Sales (net)	Profits Before income taxes[1]	After income taxes	Stock-holders' equity[2]
1952	250.2	22.9	10.7	103.7	122.0	12.9	5.5	49.8	128.0	10.0	5.2	53.9
1953	265.9	24.4	11.3	108.2	137.9	14.0	5.8	52.4	128.0	10.4	5.5	55.7
1954	248.5	20.9	11.2	113.1	122.8	11.4	5.6	54.9	125.7	9.6	5.6	58.2
1955	278.4	28.6	15.1	120.1	142.1	16.5	8.1	58.8	136.3	12.1	7.0	61.3
1956	307.3	29.8	16.2	131.6	159.5	16.5	8.3	65.2	147.8	13.2	7.8	66.4
1957	320.0	28.2	15.4	141.1	166.0	15.8	7.9	70.5	154.1	12.4	7.5	70.6
1958	305.3	22.7	12.7	147.4	148.6	11.4	5.8	72.8	156.7	11.3	6.9	74.6
1959	338.0	29.7	16.3	157.1	169.4	15.8	8.1	77.9	168.5	13.9	8.3	79.2
1960	345.7	27.5	15.2	165.4	173.9	14.0	7.0	82.3	171.8	13.5	8.2	83.1
1961	356.4	27.5	15.3	172.6	175.2	13.6	6.9	84.9	181.2	13.9	8.5	87.7
1962	389.4	31.9	17.7	181.4	195.3	16.8	8.6	89.1	194.1	15.1	9.2	92.3
1963	412.7	34.9	19.5	189.7	209.0	18.5	9.5	93.3	203.6	16.4	10.0	96.3
1964	443.1	39.6	23.2	199.8	226.3	21.2	11.6	98.5	216.8	18.3	11.6	101.3
1965	492.2	46.5	27.5	211.7	257.0	26.2	14.5	105.4	235.2	20.3	13.0	106.3
1966	554.2	51.8	30.9	230.3	291.7	29.2	16.4	115.2	262.4	22.6	14.6	115.1
1967	575.4	47.8	29.0	247.6	300.6	25.7	14.6	125.0	274.8	22.0	14.4	122.6
1968	631.9	55.4	32.1	265.9	335.5	30.6	16.5	135.6	296.4	24.8	15.5	130.3
1969	694.6	58.1	33.2	289.9	366.5	31.5	16.9	147.6	328.1	26.6	16.4	142.3
1970	708.8	48.1	28.6	306.8	363.1	23.0	12.9	155.1	345.7	25.2	15.7	151.7
1971	751.1	52.9	31.0	320.8	381.8	26.5	14.5	160.4	369.3	26.5	16.5	160.5
1972	849.5	63.2	36.5	343.4	435.8	33.6	18.4	171.4	413.7	29.6	18.0	172.0
1973	1,017.2	81.4	48.1	374.1	527.3	43.6	24.8	188.7	489.9	37.8	23.3	185.4
1973: IV	275.1	21.4	13.0	386.4	140.1	10.8	6.3	194.7	135.0	10.6	6.7	191.7
New series:												
1973: IV	236.6	20.6	13.2	368.0	122.7	10.1	6.2	185.8	113.9	10.5	7.0	182.1
1974	1,060.6	92.1	58.7	395.0	529.0	41.1	24.7	196.0	531.6	51.0	34.1	199.0
1975	1,065.2	79.9	49.1	423.4	521.1	35.3	21.4	208.1	544.1	44.6	27.7	215.3
1976	1,203.2	104.9	64.5	462.7	589.6	50.7	30.8	224.3	613.7	54.3	33.7	238.4
1977	1,328.1	115.1	70.4	496.7	657.3	57.9	34.8	239.9	670.8	57.2	35.5	256.8
1978	1,496.4	132.5	81.1	540.5	760.7	69.6	41.8	262.6	735.7	62.9	39.3	277.9
1979	1,741.8	154.2	98.7	600.5	865.7	72.4	45.2	292.5	876.1	81.8	53.5	308.0
1980	1,912.8	145.8	92.6	668.1	889.1	57.4	35.6	317.7	1,023.7	88.4	56.9	350.4
1981	2,144.7	158.6	101.3	743.4	979.5	67.2	41.6	350.4	1,165.2	91.3	59.6	393.0
1982	2,039.4	108.2	70.9	770.2	913.1	34.7	21.7	355.5	1,126.4	73.6	49.3	414.7
1983	2,114.3	133.1	85.8	812.8	973.5	48.7	30.0	372.4	1,140.8	84.4	55.8	440.4
1984	2,335.0	165.6	107.6	864.2	1,107.6	75.5	48.9	395.6	1,227.5	90.0	58.8	468.5
1985	2,331.4	137.0	87.6	866.2	1,142.6	61.5	38.6	420.9	1,188.8	75.6	49.1	445.3
1986	2,220.9	129.3	83.1	874.7	1,125.5	52.1	32.6	436.3	1,095.4	77.2	50.5	438.4
1987	2,378.2	173.0	115.6	900.9	1,178.0	78.0	53.0	444.3	1,200.3	95.1	62.6	456.6
1988	2,596.2	216.1	154.6	957.6	1,284.7	91.7	67.1	468.7	1,311.5	124.4	87.5	488.9
1989	2,745.1	188.8	136.3	999.0	1,356.6	75.2	55.7	501.3	1,388.5	113.5	80.6	497.7
1990	2,810.7	159.6	111.6	1,043.8	1,357.2	57.6	40.9	515.0	1,453.5	102.0	70.6	528.9
1991	2,761.1	99.8	67.5	1,064.1	1,304.0	14.1	7.4	506.8	1,457.1	85.7	60.1	557.4
1992[3]	2,890.2	32.5	23.2	1,034.7	1,389.8	-33.5	-23.7	473.9	1,500.4	66.0	47.0	560.8
1993	3,015.1	118.6	83.9	1,039.7	1,490.2	39.0	27.6	482.7	1,524.9	79.6	56.4	557.1
1994	3,258.4	245.3	176.6	1,110.2	1,658.7	121.7	87.7	533.6	1,599.7	123.6	88.9	576.6
1993: I[3]	717.7	11.3	11.1	1,019.5	349.5	-5.7	-1.7	464.8	368.2	17.0	12.8	554.7
II	767.4	37.6	25.2	1,035.1	381.0	15.7	9.4	479.8	386.4	21.9	15.9	555.3
III	752.5	37.7	25.0	1,047.1	368.3	16.2	11.5	492.0	384.2	21.5	13.5	555.0
IV	777.5	32.0	22.6	1,057.3	391.5	12.8	8.4	494.0	386.0	19.2	14.2	563.3
1994: I	758.0	50.2	35.5	1,072.8	384.1	23.3	16.3	504.0	373.9	26.9	19.2	568.8
II	819.7	65.1	47.0	1,094.3	421.0	36.6	26.7	522.9	398.7	28.5	20.3	571.4
III	823.2	65.6	46.9	1,120.4	412.9	30.8	22.4	541.7	410.3	34.8	24.5	578.6
IV	857.5	64.4	47.3	1,153.2	440.6	31.0	22.3	565.8	416.8	33.4	24.9	587.4
1995: I	845.4	73.5	52.6	1,194.4	432.6	36.3	26.0	589.4	412.8	37.3	26.6	605.0
II	890.4	79.4	57.2	1,233.6	456.3	39.3	29.0	614.1	434.2	40.1	28.2	619.4
III	880.9	71.3	51.2	1,252.2	445.2	30.4	21.9	625.7	435.7	40.9	29.3	626.4

[1] In the old series, "income taxes" refers to Federal income taxes only, as State and local income taxes had already been deducted. In the new series, no income taxes have been deducted.

[2] Annual data are average equity for the year (using four end-of-quarter figures).

[3] Data for 1992 (most significantly 1992:I) reflect the early adoption of Financial Accounting Standards Board Statement 106 (Employer's Accounting for Post-Retirement Benefits Other Than Pensions) by a large number of companies during the fourth quarter of 1992. Data for 1993:I also reflect adoption of Statement 106. Corporations must show the cumulative effect of a change in accounting principle in the first quarter of the year in which the change is adopted.

Note.—Data are not necessarily comparable from one period to another due to changes in accounting principles, industry classifications, sampling procedures, etc. For explanatory notes concerning compilation of the series, see "Quarterly Financial Report for Manufacturing, Mining, and Trade Corporations," Department of Commerce, Bureau of the Census.

Source: Department of Commerce, Bureau of the Census.

TABLE B–90.—*Relation of profits after taxes to stockholders' equity and to sales, all manufacturing corporations, 1947–95*

Year or quarter	Ratio of profits after income taxes (annual rate) to stockholders' equity—percent [1]			Profits after income taxes per dollar of sales—cents		
	All manufacturing corporations	Durable goods industries	Nondurable goods industries	All manufacturing corporations	Durable goods industries	Nondurable goods industries
1947	15.6	14.4	16.6	6.7	6.7	6.7
1948	16.0	15.7	16.2	7.0	7.1	6.8
1949	11.6	12.1	11.2	5.8	6.4	5.4
1950	15.4	16.9	14.1	7.1	7.7	6.5
1951	12.1	13.0	11.2	4.9	5.3	4.5
1952	10.3	11.1	9.7	4.3	4.5	4.1
1953	10.5	11.1	9.9	4.3	4.2	4.3
1954	9.9	10.3	9.6	4.5	4.6	4.4
1955	12.6	13.8	11.4	5.4	5.7	5.1
1956	12.3	12.8	11.8	5.3	5.2	5.3
1957	10.9	11.3	10.6	4.8	4.8	4.9
1958	8.6	8.0	9.2	4.2	3.9	4.4
1959	10.4	10.4	10.4	4.8	4.8	4.9
1960	9.2	8.5	9.8	4.4	4.0	4.8
1961	8.9	8.1	9.6	4.3	3.9	4.7
1962	9.8	9.6	9.9	4.5	4.4	4.7
1963	10.3	10.1	10.4	4.7	4.5	4.9
1964	11.6	11.7	11.5	5.2	5.1	5.4
1965	13.0	13.8	12.2	5.6	5.7	5.5
1966	13.4	14.2	12.7	5.6	5.6	5.6
1967	11.7	11.7	11.8	5.0	4.8	5.3
1968	12.1	12.2	11.9	5.1	4.9	5.2
1969	11.5	11.4	11.5	4.8	4.6	5.0
1970	9.3	8.3	10.3	4.0	3.5	4.5
1971	9.7	9.0	10.3	4.1	3.8	4.5
1972	10.6	10.8	10.5	4.3	4.2	4.4
1973	12.8	13.1	12.6	4.7	4.7	4.8
1973: IV	13.4	12.9	14.0	4.7	4.5	5.0
New series:						
1973: IV	14.3	13.3	15.3	5.6	5.0	6.1
1974	14.9	12.6	17.1	5.5	4.7	6.4
1975	11.6	10.3	12.9	4.6	4.1	5.1
1976	13.9	13.7	14.2	5.4	5.2	5.5
1977	14.2	14.5	13.8	5.3	5.3	5.3
1978	15.0	16.0	14.2	5.4	5.5	5.3
1979	16.4	15.4	17.4	5.7	5.2	6.1
1980	13.9	11.2	16.3	4.8	4.0	5.6
1981	13.6	11.9	15.2	4.7	4.2	5.1
1982	9.2	6.1	11.9	3.5	2.4	4.4
1983	10.6	8.1	12.7	4.1	3.1	4.9
1984	12.5	12.4	12.5	4.6	4.4	4.8
1985	10.1	9.2	11.0	3.8	3.4	4.1
1986	9.5	7.5	11.5	3.7	2.9	4.6
1987	12.8	11.9	13.7	4.9	4.5	5.2
1988	16.1	14.3	17.9	6.0	5.2	6.7
1989	13.6	11.1	16.2	5.0	4.1	5.8
1990	10.7	8.0	13.4	4.0	3.0	4.9
1991	6.3	1.5	10.8	2.4	.6	4.1
1992 [2]	2.2	−5.0	8.4	.8	−1.7	3.1
1993	8.1	5.7	10.1	2.8	1.9	3.7
1994	15.9	16.4	15.4	5.4	5.3	5.6
1993: I [2]	4.4	−1.5	9.3	1.6	−.5	3.5
II	9.7	7.8	11.4	3.3	2.5	4.1
III	9.5	9.3	9.7	3.3	3.1	3.5
IV	8.5	6.8	10.1	2.9	2.1	3.7
1994: I	13.2	12.9	13.5	4.7	4.2	5.1
II	17.2	20.4	14.2	5.7	6.3	5.1
III	16.7	16.6	16.9	5.7	5.4	6.0
IV	16.4	15.8	17.0	5.5	5.1	6.0
1995: I	17.6	17.7	17.6	6.2	6.0	6.4
II	18.6	18.9	18.2	6.4	6.4	6.5
III	16.4	14.0	18.7	5.8	4.9	6.7

[1] Annual ratios based on average equity for the year (using four end-of-quarter figures). Quarterly ratios based on equity at end of quarter only.
[2] See footnote 3, Table B–89.
Note.—Based on data in millions of dollars.
See Note, Table B–89.
Source: Department of Commerce, Bureau of the Census.

—*Common stock prices and yields, 1955–95*

Year or month	Common stock prices [1]							Common stock yields (S&P)(percent) [4]	
	New York Stock Exchange indexes (Dec. 31, 1965=50) [2]					Dow Jones industrial average [2]	Standard & Poor's composite index (1941–43=10) [2]	Dividend-price ratio [5]	Earnings-price ratio [6]
	Composite	Industrial	Transportation	Utility [3]	Finance				
1955	21.54					442.72	40.49	4.08	7.95
1956	24.40					493.01	46.62	4.09	7.55
1957	23.67					475.71	44.38	4.35	7.89
1958	24.56					491.66	46.24	3.97	6.23
1959	30.73					632.12	57.38	3.23	5.78
1960	30.01					618.04	55.85	3.47	5.90
1961	35.37					691.55	66.27	2.98	4.62
1962	33.49					639.76	62.38	3.37	5.82
1963	37.51					714.81	69.87	3.17	5.50
1964	43.76					834.05	81.37	3.01	5.32
1965	47.39					910.88	88.17	3.00	5.59
1966	46.15	46.18	50.26	90.81	44.45	873.60	85.26	3.40	6.63
1967	50.77	51.97	53.51	90.86	49.82	879.12	91.93	3.20	5.73
1968	55.37	58.00	50.58	88.38	65.85	906.00	98.70	3.07	5.67
1969	54.67	57.44	46.96	85.60	70.49	876.72	97.84	3.24	6.08
1970	45.72	48.03	32.14	74.47	60.00	753.19	83.22	3.83	6.45
1971	54.22	57.92	44.35	79.05	70.38	884.76	98.29	3.14	5.41
1972	60.29	65.73	50.17	76.95	78.35	950.71	109.20	2.84	5.50
1973	57.42	63.08	37.74	75.38	70.12	923.88	107.43	3.06	7.12
1974	43.84	48.08	31.89	59.58	49.67	759.37	82.85	4.47	11.59
1975	45.73	50.52	31.10	63.00	47.14	802.49	86.16	4.31	9.15
1976	54.46	60.44	39.57	73.94	52.94	974.92	102.01	3.77	8.90
1977	53.69	57.86	41.09	81.84	55.25	894.63	98.20	4.62	10.79
1978	53.70	58.23	43.50	78.44	56.65	820.23	96.02	5.28	12.03
1979	58.32	64.76	47.34	76.41	61.42	844.40	103.01	5.47	13.46
1980	68.10	78.70	60.61	74.69	64.25	891.41	118.78	5.26	12.66
1981	74.02	85.44	72.61	77.81	73.52	932.92	128.05	5.20	11.96
1982	68.93	78.18	60.41	79.49	71.99	884.36	119.71	5.81	11.60
1983	92.63	107.45	89.36	93.99	95.34	1,190.34	160.41	4.40	8.03
1984	92.46	108.01	85.63	92.89	89.28	1,178.48	160.46	4.64	10.02
1985	108.09	123.79	104.11	113.49	114.21	1,328.23	186.84	4.25	8.12
1986	136.00	155.85	119.87	142.72	147.20	1,792.76	236.34	3.49	6.09
1987	161.70	195.31	140.39	148.57	146.48	2,275.99	286.83	3.08	5.48
1988	149.91	180.95	134.12	143.53	127.26	2,060.82	265.79	3.64	8.01
1989	180.02	216.23	175.28	174.87	151.88	2,508.91	322.84	3.45	7.41
1990	183.46	225.78	158.62	181.20	133.26	2,678.94	334.59	3.61	6.47
1991	206.33	258.14	173.99	185.32	150.82	2,929.33	376.18	3.24	4.79
1992	229.01	284.62	201.09	198.91	179.26	3,284.29	415.74	2.99	4.22
1993	249.58	299.99	242.49	228.90	216.42	3,522.06	451.41	2.78	4.46
1994	254.12	315.25	247.29	209.06	209.73	3,793.77	460.33	2.82	5.83
1995	291.15	367.34	269.41	220.30	238.45	4,493.76	541.64	2.56	....
1994: Jan	262.11	320.92	278.29	225.15	218.71	3,868.36	472.99	2.69	....
Feb	261.97	322.41	276.67	220.85	217.12	3,905.62	471.58	2.70	....
Mar	257.32	318.08	265.68	215.45	211.02	3,816.98	463.81	2.78	5.09
Apr	247.97	304.48	250.43	210.08	208.12	3,661.48	447.23	2.90	....
May	249.56	307.58	244.75	205.77	211.30	3,707.99	450.90	2.89	....
June	251.21	308.66	246.64	206.54	215.89	3,737.58	454.83	2.84	5.67
July	249.29	307.34	244.21	205.46	210.91	3,718.30	451.40	2.87	....
Aug	256.08	316.55	244.67	211.26	214.77	3,797.48	464.24	2.78	....
Sept	257.61	322.19	239.10	204.60	211.90	3,880.60	466.96	2.80	5.91
Oct	255.22	321.53	230.71	203.35	203.33	3,868.10	463.81	2.82	....
Nov	252.48	319.33	227.45	200.13	198.38	3,792.43	461.01	2.86	....
Dec	248.65	313.92	218.93	200.02	195.25	3,770.31	455.19	2.91	6.66
1995: Jan	253.56	319.93	230.25	201.16	201.05	3,872.46	465.25	2.87	....
Feb	261.86	328.98	237.29	207.73	211.76	3,953.72	481.92	2.81	....
Mar	266.81	337.96	244.45	204.16	213.29	4,062.78	493.15	2.76	6.51
Apr	274.37	347.69	254.36	208.93	219.38	4,230.66	507.91	2.68	....
May	281.81	357.01	254.69	211.58	228.55	4,391.57	523.81	2.60	....
June	289.52	366.75	256.80	216.27	236.26	4,510.76	539.35	2.55	6.32
July	298.18	379.13	279.15	219.18	240.50	4,684.76	557.37	2.50	....
Aug	300.05	379.79	285.63	221.99	245.27	4,639.27	559.11	2.49	....
Sept	310.41	390.42	295.54	229.64	260.72	4,746.76	578.77	2.42	6.01
Oct	311.78	389.63	291.16	236.43	265.12	4,760.46	582.92	2.41	....
Nov	317.58	398.66	300.06	238.98	266.12	4,935.81	595.53	2.37	....
Dec	327.90	412.11	303.53	247.59	273.36	5,136.10	614.57	2.30	....

[1] Averages of daily closing prices, except NYSE data through May 1964 are averages of weekly closing prices.
[2] Includes stocks as follows: for NYSE, all stocks listed (more than 2,000); for Dow-Jones industrial average, 30 stocks; and for S&P composite index, 500 stocks.
[3] Effective April 1993, the NYSE doubled the value of the utility index to facilitate trading of options and futures on the index. Annual indexes prior to 1993 reflect the doubling.
[4] Based on 500 stocks in the S&P composite index.
[5] Aggregate cash dividends (based on latest known annual rate) divided by aggregate market value based on Wednesday closing prices. Monthly data are averages of weekly figures; annual data are averages of monthly figures.
[6] Quarterly data are ratio of earnings (after taxes) for 4 quarters ending with particular quarter to price index for last day of that quarter. Annual data are averages of quarterly ratios.

Note.—All data relate to stocks listed on the New York Stock Exchange.

Sources: New York Stock Exchange (NYSE), Dow Jones & Co., Inc., and Standard & Poor's Corporation (S&P).

TABLE B–92.—Business formation and business failures, 1950–95

Year or month	Index of net business formation (1967= 100)	New business incorporations (number)	Business failure rate [2]	Business failures [1] — Number of failures: Total	Under $100,000	$100,000 and over	Amount of current liabilities (millions of dollars): Total	Under $100,000	$100,000 and over
1950	87.7	93,092	34.3	9,162	8,746	416	248.3	151.2	97.1
1951	86.7	83,778	30.7	8,058	7,626	432	259.5	131.6	128.0
1952	90.8	92,946	28.7	7,611	7,081	530	283.3	131.9	151.4
1953	89.7	102,706	33.2	8,862	8,075	787	394.2	167.5	226.6
1954	88.8	117,411	42.0	11,086	10,226	860	462.6	211.4	251.2
1955	96.6	139,915	41.6	10,969	10,113	856	449.4	206.4	243.0
1956	94.6	141,163	48.0	12,686	11,615	1,071	562.7	239.8	322.9
1957	90.3	137,112	51.7	13,739	12,547	1,192	615.3	267.1	348.2
1958	90.2	150,781	55.9	14,964	13,499	1,465	728.3	297.6	430.7
1959	97.9	193,067	51.8	14,053	12,707	1,346	692.8	278.9	413.9
1960	94.5	182,713	57.0	15,445	13,650	1,795	938.6	327.2	611.4
1961	90.8	181,535	64.4	17,075	15,006	2,069	1,090.1	370.1	720.0
1962	92.6	182,057	60.8	15,782	13,772	2,010	1,213.6	346.5	867.1
1963	94.4	186,404	56.3	14,374	12,192	2,182	1,352.6	321.0	1,031.6
1964	98.2	197,724	53.2	13,501	11,346	2,155	1,329.2	313.6	1,015.6
1965	99.8	203,897	53.3	13,514	11,340	2,174	1,321.7	321.7	1,000.0
1966	99.3	200,010	51.6	13,061	10,833	2,228	1,385.7	321.5	1,064.1
1967	100.0	206,569	49.0	12,364	10,144	2,220	1,265.2	297.9	967.3
1968	108.3	233,635	38.6	9,636	7,829	1,807	941.0	241.1	699.9
1969	115.8	274,267	37.3	9,154	7,192	1,962	1,142.1	231.3	910.8
1970	108.8	264,209	43.8	10,748	8,019	2,729	1,887.8	269.3	1,618.4
1971	111.1	287,577	41.7	10,326	7,611	2,715	1,916.9	271.3	1,645.6
1972	119.3	316,601	38.3	9,566	7,040	2,526	2,000.2	258.8	1,741.5
1973	119.1	329,358	36.4	9,345	6,627	2,718	2,298.6	235.6	2,063.0
1974	113.2	319,149	38.4	9,915	6,733	3,182	3,053.1	256.9	2,796.3
1975	109.9	326,345	42.6	11,432	7,504	3,928	4,380.2	298.6	4,081.6
1976	120.4	375,766	34.8	9,628	6,176	3,452	3,011.3	257.8	2,753.4
1977	130.8	436,170	28.4	7,919	4,861	3,058	3,095.3	208.3	2,887.0
1978	138.1	478,019	23.9	6,619	3,712	2,907	2,656.0	164.7	2,491.3
1979	138.3	524,565	27.8	7,564	3,930	3,634	2,667.4	179.9	2,487.5
1980	129.9	533,520	42.1	11,742	5,682	6,060	4,635.1	272.5	4,362.6
1981	124.8	581,242	61.3	16,794	8,233	8,561	6,955.2	405.8	6,549.3
1982	116.4	566,942	88.4	24,908	11,509	13,399	15,610.8	541.7	15,069.1
1983	117.5	600,420	109.7	31,334	15,572	15,762	16,072.9	635.1	15,437.8
1984	121.3	634,991	107.0	52,078	33,527	18,551	29,268.6	409.8	28,858.8
1985	120.9	664,235	115.0	57,253	36,551	20,702	36,937.4	423.9	36,513.5
1986	120.4	702,738	120.0	61,616	38,908	22,708	44,724.0	838.3	43,885.7
1987	121.2	685,572	102.0	61,111	38,949	22,162	34,723.8	746.0	33,977.8
1988	124.1	685,095	98.0	57,097	38,300	18,797	39,573.0	686.9	38,886.1
1989	124.8	676,565	65.0	50,361	33,312	17,049	42,328.8	670.5	41,658.2
1990	120.7	647,366	74.0	60,747	40,833	19,914	56,130.1	735.6	55,394.5
1991	115.2	628,604	107.0	88,140	60,617	27,523	96,825.3	1,044.9	95,780.4
1992	116.3	666,800	110.0	97,069	68,264	28,805	94,317.5	1,096.7	93,220.8
1993	121.1	706,537	109.0	86,133	61,188	24,945	47,755.5	947.6	46,807.9
1994	125.5	741,657	86.0	71,558	50,814	20,744	28,977.9	845.0	28,132.9
1995	....	....	....	71,194	49,476	21,718	37,507.4	866.3	36,641.1
	Seasonally adjusted								
1994: Jan	125.4	61,978	....	5,784	4,043	1,741	2,556.7	66.5	2,490.2
Feb	124.9	60,680	....	5,901	4,166	1,735	2,430.8	68.8	2,362.0
Mar	127.0	64,058	....	7,133	5,107	2,026	2,181.9	82.9	2,099.1
Apr	125.2	58,992	....	5,243	3,732	1,511	1,642.5	62.6	1,579.9
May	124.7	58,528	....	6,571	4,643	1,928	2,529.9	78.4	2,451.5
June	125.6	63,097	....	6,159	4,367	1,792	2,205.6	73.6	2,132.0
July	122.7	56,380	....	5,436	3,809	1,627	2,212.8	63.7	2,149.1
Aug	125.8	64,844	....	6,476	4,556	1,920	2,106.8	76.7	2,030.1
Sept	125.3	64,564	....	6,001	4,276	1,725	3,434.0	74.3	3,359.7
Oct	124.6	60,488	....	5,915	4,327	1,588	2,023.1	72.1	1,951.0
Nov	127.9	64,542	....	5,534	3,930	1,604	2,511.8	63.7	2,448.2
Dec	127.3	62,908	....	5,405	3,858	1,547	3,141.9	61.8	3,080.1
1995: Jan	127.8	66,291	....	6,301	4,518	1,783	2,240.0	69.2	2,170.7
Feb	128.1	64,755	....	5,667	4,036	1,631	1,260.4	67.1	1,193.3
Mar	129.6	65,386	....	6,689	4,720	1,969	1,931.9	80.5	1,851.4
Apr	128.4	58,261	....	5,600	3,841	1,759	1,722.2	70.4	1,651.8
May	127.8	65,827	....	6,410	4,369	2,041	3,090.1	81.9	3,008.2
June	126.7	....	....	5,908	4,036	1,872	1,311.2	76.0	1,235.2
July	127.4	....	....	4,682	3,189	1,493	2,311.9	58.6	2,253.3
Aug	128.6	....	....	6,346	4,381	1,965	2,221.6	79.1	2,142.5
Sept	125.9	....	....	5,424	3,744	1,680	2,487.2	67.1	2,420.0
Oct	125.9	....	....	6,566	4,629	1,937	14,754.5	79.0	14,675.6
Nov	....	....	....	6,096	4,283	1,813	2,045.8	73.3	1,972.5
Dec	....	....	....	5,505	3,730	1,775	2,130.8	64.1	2,066.7

[1] Commercial and industrial failures only through 1983, excluding failures of banks, railroads, real estate, insurance, holding, and financial companies, steamship lines, travel agencies, etc.

Data beginning 1984 are based on expanded coverage and new methodology and are therefore not generally comparable with earlier data. Data for 1995 are subject to revision due to amended court filings.

[2] Failure rate per 10,000 listed enterprises.

Sources: Department of Commerce (Bureau of Economic Analysis) and The Dun & Bradstreet Corporation.

TABLE B–93.—*Farm income, 1945–95*

[Billions of dollars; quarterly data at seasonally adjusted annual rates]

Year or quarter	Income of farm operators from farming						Net farm income
	Gross farm income					Production expenses	
	Total [1]	Cash marketing receipts			Value of inventory changes [2]		
		Total	Livestock and products	Crops			
1945	25.4	21.7	12.0	9.7	−0.4	13.1	12.3
1946	29.6	24.8	13.8	11.0	.0	14.5	15.1
1947	32.4	29.6	16.5	13.1	−1.8	17.0	15.4
1948	36.5	30.2	17.1	13.1	1.7	18.8	17.7
1949	30.8	27.8	15.4	12.4	−.9	18.0	12.8
1950	33.1	28.5	16.1	12.4	.8	19.5	13.6
1951	38.3	32.9	19.6	13.2	1.2	22.3	15.9
1952	37.8	32.5	18.2	14.3	.9	22.8	15.0
1953	34.4	31.0	16.9	14.1	−.6	21.5	13.0
1954	34.2	29.8	16.3	13.6	.5	21.8	12.4
1955	33.5	29.5	16.0	13.5	.2	22.2	11.3
1956	34.0	30.4	16.4	14.0	−.5	22.7	11.3
1957	34.8	29.7	17.4	12.3	.6	23.7	11.1
1958	39.0	33.5	19.2	14.2	.8	25.8	13.2
1959	37.9	33.6	18.9	14.7	.0	27.2	10.7
1960	38.6	34.0	19.0	15.0	.4	27.4	11.2
1961	40.5	35.2	19.5	15.7	.3	28.6	12.0
1962	42.3	36.5	20.2	16.3	.6	30.3	12.1
1963	43.4	37.5	20.0	17.4	.6	31.6	11.8
1964	42.3	37.3	19.9	17.4	−.8	31.8	10.5
1965	46.5	39.4	21.9	17.5	1.0	33.6	12.9
1966	50.5	43.4	25.0	18.4	−.1	36.5	14.0
1967	50.5	42.8	24.4	18.4	.7	38.2	12.3
1968	51.8	44.2	25.5	18.7	.1	39.5	12.3
1969	56.4	48.2	28.6	19.6	.1	42.1	14.3
1970	58.8	50.5	29.5	21.0	.0	44.5	14.4
1971	62.1	52.7	30.5	22.3	1.4	47.1	15.0
1972	71.1	61.1	35.6	25.5	.9	51.7	19.5
1973	98.9	86.9	45.8	41.1	3.4	64.6	34.4
1974	98.2	92.4	41.3	51.1	−1.6	71.0	27.3
1975	100.6	88.9	43.1	45.8	3.4	75.0	25.5
1976	102.9	95.4	46.3	49.0	−1.5	82.7	20.2
1977	108.8	96.2	47.6	48.6	1.1	88.9	19.9
1978	128.4	112.4	59.2	53.2	1.9	103.3	25.2
1979	150.7	131.5	69.2	62.3	5.0	123.3	27.4
1980	149.3	139.7	68.0	71.7	−6.3	133.1	16.1
1981	166.3	141.6	69.2	72.5	6.5	139.4	26.9
1982	164.1	142.6	70.3	72.3	−1.4	140.3	23.8
1983	153.9	136.8	69.6	67.2	−10.9	139.6	14.2
1984	168.0	142.8	72.9	69.9	6.0	141.9	26.1
1985	161.2	144.1	69.8	74.3	−2.3	132.4	28.8
1986	156.1	135.4	71.6	63.8	−2.2	125.1	31.1
1987	168.3	141.8	76.0	65.8	−2.3	130.2	38.0
1988	177.3	151.2	79.6	71.6	−4.1	139.8	37.5
1989	191.9	160.8	83.9	76.9	3.8	146.9	45.0
1990	198.5	169.4	89.2	80.3	3.5	153.7	44.8
1991	191.8	167.8	85.8	82.0	−.2	153.4	38.4
1992	200.5	171.3	85.6	85.7	4.2	152.6	47.9
1993	203.0	177.1	90.0	87.1	−4.5	160.9	42.1
1994	213.5	179.7	88.1	91.6	8.7	166.7	46.7
1993: I	203.9	174.3	83.7	90.6	−8.0	158.5	45.4
II	203.4	177.2	87.9	89.3	−6.3	160.8	42.7
III	198.9	187.7	101.3	86.3	−7.4	162.6	36.3
IV	205.6	169.4	87.3	82.1	3.7	161.7	43.9
1994: I	218.8	178.8	92.0	86.8	10.6	164.3	54.5
II	206.1	169.7	82.8	86.9	10.0	166.5	39.6
III	211.8	185.8	97.6	88.2	7.8	168.5	43.3
IV	217.1	184.4	79.9	104.5	6.3	167.6	49.5
1995: I	211.4	184.4	87.5	96.9	.6	162.9	48.4
II	201.5	177.1	78.0	99.1	.6	165.3	36.3

[1] Cash marketing receipts and inventory changes plus Government payments, other farm cash income, and nonmoney income furnished by farms.

[2] Physical changes in end-of-period inventory of crop and livestock commodities valued at average prices during the period.

Note.—Data include net Commodity Credit Corporation loans and operator households.

Source: Department of Agriculture.

TABLE B–94.—Farm business balance sheet, 1950–94

[Billions of dollars]

End of year	Total assets	Real estate	Live-stock and poul-try[1]	Machin-ery and motor vehicles	Crops[2]	Pur-chased in-puts[3]	Invest-ments in cooper-atives	Other[4]	Total claims	Real estate debt[5]	Non-real estate debt[6]	Propri-etors' equity
1950	121.6	75.4	17.1	12.3	7.1		2.7	7.0	121.6	5.2	5.7	110.7
1951	136.1	83.8	19.5	14.3	8.2		2.9	7.3	136.1	5.7	6.9	123.7
1952	133.0	85.1	14.8	15.0	7.9		3.2	7.1	133.0	6.2	7.1	119.7
1953	128.7	84.3	11.7	15.6	6.8		3.3	7.0	128.7	6.6	6.3	115.7
1954	132.6	87.8	11.2	15.7	7.5		3.5	6.9	132.6	7.1	6.7	118.9
1955	137.0	93.0	10.6	16.3	6.5		3.7	6.9	137.0	7.8	7.3	121.9
1956	145.7	100.3	11.0	16.9	6.8		4.0	6.7	145.7	8.5	7.4	129.8
1957	154.5	106.4	13.9	17.0	6.4		4.2	6.6	154.5	9.0	8.2	137.3
1958	168.7	114.6	17.7	18.1	6.9		4.5	6.9	168.7	9.7	9.4	149.7
1959	173.0	121.2	15.2	19.3	6.2		4.8	6.2	173.0	10.6	10.7	151.7
1960	174.2	123.3	15.6	19.1	6.2		4.2	5.8	174.2	11.3	11.1	151.7
1961	181.4	129.1	16.4	19.3	6.3		4.5	5.9	181.4	12.3	11.8	157.3
1962	188.7	134.6	17.3	19.9	6.3		4.6	5.9	188.7	13.5	13.2	162.0
1963	196.5	142.4	15.9	20.4	7.2		5.0	5.7	196.5	15.0	14.6	166.9
1964	204.0	150.5	14.4	21.2	6.8		5.2	5.8	204.0	16.9	15.3	171.8
1965	220.6	161.5	17.6	22.4	7.7		5.4	6.0	220.6	18.9	16.9	184.8
1966	233.8	171.2	19.0	24.1	7.9		5.7	6.0	233.8	20.7	18.5	194.6
1967	245.8	180.9	18.8	26.3	7.7		5.8	6.1	245.8	22.6	19.6	203.6
1968	257.0	189.4	20.2	27.7	7.2		6.1	6.3	257.0	24.7	19.2	213.0
1969	267.6	195.3	22.8	28.6	8.1		6.4	6.4	267.6	26.4	20.0	221.2
1970	278.7	202.4	23.7	30.4	8.5		7.2	6.5	278.7	27.5	21.2	229.9
1971	301.5	217.6	27.3	32.4	9.7		7.9	6.7	301.5	29.3	24.0	248.3
1972	339.7	243.0	33.7	34.6	12.7		8.7	6.9	339.7	32.0	26.7	281.0
1973	418.3	298.3	42.4	39.7	21.1		9.7	7.1	418.3	36.1	31.6	350.6
1974[7]	449.1	335.6	24.6	48.5	22.5		11.2	6.9	449.1	40.8	35.1	373.3
1975	510.7	383.6	29.4	57.4	20.5		13.0	6.9	510.7	45.3	39.7	425.7
1976	590.7	456.5	29.0	63.3	20.6		14.3	6.9	590.7	50.5	45.6	494.6
1977	651.5	509.3	31.9	69.3	20.4		13.5	7.0	651.5	58.4	52.4	540.6
1978	767.3	601.8	50.1	68.5	23.8		16.1	7.1	767.3	66.7	60.7	639.9
1979	898.1	706.1	61.4	75.4	29.9		18.1	7.3	898.1	79.7	71.8	746.6
1980	983.2	782.8	60.6	80.3	32.7		19.3	7.4	983.2	89.7	77.1	816.4
1981	982.3	785.6	53.5	85.5	29.5		20.6	7.6	982.3	98.8	83.6	799.9
1982	944.5	750.0	53.0	86.0	25.8		21.9	7.8	944.5	101.8	87.0	755.7
1983	943.3	753.4	49.5	85.8	23.6		22.8	8.1	943.3	103.2	87.9	752.2
1984	857.0	661.8	49.5	85.0	26.1	2.0	24.3	8.3	857.0	106.7	87.1	663.3
1985	772.7	586.2	46.3	82.9	22.9	1.2	24.3	9.0	772.7	100.1	77.5	595.1
1986	724.4	542.3	47.8	81.5	16.3	2.1	24.4	10.0	724.4	90.4	66.6	567.5
1987	757.4	563.5	58.0	80.0	17.7	3.2	25.3	9.9	757.4	82.4	62.0	613.0
1988	789.6	583.7	62.2	81.2	23.6	3.5	25.1	10.3	789.6	77.8	61.7	650.0
1989	815.3	600.9	66.2	85.1	23.7	2.6	26.3	10.5	815.3	76.0	61.9	677.4
1990	838.8	618.4	70.9	85.4	23.0	2.8	27.5	10.9	838.8	74.7	63.2	700.8
1991	843.7	624.4	68.1	85.8	22.2	2.7	28.7	11.8	843.7	74.9	64.3	704.5
1992	868.4	640.6	71.0	85.6	24.2	3.9	29.4	13.6	868.4	75.4	63.6	729.4
1993	902.9	670.9	72.8	85.2	23.3	4.2	31.3	15.3	902.9	76.0	65.9	761.0
1994	933.5	703.3	68.3	85.7	23.4	5.0	32.3	15.5	933.5	77.6	69.1	786.7

[1] Excludes commercial broilers; excludes horses and mules beginning 1959; excludes turkeys beginning 1986.
[2] Non-Commodity Credit Corporation (CCC) crops held on farms plus value above loan rate for crops held under CCC.
[3] Includes fertilizer, chemicals, fuels, parts, feed, seed, and other supplies.
[4] Currency and demand deposits.
[5] Includes CCC storage and drying facilities loans.
[6] Does not include CCC crop loans.
[7] Beginning 1974, data are for farms included in the new farm definition, that is, places with sales of $1,000 or more annually.

Note.—Data exclude operator households.
Beginning 1959, data include Alaska and Hawaii.

Source: Department of Agriculture.

[1982=100]

Year	Farm output					Productivity indicators[4]	
	Total[1]	Livestock and products[2]	Crops[2]			Farm output per unit of total factor input	Farm output per unit of farm labor
			Total[3]	Feed crops	Food grains	Oil crops		
1948	51	57	48	51	44	16	54	18
1949	51	61	46	46	38	15	53	19
1950	51	63	44	47	35	18	53	20
1951	54	66	46	46	35	16	55	21
1952	55	67	48	47	44	16	56	23
1953	55	69	48	47	41	16	57	24
1954	56	71	47	48	36	18	59	25
1955	58	73	49	51	34	20	58	25
1956	58	74	49	50	35	23	59	27
1957	57	73	48	54	33	23	59	29
1958	60	74	53	58	49	28	62	32
1959	62	77	53	58	39	25	62	33
1960	63	77	55	61	47	27	64	34
1961	65	80	56	57	43	31	66	36
1962	65	81	56	58	40	31	67	36
1963	67	83	58	61	42	33	69	39
1964	67	86	56	55	46	33	70	41
1965	68	83	60	63	48	40	72	43
1966	68	84	59	62	48	43	71	46
1967	71	87	62	68	54	45	75	50
1968	72	87	63	67	57	51	77	53
1969	73	87	65	69	53	52	77	54
1970	73	90	63	64	50	52	77	55
1971	78	92	70	78	58	58	83	60
1972	78	93	70	76	56	58	83	61
1973	81	94	75	78	61	70	84	63
1974	77	92	68	66	65	56	80	64
1975	81	87	78	78	77	71	86	68
1976	83	92	77	78	77	60	85	70
1977	88	93	84	84	72	81	91	77
1978	89	93	87	91	67	86	88	81
1979	95	95	95	96	78	105	91	89
1980	91	99	86	81	87	81	87	89
1981	100	101	99	98	103	92	97	98
1982	100	100	100	100	100	100	100	100
1983	88	102	78	66	85	75	91	92
1984	99	101	97	97	94	87	103	104
1985	103	104	102	107	88	96	109	114
1986	100	104	97	102	77	88	110	117
1987	102	107	98	91	77	88	115	121
1988	95	109	86	67	70	72	111	111
1989	103	109	99	91	77	87	120	121
1990	108	111	106	94	99	87	121	126
1991	108	114	104	92	75	93	121	125
1992	116	116	115	107	93	99	129	141
1993	108	117	101	82	88	85	119	133

[1] Farm output measures the annual volume of net farm production available for eventual human use through sales from farms or consumption in farm households.

[2] Gross production.

[3] Includes items not included in groups shown.

[4] See Table B–96 for farm inputs.

Source: Department of Agriculture.

Year	Farm population, April[1] — Number (thousands)	As percent of total population[2]	Farm employment (thousands)[3] — Total	Self-employed and unpaid workers[4]	Hired workers	Crops harvested (millions of acres)[5]	Selected indexes of input use (1982=100) — Total	Farm labor	Farm real estate	Durable equipment	Energy	Agricultural chemicals[6]	Feed, seed, and purchased livestock[7]	Other purchased inputs
1948	24,383	16.6	10,363	8,026	2,337	356	95	278	92	38	65	35	55	73
1949	24,194	16.2	9,964	7,712	2,252	360	97	272	94	45	72	36	57	74
1950	23,048	15.2	9,926	7,597	2,329	345	97	261	95	52	73	44	56	74
1951	21,890	14.2	9,546	7,310	2,236	344	98	251	97	58	76	43	59	80
1952	21,748	13.9	9,149	7,005	2,144	349	98	243	98	63	79	44	58	82
1953	19,874	12.5	8,864	6,775	2,089	348	97	230	99	66	81	43	60	79
1954	19,019	11.7	8,651	6,570	2,081	346	94	224	100	69	81	44	55	75
1955	19,078	11.5	8,381	6,345	2,036	340	99	227	100	70	83	46	62	78
1956	18,712	11.1	7,852	5,900	1,952	324	98	215	101	71	83	51	64	78
1957	17,656	10.3	7,600	5,660	1,940	324	97	201	101	69	82	49	67	80
1958	17,128	9.8	7,503	5,521	1,982	324	98	192	101	68	80	50	71	83
1959	16,592	9.3	7,342	5,390	1,952	324	100	191	101	68	81	57	72	95
1960	15,635	8.7	7,057	5,172	1,885	324	99	186	101	69	82	59	71	95
1961	14,803	8.1	6,919	5,029	1,890	302	97	181	98	68	84	62	68	93
1962	14,313	7.7	6,700	4,873	1,827	295	97	179	97	67	85	56	70	94
1963	13,367	7.1	6,518	4,738	1,780	298	98	174	97	67	86	62	73	95
1964	12,954	6.7	6,110	4,506	1,604	298	96	164	97	67	88	67	71	93
1965	12,363	6.4	5,610	4,128	1,482	298	95	160	96	69	89	72	70	94
1966	11,595	5.9	5,214	3,854	1,360	294	96	149	95	71	90	83	75	95
1967	10,875	5.5	4,903	3,650	1,253	306	95	142	98	73	90	79	75	95
1968	10,454	5.2	4,749	3,535	1,213	300	94	137	96	76	90	68	76	94
1969	10,307	5.1	4,596	3,419	1,176	290	95	135	95	78	92	73	81	92
1970	9,712	4.7	4,523	3,348	1,175	293	95	133	95	78	92	76	83	89
1971	9,425	4.5	4,436	3,275	1,161	305	94	131	97	79	90	80	81	86
1972	9,610	4.6	4,373	3,228	1,146	294	95	129	95	79	89	85	83	87
1973	9,472	4.5	4,337	3,169	1,168	321	97	129	99	81	90	95	83	94
1974	9,264	4.3	4,389	3,075	1,314	328	96	120	100	85	86	100	82	99
1975	8,864	4.1	4,331	3,021	1,310	336	95	120	99	89	101	92	78	97
1976	8,253	3.8	4,363	2,992	1,371	337	98	118	100	91	113	101	82	100
1977	[8]6,194	[8]2.8	4,143	2,852	1,291	345	96	114	100	94	119	99	78	102
1978	[8]6,501	[8]2.9	3,937	2,680	1,256	338	101	110	99	96	125	109	90	119
1979	[8]6,241	[8]2.8	3,765	2,495	1,270	348	104	106	100	99	113	120	97	127
1980	[8]6,051	[8]2.7	3,699	2,401	1,298	352	105	102	102	102	110	133	102	116
1981	[8]5,850	[8]2.5	[9]3,582	[9]2,324	[9]1,258	366	103	102	102	102	106	132	97	109
1982	[8]5,628	[8]2.4	[9]3,466	[9]2,248	[9]1,218	362	100	100	100	100	100	100	100	100
1983	[8]5,787	[8]2.5	[9]3,349	[9]2,171	[9]1,178	306	97	95	93	95	97	93	102	106
1984	5,754	2.4	[9]3,233	[9]2,095	[9]1,138	348	97	95	98	91	100	106	92	109
1985	5,355	2.2	3,116	2,018	1,098	342	94	91	97	86	90	100	93	103
1986	5,226	2.2	2,912	1,873	1,039	325	91	85	95	80	84	110	94	93
1987	4,986	2.1	2,897	1,846	1,051	302	89	84	91	74	93	101	91	97
1988	4,951	2.1	2,954	1,967	1,037	297	86	86	91	70	93	92	89	86
1989	4,801	2.0	2,863	1,935	928	318	86	85	92	67	92	96	86	91
1990	4,591	1.9	2,891	2,000	892	322	89	85	91	65	92	98	93	103
1991	4,632	1.9	2,877	1,968	910	318	90	87	91	63	92	103	91	110
1992	....	....	2,810	1,944	866	317	90	82	91	61	92	103	96	114
1993	....	....	2,800	1,942	857	308	90	81	89	60	92	106	96	126
1994	....	....	2,767	1,925	842	321	......	......	......	......	......	......	......	......
1995P	....	....	2,827	1,958	869	315	......	......	......	......	......	......	......	......

[1] Farm population as defined by Department of Agriculture and Department of Commerce, i.e., civilian population living on farms in rural areas, regardless of occupation. See also footnote 8. Series discontinued in 1992.

[2] Total population of United States including Armed Forces overseas, as of July 1.

[3] Includes persons doing farmwork on all farms. These data, published by the Department of Agriculture, differ from those on agricultural employment by the Department of Labor (see Table B–31) because of differences in the method of approach, in concepts of employment, and in time of month for which the data are collected.

[4] Prior to 1982 this category was termed "family workers" and did not include nonfamily unpaid workers.

[5] Acreage harvested plus acreages in fruits, tree nuts, and farm gardens.

[6] Fertilizer, lime, and pesticides.

[7] Includes purchases of broiler- and egg-type chicks and turkey poults and livestock imports for purposes other than immediate slaughter.

[8] Based on new definition of a farm. Under old definition of a farm, farm population (in thousands and as percent of total population) for 1977, 1978, 1979, 1980, 1981, 1982, and 1983 is 7,806 and 3.6; 8,005 and 3.6; 7,553 and 3.4; 7,241 and 3.2; 7,014 and 3.1; 6,880 and 3.0; 7,029 and 3.0, respectively.

[9] Basis for farm employment series was discontinued for 1981 through 1984. Employment is estimated for these years.

Note.—Population includes Alaska and Hawaii beginning 1960.

Sources: Department of Agriculture and Department of Commerce (Bureau of the Census).

TABLE B–97.—*Indexes of prices received and prices paid by farmers, 1975–95*

[1990–92=100, except as noted]

Year or month	Prices received by farmers			Prices paid by farmers												Addendum: Average farm real estate value per acre (dollars)[3]
				All commod-ities, services, interest, taxes, and wage rates[1]	Production items											
	All farm products	Crops	Live-stock and products		Total[2]	Feed	Live-stock and poul-try	Fertil-izer	Agri-cul-tural chemi-cals	Fuels	Farm ma-chin-ery	Farm serv-ices	Rent	Wage rates	
1975	73	88	62	47	55	83	39	87	72	40	38	48		43	340
1976	75	87	64	50	59	83	47	74	78	43	43	52		48	397
1977	73	83	64	53	61	82	48	72	71	46	47	57		51	474
1978	83	89	78	58	67	80	65	72	66	48	51	60		55	531
1979	94	98	90	66	76	89	88	77	67	61	56	66		60	628
1980	98	107	89	75	85	98	85	96	71	86	63	81		65	737
1981	100	111	89	82	92	110	80	104	77	98	70	89		70	819
1982	94	98	90	86	94	99	78	105	83	97	76	96		74	823
1983	98	108	88	86	92	107	76	100	87	94	81	82		76	788
1984	101	111	91	89	94	112	73	103	90	93	85	86		77	801
1985	91	98	86	86	91	95	74	98	90	93	85	85		78	713
1986	87	87	88	85	86	88	73	90	89	76	83	83		81	640
1987	89	86	91	87	87	83	85	86	87	76	85	84		85	599
1988	99	104	93	91	90	104	91	94	89	77	89	85		87	632
1989	104	109	100	96	95	110	93	99	93	83	94	91		95	668
1990	104	103	105	99	99	103	102	97	95	100	96	96	96	96	683
1991	100	101	99	100	100	98	102	103	101	104	100	98	100	100	703
1992	98	101	97	101	101	99	96	100	103	96	104	103	104	105	713
1993	101	102	100	103	103	99	104	97	107	92	106	108	100	108	736
1994	100	105	95	106	106	105	95	106	112	84	110	113	108	111	782
1995	102	112	92	109	108	103	84	117	115	88	116	117	116	113	832
1994: Jan	105	110	98	106	106	109	100	100	110	75	109	112	108	113	782
Feb	104	110	100												
Mar	105	109	101												
Apr	102	105	100	107	107	109	100	104	109	90	114	112	108	111	
May	101	107	97												
June	100	108	94												
July	97	103	92	106	106	104	91	109	113	83	109	112	108	107	
Aug	97	101	94												
Sept	97	102	91												
Oct	95	99	89	106	105	98	87	111	114	87	108	114	108	112	
Nov	95	100	90												
Dec	98	106	90												
1995: Jan	98	103	93	108	107	97	92	115	114	84	111	116	116	116	832
Feb	97	101	94												
Mar	99	107	93												
Apr	99	113	90	108	107	100	82	122	115	92	119	115	116	112	
May	101	117	88												
June	100	113	90												
July	101	114	91	108	107	102	81	118	115	88	118	118	116	111	
Aug	102	114	92												
Sept	105	115	93												
Oct	104	114	92	111	110	112	80	114	115	88	117	119	116	114	
Nov	106	117	94												
Dec	108	118	96												

[1] Includes items used for family living, not shown separately.
[2] Includes other production items not shown separately.
[3] Average for 48 States. Annual data are: March 1 for 1975, February 1 for 1976–81, April 1 for 1982–85, February 1 for 1986–89, and January 1 for 1990–95.

Note—New series on a 1990–92 base. Data prior to 1975 are not available.

Source: Department of Agriculture.

[Billions of dollars]

Year	Exports							Imports					Agricultural trade balance
	Total[1]	Feed grains	Food grains[2]	Oil-seeds and products	Cotton	Tobacco	Animals and products	Total[1]	Crops, fruits, and vegetables[3]	Animals and products	Coffee	Cocoa beans and products	
1940	0.5	(4)	(4)	(4)	0.2	(4)	0.1	1.3	(4)	0.2	0.1	(4)	−0.8
1941	.7	(4)	0.1	(4)	.1	0.1	.3	1.7	0.1	.3	.2	(4)	−1.0
1942	1.2	(4)	(4)	(4)	.1	.1	.8	1.3	(4)	.5	.2	(4)	−.1
1943	2.1	(4)	.1	0.1	.2	.2	1.2	1.5	.1	.4	.3	(4)	.6
1944	2.1	(4)	.1	.1	.1	.1	1.3	1.8	.1	.3	.3	(4)	.3
1945	2.3	(4)	.4	(4)	.3	.2	.9	1.7	.1	.4	.3	(4)	.5
1946	3.1	0.1	.7	(4)	.5	.4	.9	2.3	.2	.4	.5	0.1	.8
1947	4.0	.4	1.4	.1	.4	.3	.7	2.8	.1	.4	.6	.2	1.2
1948	3.5	.1	1.5	.2	.5	.2	.5	3.1	.2	.6	.7	.2	.3
1949	3.6	.3	1.1	.3	.9	.3	.4	2.9	.2	.4	.8	.1	.7
1950	2.9	.2	.6	.2	1.0	.3	.3	4.0	.2	.7	1.1	.2	−1.1
1951	4.0	.3	1.1	.3	1.1	.3	.5	5.2	.2	1.1	1.4	.2	−1.1
1952	3.4	.3	1.1	.2	.9	.2	.3	4.5	.2	.7	1.4	.2	−1.1
1953	2.8	.3	.7	.2	.5	.3	.4	4.2	.2	.6	1.5	.2	−1.3
1954	3.1	.2	.5	.3	.8	.3	.5	4.0	.2	.5	1.5	.3	−.9
1955	3.2	.3	.6	.4	.5	.4	.6	4.0	.2	.5	1.4	.2	−.8
1956	4.2	.4	1.0	.5	.7	.3	.7	4.0	.2	.4	1.4	.2	.2
1957	4.5	.3	1.0	.5	1.0	.4	.7	4.0	.2	.5	1.4	.2	.6
1958	3.9	.5	.8	.4	.7	.4	.5	3.9	.2	.7	1.2	.2	(4)
1959	4.0	.6	.9	.6	.4	.3	.6	4.1	.2	.8	1.1	.2	−.1
1960	4.8	.5	1.2	.6	1.0	.4	.6	3.8	.2	.6	1.0	.2	1.0
1961	5.0	.5	1.4	.6	.9	.4	.6	3.7	.2	.7	1.0	.2	1.3
1962	5.0	.8	1.3	.7	.5	.4	.6	3.9	.2	.9	1.0	.2	1.2
1963	5.6	.8	1.5	.8	.6	.4	.7	4.0	.3	.9	1.0	.2	1.6
1964	6.3	.9	1.7	1.0	.7	.4	.8	4.1	.3	.8	1.2	.2	2.3
1965	6.2	1.1	1.4	1.2	.5	.4	.8	4.1	.3	.9	1.1	.1	2.1
1966	6.9	1.3	1.8	1.2	.4	.5	.7	4.5	.4	1.2	1.1	.1	2.4
1967	6.4	1.1	1.5	1.3	.5	.5	.7	4.5	.4	1.1	1.0	.2	1.9
1968	6.3	.9	1.4	1.3	.5	.5	.7	5.0	.5	1.3	1.2	.2	1.3
1969	6.0	.9	1.2	1.3	.3	.6	.8	5.0	.5	1.4	.9	.2	1.1
1970	7.3	1.1	1.4	1.9	.4	.5	.9	5.8	.5	1.6	1.2	.3	1.5
1971	7.7	1.0	1.3	2.2	.6	.5	1.0	5.8	.6	1.5	1.2	.2	1.9
1972	9.4	1.5	1.8	2.4	.5	.7	1.1	6.5	.7	1.8	1.3	.2	2.9
1973	17.7	3.5	4.7	4.3	.9	.7	1.6	8.4	.8	2.6	1.7	.3	9.3
1974	21.9	4.6	5.4	5.7	1.3	.8	1.8	10.2	.8	2.2	1.6	.5	11.7
1975	21.9	5.2	6.2	4.5	1.0	.9	1.7	9.3	.8	1.8	1.7	.5	12.6
1976	23.0	6.0	4.7	5.1	1.0	.9	2.4	11.0	.9	2.3	2.9	.6	12.0
1977	23.6	4.9	3.6	6.6	1.5	1.1	2.7	13.4	1.2	2.3	4.2	1.0	10.2
1978	29.4	5.9	5.5	8.2	1.7	1.4	3.0	14.8	1.5	3.1	4.0	1.4	14.6
1979	34.7	7.7	6.3	8.9	2.2	1.2	3.8	16.7	1.7	3.9	4.2	1.2	18.0
1980	41.2	9.8	7.9	9.4	2.9	1.3	3.8	17.4	1.7	3.8	4.2	.9	23.8
1981	43.3	9.4	9.6	9.6	2.3	1.5	4.2	16.9	2.0	3.5	2.9	.9	26.4
1982	36.6	6.4	7.9	9.1	2.0	1.5	3.9	15.3	2.3	3.7	2.9	.7	21.3
1983	36.1	7.3	7.4	8.7	1.8	1.5	3.8	16.5	2.3	3.8	2.8	.8	19.6
1984	37.8	8.1	7.5	8.4	2.4	1.5	4.2	19.3	3.1	4.1	3.3	1.1	18.5
1985	29.0	6.0	4.5	5.8	1.6	1.5	4.1	20.0	3.5	4.2	3.3	1.4	9.1
1986	26.2	3.1	3.8	6.5	.8	1.2	4.5	21.5	3.6	4.5	4.6	1.1	4.7
1987	28.7	3.8	3.8	6.4	1.6	1.1	5.2	20.4	3.6	4.9	2.9	1.2	8.3
1988	37.1	5.9	5.9	7.7	2.0	1.3	6.4	21.0	3.8	5.2	2.5	1.0	16.1
1989	39.9	7.7	7.1	6.3	2.3	1.3	6.4	21.7	4.2	5.1	2.4	1.0	18.2
1990	39.4	7.0	4.8	5.7	2.8	1.4	6.7	22.8	4.9	5.6	1.9	1.1	16.6
1991	39.2	5.7	4.2	6.4	2.5	1.4	7.0	22.7	4.8	5.5	1.9	1.1	16.5
1992	42.9	5.7	5.4	7.2	2.0	1.7	7.9	24.6	4.9	5.7	1.7	1.1	18.3
1993	42.6	5.0	5.6	7.3	1.5	1.3	7.9	25.0	5.0	5.9	1.5	1.1	17.6
1994	45.7	4.7	5.3	7.2	2.7	1.3	9.1	26.8	5.4	5.7	2.5	1.0	18.9
Jan–Oct:													
1994	36.0	3.6	4.2	5.4	2.0	1.0	7.3	22.1	4.5	4.8	1.9	.9	13.9
1995	45.2	6.6	5.4	7.1	2.9	1.1	9.0	25.0	4.9	5.0	2.7	.9	20.2

[1] Total includes items not shown separately.
[2] Rice, wheat, and wheat flour.
[3] Includes nuts, fruits, and vegetable preparations.
[4] Less than $50 million.

Note.—Data derived from official estimates released by the Bureau of the Census, Department of Commerce. Agricultural commodities are defined as (1) nonmarine food products and (2) other products of agriculture which have not passed through complex processes of manufacture. Export value, at U.S. port of exportation, is based on the selling price and includes inland freight, insurance, and other charges to the port. Import value, defined generally as the market value in the foreign country, excludes import duties, ocean freight, and marine insurance.

Source: Department of Agriculture.

TABLE B-99.—*U.S. international transactions, 1946–95*

[Millions of dollars; quarterly data seasonally adjusted, except as noted. Credits (+), debits (−)]

Year or quarter	Merchandise[1]			Services				Investment income			Unilateral transfers, net[3]	Balance on current account
	Exports	Imports	Net	Net military transactions[2][3]	Net travel and transportation receipts	Other services, net	Balance on goods and services	Receipts on U.S. assets abroad	Payments on foreign assets in U.S.	Net		
1946	11,764	−5,067	6,697	−424	733	310	7,316	772	−212	560	−2,991	4,885
1947	16,097	−5,973	10,124	−358	946	145	10,857	1,102	−245	857	−2,722	8,992
1948	13,265	−7,557	5,708	−351	374	175	5,906	1,921	−437	1,484	−4,973	2,417
1949	12,213	−6,874	5,339	−410	230	208	5,367	1,831	−476	1,355	−5,849	873
1950	10,203	−9,081	1,122	−56	−120	242	1,188	2,068	−559	1,509	−4,537	−1,840
1951	14,243	−11,176	3,067	169	298	254	3,788	2,633	−583	2,050	−4,954	884
1952	13,449	−10,838	2,611	528	83	309	3,531	2,751	−555	2,196	−5,113	614
1953	12,412	−10,975	1,437	1,753	−238	307	3,259	2,736	−624	2,112	−6,657	−1,286
1954	12,929	−10,353	2,576	902	−269	305	3,514	2,929	−582	2,347	−5,642	219
1955	14,424	−11,527	2,897	−113	−297	299	2,786	3,406	−676	2,730	−5,086	430
1956	17,556	−12,803	4,753	−221	−361	447	4,618	3,837	−735	3,102	−4,990	2,730
1957	19,562	−13,291	6,271	−423	−189	482	6,141	4,180	−796	3,384	−4,763	4,762
1958	16,414	−12,952	3,462	−849	−633	486	2,466	3,790	−825	2,965	−4,647	784
1959	16,458	−15,310	1,148	−831	−821	573	69	4,132	−1,061	3,071	−4,422	−1,282
1960	19,650	−14,758	4,892	−1,057	−964	639	3,508	4,616	−1,238	3,379	−4,062	2,824
1961	20,108	−14,537	5,571	−1,131	−978	732	4,195	4,999	−1,245	3,755	−4,127	3,822
1962	20,781	−16,260	4,521	−912	−1,152	912	3,370	5,618	−1,324	4,294	−4,277	3,387
1963	22,272	−17,048	5,224	−742	−1,309	1,036	4,210	6,157	−1,560	4,596	−4,392	4,414
1964	25,501	−18,700	6,801	−794	−1,146	1,161	6,022	6,824	−1,783	5,041	−4,240	6,823
1965	26,461	−21,510	4,951	−487	−1,280	1,480	4,664	7,437	−2,088	5,350	−4,583	5,431
1966	29,310	−25,493	3,817	−1,043	−1,331	1,497	2,940	7,528	−2,481	5,047	−4,955	3,031
1967	30,666	−26,866	3,800	−1,187	−1,750	1,742	2,604	8,021	−2,747	5,274	−5,294	2,583
1968	33,626	−32,991	635	−596	−1,548	1,759	250	9,367	−3,378	5,990	−5,629	611
1969	36,414	−35,807	607	−718	−1,763	1,964	91	10,913	−4,869	6,044	−5,735	399
1970	42,469	−39,866	2,603	−641	−2,038	2,330	2,254	11,748	−5,515	6,233	−6,156	2,331
1971	43,319	−45,579	−2,260	653	−2,345	2,649	−1,303	12,707	−5,435	7,272	−7,402	−1,433
1972	49,381	−55,797	−6,416	1,072	−3,063	2,965	−5,443	14,765	−6,572	8,192	−8,544	−5,795
1973	71,410	−70,499	911	740	−3,158	3,406	1,900	21,808	−9,655	12,153	−6,913	7,140
1974	98,306	−103,811	−5,505	165	−3,184	4,231	−4,292	27,587	−12,084	15,503	4 −9,249	1,962
1975	107,088	−98,185	8,903	1,461	−2,812	4,854	12,404	25,351	−12,564	12,787	−7,075	18,116
1976	114,745	−124,228	−9,483	931	−2,558	5,027	−6,082	29,375	−13,311	16,063	−5,686	4,295
1977	120,816	−151,907	−31,091	1,731	−3,565	5,680	−27,246	32,354	−14,217	18,137	−5,226	−14,335
1978	142,075	−176,002	−33,927	857	−3,573	6,879	−29,763	42,088	−21,680	20,408	−5,788	−15,143
1979	184,439	−212,007	−27,568	−1,313	−2,935	7,251	−24,565	63,834	−32,961	30,873	−6,593	−285
1980	224,250	−249,750	−25,500	−1,822	−997	8,912	−19,407	72,606	−42,532	30,073	−8,349	2,317
1981	237,044	−265,067	−28,023	−844	144	12,552	−16,172	86,529	−53,626	32,903	−11,702	5,030
1982	211,157	−247,642	−36,485	112	−992	13,209	−24,156	86,200	−56,412	29,788	−17,075	−11,443
1983	201,799	−268,901	−67,102	−563	−4,227	14,124	−57,767	85,200	−53,700	31,500	−17,718	−43,985
1984	219,926	−332,418	−112,492	−2,547	−8,438	14,404	−109,073	104,756	−74,036	30,720	−20,598	−98,951
1985	215,915	−338,088	−122,173	−4,390	−9,798	14,483	−121,880	93,677	−73,087	20,590	−22,954	−124,243
1986	223,344	−368,425	−145,081	−5,181	−8,484	19,194	−139,551	91,976	−79,095	12,881	−24,189	−150,859
1987	250,208	−409,765	−159,557	−3,844	−7,613	18,319	−152,696	100,767	−91,302	9,465	−23,107	−166,338
1988	320,230	−447,189	−126,959	−6,320	−2,591	20,546	−115,324	129,070	−115,806	13,264	−25,023	−127,083
1989	362,120	−477,365	−115,245	−6,749	4,043	26,558	−91,392	152,517	−138,858	13,659	−26,106	−103,839
1990	389,307	−498,337	−109,030	−7,599	8,002	28,633	−79,994	160,300	−139,574	20,725	−33,393	−92,661
1991	416,913	−490,981	−74,068	−5,274	17,032	32,907	−29,404	137,003	−121,892	15,111	6,869	−7,424
1992	440,352	−536,458	−96,106	−2,142	20,484	38,284	−39,480	118,425	−108,346	10,079	−32,148	−61,549
1993	456,823	−589,441	−132,618	448	19,885	37,444	−74,841	119,248	−110,248	9,000	−34,084	−99,925
1994	502,485	−668,584	−166,099	2,148	19,330	38,410	−106,212	137,619	−146,891	−9,272	−35,761	−151,245
1993:												
I	111,862	−140,821	−28,959	401	5,302	9,683	−13,573	28,950	−25,239	3,711	−7,521	−17,383
II	114,131	−147,718	−33,587	90	5,389	9,315	−18,793	29,958	−27,893	2,065	−7,609	−24,337
III	111,576	−148,181	−36,605	283	5,062	9,272	−21,988	29,931	−26,741	3,190	−8,234	−27,032
IV	119,254	−152,721	−33,467	−326	4,131	9,172	−20,490	30,412	−30,376	36	−10,722	−31,176
1994:												
I	118,445	−154,935	−36,490	−31	4,642	8,863	−23,016	30,942	−30,826	116	−7,371	−30,271
II	122,730	−164,224	−41,494	376	4,647	9,548	−26,923	32,338	−34,623	−2,285	−8,778	−37,986
III	127,384	−172,011	−44,627	1,124	4,792	9,904	−28,807	36,031	−38,564	−2,533	−8,374	−39,714
IV	133,926	−177,414	−43,488	679	5,247	10,095	−27,467	38,307	−42,878	−4,571	−11,239	−43,277
1995:												
I	138,061	−183,111	−45,050	542	5,050	10,018	−29,440	43,254	−45,215	−1,961	−7,624	−39,025
II	142,850	−191,652	−48,802	587	4,380	10,402	−33,433	45,471	−48,085	−2,614	−7,220	−43,267
III p	145,315	−188,748	−43,433	736	4,480	10,698	−27,519	44,619	−48,772	−4,153	−7,810	−39,482

[1] Adjusted from Census data for differences in valuation, coverage, and timing; excludes military.
[2] Quarterly data are not seasonally adjusted.
[3] Includes transfers of goods and services under U.S. military grant programs.

See next page for continuation of table.

TABLE B–99.—U.S. international transactions, 1946–95—Continued

[Millions of dollars; quarterly data seasonally adjusted, except as noted]

Year or quarter	U.S. assets abroad, net [increase/capital outflow (–)] Total	U.S. official reserve assets[2][5]	Other U.S. Government assets	U.S. private assets	Foreign assets in the U.S., net [increase/capital inflow (+)] Total	Foreign official assets[2]	Other foreign assets	Allocations of special drawing rights (SDRs)	Statistical discrepancy Total (sum of the items with sign reversed)	Of which: Seasonal adjustment discrepancy
1946		–623								
1947		–3,315								
1948		–1,736								
1949		–266								
1950		1,758								
1951		–33								
1952		–415								
1953		1,256								
1954		480								
1955		182								
1956		–869								
1957		–1,165								
1958		2,292								
1959		1,035								
1960	–4,099	2,145	–1,100	–5,144	2,294	1,473	821		–1,019	
1961	–5,538	607	–910	–5,235	2,705	765	1,939		–989	
1962	–4,174	1,535	–1,085	–4,623	1,911	1,270	641		–1,124	
1963	–7,270	378	–1,662	–5,986	3,217	1,986	1,231		–360	
1964	–9,560	171	–1,680	–8,050	3,643	1,660	1,983		–907	
1965	–5,716	1,225	–1,605	–5,336	742	134	607		–457	
1966	–7,321	570	–1,543	–6,347	3,661	–672	4,333		629	
1967	–9,757	53	–2,423	–7,386	7,379	3,451	3,928		–205	
1968	–10,977	–870	–2,274	–7,833	9,928	–774	10,703		438	
1969	–11,585	–1,179	–2,200	–8,206	12,702	–1,301	14,002		–1,516	
1970	–9,337	2,481	–1,589	–10,229	6,359	6,908	–550	867	–219	
1971	–12,475	2,349	–1,884	–12,940	22,970	26,879	–3,909	717	–9,779	
1972	–14,497	–4	–1,568	–12,925	21,461	10,475	10,986	710	–1,879	
1973	–22,874	158	–2,644	–20,388	18,388	6,026	12,362		–2,654	
1974	–34,745	–1,467	[4] 366	–33,643	34,241	10,546	23,696		–1,458	
1975	–39,703	–849	–3,474	–35,380	15,670	7,027	8,643		5,917	
1976	–51,269	–2,558	–4,214	–44,498	36,518	17,693	18,826		10,455	
1977	–34,785	–375	–3,693	–30,717	51,319	36,816	14,503		–2,199	
1978	–61,130	732	–4,660	–57,202	64,036	33,678	30,358		12,236	
1979	–66,054	–1,133	–3,746	–61,176	38,752	–13,665	52,416	1,139	26,449	
1980	–86,967	–8,155	–5,162	–73,651	58,112	15,497	42,615	1,152	25,386	
1981	–114,147	–5,175	–5,097	–103,875	83,032	4,960	78,072	1,093	24,992	
1982	–122,335	–4,965	–6,131	–111,239	92,418	3,593	88,826		41,359	
1983	–61,573	–1,196	–5,006	–55,372	83,380	5,845	77,534		22,179	
1984	–36,313	–3,131	–5,489	–27,694	113,932	3,140	110,792		21,331	
1985	–39,889	–3,858	–2,821	–33,211	141,183	–1,119	142,301		22,950	
1986	–106,753	312	–2,022	–105,044	226,111	35,648	190,463		31,501	
1987	–72,617	9,149	1,006	–82,771	242,983	45,387	197,596		–4,028	
1988	–100,087	–3,912	2,967	–99,141	240,265	39,758	200,507		–13,095	
1989	–168,744	–25,293	1,259	–144,710	218,490	8,503	209,987		54,094	
1990	–74,011	–2,158	2,307	–74,160	122,192	33,910	88,282		44,480	
1991	–57,881	5,763	2,911	–66,555	94,241	17,389	76,853		–28,936	
1992	–65,875	3,901	–1,661	–68,115	153,823	40,466	113,358		–26,399	
1993	–184,589	–1,379	–330	–182,880	248,529	72,146	176,383		35,985	
1994	–125,851	5,346	–322	–130,875	291,365	39,409	251,956		–14,269	
1993:										
I	–19,729	–983	467	–19,213	19,867	10,955	8,912		17,245	5,367
II	–40,933	822	–281	–41,474	51,277	17,495	33,782		13,993	154
III	–46,270	–545	–197	–45,529	77,928	19,386	58,542		–4,626	–6,353
IV	–77,657	–673	–318	–76,666	99,458	24,311	75,147		9,375	834
1994:										
I	–36,783	–59	401	–37,125	80,390	10,977	69,413		–13,336	5,274
II	–5,973	3,537	491	–10,001	46,526	9,162	37,364		–2,567	587
III	–27,940	–165	–283	–27,492	79,736	19,691	60,045		–12,082	–6,641
IV	–55,156	2,033	–931	–56,258	84,715	–421	85,136		13,718	782
1995:										
I	–75,343	–5,318	–152	–69,873	94,841	22,308	72,533		19,527	6,183
II	–100,242	–2,722	–180	–97,340	124,331	37,836	86,495		19,178	331
III [p]	–42,852	–1,893	136	–41,095	105,664	39,479	66,185		–23,330	–7,086

[4] Includes extraordinary U.S. Government transactions with India.

[5] Consists of gold, special drawing rights, foreign currencies, and the U.S. reserve position in the International Monetary Fund (IMF).

Source: Department of Commerce, Bureau of Economic Analysis.

[Billions of dollars; quarterly data seasonally adjusted]

Year or quarter	Exports							Imports						
	Total	Agricultural products	Nonagricultural products					Total	Petroleum and products	Nonpetroleum products				
			Total	Industrial supplies and materials	Capital goods except automotive	Automotive	Other			Total	Industrial supplies and materials	Capital goods except automotive	Automotive	Other
1965	26.5	6.3	20.2	7.6	8.1	1.9	2.6	21.5	2.0	19.5	9.1	1.5	0.9	8.0
1966	29.3	6.9	22.4	8.2	8.9	2.4	2.9	25.5	2.1	23.4	10.2	2.2	1.8	9.2
1967	30.7	6.5	24.2	8.5	9.9	2.8	3.0	26.9	2.1	24.8	10.0	2.5	2.4	9.9
1968	33.6	6.3	27.3	9.6	11.1	3.5	3.2	33.0	2.4	30.6	12.0	2.8	4.0	11.8
1969	36.4	6.1	30.3	10.3	12.4	3.9	3.7	35.8	2.6	33.2	11.8	3.4	4.9	13.0
1970	42.5	7.4	35.1	12.3	14.7	3.9	4.3	39.9	2.9	36.9	12.4	4.0	5.5	15.0
1971	43.3	7.8	35.5	10.9	15.4	4.7	4.5	45.6	3.7	41.9	13.8	4.3	7.4	16.4
1972	49.4	9.5	39.9	11.9	16.9	5.5	5.6	55.8	4.7	51.1	16.3	5.9	8.7	20.2
1973	71.4	18.0	53.4	17.0	22.0	6.9	7.6	70.5	8.4	62.1	19.6	8.3	10.3	23.9
1974	98.3	22.4	75.9	26.3	30.9	8.6	10.0	103.8	26.6	77.2	27.8	9.8	12.0	27.5
1975	107.1	22.2	84.8	26.8	36.6	10.6	10.8	98.2	27.0	71.2	24.0	10.2	11.7	25.3
1976	114.7	23.4	91.4	28.4	39.1	12.1	11.7	124.2	34.6	89.7	29.8	12.3	16.2	31.4
1977	120.8	24.3	96.5	29.8	39.8	13.4	13.5	151.9	45.0	106.9	35.7	14.0	18.6	38.6
1978 [1]	142.1	29.9	112.2	34.2	47.5	15.2	15.3	176.0	42.6	133.4	40.7	19.3	25.0	48.4
1979	184.4	35.5	149.0	52.2	60.2	17.9	18.7	212.0	60.4	151.6	47.5	24.6	26.6	52.8
1980	224.3	42.0	182.2	65.1	76.3	17.4	23.4	249.8	79.5	170.2	53.0	31.6	28.3	57.4
1981	237.0	44.1	193.0	63.6	84.2	19.7	25.5	265.1	78.4	186.7	56.1	37.1	31.0	62.4
1982	211.2	37.3	173.9	57.7	76.5	17.2	22.4	247.6	62.0	185.7	48.6	38.4	34.3	64.3
1983	201.8	37.1	164.7	52.7	71.7	18.5	21.8	268.9	55.1	213.8	53.7	43.7	43.0	73.3
1984	219.9	38.4	181.5	56.8	77.0	22.4	25.3	332.4	58.1	274.4	66.1	60.4	56.5	91.4
1985	215.9	29.6	186.3	54.8	79.3	24.9	27.2	338.1	51.4	286.7	62.6	61.3	64.9	97.9
1986	223.3	27.2	196.2	59.4	82.8	25.1	28.9	368.4	34.3	334.1	69.9	72.0	78.1	114.2
1987	250.2	29.8	220.4	63.7	92.7	27.6	36.4	409.8	42.9	366.8	70.8	85.1	85.2	125.7
1988	320.2	38.8	281.4	82.6	119.1	33.4	46.3	447.2	39.6	407.6	83.1	102.2	87.9	134.4
1989	362.1	42.2	319.9	91.8	138.9	34.9	54.3	477.4	50.9	426.5	84.5	112.2	87.4	142.5
1990	389.3	40.2	349.1	96.9	152.5	36.5	63.2	498.3	62.3	436.1	82.9	116.1	88.5	148.6
1991	416.9	40.1	376.8	101.7	166.5	40.0	68.6	491.0	51.7	439.2	81.2	120.8	85.7	151.5
1992	440.4	44.0	396.3	101.7	176.1	47.0	71.5	536.5	51.6	484.9	89.0	134.3	91.8	169.8
1993	456.8	43.7	413.1	105.0	182.2	52.4	73.5	589.4	51.5	538.0	101.0	152.4	102.4	182.2
1994	502.5	47.1	455.4	112.6	205.4	57.6	79.9	668.6	51.3	617.3	113.6	184.4	118.3	201.0
1993: I	111.9	10.9	100.9	25.6	44.3	12.9	18.1	140.8	12.8	128.1	23.5	35.7	25.0	43.9
II	114.1	10.9	103.2	26.0	45.8	13.2	18.2	147.7	14.3	133.4	25.0	37.7	25.5	45.2
III	111.6	10.5	101.0	26.0	44.1	12.5	18.5	148.2	12.5	135.7	26.0	38.3	25.3	46.0
IV	119.3	11.3	107.9	27.4	48.0	13.8	18.8	152.7	11.9	140.8	26.5	40.6	26.6	47.1
1994: I	118.4	11.0	107.5	26.4	48.8	13.6	18.7	154.9	10.5	144.5	27.5	42.6	26.9	47.5
II	122.7	10.9	111.9	27.1	51.0	14.1	19.7	164.2	12.9	151.4	27.7	44.9	29.0	49.8
III	127.4	11.7	115.7	29.0	51.8	14.5	20.5	172.0	15.1	156.9	28.4	47.0	30.6	50.8
IV	133.9	13.6	120.4	30.1	53.8	15.4	21.1	177.4	12.8	164.6	29.9	50.0	31.8	52.9
1995: I	138.1	14.0	124.0	32.8	54.2	15.5	21.4	183.1	13.1	170.0	31.8	51.5	32.5	54.3
II	142.9	13.4	129.4	34.9	57.8	14.7	22.1	191.7	14.6	177.1	34.6	54.8	32.1	55.5
III	145.3	14.8	130.5	34.2	58.9	15.3	22.2	188.7	14.1	174.7	31.4	57.1	30.9	55.3

[1] End-use categories beginning 1978 are not strictly comparable with data for earlier periods. See *Survey of Current Business,* June 1988.

Note.—Data are on an international transactions basis and exclude military.

In June 1990, end-use categories for merchandise exports were redefined to include reexports; beginning with data for 1978, reexports (exports of foreign merchandise) are assigned to detailed end-use categories in the same manner as exports of domestic merchandise.

Source: Department of Commerce, Bureau of Economic Analysis.

[Billions of dollars]

Item	1986	1987	1988	1989	1990	1991	1992	1993	1994	1995 first 3 quarters at annual rate[1]
Exports	223.3	250.2	320.2	362.1	389.3	416.9	440.4	456.8	502.5	568.3
Industrial countries	150.3	165.6	207.3	234.2	253.8	261.3	265.1	270.6	295.3	334.7
Canada	56.5	62.0	74.3	81.1	83.5	85.9	91.4	101.2	114.9	127.5
Japan	26.4	27.6	37.2	43.9	47.8	47.2	46.9	46.7	51.8	62.5
Western Europe[2]	60.4	68.6	86.4	98.4	111.4	116.8	114.5	111.3	115.4	129.6
Australia, New Zealand, and South Africa	7.1	7.4	9.4	10.9	11.2	11.4	12.4	11.5	13.2	15.0
Australia	5.1	5.3	6.8	8.1	8.3	8.3	8.7	8.1	9.6	10.5
Other countries, except Eastern Europe	71.0	82.3	109.1	122.2	130.6	150.4	169.5	179.8	201.8	228.2
OPEC[3]	10.4	10.7	13.8	12.7	12.7	18.4	19.7	18.7	17.1	18.2
Other[4]	60.6	71.6	95.3	109.5	117.9	132.0	149.8	161.1	184.6	210.0
Eastern Europe[2]	2.1	2.3	3.8	5.5	4.3	4.8	5.6	6.2	5.3	5.4
International organizations and unallocated	....	....	.1	.2	.6	.4	.1	.2	.1	....
Imports	368.4	409.8	447.2	477.4	498.3	491.0	536.5	589.4	668.6	751.3
Industrial countries	245.4	259.7	283.2	292.5	299.9	294.3	316.3	347.8	389.8	430.0
Canada	69.7	73.6	84.6	89.9	93.1	93.0	100.9	113.3	131.1	147.6
Japan	80.8	84.6	89.8	93.5	90.4	92.3	97.4	107.2	119.1	127.2
Western Europe[2]	89.0	96.1	102.6	102.4	109.2	102.0	111.4	120.9	132.9	147.9
Australia, New Zealand, and South Africa	5.9	5.4	6.2	6.6	7.3	7.0	6.6	6.4	6.7	7.2
Australia	2.6	3.0	3.5	3.9	4.4	4.1	3.7	3.3	3.2	3.5
Other countries, except Eastern Europe	121.1	148.2	161.8	182.8	196.1	194.9	218.2	238.1	272.9	313.9
OPEC[3]	18.9	24.4	23.0	29.2	37.0	33.4	32.4	32.6	31.7	35.3
Other[4]	102.2	123.8	138.8	153.6	159.1	161.5	185.8	205.4	241.2	278.6
Eastern Europe[2]	2.0	1.9	2.2	2.1	2.3	1.8	2.0	3.5	5.8	7.5
International organizations and unallocated	....	....	....	....	....	....	....	....	....	....
Balance (excess of exports +)	−145.1	−159.6	−127.0	−115.2	−109.0	−74.1	−96.1	−132.6	−166.1	−183.0
Industrial countries	−95.1	−94.1	−75.9	−58.2	−46.1	−33.0	−51.2	−77.2	−94.5	−95.3
Canada	−13.2	−11.6	−10.3	−8.8	−9.6	−7.1	−9.5	−12.2	−16.2	−20.1
Japan	−54.4	−56.9	−52.6	−49.7	−42.6	−45.0	−50.5	−60.5	−67.3	−64.6
Western Europe[2]	−28.6	−27.5	−16.2	−4.0	2.2	14.8	3.1	−9.7	−17.6	−18.4
Australia, New Zealand, and South Africa	1.1	2.0	3.2	4.2	3.9	4.4	5.8	5.2	6.6	7.8
Australia	2.5	2.3	3.3	4.2	3.9	4.2	5.0	4.8	6.4	7.0
Other countries, except Eastern Europe	−50.1	−65.8	−52.7	−60.6	−65.5	−44.5	−48.7	−58.3	−71.2	−85.7
OPEC[3]	−8.5	−13.7	−9.2	−16.6	−24.3	−15.0	−12.7	−14.0	−14.6	−17.1
Other[4]	−41.6	−52.1	−43.5	−44.1	−41.2	−29.5	−36.0	−44.3	−56.6	−68.6
Eastern Europe[2]	.1	.3	1.6	3.5	2.1	3.0	3.7	2.7	−.5	−2.1
International organizations and unallocated	....	....	.1	.2	.6	.4	.1	.2	.1	....

[1] Preliminary; seasonally adjusted.
[2] The former German Democratic Republic (East Germany) included in Western Europe beginning fourth quarter 1990 and in Eastern Europe prior to that time.
[3] Organization of Petroleum Exporting Countries, consisting of Algeria, Ecuador (through 1992), Gabon, Indonesia, Iran, Iraq, Kuwait, Libya, Nigeria, Qatar, Saudi Arabia, United Arab Emirates, and Venezuela.
[4] Latin America, other Western Hemisphere, and other countries in Asia and Africa, less members of OPEC.

Note.—Data are on an international transactions basis and exclude military.

Source: Department of Commerce, Bureau of Economic Analysis.

TABLE B-102.—U.S. international trade in goods on balance of payments (BOP) and Census basis, and trade in services on BOP basis, 1974-95

[Billions of dollars; monthly data seasonally adjusted]

Year or month	Goods: Exports (f.a.s. value) [1][2] — Census basis (by end-use category)							Goods: Imports (customs value, except as noted) [5] — Census basis (by end-use category)							Services (BOP basis)	
	Total, BOP basis [3]	Total, Census basis [3][4]	Foods, feeds, and beverages	Industrial supplies and materials	Capital goods except automotive	Automotive vehicles, parts, and engines	Consumer goods (nonfood) except automotive	Total, BOP basis	Total, Census basis [4]	Foods, feeds, and beverages	Industrial supplies and materials	Capital goods except automotive	Automotive vehicles, parts, and engines	Consumer goods (nonfood) except automotive	Exports	Imports
	F.a.s. value [2]							F.a.s. value [2]								
1974	98.3	99.4						103.8	103.3						22.6	21.4
1975	107.1	108.9						98.2	99.3						25.5	22.0
1976	114.7	116.8						124.2	124.6						28.0	24.6
1977	120.8	123.2						151.9	151.5						31.5	27.6
1978	142.1	145.8						176.0	176.1						36.4	32.2
1979	184.4	186.4						212.0	210.3						39.7	36.7
1980	224.3	225.6						249.8	245.3						47.6	41.5
								Customs value								
1981	237.0	238.7						265.1	261.0						57.4	45.5
1982	211.2	216.4	31.3	61.7	72.7	15.7	14.3	247.6	244.0	17.1	112.0	35.4	33.3	39.7	64.1	51.7
1983	201.8	205.6	30.9	56.7	67.2	16.8	13.4	268.9	258.0	18.2	107.0	40.9	40.8	44.9	64.3	55.0
1984	219.9	224.0	31.5	61.7	72.0	20.6	13.3	332.4	6 330.7	21.0	123.7	59.8	53.5	60.0	71.2	67.7
1985	215.9	7 218.8	24.0	58.5	73.9	22.9	12.6	338.1	6 336.5	21.9	113.9	65.1	66.8	68.3	73.2	72.9
1986	223.3	7 227.2	22.3	57.3	75.8	21.7	14.2	368.4	365.4	24.4	101.3	71.8	78.2	79.4	86.5	81.0
1987	250.2	254.1	24.3	66.7	86.2	24.6	17.7	409.8	406.2	24.8	111.0	84.5	85.2	88.7	98.5	91.7
1988	320.2	322.4	32.3	85.1	109.2	29.3	23.1	447.2	441.0	24.8	118.3	101.4	87.7	95.9	111.1	99.5
1989	362.1	363.8	37.2	99.3	138.8	34.8	36.4	477.4	473.2	25.1	132.3	113.3	86.1	102.9	127.4	103.5
1990	389.3	393.6	35.1	104.4	152.7	37.4	43.3	498.3	495.3	26.6	143.2	116.4	87.3	105.7	147.8	118.8
1991	416.9	421.7	35.7	109.7	166.7	40.0	45.9	491.0	488.5	26.5	131.6	120.7	85.7	108.0	164.3	119.6
1992	440.4	448.2	40.3	109.1	175.9	47.0	51.4	536.5	532.7	27.6	138.6	134.3	91.8	122.7	178.6	122.0
1993	456.8	465.1	40.6	111.8	181.7	52.4	54.7	589.4	580.7	27.9	145.6	152.4	102.4	134.0	187.8	130.0
1994	502.5	512.6	41.9	121.4	205.2	57.6	60.0	668.6	663.3	31.0	162.0	184.4	118.3	146.3	198.7	138.8
1994: Jan	38.9	39.7	3.4	9.0	16.2	4.5	4.6	50.3	49.9	2.4	11.7	14.0	8.5	11.6	15.4	11.0
Feb	37.4	38.2	3.2	8.7	15.4	4.5	4.5	51.1	50.3	2.3	11.9	14.0	8.9	11.6	15.6	11.6
Mar	42.1	42.8	3.4	10.6	17.3	4.7	4.9	53.6	52.5	2.6	12.6	14.5	9.4	11.5	16.7	11.7
Apr	40.4	41.1	3.2	9.6	16.8	4.8	4.8	53.8	53.2	2.5	12.7	14.7	9.4	11.9	16.0	11.4
May	40.4	41.3	3.3	9.9	16.6	4.6	4.9	54.5	54.0	2.5	13.1	14.9	9.6	12.1	16.4	11.5
June	41.9	42.8	3.2	9.8	17.6	4.7	5.2	55.9	55.7	2.6	14.0	15.2	10.0	12.1	16.7	11.6
July	40.4	41.2	3.1	10.2	16.3	4.3	4.9	56.3	56.0	2.6	14.4	15.3	9.9	12.1	16.6	11.6
Aug	43.7	44.7	3.6	10.7	17.6	5.1	5.2	57.9	57.6	2.7	14.7	15.4	10.7	12.4	16.6	11.7
Sept	43.3	44.1	3.7	10.3	17.8	5.0	5.1	57.8	57.6	2.7	14.2	16.3	10.0	12.5	17.7	11.8
Oct	43.3	44.3	3.8	10.7	17.0	4.9	5.2	58.2	58.0	2.7	13.9	16.4	10.3	12.8	16.7	11.6
Nov	44.4	45.3	4.0	10.7	18.0	5.0	5.4	59.7	59.5	2.6	14.5	16.8	10.7	12.9	17.3	11.7
Dec	46.2	47.2	4.2	11.3	18.7	5.5	5.3	59.4	59.2	2.7	14.2	16.8	10.8	12.9	17.0	11.6
1995: Jan	44.9	45.6	3.9	11.6	17.1	5.5	5.1	60.7	60.5	2.8	14.5	17.1	11.0	13.3	17.3	11.8
Feb	45.6	46.3	3.9	11.7	17.9	5.3	5.3	59.9	59.7	2.8	14.4	16.9	10.8	13.1	16.5	11.7
Mar	47.9	48.7	4.1	12.6	19.2	5.1	5.4	62.5	61.6	2.9	15.3	17.6	10.7	13.3	17.4	12.1
Apr	47.2	47.8	4.2	12.3	18.8	5.1	5.3	63.5	62.6	2.7	15.5	18.0	11.0	13.6	17.2	12.1
May	48.3	49.1	4.0	12.4	19.4	5.1	5.6	64.3	63.1	2.7	15.8	18.1	10.7	13.8	17.3	12.1
June	47.4	48.2	3.9	12.7	19.5	4.5	5.4	63.9	63.0	2.8	15.7	18.7	10.4	13.4	17.3	12.2
July	46.4	47.1	4.2	11.8	19.0	4.4	5.2	62.6	62.4	2.7	15.3	18.9	10.0	13.5	17.3	12.1
Aug	49.1	49.8	4.5	12.1	20.0	5.3	5.5	62.6	62.4	2.8	14.9	18.9	10.4	13.5	17.3	12.1
Sept	49.8	50.5	4.8	12.4	19.7	5.6	5.5	63.5	63.3	2.8	15.3	19.3	10.4	13.5	17.7	12.2
Oct	49.0	49.8	4.4	12.6	20.3	4.8	5.5	62.7	62.3	2.8	14.7	19.7	9.5	13.3	17.8	12.2
Nov p	49.4	50.2	4.4	11.8	20.8	4.9	5.5	61.9	61.6	2.7	14.9	19.3	9.6	12.9	17.9	12.5

[1] Department of Defense shipments of grant-aid military supplies and equipment under the Military Assistance Program are excluded from total exports through 1985 and included beginning 1986.

[2] F.a.s. (free alongside ship) value basis at U.S. port of exportation for exports and at foreign port of exportation for imports.

[3] Includes undocumented exports to Canada through 1988. Beginning 1989, undocumented exports to Canada are included in the appropriate end-use category.

[4] Total includes "other" exports or imports, not shown separately.

[5] Total arrivals of imported goods other than intransit shipments.

[6] Total includes revisions not reflected in detail.

[7] Total exports are on a revised statistical month basis; end-use categories are on a statistical month basis.

Note.—Goods on a Census basis are adjusted to a BOP basis by the Bureau of Economic Analysis, in line with concepts and definitions used to prepare international and national accounts. The adjustments are necessary to supplement coverage of Census data, to eliminate duplication of transactions recorded elsewhere in international accounts, and to value transactions according to a standard definition.

Data include trade of the U.S. Virgin Islands.

Source: Department of Commerce (Bureau of the Census and Bureau of Economic Analysis).

TABLE B–103.—*International investment position of the United States at year-end, 1986–94*

[Billions of dollars]

Type of investment	1986	1987	1988	1989	1990	1991	1992	1993	1994
NET INTERNATIONAL INVESTMENT POSITION OF THE UNITED STATES:									
With direct investment at current cost	45.0	−11.1	−134.5	−250.3	−251.1	−355.1	−515.7	−545.3	−680.8
With direct investment at market value	136.4	71.3	14.8	−77.1	−211.7	−349.0	−570.6	−453.9	−584.0
U.S. ASSETS ABROAD:									
With direct investment at current cost	1,479.1	1,637.1	1,784.1	1,979.3	2,066.4	2,131.7	2,142.2	2,393.6	2,477.7
With direct investment at market value	1,577.7	1,722.3	1,949.7	2,251.4	2,178.1	2,314.9	2,282.9	2,708.7	2,765.2
U.S. official reserve assets	139.9	162.4	144.2	168.7	174.7	159.2	147.4	164.9	163.4
Gold [1]	102.4	127.6	107.4	105.2	102.4	92.6	87.2	102.6	100.1
Special drawing rights	8.4	10.3	9.6	10.0	11.0	11.2	8.5	9.0	10.0
Reserve position in the International Monetary Fund	11.7	11.3	9.7	9.0	9.1	9.5	11.8	11.8	12.0
Foreign currencies	17.3	13.1	17.4	44.6	52.2	45.9	40.0	41.5	41.2
U.S. Government assets other than official reserves	89.6	88.9	86.1	84.5	82.0	79.1	80.7	81.0	81.3
U.S. credits and other long-term assets	88.7	88.1	85.4	83.9	81.4	77.4	79.0	79.0	79.2
Repayable in dollars	87.1	86.5	83.9	82.4	80.0	76.2	77.9	78.0	78.3
Other	1.6	1.6	1.5	1.5	1.3	1.2	1.1	1.0	.9
U.S. foreign currency holdings and U.S. short-term assets	.9	.8	.7	.6	.6	1.6	1.7	2.0	2.1
U.S. private assets:									
With direct investment at current cost	1,249.6	1,385.9	1,553.8	1,726.1	1,809.7	1,893.4	1,914.0	2,147.6	2,233.0
With direct investment at market value	1,348.2	1,471.0	1,719.4	1,998.2	1,921.5	2,076.7	2,054.8	2,462.7	2,520.5
Direct investment abroad:									
At current cost	431.5	505.1	526.8	560.4	620.0	644.3	657.9	706.6	761.0
At market value	530.1	590.2	692.5	832.5	731.8	827.5	798.6	1,021.7	1,048.4
Foreign securities	143.4	154.0	176.0	217.6	228.7	302.4	333.8	542.9	538.6
Bonds	80.4	84.3	90.0	97.8	118.7	143.6	155.8	245.2	224.7
Corporate stocks	63.0	69.6	86.0	119.9	110.0	158.8	178.1	297.7	313.9
U.S. claims on unaffiliated foreigners reported by U.S. nonbanking concerns	167.4	177.4	197.8	234.3	265.3	256.3	254.3	250.4	286.8
U.S. claims reported by U.S. banks, not included elsewhere	507.3	549.5	653.2	713.8	695.7	690.4	668.0	647.7	646.7
FOREIGN ASSETS IN THE UNITED STATES:									
With direct investment at current cost	1,434.2	1,648.2	1,918.6	2,229.7	2.317.5	2,486.8	2,657.9	2,938.9	3,158.6
With direct investment at market value	1,441.3	1,650.9	1,935.0	2,328.5	2,389.8	2,664.0	2,853.5	3,162.5	3,349.2
Foreign official assets in the United States	241.2	283.1	322.0	341.9	375.3	401.7	442.7	516.7	545.3
U.S. Government securities	178.9	220.5	260.9	263.7	295.0	315.9	335.7	388.3	414.9
U.S. Treasury securities	173.3	213.7	253.0	257.3	287.9	307.1	323.0	371.2	393.4
Other	5.6	6.8	8.0	6.4	7.1	8.8	12.7	17.1	21.5
Other U.S. Government liabilities	18.0	15.7	15.2	15.4	17.2	18.6	20.8	22.5	24.7
U.S. liabilities reported by U.S. banks, not included elsewhere	27.9	31.8	31.5	36.5	39.9	38.4	55.0	69.8	72.7
Other foreign official assets	16.4	15.0	14.4	26.3	23.2	28.7	31.3	36.1	32.9
Other foreign assets in the United States:									
With direct investment at current cost	1,193.0	1,365.1	1,596.6	1,887.8	1,942.2	2,085.1	2,215.2	2,422.2	2,613.3
With direct investment at market value	1,200.1	1,367.9	1,612.9	1,986.6	2,014.4	2,262.3	2,410.8	2,645.9	2,803.9
Direct investment in the United States:									
At current cost	265.8	313.5	375.2	435.9	467.3	491.9	498.6	535.8	580.5
At market value	273.0	316.2	391.5	534.7	539.6	669.1	694.2	759.5	771.1
U.S. Treasury securities	96.1	82.6	100.9	166.5	162.4	189.5	224.8	253.3	265.6
U.S. securities other than U.S. Treasury securities	309.8	341.7	392.3	482.9	467.4	559.2	620.0	732.2	755.7
Corporate and other bonds	140.9	166.1	191.3	231.7	245.7	287.3	319.9	392.1	417.8
Corporate stocks	168.9	175.6	201.0	251.2	221.7	271.9	300.2	340.0	337.9
U.S. liabilities to unaffiliated foreigners reported by U.S. nonbanking concerns	90.7	110.2	144.5	167.1	213.4	208.9	220.7	229.0	225.1
U.S. liabilities reported by U.S. banks, not included elsewhere	430.6	517.2	583.7	635.5	631.6	635.6	651.0	671.9	786.3

[1] Valued at market price.

Note.—For details regarding these data, see *Survey of Current Business*, June issues 1991–1995.

Source: Department of Commerce, Bureau of Economic Analysis.

TABLE B–104.—*Industrial production and consumer prices, major industrial countries, 1970–95*

Year or quarter	United States	Canada	Japan	European Union¹	France	Germany²	Italy	United Kingdom
	Industrial production (1987=100)³							
1970	61.4	59.0	55.0	73.1	72	75.5	68.3	78.9
1971	62.2	62.3	56.5	74.7	77	77.0	68.0	78.5
1972	68.3	67.8	59.6	78.0	81	79.9	70.8	79.9
1973	73.8	75.8	69.0	83.7	87	85.0	77.7	87.0
1974	72.7	77.3	66.3	84.3	90	84.8	81.2	85.4
1975	66.3	71.6	59.3	78.7	83	79.6	73.7	80.8
1976	72.4	76.5	65.9	84.5	90	86.8	82.9	83.4
1977	78.2	79.0	68.6	86.6	92	88.0	83.8	87.6
1978	82.6	81.8	73.0	89.0	94	90.4	85.4	90.1
1979	85.7	85.7	78.2	93.1	99	94.7	91.1	93.6
1980	84.1	82.8	81.8	92.8	98.9	95.0	96.2	87.0
1981	85.7	84.5	82.6	91.1	98.3	93.2	94.7	84.2
1982	81.9	76.2	83.0	89.9	97.3	90.3	91.7	85.8
1983	84.9	81.2	85.5	90.8	96.5	90.9	88.9	88.9
1984	92.8	91.0	93.5	92.8	97.1	93.5	91.8	89.0
1985	94.4	96.1	96.9	95.8	97.2	97.7	92.9	93.9
1986	95.3	95.4	96.7	98.0	98.0	99.6	96.2	96.2
1987	100.0	100.0	100.0	100.0	100.0	100.0	100.0	100.0
1988	104.4	105.3	109.4	104.2	104.6	103.9	105.9	104.8
1989	106.0	105.2	115.7	108.2	108.9	108.8	109.2	107.0
1990	106.0	101.7	120.6	110.4	111.0	114.5	109.4	106.7
1991	104.2	97.4	122.9	109.6	111.0	118.7	108.4	102.8
1992	107.7	98.5	115.8	108.4	109.7	116.3	108.2	102.7
1993	111.5	102.9	111.0	104.9	105.6	107.4	105.5	104.7
1994	118.1	109.6	112.3	109.8	111.0	110.8	110.7	110.0
1995ᴾ	121.9	....	115.8	....	....	....	....	....
1994: I	115.5	105.4	110.1	106.5	105.6	107.9	105.4	107.5
II	117.5	108.4	110.7	109.1	108.3	110.1	110.0	109.9
III	118.8	111.3	113.5	111.0	110.3	111.4	113.0	111.4
IV	120.6	113.3	114.5	111.9	110.5	112.8	114.7	111.2
1995: I	121.8	114.2	116.1	112.5	111.8	110.5	115.2	112.1
II	121.4	113.6	116.3	113.1	111.9	111.8	116.5	112.2
III	122.3	114.0	114.2	....	....	110.8	120.0	112.9
IVᴾ	122.6	....	116.4	....	....	....	....	....
	Consumer prices (1982–84=100)							
1970	38.8	35.1	38.5	26.6	28.7	52.9	16.8	21.8
1971	40.5	36.1	40.9	28.3	30.3	55.6	17.6	23.8
1972	41.8	37.9	42.9	30.1	32.2	58.7	18.7	25.5
1973	44.4	40.7	47.9	32.7	34.5	62.8	20.6	27.9
1974	49.3	45.2	59.0	37.4	39.3	67.2	24.6	32.3
1975	53.8	50.1	65.9	42.8	43.9	71.2	28.8	40.2
1976	56.9	53.8	72.2	47.9	48.1	74.2	33.6	46.8
1977	60.6	58.1	78.1	53.8	52.7	76.9	40.1	54.2
1978	65.2	63.3	81.4	58.7	57.5	79.0	45.1	58.7
1979	72.6	69.1	84.4	65.1	63.6	82.2	52.1	66.6
1980	82.4	76.1	91.0	74.0	72.3	86.7	63.5	78.5
1981	90.9	85.6	95.3	83.2	82.0	92.2	75.3	87.9
1982	96.5	94.9	98.0	92.2	91.6	97.1	87.7	95.4
1983	99.6	100.4	99.8	100.2	100.5	100.3	100.8	99.8
1984	103.9	104.8	102.1	107.4	107.9	102.7	111.5	104.8
1985	107.6	108.9	104.1	114.0	114.2	104.8	121.1	111.1
1986	109.6	113.4	104.8	118.2	117.2	104.7	128.5	114.9
1987	113.6	118.4	104.9	122.2	120.9	104.9	134.4	119.7
1988	118.3	123.2	105.7	126.7	124.2	106.3	141.1	125.6
1989	124.0	129.3	108.0	133.3	128.6	109.2	150.4	135.4
1990	130.7	135.5	111.4	140.8	133.0	112.2	159.5	148.2
1991	136.2	143.1	115.0	148.0	137.2	116.2	169.8	156.9
1992	140.3	145.2	116.9	154.2	140.6	120.9	178.8	162.7
1993	144.5	147.9	118.5	159.4	143.5	125.2	186.3	165.3
1994	148.2	148.2	119.3	164.2	145.9	128.6	193.6	169.3
1995ᴾ	152.4	151.4	119.2	....	148.4	130.8	204.0	175.2
1994: I	146.7	148.0	118.9	162.5	144.9	127.5	191.2	166.8
II	147.6	147.5	119.4	164.2	145.8	128.3	192.8	169.8
III	148.9	148.3	119.1	164.8	146.0	129.1	194.2	169.9
IV	149.6	148.8	119.7	165.6	146.6	129.1	196.5	171.0
1995: I	150.9	150.4	119.0	167.3	147.4	130.1	199.5	172.5
II	152.2	151.5	119.5	169.1	148.2	130.8	203.4	175.6
III	152.9	151.8	119.1	170.0	148.6	131.3	205.4	176.1
IVᴾ	153.6	151.9	119.1	....	149.5	131.1	208.0	176.4

¹ Consists of Belgium-Luxembourg, Denmark, France, Greece, Ireland, Italy, Netherlands, United Kingdom, Germany, Portugal, and Spain. Data exclude Austria, Finland and Sweden which became members January 1, 1995. Industrial production includes data for Greece beginning 1981; data for Portugal and Spain are included beginning 1982.
² Data are for West Germany only.
³ All data exclude construction. Quarterly data are seasonally adjusted.

Sources: National sources as reported by Department of Commerce (International Trade Administration, Office of Trade and Economic Analysis), Department of Labor (Bureau of Labor Statistics), and Board of Governors of the Federal Reserve System.